Readings in

APPLIED

ENGLISH LINGUISTICS

Readings in

APPLIED

ENGLISH LINGUISTICS

Edited by
HAROLD B. ALLEN
UNIVERSITY OF MINNESOTA

New York

APPLETON-CENTURY-CROFTS, Inc.

Preface

WHEN THE IDEA of this collection of readings on linguistics was first suggested to me, I was chagrined at not having thought that the increasingly serious problem I had been facing for several years was almost surely a problem for others as well, and that therefore it would be most helpful to publish such a volume for all those interested in the field.

Not many years ago it seemed enough for a person concerned with the teaching of English to know something of a fairly settled corpus of information about the language. For the secondary school teacher this usually meant a compact presentation of systematic traditional grammar, with perhaps—if he were lucky—a brief history of the English language. For the college teacher this meant Old English grammar, with perhaps some attention to early Germanic phonology and the grammar of Gothic or Old Norse and such ancillary language data as would inhere in the study of Chaucer and Shakespeare. The undergraduate English major not headed for teaching rarely was expected to acquire any organized knowledge of his language at all, except for the unrealistic grammatical rules of his freshman English handbook.

This ostensibly happy situation no longer exists. The far-reaching advances in the relatively new discipline of linguistics in the past few years are now being matched by specific developments in the study of our own language. The general English major and the undergraduate and the graduate student preparing to teach English are beginning to find that some knowledge of English linguistics is basic to their understanding of usage, to composition, and even to the criticism of literature. Further, so active are workers in English linguistics today, so rapid are the advances, that the student needs not only the synthesized information in a textbook or a series of lectures but also the content and points of view in current articles by these workers and by those seeking to apply their findings.

Experience over more than a dozen years has convinced me of the value of sending students to these current articles. While a teacher, or a single textbook, carries a certain weight in persuading the student of the validity of materials which may contradict deeply entrenched but uncritically accepted attitudes, the weight is multiplied when the student reads article after article presenting additional evidence and further cogent analysis. When a student is confronted with a new approach, he is entitled to know whether it is only the individualistic bent of his instructor or of his single textbook or whether, on the contrary, it is that of contemporary scholars in the field. He is, in brief, entitled to learn what is going on in that part of the world of study and teaching in which he expects to do his own work.

But the student cannot easily learn this when the library lacks some of the needed publications, when a number of other students are trying to read the same articles in the publications it does have, when his time in the library is limited and current journals may not be removed, and when the library's having only one copy of a given journal prevents his reading articles in any kind of reasonable sequence. And with the recent rapid increase in the quantity of desirable articles which the student should read, the problem has become more and more serious. Hence this collection as a workable solution.

In this collection the student will find some duplication and overlapping. This use of printing space is deliberate, in the belief that desirable enforcement of understanding will result. The student will find also some disagreement among the authors. One writer, reluctant to cast aside completely notions long cherished, accepts the findings of linguistics only with reservations; others, accepting the basic premises of the linguist, differ among themselves in the use and presentation of linguistic findings. Such differences are natural in the rapid development of a young and lively science; and becoming aware of them is an aid, not a deterrent, in understanding the useful implications of that science.

Choice of the selections has been governed largely by their expected use and by the need to keep within reasonable limits. They are all within the broad framework of modern linguistic science, and a significant number deal particularly with structural linguistics. They are largely derivative and secondary articles, not statements of linguistic theory or reports of original research. Some are concerned with the explanation of the structural approach to the study of present-day English and with the resulting impact upon the teaching of composition and upon literary criticism; others concern structural correlations with the study of language usage and with the regional distribution of language variants in the United States. But except for Charles C. Fries's article explaining the linguist's attitude toward the study of verbal meaning and for such attention to vocabulary usage as is given in Robert J. Geist's discussion of *disinterested* the whole area of semantics (to say nothing of general semantics) has had to be omitted from consideration here.

Help in determining the contents of this book came from various colleagues known to be interested in the acquisition of sound linguistic information by those who teach English. To twenty was sent a suggested list of eighty-two articles. Critical comments from eighteen of them led to dropping twenty-four titles and adding seven others, making the present total of sixty-five. For these friendly suggestions I am grateful to the following: Virginia Alwin, Richard Beal, Margaret M. Bryant, MacCurdy Burnet, Dwight Burton, Frederic G. Cassidy, Thomas F. Dunn, Karl W.

Dykema, George P. Faust, Alfred H. Grommon, Archibald A. Hill, Sumner Ives, Albert R. Kitzhaber, Donald J. Lloyd, Jessie R. Lucke, Francis Shoemaker, Erwin Steinberg, and Russell Thomas. I am also, and especially, grateful to the authors and publishers who have generously granted permission to reprint these sixty-five articles in this collection.

H.B.A.

University of Minnesota

Foreword to Students

FOR NEARLY A CENTURY and a half a growing number of scholars have been carrying on studies of language and languages according to the basic principles of what is now known as linguistics or linguistic science. As these studies progressed, they contributed more and more to a body of theory and of data which stood in direct contrast to notions of language handed down from classical philosophers. Especially as these studies threw more light upon the history and the structure of our own language did they come into conflict with long-accepted beliefs about the nature and the use of English.

Linguists for several decades have from time to time called attention to the fact that in the teaching of English, however, there was little or no recognition of the findings of linguistic science, and asserted that uncritical adherence to the older body of material constituted a serious "cultural lag." A decade ago it even seemed that this cultural lag would be widened, rather than narrowed, because of the progress of research in that area of language investigation generally called structural linguistics, again particularly with respect to the study of English.

But quite recently the picture has changed. Leadership in the National Council of Teachers of English and its constituent group, the Conference on College Composition and Communication, and in the College English Association has in one way or another created a growing ferment of interest in the potential utility of structural linguistics in the teaching of English. Each of these organizations has committes concerned with this subject. National conventions of each have given lively attention to it in terms of papers, discussions, and continuing workshops. Regional and local meetings of teachers in various parts of the country have shown similar curiosity and interest. Journals and reports of various kinds have dealt with the subject. Furthermore, new textbooks in linguistics and in the application of linguistics in the teaching of composition are at last appearing, with others now under contract for publication within a year or two.

It may already be insisted upon that no prospective teacher of English should honestly consider himself prepared for his job unless he has some clear understanding of linguistic principles and some awareness of the implication of linguistics for his teaching of pronunciation, grammar, vocabulary, spelling, composition, and literature.

To aid in acquiring this understanding and this awareness selected recent articles have been brought together in this book. They will introduce you to some of the leaders who in one way or another are applying the findings of linguistics to the teaching of English, who through writing and speaking and teaching are trying to reduce that cultural lag. This collection may be used as a text or as a supplement to a class textbook by revealing in greater detail some of the thinking of these leaders and by suggesting—through demonstration of points of difference—further constructive and critical thinking upon your part.

Although it is not imperative that the order of the articles be followed and it is true that some cross-reference will be necessary, still it has seemed reasonable to arrange them in seven major groups: the historical background, the present state of linguistics in the United States, the contribution of linguistic geography, linguistics and usage, linguistics and the teaching of grammar and composition, linguistics and the dictionary, and, finally, linguistics and literary study.

H.B.A.

University of Minnesota

Contents

Part IV. LINGUISTICS AND USAGE

Part V. LINGUISTICS AND THE TEACHING
OF GRAMMAR AND COMPOSITION

Part VI. LINGUISTICS AND THE DICTIONARY

Part VII. LINGUISTICS AND THE STUDY OF LITERATURE

Part I

THE HISTORICAL BACKGROUND

INTRODUCTION

ANTHROPOLOGISTS tell us that widespread among both primitive and non-primitive people is the belief that language is something mystical if not sacrosanct. It may well be that persistence of this notion among speakers of the European languages is supported in part by the absence of easily available information about the variegated, if not shady, history of the grammatical ideas still commonly accepted.

Perhaps the best conspectus of this complex history is that by M. H. Robins, *Ancient and Mediaeval Grammatical Theory in Europe* (Bell, London, 1951). Robins, a lecturer in linguistics in the School of Oriental and African Studies of the University of London, excellently provides in this volume an overview through the eyes of a modern linguist. For the teacher a good synoptic treatment is included in Robert C. Pooley's recent *Teaching English Grammar* (Appleton-Century-Crofts, 1957). In the present collection Dykema opens Part I with an interpretive summary of the history of grammar in terms of its relation to the generally accepted corpus of knowledge in the schools.

McMillan then goes on to look briefly at the chief accomplishments of the first century of modern linguistic science. Although several general books on linguistics provide fuller summaries of nineteenth-century developments (notably Leonard Bloomfield's *Language,* Holt, 1933 and Louis H. Gray's *Foundations of Language,* 1939), the most detailed history is John Spargo's translation of Holger Pedersen's book, *Linguistic Science in the Nineteenth Century* (Harvard University Press, 1931). One matter referred to by McMillan, the persistent confusing of philology and linguistics, has been carefully treated by George Melville Bolling in "Linguistics and Philology," *Language,* 5.27–32 (1928), and a related topic, the curricular problem arising from that confusion, is briefly dealt with by R. C. Simonini, Jr., in "Linguistics in the English Curriculum," *College English,* 19.163–165 (January, 1958).

1

Although Dwight Whitney in the nineteenth century and Franz Boas in the early twentieth were great pioneers in linguistic progress in the United States, it is to Edward Sapir and his successor at Yale, the late Leonard Bloomfield, that contemporary scholars look as the immediate leaders in linguistic science in this country. Sapir's *Language* (Harcourt, Brace, 1921) and Bloomfield's *Language* are still the basic texts any student in linguistics must thoroughly know before proceeding to graduate research in the field.

A brief detailed statement of the proliferation of linguistic study during the past quarter-century is that by C. M. Wise and Ruth Hirsch, "Directions in Linguistics," *Quarterly Journal of Speech,* 39. 225–231 (1953); the best comprehensive study is that of Robert A. Hall, Jr., "American Linguistics, 1925–50," *Archivum Linguisticum,* 3.101–125 (1951) and 4.1–16 (1952). For this Part it seemed desirable to choose Hill's article because of its careful treatment of the structural developments even though Hill admittedly has slighted or even ignored the work of scholars in other linguistic areas. Indeed, so much does the article limit itself to the research of the Smith-Trager group that for full comprehension the reader may want to return to it after reading the explanations in Part II of this collection.

Historical Development of the Concept of Grammatical Properties*

KARL W. DYKEMA

LAST CHRISTMAS my daughter brought me this little book as a perhaps slightly ironic gift for her pedant father. It is entitled *A Short Introduction of Grammar,* and was published "At the Theater, Oxford, 1699." Since we are going to do a lot of talking about grammar during our three sessions here, it is appropriate that we begin with a passage from a grammar. Here then are some excerpts from the Preface:

> Although the very great importance of having the first Rudiments of Grammar well laid, in order to all future progress in learning, is a thing manifest in its self, and acknowledged by all sober men; (those Empiricks who have pretended to a compendious art of teaching without Rule or Method, having been abundantly confuted by their shamful misadventures:) Yet the particular

* Originally a paper read at the meeting of the Conference on College Composition and Communication in St. Louis, in 1954, this article is here reprinted by permission of author and publisher from *College Composition and Communication,* 5.135–140 (December, 1954).

Conduct of Grammatical Institution has in all times been variously discours'd, and no less diversly pursued . . . Grammar is the Sacrist, that bears the Key of Knowledge, by whom alone admittance can be had into the Temple of the Muses, and treasures of Arts; even whatever can enrich the Mind, and raise it from the level of a Barbarian and Idiot, to the dignity of an Intelligence. But this Sacrist is a severe Mistress, who being once contemned, will certainly revenge the Injury, it being evident that no Person ever yet despised Grammar, who had not his fault return'd upon him; . . . It would be observed farther that Grammar, as she is a severe Mistress, is also a coy one; and hardly admits any courtship but of the youthful votary. There are indeed many who by great industry, have redeem'd the want of early Institution but in the performances of such, there still appears somewhat of stiffness and force; and what has more in it of Art than Nature;

I think you recognize in these words a very familiar attitude, still frequently expressed or implied in some grammars today, though not usually in quite so arresting a style. But today the grammar which is referred to is that of English; whereas the final sentences of his Preface make it clear that this author was thinking of quite other things.

When on the other side he that begins an early Court, has greater assurances of favour; with little difficulty becomes a Denison of Rome and Athens, in whatsoever Climate he happens to be born; and makes their Languages his mother tongue; thereby obtaining a free address to all the wisdom of precedent ages, and the friendship of the Heroes of them; to treat familiarly with Xenophon and Caesar, Demosthenes and Cicero, Thucydides and Livy, or whomsoever else he chuses for an acquaintance. He first will read; then equal their Atchievements; and having fill'd his head with their arts and knowledge, will crown it also with their Laurels.

Whom these temptations cannot move to study, let him throw away his book, and like an illiterate criminal perish for not reading in it; let him live a fool, and dye a brute.

And the full title of the book reads: A Short Introduction of Grammar, Generally To Be Used: Compiled and set forth for the bringing up of all those that intend to attain to the Knowledge of the Latin Tongue.

This book is a reprint of William Lily's famous Latin grammar with considerable annotation both of the English Introduction and the Latin grammar itself. The validity of the views I have just read will be examined by some of the following speakers, who will expose them to the conclusions of linguistics. But since these views show such admiration for the "Denisons" of the ancient world, it may also be useful first to compare the attitudes expressed with those of the Greeks and Romans themselves, because the contrast is so remarkable.

Modern discussions of the attitudes of the ancients toward language are not numerous, and since I am no classicist myself, I must lean heavily on the few classicists, mostly French and German, who have discussed the matter during the last hundred years.[1] The history of grammar has, perhaps understandably, been pursued by a limited number of scholars, partly, no doubt, because it is not a superficially glamorous subject, but also because the evidence is scanty and fragmentary.

It can, however, be stated that the educational institutions of Greece during the period of her glory had no place for grammar in them for the very simple reason[2] that it had not yet been invented. An attempt to formulate a grammatical theory and terminology is apparent here and there in Plato and Aristotle, and there was apparently a good deal of grammatical theorizing in the third century B.C. But the earliest extant Greek grammar, that of Dionysius Thrax, did not appear until the second century B.C. Yet the study of grammar did not become a part of either Hellenistic or Roman education since it had been developed as a part of the Greek intellectual passion for systematic analysis and description of every significant phenomenon, not as a pedagogical device. And it seems to have remained mainly a matter of speculation and controversy among the not inconsiderable group of thinkers who had inherited the name of grammarian from their teaching duties as instructors of reading and writing, i.e., teachers of letters.[3]

But somewhere in the development of Western culture, grammar became a tool for teaching a foreign language. Early in the sixth century Priscian used grammar to teach Latin in Constantinople;[4] but for the most part grammar was a part of the textual analysis of the classics, of works in the Greek or Latin which was still the student's own language. Perhaps as the student's knowledge of those classical languages became more uncertain, grammar somehow was used as a means of teaching him the language itself. At any rate in early modern times it is firmly established as the foundation for the study of the classical languages, and among the earliest books printed in fifteenth century Italy are grammars of Greek and Latin.[5]

The author of the book I quoted is well aware of the ancient grammarians. He cites Priscian, Donatus, and Varrus in his notes.[6] And it can hardly be doubted that all well-educated men of his time were aware of the classical provenience of the grammar they had studied. It must have seemed axiomatic to them that the method of learning Latin and Greek through formal grammar represented a tradition going back to the ancients

---

[1] Particularly H. Steinthal, *Geschichte der Sprachwissenschaft bei den Griechen und Römern* (Berlin, 1863); Th. Benfey, *Geschichte der Sprachwissenschaft und orientalischen Philologie in Deutschland* (München, 1869); and H. I. Marrou, *Histoire de l'Éducation dans l'Antiquité* (Paris, 1948).

[2] Marrou, p. 236.

[3] *Ibid.*, p. 236.

[4] *Ibid.*, p. 372.

[5] J. E. Sandys, *A History of Classical Scholarship* (Cambridge, 1908), Vol. 2, pp. 61, 71, 77.

[6] *A Short Introduction* . . . pp. 21, 23, 28.

themselves. The prestige of everything classical was so great, particularly in the eighteenth century, that this association of grammar with ancient literature gave it a fundamental place in educational practice.

It was against such a background that the vernacular began gradually to claim a place for itself in the curriculum. Inevitably a grammatical treatment of it came to be prescribed, though there are protests, like Sidney's in his *Apologie for Poetrie,* where he writes:

> Another will say it wanteth Grammar. Nay truly, it hath that prayse, that it wanteth not Grammar: for Grammer it might have, but it needes it not; beeing so easie of itselfe, and so voyd of those cumbersome differences of Cases, Genders, Moodes, and Tenses, which I thinke was a peece of the Tower of Babilons curse, that a man should be put to schoole to learne his mother-tongue.[7]

But even so intelligent and emancipated an educator as Comenius, who first published his *Great Didactic* in his native Czech (1628–32), wanted to teach the children in his Vernacular School "to write . . . in accordance with the grammatical rules of the mother-tongue." (ch. 29, 6 ii.)[8] Perhaps Comenius's rules for Czech would have been more than a slavish translation of Latin grammar into the vernacular, since his approach to language teaching was based on a good deal more intelligent analysis of the problem than was common in his day. Most of the grammatical analysis of the vernacular was, however, based on the already existing works which had been devised to introduce students to Latin grammatical concepts by approximating them in English translation. These works now became the foundation for grammars of the vernacular whose purpose was to prescribe the correct use of English, for example, with the same authority and simplicity as was done for Latin in the standard school grammars.

The eighteenth century grammarian of English faced enormous difficulties, of most of which he was probably unaware. First, he was faced with the mass of material that a total living language with all its dialects presents, though of course he did not recognize that he had this problem. Second, he was totally unprepared to make an original and independent analysis of any language because he had never been confronted with the problem of analyzing a language for which no formal description existed; that is, he had no acquaintance with a methodology of linguistic analysis. Third, he was fatally handicapped by an intimate acquaintance with the concepts of classical grammar, concepts which had come to be accepted as universals, though many of them had little relevancy to English; these preconceptions also prevented him from noticing many grammatical phenomena peculiar to English. Fourth, the cultural atmosphere in which he

---

[7] Sir Philip Sidney, *An Apologie for Poetrie,* p. 70 (London: A. Constable & Co., 1905).

[8] J. A. Comenius, *The Great Didactic.* Translated and edited by M. W. Keating (London, 1896) p. 420.

worked tended to make him look upon English as an inferior or at best
a defective language; he therefore considered himself as in duty bound to
improve and—as the expression was—to ascertain the language. Fifth, he
found himself in a position never enjoyed by his classical predecessors, the
position of enjoying a large audience, made up principally of members of
the middle class who had social aspirations. This last point is of tremendous
importance because it explains how formal English grammar got itself so
firmly established in the schools. For we must not forget that especially
during the past century and a half a very important function of the schools
has been felt to be that they should help the ambitious to push their way
socially upward into a class where control of a particular variety of English was an important means of admission.

How much effect the teaching of grammar has had on the actual
language habits of those who have been exposed to it during the last 200
years is a moot point which deserves much fuller study than it has received.
But one tremendous success the teaching of formal grammar has certainly
had. It has instilled a well-nigh universal faith in its efficacy for curing all
manner of linguistic ills. Like many another faith it prescribes a regimen
that few of the faithful are willing to submit to. Perhaps for that very
reason—for the reason that few have really tested it—the faith remains
nearly as strong as ever among the people as a whole. And therefore like all
attacks on a faith, those who question it are looked upon as heretics, though
fortunately the punishment for grammatical heresy is somewhat milder
than burning at the stake. Still, the grammarian's fate is a precarious one.
Though Dante counts Donatus among the blessed, he consigns Priscian to
Hell for sodomy. Professor Curtius has tried to unravel the threads of
medieval tradition which moved Dante to treat the two grammarians so
differently, but has been unable to discover more than a misinterpretation
of Priscian's dedication of his work to a patriarch named Julian. Later
writers confused this Julian with the more famous Roman emperor, Julian
the Apostate, and thereby prepared the way for Priscian's damnation.[9]
Perhaps some of you will consign us to a similar fate by interpreting our
labors here as dedicated to some horrible linguistic apostasy whereas we
are really dedicating ourselves to a better understanding of the true nature
of language.

The eighteenth century grammarian worked, then, under almost in-
superable handicaps, and were it not for the unfortunately tremendous
influence his work has had we could examine it more coolly and recognize
his often considerable contributions. He is certainly not to be condemned
for the honesty with which he described his purpose. Unlike many present-
day grammarians he usually stated quite frankly that he didn't like the
language as it was and had written his grammar to reform it. Today many

[9] Ernst Robert Curtius, *Europaeische Literatur und lateinisches Mittelalter* (Bern,
1953) p. 51, note 1.

a grammar states in its preface that it will describe the language of cultivated writers while it actually reproduces with only minor revision the
prescriptive grammar of the eighteenth century.

I have attempted to trace briefly the Western grammatical tradition from
its origin down to our own day with some interpretive comments intended
to show that the use to which grammar has been put in the last several
hundred years is one which its originators never dreamed of and one which
has had some rather unhappy results. I should like to add a word more
about this intellectual and social phenomenon which has had such an effect
on Western culture.

Dionysius Thrax's little *techne*, as he named it, has been called the most
influential book in the Western culture after the Bible.[10] In it are to be
found virtually all the standard grammatical terms, and the classifications
which he presented remain those of all standard grammar books. Yet his
little book represents the latest and one of the least of Greek intellectual
achievements. Still it might have been otherwise if the Greeks had not been
so certain that they had nothing to learn from another culture. Alexander
the Great introduced them to India, where one of the most penetrating
schools of descriptive grammar had culminated nearly a century earlier
in the work of Panini (c. 400 B.C.). But grammatical analysis like all other
Greek intellectual achievements was to be a purely native development,
and perhaps because it came as a sort of after-thought in the evening of the
Greek mind, it is a lesser accomplishment, legitimately ignored in our usual
study of Greek thought. From this already modest achievement the Romans
derived their even less original grammar of Latin, which was in no way
improved during the Middle Ages by being mixed with a large portion of
philosophy.[11] Finally this inadequate framework was used to describe the
Modern European vernaculars and proved a very incomplete and dis-
torting basis for our modern grammars. You may feel that these are hard
words, that though there may be weaknesses in our traditional grammars,
on the whole what they describe is recognizable in the language itself. It
is, of course. Greek and English are both Indo-European languages and
will therefore have a great deal in common, especially when compared to a
non-Indo-European tongue. To this extent a common grammatical pattern
will do to describe both languages. But Greek is quite incomprehensible to
one who knows only English; the languages as living media of communication are very different. A comprehensively descriptive grammar will be
as much concerned with the differences as with the similarities, and it is in
describing these differences that classical grammar fails, as I think the
structuralists have conclusively demonstrated. It is also true that a foreign

---

[10] Franz Susemihl, *Geschichte der griechischen Literatur in der Alexandrinerzeit*
(Leipzig, Vol. 2, 1892) p. 172.
[11] R. H. Robins, *Ancient and Medieval Grammatical Theory in Europe* . . . (London, 1951), Ch. III.

language can be learned after a fashion through the medium of modern ad-
aptations of classical grammar, as all of you know from experience, generally sad. It does work after a fashion, as did also the Ptolemaic system of
astronomy. But what we master of a foreign language through such a grammar is a very creaky and inflexible structure indeed.

This, then, is what has happened. Western grammar starts as a phase
of Greek intellectual exploration. It is a late phase, a part of the dusky
Hellenistic afterglow, and is inadequate even as an analysis of Greek. Its
adaptation to Latin weakens it, it is confused with philosophy in its trans-
mission to modern Europe, and for us it finally becomes the basis for a
rigidly prescriptive treatment of English. This astonishing transformation
of a speculative intellectual exercise into an almost universally accepted
pedagogical device came about because of the enormous prestige of the
classical tradition, the great age of that tradition, and the almost complete
ignorance until very recently of what we now call linguistics. Grammar
became so integral a part of Western educational practice that a faith in it
was acquired with the education itself. It is hardly strange that as part of
our educational experience we should all have acquired an implicit faith in
grammar just as all our ancestors a few centuries ago accepted the Ptolemaic description of the sun revolving about the earth. The Ptolemaic hypothesis, not much younger than Greek grammar and a product of the
same Hellenistic culture, maintained its hold on Western thought for much
the same reasons that Western grammar still does.

It is necessary for the perpetuation of our culture that we accept the
traditional unless and until it is proved useless or invalid. I have tried to
suggest that there is in the history of the Western grammatical tradition
itself much that will bring into question both the utility and validity of
classical grammar as an approach to language. Through no fault of its
devisers, it has created a state of confusion in many of us not unlike that
of that Rat in Kenneth Grahame's *Wind in the Willows:*

> The Toad, having finished his breakfast, picked up a stout stick and swung
> it vigorously, belaboring imaginary animals. "I'll learn 'em to steal my house!"
> he cried. "I'll learn 'em, I'll learn 'em!"
>
> "Don't say learn 'em, Toad," said the Rat greatly shocked. "It's not good
> English."
>
> "What are you always nagging at Toad for?" inquired the Badger peevishly.
> "What's the matter with his English? It's the same what I use myself, and if
> it's good enough for me, it ought to be good enough for you!"
>
> "I'm very sorry," said the Rat humbly. "Only I think it ought to be 'teach'
> 'em, not learn 'em."
>
> "But we don't *want* to teach 'em," replied the Badger. "We want to *learn*
> 'em—learn 'em, learn 'em! and what's more, we're going to *do* it, too!"
>
> "Oh, very well, have it your own way," said the Rat. He was getting rather
> muddled about it himself, and presently he retired into a corner, where he

could be heard muttering, "Learn 'em, teach 'em, teach 'em, learn 'em!" till the Badger told him rather sharply to leave off.[12]

I hope when all eight of us are through with you, you will not depart with comparable incoherent mutterings.

Summary of Nineteenth-Century Historical and Comparative Linguistics*

JAMES B. McMILLAN

THE MAIN DEVELOPMENTS in the study of language in our culture during the last century can be summarized, it seems to me, under three heads. Two are positive: (1) a drastic revision of the orthodox concept of language to include such assumptions as (a) language is speech, (b) language has system, (c) language has variety, and (d) language changes, and (2) an accumulation of an enormous mass of facts about the English language and the refinement of methods for collecting and classifying facts. One is negative: there was a confusion of levels of discourse (failure to separate linguistics and rhetoric), a confusion of description and history, and a confusion of linguistics and psychology.

Before elaborating, I wish to stipulate several definitions in the interest of clear communication. (1) A language is an arbitrary system of vocal signals by means of which groups of human beings interact. This definition excludes writing, gesture, animal noises, and visual and auditory and tactile code systems, and it does not limit language to particular groups or kinds of human beings. (2) Linguistics is the scientific study of language. It is inductive, objective, tentative, and systematic; it is concerned with reportable facts, methods, and principles; it works by means of observations, hypotheses, experiments, postulates, and inferences; its products are descriptive verbal or algebraic statements about language. Strict linguistics does not include statements about physiology or non-verbal culture. The correlation of linguistic statements with statements about non-verbal culture belongs in a discipline which has been called metalinguistics or exolinguistics. (3) Philology is the study of written documents (usually belletristic writings) to determine authorship, authenticity, provenience, dating, or meaning. Philology may use linguistic statements, just as it may

---

[12] Kenneth Grahame, *The Wind in the Willows* (London, 1908), Ch. XI.

* A paper given at the CCCC Spring Meeting, 1954, in St. Louis, as part of a panel discussion on the general subject, "Modern Linguistics and the Teaching of Freshman English." Reprinted, by permission, from *College Composition and Communication* 5.140–149 (December, 1954).

use paleographic, bibliographic, astrological, and archaeological statements, but philology as here used is not co-extensive with linguistics. (4)
Rhetoric is the art of speaking or writing effectively. It may be the practical
art of communication (with experimental tests) or the fine art of speaking
or writing with aesthetic effects. Rhetoric may include and use linguistic
statements. But these statements come from workers in separate disciplines
and must be authenticated by different means (although it is common for
one person to work as an expert in more than one discipline).

In addition to stipulating definitions, I would insist that to talk sense we
must discriminate levels of discourse, just as we discriminate physics,
chemistry, and biology, or as we discriminate novels, prose fiction, and
prose. In the hierarchy philology and rhetoric may be considered above
linguistics, since they include bigger units of phenomena, just as biology
may be considered above chemistry. Or, to put it differently, linguistics is
more basic than rhetoric in the sense that chemistry is more basic than
biology.

For example, the sentence *It ain't hisn!* may be examined by a rhetorician
for its communicability, its appropriateness, or its aesthetic effect. He may
ask the linguist for a full statement about the utterance, and the linguist
can find and report many facts about the phonology, morphology, syntax,
and lexicography involved (in terms of the same and other utterances by
the same speaker or other speakers), but the linguist cannot *on linguistic
grounds* make philological or rhetorical statements or judgments about a
locution. Just as a physician can ask a pharmacist whether a certain powder
can be dissolved in water, so can the rhetorician ask the linguist about the
intraverbal characteristics of *It ain't hisn;* but just as the pharmacist would
not venture an opinion on whether the powder would be good for a patient,
so the linguist has no right *as a linguist* to say that the locution is good or
bad. Sometimes, of course, the physician is his own pharmacist, and very
frequently the rhetorician is his own linguist, but the levels of operation
and discourse need not be blurred by this overlapping. In considering the
contributions of the nineteenth century, we must remember that science
operates through specializations, compartments, and hierarchies.

✽   ✽   ✽

Now to look specifically at what language study in the last century was
and what it contributed to us as teachers. The study of language was made
a science in the nineteenth century. The development of this science has
been related by Pedersen, and it was codified by Hermann Paul in his
Prinzipien der Sprachgeschichte (1800), which was translated into English by H. A. Strong in 1889. Benjamin Ide Wheeler, in the preface to the
American edition of Paul, said, "The rapid increase of the materials for a
science of language within the last few decades has acted on the one hand
to repress amateurism, and on the other to check arbitrariness of method

on the part of professional linguists." The method applied was that of observation, collection, classification, hypotheses, postulates, and systematic statements. Paul, at least, saw the necessity for strict attention to the pertinent materials. He said (p. 11), "The picture of a particular condition of language is often blurred when the beholder happens to be acquainted with a language nearly related to the object of his consideration, or with an older or more recent stage of its development. The greatest care . . . is necessary to prevent the intrusion of any foreign material." The confusion of linquistic and extra-linguistic facts and the confusion of linguistics, rhetoric, and philology was not unnoticed in 1880.

The definition of language as speech (vocal signals) was explicit; Paul said (p. 433), "No philologist should ever disregard the fact that whatever is written is not language itself; that speech rendered into writing always needs to be rendered back into speech before it can be dealt with." And (p. 37) "A further source of deception is the habit of starting not from the spoken, but from the written word." Again (p. 39) "A word is not a united compound of a definite number of independent sounds, of which each can be expressed by an alphabetical sign; but it is essentially a continuous series of infinitely numerous sounds, and alphabetical symbols do no more than bring out certain characteristic points of this series in an imperfect way." Contemporary stump-speakers who decry the linguists' definition of language as speech obviously have not done their home-work in classical nineteenth century philology.

The definition of language as structured (a system) was elemental in 1880, and formal (as opposed to semantic) classification was common. Quoting Paul (p. 406): "The division into parts of speech most capable of being systematically carried out is that which starts from the mode of flexion." And (p. 417) "The formation of a comparative and superlative may be regarded as a test for the transformation of the participle into an adjective pure and simple."

Nineteenth century scientific language study rejected the arm-chair notion of a standard norm, and recognized variety in language. Paul insisted (p. 21) that ". . . we have, strictly speaking, to differentiate as many languages as there are individuals . . . at any given moment within any given community there are as many dialects spoken as there are individuals to speak them . . . each having its own historical development." The term *idiolect* had not been coined, but the concept was there, clean and sharp.

The eighteenth-century notion of "fixing" a language was rejected in the nineteenth century. Paul said that each individual's dialect (p. 21) is ". . . in a state of perpetual change." And (p. 481) "A written language to serve any practical purpose must change with the times, just like a living dialect." Professional students of language have not just recently invented the notion that language by its nature cannot remain static; the fact was commonplace and never seriously debated in professional circles in nineteenth century philology. (The practice of textbook writers is, of course, something else; rarely did they seem aware that language was being studied.) Because value-judgments and ethnolinguistic statements were not rigidly excluded from linguistic statements, the notion that change was "corruption" lingered for many years, but the fact of change was universally recognized. Grimm, Verner, Grassmann, and other historical and comparative philologists discovered the regularity of linguistic change and, as a correlate, the regularity and system making the structure.

The first great contribution of historical and comparative study, then, was the recognition of linguistics as a science, and the changed concept of language that scientific study produced.

The second great contribution was the great quantity of ordered and classified information about English, both past and present. We need recall merely the Oxford Dictionary, the works on phonetics of Ellis, Sweet, Sievers, and others, the grammars of Sweet, Jespersen, Luick, Poutsma, Curme, and Kruisinga, and the countless special treatises that are recorded in Kennedy's bibliography to realize the amount of data that was produced. Some of this work was written, or at least published, in the twentieth century, but most of our recording and classification was a product of nineteenth century language study. Much of the misinformation epidemic in textbook was produced in the last century, granted, but not in the framework of professional linguistics or philology.

The third bequest of the last century was a set of handicaps. First, historical philologists simply could not divorce language from language history. Paul said (p. xlvi), "What is explained as an unhistorical and still scientific observation of language is at bottom nothing but one incompletely historical . . ." And ". . . it is the task of science not merely to determine what reciprocally corresponds in the different languages or dialects, but as far as possible to reconstruct the fundamental forms and meanings which have not come down to us." Paul and his contemporaries realized that diachronic statements must be based on full and accurate synchronic statements, but they insisted on regarding the descriptive statements as subordinate and not worth making for their own sake.

Second, the dominant workers insisted on explaining linguistic phenomena in terms of psychology. True, they gave up logic, but they merely substituted psychology. Although Paul noted that observed speech is the only datum we can use without inferences, he repeatedly used such definitions as the following (p. 111): "The sentence is the linguistic expression or symbol, denoting that the combination of several ideas or groups of ideas has been effected in the mind of the speaker." Similar remarks occur on page after page of his work, but not one of his psychological explanations is actually useful in attempting to describe or account for linguistic phenomena.

The third handicap was the failure of philology to distinguish itself explicitly and formally from linguistics and from rhetoric. Probably because the same people studied language and rhetoric, and probably because the three disciplines have much overlapping terminology, confusion was deepseated and widespread. Because a man had studied the history and structure of English and also taught people rhetoric it was perhaps inevitable that he should find it hard to keep his linguistics and his rhetoric separate. The confusion was further compounded when people brought up on an authoritarian doctrine of correctness found that they could use the terminology of linguistics and philology to phrase their *dicta* and so (perhaps unintentionally) claimed undeserved sanctions. Let us consider a typical example. When a rhetorician considers a sentence like "The president knowed that the senator had broke his promise" he may want to tell the writer to change *knowed* to *knew* and *broke* to *broken*, and he has a perfect right to do so. But if he cites linguistics or the English language as his authority, he is confusing levels of discourse. The linguist knows and will report that both *knowed* and *broke* are formed normally within the structure of English, that they do not prevent communication, and that they are not structurally ambiguous. He can find the history of each form and he can relate each to other regular forms of the same classes. If we keep our levels of discourse straight, there is no reason *derived from English grammar* to object to these locutions. But if the rhetorician tries correlating *knowed* (pret.) and *broke* (past ptc.) with non-linguistic phenomena (such as the education and socio-economic status of people who use and who do not use the forms), he will certainly find reasons to advise the writer. These reasons are based on metalinguistic (or exolinguistic or ethnolinguistic) facts that are irrelevant to linguistics.

This is as simple and easy-to-apply a distinction as that between medicine and pharmacy, but it has profound implications, is potentially of tremendous use to the teaching of composition, and is the source of the senseless arguments between linguists and "traditionalists." When rhetoricians generally learn that linguists do not object to their conclusions but violently object to misstatements about language to justify those conclusions, both linguistics and rhetoric will profit, become mutually more agreeable, and finally throw off the handicap imposed a hundred years ago.

Linguistics since Bloomfield*

Archibald A. Hill

Leonard Bloomfield, more even than his two great near-contemporaries, Franz Boas and Edward Sapir, is the real founder of American linguistics. From Boas, Bloomfield got the realization of the importance of so-called primative languages as the laboratories in which the principles of investigation later applied to English could be worked out. From Sapir came the notion of patterning; yet to Bloomfield belongs the real credit for formulating the American approach to phonemics, and for giving all of American linguistics its firmly non-mentalistic basis; that is, the belief that formal differences are what give differences in meaning, and that consequently meaning must be investigated through formal differences. The contrary assumption, held of course by most non-linguists, is that differences in meaning make the formal differences, so that formal differences should be investigated only in terms of meanings. With this position linguists disagree, holding that to use meaning as a tool in analysis results in circularity and confusion. Our disagreement unfortunately has resulted in much misunderstanding, and the false accusation that linguists are not interested in meaning—which is what the Semanticists say of us, for instance.

Since Bloomfield's monumental book *Language,* there have been advances in several important fields. The first of these is in phonetic and phonemic accuracy. Bloomfield's phonetics was necessarily a phonetics of words in isolation, as the phonetics of such pioneers as Henry Sweet, Otto Jespersen, and Daniel Jones had been. Later phoneticians, greatly aided by modern recording devices, have worked with utterances as complete and as natural as possible. A chief result of such phonetics has been to call attention to the various phenomena of transition—the junctures. These are of several sorts, the ones on which there is the greatest convergence being the terminal junctures, variations in which can be illustrated by these two utterances:

What's that in the road ahead?
What's that in the road? A head?

The juncture on which there has been most disagreement is the internal, or plus juncture, the entity that makes the difference between two phrases

* Reprinted by permission from *Quarterly Journal of Speech,* 41.253–260 (October, 1955).

like *that's tough* and *that stuff*. The junctures were first described in an important article by Bernard Bloch and George L. Trager in *Language*, fifteen years ago. Unfortunately Bloch later repudiated the article, and there has been much disagreement, though most linguists (perhaps even Bloch) would now accept the phonemic status of the plus. The terminal junctures have long been defined to everyone's satisfaction as partly time and partly pitch phenomena. It was, however, a great contribution when Martin Joos, as the result of investigations with the sound spectrograph which are still unpublished, was able to define plus as a phenomenon of time alone. It is interesting that Joos' definition applies to juncture in other languages, such as Latin, as well. Other instances of increased accuracy have been the establishing of four stress phonemes, instead of the traditional three. Thus we can now set up a series like *bríefly*, *bríefcàse*, and *brîef cáse*, in which all four grades are employed, and all in contrast, from the weakest on the second syllable of *briefly*, the tertiary on the second syllable of *briefcase*, the secondary on the first of *brief case*, to the primary on the first syllables of *briefly* and *briefcase*. Further, once the terminal pitches had been satisfactorily isolated from the pitch pattern of the rest of the sentence, Rulon S. Wells and Kenneth L. Pike were able to identify four pitch phonemes, analogous to the four stresses.

In phonemic theory, perhaps the chief advance has been the elimination of an error on Bloomfield's part. Bloomfield, in his discussion of the unstressed central vowel of English, the schwa, said that the schwa was the unstressed representative of most of the vowel phonemes which appear in stressed syllables. This introduced a theory of phonemic overlapping, which had the unfortunate result of making the boundaries between phonemes arbitrary, and the whole analysis confusing. Bloch is primarily responsible for recognizing this danger, and countering it with the postulate that identical sounds must always belong to the same phoneme. It is this axiom which denies such statements as this about Icelandic: "though /n/ and /ŋ/ contrast, when /n/ becomes /ŋ/ in a proper name like Jon Grimsson, the /ŋ/ is serving as an allophone of /n/." All such statements are now shown to be a result of mixing of levels. The variation is non-significant, of course, but belongs on the morphemic rather than the phonemic level.

Of very great general and theoretic importance has been the steadily growing weight given to structure and pattern in language. Bloch and Trager, and later Trager and Henry Lee Smith, working along lines similar to those of the Prague School in Europe, have been able to reduce English phonemes to statable patterns, and use these patterns for prediction, in many ways similar to the prediction in natural science. For instance, the phonemic pattern of vowels in 1930 was essentially that of the IPA, usually with thirteen vowels arranged in two dimensions, close-open, and front-back, but giving an unsymmetrical pattern. The Bloch-Trager-Smith pattern reduced these to eight, arranged in three rows and three columns, except for the top central position, which was empty. The empty position strongly suggested a ninth vowel. Accordingly /ɨ/ was predicted, and later verified by return to the data, giving us a vowel totally unsuspected as long as we worked in the IPA frame.

The reduction from thirteen to nine vowels, described above, was also accomplished largely by working through pattern. It was an old observation, going back as far as Sweet, that the so-called long vowels of *beet* and *boot* were really diphthongs, analyzable as /i/ followed by /y/, and /u/ followed by /w/. The difficulty was with words like *idea* and the /r/-less pronunciations of words like *beard*. All agreed that these contained a centering off-glide which is parallel to the fronting off-glide in *beet*, and the backing off-glide of *boot*. In a step which seemed radical, Bloch and Trager identified this centering off-glide as a post-vocalic allophone of the [h] of *home*, as they had identified the off-glide of *beet* with the pre-vocalic [y] of *yes*. The step was justified by two facts. The [h] of *home* is in complementary distribution with the off-glide of *idea*, and the necessary physical similarity is found in the gliding quality of both sounds. Objections have largely turned on the difference in voice, since pre-vocalic /h/ is usually voiceless, the post-vocalic glide usually voiced. Further structural studies, however, have shown that voice is not a distinctive feature either of initial /h/ or of glides. Once again Bloch repudiated his own formulation, but this time dramatically readopted it, in a class lecture at the Indiana Linguistic Institute, during which he summed up the arguments on both sides and changed the opinion with which he had entered the classroom.

If we carry pattern congruities still further, we can find unsuspected symmetry in consonants as well. The usual pattern for stops and spirants is as follows (I leave out /c/ and /j/, since these composite or affricate stops are by some analyzed as clusters):

$$
\begin{array}{llll}
p & t & k \\
b & d & g \\
\quad f\,\theta & s & \check{s} \\
\quad v\,\eth & z & \check{z}
\end{array}
$$

This arrangement is phonetically accurate, since the spirants do not, except for /s/ and /z/, occur at the same articulatory position as the stops. But it is possible to make a structural restatement, which gives perfect symmetry if we now include /c/ and /j/.

The new figure is:

$$
\begin{array}{llll}
p & t & c & k \\
b & d & j & g \\
f & \theta & s & \check{s} \\
v & \eth & z & \check{z}
\end{array}
$$

The figure is not meant to imply that the positions for stops and spirants are alike, merely that the four positions for the two sets are structurally analogous. As can be seen, it is a structural argument against analyzing /c/ and /j/ as clusters.

The use of patterning led directly to still another radical formulation, this time in the work of Trager and Smith. Phonemes had previously been thought of as contrasts existing only in the speech of a single individual. Sounds which existed in the speech of different individuals could never contrast. But pattern investigation showed that sounds which had been predicted on the basis of partially symmetrical individual patterns could be found in the expected pattern positions only if individual speech was compared with other individual speech. Thus for instance, not all speakers of English have the predicted /ɨ/. It occurs commonly in the restressed form of such a phase as "just a minute," where it is often written *jist* or *jest*, though the form which these writings indicate contrasts with *just*, *gist*, and *jest*. If you have these contrasts you have the /ɨ/. If you don't, you may still have a "barred eye" elsewhere, or you may lack it. The new formulation which takes such differences into account states that speech communities are characterized by a symmetrical arrangement of the total possibilities of contrast, called an over-all frame. From this frame each individual and each dialect select some but not all of the possibilities. The formulation here given has resulted in a modification of the definition of the phoneme. The old concept of the phoneme turned on individual speech, the idiolect. Individual phonemic structures are therefore structures of idiophonemes. The newer concept turns on dialects, and to revive and modify a term used by Jones, can be called a structure of diaphonemes. The over-all frame is not yet universally accepted—Einar Haugen and Hans Kurath are among the objectors—but it has already given interesting results in historical study. For instance, a simple example can be found in the history of such words as *day* and *blow*. The great majority of historical students, Karl Luick, Eilert Ekwall, Wilhelm Viëtor, Wilhelm Horn, H. C. Wyld, R. E. Zachrisson, and Helge K. A. Kökeritz, with only Jespersen and Joseph Wright dissenting, have assumed that the Middle English diphthongs of these words were simplified to long simple vowels in Early Modern English, and were then again diphthongized in the nineteenth century. A frame which analyzes all long vowels as diphthongs, even when they occur in Early Modern English or Middle English, obviously avoids such contradictory views of sound change, with sounds developing in a new direction, and then back again to their starting point.

Structuralism, once worked out on the phonemic level, forced recognition that there were separate and higher levels, in the hierarchy of language symbols. This had of course been stated by Bloomfield, but it was the work of men like Zellig S. Harris, Charles F. Hockett, Trager, and Smith to set up what W. Freeman Twaddell has called the "eme" and the "allo" as general terms applicable in a like fashion to all levels of language. At present Smith and others are working on syntax, setting up taxemes or units of order, which hold considerable promise for a syntax firmly based on phonology and morphology, and free from the mentalism of traditional sentence analysis. Understanding of the levels also gives us interesting pictures of the areas lying between the levels. Between phonemics and morphemics is the area of phonotactics, the sequences of phonemes. Between morpheme and word is the area of morphotactics or the sequences of morphemes. Between the word and phrase (and clause) is logotactics. These areas have not as yet received like amounts of attention. The phonotactics of English has been at least tentatively described in work as yet unpublished. Charles C. Fries' work on English structure is largely in the area of logotactics, and is obviously important.

The final area in which one could at least hope for advance of the sort previously described is that of the relation of language to other cultural phenomena. This is a field, however, in which we must report promise rather than solid achievement. First, the late Benjamin Lee Whorf set up a hypothesis which is still reverberating in linguistic circles. This is the theory held long ago by Karl Wilhelm von Humboldt, that language structure influences both nonlinguistic activity and the individual's view of reality. It is being actively discussed, and must at present be labeled unproved. Many of Whorf's examples, such as that Hopi uses ordinal numbers—first, second, third, etc.—to count days, and that this suggests that the Hopi think of days as reappearances of the same entity, rather than separate entities, have recently been shown to be rather hasty. Thus it has been argued that if Englishmen refer to George the first, the second, and so on, Whorf's seasoning would force us to the conclusion that they think of these kings as successive reincarnations of the same man. Yet in spite of all objections that can be brought, it is certainly possible that the hypothesis will yet be established, and the effects of language behavior may one day be measured. In an important article, Eric Lenneberg has devised an experimental measure of the effect of language entities on color perception, the first such test which has yet been devised for the Whorf theory. Whorf's theory, also, has recently been discussed at length in a volume published as a supplement to the *American Anthropologist*.

A less controversial, and more programmatic, statement was that of Trager in his pamphlet, *The Field of Linguistics*. The work, like similar analyses by Joos and Bloch, established that there are three levels in language, called by Trager *prelinguistics*, the level of language sounds considered simply as noise, *microlinguistics*, the area of phonemics, morphemics, syntax and so on, and *metalinguistics*, the area beyond, consisting ultimately of the non-linguistic objects and behavior with which language corresponds. If this metalinguistic area can be shown to have structure, and if this structure can be stated, there is at least a hope of stating correspondence between the two structures, and so solving the problem of meaning. There have been some attempts in this direction. Murray Emeneau was able to show correlation between the elaborately structured social status levels of Indochina and the lexical structure of the terms of address. Harry Hoijer brought forward evidence for correlation between the constantly moving, nomadic life of the Navajos and their sentence structure, which says typically, not "Here is a ball," but "Ball moves in round object fashion." Finally Harris in work on discourse analysis which he has only partially published, was able to show that there was correlation between the pattern of sentences in a bit of writing, and the author's set of values and political beliefs.

But correlation between symbol and non-symbol is not the only way in which we can investigate the field which we can broadly call meaning. In our daily living we do not react to speech events in terms of their discrete components, but primarily to their totality. In this sense, it is the total speech act which has meaning and which calls forth a response; lexical descriptions of words and morphemes are only abstractions. It follows that the more we can find out about the accompaniments of words and morphemes, the more we find out about the total meanings of utterances. When linguists were able to formulate the phonemic difference between the patterns of pitch 2-3-1 and 2-3-2 (that is, mid-high-low, and mid-high-mid), they were able to formulate also the difference in response between these sentences:

> *He has a very pleasant personality.*   [2-3-1]
> *He has a very pleasant personality.*   [2-3-2]

The sentence is one I owe to Smith. The difference in response is obvious. The second is a kind of insult.

A second such advance was Smith's analysis of the vocal qualifiers, the sorts of things that can be called *overloudness* and *oversoftness,* to name only two. Each (but not both) can be added to the sentence we have quoted above, and each modifies the response sharply, though I would not attempt to write definitions for such qualifiers. Still another important exploration was that of Ray Birdwhistell into the patterned body movements which accompany speech. This area—kinesics—is not concerned primarily with the formalized gestures, like the crooked finger which means "come here," but with the smiles and nods and eyebrow-lifting which accompany all speech. The importance of these things is a commonplace in our folk speech. We all remember Owen Wister's "When you call me that, *smile!*" All of these things, once thought to be instinctive, can now be shown to be learned behavior which differs from culture to culture. For instance, the kind of giggling which in our society is a form of laughter, in Japan is a reaction of embarrassment and frustration, and when we interpret a Japanese giggle as being laughter, we are seriously mistaken.

All of these accompaniments of speech are important for the study of meaning, not only because they modify it, and thus contribute to it, but also because the way in which language correlates with these metalinguistic activities will probably turn out to be a fairly exact model of the way language correlates with patterned activities farther from symbolism than are vocal qualifiers and kinesics.

Consideration of total meaning brings me naturally to a discussion of literature. One definition of literature—this one belongs to Hockett—is that it is a long idiom. That is to say, an utterance whose total meaning can not be arrived at from a knowledge of its linguistic components. The investigation of literature has, then, for one of its principal tasks, though not of course its only task, the identification of the metalinguistic components of literature which are peculiar to it, and which contribute to its total meaning in a way similar to the contribution of a smile to the total meaning of a non-literary utterance. For lyric poetry at least, some of these components can be pointed to, and some conclusions drawn. It is a commonplace that lyric poetry is distinguished by meter and rhyme, and it is equally commonplace to say that meter and rhyme are parts of the poetic structure, not of the underlying linguistic structure. What is not quite so commonplace is to point out that both meter and rhyme have analogues in the entities of language. English meter is composed of stress patterns, similar to the stress patterns of speech, but differing from them. Verse stress has only two levels, a strong and a weak, while speech has four. As a result of this reduction, the middle grades of speech stress vary in verse, being either poetic strongs or weaks according to whether they are surrounded by stresses weaker or stronger than themselves. The verse patterns are also longer than those of speech. They are a sort of long stress morph, imposed on the stress morphemes of speech, and, ideally at least, not in conflict with them. The various verse patterns distinguish the various types of verse, in much the same way that the pattern tertiary-primary distinguishes the verb *hòok úp,* from the noun *hóok-ùp,* with primary-tertiary. The metalinguistic stress morphs of poetry are again like stress morphemes of speech in that both have many allomorphs, since, in both, the number and position of weak syllables vary. The speech analogue for rhyme can be found in the process that Bloomfield called selection. A typical example of selection is that a third person sigular subject selects a third person singular ending in the accompanying verb. In poetry the occurrence of *June* in the tenth syllable selects the occurrence of *moon* in the twentieth. More exactly, a sequence /-uwn/ selects recurrence at statable intervals.

These processes are not in themselves meaningful, any more than overloudness is meaningful. They do, however, contribute to the total esthetic impression, which is the meaning of the poem. They are metalinguistic elaborations of speech, having the peculiarity of being very like normal speech processes. They have a further peculiarity, in which they are different from speech entities. I have defined rhyme and meter as being metalinguistic entities which are on the same level as morphemes in speech. Morphemes, however, always form parts of larger structures which are meaningful, and to which the meaning of morphemes directly contributes. With the poetic morphs, on the other hand, there are no such larger entities of which they form a part, and to arrive at the larger poetic entities one must return to the normal language content of the poem, which is then elaborated afresh in a different way. There is some parallel in the way other metalinguistic structures act. Vocal qualifiers are elaborations of speech, which contribute to its total meaning, but they are not parts of larger metalinguistic structures; that is, there are vocal qualifier morphs, but no vocal qualifier words and phrases. The fact that verse stress morphs do not form larger wholes comparable to words and phrases, is a theoretical reason why the perennial attempt to say that certain kinds of meter are appropriate to certain kinds of poetic discourse is one which seems likely always to be unsuccessful.

I am extremely hesitant to dogmatize at this point, but such work as I have lately been doing in the analysis of poetry leads me to hazard the guess that in lyric poetry words, phrases, and sentences are typically cast into statements of four basic shapes (there may, of course, be others):

1. Equations. Two things are stated to be the same. "Beauty is Truth, Truth Beauty."

2. Analogies. A is to B, as C is to D. *The Fall of the House of Usher* speaks of "vacant eye-like windows." Eyes are to face as windows are to house.

3. Sums. Something plus something else gives something new.

> Stone walls do not a prison make
> Nor iron bars a cage:
> Minds innocent and quiet take
> That for an hermitage.

That is, stone walls, plus iron bars, plus quiet mind, become hermitage.

4. Affects. Something does something, usually to something else. "Jennie kissed me."

In these terms, the forms of Blake's little poem *London* can be given as, first, three affects:

> I wander through each
>   charter'd street   [affect 1]
> Near where the charter'd Thames
>   does flow
> And mark in every face
>   I meet   [affect 2]
> Marks of weakness, marks
>   of woe.

> In every cry of
>   every Man
> In every Infant's cry
>   of fear
> In every voice, in every
>   ban
> The mind-forg'd manacles
>   I hear.   [affect 3]

These again are followed by three powerful analogies: as chimney sweeper is to church, so soldier is to palace, and so harlot is to home.

> How the chimney-sweeper's
>   cry
> Every black'ning Church
>   appalls:
> And the hapless soldier's
>   sigh
> Runs in blood down Palace
>   walls.
> But most through midnight streets
>   I hear
> How the youthful Harlot's
>   curse
> Blasts the new born infant's
>   tear
> And blights with plagues the marriage
>   hearse.

I do not wish to press this sort of analysis further at present, but one of the most interesting implications (for me at least) is that just as these forms overlap, and contain other forms—for instance, "mind-forg'd manacles" is an analogy contained in a sentence in affect form—so these poetic components give Empson-like ambiguities and new meanings as one pursues them farther out into the metalinguistic and metaliterary sphere. Again these components give the total content-pattern of the poem, and other things being equal, the more symmetrical the arrangement, the more effective the poem. Thus here it is primarily the symmetry between the successive analogies which justifies the mixed metaphor of a sigh which runs in blood. These components which thus build up the content pattern, are therefore apparently on the linguistic level of such main sentence components as subject, predicator, and complement, which taken together give the pattern of the sentence.

Investigation of this type is certainly in its infancy, and you may not think it is very promising. Yet since literature is the use of language most characterized by special structural characteristics of its own, it promises a way of investigating structure which should be extremely repaying for linguistics. At the same time we can say that linguistics, which has been amply rewarding in the investigation of other types of utterance, holds some hope of illuminating the area of language in which man's values are most deeply embedded, the literature which has been the constant creation, companion, and model of his spirit.

Part II

LINGUISTICS TODAY

INTRODUCTION

STRICTLY SPEAKING, the first article in this Part, that by the late Benjamin Lee Whorf, is not aimed at English language study, but, as Hill hints (p. 18), Whorf's daring theories of language and nonlanguage cultural relationships are already affecting English linguistic research and even the preparation of materials for freshman courses in communication. Controversial to many, who either reject his thesis out of hand or accept it in part as resting upon overstatements, this brilliant student of Sapir has certainly provoked wide interest in the question of the dependence of the individual upon his own language for his comprehension of the world around him. The first full-scale attempt to determine correlations between language structure and the structure of other human activity is that of Kenneth L. Pike, *Language: In Relation to a Unified Theory of the Structure of Human Behavior,* Summer Institute of Linguistics, Glendale, California, Part I (1954), Part II (1955).

Since this relationship has been brought to classroom attention recently through the use of one of the Ways of Mankind recordings, *A Word in Your Ear,* perhaps it should be said that a miscomprehending attack by Ernst Pulgram ("Language and National Character," *Quarterly Journal of Speech,* 40.393–400, 1954) was answered by the speaker himself, Walter Goldschmidt, in "Language and Culture: A Reply," *Quarterly Journal of Speech,* 41.279–283 (1955).

Although a passing reference to Charles Carpenter Fries appears in Hill's article, actually Fries's contributions to the study of English are better known and probably more influential among American teachers of English than are those of any other scholar. Following his earlier quantitative study of usage, *American English Grammar* (Appleton-Century-Crofts, 1940), his *Structure of English* (Harcourt, Brace, 1952) appeared as the first published structural analysis of Modern English syntax. Dykema here offers a brief description of Fries's analysis, without seeking such a minute criticism as that of Sledd.

It will be much less difficult to read Sledd's review, however, if the student first digests Francis's introductory article, orginally prepared as a talk to a businessmen's group, and then goes on to the series of three articles by Faust. Faust's purpose is to explain linguistic principles to nonlinguistically-trained freshman English teachers, but he does not go into a discussion of syntax, the area studied by Fries.

Sledd with dispassionate care offers what is probably the most enlightened critical review of Fries's *Structure,* concluding that, although the two proceed from somewhat different premises, this study and the Smith-Trager *Outline of English Structure* so effectively complement each other that together they constitute the *unum necessarium* for the student of present-day English. It is the *Outline* that Faust drew upon for his explanations; a review of it by Whitehall appears in Part VII.

One deprecatory criticism which Sledd and others make is that Fries analyzes in terms of the written language (even though his corpus of material is recorded conversation) and resorts to oral phenomena such as stress and intonation only to resolve ambiguities. How intonation alteration can materially change the meaning of an utterance is the point of the note by Bolinger. Dykema, also dealing with the spoken language, insists that grammatical analysis itself would produce quite different results if writing and speaking are studied separately, hence any grammatical statement should be accompanied by indication of its reference to either speech or to writing.

A present frontier in linguistic research is that where structural analysis touches upon lexical meaning. Partly in reaction to the traditional mentalistic approach to language study and to the meaning-oriented analysis of the medieval grammarians, but largely because of their insistence of rigorous objective data as alone consistent with scientific method, linguists have sought to produce results in terms of contrasting features of form and arrangement. This deliberate abstention from dealing with lexical meaning —which is what "language" chiefly seems to suggest to the layman—has given rise to some misapprehension of the linguist's real position. Fries here defines that position vis-à-vis sound and unsound uses of meaning in linguistic analysis, making clear that the linguist has no business employing meaning itself as a basis for classification of language materials.

Following Fries, three writers offer illustrations of recent applications of structural analysis in solving specific syntactic problems where meaning is involved. These three articles also serve to suggest what a student himself might do on a smaller scale to acquire inductively an appreciation of these or similar problems. Francis finds that one ambiguous construction in English cannot be ultimately resolved by structural analysis but must be explained rather upon the basis that it is statistically more likely that a word with a certain meaning will occur with certain other words than not. Marchand deals with the difficult question of compounds in terms of stress as the feature which distinguishes a mere syntactic group such as *college president* from a true compound like *opera director*, although he admits the possibility of then classifying compounds according to notional or functional criterions. (The student might well discover for himself how many linguistic compounds he can find in a given passage and then relate his discoveries to the number which might be found if typographical features alone are used as the basis for determination.) Anthony's recent dissertation on the verb-*up* combination—that which Fries in his *Structure* said was too involved for consideration there—here offers a starting-point for an investigation of other word clusters, with implications similar to the conclusion of Francis, namely, that probability of occurrence is sometimes the only method of resolving ambiguity. Their agreement upon this particular limit of structural analysis is a recognition of the need to keep analysis upon different levels as one proceeds from morphemics to syntax and to discourse as a whole.

Because language—principally in the areas of semantics and grammatical usage—has wide popular interest, a good market has existed for some time for popularizations of language information. Buell's review of one such popularization evidences the need for student and teacher to be wary of the information (or misinformation) they contain. Such books as Pei's, as well as the earlier *Loom of Language* by Frederick Bodmer and *Mark My Words* by John B. Opdycke make even more difficult the job of the teacher who is trying to inculcate sound attitudes toward language in his students. Bodmer's book was scathingly indicated by Leonard Bloomfield in *American Speech* in October, 1944, and Opdycke's adversely reviewed by Karl W. Dykema in *American Speech* in February, 1950.

For the student who would like to go on from these articles to a really comprehensive description of the current status of linguistic studies in the United States there is no single source better than John B. Carroll's *The Study of Language* (Harvard University Press, 1953).

Science and Linguistics*

NOTIONS ABOUT TALKING AND THINKING, WHICH COMPOSE A SYSTEM
OF NATURAL LOGIC, GO WRONG IN TWO WAYS; HOW WORDS
AND CUSTOMS AFFECT REASONING

BENJAMIN LEE WHORF

EVERY NORMAL PERSON in the world, past infancy in years, can and does talk. By virtue of that fact, every person—civilized or uncivilized—carries through life certain naive but deeply rooted ideas about talking and its relation to thinking. Because of their firm connection with speech habits that have become unconscious and automatic, these notions tend to be rather intolerant of opposition. They are by no means entirely personal and haphazard; their basis is definitely systematic, so that we are justified in calling them a system of natural logic—a term that seems to me preferable to the term common sense, often used for the same thing.

According to natural logic, the fact that every person has talked fluently since infancy makes every man his own authority on the process by which he formulates and communicates. He has merely to consult a common substratum of logic or reason which he and everyone else are supposed to possess. Natural logic says that talking is merely an incidental process concerned strictly with communication, not with formulation of ideas. Talking, or the use of language, is supposed only to "express" what is essentially already formulated nonlinguistically. Formulation is an independent process, called thought or thinking, and is supposed to be largely indifferent to the nature of particular languages. Languages have grammars, which are assumed to be merely norms of conventional and social correctness, but the use of language is supposed to be guided not so much by them as by correct, rational, or intelligent *thinking*.

Thought, in this view, does not depend on grammar but on laws of logic or reason which are supposed to be the same for all observers of the universe—to represent a rationale in the universe that can be "found" independently by all intelligent observers, whether they speak Chinese or Choctaw. In our own culture, the formulations of mathematics and of formal logic have acquired the reputation of dealing with this order of

* First published in *The Technology Review*, 42.229–231, 247–248 (April, 1940), this article is here reprinted by permission from a collection of Whorf's writings titled *Language, Thought, and Reality* (copyright © 1956 by Massachusetts Institute of Technology and published jointly by The Technology Press and John Wiley & Sons, Inc.)

things, i.e., with the realm and laws of pure thought. Natural logic holds that different languages are essentially parallel methods for expressing this one-and-the-same rationale of thought and, hence, differ really in but minor ways which may seem important only because they are seen at close range. It holds that mathematics, symbolic logic, philosophy, and so on, are systems contrasted with language which deal directly with this realm of thought, not that they are themselves specialized extensions of language. The attitude of natural logic is well shown in an old quip about a German grammarian who devoted his whole life to the study of the dative case. From the point of view of natural logic, the dative case and grammar in general are an extremely minor issue. A different attitude is said to have been held by the ancient Arabians: Two princes, so the story goes, quarreled over the honor of putting on the shoes of the most learned grammarian of the realm; whereupon their father, the caliph, is said to have remarked that it was the glory of his kingdom that great grammarians were honored even above kings.

The familiar saying that the exception proves the rule contains a good deal of wisdom, though from the standpoint of formal logic it became an absurdity as soon as "prove" no longer meant "put on trial." The old saw began to be profound psychology from the time it ceased to have standing in logic. What it might well suggest to us today is that if a rule has absolutely no exceptions, it is not recognized as a rule or as anything else; it is then part of the background of experience of which we tend to remain unconscious. Never having experienced anything in contrast to it, we cannot isolate it and formulate it as a rule until we so enlarge our experience and expand our base of reference that we encounter an interruption of its regularity. The situation is somewhat analogous to that of not missing the water till the well runs dry, or not realizing that we need air till we are choking.

For instance, if a race of people had the physiological defect of being able to see only the color blue, they would hardly be able to formulate the rule that they saw only blue. The term blue would convey no meaning to them, their language would lack color terms, and their words denoting their various sensations of blue would answer to, and translate, our words light, dark, white, black, and so on, not our word blue. In order to formulate the rule or norm of seeing only blue, they would need exceptional moments in which they saw other colors. The phenomenon of gravitation forms a rule without exceptions; needless to say, the untutored person is utterly unaware of any law of gravitation, for it would never enter his head to conceive of a universe in which bodies behaved otherwise than they do at the earth's surface. Like the color blue with our hypothetical race, the law of gravitation is a part of the untutored individual's background, not something he isolates from that background. The law could not be formulated until bodies that always fell were seen in terms of a wider astronomical world in which bodies moved in orbits or went this way and that.

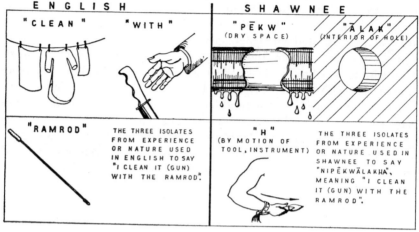

del. J. Martin Rosse

Fig. 1

Languages dissect nature differently. The different isolates of meaning (thoughts) used by English and Shawnee in reporting the same experience, that of cleaning a gun by running the ramrod through it. The pronouns "I" and "it" are not shown by symbols, as they have the same meaning in each case. In Shawnee "ni-" equals "I"; "-a" equals "it."

Similarly, whenever we turn our heads, the image of the scene passes across our retinas exactly as it would if the scene turned around us. But this effect is background, and we do not recognize it; we do not see a room turn around us but are conscious only of having turned our heads in a stationary room. If we observe critically while turning the head or eyes quickly, we shall see, no motion it is true, yet a blurring of the scene between two clear views. Normally we are quite unconscious of this continual blurring but seem to be looking about in an unblurred world. Whenever we walk past a tree or house, its image on the retina changes just as if the tree or house were turning on an axis; yet we do not see trees or houses turn as we travel about at ordinary speeds. Sometimes ill-fitting glasses will reveal queer movements in the scene as we look about, but normally we do not see the relative motion of the environmnt when we move; our psychic make-up is somehow adjusted to disregard whole realms of phenomena that are so all-pervasive as to be irrelevant to our daily lives and needs.

Natural logic contains two fallacies: First, it does not see that the phenomena of a language are to its own speakers largely of a background character and so are outside the critical consciousness and control of the speaker who is expounding natural logic. Hence, when anyone, as a natural logician, is talking about reason, logic, and the laws of correct thinking, he is apt to be simply marching in step with purely grammatical facts that have somewhat of a background character in his own language or family of languages but are by no means universal in all languages and in no sense a common substratum of reason. Second, natural logic confuses agreement about subject matter, attained through use of language, with knowledge of the linguistic process by which agreement is attained, i.e., with the province of the despised (and to its notion superfluous) grammarian. Two fluent speakers, of English let us say, quickly reach a point of assent about the subject matter of this speech; they agree about what their language refers to. One of them, A, can give directions that will be carried out by the other, B, to A's complete satisfaction. Because they thus understand each other so perfectly, A and B, as natural logicians, suppose they must of course know how it is all done. They think, e.g., that it is simply a matter of choosing words to express thoughts. If you ask A to explain how he got B's agreement so readily, he will simply repeat to you, with more or less elaboration or abbreviation, what he said to B. He has no notion of the process involved. The amazingly complex system of linguistic patterns and classifications which A and B must have in common before they can adjust to each other at all, is all background to A and B.

These background phenomena are the province of the grammarian— or of the linguist, to give him his more modern name as a scientist. The word linguist in common, and especially newspaper, parlance means something entirely different, namely, a person who can quickly attain agreement about subject matter with different people speaking a number of different languages. Such a person is better termed a polyglot or a multilingual. Scientific linguists have long understood that ability to speak a language fluently does not necessarily confer a linguistic knowledge of it, i.e., understanding of its background phenomena and its systematic processes and structure, any more than ability to play a good game of billiards confers or requires any knowledge of the laws of mechanics that operate upon the billiard table.

The situation here is not unlike that in any other field of science. All real scientists have their eyes primarily on background phenomena that cut very little ice, as such, in our daily lives; and yet their studies have a way of bringing out a close relation between these unsuspected realms of fact and such decidedly foreground activities as transporting goods, preparing food, treating the sick, or growing potatoes, which in time may become very much modified simply because of pure scientific investigation in no way concerned with these brute matters themselves. Linguistics is in quite similar case; the background phenomena with which it deals are involved in all our foreground activities of talking and of reaching agreement, in all reasoning and arguing of cases, in all law, arbitration, conciliation, contracts, treaties, public opinion, weighing of scientific theories, formulation of scientific results. Whenever agreement or assent is arrived at in human affairs, and whether or not mathematics or other specialized symbolisms are made part of the procedure, *this agreement is reached by linguistic processes, or else it is not reached.*

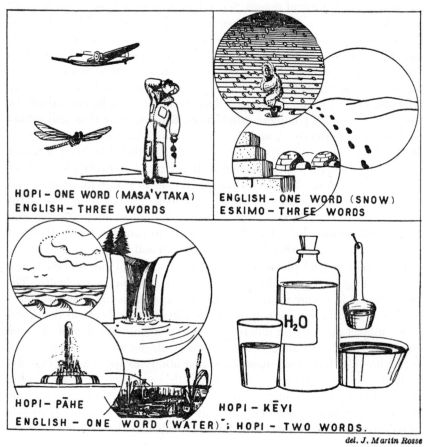

HOPI – ONE WORD (MASA'YTAKA)
ENGLISH – THREE WORDS

ENGLISH – ONE WORD (SNOW)
ESKIMO – THREE WORDS

HOPI – PĀHE
ENGLISH – ONE WORD (WATER); HOPI – TWO WORDS.

HOPI – KĒYI

del. J. Martin Rosse

Fig. 2

Languages classify items of experience differently. The class corresponding to one word and one thought in language A may be regarded by language B as two or more classes corresponding to two or more words and thoughts.

As we have seen, an overt knowledge of the linguistic processes by which agreement is attained is not necessary to reaching some sort of agreement, but it is certainly no bar thereto; the more complicated and difficult the matter, the more such knowledge is a distinct aid, till the point may be reached—I suspect the modern world has about arrived at it—when the knowledge becomes not only an aid but a necessity. The situation may be likened to that of navigation. Every boat that sails is in the lap of planetary forces; yet a boy can pilot his small craft around a harbor without benefit of geography, astronomy, mathematics, or international politics. To the captain of an ocean liner, however, some knowledge of all these subjects is essential.

When linguists became able to examine critically and scientifically a large number of languages of widely different patterns, their base of reference was expanded; they experienced an interruption of phenomena hitherto held universal, and a whole new order of significances came into their ken. It was found that the background linguistic system (in other words, the grammar) of each language is not merely a reproducing instrument for voicing ideas but rather is itself the shaper of ideas, the program and guide for the individual's mental activity, for his analysis of impressions, for his synthesis of his mental stock in trade. Formulation of ideas is not an independent process, strictly rational in the old sense, but is part of a particular grammar and differs, from slightly to greatly, as between different grammars. We dissect nature along lines laid down by our native languages. The categories and types that we isolate from the world of phenomena we do not find there because they stare every observer in the face; on the contrary, the world is presented in a kaleidoscopic flux of impressions which has to be organized by our minds—and this means largely by the linguistic systems in our minds. We cut nature up, organize it into concepts, and ascribe significances as we do, largely because we are parties to an agreement to organize it in this way—an agreement that holds throughout our speech community and is codified in the patterns of our language. The agreement is, of course, an implicit and unstated one, *but its terms are absolutely obligatory;* we cannot talk at all except by subscribing to the organization and classification of data which the agreement decrees.

This fact is very significant for modern science, for it means that no individual is free to describe nature with absolute impartiality but is constrained to certain modes of interpretation even while he thinks himself most free. The person most nearly free in such respects would be a linguist familiar with very many widely different linguistic systems. As yet no linguist even is in any such position. We are thus introduced to a new principle of relativity, which holds that all observers are not led by the same physical evidence to the same picture of the universe, unless their linguistic backgrounds are similar, or can in some way be calibrated.

This rather startling conclusion is not so apparent if we compare only our modern European languages, with perhaps Latin and Greek thrown in for good measure. Among these tongues there is a unanimity of major pattern which at first seems to bear out natural logic. But this unanimity exists only because these tongues are all Indo-European dialects cut to the same basic plan, being historically transmitted from what was long ago one speech community; because the modern dialects have long shared in building up a common culture; and because much of this culture, on the more intellectual side, is derived from the linguistic backgrounds of Latin and Greek. Thus this group of languages satisfies the special case of the clause beginning "unless" in the statement of the linguistic relativity principle at the end of the preceding paragraph. From this condition follows the unanimity of description of the world in the community of modern scientists. But it must be emphasized that "all modern Indo-European-speaking observers" is not the same thing as "all observers." That modern Chinese or Turkish scientists describe the world in the same terms as Western scientists means, of course, only that they have taken over bodily the entire Western system of rationalizations, not that they have corroborated that system from their native posts of observation.

When Semitic, Chinese, Tibetan, or African languages are contrasted with our own, the divergence in analysis of the world becomes more apparent; and when we bring in the native languages of the Americas, where speech communities for many millenniums have gone their ways independently of each other and of the Old World, the fact that languages dissect nature in many different ways becomes patent. The relativity of all conceptual systems, ours included, and their dependence upon language stand revealed. That American Indians speaking only their native tongues are never called upon to act as scientific observers is in no wise to the point. To exclude the evidence which their languages offer as to what the human mind can do is like expecting botanists to study nothing but food plants and hothouse roses and then tell us what the plant world is like!

Let us consider a few examples. In English we divide most of our words into two classes, which have different grammatical and logical properties. Class 1 we call nouns, e.g., "house," "man"; Class 2, verbs, e.g., "hit," "run." Many words of one class can act secondarily as of the other class, e.g., "a hit," "a run," or "to man" the boat, but on the primary level the division between the classes is absolute. Our language thus gives us a bipolar division of nature. But nature herself is not thus polarized. If it be said that strike, turn, run, are verbs because they denote temporary or short-lasting events, i.e., actions, why then is fist a noun? It also is a temporary event. Why are lightning, spark, wave, eddy, pulsation, flame, storm, phase, cycle, spasm, noise, emotion, nouns? They are temporary events. If man and house are nouns because they are long-lasting and stable events, i.e., things, what then are keep, adhere, extend, project, continue, persist, grow, dwell, and so on, doing among the verbs? If it be objected that possess, adhere, are verbs because they are stable relationships rather than stable percepts, why then should equilibrium, pressure, current, peace, group, nation, society, tribe, sister, or any kinship term, be among the nouns? It will be found that an "event" to *us* means "what our language classes as a verb" or something analogized therefrom. And it will be found that it is not possible to define event, thing, object, relationship, and so on, from nature, but that to define them always involves a circuitous return to the grammatical categories of the definer's language.

In the Hopi language, lightning, wave, flame, meteor, puff of smoke, pulsation, are verbs—events of necessarily brief duration cannot be anything but verbs. Cloud and storm are at about the lower limit of duration for nouns. Hopi, you see, actually has a classification of events (or linguistic isolates) by duration type, something strange to our modes of thought. On the other hand, in Nootka, a language of Vancouver Island, all words seem to us to be verbs, but really there are no Classes 1 and 2; we have, as it were, a monistic view of nature that gives us only one class of word for all kinds of events. "A house occurs" or "it houses" is the way of saying "house," exactly like "a flame occurs" or "it burns." These terms seem to us like verbs because they are inflected for durational and temporal nuances, so that the suffixes of the word for house event make it mean long-lasting house, temporary house, future house, house that used to be, what started out to be a house, and so on.

Hopi has a noun that covers every thing or being that flies, with the exception of birds, which class is denoted by another noun. The former noun may be said to denote the class (FC–B)—flying class minus bird. The Hopi actually call insect, airplane, and aviator all by the same word, and feel no difficulty about it. The situation, of course, decides any possible confusion among very disparate members of a broad linguistic class, such as this class (FC–B). This class seems to us too large and inclusive, but so would our class "snow" to an Eskimo. We have the same word for falling snow, snow on the ground, snow packed hard like ice, slushy snow, wind-driven flying snow—whatever the situation may be. To an Eskimo, this all-inclusive word would be almost unthinkable; he would say that falling snow, slushy snow, and so on, are sensuously and operationally different, different things to contend with; he uses different words for them and for other kinds of snow. The Aztecs go even farther than we in the opposite direction, with cold, ice, and snow all represented by the same basic word with different terminations; ice is the noun form; cold, the adjectival form; and for snow, "ice mist."

What surprises most is to find that various grand generalizations of the Western world, such as time, velocity, and matter, are not essential to the construction of a consistent picture of the universe. The psychic experiences that we class under these headings are, of course, not destroyed; rather, categories derived from other kinds of experiences take over the rulership of the cosmology and seem to function just as well. Hopi may be called a timeless language. It recognizes psychological time, which is much like Bergson's "duration," but this "time" is quite unlike the mathematical time, T, used by our physicists. Among the peculiar properties of Hopi time are that it varies with each observer, does not permit of simultaneity, and has zero dimensions, i.e., it cannot be given a number greater than one. The

<table>
OBJECTIVE FIELD	SPEAKER (SENDER)	HEARER (RECEIVER)	HANDLING OF TOPIC RUNNING OF THIRD PERSON
SITUATION I a.			ENGLISH..."HE IS RUNNING". HOPI ... "WARI". (RUNNING, STATEMENT OF FACT.)
SITUATION I b. OBJECTIVE FIELD BLANK DEVOID OF RUNNING			ENGLISH..."HE RAN". HOPI ... "WARI". (RUNNING, STATEMENT OF FACT.)
SITUATION 2.			ENGLISH HE IS RUNNING HOPI ..."WARI". (RUNNING, STATEMENT OF FACT)
SITUATION 3. OBJECTIVE FIELD BLANK			ENGLISH..."HE RAN". HOPI ... "ERA WARI". (RUNNING, STATEMENT OF FACT FROM MEMORY)
SITUATION 4. OBJECTIVE FIELD BLANK			ENGLISH..."HE WILL RUN". HOPI ... "WARIKNI", (RUNNING, STATEMENT OF EXPECTATION.)
SITUATION 5. OBJECTIVE FIELD BLANK			ENGLISH..."HE RUNS". (E.G. ON THE TRACK TEAM.) HOPI ..."WARIKNGWE". (RUNNING, STATEMENT OF LAW.)
</table>

del. J. Martin Rosse

Fig. 3

Contrast between a "temporal" language (English) and a "timeless" language (Hopi). What are to English differences of time are to Hopi differences in the kind of validity.

Hopi do not say, "I stayed five days," but "I left on the fifth day." A word referring to this kind of time, like the word day, can have no plural. The puzzle picture in Figure 3 will give mental exercise to anyone who would like to figure out how the Hopi verb gets along without tenses. Actually, the only practical use of our tenses, in one-verb sentences, is to distinguish among five typical situations, which are symbolized in the picture. The timeless Hopi verb does not distinguish between the present, past, and future of the event itself but must always indicate what type of validity the *speaker* intends the statement to have: (a) report of an event (situations 1, 2, 3 in the picture); (b) expectation of an event (situation 4); (c) generalization or law about events (situation 5). Situation 1, where the speaker and listener are in contact with the same objective field, is divided by our language into the two conditions, 1a and 1b, which it calls present and past, respectively. This division is unnecessary for a language which assures one that the statement is a report.

Hopi grammar, by means of its forms called aspects and modes, also makes it easy to distinguish between momentary, continued, and repeated occurrences, and to indicate the actual sequence of reported events. Thus the universe can be described without recourse to a concept of dimensional time. How would a physics constructed along these lines work, with no T (time) in its equations? Perfectly, as far as I can see, though of course it would require different ideology and perhaps different mathematics. Of course V (velocity) would have to go too. The Hopi language has no word really equivalent to our "speed" or "rapid." What translates these terms is usually a word meaning intense or very, accompanying any verb of motion. Here is a clew to the nature of our new physics. We may have to introduce a new term I, intensity. Every thing and event will have an I, whether we regard the thing or event as moving or as just enduring or being. Perhaps the I of an electric charge will turn out to be its voltage, or potential. We shall use clocks to measure some intensities, or, rather, some *relative* intensities, for the absolute intensity of anything will be meaningless. Our old friend acceleration will still be there but doubtless under a new name. We shall perhaps call it V, meaning not velocity but variation. Perhaps all growths and accumulations will be regarded as V's. We should not have the concept of rate in the temporal sense, since, like velocity, rate introduces a mathematical and linguistic time. Of course we know that all measurements are ratios, but the measurements of intensities made by comparison with the standard intensity of a clock or a planet we do not treat as ratios, any more than we so treat a distance made by comparison with a yardstick.

A scientist from another culture that used time and velocity would have great difficulty in getting us to understand these concepts. We should talk about the intensity of a chemical reaction; he would speak of its velocity or its rate, which words we should at first think were simply words for intensity in his language. Likewise, he at first would think that intensity was simply our own word for velocity. At first we should agree, later we should begin to disagree, and it might dawn upon both sides that different systems of rationalization were being used. He would find it very hard to make us understand what he really meant by velocity of a chemical reaction. We should have no words that would fit. He would try to explain it by likening it to a running horse, to the difference between a good horse and a lazy horse. We should try to show him, with a superior laugh, that his analogy also was a matter of different intensities, aside from which there was little similarity between a horse and a chemical reaction in a beaker. We should point out that a running horse is moving relative to the ground, whereas the material in the beaker is at rest.

One significant contribution to science from the linguistic point of view may be the greater development of our sense of perspective. We shall no longer be able to see a few recent dialects of the Indo-European family, and the rationalizing techniques elaborated from their patterns, as the apex of the evolution of the human mind; nor their present wide spread as due to any survival from fitness or to anything but a few events of history —events that could be called fortunate only from the parochial point of view of the favored parties. They, and our own thought processes with them, can no longer be envisioned as spanning the gamut of reason and knowledge but only as one constellation in a galactic expanse. A fair realization of the incredible degree of diversity of linguistic system that ranges over the globe leaves one with an inescapable feeling that the human spirit is inconceivably old; that the few thousand years of history covered by our written records are no more than the thickness of a pencil mark on the scale that measures our past experience on this planet; that the events of these recent millenniums spell nothing in any evolutionary wise, that the race has taken no sudden spurt, achieved no commanding synthesis during recent millenniums, but has only played a little with a few of the linguistic formulations and views of nature bequeathed from an inexpressibly longer past. Yet neither this feeling nor the sense of precarious dependence of all we know upon linguistic tools which themselves are largely unknown need be discouraging to science but should, rather, foster that humility which accompanies the true scientific spirit, and thus forbid that arrogance of the mind which hinders real scientific curiosity and detachment.

Progress in Grammar*

Karl Dykema

Charles Carpenter Fries in *The Structure of English*[1] has made significant progress in English grammar, though the term "grammar" is probably intentionally avoided in the title because it has become so ambiguous.

Grammar illustrates one of those etymons which in most European languages still show their Greek form. But for *Grammar* we have not only preserved much of the Greek spelling but also much of the Greek descriptive system that the word came to denote. Our modern Western culture is grammar-conscious, and the present complex of concepts for which *gram-*

* Reprinted by permission from *College English,* 14.93–100 (November, 1952).
[1] New York: Harcourt, Brace & Co., 1952. Pp. x+304.

mar stands in the minds of Western people had its origin more than two thousand years ago in ancient Greek culture.

If grammar means different things to different people today, it is hardly surprising because it was conceived in varying ways within a few centuries of its birth. Grammatical terminology had its origin in the philosophical speculations of Greek thinkers; at first it had neither normative nor pedagogical implications or applications. Gradually, however, linguistic speculation became a systematic field, and grammar—in our sense—became a part of the curriculum of Hellenic Greece and Rome.

It is not clear just where and when in the Western cultural tradition grammar became primarily a means of learning the correct use of a language—at first usually a foreign one—and ceased to be a part of logic and hence of philosophy. The break, of course, was never complete, and the Middle Ages continued the idea of grammatical concepts as universals. But certainly in the period since ancient times grammar has generally come to be thought of as the means of achieving correctness in language. And since Western culture accepts correctness in language as vastly important, Western culture is preoccupied with grammar.

But the ancient difference in objective lingers on. There are grammarians who are primarily concerned with the essential structure of a language, and there are grammarians who are primarily concerned with the correct use of a language. Both kinds, to be sure, are likely to give some attention to the primary concern of the other. The latter, the normative grammarian, must get his prescriptive system somewhere, and, though he generally inherits it from an earlier grammarian, he usually makes some attempt to show a relationship between his system and the way people actually do talk. The former, the descriptive grammarian, discovering discrepancies between what he observes and what the prescriptionist teaches, is often exasperated to the point of trying to get his grammar applied to the teaching of correctness.

For many hundreds of years the speculative and descriptive grammarian had no place in Western culture. To the medieval scholar no language except Latin was worth serious attention, and he had inherited authoritative grammars of that language which made further investigation of it unnecessary. Latin and grammar became often synonymous terms; to know one's grammar was to know Latin. By implication, then, Latin grammar was a complete and perfect description of the Latin language itself. And this conviction that a book labeling itself a grammar of a language was a complete and perfect description of that language was carried over to the vernacular languages when grammars of them were devised on the model of classical grammar.

When the nineteenth-century scholars began to examine languages as phenomena, they were confronted with these grammars of the vernacular constructed on the classical model and sometimes as much as two centuries old. Only gradually did they discover the inadequacy of the classical system for describing languages other than Greek. Acquaintance with the works of the ancient grammarians of Sanskrit was a revelation as was also the impossibility of fitting some non-Indo-European languages into the classical system. Still the nineteenth century made relatively few innovations in grammatical description because of the tremendous task of gathering and systematizing historical phonological and morphological material.

The crucial problem in grammar is syntax; that is, the crucial problem in understanding how a language works—and also simply in understanding it—is to grasp the structure of that language. In English, at least, it is apparent that we have two kinds of linguistic units. The first can be quite easily identified and even, by the convenient if arbitrary system of spelling, classified for ready reference in a dictionary. But words as isolated units are insufficient for communication; they must be part of another unit which we have agreed to call a sentence. It is this unit that reveals the essential structure of English.

But what is a sentence? Fries is at some pains to show that careful descriptive grammarians have failed to give a satisfactory definition.[2] He believes that the reason for their failure is their dependence on meaning as a criterion. In the earliest Western grammar extant, that of Dionysius Thrax (b. *ca.* 146 B.C.), the sentence is defined as "a combination of words, either in prose or verse, making complete sense."[3] But the decision as to what complete sense is, is a subjective one and therefore one on which no satisfactory agreement can be reached. Fries determines to reject meaning as a criterion. His book is a description of his methods and procedures for identifying the sentence. It is therefore a formal grammar of English but strictly in the sense of formal as a description of form and structure.

For perhaps two centuries now, English-speaking students have been taught to believe that the classical formal grammars of English give us an accurate description of the structure of our language. In the past twenty years—say, since Leonard's *Current English Usage* (1932)—there has been some doubt as to the accuracy in detail of this formal grammar, and in the practical matter of teaching correctness it has in varying degrees been abandoned in favor of what is now often called the grammar of usage or just usage. But, as Fries points out,[4] an acceptance of usage as the basis for teaching correctness does not necessarily mean the abandonment of faith in the essential adequacy of classical grammar as a description of English. An examination of the more recent college handbooks will verify this assertion. In varying degrees they all accept the conclusions on good

[2] *Ibid.,* pp. 9–19.
[3] "The Grammar of Dionysius Thrax, Translated from the Greek by Thos. Davidson," *Journal of Speculative Philosophy,* VIII (1874), 326–29.
[4] Fries, *op. cit.,* pp. 275–77.

usage of the various studies of the last two decades, particularly Leonard's. But also in varying degrees they give some account of the classical formal grammar of English.

Professor Fries believes that this position is untenable. The rigorously descriptive technique has been applied with devastating effect to individual usage items. Scarcely a handbook any longer argues, for instance, that *It's me* is wrong. The handbook writers have been forced to bow to the overwhelming evidence of the descriptive approach. This has been the easier for them to do because the pedagogical descriptionists have for the most part concerned themselves only with minute aspects of the total structure of the language and have seldom insisted upon the relationship of the particular item to the total structure. The classical formal grammar has therefore been tacitly left unchallenged.

Professor Fries now challenges it. He believes that this same rigorous descriptive approach when applied to the total structure of English will have as devastating an effect as it did with individual usage items. "From the point of view underlying this study, the principles, the procedures, the definitions, of 'formal grammar' are unsound. [It] is, like the Ptolemaic astronomy, falsely oriented . . . [and] . . . cannot be expected to provide any satisfactory insight into the mechanisms of our language or any grasp of the processes by which language functions."[5]

A strong statement, indeed! Yet largely true. But he does seem to forget sometimes how heavily he leans on the thousands of grammarians who are his predecessors. The statements quoted above might suggest that Fries has completely rejected the principles, procedures, and definitions of formal grammar. Not at all. Many of them he finds useful, as far as they go. But they don't go far enough. They are insufficient. His quarrel with classical formal grammar is that it is unsound because falsely oriented. False orientation may result not only from false description but from incomplete description. The trouble with classical formal grammar as a description of English is not so much that it is wrong as that it is incomplete. Worst of all, it is an incomplete description which pretends to completeness, and that is its fatal weakness.

Fries accepts the traditional system to the extent that it applies to the phenomena he finds in English. He finds, for example, that the concept of parts of speech can be applied to four kinds of words. But the traditional means of defining parts of speech are undependable because inconsistent in vacillating between function and form, on the one hand, and meaning, on the other. Fries rejects meaning, finding that on the basis of structural considerations alone four parts of speech emerge. I shall equate these with nouns, verbs, adjectives, and adverbs, though Fries quite rightly insists that there is necessarily no exact correspondence because

[5] *Ibid.*, p. 277.

his definitions do not apply to words except in actual utterances.[6] Similarly
he uses terms such as "subject," "object," "appositive," "modifier," etc.,
in a structural sense which is much more narrowly definable than the
traditional one because he eliminates meaning entirely as an identifying
factor and relies entirely on "contrasting formal arrangements."

Fries begins his quest of the sentence by isolating an *utterance unit:*
"any stretch of speech by one person before which there was silence on his
part and after which there was also silence on his part."[7] He then defines a
sentence as "a single free utterance, minimum or expanded; i.e., that it is
free in the sense that it is not included in any larger structure by means
of any grammatical device."[8] Here is the significant addition which Fries
has made to the classical procedure. Dionysius depends on meaning to
identify his group of words as a sentence; Fries rejects meaning and depends entirely on formal considerations.

Fries's sentence is, then, a word or group of words performing a linguistic function but having no grammatical connection with other linguistically functioning words. Here we find two limitations on the classical procedure. First, he never invents his material, as older grammarians
have been all too prone to do when they wanted a convenient illustration
of a point. In fact, he feels that objectivity can be achieved only by using
recordings of speech which was spoken solely to perform its linguistic
function.[9] Second, the sentence is identified by its having no connections
with other words through formal grammatical devices. The bulk of Fries's
book is devoted to describing the grammatical devices which English
uses to show the relations of words in sentences. "The grammar of a language consists of the devices that signal structural meanings."[10]

Fries's book makes significant progress in English grammar because of
a number of important procedures which he carries through more rigorously and systematically than have others. First, he follows most rigorously the principle so much insisted on by the nineteeth-century linguistic
scholars that the grammatical description of a particular language must be
derived solely from it, not imposed upon it through preconceived grammatical categories derived from another system. This is a simple injunction
but almost impossible to follow because grammarians have always absorbed classical grammar in the course of their regular education and
tend therefore to find examples of the classical grammatical concepts in
the language they are studying. Fries feels that, though he can go so far
as to name four groups of words parts of speech, each individual group
is best labeled by a number rather than noun, verb, adjective, adverb. The

[6] *Ibid.,* p. 140.
[7] *Ibid.,* p. 23.
[8] *Ibid.,* p. 25.
[9] *Ibid.,* p. 3 n.
[10] *Ibid.,* p. 56.

remaining words he refuses even to call parts of speech. Instead he labels them "function words" and classifies them into fifteen subdivisions.

Second, he depends entirely upon living language. The material of his study is mechanical recordings of "some fifty hours of . . . conversations on a great range of topics—conversations in which the participants were entirely unaware that their speech was being recorded."[11] The author believes that this record of 250,000 words of three hundred different speakers[12] supplies a body of material sufficient to permit an analysis which will be an "an *introduction* to the structure of English utterances— not a complete descriptive treatment of all the features of that structure."[13] This use of nonliterary material as the basis for grammatical analysis may at first be disturbing, but, though the literary artist's use of language is that which most impresses us, his use of it must be based on the same foundations as our own, or we could not understand him. The essential structure of a language is to be found therefore in the practice of the ordinary user, preferably in his spontaneous, unedited oral practice. Throughout the history of Western grammatical analysis, the grammarian has found it difficult to get at the essential grammatical structure of the language because he has had to use as his material the consciously contrived written products of the literary artist.[14] Dionysius in his definition of grammar went so far as to exclude by implication the structure of the spoken language: "the usages of the language as generally current among poets and prose writers."[15] Nevertheless, grammarians have recognized the weakness of their dependence both on literary material and on the transcription of the language,[16] but they have not been able to obtain a usable body of spoken language in any sense comparable to the inexhaustible supply of printed material. By using modern recording equipment to provide him with the material, Fries is able to base his study exclusively on spoken English—on a record which faithfully reproduces every characteristic of the original, undistorted by editors or the vagaries and inadequacies of English spelling.

Third, he recognizes grammatical structure only in sentences. For example, in the sentence *The bird flies after flies,* the two *flies* have identical phonetic form and are therefore formally ambiguous as isolated units. To isolate them is therefore to give an incomplete grammatical description of them; only in the sentence can their structural meaning be properly an-

---

11 *Ibid.,* p. 3.

12 *Ibid.,* p. viii.

13 *Ibid.,* p. 3.

14 This problem is discussed in my paper read before English Group XIII of the Modern Language Association in 1948 and published as "The Grammar of Spoken English: Its Relation to What Is Called English Grammar," *American Speech,* XXIV (1949), 43–48.

15 "The Grammar of Dionysius Thrax," *op. cit.*

16 Harold E. Palmer, *A Grammar of Spoken English on a Strictly Phonetic Basis* (Cambridge, 1924), and C. C. Fries, *American English Grammar* (New York, 1940).

alyzed. "Another of the basic assumptions of our approach here to the grammatical analysis of sentences is that the formal signals of structural meanings operate in a system—that is, that the items of form and arrangement have signalling significance only as they are parts of patterns in a structural whole."[17] The temptation to make morphology a separate part of grammatical analysis results, no doubt, from the sets of paradigms so familiar to students of Latin, though even in Latin many of the inflected forms are ambiguous except in structural units. Fries insists that structural devices are significant only in contexts, and he holds rigorously to this principle.

Fourth, he uses evidence which is apparent only to the ear, which would not be indicated in a transcription in ordinary spelling. He points out, for example, that intonation is sometimes a structural signal.[18] In the phrase *a moving van*, the nature of the modification of *van* by *moving* is shown (*a*) by a rising intonation on the first syllable of *moving*, a falling intonation on the second syllable; and (*b*) a rising intonation on *moving* not falling until *van*; (*a*) means a van that does moving, (*b*) means a van in motion.[19] Also occasionally he uses phonetic transcription to make clear structural differences which are apparent to the ear but are not reflected in our spelling. [sɛpərət, sɛpəret] for *separate*.[20]

Fifth, and most important, he rejects meaning as a method of analysis. The simplest way to illustrate the fruitfulness of this approach is to cite his first example, Lewis Carroll's "Jabberwocky." As he points out, since this poem is nonsense, it cannot be analyzed on the basis of its meaning. Yet "any speaker of English will recognize at once the frames in which [the nonsense] words appear."[21] Evidently there is a structural framework which has a grammatical meaning independent of the lexical meanings of the words which are fitted into it; the structural meanings of a sentence plus the lexical meanings of its word units make what Fries calls the total linguistic meaning of the sentence.[22] This is one of the most interesting and revealing chapters in the book and should demolish once and for all the notion that such languages as Latin have far more grammatical resources than does English.

The results of Fries's procedures are many and illuminating. Any proper appreciation of them, however, must be gained from firsthand acquaintance with his book. One of them may perhaps be suggested, since I have already touched upon it more than once. The traditional parts of speech are redefined, always, of course, in a functioning structure. Words are first divided into two groups of extremely unequal numbers: parts

[17] Fries, *Structure*, pp. 59–60.
[18] *Ibid.*, pp. 26–28.
[19] *Ibid.*, p. 221 n.
[20] *Ibid.*, p. 130.
[21] *Ibid.*, p. 70.
[22] *Ibid.*, p. 56.

of speech and function words. The former, for the sake of brevity, may be roughly equated with nouns, verbs, adjectives, and adverbs.[23] The latter, which in his material totaled only 154, are the kind of words which, along with such other structural devices as inflections, intonation, and position, make the grammar of "Jabberwocky" and the rest of English clear.[24] Unlike the parts of speech, which are normally identified by various formal aspects, the function words are memorized by the native speaker of English, and their function is recognized from the word itself.

Much of the approach in this book is not original with Fries, and readers of *Language, Journal of the Linguistic Society* will find much in it that is familiar. Fries himself frankly recognizes his great indebtedness to others.[25] And there are many matters of style, method, and detail to object to. But none of these matters is of much importance compared to the fact that Fries has presented to the "educated lay reader, [including] teachers in our schools and colleges,"[26] a description of the structure of English which that lay reader can read and which will give him a considerably more complete understanding of how English works than any comparable book. To be sure, he'll find the going pretty hard; grammars are never easy reading, and Fries's book is harder than other grammars because the approach is new and the concepts often difficult. But no teacher who pretends to any acquaintance with the grammar of English can honestly ignore this book.

Any systematic study of a phenomenon inevitably raises the question of what is the use of it. About grammar the question has been asked with particular insistence of late. Fries does not shirk answering it. His final chapter, "Practical Applications," suggests six possible uses for his grammar. No criticism of his suggestions can be very meaningful except in the light of a rather full acquaintance with his system. It seems to me that his first suggestion, that his grammar should prove helpful in the teaching of English as a foreign language, is entirely plausible.[27] The other points, however—except the last—are much less persuasive and entirely too reminiscent of the exaggerated claims made for the traditional prescriptive grammar: avoidance of ambiguous constructions,[28] more accurate punctuation,[29] greater variety in sentence structure,[30] and better grasp of the devices for communicating meaning.[31] In fact, he appears to contradict himself because just before presenting these points he has em-

[23] *Ibid.*, pp. 65–86.
[24] *Ibid.*, pp. 87–109.
[25] *Ibid.*, p. ix.
[26] *Ibid.*, p. 7.
[27] *Ibid.*, pp. 279–80.
[28] *Ibid.*, pp. 280–81.
[29] *Ibid.*, pp. 281–90.
[30] *Ibid.*, pp. 290–93.
[31] *Ibid.*, pp. 293–96.

phasized that native speakers of English master the grammar of their language at an early age, unaware of what they are doing, and that they use that grammar unconscious of the varied and complex materials they are utilizing.

His final point occupies only a brief paragraph on the last page. It is so important that I shall quote it in full:

> The chief use and value of a descriptive analysis of the structure of English, however, does not seem to me to lie in any of the five matters just discussed, or in all of them together. I believe fundamentally in *education* as distinct from *training*. Training seems to measure usefulness or value in terms of output or product, with the individual person as the means. His skills are developed so that he can do things. Education, in contrast with training, seems to stress the individual himself as the end, and measures usefulness and value in terms of contribution to the freedom and development of individual personality. From this point of view, I should insist that the chief value of a systematic analysis and description of the signals of structural meaning in English is the insight it can give concerning the way our language works, and, through English, into the nature and functioning of human languages.[32]

This point of view is a reaffirmation of the original Greek philosophical approach to language, a curiosity about the nature of things, a desire for the liberation of the spirit through knowledge, of freedom from the bondage of authoritarianism in language. It is indeed progress in grammar if the author can help the educated lay reader to realize that language is his servant; that it is no tyrant that he must fear and subserve.

Revolution in Grammar*

W. NELSON FRANCIS

I

A LONG OVERDUE revolution is at present taking place in the study of English grammar—a revolution as sweeping in its consequences as the Darwinian revolution in biology. It is the result of the application to English of methods of descriptive analysis originally developed for use with languages of primitive people. To anyone at all interested in language, it is challenging; to those concerned with the teaching of English (including parents), it presents the necessity of radically revising both the substance and the methods of their teaching.

* Reprinted by permission from *Quarterly Journal of Speech*, 40.299–312 (October, 1954).

[32] *Ibid.*, p. 296.

A curious paradox exists in regard to grammar. On the one hand it is felt to be the dullest and driest of academic subjects, fit only for those in whose veins the red blood of life has long since turned to ink. On the other, it is a subject upon which people who would scorn to be professional grammarians hold very dogmatic opinions, which they will defend with considerable emotion. Much of this prejudice stems from the usual sources of prejudice—ignorance and confusion. Even highly educated people seldom have a clear idea of what grammarians do, and there is an unfortunate confusion about the meaning of the term "grammar" itself.

Hence it would be well to begin with definitions. What do people mean when they use the word "grammar"? Actually the word is used to refer to three different things, and much of the emotional thinking about matters grammatical arises from confusion among these different meanings.

The first thing we mean by "grammar" is "the set of formal patterns in which the words of a language are arranged in order to convey larger meanings." It is not necessary that we be able to discuss these patterns self-consciously in order to be able to use them. In fact, all speakers of a language above the age of five or six know how to use its complex forms of organization with considerable skill; in this sense of the word—call it "Grammar 1"—they are thoroughly familiar with its grammar.

The second meaning of "grammar"—call it "Grammar 2"—is "the branch of linguistic science which is concerned with the description, analysis, and formulization of formal language patterns." Just as gravity was in full operation before Newton's apple fell, so grammar in the first sense was in full operation before anyone formulated the first rule that began the history of grammar as a study.

The third sense in which people use the word "grammar" is "linguistic etiquette." This we may call "Grammar 3." The word in this sense is often coupled with a derogatory adjective: we say that the expression "he ain't here" is "bad grammar." What we mean is that such an expression is bad linguistic manners in certain circles. From the point of view of "Grammar 1" it is faultless; it conforms just as completely to the structural patterns of English as does "he isn't here." The trouble with it is like the trouble with Prince Hal in Shakespeare's play—it is "bad," not in itself, but in the company it keeps.

As has already been suggested, much confusion arises from mixing these meanings. One hears a good deal of criticism of teachers of English couched in such terms as "they don't teach grammar any more." Criticism of this sort is based on the wholly unproved assumption that teaching Grammar 2 will increase the student's proficiency in Grammar 1 or improve his manners in Grammar 3. Actually, the form of Grammar 2 which is usually taught is a very inaccurate and misleading analysis of the facts of Grammar 1; and it therefore is of highly questionable value in improving a person's ability to handle the structural patterns of his language. It is hardly reasonable to expect that teaching a person some inaccurate grammatical analysis will either improve the effectiveness of his assertions or teach him what expressions are acceptable to use in a given social context.

These, then, are the three meanings of "grammar": Grammar 1, a form of behavior; Grammar 2, a field of study, a science; and Grammar 3, a branch of etiquette.

II

Grammarians have arrived at some basic principles of their science, three of which are fundamental to this discussion. The first is that a language constitutes a set of behavior patterns common to the members of a given community. It is a part of what the anthropologists call the culture of the community. Actually it has complex and intimate relationships with other phases of culture such as myth and ritual. But for purposes of study it may be dealt with as a separate set of phenomena that can be objectively described and analyzed like any other universe of facts. Specifically, its phenomena can be observed, recorded, classified, and compared; and general laws of their behavior can be made by the same inductive process that is used to produce the "laws" of physics, chemistry, and the other sciences.

A second important principle of linguistic science is that each language or dialect has its own unique system of behavior patterns. Parts of this system may show similarities to parts of the systems of other languages, particularly if those languages are genetically related. But different languages solve the problems of expression and communication in different ways, just as the problems of movement through water are solved in different ways by lobsters, fish, seals, and penguins. A couple of corollaries of this principle are important. The first is that there is no such thing as "universal grammar," or at least if there is, it is so general and abstract as to be of little use. The second corollary is that the grammar of each language must be made up on the basis of a study of that particular language —a study that is free from preconceived notions of what a language should contain and how it should operate. The marine biologist does not criticize the octopus for using jet-propulsion to get him through the water instead of the methods of a self-respecting fish. Neither does the linguistic scientist express alarm or distress when he finds a language that seems to get along quite well without any words that correspond to what in English we call verbs.

A third principle on which linguistic science is based is that the analysis and description of a given language must conform to the requirements laid down for any satisfactory scientific theory. These are (1) simplicity, (2) consistency, (3) completeness, and (4) usefulness for predicting the behavior of phenomena not brought under immediate observation when the theory was formed. Linguistic scientists who have recently turned their attention to English have found that, judged by these criteria, the traditional grammar of English is unsatisfactory. It falls down badly on the first two requirements, being unduly complex and glaringly inconsistent within itself. It can be made to work, just as the Ptolemaic earth-centered astronomy can be, but at the cost of great elaboration and complication. The new grammar, like the Copernican sun-centered astronomy, solves the same problems with greater elegance, which is the scientist's word for the simplicity, compactness, and tidiness that characterize a satisfactory theory.

III

A brief look at the history of the traditional grammar of English will make apparent the reasons for its inadequacy. The study of English grammar is actually an outgrowth of the linguistic interest of the Renaissance. It was during the later Middle Ages and early Renaissance that the various vernacular languages of Europe came into their own. They began to be used for many kinds of writing which had previously always been done in Latin. As the vernaculars, in the hands of great writers like Dante and Chaucer, came of age as members of the linguistic family, a concomitant interest in their grammars arose. The earliest important English grammar was written by Shakespeare's contemporary, Ben Jonson.

It is important to observe that not only Ben Jonson himself but also those who followed him in the study of English grammar were men deeply learned in Latin and sometimes in Greek. For all their interest in English, they were conditioned from earliest school days to conceive of the classical languages as superior to the vernaculars. We still sometimes call the elementary school the "grammar school"; historically the term means the school where Latin grammar was taught. By the time the Renaissance or eighteenth-century scholar took his university degree, he was accustomed to use Latin as the normal means of communication with his fellow scholars. Dr. Samuel Johnson, for instance, who had only three years at the university and did not take a degree, wrote poetry in both Latin and Greek. Hence it was natural for these men to take Latin grammar as the norm, and to analyze English in terms of Latin. The grammarians of the seventeenth and eighteenth centuries who formulated the traditional grammar of English looked for the devices and distinctions of Latin grammar in English, and where they did not actually find them they imagined or created them. Of course, since English is a member of the Indo-European family of languages, to which Latin and Greek also belong, it did have many grammatical elements in common with them. But many of these had been obscured or wholly lost as a result of the extensive changes that had taken place in English—changes that the early grammarians inevitably conceived of as degeneration. They felt that it was their function to resist further change, if not to repair the damage already done. So preoccupied were they with the grammar of Latin as the ideal that they overlooked in large part the exceedingly complex and delicate system that English had substituted for the Indo-European grammar it had abandoned. Instead they stretched unhappy English on the Procrustean bed of Latin. It is no wonder that we commonly hear people say, "I didn't really understand grammar until I began to study Latin." This is eloquent testimony to the fact that the grammar "rules" of our present-day textbooks are largely an inheritance from the Latin-based grammar of the eighteenth century.

Meanwhile the extension of linguistic study beyond the Indo-European and Semitic families began to reveal that there are many different ways in which linguistic phenomena are organized—in other words, many different kinds of grammar. The tone-languages of the Orient and of North America, and the complex agglutinative languages of Africa, among others, forced grammarians to abandon the idea of a universal or ideal grammar and to direct their attention more closely to the individual systems employed by the multifarious languages of mankind. With the growth and refinement of the scientific method and its application to the field of anthropology, language came under more rigorous scientific scrutiny. As with anthropology in general, linguistic science at first concerned itself with the primitive. Finally, again following the lead of anthropology, linguistics began to apply its techniques to the old familiar tongues, among them English. Accelerated by the practical need during World War II of teaching languages, including English, to large numbers in a short time, research into the nature of English grammar has moved rapidly in the last fifteen years. The definitive grammar of English is yet to be written, but the results so far achieved are spectacular. It is now as unrealistic to teach "traditional" grammar of English as it is to teach "traditional" (i.e. pre-Darwinian) biology or "traditional" (i.e. four-element) chemistry. Yet nearly all certified teachers of English on all levels are doing so. Here is a cultural lag of major proportions.

IV

Before we can proceed to a sketch of what the new grammar of English looks like, we must take account of a few more of the premises of linguistic science. They must be understood and accepted by anyone who wishes to understand the new grammar.

First, the spoken language is primary, at least for the original study of a language. In many of the primitive languages,[1] of course, where writing is unknown, the spoken language is the *only* form. This is in many ways an

---

[1] "Primitive languages" here is really an abbreviated statement for "languages used by peoples of relatively primitive culture"; it is not to be taken as implying anything simple or rudimentary about the languages themselves. Many languages included under the term, such as native languages of Africa and Mexico, exhibit grammatical complexities unknown to more "civilized" languages.

advantage to the linguist, because the written language may use conventions that obscure its basic structure. The reason for the primary importance of the spoken language is that language originates as speech, and most of the changes and innovations that occur in the history of a given language begin in the spoken tongue.

Secondly, we must take account of the concept of dialect. I suppose most laymen would define a dialect as "a corrupt form of a language spoken in a given region by people who don't know any better." This introduces moral judgments which are repulsive to the linguistic scholar. Let us approach the definition of a dialect from the more objective end, through the notion of a speech community. A speech community is merely a group of people who are in pretty constant intercommunication. There are various types of speech communities: local ones, like "the people who live in Tidewater Virginia"; class ones, like "the white-collar class"; occupational ones, like "doctors, nurses, and other people who work in hospitals"; social ones, like "clubwomen." In a sense, each of these has its own dialect. Each family may be said to have its own dialect; in fact, in so far as each of us has his own vocabulary and particular quirks of speech, each individual has his own dialect. Also, of course, in so far as he is a member of many speech communities, each individual is more or less master of many dialects and shifts easily and almost unconsciously from one to another as he shifts from one social environment to another.

In the light of this concept of dialects, a language can be defined as a group of dialects which have enough of their sound-system, vocabulary, and grammar (Grammar 1, that is) in common to permit their speakers to be mutually intelligible in the ordinary affairs of life. It usually happens that one of the many dialects that make up a language comes to have more prestige than the others; in modern times it has usually been the dialect of the middle-class residents of the capital, like Parisian French and London English, which is so distinguished. This comes to be thought of as the standard dialect; in fact, its speakers become snobbish and succeed in establishing the belief that it is not a dialect at all, but the only proper form of the language. This causes the speakers of other dialects to become self-conscious and ashamed of their speech, or else aggressive and jingoistic about it—either of which is an acknowledgment of their feelings of inferiority. Thus one of the duties of the educational system comes to be that of teaching the standard dialect to all so as to relieve them of feelings of inferiority, and thus relieve society of linguistic neurotics. This is where Grammar 3, linguistic etiquette, comes into the picture.

A third premise arising from the two just discussed is that the difference between the way educated people talk and the way they write is a dialectal difference. The spread between these two dialects may be very narrow, as in present-day America, or very wide, as in Norway, where people often speak local Norwegian dialects but write in the Dano-Norwegian *Riksmaal*,

The extreme is the use by writers of an entirely different language, or at least an ancient and no longer spoken form of the language—like Sanskrit in northern India or Latin in western Europe during the Middle Ages. A corollary of this premise is that anyone setting out to write a grammar must know and make clear whether he is dealing with the spoken or the written dialect. Virtually all current English grammars deal with the written language only; evidence for this is that their rules for the plurals of nouns, for instance, are really spelling rules, which say nothing about pronunciation.

This is not the place to go into any sort of detail about the methods of analysis the linguistic scientist uses. Suffice it to say that he begins by breaking up the flow of speech into minimum sound-units, or phones, which he then groups into families called phonemes, the minimum significant sound-units. Most languages have from twenty to sixty of these. American English has forty-one: nine vowels, twenty-four consonants, four degrees of stress, and four levels of pitch. These phonemes group themselves into minimum meaningful units, called morphemes. These fall into two groups: free morphemes, those that can enter freely into many combinations with other free morphemes to make phrases and sentences; and bound morphemes, which are always found tied in a close and often indissoluble relationship with other bound or free morphemes. An example of a free morpheme is "dog"; an example of a bound morpheme is "un-" or "ex-." The linguist usually avoids talking about "words" because the term is very inexact. Is "instead of," for instance, to be considered one, two, or three words? This is purely a matter of opinion; but it is a matter of fact that it is made up of three morphemes.

In any case, our analysis has now brought the linguist to the point where he has some notion of the word-stock (he would call it the "lexicon") of his language. He must then go into the question of how the morphemes are grouped into meaningful utterances, which is the field of grammar proper. At this point in the analysis of English, as of many other languages, it becomes apparent that there are three bases upon which classification and analysis may be built: form, function, and meaning. For illustration let us take the word "boys" in the utterance "the boys are here." From the point of view of form, "boys" is a noun with the plural ending "s" (pronounced like "z"), preceded by the noun-determiner "the," and tied by concord to the verb "are," which it precedes. From the point of view of function, "boys" is the subject of the verb "are" and of the sentence. From the point of view of meaning, "boys" points out or names more than one of the male young of the human species, about whom an assertion is being made.

Of these three bases of classification, the one most amenable to objective description and analysis of a rigorously scientific sort is form. In fact, many conclusions about form can be drawn by a person unable to understand or speak the language. Next comes function. But except as it is revealed by form, function is dependent on knowing the meaning. In a telegraphic sentence like "ship sails today"[2] no one can say whether "ship" is the subject of "sails" or an imperative verb with "sails" as its object until he knows what the sentence means. Most shaky of all bases for grammatical analysis is meaning. Attempts have been made to reduce the phenomena of meaning to objective description, but so far they have not succeeded very well. Meaning is such a subjective quality that it is usually omitted entirely from scientific description. The botanist can describe the forms of plants and the functions of their various parts, but he refuses to concern himself with their meaning. It is left to the poet to find symbolic meaning in roses, violets, and lilies.

At this point it is interesting to note that the traditional grammar of English bases some of its key concepts and definitions on this very subjective and shaky foundation of meaning. A recent English grammar defines a sentence as "a group of words which expresses a complete thought through the use of a verb, called its predicate, and a subject, consisting of a noun or pronoun about which the verb has something to say."[3] But what is a complete thought? Actually we do not identify sentences this way at all. If someone says, "I don't know what to do," dropping his voice at the end, and pauses, the hearer will know that it is quite safe for him to make a comment without running the risk of interrupting an unfinished sentence. But if the speaker says the same words and maintains a level pitch at the end, the polite listener will wait for him to finish his sentence. The words are the same, the meaning is the same; the only difference is a slight one in the pitch of the final syllable—a purely formal distinction, which signals that the first utterance is complete, a sentence, while the second is incomplete. In writing we would translate these signals into punctuation: a period or exclamation point at the end of the first, a comma or dash at the end of the second. It is the form of the utterance, not the completeness of the thought, that tells us whether it is a whole sentence or only part of one.

Another favorite definition of the traditional grammar, also based on meaning, is that of "noun" as "the name of a person, place, or thing"; or, as the grammar just quoted has it, "the name of anybody or anything, with or without life, and with or without substance or form."[4] Yet we identify nouns, not by asking if they name something, but by their positions in expressions and by the formal marks they carry. In the sentence, "The slithy toves did gyre and gimble in the wabe," any speaker of English knows that "toves" and "wabe" are nouns, though he cannot tell what they name, if indeed they name anything. How does he know? Actually because they have

---

[2] This example is taken from C. C. Fries, *The Structure of English* (New York, 1952), p. 62. This important book will be discussed below.

[3] Ralph B. Allen, *English Grammar* (New York, 1950), p. 187.

[4] *Ibid.*, p. 1.

certain formal marks, like their position in relation to "the" as well as the whole arrangement of the sentence. We know from our practical knowledge of English grammar (Grammar 1), which we have had since before we went to school, that if we were to put meaningful words into this sentence, we would have to put nouns in place of "toves" and "wabe," giving something like "The slithy snakes did gyre and gimble in the wood." The pattern of the sentence simply will not allow us to say "The slithy arounds did gyre and gimble in the wooden."

One trouble with the traditional grammar, then, is that it relies heavily on the most subjective element in language, meaning. Another is that it shifts the ground of its classification and produces the elementary logical error of cross-division. A zoologist who divided animals into invertebrates, mammals, and beasts of burden would not get very far before running into trouble. Yet the traditional grammar is guilty of the same error when it defines three parts of speech on the basis of meaning (noun, verb, and interjection), four more on the basis of function (adjective, adverb, pronoun, conjunction), and one partly on function and partly on form (preposition). The result is that in such an expression as "a dog's life" there can be endless futile argument about whether "dog's" is a noun or an adjective. It is, of course, a noun from the point of view of form and an adjective from the point of view of function, and hence falls into both classes, just as a horse is both a mammal and a beast of burden. No wonder students are bewildered in their attempts to master the traditional grammar. Their natural clearness of mind tells them that it is a crazy patchwork violating the elementary principles of logical thought.

V

If the traditional grammar is so bad, what does the new grammar offer in its place?

It offers a description, analysis, and set of definitions and formulas—rules, if you will—based firmly and consistently on the easiest, or at least the most objective, aspect of language, form. Experts can quibble over whether "dog's" in "a dog's life" is a noun or an adjective, but anyone can see that it is spelled with " 's " and hear that it ends with a "z" sound; likewise anyone can tell that it comes in the middle between "a" and "life." Furthermore he can tell that something important has happened if the expression is changed to "the dog's alive," "the live dogs," or "the dogs lived," even if he doesn't know what the words mean and has never heard of such functions as modifier, subject, or attributive genitive. He cannot, of course, get very far into his analysis without either a knowledge of the language or access to someone with such knowledge. He will also need a minimum technical vocabulary describing grammatical functions. Just so the anatomist is better off for knowing physiology. But the grammarian, like the anatomist, must beware of allowing his preconceived notions to lead him into the error of interpreting before he describes—an error which often results in his finding only what he is looking for.

When the grammarian looks at English objectively, he finds that it conveys its meanings by two broad devices: the denotations and connotations of words separately considered, which the linguist calls "lexical meaning," and the significance of word-forms, word-groups, and arrangements apart from the lexical meanings of the words, which the linguist calls "structural meaning." The first of these is the domain of the lexicographer and the semanticist, and hence is not our present concern. The second, the structural meaning, is the business of the structural linguist, or grammarian. The importance of this second kind of meaning must be emphasized because it is often overlooked. The man in the street tends to think of the meaning of a sentence as being the aggregate of the dictionary meanings of the words that make it up; hence the widespread fallacy of literal translation—the feeling that if you take a French sentence and a French-English dictionary and write down the English equivalent of each French word you will come out with an intelligible English sentence. How ludicrous the results can be, anyone knows who is familiar with Mark Twain's retranslation from the French of his jumping frog story. One sentence reads, "Eh bien! I no saw not that that frog has nothing of better than each frog." Upon which Mark's comment is, "if that isn't grammar gone to seed, then I count myself no judge."[5]

The second point brought out by a formal analysis of English is that it uses four principal devices of form to signal structural meanings:

1. Word order—the sequence in which words and word-groups are arranged.

2. Function-words—words devoid of lexical meaning which indicate relationships among the meaningful words with which they appear.

3. Inflections—alterations in the forms of words themselves to signal changes in meaning and relationship.

4. Formal contrasts—contrasts in the forms of words signaling greater differences in function and meaning. These could also be considered inflections, but it is more convenient for both the lexicographer and the grammarian to consider them separately.

Usually several of these are present in any utterance, but they can be separately illustrated by means of contrasting expressions involving mini-

[5] Mark Twain, "The Jumping Frog; the Original Story in English; the Retranslation Clawed Back from the French, into a Civilized Language Once More, by Patient and Unremunerated Toil," 1601 . . . and Sketches Old and New (n.p., 1933), p. 50.

mum variation—the kind of controlled experiment used in the scientific laboratory.

To illustrate the structural meaning of word order, let us compare the two sentences "man bites dog" and "dog bites man."—The words are identical in lexical meaning and in form; the only difference is in sequence. It is interesting to note that Latin expresses the difference between these two by changes in the form of the words, without necessarily altering the order: "homo canem mordet" or "hominem canis mordet." Latin grammar is worse than useless in understanding this point of English grammar.

Next, compare the sentences "the dog is the friend of man" and "any dog is a friend of that man." Here the words having lexical meaning are "dog," "is," "friend," and "man," which appear in the same form and the same order in both sentences. The formal differences between them are in the substitution of "any" and "a" for "the," and in the insertion of "that." These little words are function-words; they make quite a difference in the meanings of the two sentences, though it is virtually impossible to say what they mean in isolation.

Third, compare the sentences "the dog loves the man" and "the dogs loved the men." Here the words are the same, in the same order, with the same function-words in the same positions. But the forms of the three words having lexical meanings have been changed: "dog" to "dogs," "loves" to "loved," and " man" to "men." These changes are inflections. English has very few of them as compared with Greek, Latin, Russian, or even German. But it still uses them; about one word in four in an ordinary English sentence is inflected.

Fourth, consider the difference between "the dog's friend arrived" and "the dog's friendly arrival." Here the difference lies in the change of "friend" to "friendly," a formal alteration signaling a change of function from subject to modifier, and the change of "arrived" to "arrival," signaling a change of function from predicate to head-word in a noun-modifier group. These changes are of the same formal nature as inflections, but because they produce words of different lexical meaning, classifiable as different parts of speech, it is better to call them formal contrasts than inflections. In other words, it is logically quite defensible to consider "love," "loving," and "loved" as the same word in differing aspects and to consider "friend," "friendly," "friendliness," "friendship," and "befriend" as different words related by formal and semantic similarities. But this is only a matter of convenience of analysis, which permits a more accurate description of English structure. In another language we might find that this kind of distinction is unnecessary but that some other distinction, unnecessary in English, is required. The categories of grammatical description are not sacrosanct; they are as much a part of man's organization of his observations as they are of the nature of things.

If we are considering the spoken variety of English, we must add a fifth device for indicating structural meaning—the various musical and rhythmic patterns which the linguist classifies under juncture, stress, and intonation. Consider the following pair of sentences:

> Alfred, the alligator is sick
> Alfred the alligator is sick.

These are identical in the four respects discussed above—word order, function-words, inflections, and word-form. Yet they have markedly different meanings, as would be revealed by the intonation if they were spoken aloud. These differences in intonation are to a certain extent indicated in the written language by punctuation—that is, in fact, the primary function of punctuation.

VI

The examples so far given were chosen to illustrate in isolation the various kinds of structural devices in English grammar. Much more commonly the structural meaning of a given sentence is indicated by a combination of two or more of these devices: a sort of margin of safety which permits some of the devices to be missed or done away with without obscuring the structural meaning of the sentence, as indeed anyone knows who has ever written a telegram or a newspaper headline. On the other hand, sentences which do not have enough of these formal devices are inevitably ambiguous. Take the example already given, Fries's "ship sails today." This is ambiguous because there is nothing to indicate which of the first two words is performing a noun function and which a verb function. If we mark the noun by putting the noun-determining function-word "the" in front of it, the ambiguity disappears; we have either "the ship sails today" or "ship the sails today." The ambiguity could just as well be resolved by using other devices: consider "ship sailed today," "ship to sail today," "ship sail today," "shipping sails today," "shipment of sails today," and so on. It is simply a question of having enough formal devices in the sentence to indicate its structural meaning clearly.

How powerful the structural meanings of English are is illustrated by so-called "nonsense." In English, nonsense as a literary form often consists of utterances that have a clear structural meaning but use words that either have no lexical meanings, or whose lexical meanings are inconsistent one with another. This will become apparent if we subject a rather famous bit of English nonsense to formal grammatical analysis:

> All mimsy were the borogoves
> And the mome raths outgrabe.

This passage consists of ten words, five of them words that should have lexical meaning but don't, one standard verb, and four function-words. In so far as it is possible to indicate its abstract structure, it would be this:

All .... y were the .... s
And the ... ... s ....

Although this is a relatively simple formal organization, it signals some rather complicated meanings. The first thing we observe is that the first line presents a conflict: word order seems to signal one thing, and inflections and function-words something else. Specifically, "mimsy" is in the position normally occupied by the subject, but we know that it is not the subject and that "borogroves" is. We know this because there is an inflectional tie between the form "were" and the "s" ending of "borogroves," because there is the noun-determiner "the" before it, and because the alternative candidate for subject "mimsy," lacks both of these. It is true that "mimsy" does have the function-word "all" before it, which may indicate a noun; but when it does, the noun is either plural (in which case "mimsy" would most likely end in "s"), or else the noun is what grammarians call a mass-word (like "sugar," "coal" "snow"), in which case the verb would have to be "was," not "were." All these formal considerations are sufficient to counteract the effect of word order and show that the sentence is of the type that may be represented thus:

All gloomy were the Democrats.

Actually there is one other possibility. If "mimsy" belongs to the small group of nouns which don't use "s" to make the plural, and if "borogroves" has been so implied (but not specifically mentioned) in the context as to justify its appearing with the determiner "the," the sentence would then belong to the following type:

(In the campaign for funds) all alumni were the canvassers.
(In the drought last summer) all cattle were the sufferers.

But the odds are so much against this that most of us would be prepared to fight for our belief that "borogroves" are things that can be named, and that at the time referred to they were in a complete state of "mimsyness."

Moving on to the second line, "and the mome raths outgrabe," the first thing we note is that the "And" signals another parallel assertion to follow. We are thus prepared to recognize from the noun-determiner "the," the plural inflection "s," and the particular positions of "mome" and "outgrabe," as well as the continuing influence of the "were" of the preceding line, that we are dealing with a sentence of this pattern:

And the lone rats agreed.

The influence of the "were" is particularly important here; it guides us in selecting among several interpretations of the sentence. Specifically, it requires us to identify "outgrabe" as a verb in the past tense, and thus a "strong" or "irregular" verb, since it lacks the characteristic past-tense ending "d" or "ed." We do this in spite of the fact that there is another strong candidate for the position of verb: that is, "raths," which bears a regular verb inflection and could be tied with "mome" as its subject in the normal noun-verb relationship. In such a case we should have to recognize "outgrabe" as either an adverb of the kind not marked by the form-contrast "ly," an adjective, or the past participle of a strong verb. The sentence would then belong to one of the following types:

> And the moon shines above.
> And the man stays aloof.
> And the fool seems outdone.

But we reject all of these—probably they don't even occur to us—because they all have verbs in the present tense, whereas the "were" of the first line combines with the "And" at the beginning of the second to set the whole in the past.

We might recognize one further possibility for the structural meaning of this second line, particularly in the verse context, since we are used to certain patterns in verse that do not often appear in speech of prose. The "were" of the first line could be understood as doing double duty, its ghost or echo appearing between "raths" and "outgrabe." Then we would have something like this:

> All gloomy were the Democrats
> And the home folks outraged.

But again the odds are pretty heavy against this. I for one am so sure that "outgrabe" is the past tense of a strong verb that I can give its present. In my dialect, at least, it is "outgribe."

The reader may not realize it, but in the last four paragraphs I have been discussing grammar from a purely formal point of view. I have not once called a word a noun because it names something (that is, I have not once resorted to meaning), nor have I called any word an adjective because it modifies a noun (that is, resorted to function). Instead I have been working in the opposite direction, from form toward function and meaning. I have used only criteria which are objectively observable, and I have assumed only a working knowledge of certain structural patterns and devices known to all speakers of English over the age of six. I did use some technical terms like "noun," "verb," and "tense," but only to save time; I could have got along without them.

If one clears his mind of the inconsistencies of the traditional grammar (not so easy a process as it might be), he can proceed with a similarly rigorous formal analysis of a sufficient number of representative utterances in English and come out with a descriptive grammar. This is just what

Professor Fries did in gathering and studying the material for the analysis he presents in the remarkable book to which I have already referred, *The Structure of English*. What he actually did was to put a tape recorder into action and record about fifty hours of telephone conversation among the good citizens of Ann Arbor, Michigan. When this material was transcribed, it constituted about a quarter of a million words of perfectly natural speech by educated middle-class Americans. The details of his conclusions cannot be presented here, but they are sufficiently different from the usual grammar to be revolutionary. For instance, he recognizes only four parts of speech among the words with lexical meaning, roughly corresponding to what the traditional grammar calls substantives, verbs, adjectives and adverbs, though to avoid preconceived notions from the traditional grammar Fries calls them Class 1, Class 2, Class 3, and Class 4 words. To these he adds a relatively small group of function-words, 154 in his materials, which he divides into fifteen groups. These must be memorized by anyone learning the language; they are not subject to the same kind of general rules that govern the four parts of speech. Undoubtedly his conclusions will be developed and modified by himself and by other linguistic scholars, but for the present his book remains the most complete treatment extant of English grammar from the point of view of linguistic science.

VII

Two vital questions are raised by this revolution in grammar. The first is, "What is the value of this new system?" In the minds of many who ask it, the implication of this question is, "We have been getting along all these years with traditional grammar, so it can't be so very bad. Why should we go through the painful process of unlearning and relearning grammar just because linguistic scientists have concocted some new theories?"

The first answer to this question is the bravest and most honest. It is that the superseding of vague and sloppy thinking by clear and precise thinking is an exciting experience in and for itself. To acquire insight into the workings of a language, and to recognize the infinitely delicate system of relationship, balance, and interplay that constitutes its grammar, is to become closely acquainted with one of man's most miraculous creations, not unworthy to be set beside the equally beautiful organization of the physical universe. And to find that its most complex effects are produced by the multi-layered organization of relatively simple materials is to bring our thinking about language into accord with modern thought in other fields, which is more and more coming to emphasize the importance of organization—the fact that an organized whole is truly greater than the sum of all its parts.

There are other answers, more practical if less philosophically valid. It is too early to tell, but it seems probable that a realistic, scientific grammar should vastly facilitate the teaching of English, especially as a foreign language. Already results are showing here; it has been found that if intonation contours and other structural patterns are taught quite early, the student has a confidence that allows him to attempt to speak the language much sooner than he otherwise would.

The new grammar can also be of use in improving the native speaker's proficiency in handling the structural devices of his own language. In other words, Grammar 2, if it is accurate and consistent, *can* be of use in improving skill in Grammar 1. An illustration is that famous bugaboo, the dangling participle. Consider a specific instance of it, which once appeared on a college freshman's theme, to the mingled delight and despair of the instructor:

> Having eaten our lunch, the steamboat departed.

What is the trouble with this sentence? Clearly there must be something wrong with it, because it makes people laugh, although it was not the intent of the writer to make them laugh. In other words, it produces a completely wrong response, resulting in total breakdown of communication. It is, in fact, "bad grammar" in a much more serious way than are mere dialectal divergences like "he ain't here" or "he never seen none," which produce social reactions but communicate effectively. In the light of the new grammar, the trouble with our dangling participle is that the form, instead of leading to the meaning, is in conflict with it. Into the position which, in this pattern, is reserved for the word naming the eater of the lunch, the writer has inserted the word "steamboat." The resulting tug-of-war between form and meaning is only momentary; meaning quickly wins out, simply because our common sense tells us that steamboats don't eat lunches. But if the pull of the lexical meaning is not given a good deal of help from common sense, the form will conquer the meaning, or the two will remain in ambiguous equilibrium—as, for instance, in "Having eaten our lunch, the passengers boarded the steamboat." Writers will find it easier to avoid such troubles if they know about the forms of English and are taught to use the form to convey the meaning, instead of setting up tensions between form and meaning. This, of course, is what English teachers are already trying to do. The new grammar should be a better weapon in their arsenal than the traditional grammar since it is based on a clear understanding of the realities.

The second and more difficult question is, "How can the change from one grammar to the other be effected?" Here we face obstacles of a formidable nature. When we remember the controversies attending on revolutionary changes in biology and astronomy, we realize what a tenacious hold the race can maintain on anything it has once learned, and the resistance it can offer to new ideas. And remember that neither astronomy nor biology was taught in elementary schools. They were, in fact, rather specialized subjects in advanced education. How then change grammar, which is taught to everybody, from the fifth grade up through college? The vested interest represented by thousands upon thousands of Engish and Speech teachers who have learned the traditional grammar and taught it for many years is a conservative force comparable to those which keep us still using the chaotic system of English spelling and the unwieldy measuring system of inches and feet, pounds and ounces, quarts, bushels, and acres. Moreover, this army is constantly receiving new recruits. It is possible in my state to become certified to teach English in high school if one has had eighteen credit hours of college English—let us say two semesters of freshman composition (almost all of which is taught by people unfamiliar with the new grammar), two semesters of a survey course in English literature, one semester of Shakespeare, and one semester of the contemporary novel. And since hard-pressed school administrators feel that anyone who can speak English can in a pinch teach it, the result is that many people are called upon to teach grammar whose knowledge of the subject is totally inadequate.

There is, in other words, a battle ahead of the new grammar. It will have to fight not only the apathy of the general public but the ignorance and inertia of those who count themselves competent in the field of grammar. The battle is already on, in fact. Those who try to get the concepts of the new grammar introduced into the curriculum are tagged as "liberal" grammarians—the implication being, I suppose, that one has a free choice between "liberal" and "conservative" grammar, and that the liberals are a bit dangerous, perhaps even a touch subversive. They are accused of undermining standards, of holding that "any way of saying something is just as good as any other," of not teaching the fundamentals of good English. I trust that the readers of this article will see how unfounded these charges are. But the smear campaign is on. So far as I know, neither religion nor patriotism has yet been brought into it. When they are, Professor Fries will have to say to Socrates, Galileo, Darwin, Freud, and the other members of the honorable fraternity of the misunderstood, "Move over, gentlemen, and make room for me."

Basic Tenets of Structural Linguistics*

GEORGE P. FAUST

IN WRITING about structural linguistics, I am making two assumptions to begin with: that so far some readers know the subject only by name, and that the great majority are looking for explanation from someone who, like me, is a teacher rather than a professional linguist. For the first group I should make the point clear that structural linguistics can be applied to any language, not just English, though English will be our concern here. The simplest possible definition is that structural linguistics analyzes a language into its significant sounds, the patterns of sound we call words (for English), and the patterns of words we call phrases, clauses, and sentences. This means that structural linguistics sets up an alternative grammar to the one we learn in school. It has a different basis, it is constructed differently, and its results coincide only in part with those of traditional grammar.

Before we go further, it will be well to take care of possible sources of misunderstanding. To all but perhaps the youngest teachers, linguistics mostly has to do with history, or at least with historical explanations. Structural linguistics is different. Its aim is to come as close as possible to describing the characteristics of a language at a given time. History is simply beside the point. Now this is certainly not fully understood. In *Our Language*, a recent British book along traditional lines, Simeon Potter says at one point: "No one who is acquainted only with the living language as it is, or, to use the more fashionable expression, no one who studies [the example] synchronically (and not diachronically or historically), would venture to say which of these three uses [of *while*] is the original one. . . ." Certainly not, but it is hard to see why an account of present structure should be concerned with the history implied in "the original one." Historical (diachronic) linguistics is an honorable field of study; so is structural (synchronic) linguistics. They serve different purposes, and while they can be useful to each other, they properly do not use the same methods.

One more possible misunderstanding. Structuralism is such a novelty to most of us that we may fail to realize that every paradigm in any gram-

* This article and the two following ones are developed from a panel discussion during the meeting of Conference on College Composition and Communication in Chicago, 1953. Reprinted by permission from *College Composition and Communication*, 4.122–125 (December, 1953).

mar has been presented as a structural set, though not necessarily the most valid or useful one. In the last generation or so, much more rigorous analyses have been made of many languages, especially the so-called primitive ones that had no system of writing and so had to be treated synchronically. Structural analysis has been focused on English partly in connection with the teaching of English to foreigners, where it has been reassuringly successful. However, a language like ours, with a tradition of writing and a considerable number of dialects, is very complex, and the study of it is not complete. This does not imply that what has been learned is not usable already. The basic structural techniques have been proved by trial, and there is no reason to suppose that they are not applicable to English.

The prestige of our literature accounts for at least one of the two major differences between the traditional and structural ways of looking at language. These differences are in the view we take of the relation between spoken and written English and in our thinking about the correspondences between meaning and form. The writing we deal with in the classroom is in standard English; at the same time we are all keenly aware of nonstandard speech around us. In addition, writing and speaking seem to represent extremes of permanence and evanescence. From these experiences and from our training in literary studies, it is only natural that we should tend to regard writing as superior to speech. As a result, we tend to think of writing as a norm instead of a specialized form of language.

For the structuralist, writing is secondary to speech. This position is not taken arbitrarily or for the sake of irritating others. It seems to have much to justify it. For instance, children learn to speak long before they learn to write. Again, grammars traditionally introduce students first to the sounds and pronunciations of a language. It is strong circumstantial evidence that every script presupposes a spoken language; and the fact that no human community has been found without a language fully developed for the purposes of its users is an even more powerful argument that speech preceded writing by a very long time. The point is that without speech there can be no writing.

Insistence on the primacy of speech is not an esthetic judgment. A linguist *qua* linguist is interested in all forms of language, but he takes each on its own terms. "Better" and "worse" have no linguistic meaning, except better or worse for analysis. Our conventional writing does not show unambiguously the patterns of accent and intonation that we have to use when we speak. Since these turn out to be grammatically important, speech is better for analysis than writing, from which different patterns may sometimes be inferred by different readers. Also, some grammatical arrangements are actually used in speech which would be ambiguous or misunderstood in writing. "Thank whoever put my slippers there for me" (with a break after *there* and a primary accent on *for*) clearly means "Thank for me . . .," but cannot be used in normal writing. We make some such substitution as "Give my thanks to . . ."

Knowledge of what happens in speech helps a teacher explain the ways of edited English. For instance, many Kentuckians regularly say "I'll have him to stop in" and "I'd like for you to wait." Merely telling them that the *to* and *for* are errors is likely to produce one or both of two effects: They come to feel that their speech is inferior, or they decide that classroom English has little or nothing to do with realities outside of teacherdom. If, on the other hand, they can be shown that edited English is based on a dialect different from theirs, but not better, they can understand without resentment or possible loss of self-respect why they should not reflect their own speech in general writing. Punctuation, too, can be simplified by approaching it through spoken English. For years I taught the difference between restrictive and non-restrictive by using "My brother, who lives in . . ." and then going on to a rather complicated explanation involving the size of the family I grew up in. Of course I repeated the sentence over and over, with and without the comma, so to speak. But I never suspected until last year that if my students learned anything, it was from listening to my intonation, not my explanation. Now I teach them to listen for the cadence, and decide their punctuation on that basis. With a very few restrictions to take care of arbitrary editorial practice, the system works, and the students are spared the details of my family.

In addition to seeing in speech an importance unfamiliar to most of us, structural linguists strike us as practically ignoring meaning if not denying its existence. We are mistaken. No linguist would think of denying the constantly certified fact that language conveys meaning. The basic difference seems to be that we tend to think of language as produced by meaning, and the structuralists regard it as a medium for transmitting "messages." They discriminate between lexical and grammatical meaning, for instance, and concentrate on the grammatical. What this means is that if a student presented a paper with the title "The Sprillickams Grapchids," you would be completely in the dark about lexical meaning, but you would feel an impulse to indicate that an apostrophe was needed in *Sprillickams*. And you would be right, for you would have understood the grammatical signals: In English the form could hardly be anything except a possessive. What is the conclusion? To me it is that much of the heat of fruitless controversy would be dissipated if we all recognized that the term language is used with different emphases—the familiar one that stresses general or referential meaning and the novel one that limits itself at present to the mechanisms.

The structural objection to the traditional use of *language* is that the account of the mechanisms becomes distorted beyond reason. Not long ago I found on a blackboard the legend MEANING DETERMINES FORM. Put *grammatical* before each noun, and the linguist would *reverse the legend.* An individual may be able to choose from among current forms, but meaning cannot possibly determine obsolete or non-existent forms. English once had dual forms of personal pronouns, and it is pretty safe to assume that speakers have never stopped meaning "we two" and "you two." But the dual forms have disappeared and cannot now be revived. Or again, *we* sometimes includes the listener, sometimes excludes him. Some other languages have separate forms for the two meanings, but not English. Here again meaning cannot and does not determine form. On the other hand, if we use forms like *boys* and *children,* we can't help meaning what we call plural. We say *one car, several cars;* we do not say *one cars, several car.*

Traditional grammar often produces semantic whirlpools: In "He wore a blue tie," *blue* is the name of a color, yet we do not call it a noun. Structural linguistics, on the other hand, takes its cues from signs that are either overlooked or taken for granted in traditional teaching, and its explanations in terms of linguistic behavior are more accurate and easier to understand. Let me offer an incomplete but serviceable illlustration.

Comma splices and sentence fragments are the result of a student's inability to classify the connective between two clauses. The result of appeals to the meanings of the words, or to "sentence sense," or even to dictionary classification, often is confusion. The student continues to be unable to see the "essential" difference of meaning between *so* and *therefore,* and anyway the dictionary lists *therefore* as a conjunction. One teacher proclaimed that a comma before *therefore* produces a reader block—and this to a class which had been guessing wildly at what was wrong with a sentence that read all right to them. I am told that in some quarters comma splices are still regarded as signs of iniquity, and the student must be flunked. Of course most of us are far beyond that stage. Still, we prefer editorial orthodoxy.

How can a student find out for sure whether a connective is a conjunction or a conjunctive adverb? By using a set of linguistic frames and trying a test. The formula for such frames is $Cl_1 + X + Cl_2$, in which Cl stands for *clause* and X for the connective to be identified.[1] Here is one frame which can be used for a restricted list of forms:

Cl_1	X	Cl_2
Jack came		the others were gone

Now suppose a student wants to try out *but* and *however.* With his automatically appropriate intonation patterns he can use them both in the frame and produce utterances that his friends will agree are English. The test lies in trying each connective also between the subject and verb

[1] This formula assumes that *clause* is known. I myself prefer SVC_1 X SVC_2, in which SVC stands for subject-verb-complement(s).

of the second clause. The resulting pairs, together with my reaction to each utterance, are these:

1. Jack came but the others were gone (Yes)
2. Jack came the others but were gone (No)
3. Jack came however the others were gone (Yes)
4. Jack came the others however were gone (Yes)

The "No" after 2 classifies *but* as a conjunction; the "Yes" after 4 classifies *however* as a conjunctive adverb.[2]

Formulas like Cl_1+X+Cl_2 are sometimes objected to as cardinal pomposities of structural linguistics, on a par with advertising's "Scientists say . . ." They are certainly discomforting at first, because they are unfamiliar, but after you have worked with them a while, you come to realize the advantages of their brevity, clarity, and immediacy. Students like them. As for their making language seem too mechanical, the insistence of structural linguistics is precisely that language is a complex set of mechanisms. This should not be a shock—but it is—to those of us who maintain that *person* should be mechanically referred to by pronoun forms related to *he*. To which the structural objection is that the formula is not consistent with the facts of language.

Beneath any haggling over individual points lies the difference in approach. Traditionally we have started out armed with canonical lists of conjunctions and conjunctive adverbs, and with definitions designed to justify the lists. If such a test as the one proposed here supports the lists, it is acceptable; if not, it is inadequate. On the contrary, the structuralists first observe the facts and formulate definitions to match the facts. Many prefer to express the definitions as formulas, though formulas are no more essential in linguistics than they are in chemistry, where every formula could be verbalized. Classification is based on such definitions and produces results which can be expressed as lists. Thus the starting point of the traditionalist is the end point of the structuralist. Which is better, then, to start with the facts—including the facts about edited English—and work to the lists, or to start with the lists and try to bend the facts? In the long run, I am afraid, we will look a little foolish if we refuse to face the linguistic facts.

[2] It goes without saying that the test applies only to connectives between clauses in the student's own writing or his reading of contemporary American English. Some previous preparation is assumed. For instance, the student must have learned to notice the differences between *however* followed by a break in intonation and *however* without a break. Otherwise he might be confused by something like "Make your corrections however you like."

Terms in Phonemics*

George P. Faust

By means of phonemic analysis, structural linguists try to discover the sound-system of a language as it is consciously or subsconsciously meaningful to the speakers. A new set of terms (and symbols) is forced upon them partly because they have formed new categories and developed new techniques and partly because the familiar terms have an aura of association that would act to block understanding if they were used in new senses. The difficulty is that the new terms themselves have blocked understanding between structuralists and teachers. The problem of this article is to remove some of the barriers and show some of the uses teachers can make of the present knowledge of English structure, with no attempt to go beyond phonemics.[1]

But the barriers will not fall automatically with the explanation of a few technical tems. As I have tried to say earlier,[2] we must first persuade ourselves to accept two basic tenets: (1) that speech is the primary form of language and underlies all writing, and (2) that the concern of structuralists is with the mechanisms of language as a medium, not with the "message" (meaning) carried by the medium.

These two tenets accepted, let us start by fastening attention on the *p*-sounds in the possible expression 'rapid pup.' We will follow the general practice of putting phonetic symbols in brackets, e.g., [p], and phonemic symbols between slashes, e.g., /p/. In a phonemic transcription of my speech without stress and intonation marked, we can set our expression down as /ræpid pəp/. This is not phonetic, for among other things any competent phonetician could hear differences among the *p*-sounds as he listened to me. If he took the first as a phonetic norm, he might transcribe them in order as [p], [p'], and [p'], with ['] standing for aspiration (a puff of air that can be felt on the back of the hand held close to the mouth)

---

* Reprinted by permission from *College Composition and Communication*, 5.30–34 (February, 1954).

[1] In general, this article will follow the analysis in George L. Trager and Henry Lee Smith, Jr., *An Outline of English Structure* (Studies in Linguistics: Occasional Papers No. 3), 1951. This is a thoroughly technical piece of work *not* recommended for beginners. The best available starting point is Robert A. Hall's *Leave Your Language Alone* (Linguistica: Ithaca, N.Y.), 1950. If you don't like the social attitudes expressed, ignore them and concentrate on the very able exposition of linguistics.

[2] "Basic Tenets of Structural Linguistics," *CCC*, December, 1953, pages 122–126.

2

and ['] indicating no release by reopening the lips. All three varieties are called allophones.

To put it as untechnically as I can, ALLOPHONES are phonetically similar sounds that never get in each other's way. As native speakers of English, we have learned to use the proper allophones automatically and to ignore them completely in our own speech and in the speech of others. This means that *if you know that a word has two pronunciations, they differ phonemically, not allophonically.* It is only when a foreigner fails to use the right allophones that we become vaguely conscious that something is wrong: The foreigner, we say, speaks English with an accent. In all this we are reacting quite normally, and no phonetically untrained reader should be disturbed if he fails to hear allophonic differences.

Allophones have COMPLEMENTARY DISTRIBUTION, the technical term that corresponds to "never get in each other's way." This is a tricky term to handle. Allophones tend to be restricted. That is, [p'] simply cannot appear at the beginning of a word because we have to reopen our lips to get on with the word. On the other hand, [p'] does on occasion replace [p'] at the end of a word. But we speakers react to /pəp/ as the "same" word, no matter which allophone is used, and any sense of difference here is likely to be referred to the speaker's attitude, not his dialect. Therefore, the allophones never collide, even when they alternate with one another, and they complement one another in such a way that in sum they take care of all the situations in which their phoneme occurs.

Complementary distribution is one side of the coin, CONTRASTIVE DISTRIBUTION the other. Sounds contrast most obviously when the difference produces different words. Thus /p/ and /f/ contrast because 'pup' is not 'puff' (/pəf/). *And one contrast anywhere in the language is enough to establish separate phonemes everywhere in the language.* It is known quite definitely that [p] between vowels is voiced in normal American speech and is thus very close to [b] in the same situation—at least as close to [b] phonetically as to initial [p']. But since [p] and [b] are assigned by speakers to different phonemes (cf. the contrast between /pet/ and /bet/), the phonetic similarity is inconsequential. You can test this for yourself. Just invite a friend to pat your 'rabid pup' and see whether his reactions are like those of the friends you have invited to pat your 'rapid pup.'

Here it is necessary to insist that the difference in meaning is the *result* of the difference in sound. Strangers who hear my weakly aspirated initial /p/ (an individual peculiarity) quite easily "misunderstand" me and think, for instance, that my middle initial is B instead of P. The sense of "misunderstand" here is that they have misclassified a sound, with resultant change of meaning.

An error of this sort points up one extremely important difference between phonetics and phonemics. In phonetics a sound can be between a

/p/ and a /b/ in the sense that it can have certain characteristics of each, such as the voicelessness of an initial /p/ and the relatively weak aspiration of an initial /b/. The phonetician tries to describe the sound actually produced. But in phonemics there are no gradations. *A sound is assigned to one phoneme or another, and there is no in-between stage.* The linguistic evidence goes to show that we hear in terms of phonemes and listen to only as much of a sound as we need to in order to assign it to an established phoneme. This is a fundamental reason why phonemic transcriptions don't need to distinguish among allophones.

We should now be ready for some definitions. A sound produced is a PHONE. It is a unique historical event, in theory as individual as a fingerprint. Obviously, only a microscopic sample of the phones produced ever get recorded, and yet the patterning of language is such that linguists can classify as confidently as though they had a statistically large sample. In great measure, this is because they have occasion to concentrate on only a few variations. The subclasses into which phones are fitted are ALLOPHONES, each of which, though in complementary distribution, is distinct from all others by at least one phonetic feature. At this level we are still in a region where sounds may be symbolized in phonetic transcription. Next, the allophones are gathered into one class, a PHONEME, which is distinguished by the phonetic similarity of its members and by its contrastive distribution with other phonemes.

To tie all three together, any phone may be called a phone (i.e., an individual sound) or an allophone (i.e., a member of an allophone) or a phoneme (i.e., a member of a phoneme). Imagine that I now hear you say 'pup.' The first sound was a phone, already past history. As long as it remains unclassified, I can call it nothing but a phone. Probably I will next classify it as a member of the phoneme /p/, and now I can call it either a phone or a phoneme. When finally I group it with other members of /p/ that have aspiration, I can also call it an allophone of /p/, and I can describe that allophone phonetically as [pʻ]. In the same kind of way, all other vowel-like or consonant-like phones can be identified as belonging to one or another of the thirty-three phonemes that make up this part of the English sound-system.

For teachers, the usefulness of having a working acquaintance with these phonemes is that it sheds valuable light on many spelling problems. All of us already know, in a relatively unsystematic way, that our students tend to reflect their pronunciations in their writing, but the remedies we have offered have sometimes been unrealistic, to a considerable extent because we have confused letters and sounds. One pronunciation of *often*, now well established, is supposed to be due to the letter *t* in the spelling—some people, apparently, never thought of *soften*. Once we realize that *used to* is regularly pronounced /yuwstuw/, not /yuwzd tuw/, we may be more sympathetic to the spelling *use to*, which is really very sensible, if not orthodox. Of course we should try to impress the conventional spelling but not, I suggest, at the cost of a pronunciation which may be unforced for some speakers but which I never happen to have heard attempted except by teachers. Again, probably many of us tear our hair over students who seem unable to pluralize words like *scientist*. But a great many standard speakers have /-s/ at the end of such words instead of /-st/, and to them the plural presumably sounds just like the singular.[3] It would strike an informed teacher as unreasonable to attempt to modify a standard pronunciation; it would be better to show the students that for spelling such words they cannot trust their ears. This is the type of situation which a knowledge of phonemics enables a teacher to handle sensibly.

To return to the sound-system, the set of phonemes referred to so far are called SEGMENTAL PHONEMES to distinguish them from another more recently discovered set, the SUPRASEGMENTAL PHONEMES. These consist of stresses, pitches, and junctures—the last being modes of transition from one speech-segment to another. Of course the fact of their existence is not news; the recent knowledge is of their contrastive distribution into phonemes, which has been worked out in considerable detail during the last ten years by Kenneth Pike and others.

STRESS is familiar as what we call accent in dictionaries, where only three relative degrees are necessary, counting the unmarked as weak. (However, you should not expect dictionaries to be accurate on stress. For example, they leave the second syllable of *cargo* unmarked, though it definitely has more stress than the second syllable of *sofa*—as much, in my speech, as the marked second syllable of *blackbird*.) Connected speech has a fourth degree of stress which overrides the others and which we use to establish word-groups. Customary symbols of stress are

$$/ \ ' \ , \ \hat{} \ , \ \grave{} \ , \ \breve{} \ /,$$

called primary, secondary, tertiary, and weak.

Whêre's thĕ cárgò

illustrates the four phonemic stresses.

The very idea that relative levels of PITCH are contrastive is a novelty. Here there is nothing like a familiar dictionary to fall back on, and since the proof is somewhat complicated, about all that can be done here is to make the flat assertion that English has four phonemic pitches. The joke 'What are we having for dinner? Mother?' depends on the misuse of pitch levels. In the commonplace 'What are we having for dinner, Mother?' the vocative can be either at the lowest pitch or the next above, but it can never be at either of the two highest pitches. With next-to-top pitch, as in the joke, 'mother' becomes a separate question.[4]

---

[3] A structurally more accurate way of putting this is that the final consonant cluster /-sts/ is non-existent in the speech of many Americans.

[4] I am indebted to H. L. Smith, Jr., for this passage, joke included.

Pitches are usually symbolized by numbers: $/^{1,2,3,4}/$. Unfortunately, there are two systems in use, one that numbers from the top and one that begins at the bottom. Other devices, like dotted lines above and below the text, are also in use.

The phonemes of JUNCTURE, or TRANSITION, are classes of the ways we use to pass from one bit or stretch of linguistic material to the next. If this merely seems a clumsy way of saying something like "get from one phrase or sentence to the next," the reason is that the use of juncture helps to define terms like *phrase* and *sentence*. Therefore we cannot, without circular reasoning, use the terms in describing juncture. As a minor digression, let me point out that our standard practice has been to use circularity, though often at one or two removes. We may use *sentence* to help define *verb*, and then turn around and use *verb* to help define *sentence*. The structuralists try very hard not to fall into this sort of trap.

The four phonemes of juncture are symbolized by $/+, |, ||, \#/$, called plus juncture, single bar juncture, double bar juncture, and double cross juncture respectively. PLUS JUNCTURE, which classically distinguishes 'night rate' from 'nitrate,' can be left behind with the observation that it always occurs at least between secondary stresses, and between a secondary and primary, unless one of the other three junctures is there. (This, of course, like all that follows, is a rule of the language, not of the structuralists; it is a phenomenon observed, not created.) The remaining junctures can be thought of as major, for they serve to establish what is probably the basic rule of English grammar: There is always one, and only one, primary stress between any pair of $/|, ||, \#/$. This rule is completely accurate if the silence before speech is counted as a major juncture and if the speaker is not interrupted. For example, both these versions are accepted by listeners as normal English:

> My ôlder brôther is a plúmber.
> My ôlder brôther | is a plúmber.

SINGLE BAR JUNCTURE can be read as transition across a fairly minor break with pitch sustained to the point of juncture. It is never an uninterrupted speaker's final juncture. DOUBLE BAR JUNCTURE is familiar to us as the rising "question intonation," a thoroughly misleading term. The questions that end in double bar are those without question words, like 'Are you going?' and 'He's here?' In all but perhaps a very few dialects, questions like 'Where are you going?' do not end in double bar. Polite vocatives always end with double bar: 'I'm going, Mother.' Especially in rather slow speech, the rise of double bar is common within the conventional sentence:

> The sôldiers in Koréa || wânted to gêt hóme.

DOUBLE CROSS JUNCTURE is marked by voice fade-out, and usually a lowering of pitch. It appears where periods have been used in the examples, and at the end of 'Where are you going?' It also appears, at least in some reading styles, before what we have been trained to call a non-restrictive subordinate clause at the end of a sentence.

The implications of the suprasegmental phonemes for teachers are important. Almost all marks of punctuation are juncture signals, as we demonstrate again and again by reading aloud mispunctuated student sentences to show that they sound queer. Some of us, perhaps, sometimes even deliberately misread the student's punctuation because it violates an editorial rule, not a linguistic principle. But almost nobody, within my knowledge, is equipped to give students a sensible explanation of punctuation in terms of major junctures and the arbitrary rules of editors.[5]

Reading styles differ within rather narrow limits, but for the sake of illustration we can arbitrarily pick one in which /#/ is symbolized by a period and /|||/ by a comma. No other junctures are marked by punctuation. If the student gives the reading 'He wasn't there /|||/ therefore I didn't see him,' the comma before *therefore* is right linguistically, however wrong it may be editorially. If he reads 'I didn't go to the dance /#/ because I was too tired,' the proper punctuation linguistically is into two sentences. In the past year and a half, I have marked comma faults and fragments RA for "Read aloud." When the student's reading has been right linguistically, I have been able to show him how to identify the situations in which he cannot trust to his ear for punctuation. Without claiming perfect results, I can say that I have been astonished at how readily students of all levels have taken to my explanations and how often they have asked me why punctuation was never explained to them that way in high school.

Over and above such editorial errors in punctuation, the suprasegmental phonemes are important in helping students understand why we group words as we do and how it happens that writing produced by the unwary is often ambiguous. Students can see (and hear) that junctures enclose word groups, and when they understand that the number of junctures increases as the pace of reading slows, they can more and more guard their readers against misunderstanding. 'After eating the baby fell asleep' (which I owe to a former colleague) tends to disappear. This is not simply a matter of punctuation, for often the student either alters the word order ('The baby fell asleep after eating') or makes a substitution ('After its meal the baby fell asleep'). The reason it disappears is that the student has discovered that

After êating the báby . . .

is a possible alternative to

After éating . . .

[5] By far the best available explanation is that by A. H. Marckwardt in the Thorndike-Barnhart *Comprehensive Desk Dictionary* (Doubleday, 1951), pp. 21–24.

The sound system of English, then, has a rather direct bearing on what teachers do in the classroom. In particular, familiarity with the segmental phonemes should make for an understanding of spelling difficulties due to dialect and should kill once and for all the notion that unconventional phonemic spelling is a sign that the speller "doesn't speak good English" or "doesn't enunciate his words clearly": When the snow is deep, many of the best people wear

/ártĭks/, not /árk+tĭks/.

And second, acquaintance with the suprasegmental phonemes can help us realize why naive students punctuate as they do and manage to produce some of their howlers. It is not a question of studying speech for its own sake; it is a question of being able to put our fingers quite precisely on what is amiss and of being in a position to help each student accommodate himself to our traditional writing system and its editorial expectations.

Something of Morphemics*

GEORGE P. FAUST

THE TWO PREVIOUS ARTICLES of this series have mainly tried to explain (1) that the structural linguists give priority to speech over writing for purposes of analysis and concern themselves with language as a medium of communication, and (2) what the most essential terms in phonemics are and how they are used. The present article will by necessity use the earlier two as background, assuming acquaintance with the phonemes of English and some ability to read phonemic transcription. I hope that is not too forbidding.

As we approach morphemics, new terms will concern us, but they will seem like so much abracadabra unless the occasion for them is clear. I myself do not see how they could be dispensed with. Again, familiar terms used in new ways are sure to be traps unless the redefinitions of them are observed and absorbed. But as Professor Fries has observed, "The difference between the [structural] approach used here and the older approach lies much deeper than a mere matter of terminology."[1] There should be no worship of terms, nor fear either, for the terms themselves are not central except as they operate as tools. In general, the structuralists seem to care relatively little for the terms and a great deal for accurate

* Reprinted by permission from *College Composition and Communication*, 5.65–69 (May, 1954).
[1] *The Structure of English* (Harcourt, Brace and Co., 1952), p. 2.

definition and consistent use. What is important is the discovery of a pattern or of a tool, a method, for bringing patterns to light.

MORPHEMICS, which includes everything in language (narrowly defined) from the smallest unit of meaning to the construction of the sentence, takes its name from a useful tool, the morpheme. The first stages of morphemics, up to syntax, are called MORPHOLOGY, and the first two steps in morphology are to identify morphs and classify them. A MORPH can be over-simply defined as an individual linguistic form which is an indivisible unit of meaning. Someone who says 'scramble' has used a morph. It seems to contain several forms—*am, ram, scram, ramble, amble*. But if any one of them is taken out, the remainder of the sounds is meaningless. We are forced to conclude that the 'scramble' we heard is indivisible.

Any morph can be recorded as a phoneme or a pattern of phonemes. (Here it should be emphasized that no phoneme *qua* phoneme is a morph. To be a morph, a phoneme must in addition carry meaning.) Suppose you render the line "A rose is a rose is . . ." Each occurrence of *a* /ə/, *rose* /rowz/, and *is* /iz/ is a morph, but the second occurrence is not the same morph as the first, for, strictly speaking, no morph is ever repeated. This only means, of course, that the first pin of the paper is never the second, no matter how much alike they may be.

Determining whether a form is meaningful is a technical process that cannot be described here, but it is important to note that the structuralist does not need to be able to put his finger on the meaning. He only needs to know that it is there. And here is a good place to make, briefly, some distinction between referential meaning, which belongs to semantics, and differential meaning, which is a tool of structural linguistics. Given the knowledge that a form has meaning, it *is* important to the linguist to know whether its meaning is "same" or "different" as compared with another form. So, if he hears

'He's still' /hiyz stíl/

on one occasion and

'He's still here' /hiyz stíl híhr/

on another, he will want to find out whether the two forms he has recorded as /stíl/ are "same" or "different." (As a native speaker, I say, "Different." Do we agree?)

Broadly speaking, structuralists arrive at morphemes by comparing morphs. A MORPHEME can be defined, again oversimply, as a class of morphs that are semantically similar and contrast with morphs belonging to other morphemes. Semantic similarity by itself might gather /red/, /yelow/, /blɪw/[2] into one morpheme of color, but since they all contrast before /dres/, say, they belong to different morphemes.

---

2 /ɪ/ represents the high central vowel.

Often there are differences among the members of a morpheme, usually phonemic, and it is useful to recognize subclasses, called allomorphs. An ALLOMORPH consists of like morphs that are in complementary distribution with all other members of their morpheme. For example, English has a morpheme of plurality which has a great many allomorphs. To take the three simplest and most obvious variants, consider *coats* /kowts/, *gloves* /gləvz/, and *dresses* /dresɪz/. In each case a member of the plural morpheme is present, as we can learn from experiment. The forms /s, z, ɪz/ differ phonemically but are in complementary distribution. That is, we do not say /kowtɪz/, and with our training, we probably cannot say /kowtz/. These three, along with many others also in complementary distribution, are set up as allomorphs of the plural morpheme. (The morpheme itself is recorded for convenience as /Z₁/[3]; every such "cover symbol" should be described in full somewhere.) *Allomorph* is so convenient a term that even morphemes with a single phonemic shape are said to have one allomorph.

The parallel of *morph, allomorph,* and *morpheme* with *phone, allophone,* and *phoneme* is obvious. Any morph may be called a morph (i.e., an individual linguistic form which is an indivisible unit of meaning) or an allomorph (i.e., a member of an allomorph) or a morpheme (i.e., a member of a morpheme). If I hear you say 'Take your coats,' the last meaningful unit, /s/, is a morph that immediately becomes past history. By comparison with other examples of /s/ with the same kind of meaning, I can set up what I think is a class. But a trained structuralist would very soon discover that my supposed class was only a subclass, an allomorph, of a morpheme that has many allomorphs.

The material considered so far has all consisted of segmental phonemes and has given us SEGMENTAL MORPHEMES. The suprasegmental phonemes produce SUPRASEGMENTAL MORPHEMES, whose meanfulness is harder for us to grasp, partly—at a guess—because they have only recently been discovered. But apparently it is impossible for us to say anything in English without using at least three morphemes: one segmental, one of stress, and one of intonation (pitch and major juncture).[4] The full phonemic transcription of one way of saying 'Go' is

$$/^3\text{gów}^1\#/.$$

One morpheme is the segmental material, /gow/; one is the stress, /'/; and one is the intonation pattern, /³ ¹#/. The suprasegmental morphemes need not be examined here; their greatest value is in syntactic analysis.

---

[3] For simplicity, the customary brackets for morphemes are not used in this article. The subscript distinguishes the plural morpheme from any others that may have any of the same phonemic shapes.

[4] See G. L. Trager and H. L. Smith, Jr., *An Outline of English Structure* (Studies in Linguistics: Occasional Paper No. 3). Pitch is represented /4 (highest), 3, 2, 1 (lowest)/.

After the morphemes are accounted for, the next step in morphology is to classify the segmental morphemes in what might be called "the grammar of the word." Briefly, the segments can be grouped into BASES, PREFIXES, and SUFFIXES. Bases are usually "free forms" like *sweet*—forms that occur without any prefix or suffix—but some are not, like *-ceive*, which always occurs with a prefix. Prefixes, which like suffixes are never free forms, need no comment. There are two kinds of suffixes, DERIVATIONAL and GRAMMATICAL. Derivational suffixes, like the *-ness* of *coolness*, tend to limit forms to a particular part of speech. (Does this account for our widespread objection to the use of *suspicion* as a verb?) Grammatical suffixes give us the inflections of the few remaining paradigms in English. Disregarding suprasegmental features, the WORD can now be defined as a single base with or without prefixes and suffixes. By this definition, *incompatibility*, with its single base, is a word; *shotgun*, with two bases, is not. *It is of no linguistic importance that* shotgun *is written solid.*

The final step in morphology is the establishment of PARADIGMS, which can be viewed as sets of grammatical suffixes. These suffixes follow the base and derivational suffixes (e.g., either *help* or *helpfulness*). English has paradigms for pronouns, nouns, verbs, and adjectives. In at least the last three, "no suffix" must be recognized as a characteristic ending by contrast with the suffixes used. It is a peculiarity of the language that the noun suffixes for "plural" and "possessive" coalesce when they are both present and the plural morpheme is one of /s, z, ɪz/. Thus we get /kidz/ (alongside /menz/) where we might have expected /kidzɪz/.

The paradigm for MORPHOLOGICAL PRONOUNS, a notoriously irregular set, has been the occasion for a good deal of experimenting. The presentation we grew up with emphasizes person, number, gender and case in that order. One of the structural presentations re-works the order to gender, case, person, and number, with really no attention to the last two. The order of cases is also modified to subject, object, 1st possessive, 2nd possessive. Here is the paradigm: *Without Gender:* I, me, my, mine; we, us, our, ours; you, you, your, yours; they, them, their, theirs. *With Gender:* he, him, his, his; she, her, her, hers; it, it, its,—. (Whether the forms of *who* are included is a matter of personal preference.)

The paradigm for NOUNS is: *Common Case:* Sg. (no suffix) /layf/, Pl. (/-Z_1/) /layvz/; *Possessive Case:* Sg. (/-Z_2/) /layfs/, Pl. (/-Z_1/ and /-Z_2/ merged) /layvz/.

The paradigm for VERBS is: *Infinitive and General Present:* (no suffix) /liv/, /rayz/; *3rd Singular Present:* (/-Z_3/) /livz/, /rayzɪz/; *Past:* (/-D_1/) /livd/, /rowz/; *Past Participle:* (/-D_2/) /livd/, /rizɪn/; *Present Participle:* ('-ing') 'living,' 'rising.'

The paradigm for ADJECTIVES is: *Positive:* (no suffix) /layv/; *Comparative:* (/-ər/) /layvər/; *Superlative:* (/-ɪst/) /layvɪst/.

The reason for going into the paradigms fully is that they serve as defi-

nitions of parts of speech at the morphological level. If an item is inflectible within a paradigm—that is, if it appears with at least two appropriate
suffixes (including "no suffix")—it is a member of the part of speech defined by the paradigm.[5] Every item must qualify by this test to be included, which means that *poor* (*poorer, poorest*) is a MORPHOLOGICAL
ADJECTIVE, but *excellent* remains unassigned. A MORPHOLOGICAL NOUN is
defined as a linguistic item which is inflectible for singular/plural, or for
common case/possessive, or for both. Similarly, a MORPHOLOGICAL VERB is
inflectible for present/past, etc. *Man* is a noun because of what we write
man's as well as because of *men;* it is also a verb because of *manned* and
other verbal suffixation. What any one occurrence of the form *man* itself
may be is a question of assigning it to a paradigm.

Roughly speaking, structural linguistics offers the same list of nouns
and verbs as traditional grammar. It is not important why this is so. It is not
even important what particular words, like *other* (cf. *others*), are included
among nouns, say. What is important is the basis for the classification. We
are thoroughly used to a system that often starts with philosophical definitions, and freshmen still know that "A noun is the name of . . ."
At this point it is hard for me to see why, *philosophically* speaking, *rain*
is not just as much of a noun in 'It rained during the night' as in 'Rain fell
during the night.' The difference to me now is purely linguistic. In the first,
rain has a suffix that belongs distinctly to the paradigm labeled *verb;* in
the second, *rains*, with the plural morpheme, can be substituted for *rain*
and produce an English sentence.

Structural definitions are no panacea in teaching, but my experience
with using them has been encouraging. For the present, students who have
mastered traditional grammar had better be left alone, unless they are
exceptionally bright. But among those who never "learned grammar" in
high school, I have found some who can match forms more easily than
grasp the traditional definitions.

When we leave morphology for syntax, we come to an area where much
has been done and much remains to be done. Professor Fries's analysis is
so well known and speaks so adequately for itself that I need do no more
than allude to *The Structure of English*. The highly technical Trager-
Smith *Outline of English Structure*, which I have been more or less following (but any mistakes are mine), is simply unreadable without training in
structural linguistics. Yet it has been extraordinarily influential among
structuralists, especially for its insistence on a separation of "levels" in
analysis and for its report on how we use suprasegmental morphemes to
determine constructions.

[5] It is not true, as sometimes claimed, that morphological parts of speech cannot be
identified without the help of syntax. Without anything to go on but 'Boys will be boys'
a linguist could find out from a completely naive informant that *boys* is the plural of
boy. Contrast 'Fuzz will be fuzz.' If the linguist already knows that *they* is plural, he
can take a short cut by trying 'They will be boys.'

Separation of levels means, among other things, that parts of speech morphologically defined are not the same as parts of speech syntactically defined. If you hear 'Today is Sunday,' 'Today's paper just came,' and 'He just came today,' you can tell from the forms in the first two that *today* is a morphological noun. But in the second it is in some respects a SYNTACTIC ADJECTIVE, and in the last, fully a SYNTACTIC ADVERB.[6] It is only at the syntactic level that adverbs, prepositions, conjunctions, question words (e.g., *when, why, what*), some auxiliaries, and some adjectives can be assigned to parts of speech. To avoid confusion, it is always best to prefix either *morphological* or *syntactic,* whichever is proper, to the name of the part.

Traditional definitions have been by meaning, by form, and by function. Definition by meaning is demonstrably unnecessary. By the separation of levels, it is now possible to take care of difficulties and confusions growing out of using definition by form and definition by function simultaneously. As a resultant, we may well expect an end of such descriptions as "noun used as adjective" (e.g., in *state highway*) and "noun used as adverb" or "adverbial noun" (e.g., *home* in 'He went home'). If the cleavage between levels were consistently represented in our schoolbooks, I feel sure we would be able to teach it easily.

Suprasegmental morphemes are either SUPERFIXES, patterns of stress with or without plus juncture intervening, or INTONATION PATTERNS, patterns of pitch and major juncture. Several superfixes have been discovered to be "phrase-making":

$$/\,'+\,'/,\ /\,'+\,\backslash/,\ \text{and}\ /\,'+\wedge/.$$

($/\wedge+\,'/$ does not make phrases.) Noun compounds have superfixes and are syntactic phrases (e.g., *shotgun*—shót+gùn—which was rejected as a morphological word). 'A blackboard [blâck+bôard] isn't just a black board [blâck+bóard]' illustrates the difference between phrase and non-phrase, and so does 'It's a come-down' (cóme+dôwn) in contrast with 'He's come down' (côme+dówn). Intonation patterns make a number of distinctions, only one of which can be illustrated here. '²He's ³góing¹#' uses the commonest morpheme, which can be described as "statement unless qualified by other signals." It contrasts with '²Is he ³góing³||', a pattern associated with questions that use no questionword. ('²He's ³góing³||' is a question because of the pattern; '²Where is he ³góing¹#' is a question because the pattern is qualified by the use of *where.*) Generally speaking, superfixes apply to phrases, while intonation patterns apply to larger constructions that might be called intonation clauses.

It has proved impossible to cover the ground of morphemics in even a

---

[6] In terminology, the Trager-Smith analysis distinguishes less clumsily, but introduces more new terms: *morphological adjective=adjective; syntactic adjective=adjectival.* There are no *adverbs*—only *adverbials.*

simplified way. My apologies are due the reader for a crowded article which has found little room to point to applications useful to us as teachers. One thing is reasonably certain, and that is that many uses will be found as we gather a corps of middlemen—structuralists who know something about our teaching problems and teachers who are at home with structural linguistics.

Fries's *Structure of English:* A Review*

JAMES H. SLEDD

EDITOR'S NOTE:

[In the first and longer portion of this critical review the author dealt with the significant study, *An Outline of English Structure*, by George L. Trager and Henry Lee Smith, Jr., 1951. There, after identifying himself as "neither a linguist nor a man of letters, but a Ph.D. in English," Sledd provided a keen and cogent criticism, somewhat too long and technical for inclusion here, and ended with the appraisal that, because of the Smith-Trager analysis, "With luck, the average freshman in the next generation will know far more about English than the average teacher knows today, and the average teacher will know what the superior freshman OUGHT to know."]

Thanks also will be due to Fries for his *Structure of English*, an excellent if somewhat old-fashioned book which has already been hailed as revolutionary.[1] One of the relatively few philologists who have not only

* *The structure of English: An Introduction to the Construction of English Sentences.* By Charles Carpenter Fries. Pp. ix, 304 (New York: Harcourt, Brace and Company, 1952). Review reprinted with permission of author and publisher, from *Language*, 31.312–345 (1955). Only pages 335–345 are reproduced here.

[1] Earlier reviews of the *Structure* include those by Max Bertschinger, *English studies* 34.300–4 (1953); James W. Downer, *Language learning* 4.133–7 (1952–3); Karl Dykema, *College English* 14.93–100 (1952); Norman E. Eliason, *MLN* 69.66–8 (1954); Nils Erik Enkvist, *Neuphilologische Mitteilungen* 55.149–51 (1954); W. Nelson Francis, *Quarterly journal of speech* 40.299–312 (1954); Otto Funke, *Sprachgeschichte und Wortbedeutung* 141–50 (Bern, 1954); Funke, *Archivum linguisticum* 6.1–19 (1954); Edna Lue Furness, *Modern language journal* 38.57–8 (1954); Archibald A. Hill, *JEGP* 51.591–3 (1952); Robert C. Pooley, *Am. speech* 28.35–40 (1953); J. A. Sheard, *MLR* 49.220–1 (1954); James Sledd, *MP* 50.138–41 (1952); Harry R. Warfel, *Who killed grammar?* (Gainesville, Fla., 1952); and R. W. Zandvoort, *Museum* 58.250–4 (1953). Judgments have ranged from hysterical condemnation to ecstatic praise, but in general the reception has been favorable, particularly in the United States, where Fries has a large following among teachers on the fringes of linguistics. Perhaps these educated laymen, of whom the present reviewer makes one, have been a bit on the enthusiastic side. Readers less familiar with Fries's work might wish to consult some of his earlier studies; for example, The periphrastic future with *shall* and *will* in modern

kept up with modern linguistics but have contributed actively to its development, Fries has always been interested in the APPLICATION of linguistic science; and although his original contributions have been solid and
extensive, his practical bent and his frequent choice of a semipopular
audience have restricted his theoretical excursions and his use of new
techniques. His repute as an innovator, it might almost be said, has been
earned by his abstaining from innovation.

Fries's theory and analysis of meaning and meanings are excellent examples of the methods which have made him a radical for some readers
and a reactionary for others. Although he says in a footnote (32) that he
has his psychological fingers crossed and makes no 'psychological assumptions or assertions whatever,' the results of his theory of meaning in
his work are just the same as if he defended the behavioristic assumptions
which he uses. For Fries, 'the "meaning" of any speech signal must consist . . . not only of the practical situation which stimulates the making
of the particular speech sounds but also of the practical response which
these particular speech sounds (through language) produce in another
individual' (34). This is familiar doctrine, propagated long ago by Bloomfield, but it leads to gaudy contradiction. If Fries's definition were sound,
his readers could not understand the recorded telephone conversations
which are the materials of his book, and readers of LANGUAGE would not
understand one word of the sentence which is now before their eyes; the
readers in neither case would have the necessary information about
speakers, hearers, situations, and responses. Indeed, since the definition
makes interpretation impossible and puts meaning beyond discussion,
Fries could never have written an analysis to which, he says, control of
differential meaning was essential.

In this very matter of the use of meaning in linguistic analysis, Fries en-
tangles himself in another contradiction. Quite uncompromisingly, he insists that 'any use of meaning is unscientific whenever the fact of our
knowing the meaning leads us to stop short of finding the precise formal
signals that operate to convey that meaning' (8, fn. 6); but from time to
time he refuses to accept his own excellent advice. Thus whenever he uses
'letter exponents' in his formulas to indicate that two or more words have
the same or different referents, he is cheating; for if the superscripts are
necessary to the identification of the various structures, then the structures are formally indefinable and have no place in Fries's grammar. It may
well be true that the linguist, as Fries has argued, must control differential
meaning; he must know, for example, that *cot* and *lot* are significantly dif-

English, *PMLA* 40.960–1040 (1925); The rules of the common school grammars,
PMLA 42.221–37 (1927); *The teaching of the English language* (New York, 1927);
American English grammar (New York, 1940); *Teaching and learning English as a
foreign language* (Ann Arbor, 1945); *Have* as a function-word, *Language learning*
1.4–8 (1948); Meaning and linguistic analysis, *Lg.* 30.57–68 (1954).

ferent. But if, when he encounters the sentence *Tonight that cot is my lot,* the linguist insists that he must know whether *cot* and *lot* have the same referent, he has broken down all barriers to the use of meaning in his analysis. For him, it has become legitimate to ask, in every instance, whether or not one nominal has the same referent as another; and with a question in that form, he can push his semantic inquiries as far as the most conservative grammarian might wish to do. Fries's introduction proclaims a revolution which his text subverts—and that not once, but repeatedly.

The subversion is not only theoretical. Almost any reader must sometimes be puzzled by Fries's remarks about the meanings of specific structures, partly because a few of them are singularly empty, partly because somewhat more of them are wrong in fact. Emptiness reaches the extreme of pure tautology in the pronouncement that 'the structural meaning of "performer"' in a particular kind of subject 'includes *everything that is linguistically grasped in the pattern of performer*' (178). To be sure; a thing means what it means, but why bother to say so? Factual error appears in the statment that when a past participle modifies a noun, the noun 'represents the "undergoer of the action" indicated in the "modifier"' (220). Anyone could immediately think of several contrary examples, like *the vanished buffalo, the newly arrived teacher, the risen Lord,* and so on; and no one would have much trouble finding other mistakes about the meanings of individual constructions. As a contribution to English semantics, *The Structure of English* is not a distinguished book. Fries is certainly right that the linguist must sooner or later face semantic questions, call them metalinguistic or not, and Pike may be right that he must face them sooner; but it must be added that when the linguist puts on his semantic hat, he must not put off his high standards of method and result.

Perhaps, then, *The Structure of English* will owe some of its strength as propaganda not only to its general strength, but to its occasional weakness, as linguistic science: it exemplifies the conflict which most of its readers must undergo in trying to free themselves from an outworn grammatical tradition. Already in his introduction, Fries lost perhaps his most serious skirmish with himself, and the consequences are so bad that, in the reviewer's opinion, they frustrate Fries's intent 'to provide the fundamental descriptive analysis upon which . . . practical textbooks can be built.' Fries has created much of the demand for better textbooks, and he will provide, as the reviewer is glad to testify, much of the material for them; but extensive corrections and additions will have to be made to Fries's statements if the new texts are not to perpetuate old difficulties. One counsel of perfection is that the textbook-makers should remember that neither the English language nor the scholarly study of it is confined to the United States. More immediately relevant is the suggestion that without the phonology, not even a good elementary description of English structure can be written, so that popularizers must draw heavily on the linguists who have most vigorously argued this proposition—on Trager, Smith, and their phonologically-minded colleagues and predecessors. The popularizers cannot get their phonology from Fries, who chooses to minimize it, partly 'because the use of even simplified phonemic notation would probably put the book beyond the patience of many lay readers' (7). The gains from a strategic retreat at this point are not worth the losses.

Just how great the losses are, appears from the fact that a summary of *The Structure of English* is almost prerequisite to their full statement. After the introduction, whose most important contents have already been noted, Fries boxes a noisy but inconclusive round with the question what is a sentence. Here and elsewhere in his book, he gets in his best licks when he criticizes the familiar attempts at semantic definitions of formal categories; but his positive contribution, in this and the third chapter, which deals with 'kinds of sentences,' is limited. Several reasons may justify this mildly negative judgment. Even for a grammarian, Fries is no stylist; the traditional grammars which he berates so convincingly are not the best available alternatives to his own system; and he says so little about his methods that some readers grow suspicious of his results. The reviewer, who suspects that Fries has no definition of the sentence, naturally does not know how sentences were isolated in Fries's materials; and he notes at least occasional overlapping in Fries's nonlinguistic classification of sentences into greetings, calls, and questions (all regularly eliciting oral responses); commands or requests (with 'action' responses); and statements (provoking continuous attention to continuous discourse).

Chapter 4, which pummels semantic definitions again and makes the transition to Fries's analysis of the parts of speech, is notable for its insistence that the forms which signal structural meanings operate in a system. Linguists, of course, need not be told that since 'an English sentence is . . . not a group of words as words but rather a structure made up of form-classes,' it must be described 'in terms of the selection of these large form-classes and the formal arrangements in which they occur' (64); but to the educated American layman, there is considerable novelty in the idea that languages must be described systematically if at all. The great advantage of Fries's *Structure* over the Trager-Smith *Outline* is precisely that Fries, although he too has pretty much to assume a nonexistent morphological analysis, comes much closer to a relatively complete statement of the essentials of English syntax than Trager and Smith do; his omission of considerable material on the verbal system is deliberate. Less fortunate, in the reviewer's opinion, is Fries's decision to replace the usual labels, *noun, verb, adjective,* and *adverb,* with the more scientific-looking *Class 1, Class 2, Class 3,* and *Class 4.* Since the great majority of his Class 1 words, for example, would be nouns in any freshman handbook, it seems wiser to take advantage of this overlap and to preserve the traditional names, despite the risk of confusion between the old and new definitions, than to excite unnecessary irritation. There will be irritation enough in Chapter 6, with its fifteen somewhat messy groups of 'function words.' Chapter 7 concludes the discussion of parts of speech by listing morphological and syntactic characteristics of each of the four classes.

In the eighth chapter, the parts of speech and function words are put to work as Fries attempts 'to describe the distinctive contrasts of pattern that mark the various kinds of sentences [statements, questions, and commands], not apart from, but within the various primary intonation contours' (143); the centering of attention 'upon the devices and patterns of structure other than intonation' is characteristic of his method. Proceeding further in his classification and analysis, in his ninth chapter he discusses the structural meanings of subjects and objects. He puts together, from the numerical and alphabetical symbols for his four classes and fifteen groups, a series of formulas to express the significant contrasts which identify these structures; and he employs the same symbols, in Chapter 10, in a discussion of structures of modification and their meanings. At least for native speakers, the formulaic presentation, like the use of jabberwocky sentences, seems to the reviewer to be a teaching device of considerable value, which he would hope and expect to see rather generally adopted.

Three more chapters complete *The Structure of English*. The eleventh begins with an examination of 'sequence sentences,' the sentences after the first sentence in a stretch of uninterrupted talk with which a speaker opens a conversation, and ends with a discussion of the devices 'by which word-groups having the formal characteristics of free utterance units are included in larger sentence units' (252–53). 'Included sentences' raise the problem of immediate constituents to which Chapter 12 is devoted. Accepting the dogma that 'in English a layer of structure has usually only two members' (264), Fries lists 'a series of steps for the analysis of present-day English sentences that seem to reveal the immediate constituents of each structure in its proper structural layer and thus the relation of structure to structure' (266). 'For this type of analysis,' he insists as he introduces examples of its working, 'it is not necessary to know the lexical meanings of the words nor to know what a sentence is about' (268); 'it is formal analysis of formal units' (Trager-Smith, *Outline* 68). The thirteenth chapter concludes the book with some suggestions concerning practical applications and with a statement of the intrinsic value of linguistic study.

From this summary, it should be clear that Fries has dealt systematically with basic facts and problems of English syntax, and none of the criticisms which the reviewer has made or will make should obscure his conviction that Fries's results are of the first importance. His is the first serious book-length attempt to treat the English sentence from the structural point of view; much of his analysis is solid and will have to be incorporated into future descriptions; and although at times his writing vexes academic readers, he has tried hard to make his material comprehensible and useful to nonlinguists. It was, indeed, Fries's estimate of educated laymen, including teachers of English and foreign languages 'in our schools and colleges' (7), which prompted him to present his evidence in 'conventional spelling,' not 'phonemic notation,' though one suspects that there may also be deeper causes for his neglect of the phonology. With the outline of his book in mind, the consequences of that neglect may now be detailed.

Bluntly, the neglect of phonology made it certain that Fries would have difficulty in defining the sentence, that some of his form-classes would be hopelessly heterogeneous, that his discussion of certain structures, such as modification, would be misleading, and that he would invite the very confusion of speech with writing which he exhorts his reader to avoid. Of the definition of the sentence, it is enough to say that after grandly berating the traditional grammars, Fries himself leaves the sentence as undefined as he found it. 'Each sentence,' he says, quoting Bloomfield, 'is an independent linguistic form, not included by virtue of any grammatical construction in any larger linguistic form' (21); but Fries leaves the concepts of independence and inclusion more than a little ambiguous. One would like to know, for example, and to know in some detail, what are the specific signs that mark a form as independent or included and why Fries's 'sequence signals' are not to be taken as grammatical constructions marking the inclusion of two smaller units in a larger one; and until this information is provided, one can only judge that 'sequence sentences' really are no sentences at all but are included, with the so-called sentences that precede them, in some larger construction on whose size Fries sets no upper limit. Fries only makes the difficulty worse when he notes that almost all a speaker's sentences, after the one with which he begins a conversation, 'contain some type of sequence signal' and that 'the "response utterances" of a second speaker continuing the conversation also have them' (251). The same problem arises with questions and answers, if 'the question itself is part of the frame in which the answer as an utterance operates' (165). *Is Mr. L—— there?* a speaker asks, and gets the answer, *No, he's not right now,* in which the pronoun might be taken as one signal of inclusion. In all this obscurity, Fries makes no use of possible phonological markers of the sentence but in a single footnote dismisses, as fruitless experiment, his attempts at segmentation by 'the marking of pauses, and of intonation sequences' (36, fn. 12). It might not be impertinent to ask precisely how good his recordings of telephone conversations are and whether he himself transcribed them phonemically or simply had a secretary prepare a conventional typscript.

If Fries's treatment of the whole sentence suffers from his neglect of the phonology, so do his discussions of word-classes and of structures within the sentence. An obvious example is Group E of his function words, which includes *and, or, not, nor, but,* and *rather than*—this last a very peculiar item to appear with the label *word,* though no more peculiar than the similarly labeled *in order that* (253). The testing frame for Group E, in which superfixes and intonation patterns are as usual left unmarked, is a rather long sentence: 'The concerts *and* the lectures are *and* were interesting *and* profitable now *and* earlier' (94). If the reader shortens the frame a little and substitutes *not* for *and*, as he is assured he may do, a startling difference on the suprasegmental level immediately appears:

^{2}Thĕ + côncèrts + ănd + thĕ + ^{3}léctŭres^2 |
$\qquad\qquad\qquad$ ^{2}ăre + ìnteřestĭng + ănd + ^{3}prófĭtăblĕ^1 #
^{2}Thĕ + ^{3}cóncèrts^2 || ^{1}nòt + thĕ + ^{2}léctŭres^1 |
$\qquad\qquad\qquad$ ^{2}ăre + ^{3}ìnteřestĭng^2 || ^{2}nòt + ^{3}prófĭtăblĕ^1 #

Fries's Group E, that is to say, is not one group at all, but several groups; for patterns of pitch and stress are just as much a part of a testing frame as the words that they accompany, and if classes are defined by occurrence in frames, a change of frames means a different class.

Suprasegmental morphemes are as essential to the definition of structures like subject and object as they are to the specification of testing frames; but Fries neglects them in the one undertaking as in the other. As a result, he must rely on the listing of special verbs and on the surreptitious introduction of referential meaning in order to define the 'predicate nominative'; but in at least one instance, the superfixes seem to provide a useful clue. Fries contrasts these sentences:

$\qquad\qquad$ ^{2}The + mân + sèemed + him^{3}sélf^1 #
$\qquad\qquad$ ^{2}The + mân + ^{3}húrt + himsèlf^1 #

Although the reviewer cannot pretend to have studied the matter thoroughly, the contrast in the position of the primary stress indicates a line of inquiry which ought to be followed to the end before any decisions are based on identity of referential meanings.

Fries's unwillingness to engage in such inquiry has given some of his less sympathetic reviewers an unnecessarily easy triumph. Otto Funke is one who questions the possibility of formal analysis without the use of lexical meanings; and he chooses, as a prime example, one of Fries's 'structures of modification.' Discussing the phrase *an insane asylum*, Fries says that only 'lexical incompatibility' prevents the structure from being ambiguous. Funke leaps triumphantly on this admission—but lands face down on a sharp superfix. He simply does not know the difference between an asylum for the insane, which is an /^{2}in^{3}séynŏsàylŏm^1|||/, and an asylum irresponsibly managed, which is an /^{2}ĭnsêyn + ŏ^{3}sáylŏm^1 # /. And Funke does not know the difference because native speakers like Fries have neglected to tell him. When Fries forgets his own lesson, that meanings are formally signalled, and when he forgets that the signals in speech must escape the student who operates only with marks on paper, he finds a mare's nest of spurious ambiguities to bewilder the simpleminded.

In Fries's discussion of modification this is particularly true. There, his neglect of superfixes prevents him from making the distinction between a *criminal láwyer* and *a criminal lâwyer, a Spânish stúdent* and *a Spánish stûdent, a dêaf and dûmb téacher* and *a dèaf and dúmb têacher;* and the inevitable result will be that readers like Funke are encouraged to persist in their confusion of speech with writing. The choice of newspaper headlines as sources of alleged ambiguities is peculiarly unfortunate in this respect. All that many of Fries's headlines prove is that if enough of the signals are filtered out, the remainder will not be clear. One of his headlines is *Vandenberg Reports Open Forum* (62). Fries calls this headline structurally ambiguous, but if read aloud, it is perfectly plain. If Senator Vandenberg was reporting an open forum, then the headline is

$$\text{³Vándĕnbèrg² } || \text{ ²rĕpôrts } + \text{ ôpĕn } + \text{ ³fórŭm¹ } \#$$

If reports by Senator Vandenberg opened a forum, then it is

$$\text{³Vándĕnbèrg } + \text{ rĕpôrts² } || \text{ ²ôpĕn } + \text{ ³fórŭm¹ } \#$$

Any native speaker makes and hears such distinctions every day; but once the innocent observer gets himself involved in a defective writing system, he is likely to lose his common sense and try to argue that the trouble is in the language itself. 'What,' asks one reviewer, 'would structural analysis alone do with 'Professor Rakes Leaves after College Commencement'?' The answer: read it aloud and note the formal distinctions which orthography does not record:

$$\text{²Prŏfèssŏr} + \text{³Rákes² } | \text{ ²Lêaves} + \text{àftĕr} + \text{Côllĕge} + \text{Cŏm³méncemĕnt¹ } \#$$
$$\text{²Prŏ³féssŏr² } | \text{ ²Râkes} + \text{Lêaves} + \text{àftĕr} + \text{Côllĕge} + \text{Cŏm³méncemĕnt¹ } \#$$

In linguistic matters, the educated layman would be better off if he were really literate or really illiterate; his middle ground is untenable.

The conflict between tradition and innovation which appears in Fries's treatment and use of meaning and in his neglect of the phonology does not appear so clearly in other aspects of his establishment of his four major form-classes and his fifteen groups of function words; but here, too, there are difficulties. In principle, the grammarian should recognize an array of classes such that with them he can account for most utterances of the language and that the recognition of further classes would show a sharp diminution of returns in his power to do so. A very great number of classes, however, actually exist in the utterances, so that the choice of defining characteristics is extremely difficult. The methods of Trager and Smith might lead to the establishment of classes on three levels: first, bases or stems classified by their distribution with respect to inflectional suffixes; second, bases or stems classified by their distribution with respect to derivational suffixes; third, morphemic words or phrases classified by their occurrence in environments larger than the morphemic word. Mixing levels might lead to the establishment of further classes, with defining characteristics drawn from any two of the three levels, from all three levels, from either of any two, or from any of all three; and of course on each level the specified environments might be either single or multiple and the forms to be classified might be treated in isolation (which would necessitate statements of total distribution and would thus multiply classes) or only as they occur in actual utterances (which would amount to labeling positions in the first instance and forms only as they fill those positions). It has already been suggested that if bases and stems are classified by their inflections, mixing levels is an almost automatic reaction: *man* is a noun, because it occurs with the inflectional suffixes for the plural and the possessive, but *men's* is not a noun, since no further suffixes can be added. If now *men's* is to be classified syntactically, by its occurrence in larger environments, the choice of testing frames will determine whether it is to be adjectival or nominal; and even if it is arranged that *men's* should be nominal in most or all of its occurrences, there will still be some instances in which a noun (or a complex of a noun plus an inflectional suffix) will not be nominal, a verb (or verb-plus-inflection) not verbal, etc. In a jungle like this, the reviewer would welcome a little more tradition to fight or follow.

It is not quite clear what solutions Fries proposes. Apparently, his fifteen groups of function words are purely syntactic. They are discovered by finding what words will fill certain positions in sentences, and they may be said to be defined either by stating the distinctive position or positions for each group or by simple listing. Fries emphasizes that 'there are no formal contrasts by which we can identify the words of these lists. They must be remembered as items' (109). The four classes, on the other hand, are by no means purely syntactic. If the reader asks what are the necessary and sufficient conditions for inclusion in one of them, Fries answers that there are no necessary conditions and that sufficient conditions may be either syntactic or morphological. 'There is no single characteristic,' he says, 'that all the examples of one part of speech must have in the utterances of English' (73); and the 'significant markings within an utterance' may 'consist of relative positions, accompanying function words, contrastive patterns of the shapes or forms of the words themselves, corresponding forms of other words, [or] substitute forms with which the words themselves correlate' (141, fn. 18). Of these distinctive features, some are always sufficient to mark the inclusion of an item in a given class. For example, 'all compounds of which the last unit is *one*, or *body*, or *thing*, or *self/selves*' are Class 1, and so are 'all words marked by one of the "determiners"' (116,118). Some other characteristics, however, are neither necessary nor invariably sufficient conditions for membership in a class, and since 'in general, "position" markers in any particular sentence supercede [sic, repeatedly] morphological or form markers' (141), these weaker criteria are likely to be morphological rather than syntactic. An example is furnished by the sentence *The poorest are always with us,* in which *poorest,* despite its inflection, is marked as Class 1 by the determiner *the* (140, 141).

The reviewer's difficulty with all this is not primarily that Fries mixes levels (as he does, quite happily), but that his specific assignments to his four classes are baffling and that his fifteen groups are neither well chosen nor clearly defined. For one instance, *afternoon* (or perhaps *Thursday afternoon*) is called Class 4 in the question-and-answer, *When is the service? Thursday afternoon* (171). Presumably, one should make the same classification in the sentence, *The service is Thursday afternoon;* but in the sentence *The committee approved the request last Wednesday,* Fries calls *Wednesday* Class 1, and similarly in *The abstract came Wednesday* (186, 229). The reviewer does not see why *Wednesday* is Class 1 in *The abstract came Wednesday,* but *Thursday* is Class 4 in *The service is Thursday.* One more of many examples is the word *burning* in *A burning fire is in the fireplace.* The word fits Fries's testing frame for Class 3 and is replaceable by words like *hot, good, bright,* or *cozy,* yet he does not call it Class 3. Although he has said that position markers supersede morphological markers, he calls *burning* Class 2 (208). This sort of thing happens so often that the reviewer loses all confidence in his ability to apply Fries's system.

The situation is even worse with the function words. Group A, to begin with, is defined as including 'all the words that can occupy the position of *the*' in the frame *The concert was good.* Since Fries himself, among his determiners, lists *this, that, John's,* and the numerals from *one* through *ninety-nine* (89), he must intend that stress should be ignored in making the classification; but if stress is ignored, and if other items which are not mutually exclusive with *the* are listed, then the door is open for the inclusion of a great variety of words among the determiners—*organ, unrehearsed, pops, often, old, amusing, then,* etc. To say that the substitution of most of these items would change the structural meaning of the frame is hardly possible. The reply would be that the structural meaning seems to change when *the* is replaced by *both, few, one, four, many, all,* and the like, which do not occupy the same set of positions as *the;* yet Fries puts all of these in Group A.

Group B also promises to expand uncontrollably. *Has to* is included in it (with no phonemic transcription), because *has to* fills the slot in *The concert has to be good there* (90). The same test would apparently justify including *better, ought to,* and *promises to. Got* is included because it fills the slot in *The class got moved;* but if *got* belongs to Group B, it might be hard to rule out *looked, seemed, felt,* or *appeared.* When *kept* is included, finally, on the basis of *The class kept moving,* the bars are down for *began, continued, disliked, quit, stopped, tried,* or *wanted,* and the group has become a semantic catch-all. Though Fries undoubtedly intends no such result, his own exposition provides no way to avoid it. The consequences for the rest of his book are obvious.

Two more points, and the reviewer will have finished the ungracious task of listing what he takes to be the major defects in a valuable book. The first is that Fries's rules for IC-analysis are severely limited, neither consistent nor complete. Fries calls them 'a series of steps for the analysis of present-day English sentences that seem to reveal the immediate constituents of each structure in its proper structural layer' (266); but his claim is hardly justified. The most obvious question, of course, is what becomes of the superfixes and intonation-patterns in the course of the analysis; unless good reason is given for a different procedure, at some stage they must be treated as constituents, not simply neglected. Waiving that objection, one may doubt that Fries's steps would carry him through the analysis even of the sentences in his own book. A fragment of a conversation recorded on pp. 50–51 runs as follows: *he suggested that we go down and get Mrs. R—— and tell her who we are and that he sent us and try the fourteen-inch typewriters and see if our stencils would work with such type and if we can use them to get them right away because they have those in stock and we won't have to wait.* This normal academic conversation sounds remarkably like the 'Vulgar English sentences' which Fries describes on p. 292: 'many of the Vulgar English sentences are either the very brief statements of "constituents" without any representation of the different layers in which these "constituents" belong, or the very long sentences in which these "constituents" are added in loose succession, without any grasp of the layers of structure in which the "constituents" function.' Precisely, since the 'vulgar' write as most of us talk; but what do such sentences do to Fries's rules and to the doctrine of bipartite structure? To the reviewer, it would appear that in the quoted sentence (50–1) the first *we* is the subject of six verbs. All of them are connected by *and,* but the sixth is marked as an infinitive by *to;* and this shifted construction increases the difficulty of discovering only two constituents where there seem clearly to be six. It might not be too rash a conclusion that the patterns of literary language control the grammarian's procedures even when he is studying recorded speech, and that he will never rightly understand the relationships between talk and book-talk until he finds a method that will be applicable to both without distortion or until he specifies the differences in method which the different materials require.

From IC-analysis to propaganda for linguistics is no great distance in *The Structure of English,* since Fries believes that 'most of the failures of communication seem to be tied up, in one way or another, with the problems of immediate constituents' (262). A final major objection to his book might be that as a propagandist he often rides his horse too hard and sometimes stumbles into plain mistakes. He is mistaken, for example, when he tries (281 ff.) to establish too close a connection between intonation and punctuation. Thus he recommends that the contour after *afterward,* in the following sentence, might have a comma as its graphic substitute: *The discussion afterward, proved the success of the talk.* Unfortunately, his punctuation violates the rather widely observed custom that a comma should not be used to separate subject and predicate. In his capacity as spelling reformer (if that is what a reformer of punctuation is), Fries has neglected the fact that speech and writing are partially independent systems and that the conventions of writing, in writing, are no more and no less binding than the conventions of speech in speech. It is doubtful, however, that the mistake will alienate many more readers than the over-emphasis on the principle of immediate constituents, which Fries applies to such diverse materials as baseball and the marking off of paragraphs.

That any readers should be alienated is as much a criticism of them as it is of Fries. Like the *Outline of English Structure, The Structure of English* should be required reading for teachers of language and languages, English and foreign, in our schools, colleges, and universities. There are, to be sure, striking differences between the two books. The *Outline,* highly technical and theoretical, is part of an elaborate scheme for the organization of knowledge; the *Structure* is placed in no such framework and is addressed to the educated layman. Whereas Trager and Smith almost seem to care more for method than for results, Fries proceeds at times with a lighthearted carelessness, mixing levels and using referential meaning in the most heretical fashion. Numerous differences in detail may be traced to these more general differences. On the other hand, the broad backgrounds of knowledge and method from which the *Outline* and the *Structure* have emerged are very similar, so that the reviewer has been able to apply to Fries (at least to the ideal Fries) a statement with which Trager and Smith describe their work: 'it is formal analysis of formal units.' Moreover, since Trager and Smith pay most attention to the phonology, which Fries neglects, and since Fries rather carefully develops the syntax, which is only hinted at by Trager and Smith, the *Outline* and the *Structure* supplement one another. Together, they give the popularizer of modern linguistics a not unimpressive exhibit, though he may be a little worried by the freedom with which the specimens thumb their noses at the spectators.

The reviewer would beg leave to conclude, however, by cocking his own snook at some of the stuffier onlookers. In the last twenty-five years or so, departments of English have ceased to be the centers for the study of English linguistics which they once were; but as they have grown less hospitable to the linguist, they have grown more friendly to the critic, especially to the kind of critic who makes language central to his study of literature. The result, in some quarters, has been the reduction of literary study to a linguistic undertaking by men who are not linguists, so that the wildest nonsense can be accepted as evidence of the finest insight. Even the conservative literary scholar may be perfectly willing that he and his students should pontificate on matters which they do not understand. An excellent illustration can be drawn from the recent presidential address of A. S. P. Woodhouse to the Royal Society of Canada (The Nature and Function of the Humanities, *Transactions of the Royal Society of Canada,* Vol. 46, Ser. 3, Sec. 2 [June, 1952]). Discussing 'the nature and function of the humanities', Woodhouse somewhat carelessly bewailed 'the modern flight from linguistic studies'—carelessly, because he should have said 'the flight from linguistic studies as conducted by humanists.' Only in 1950 Einar Haugen had told the Linguistic Society that 'within our generation a vast expansion of linguistic study has taken place' (*Lg.* 27.219). Woodhouse might very usefully have asked, if he had read Haugen, why Haugen's analysis of the situation differed so radically from his; but instead he conducted his discussion of linguistics through two thin paragraphs to an eloquently mistaken conclusion. 'It is a question,' he said, 'whether philologists should ever be allowed to teach English composition: with them, whatever is is right.' The most cherished values of some humanists, it might almost appear, are ignorance and brutal dogmatism; for at almost the same time that Woodhouse was assuming the god, Fries was denouncing, as an antique delusion, the belief that philologists and linguists 'have no standards' (*Structure of English* 5). Let it be added, for the benefit of humanists, that the refutation of Woodhouse does not depend merely on Fries's assertion. Random examination of any moderately well stocked bookshelf will show that even 'advanced' American linguists, as a group, do not believe that in language whatever is is right, and that British and Continental linguists are likely to be yet more conservative in this matter than Americans. Woodhouse, however, would base his educational policy on injustice and vulgar error. He would check the 'flight from linguistics' with the declaration that a young man who knows anything much about the English language (a philologist) is unemployable by an English department (since if he cannot begin by teaching composition, he has precious little chance of beginning to teach). For such statements, and for the attitudes that prompt them, the reviewer has nothing but contempt. If men of letters want to debate the value of linguistics in literary study, they should learn some linguistics; Fries's book would be a good one to begin with. If they want to talk about prosody and metrics or about stylistics, they would profit from reading Trager and Smith. If, on the other hand, they want to see the study of language and languages move from the humanities to the social sciences, they have only to go on as they are going. At the end of that road, the coroner's verdict will be Suicide While the Balance of the Mind was Disturbed.

The *What* and the *Way**

DWIGHT L. BOLINGER

THE PRIMACY of the *spoken* language is one of those re-orientations of thinking comparable to the shift from a geocentric to a heliocentric system, or that from creation to evolution. Once the shift is made, everything takes on a different perspective. The inconsistencies that forced the change of view are automatically solved, and it seems impossible that anyone could have believed in the former error.

Like all views that are grounded in popular belief, however, the ramifications of the error are legion, and have to be rooted out one by one. It was not enough to say, once and for all, that the sun was central; it had to be pointed out, patiently, over whole generations, that the earth was only one of many planets; that the earth rotates; that the year is determined by the earth's revolution about the sun—and a hundred other facts as readily deduced from the one grand thesis but not obvious until separately observed and driven home.

The ramifications of written language as "the" language are just as numerous and may take as long to eradicate. It follows, from the main thesis of the primacy of the spoken language, that the distinction of "correct" language, so far as it depends on most-written forms, is unfounded; that outworn spellings are pernicious; that etymological word-divisions (*all right* versus *altogether*) need to be revised; but each of these and manifold others have to be tackled separately.

One such bit of folk-lore is that which is often expressed in the phrase "What you say is all right, but I don't like the way you say it." It is obvious from the main thesis that in any sound brought forth by the human vocal mechanism there is no part that can be singled out as a "thing" while other parts are merely ways of doing that thing. All is either thing or manner.

What one encounters here is a reflexion, back into the spoken language, of the superstition of the importance of written language: the traditionally *writable* features of the sound are regarded as more substantial than the features for which the letter signs are not used. They may be variously shown on the page, of course; italics, punctuation marks, and even (as in Mark Twain's setting of the elocutionary speech) wavy lines; but the "words themselves" are always conceived of as the firm substratum, with the residue as ephemeral and relatively unimportant ornamentation.

* Reprinted by permission from *Language Learning*, 2.86–88 (July–September, 1949).

This ramification, the false dichotomy of "what" versus "way," has enough basis in fact to keep it going beyond the span of life of the other ramifications of the error. Certain features of sound are more important, in most situations, than others. The features that distinguish *wheat* from *oats* are more urgent as a rule than those which distinguish oats-liked from oats-disliked; the features that distinguish *ear* from *year* in some dialects may cause difficulties of communication that compel us to note them, but the variations of resonance that distinguish haughty from humble speech are left to the novelist, and find no place in public documents or courts of law. In addition, the disability of not having all features of the sound writable has been partly overcome by other means: descriptive terms (the *haughty* and *humble* just used), circumlocution, etc., so that we are frequently unaware of the insufficiency of the written formula; there is even a kind of vested interest in these halting substitutes.

It takes little imagination, however, to discover situations in which the supposed unimportance of the "way" becomes damaging. In quoting another's discourse, for example, it becomes possible for a speaker to distort completely the meaning of the original, and still imagine that he is reporting truthfully. A lawyer confronts a defendant with the question: Did you or did you not say to Mr. W. on this occasion, "I could kill you for what you've done?" How many wretches have had to answer "yes" to such a question, and suffered for it, when the words were actually uttered upon an intonation profile that clearly implied (and could never imply anything else) that the action set forth was precisely one which the speaker did not intend to carry out? How pervasive is the error one sees in this very exposition, where I fall into the use of *implies* rather than *says;* for *to say* has usually the connotation of that "what," and *to imply* has that of the "way."

So much, too, for the question of truth and falsity. The "yes" of the courtroom scene was a lying answer, though the victim was not clever enough to see it. Truth and falsehood as a moral issue have been made to adhere completely to the "what" of language. Any one of us can recall a dozen anecdotes or episodes in our own lives when we have cleverly "evaded" an embarrassing question, and have thereby saved ourselves an attack of conscience; while few but can recall at least one or two instances when we have been cornered, have said *yes* when the situation demanded *no,* and have gone about with inner gnawings afterward. If language had been completely described, and if our sense of guilt were made to adhere to the whole of it, there would be very few answers that could be regarded as truthful unless they gave the precise information that the questioner wanted; there would still be mistakes, for people can misunderstand, but if the intent of a question were understood, the person questioned would have to regard it as adequately symbolized and answer accordingly. Instead, we go childishly about our verbal gymnastics with the "what," and feel no remorse at lying with every element of language except our words. As with *imply* and *say*, the what-way dichotomy is reflected in this sphere as *to evade* and *to lie*.

And what of the language teachers, who ought to know the medium they deal with? I will instance a pet of theirs, the well-known Misplaced Modifier. To use *I just want one* (they say) is wrong, because *just* modifies *one* and accordingly should go next to it. Now this prescriptive argument supposes that the hearer will misunderstand when the *just* is misplaced; the "what," the words, are spatially conceived, and all discriminative elements of speech except those of temporal order are ignored. Actually no such expression, if naturally spoken, would ever be misunderstood, for the intonation, part of the "way," clearly shows that *just* is the companion of *one*.

The importance, socially, of the "unimportant" features may be gauged by the fact that the majority of our emotional misunderstandings as a result of misquoting are probably traceable not to misquoted words but to misquoted "ways." With the "way" the reporter is apt to feel that he may do as he pleases, so that communication features such as gesture and intonation get completely out of control.

In short, the Virginian had the correct measures of the oneness of the communication-complex when he said, "When you call me that, smile."

The Grammar of Spoken English: Its Relation to What Is Called English Grammar*

KARL W. DYKEMA

WHAT LITTLE we know of the grammar of spoken English is based on unsystematic impressions of what we hear and on the unsubstantiated assumption that the grammar of the spoken language must be essentially that of the written. Before we can hope to get an authentic grammar of spoken English there are two steps we must take. One of them is obvious: we must have a sufficient body of recorded evidence of actual spoken usage to permit systematic analysis. The other step is less apparent, but a necessary prerequisite. The grammar of spoken English must be based on a far more objective analysis of the evidence than has characterized the analysis of written English. I shall attempt, therefore, to substantiate my assertion that much of the best scholarly work in English grammatical analysis has lacked that necessary objectivity.

* This paper was read before the Present-Day English Group of the Modern Language Association, New York, December 28, 1948.

By the grammar of spoken English I mean a complete and consistent description of every aspect and variety of the spoken English language. Since the preparation of such a description seems not only improbable but impossible, I must explain why I postulate such a conception.

The fundamental reason is this: if we assume that the function of language is communication, we must conclude that that is language which performs this function, and that is not language but a mere counterfeit which fails to perform this function. Let me hasten to illustrate my definition. Such examples as 'I seen the bothen of 'm,' 'Them dogs are us'n's,' 'I'll call you up, without I can't,'[1] all performed the required function for me and must therefore be explained by our ideal grammar. On the other hand, the utterances of those to whom English is not vernacular are sometimes so un-English in their arrangements of sounds and words as to be quite incomprehensible. Such language we need not consider and may dismiss as counterfeit.

I must now amplify the definition of grammar as the systematic description of a language. A description which merely enumerates is of little value. The parts list for an automobile does in a sense describe the car, but it is only the engineer's blueprint, in which all those parts are assembled into a working unit, that truly describes the automobile. It describes it in the sense that for those who can read blueprints it becomes apparent how all the seemingly unrelated particles contribute necessarily to the operating whole. A true grammar must bring all the parts of a language together into a coherent whole and show how they function. The system of description must account for every sense unit of the spoken language. If it will not fit, there is something wrong with the system of description. This means that there can be no arbitrary exclusions on the basis of levels. The examples I cited earlier must fit into the analysis just as completely as the so-called 'standard' constructions. The only basis for exclusion will be incomprehensibility—the counterfeit language I referred to above.

I assume that language is a natural phenomenon and like all natural phenomena capable of being described by what, on the analogy of the natural sciences, may be called laws. The difficulty of the task is of course apparent, but I wish to suggest that perhaps the greatest difficulty is the one which we are too little aware of—our failure, at least in part, to approach the task with sufficient objectivity.

Mr. Mencken has remarked that we have had more searching studies of the grammars of certain esoteric languages than of the grammar of our own common speech,[2] and he may well be right. The foreign student of a language, especially of a nonliterary one, enters upon his task of describing it with the enormous advantage of a complete absence of any of the linguistic prejudices which the speakers of the language itself may

[1] H. L. Mencken, *The American Language: Supplement II* (New York, 1948), p. 394.
[2] *Ibid.*, p. 332.

have. His sole handicap is then an ignorance of the language; and I am inclined to believe that this is a minor one compared to the mighty millstone of inherited attitudes that burdens the English-speaking student of English. For many years I have been disturbed by what appear to me, at least, to be stultifyingly contradictory statements about language in the works of some of our leading linguistic scholars. And I should like to cite a few to support my point.

On the whole, they seem to follow an easily explicable pattern: the statement of general principles is scientifically objective; the analysis of specific problems is traditionally prescriptive.

I shall begin with one of the earliest of our great linguistic scholars, William Dwight Whitney (1827–94), of Yale University. At the end of the opening lecture of his *Language and the Study of Language,* he makes an eloquent statement about the necessary relationship of inevitable linguistic change and continued vitality in a language, and concludes with the assertion that a recognition of this 'is the fundamental fact upon which rests the whole method of linguistic study.'[3] But his failure to apply this general principle to specific cases is apparent in many passages in his later essay on the 'Elements of English Pronunciation.'[4] He makes such a remark as this: '. . . a region where the proper distinction of *shall* and *will* was strictly maintained. . . .'[5] And personal taste in pronunciation is very strongly expressed, as in his liking for the short *o* in words like *whole, stone, coat,*[6] or his preference of [duz] to [dʌz] for *does.*[7] On the other hand, the pronunciations [tʃaɪˈniz], [ˈguzbɛrɪ], and [pəˈzɛs] instead of [tʃaɪˈnis], [ˈgusbɛrɪ], and [pəˈsɛs] he considers an 'abomination to his native ear.'[8] And [kjaɪnd], [gjɑɚd], and [gjɚd], and [gjɚl] for *kind, guard,* and *girl* are to him 'one of the latest downward steps in English orthoepy.'[9] Whitney states that part of his object in this essay is 'to furnish a small contribution to the subject of English dialectic utterance . . .'[10] Though he certainly succeeds in making his intended contribution, he also reveals an approach which is out of place in what purports to be a scientific report; he reveals a very strong personal attitude toward a number of linguistic items and thus makes us suspect that the selection of the items included in his essay is more a matter of subjective reaction than of objective observation.

In George Lyman Kittredge's *Some Landmarks in the History of English Grammar* is a terrifying passage. After quoting with approval Ben

---

[3] *Language and the Study of Language* (New York, 1867), p. 33.
[4] *Oriental and Linguistic Studies,* 2d series (New York, 1874), pp. 202–76.
[5] *Ibid.,* p. 203.
[6] *Ibid.,* p. 216.
[7] *Ibid.,* p. 217.
[8] *Ibid.,* pp. 260–61.
[9] *Ibid.,* p. 252.
[10] *Ibid.,* p. 203.

Jonson's declaration that his *English Grammar* was 'made . . . out of his observation of the English language now spoken, and in use,' and Quintilian's statement that custom is 'the surest mistress of speech,' Kittredge makes this comment:

> The lesson of this passage seems very hard to learn. Scholars have always consistently averred that good usage is the only conceivable criterion of good English, but most people still clamor for a heaven-sent 'standard' to measure their words by. The best established idioms are continually put upon their defence merely because, since they *are* idioms, they differ from somebody's preconceived and ill-instructed notions of what ought to be correct.[11]

I call it a terrifying passage because if Kittredge could forget this statement of 1906 in a matter of seven years, what cannot the rest of us do! And that he must have forgotten it seems evident from any number of passages in the *Advanced English Grammar* published by Kittredge and Farley in 1913. For example, they insist that the correct construction is *It is I*, not *It is me*.[12] This statement in the Kittredge-Farley work puts Professor Kemp Malone in the position of suggesting that the two authors are pseudo-refined, for in *Modern Language Notes* Malone wrote that *It is I* 'in my opinion, should be classed as an archaism, inappropriate for contemporary conversation except in the mouths of the pseudo-refined.'[13] And Kittredge-Farley could hardly justify their insistence on *It is I* as an archaism since Henry Sweet, in his *New English Grammar*, a book which one would expect the authors of an advanced English grammar to have consulted, had pointed out in 1891 the establishment of *It is me* in the spoken language.[14]

The ineradicable influence of the normative approach is well exemplified in George H. McKnight, who in his *Modern English in the Making* recorded many of the absurdities of the prescriptionists. Yet in a curiously unsympathetic review of Fries's *American English Grammar*, McKnight concludes with a paragraph in which he clearly implies that the task of the grammarian is 'a double one, that of registering the facts of language as they are observed in cultivated use, and that of giving some direction to the changes that are constantly going on.'[15]

This conviction concerning the function of the grammarian is apparent also in the work of the man who has given us the most detailed grammar of English produced in this country, George O. Curme. His volume on *Syntax* opens with the statement that his purpose is 'to present a systematic

[11] *Some Landmarks in the History of English Grammar* (Boston, n.d.), pp. 6–7. S. A. Leonard, in his *The Doctrine of Correctness in English Usage, 1700–1800* (Madison, Wis., 1929), p. 325, gives its date as 1906.

[12] George Lyman Kittredge and Frank Edgar Farley, *An Advanced English Grammar* (Boston, 1913), p. 58.

[13] *Modern Language Notes*, LVII (February, 1942), 142.

[14] Henry Sweet, *A New English Grammar* (Oxford, 1891), I, 341.

[15] *Journal of English and Germanic Philology*, XL (July, 1941), 455.

and rather full outline of English syntax based upon actual usage.'[16] He asserts his emancipated position when he insists that 'the lesser grammarians, who so generally present only one form of English, not only show their bad taste, but do a great deal of harm in that they impart erroneous ideas of language.' And also: 'Those who always think of popular speech as ungrammatical should recall that our present literary grammar was originally the grammar of the common people of England.' Yet he himself apparently fails to recall it on the very next page where he says: 'Left entirely to the common people the English language would soon deteriorate.' The reason for this inconsistency is revealed three pages later in this passage:

> The author defends in this book the recommendations of conservative grammarians wherever they contend against the tendencies of the masses to disregard fine distinctions in the literary language already hallowed by long usage. On the other hand, the author often takes a stand against these conservative grammarians wherever they cling to the old simply because it is old and thus fail to recognize that English grammar is the stirring story of the English people's long and constant struggle to create a fuller and more accurate expression of their inner life.[17]

What this passage means in practice can be succinctly demonstrated from Curme's brief *Principles and Practice of English Grammar*, published two years ago. He is with the conservatives, for example, in the form of the interrogative pronoun. He dislikes *Who did you meet?* and *Who did you give it to?*, and says 'We should withstand the very strong drift here toward the modern forms and use the more expressive older ones.'[18] He also requires *It is he.* [19] But he is against the conservatives here:

> The present literary passive is the weakest part of our language, since it cannot express our thought accurately. In our colloquial speech, where we are not as much under restraint as in the literary language, we often yield here to the impulse to express ourselves more precisely and use the copula *get* instead of *be:* Our house *gets painted* every year. John tried to cheat, but he *got caught* at it. . . . This fine construction deserves to be carried into the literary language.[20]
>
> . . . Though the use of *like* as a conjunction has become very common in colloquial speech, our literary language still requires the colorless, less expressive *as.*[21]

Subjectivity is also apparent in such statements as Curme's that in our present English 'there has been much progress also toward greater ac-

[16] *Syntax* (Boston, 1931), p. v.
[17] *Ibid.*, pp. vi-x.
[18] *Principles and Practice of English Grammar* (New York, 1947), p. 49.
[19] *Ibid.*, p. 113.
[20] *Ibid.*, p. 53.
[21] *Ibid.*, p. 180.

curacy of expression. For a long while the trend has been toward better things.'[22] Against this could be set Abbott's concluding words in the Introduction to his *Shakespearian Grammar* where after extravagantly praising the superiority of Elizabethan English he says:

> We may perhaps claim some superiority in completeness and perspicuity for modern English, but if we were to appeal on this ground to the shade of Shakespeare in the words of Antonio in the *Tempest,*—
> 'Do you not hear us speak?'
> we might fairly be crushed with the reply of Sebastian—
> 'I do; and surely
> It is a sleepy language.'[23]

What neither man seems to recollect is that he is comparing noncomparable things. No one, excepting perhaps Virginia Woolf's Orlando, could make such comparisions because he would have to have been a part of the culture which produced each language. The English of 1600 met the needs of the Englishman of that age. It was not the English of 1900; we cannot even say it would not meet the needs of 1900; all we can say is that if the English speaker of 1900 tried to express himself in what he conceived to be the English of 1600 he would find it an inadequate language. And of course we can persuade ourselves as Abbott has done that Sebastian would find ours a sleepy language. It is the same endless and futile argument about the relative merits of English and Latin, English and French, etc. English is the best medium to express English concepts, French to express French concepts; if anyone honestly asserts that he finds another language more satisfactory for the expression of his ideas, he means that his ideas are no longer native ideas. Those who assert that our language is sadly lacking because we have no word corresponding to French *esprit* or German *Sehnsucht* forget that that is simply because we possess no *esprit* and suffer from no *Sehnsucht*.

I shall conclude with a few fairly obvious but necessary points. Written and spoken English are two pretty different things, at least to the extent that they have been studied; but modern recording devices should soon make it possible to collect authentic evidence of the unstudied speech of every type of speaker of English. With a microphone under his lapel and his recording apparatus successfully concealed, the student of the spoken language should be able to gather unlimited evidence of the speech of bank president or bank charwoman. It might, however, be impossible to gather any evidence as to the written English of either individual because the charwoman may be illiterate and the bank president may dictate to a secretary everything that passes for his written work. Our grammars of written English, therefore, necessarily represent the usage of a limited group, perhaps only a small minority. Then there is so much in the spoken

---

[22] *Parts of Speech and Accidence* (Boston, 1935), pp. vi-vii.
[23] E. A. Abbott, *A Shakespearian Grammar* (London, 1870), p. 16.

language that can find no satisfactory representation in conventional writing, as the necessity for recreating a play from the written dialogue sufficiently proves. And finally, the conventions of the written language, both mechanical and rhetorical, are learned late, mostly in school, often unwillingly and hence imperfectly.

What are called English grammars have of necessity been based mainly on the written language because it represented the only readily accessible, substantial, and verifiable body of material. But for the obvious reasons I have just enumerated, what we call English grammar gives us very little reliable knowledge of the grammar of spoken English. Our knowledge of that grammar must be based on a complete and consistent description of every aspect and variety of the spoken language. And such a description is impossible so long as we attack the problem from the subjective viewpoint which has in the past characterized so much of the best grammatical analysis of English.

Meaning and Linguistic Analysis*

CHARLES C. FRIES

MANY WHO HAVE READ the materials of present-day American linguists and have listened to their discussions have gained the impression that these linguists have cast out 'meaning' altogether.[1] The two statements following are typical.

> Certain leading linguists especially in America find it possible to exclude the study of what they call 'meaning' from scientific linguistics, but only by deliberately excluding anything, in the nature of mind, thought, idea, concept. 'Mentalism' is taboo.[2]

> A general characteristic of the methodology of descriptive linguistics, as practised by American linguists today, is the effort to analyze linguistic structure without reference to meaning.[3]

* Reprinted by permission from *Language*, 30.57–68 (January–March, 1954).

[1] When I set out to challenge anew the conventional uses of meaning as the basic tool of analysis in sentence structure and syntax—the area of linguistic study in which it has had its strongest hold—I felt very keenly an obligation to state as fully and as accurately as I could just what uses I did make of meaning in my procedures. This paper represents the result. Although the materials presented here use general terms, I should like to point out that my experience has dealt primarily with English. This statement of the principles and assumptions that have underlain and guided my studies of English may not have equal relevance to the problems presented by other languages.

[2] J. R. Firth, "General Linguistics and Descriptive Grammar," *Transactions of the Philological Society*, 1950.82 (London, 1951).

[3] John B. Carroll, *A Survey of Linguistics and Related Disciplines* 15 (Cambridge, Mass., 1950).

One can point to a variety of quotations from the writings of our American linguists, that seem to substantiate the views that these linguists not only condemn the 'use of meaning' in linguistic analysis (as indicated in the quotation from Carroll), but (as indicated in the quotation from Firth) even refuse to treat 'meaning.'

Concerning the supposed refusal to treat 'meaning', quotations such as the following have sometimes been offered in evidence.

> The situations which prompt people to utter speech include every object and happening in the universe. In order to give a scientifically accurate definition of meaning for every form of a language, we should have to have a scientifically accurate knowledge of everything in the speakers' world. The actual extent of human knowledge is very small, compared to this.
>
> The statement of meanings is therefore the weak point in language-study, and will remain so until human knowledge advances very far beyond its present state.
>
> The signals can be analyzed but not the things signaled about. This reinforces the principle that linguistic study must always start from the phonetic form and not from meaning. . . . the meanings . . . could be analyzed or systematically listed only by a well-nigh omniscient observer.[4]

Concerning the alleged condemnation of the 'use of meaning' in linguistic analysis the evidence usually consists of quotations like the following.

> Theoretically it would be possible to arrive at the phonemic system of a dialect entirely on the basis of phonetics and distribution, without any appeal to meaning—provided that in the utterance of the dialect not all the possible combinations of phonemes actually occurred.
>
> . . . our approach differs in some respects from Bloomfield's—chiefly in that Bloomfield invokes meaning as a fundamental criterion . . .[5]
>
> In the present state of morphemic analysis it is often convenient to use the meanings of utterance fractions as a general guide and short-cut to the identification of morphemes. This is especially so in the case of languages that are more or less well known to the analyst, and has been true for most morphemic work done up to now. When we are confronted, however, with a language that we know little about in terms of the relations of the linguistic behavior, it becomes clear that meaning can be of little help as a guide. The theoretical basis of analysis then becomes evident: it consists of the recognition of the recurrences and distributions of similar patterns and sequences. The analyst must therefore constantly keep in mind this theoretical basis, and must be aware that his hunches about what goes with what are really short-cut conclusions about distributional facts.[6]

[4] Leonard Bloomfield, *Language*, pp. 139, 140, 162 (New York, 1933).
[5] Bernard Bloch, "A Set of Postulates for Phonemic Analysis, *Lg.* 24.5 note 8, 24.6 (1948).
[6] George Trager and Henry Lee Smith Jr., *An Outline of English Structure*, p. 54 (Oklahoma, 1951).

In exact descriptive linguistic work . . . considerations of meaning can only be used heuristically, as a source of hints, and the determining criteria will always have to be stated in distributional terms. The methods presented in the preceding chapters offer distributional investigations as alternatives to meaning considerations.[7]

Some who are counted among our linguistic scholars have so vigorously condemned all 'uses of meaning' that for many linguistic students the word *meaning* itself has almost become anathema.

On the other hand, those who oppose the recent developments in the methods of linguistic study nearly all assume, as a matter of course, that all use of every type of meaning has been rigidly excluded from the linguistic studies made in accord with these methods, and often make that assumed fact the basis of their opposition and criticism.

Sometimes it is insisted that the so-called 'repudiation of meaning' in the work of American linguists stems from Leonard Bloomfield. This view rests not upon what Bloomfield has said about meaning (which seems to have been overlooked) but upon inferences drawn from a somewhat superficial reading of his discussions of mentalism and mechanism. Thus concerning Bloomfield there have been such assertions as the following.

Mechanists cannot successfully speak of meaning because they undertake to ignore certain phases of human response.

The mechanist cannot consider the ethnologic features of meaning, such as connotative colorings or social levels.

The mechanists' definition of a plant-name . . . cannot . . . extend beyond the definition which appears in a handbook of botany: it cannot deal with ethnically conditioned features of meaning.

Bloomfield's physicalism (mechanism, anti-mentalism), as it is expressed in his linguistic writings, was not a philosophy of the universe nor a psychological system, but solely, as he insisted over and over again, a matter of the method of scientific descriptive statement:

An individual may base himself upon a purely practical, an artistic, a religious, or a scientific acceptance of the universe, and that aspect which he takes as basic will transcend and include the others. The choice, at the present state of our knowledge, can be made only by an act of faith, and with this the issue of mentalism should not be confounded. It is the belief of the present writer that the scientific description of the universe, whatever this description may be worth, requires none of the mentalistic terms, because the gaps which these terms are intended to bridge exist only so long as language is left out of account.[8]

Bloomfield strove vigorously to avoid mentalistic terms (*concept, idea,* etc.) in the statement of his linguistic materials and believed that every

[7] Zellig S. Harris, *Methods in Structural Linguistics*, p. 365, note 6 (Chicago, 1951).
[8] Bloomfield, *Linguistic Aspects of Science*, p. 12 (Chicago, 1944).

truly 'scientific statement is made in physical terms.'[9] But his efforts to
achieve statements in physical rather than 'mentalistic' terms do not lead
to the conclusion that he 'ignores meaning' or that 'he takes no account of
meaning.' He and many of his followers have pointed to certain uses of
meaning in linguistic analysis as constituting unscientific procedures, but
he and many of his followers have constantly insisted that meaning cannot
be ignored. Pertinent quotations from Bloomfield's *Language* are abundant:

> Man utters many kinds of vocal noise and makes use of the variety: under
> certain types of stimuli he produces certain vocal sounds, and his fellows,
> hearing these same sounds, make the appropriate response. To put it briefly,
> in human speech, different sounds have different meanings. To study this
> coordination of certain sounds with certain meanings is to study language.
> (27)
>
> The study of significant speech-sounds is phonology or practical phonetics.
> Phonology involves the consideration of meanings. (28)
>
> Only two kinds of linguistic records are scientically relevant. One is a me-
> chanical record of the gross acoustic features, such as is produced in the pho-
> netics laboratory. The other is a record in terms of phonemes, ignoring all
> features that are not distinctive in the language. Until our knowledge of
> acoustics has progressed far beyond its present state, only the latter kind of
> record can be used for any study that takes into consideration the meaning
> of what is spoken. (85)
>
> It is important to remember that practical phonetics and phonology pre-
> suppose a knowledge of meaning: without this knowledge we could not as-
> certain the phonemic features. (137)
>
> Only in this way will a proper analysis (that is, one which takes account of
> the meanings) lead to the ultimate constituent morphemes. (161)

Let me add to these quotations an excerpt from a letter dated 29 January
1945, written by Bloomfield to a friend of mine:

> It has become painfully common to say that I, or rather, a whole group of
> language students of whom I am one, pay no attention to meaning or neglect
> it, or even that we undertake to study language without meaning, simply as
> meaningless sound. . . . It is not just a personal affair that is involved in the
> statements to which I have referred, but something which, if allowed to de-
> velop, will injure the progress of our science by setting up a fictitious con-
> trast between students who consider meaning and students who neglect or
> ignore it. The latter class, so far as I know, does not exist.

With Bloomfield, no serious study of human language can or does
ignore 'meaning'. It is my thesis here that on all levels of linguistic analysis

[9] Bloomfield, "Language or Ideas?," *Language*, 12.92 note 6. Bloomfield followed
Weiss in objecting to the term *behaviorism* and believed that *physicalism* indicated
much better the essential quality of the kind of descriptive statements he sought.

certain features and types of meaning furnish a necessary portion of the apparatus used. In what I shall say, however, I do not mean to defend the common uses of meaning as the BASIS of analysis and classification, or as determining the content of linguistic definition and descriptive statement, though such uses have characterized much of the study of language since the time of the Greeks. The issue is not an opposition between NO use of meaning whatever, and ANY and ALL uses of meaning.

With many others, I believe that certain uses of meaning in certain specific processes of linguistic analysis and in descriptive statement are unscientific, that is, that they do not lead to satisfactory, verifiable, and useful results. The more one works with the records of actual speech the more impossible it appears to describe the requirements of sentences (for example) in terms of meaning content. The definitive characteristics distinguishing those expressions which occur alone as separate utterances from those which occur only as parts of larger units are not matters of content or meaning, but matters of form, different from language to language. In the defining of 'subjects' and 'objects,' of the 'parts of speech,' of 'negation,' we have not successfully approached the problems by seeking criteria of meaning content. Only as we have been able to find and to describe the contrastive formal characteristics have we been able to grasp grammatical structures in terms that make prediction possible. Structures do signal meanings, it is true, and these meanings must be described. But the meanings cannot serve successfully to identify and distinguish the structures. Not only does each structure usually signal several different meanings, but—what is more important—there is probably in present-day English no structural meaning that is not signalled by a variety of structures.[10]

This challenging of certain uses of meaning, as I have said, does not constitute a repudiation of all meaning in linguistic analysis. Meaning of some kind and of some degree always and inevitably constitutes part of the framework in which we operate. If that is so, then for clarity and understanding, as well as for rigorous procedure on each level of analysis,

---

[10] The meaning 'performer of the action' is one of the meanings signaled by the structure we call 'subject.' We cannot, however, expect to DEFINE the structure 'subject' as 'performer of the action,' for this meaning is signaled by a variety of other structures that are not 'subjects.' For example, in each of the following sentences, the word *committee* has the meaning 'performer of the action (of recommending)'; but only in the first sentence is this word in the structure of 'subject': *The committee recommended his promotion; His promotion was recommended by the committee; The recommendation of the committee was that he be promoted; The committee's recommendation was that he be promoted; The action of the recommending committee was that he be promoted.* The structure of 'subject,' on the other hand, signals at least five different meanings—four in addition to that of 'performer'—each distinguished by special formal arrangements. See C. C. Fries, *The Structure of English*, pp. 176–83 (New York, 1952).

we must state as completely as possible the precise uses of each type of meaning that our procedures require and assume.[11]

How much and just what of linguistic analysis can be accomplished without the use of any kind or degree of meaning at all? Certain meanings seem essential to making the very first step—the setting up of the material to be worked with, to be analyzed and described. There must be a 'meaning frame' within which to operate. We must know or assume, for example, (a) that the sound sequences we attempt to analyze are indeed real language utterances and the utterances of a single language, not those of several languages—a dozen or a hundred; (b) something of the range of possibilities in human language behavior and the significance of certain techniques or methods of procedure for linguistic analysis; and (c) a practical control of a language (usually another language) in which to grasp and record the processes and the results of the analysis. (Many difficulties arise from the fact that often the language of the descriptive record of the analysis differs greatly in its range of meanings and way of grouping experience from that of the language being analyzed.)

Under (b), for example, we assume that all languages have some type of meaningful units—morphemes; that all languages have bundles of contrasts of sound that function in separating or marking out or identifying these morphemes; that generally the lexical items have some contrastive formal features that make possible their classification into structurally functioning units; that all languages have formal arrangements of some sort of these structurally functioning units into contrastive patterns that have significance as structural signals of certain features of meaning; and that the linguistically significant patterns of structural arrangement are limited, much fewer than the total number of morphemes.

We must approach every linguistic analysis with a large body of 'meaning' in hand. The question is not, then, whether we can dispense with

[11] To accuse linguists of deliberately refusing to treat meaning at all is to ignore the facts. The number of thoroughly trained linguists is very small indeed, and, although there are more positions for such linguists in the academic world than there were twenty years ago, there are not enough such positions to support a sufficient number of linguists to carry on the linguistic studies that are needed in every part of the field. For the past twenty-five years the really live issues that have claimed the attention of linguists have centered about linguistic structure. The new views of the significance of structure and the success of new procedures of structural analysis applied to various aspects of language have aroused such enthusiasm that most linguists have devoted their studies to these matters. Although the present center of liveliest interest in linguistics is structure rather than meaning, some portions of the general problems of meaning have received attention. (See for example Bloomfield's *Linguistic Aspects of Science*, 1939; *Philosophical Aspects of Language*, 1942; Language or Ideas?, *Lg.* 12.89–95 [1936]; Meaning, *Monatshefte für deutschen Unterricht* 35.101–6 [1943].)

Even with respect to the lexicon, we should, for the record, note that the American linguists whose center of interest has been the English language have given constant support to the labors of those who have been struggling with the problems of producing the various period dictionaries proposed by Sir William Craigie. The *Oxford Dictionary* itself was an effort to apply practically what was at that time called the 'new philological science.'

all meaning in linguistic analysis but rather, more specifically, whether we can proceed with a valid and useful analysis without some knowledge or some control (e.g. through an informant) of the meanings of the language forms which we are analyzing.

In respect to this specific question, we must face the problem of distinguishing, with some precision if possible, several varieties of meaning. I do not refer especially to the tremendous diversity of meanings which ·Z attach to the word *meaning*[12] itself, although that diversity often prevents fruitful discussion. A few quotations will show a little of this diversity:

> The meaning of any sentence is what the speaker intends to be understood from it by the listener.[13]

> By the meaning of a proposition I mean . . . the ideas which are called to mind when it is asserted.[14]

> What we call the meaning of a proposition embraces every obvious necessary deduction from it.[15]

> Meaning is a relation between two associated ideas, one of which is appreciably more interesting than the other.[16]

> To indicate the situation which verifies a proposition is to indicate what the proposition means.[17]

> The meaning of anything whatsoever is identical with the set of expectations its presence arouses.[18]

> Meaning is the fact of redintegrative sequence . . . the evocation of a total response by a partial stimulus.[19]

> . . . the word 'meaning' has established itself in philosophical discourse because it conveniently covers both reason and value.[20]

> The meaning of certain irregularities in the motion of the moon is found in the slowing up of the motion of the earth around its axis.[21]

> 'Meaning' signifies any and all phases of sign-processes (the status of being

[12] See Leo Abraham, What is the theory of meaning about?, *The Monist* 46.228–56 (1936). In this article are gathered more than fifty typical quotations from philosophical and psychological writers, in each of which the term *meaning* is used in a different sense. At the end of these quotations he concludes, 'There is clearly nothing both common and peculiar either to all the various disparate senses, or to only the more familiar among them, which itself bears, or should bear, the name "meaning" . . . A subject matter for the "theory of meaning" cannot, accordingly, be obtained by abstraction from all or some of the entities revealed by the linguistic phenomenology of the term "meaning".'

[13] A. Gardiner, "The Definition of the Word and the Sentence, "*British Journal of Psychology*, 1922.361.

[14] N. Campbell, *Physics: The Elements*, p. 132 (1920).

[15] C. S. Peirce, *Collected Papers*, 5.165 (1934).

[16] F. Anderson, "On the Nature of Meaning," *Journal of Philosophy*, 1933.212

[17] A. J. Ayer, "Demonstration of the Impossibility of Metaphysics," *Mind*, 1934.333.

[18] C. W. Morris, "Pragmatism and Metaphysics," *Philosophical Review*, 1934.557.

[19] H. L. Hollingworth, "Meaning and the Psycho-physical Continuum," *Journal of Philosophy*, 1923.440.

[20] W. E. Hocking, *Philosophical Review*, 1928.142.

[21] M. R. Cohen, *Reason and Nature*, p. 107 (1931).

a sign, the interpretant, the fact of denoting, the signification) and frequently suggests mental and valuational processes as well.[22]

We come then to the conclusion that meaning is practically everything. We always see the meaning as we look, think in meanings as we think, act in terms of meaning when we act. Apparently we are never directly conscious of anything but meanings.[23]

As speakers of English have employed it, the word *meaning* has thus represented a great range of content. In English usage the word *meaning* has signified such diverse matters as 'the denotation of a name,' the connotation of a symbol,' 'the implications of a concept,' 'the neuro-muscular and glandular reactions produced by anything,' 'the place of anything in a system,' 'the practical consequences of anything,' 'the usefulness of anything,' 'that to which the interpreter of a symbol does refer,' 'that to which the interpreter of a symbol ought to be referring,' 'that to which the user of a symbol wants the interpreter to infer,' 'any object of consciousness whatever.' This great diversity of statement arises out of an attempt to describe the specific content of the situations in which the word *meaning* appears. Even more difficult and controversial has been the effort to classify and define the various kinds of meaning in terms of the meaning content of utterances in general. Often these various 'meanings' are grouped under two general headings: (1) the scientific, descriptive, representative, referential, denotive, cognitive kind of meaning, and (2) the emotive, expressive, noncognitive kind of meaning.[24]

The following quotation summarizes a portion of an analysis of utterances in terms of meaning content.

Thus in the case of certain sorts of indicative, interrogative, imperative, and optative sentence-utterances . . . it seems possible to disinguish a number of factors, each of which may be and has been referred to as the meaning or part of the meaning of the utterance. These are: (1) the primary conceptual content symbolized, i.e. presented and evoked; (2) the propositional attitude (with regard to this) expressed and evoked; (3) the secondary conceptual content presented and evoked; (4) the propositional attitudes (regarding this) expressed and evoked; (5) the emotions and conative attitudes expressed; (6) the emotional tone; (7) the emotions and attitudes revealed; (8) other kinds of effects; (9) the purpose.[25]

[22] C. W. Morris, *Signs, Language, and Behavior,* p. 19 (New York, 1946).
[23] W. B. Pillsbury, "Meaning and Image," *Psychological Review,* 1908.156.
[24] C. L. Stevenson, *Ethics and Language,* p. 33 (New Haven, 1944): 'The emotive meaning of a word is the power that the word acquires, on account of its history in emotional situations, to evoke or directly express attitudes, as distinct from describing or designing them.' Id. 73: 'The independence of emotive meaning can be roughly tested by comparing descriptive synonyms which are not emotive synonyms. Thus to whatever extent the laudatory strength of "democracy" exceeds that of "government where rule is by popular vote," the emotive meaning of the former will be independent.'
[25] William Fankena, "Cognitive and Non-cognitive Aspects of Language," *Language and Symbolism* [unpublished tentative report] 5.27, 28 (1952).

Let me turn away from these attempts to classify and describe the different kinds of meaning in terms of the meaning content itself to a classification based upon the kinds of signals a language uses in fulfilling its social function. I am concerned here solely with language as it provides a connection between two nervous systems. Such a use of language is not by any means limited to the communication of knowledge; but it provides for all the ways in which the members of a group interact.

A well-known diagram (slightly modified) will furnish a simplified frame for some comments concerning my use here of the term *meaning* as it applies to language content. This diagram must not be taken as implying any psychological theory whatever.

	INDIVIDUAL A	INDIVIDUAL B	
S ⟶	r . . . . s	⟶ R
Effective field of the stimulus	Sounds as produced	Sounds as heard	The practical response

The particular speech act which
becomes an effective stimulus
for B through language

The speech act consists of both r, the succession of sound waves as produced by individual A, and s, the succession of sound waves as heard by individual B. Broadly speaking, there never is or can be an exact repetition of any particular succession of sound waves as produced and as heard: precise measurements and accurate recordings always reveal some differences. But in a linguistic community two or more physically different speech acts may fit into a single functioning pattern and thus may be functionally the 'same.'[26] Basically, then, the material that constitutes language must be recurring 'sames' of speech acts. The sum of the speech acts of a community does not, however, constitute its language. Only as sequences of vocal sounds are grasped or recognized[27] as fitting into recurring patterns do they become the stuff of language—only when they

[26] These 'sames' must not be taken as the engineer's 'norms' with margins of tolerance —statistical norms clustering around averages; see Martin Joos, Language design, *Journal of the Acoustical Society* 22.701–8 (1950). They are 'sames' as the various types of 'strike' in baseball are functionally the same; see Fries, *The Structure of English*, pp. 60–1.

[27] I take *recognition* here to mean not a conscious act of identification, but rather an automatic conditioned response connecting the patterns of vocal sound with recurrent features of experience. Rcognition is itself a 'meaning' response. I am assuming that every kind of meaning has this kind of process. On every level, it seems to me, shapes, colors, sizes, smells, tastes have meaning only as they fit into patterns that connect them in some way with recurring features of experience. When stimuli do not fit such patterns of recurring experience they are 'meaningless,' and confuse us. As a matter of fact it is usually the case that only features that do fit such patterns are reacted to at all; the others do not become effective features of stimuli. For adults there seems to be no such thing as 'raw' observation unrelated to any pattern of experience.

are correlated with recurring practical situations in man's experience and thus become the means of eliciting predictable responses.

The schematic formula above helps to direct attention to three aspects of meaning in language. First, there is the recognition of a sequence of vocal sounds as fitting into some pattern of recurring sames. Second, there is the recognition of the recurring sames of stimulus-situation features with which these sames of vocal sounds occur. Third, there is the recognition of the recurring sames of practical response features which these sames of vocal sounds elicit. A language, then, is a system of recurring sequences or patterns of sames of vocal sounds, which correlate with recurring sames of stimulus-situation features, and which elicit recurring sames of response features.[28]

In general, for linguists,[29] the 'meanings' of an utterance consist of the correlating, regularly recurrent sames of the stimulus-situation features, and the regularly elicited recurring sames of response features.[30] These meanings are tied to the patterns of recurring sames of vocal sounds. In other words, the patterns of recurring sound sequences are the signals of the meanings. The meanings can be separated into various kinds or layers in accord with the several levels of patterns in the recurring sound sequences which do the signaling. Utterances will have then at least the following types or 'modes' of meaning.

(a) There is the automatic recognition of the recurrent sames that constitute the lexical items. The lexical items selected for a particular utterance are distinguished from others that might have been selected by sharp patterns of sequences of sound contrasts. One layer of the mean-

---

[28] A linguistic community consists of those individuals that make the 'same' regular and predictable responses to the 'same' patterns of vocal sounds. The language function is fulfilled only in so far as it is possible to predict the response features that will regularly be elicited by the patterns of vocal sound. For the discussion here I am not concerned with what might be called 'personal' meaning—the special non-recurrent or not regularly recurring response features that mark individual differences.

[29] For many others the meaning of a text or a sequence of utterances has often been considered a function of (a) the 'words' (as items of sound patterns which experience has connected in some way with reality), and (b) the 'context.' This context has included both the so-called 'verbal context' or linguistic context (not specified further) and the 'context of situation'—the circumstances in which the utterance occurs. Firth has pushed the analysis of 'context' much farther in his dealing with 'formal scatter' and 'meaning by collocation.' See his Modes of meaning, *Essays and studies* (English Assn.) 1951.118–49, and General linguistics and descriptive grammar, *Transactions of the Philological Society*, 1951.85–7; cf. his earlier "Technique of Semantics," *Trans. Philol. Soc.* 1935.36–72, and "Personality and Language in Society," *Sociological Review*, 1950.

[30] In the study of the language records of a former time we have, because of the nature of the evidence, usually had to try to arrive at the meanings of the language forms by connecting them with recurring elements of the situations in which they were used. In the study of living languages it is often possible to observe directly the responses which particular language forms elicit in a speech community. We assume that if a particular response regularly follows the utterance of a language pattern, then this pattern 'means' this response. Upon such regular recurrences rests the kind of prediction that makes possible the social functioning of language.

ing of the utterance is determined and signaled by the particular lexical items selected and thus recognized. This recognition covers both the identi- fication of the item itself by its contrastive shape, and the situation and response features with which this shape correlates in the linguistic com- munity. If the stress and intonation, as well as the social-cultural situation, are kept constant, the meaning of the utterance *The point of this pen is bent over* differs from that of each of the following only because the lexical items differ: *The point of this pin is bent over, The cover of this pan is bent over, The top of that pen was sent over.* One of the separable layers of the meanings signaled by our utterances is thus the lexical meanings.

One other feature of lexical meaning must be noted. In addition to the recognition of the shape or forms of the lexical item itself, identified by contrastive patterns of sound sequences, there is also the automatic (and sometimes more conscious) recognition of the distribution of each lexical item with 'sets' of other lexical items as they occur in the complete utter- ance unit.[31] There is a 'lexical scatter' as well as a 'formal scatter.' It is this recognition of the particular set in which the lexical item occurs[32] that stimulates the selection of the specific 'sense' in which that item is to be taken, the specific stimulus-response features for that utterance.

(b) In addition to the layer of lexical meaning there is the automatic recognition of the contrastive features of arrangement in which the lexical items occur.[33] These contrastive features of arrangement regularly cor- relate with and thus signal a second layer of meanings—structural mean- ings. The difference in meaning between the following sentences depends solely upon the contrastive features of arrangement, assuming that the stress and intonation as well as the social-cultural situation are kept con- stant: *There is a book on the table, Is there a book on the table.* Structural meanings are not vague matters of 'context,' so called. They are sharply de- fined and specifically signaled by a complex system of contrastive patterns.

Together, LEXICAL MEANINGS and STRUCTURAL MEANINGS constitute the LINGUISTIC MEANING of our utterances. Linguistic meaning thus consists of lexical meanings within a frame of structural meanings—that is, of the

---

[31] 'Complete utterance unit' here means the total span of talk of one person in a single conversation or discourse.

[32] As we record more specifically the details of the experience of language learning, we realize increasingly that we 'learn' not only the shape of a lexical item and the recur- rent stimulus-response features that correlate with it, but also the sets of other lexical items with which it usually occurs. Perhaps when psychologists explore the 'free asso- ciation' of words for an individual, they are really dealing with these sets of lexical distribution.

[33] In English the functioning units of the contrastive arrangements that signal mean- ings are not lexical items as such, but rather classes of these items. A variety of formal features make possible the classification of lexical items into a very small number of form classes the members of which each function as structurally the same. Linguistic analysis must discover and describe these form classes as a means of dealing with the structures themselves.

stimulus-response features that accompany contrastive structural arrangements of lexical items.

But the linguistic meaning is only part of the total meaning of our utterances. In addition to the regularly recurring responses to the lexical
items and structural arrangements there are also throughout a linguistic
community recurring responses to unique whole utterances or sequences
of utterances. Rip Van Winkle's simple utterance, *I am a poor quiet man,
a native of the place, and a loyal subject of the King, God bless him!*, almost caused a riot, not because of the linguistic meaning signaled by the
lexical items and structures, but because the unique utterance as a whole,
now, after the Revolution, meant to the group that he was a confessed
enemy of the newly established government. The statement, *Bill Smith
swam a hundred yards in forty-five seconds*, would have not only the linguistic meaning attaching to the lexical items and the structures, but also
the significance of the unique utterance as a whole, that this man had
achieved a new world record. The petulant child's insistence at bed-time
that he is hungry often means to the mother simply that he is trying to delay the going to bed. Meanings such as these I call 'social-cultural' meanings.[34] Linguistic meaning without social-cultural meaning constitutes
what has been called 'mere verbalism.' The utterances of a language that
function practically in a society therefore have both linguistic meaning
and social-cultural meaning.

In general the meanings of the utterances are tied to formal patterns
as signals.[35] In respect to linguistic meanings, I have assumed as a basis for
study, that all the signals are formal features that can be described in
physical terms of form, arrangement, and distribution. As I see it, the
task of the linguistic analyst is to discover, test, and describe, in the system
in which they occur, the formal features of utterances that operate as
signals of meaning—specifically, (1) the contrastive features that constitute the recurrent sames of the forms of lexical units—the bundles of
contrastive sound features by which morphemes are identified, (2) the
contrastive markers by which structurally functioning groups of morphemes can be identified, and (3) the contrastive patterns that constitute
the recurrent sames of the structural arrangements in which these structurally functioning classes of morphemes operate. In describing the results
of the analysis, only verifiable physical terms of form, of arrangement, and
of distribution are necessary. Whenever descriptive statements must de-

---

[34] The term 'social-cultural meaning' is not wholly satisfactory, but it is the best I
have found to cover all the varieties of predictable meaning other than linguistic meaning. As indicated above, I have excluded from the discussion here the personal meaning
of individual differences.

[35] This is true even of many of the varieties of social-cultural meaning—for example,
the set of deviations from the norm of the sound segments that signal the meaning that
a speaker is drunk, the whispering of an utterance that signals the meaning that the
content of it is secret, and the unusual distribution that is the cue to a metaphor.

part from such formal matters, the fact is evidence of unsolved problems.

In the process of discovering just what formal features constitute the linguistic signals I can see no merit in denying ourselves access to any sources of suggestions concerning the nature of the materials that are significant. The more we know of the diverse characteristics of languages in general and of the processess that have marked language history, the more fruitfully prolific will be our suggestions. The less we know about language, the more frequently we may be led into blind alleys or follow the superstitions of the past.

In the process of testing these suggestions, however, and of proving the validity of our insights concerning the precise formal features that are significant, we need all the rigor that scientific procedure can offer. The real question centers upon the validity of the procedures through which we use techniques of distribution and of substitution. There must be some rigorous way of establishing 'sameness' of frame and 'sameness' of focus, as well as what constitutes 'difference' in each case.

In carrying out these tasks certain uses of particular kinds of 'meaning' within the utterance seem necessary and legitimate. (1) In testing the contrastive features that constitute the recurrent sames of lexical forms it is necessary to control in some way enough of the lexical meaning to determine whether forms showing certain differences of sound features are, for the particular language, 'same' or 'different.'[36] (2) In testing the contrastive patterns that constitute the recurrent sames of structural arrangements it is necessary to control in some way enough of the structural meaning to determine whether particular variants are substitutable, leaving the arrangement the 'same' for the language, or constitute such a change as to make the arrangement 'different.' Note that lexical meaning does not form part of the apparatus in which to test structural arrangements.

Social-cultural meanings which attach to the unique utterance as a whole or to a sequence of utterances do not seem to form any part of the frames in which to test either lexical forms or structural forms. Although a certain control of specific kinds of meaning seems to me essential for the various parts of linguistic analysis I should like to insist that as a general principle any use of meaning is unscientific whenever the fact of our knowing the meaning leads us to stop short of finding the precise formal signals that operate to convey that meaning.

[36] Sometimes it is insisted that we use 'differential' meaning, not 'referential' meaning. Perhaps this statement means that the linguistic analyst seeks basically to establish the fact whether two instances differ in meaning content or not. He does not need to know what that content is or in what ways the two may differ. If they differ in meaning he assumes that there must be some difference in formal features, and sets out to find, prove, and describe that difference.

Resolution of Structural Ambiguity by Lexical Probability: The English Double Object*

W. Nelson Francis

THE DOCTRINE that lexical meaning must not be used in linguistic analysis has been a necessary and fruitful corrective against the indiscriminate resort to meaning in the traditional grammar. But it should be remembered that the total exclusion of meaning produces an artificial linguistic situation, useful for laboratory purposes but not characteristic of the normal communicative use of language. It is true that a listener is primarily concerned with deriving meaning by decoding structural clues, but it should not be overlooked that the reverse process goes on also. Certain structural meanings are interpreted in the light of the lexical meaning of a whole passage or its components. This type of interpretation is resorted to whenever a passage is structurally ambiguous. What happens is that one of two or more possible structural meanings is selected on the ground that it supplies a more probable total meaning. The decision as to probability is based on a delicate weighing of the context, both linguistic and nonlinguistic, and the semantic alternatives permitted by the words involved. When there is no preponderance of probability either way, the passage remains totally ambiguous; that is, its ambiguity is both structural and lexical.

In English, changes which have taken place over the last thousand years may well have increased certain possibilities of structural ambiguity. The disappearance of noun and adjective inflections has shifted the syntactic burden from the devices of government and concord, which are natural to inflected languages, and placed it upon word order, intonation, and the refined use of various determiners and markers. Since the permutations of word order are fewer than those of a multicase inflectional system, the number of structures showing potential structural ambiguity is large. The other formal devices mentioned above—intonation and function words—do not resolve them all. A good deal of the resolution of potential ambiguity is left to be done by lexical probabilities and compatibilities.

This point can be illustrated by many Engish constructions. One of the clearest examples is the structure involving a transitive verb followed by two nouns: schematically $NVDN(D)$ N, where D stands for a noun-

* Reprinted by permission from *American Speech*, 31.102–106 (May, 1956).

determiner such as *a/an, the, my.* Substituting nonsense words in the key positions gives us something like:

He darbed the vellig (a) harnip.

The most common constructions of the two nouns in object position here are four:

1. Noun-adjunct modifying direct object (noun-adjunct construction):

He opened an automobile agency.

2. Direct object followed by appositive (appositive construction):

He introduced his father, a doctor.

3. Indirect object and direct object (indirect-object construction):

He wrote his brother a letter.

He sent his brother money.

4. Direct object and object complement (object-complement construction):

He considered his life a failure.

The governor appointed my uncle coroner.

We should note first that some of these potential ambiguities are obviated by purely structural means.[1] Thus the presence of a determiner with the second noun eliminates the possibility of the noun-adjunct construction, since a determiner cannot come between a noun-adjunct and its head. Similarly, the absence of a determiner in this position largely eliminates the appositive construction, since a simple appositive (except the close appositive) always has a determiner. (We cannot here go into the case of the complex appositive, as in *He introduced his father, dean of men at Podunk.*)

Further discriminations are made by intonation. Thus a single-bar or double-cross juncture between the nouns is a clear mark of the appositive construction:[2]

/²hiy+intrədûwst+iz+³fáhðər²|²ə+³dáktər¹‡/
/²hiy+kɔ̂hld+iz+³brə̂ðər¹‡²ə+pə³líysmən¹‡/

A rise to pitch /3/ on the first noun, with or without primary stress on that noun and without a terminal juncture after it, discriminates the noun-

---

[1] A fifth possibility is the adverbial object construction, as in *He gave a speech this morning.* Although inclusion of this relatively rare construction would further illustrate the point being made in this article, it is omitted for the sake of simplicity.

[2] The phonemic transcriptions that follow are of my own East Midland (Philadelphia area) dialect, reported according to the system of Trager and Smith (*Outline of English Structure,* 1951).

adjunct structure from the potentially ambiguous indirect-object and object-complement constructions:

/^{2}hỉy+ôwpənd+ən+ɔ́htəmə^{3}bíyl+êyjỉnsiy^1‡/
/^{2}hỉy+kɔ́hld+ỉz+^{3}brɔ̂ðər+pəlíysmən^1‡/

Intonation thus combines with the distribution of noun-determiners to prevent the noun-adjunct and appositive constructions from being structurally ambiguous. We are left with the indirect-object and object-complement structures, which can together be called the double-object construction. These are formally identical. Applying intonational markers to the schematic and nonsense representations, we get:

^{2}Ǹ V̂ D N̂ (D) ^{3}Ń^1‡
^{2}hè dârbed the vêllig (a) ^{3}hárnip^1‡

Unambiguous examples of both have already been cited:

^{2}hè wrôte his brôther a ^{3}letter^1‡ (Indirect-object construction)
^{2}hè consỉdered his lỉfe a ^{3}failure^1‡ (Object-complement construction)

A totally ambiguous example is:

^{2}he câlled his brôther a po^{3}líceman^1‡

Structurally, this is no more ambiguous than the preceding examples. But it is totally ambiguous because the meanings of the words involved are compatible with either the indirect-object construction or the object-complement construction. That is, it can be translated either as 'He summoned a policeman for his brother' or 'He said that his brother is a policeman.' The lexical probabilities are more or less evenly balanced (depending, of course, on context), so that the structural ambiguity is unresolved.

Fries solves this problem by what amounts to a covert appeal to meaning:

> In statement sentences, whenever two Class 1 words follow a Class 2 word, and the referents of the Class 1 words are different . . . and there is no function word of Group E between the last two Class 1 words, then the first of these Class 1 words is 'indirect object' and the second, 'direct object.' . . . [When] the two Class 1 words following the Class 2 word have the same referent . . . the first of the two Class 1 words is 'direct object' and the second is 'object complement.'[3]

But this really begs the question. How can we know whether or not the referents of the two nouns are the same or different until we know the total meaning of the structure? Fries correctly recognizes that the resolution of this ambiguity is lexical, but he states it in what might be called 'pseudo-structural' terms.

---

[3] Charles Carpenter Fries, *The Structure of English* (New York, 1952), pp. 193–94.

It is apparent, then, that the two double-object constructions are formally identical and that the distinction between them is made on lexical grounds. The two principal points where lexical signals of structure enter in are the verb and the second object. The discrimination between the two constructions is made at one of these points if it is made at all. Looking first at the verb, we may note that the verbs which can appear in this structure can be divided into three groups: (1) those that characteristically signal the indirect-object construction; (2) those that characteristically signal the object-complement construction; and (3) those that may appear with either. Typical examples of these groups are the following:

1. *Only with Indirect Object*	2. *Only with Object Complement*	3. *Ambiguous*
give	consider	make
get	classify	call
hire	think	appoint
send	license	choose

If a verb from either group 1 or group 2 appears, the completed structure will not be ambiguous. Compare.

> He sent the vellig a harnip. (Indirect-object construction)
> He considered the vellig a harnip. (Object-complement construction)

But if one of the ambiguous verbs appears, the ambiguity of the structure will be resolved, if at all, by the second object. Its meaning, taken in the light of the meanings of the verb and first object, will swing the hearer's interpretation of the syntax of the structure one way or the other. Thus certain nouns, following specific verbs and first objects, will identify themselves as direct objects, others as object complements, and a third group will remain ambiguous. Since the lists are semantically determined, they will vary with each verb and first object. Thus:

		Direct Object	Object Complement	Ambiguous
He called	my brother a	waitress	gambler	policeman
		taxi	liar	friend
	my sister a	policeman	gambler	waitress
		taxi	liar	friend
He made	my brother a(n)	offer	policeman	friend
		position	prisoner	wreck
He chose	my brother a(n)	home	director	helper
		wife	executor	agent

It should be emphasized that these lists reflect not clear-cut distinctions but varying degrees of probability. Since the syntax permits any noun to appear in either structure, it is only the speaker's and hearer's agreement as to the probabilities of the context that resolves the ambiguity.

Contexts are conceivable in which one man might say to another, 'You taxi!' or 'I'll call a liar for you,' so that *He called my brother a taxi* would be the object-complement construction[4] and *He called my brother a liar,* the indirect-object construction. It is only the improbability of such contexts occurring that leads us to classify these second objects as unambiguous. Here, then, is a clear case of a structural ambiguity which is habitually resolved in the stream of speech by largely unconscious recourse to lexical probability.

Notes on Nominal Compounds in Present-Day English*

Hans Marchand

1.1. When two or more words are combined into a morphological unit, we speak of a compound. The principle of combining two words arises from the natural human tendency to see a thing identical with another one already existing and at the same time different from it. If we take the word *rainbow,* for instance, identity is expressed by the basic *bow:* the phenomenon of a rainbow is fundamentally a bow. But it is a bow connected with the phenomenon rain: hence the differentiating part *rain.* The compound is thus made up of a determining and a determined part. In the system of languages to which English belongs the determinant generally precedes the determinatum. The types which do not conform to this principle are either syntactical compounds (e.g. *father-in-law*) or loan-compounds (e.g. *MacDonald, Fitzerald*) with the "inner form" of a non-English language. The determinatum is the grammatically dominant part which undergoes the changes of inflection. On the other hand, its semantic range is considerably narrowed as the second word of a compound, determined as it is by the first word.

1.2. A compound, we have said, has two constituent elements, the determinatum and the determinant. There are, however, many combinations which do not seem to fulfill this condition. The essential part of the de-

---

[4] After this was written, this conjecture was corroborated by an anecdote in the London *Times Literary Supplement* for August 26, 1955, concerning Joseph H. Choate when he was ambassador to the Court of St. James's. 'Of his [Choate's] wit many instances must be on record, instances more scintillating than his unforgotten "You are a cab!" repartee to a much-bemedalled "brass hat" who, mistaking him for a member of the domestic staff at Buckingham Palace after some royal function, had said to him curtly, "Call me a cab!" '

* Reprinted by permission from *Word,* 11.216–227 (August, 1955), with minor changes by the author.

terminatum as a formal element is obviously missing in such types as *pick-pocket, runabout, overall, blackout, dugout,* the bahuvrihi types *hunch-back, paleface, fivefinger, scatterbrain.* A pickpocket is neither a pick nor a pocket, a hunchback is neither a hunch nor a back, and so on. In all of the preceding combinations the basis, the determinatum, is implicitly under-stood, but not formally expressed. The combinations are compounds with a zero determinatum (also called exocentric compounds, as the determina-tum lies outside the combination).

1.3. A similar concept underlies combinations of the type *householder.* The analysis of *householder* is parallel to that of *pickpocket:* 'one who holds a house.' The difference is that *householder* has a formal determina-tum (*-er*) whereas *pickpocket* has not. However, the conceptual analysis clashes with a word-forming principle in English. *Householder* cannot be considered a suffixal derivative from the basis *household* in the way that *old-timer* or *four-wheeler* are derived from *old time* (*s*) or *four-wheel* (*s*), as there is no compound verb * *to household* in English. The modern type *to brainwash* is of quite recent development and is not nearly so well es-tablished as the type *householder,* which is very old (in its present form, extended by *-er,* it goes back to late Old English, while the original OE type *man-slaga* 'man-killer' is Indo-European; cf. Latin *armiger, signifer, artifex*). The idea of verb/object relation could combine with the concept of agent substantive only by way of joining an agent noun created ad hoc as a pseudo-basis to a common substantive. We are thus faced with the fact that an analysis which considers the underlying concept only may be disavowed by the formal pattern. The formative basis of combinations of the type *householder* is the agent substantive, however artificial the an-alysis may sometimes appear. A *skyscraper,* though not naturally analyz-able as 'a scraper of the sky' but '(a building which) scrapes the sky,' from the formative point of view must be understood as a compound with *scraper* as the basis. This type of compound therefore is not the primary one which arises from combining two fully independent common sub-stantives (as in the type *rainbow*). Because of their 'forcible' character, such compounds have been termed synthetic compounds (in German they are called *Zusammenbildungen*).

1.4. Parallel to *householder* are the types *housekeeping* (sb.) and *heart-breaking* (adj.). The second words of such combinations do not often exist as independent words: *holder, keeping, breaking* are functional de-rivatives, being respectively the agent substantive, the action substantive, and the first participle of the underlying verbs. Strictly speaking, they should not figure in a dictionary, which is an assemblage of semantic units. The lexical value of, say, the word *crasher* is nil, as the word represents nothing but the aspect of actor of the verb *crash,* whereas *gate-crasher* is a lexical unit. In the same sense, the second elements of most compound impersonal substantives of the type *housekeeping* and of most compound participles of the type *heartbreaking* are semantic units only in conjunction with their first words, *house* and *heart*. In a similar way, other combinations with participles as second words are synthetic compounds: *cooking, going, working* are not adjectives, but preceded by adjectives or locative particles they form compounds (*quick-cooking, easy-going, hard-working; forthcoming, inrushing, outstanding*). *Eaten, bred, borne, baked, flown, spread* are nothing but participles, but *moth-eaten, home-bred, air-borne* or *fresh-baked, high-flown, widespread* are compounds.

1.5. The non-compound character of extended bahuvrihi combinations is manifest. *Hunchbacked, palefaced, five-fingered, knock-kneed* are not analyzable into the immediate constituents *hunch+backed, pale+faced,* etc.; the determinatum is always -*ed* while the preceding compound basis is the determinant. Extended bahuvrihi adjectives therefore are suffixal derivatives from compounds or syntactic groups. Exactly parallel are combinations of the types *old maidish* and *four -wheeler*.

1.6. One of the constituent members of a compound may itself be a compound. In German, the determinant as well as the determinatum occur as compounds (*Rathaus-keller, Berufsschul-lehrer; Stadt-baurat, Regierungs-baumeister*). The regular pattern in English, however, is that of the determinant being a compound (*aircraft carrier, traffic signal controller, flower pot stand, plainclothes man, milk truck driver* etc.), whereas in the event of a compound determinatum the whole combination becomes a two-stressed syntactic group (*níght wátchman, víllage schoólmaster, hoúse doórkeeper*). The only case of a compound determinatum in English I can think of is one in which the second constituent is a preparticle compound, as in *báby oùtfit, húnting oùtfit*.

2.1. What is the criterion of a compound? Many scholars have claimed that a compound is determined by the underlying concept; others have advocated stress; some even seek the solution of the problem in spelling. H. Paul says that "the cause which makes a compound out of a syntactic phrase is to be sought in the fact that the compound is in some manner isolated as compared to its elements."[1] By isolation he understands difference in meaning from a syntactic group with the same words, and treats as compounds such phases as *dicke Milch* or *das goldene Vliess*, which are what Bally terms *groupes locutionnels*. H. Koziol[2] holds that the criterion of a compound is the psychological unity of a combination, adding that there "seems to be" a difference of intonation between a compound and a syntactic group which it is, however, difficult to describe. W. Henzen,[3]

[1] H. Paul, *Deutsche Grammatik*. Band V, Teil IV: Wortbildungslehre (Halle, 1920) 4.

[2] H. Koziol, *Handbuch der englischen Wortbildungslehre* (Heidelberg, 1927) 46 f.

[3] W. Henzen, *Deutsche Wortbildung* (Halle, 1947) 44.

who discusses at some length the diverse definitions, decides for "the impossibility of a clear-cut distinction" between a compound and a syntactic group and hesitatingly proposes to consider a compound as "the multi-stem expression of a conceptual unit which is written together." This is a very weak definition and he admits that the German separable verbs do not fit it. Bloch and Trager[4] do not treat the question in detail; they call a compound "a word made up wholly of smaller words," specifying that both of the immediate constituents must be free forms.

2.2. Stress also has been advocated as a criterion. "Wherever we hear lesser or least stress upon a word which would always show high stress in a phrase, we describe it as a compound member: *ice-cream* |ajs-|krijm is a compound, but *ice cream* |ajs |krijm is a phrase, although there is no denotative difference of meaning."[5] Kruisinga[6] makes no difference at all between a compound and a syntactic group, at the same time feeling the need to maintain the traditional concept of compound. He defines the compound as "a combination of two words forming a unit which is not identical with the combined forms or meanings of its elements." In a similar way, Bally defines the compound as a syntagma expressive of a single idea.[7] Jespersen also introduces the criterion of concept, and rejects Bloomfield's criterion of stress. "If we stuck to the criterion of stress, we should have to refuse the name of compound to a large group of two-linked phrases that are generally called so, such as *headmaster* or *stone wall*." This is certainly no argument, nor is the objection that words such as *subcommittee, non-conductor* have forestress according to Jones, but level stress according to Sweet. The first elements are not independent morphemes, anyway. For this reason it is wrong to argue that "the prefixes *un-* (negative) and *mis-* are often as strongly stressed as the following element; are they, then, independent words?"[8] If it rains, the ground becomes wet. But if the ground is wet, we are not entitled to the conclusion that it has rained. As for the criterion of stress, we shall see that it holds for certain types only.

2.3. That spelling is no help in solving the problem I will add for the sake of completeness only. A perusal of the book *Compounding in the English Language*,[9] which is a painstaking investigation into the spelling variants of dictionaries and newspapers, shows the complete lack of uniformity.

[4] B. Bloch and G. L. Trager, *Outline of Linguistic Analysis* (Baltimore, 1942), 54, 68.

[5] L. Bloomfield, *Language* (New York, 1933) 228.

[6] E. Kruisinga, *A Handbook of Present-Day English*, Part II: Accidence and Syntax 3. Fifth edition (Groningen, 1932) 1581.

[7] Ch. Bally, *Linguistique générale et linguistique française*, second edition (Bern, 1944) 94.

[8] O. Jespersen, *A Modern English Grammar on Historical Principles*, Part VI: Morphology (Copenhagen, 1942) 8.12.

[9] A. M. Ball, *Compounding in the English Language* (New York, 1939) and *The Compounding and Hyphenation of English Words* (New York, 1951).

2.4. For a combination to be a compound there is one condition to be fulfilled: the compound must be morphologically isolated from a parallel syntactic group. However much *the Holy Roman Catholic Church* or *the French Revolution* may be semantic or psychological units, they are not morphologically isolated: they are stressed like syntactic groups. *Bláckbìrd* has the morphophonemic stress pattern of a compound, *bláck márket* has not, despite its phrasal meaning; the latter therefore is a syntactic group, morphologically speaking. Stress *is* a criterion here. The same distinction keeps apart the types *strónghòld* and *lóng waít*, the types *shárpshoòter* and *goód ríder*, the types *búll's-eỳe* and *rázor's édge*, the types *wríting-tàble* and *fólding doór*.

2.5. On the other hand, there are many combinations with double stress which are undoubtedly compounds. Most combinations with participles as second elements belong here: *eásy-góing, hígh-bórn, mán-máde*. We have already pointed out their synthetic character. Being determined by first elements which syntactically could not be their modifiers, they must be considered compounds. The type *gráss-greén* has two heavy stresses, but again the criterion is that an adjective cannot syntactically be modified by a preceding substantive (the corresponding syntactic construction would be *green as grass*). The adjectival type *ícy-cóld* is isolated in that syntactically the modifier of an adjective can only be an adverb. The corresponding coordinative type *Gérman-Rússian* (*war*) is likewise morphologically distinct. The corresponding syntactic construction would be typified by *long, grey* (*beard*), with a pause between *long* and *grey*, whereas the combination *German-Russian* is marked by the absence of such a pause.

3.1. The most important type in which stress is morphophonemic is *raínbòw*. As it has been the object of much discussion, it will here be given a somewhat detailed treatment. English has at all periods known and made use of this Germanic type of word formation. The possibility of combining substantives is today as strong as ever. On the other hand, English has, for at least three centuries, been developing the syntactic group of the type *stóne wáll*,[10] which has two stresses. While the coining of forestressed compounds continues, a new syntactic type has arisen which challenges the privileged position of the type *rainbow*. Though the co-existence of two types of substantive+substantive combination has long been recognized, the conditions under which a combination enters the compound type, *raínbòw*, or the syntactic group type, *stóne wáll*, do not seem to have been studied. Sweet, in his chapter on the stressing of compounds,[11] has a few remarks on the subject, but otherwise the problem has not received attention. The following, therefore, can be an attempt only.

[10] O. Jespersen, *A Modern English Grammar on Historical Principles* (Heidelberg, 1909–1914) 1. 5. 33–37 and 11. 13.
[11] H. Sweet, *A New English Grammar* (Oxford, 1892) 889–932.

3.2. The most important factor is the underlying concept. Some concepts are invariably tied up with forestress pattern. The concept may be grammatical: when the verb/object or subject/verb relation is present, the combination receives forestress. Therefore the following are types of stable compounds: *hoúsehòlder, skyscraper, doorkeeper, caretaker; hoúsekeèping, sightseeing, mindreading, childbearing; ráttlesnàke, popcorn, sobsister, crybaby.* The first element is the object in the verbal nexus substantives *householder* and *housekeeping.* There are also combinations in which the underlying relation is the same though the formal type be different (*geógraphy teàcher, árt crìtic, cár thìef*) and related contructions such as *teá mèrchant, clóth deàler, leáther wòrker, stéel prodùction, tráffic contròl, móney restrìctions, fúr sàle, graín stòrage.* If the second element has acquired the status of an independent word, the predicate/ object nexus may have come to be blurred, as in *párty leáder, fúneral diréctor,* which are stressed as syntactic groups. Again, a combination may step out of line, either because the verbal nexus is blurred or because the combination is too long: *cóntract violátions, búsiness administrátion, cóncert perfórmance* always have two stresses.

3.3. As a rule, combinations in which a verbal nexus is expressed have forestress. Most combinations with a verbal stem therefore are compounds: *shówroòm, paýdày, dánce floòr, plaỳboỳ, sweátshòp.* But in cases where the verbal stem is used in adjunctal function, i.e. has become a quasi-adjective, equivalent to a past participle, a situation similar to that in *stone wall* has arisen: the two constituents receive full stress. We say *roást beéf, roást mútton,* etc., and *wáste páper, wáste lánd* are often heard though many speakers always give to these combinations the compound stress. The case is the same with combinations whose first constituents are *-ing* forms of a verb. Most combinations of type *wríting-tàble* are compounds because the underlying concept is that of destination (*looking-glass, frying-pan,* etc.). But when the verbal *-ing* is apprehended as an adjunct, i.e. a participle, the combination is susceptible of being treated as a syntactic group: *Flýing Dútchman, flýing saúcers, revólving doór.* However, other combinations have forestress owing to the idea of implicit contrast: *húmming-bìrd,* with the frequent constituent *bird,* receives forestress to distinguish it from *bláckbìrd, bluébìrd, mócking-bìrd.*

3.4. Other relations are of a purely semantic nature. The following cases involve forestress pattern:

The underlying concept is that of purpose, destination: *theater ticket, freight train, bread basket, paper clip, reception room, concert hall, windshield, toothbrush.*

The signifié of the second element is naturally dependent on that of the first: *windmill, watermill, water clock, motorcar, motorboat, steam engine, mule cart, sea bird, water rat, lap dog.*

The first element denotes the originator of what is expressed by the second: *rainwater, rainbow, bloodstain, birth right, pipe smoke, smoke screen.*

The underlying concept is that of resemblance: *blockhead, bellflower, goldfish, horse-fish, iron-weed, silkweed, wiregrass.*

3.5. There are other, quite external factors conducive to forestress. The frequent occurrence of a word as second constituent is apt to give combinations with such words compound character. The most frequent word of this kind is probably *man* (the reduction of the vowel and the loss of stress of *man* as a second element is another result of the same phenomenon: *policeman, congressman, gunman, postman, milkman.* A few other words frequent as second constituents of compounds are *ware* (*houseware, hardware, silverware*), *work* (*woodwork, network, wirework*), *shop* (*giftshop, candyshop, hatshop*), *store* (*bookstore, drugstore, foodstore*), *fish* (*bluefish, goldfish, jellyfish*). The forestress of such combinations is thus due to implicit contrast: each *-man, -shop, -store* word is automatically stressed on the first member to distinguish the combination from others of the same series. The case of *-girl* combinations is particularly interesting in this connection. Appositional combinations are usually syntactic groups with two stresses in English (*boy king, woman writer, gentleman farmer*), but *servant girl, slave girl, peasant girl, gipsy girl* have contrastive forestress.

4.1. The criterion of the underlying concept may now be applied to the syntactic group type *stóne wáll.* The grammatical concept which involves syntactic stressing is that of adjunct/primary. All coordinative combinations, additive as in *king-emperor, secretary-stenographer,* or appositional as in *gentleman-farmer, prince consort,* have two heavy stresses. The only copulative combination I know that has forestress is *fíghter-bòmber,* the stress obviously being due to contrast with common bombers. Here belong combinations with sex or age denoting first constituents as *man, woman, boy, girl, baby, embryo,* except that owing to contrast, *boy friend, girl friend, manservant, maidservant* have developed forestress. (It is perhaps interesting to point out that the sex-denoting pronouns *he, she,* as in *he-goat, she-dog,* form forestressed compounds, despite Sweet 904.) Combinations with first constituents denoting relational position, as *top, bottom, average, brother, sister, fellow* likewise have the basic stress pattern of the syntactic group under discussion.

4.2. Combinations with a first member denoting material are treated as adjunct/primary groups and receive two stresses: *gold watch, silver chain, steel door, iron curtain, cotton dress, silk stocking, leather glove, straw hat, paper bag.*

4.3. Incidentally, the treatment of adjunct/primary combinations consisting of two substantives has a parallel in Turkish. Determinative substantive

+substantive combinations all receive the determinative group suffix whereas coordinative combinations made up of two substantives do not. Turkish morphologically opposes *kadın terzi-si* (*kadın* 'woman', *terzi* 'tailor, dressmaker', *-si* = the determinative group suffix), women's tailor' to *kadın terzi* '(woman) dressmaker'. Coordinative groups in both languages are treated like syntactic groups of adjective+substantive.

5.1. Often two contradictory principles are at work; then one has to give way. Though material denoting first constituents usually makes a combination into a syntactic group, a frequently used second element may obviate the result, as in *tínwàre, íronwàre, sílverwàre,* or contrastive stress may interfere with the normal two-stress pattern of coordinative combinations, as in *fíghter-bòmber, gírl frìend, bóy frìend.*

5.2. When a substantive can also be interpreted as adjective, changed analysis may lead to change in the stress pattern. Though a hospital can be neither mental nor animal, we stress *méntal hóspital, ánimal hóspital,* as against *síck roòm, poór hoùse.* Similar shifts occur also in a more amply inflected language such as German: *ein deutsches Wörterbuch, ein lateinisches Heft, die französische Stunde.*

5.3. Many forestressed compounds denote an intimate, permanent relationship between the two signifiés to the extent that the compound is no longer to be understood as the sum of the constituent elements. A summerhouse, for instance, is not merely a house inhabited in summer, but a house of a particular style and construction which make it suitable for the warm season only. Two-stressed combinations of type *stóne wáll* never have this character. A syntactic group is always analyzable as the additive sum of its elements. It is an informal, noncommittal meeting, never a union of the constituents. This is a great advantage which English enjoys, for instance, over German. German cannot express morphologically the opposition 'permanent, intimate relationship' ∾ 'occasional, external connection' instanced by *súmmer-hoùse* ∾ *súmmer résidence, Chrístmas trèe* ∾ *Chrístmas tráffic.* English, therefore, has acquired a substantive+substantive combination of a looser, casual kind for groups in which an intimate, permanent relationship between the signifiés is not meant to be expressed: *field artillery, world war, country gentleman, village constable, parish priest, city court, state police, home town, district attorney,* and countless other combinations.

5.4. On the one hand, the possibilities of coining compounds are much more restricted than in German, where any occasional combination of two substantives automatically becomes a forestressed compound. On the other hand, English compounds are much closer morphologic units which cannot be split up the way German compounds are. In German, it is possible to say, for instance, *Hand- und elektrische Modelle* (*Weltwoche,* Sept. 26,

1947), clipping the *rainbow* type compound and leaving the adjective/ substantive syntactic group intact. However, in English as well as in German, serial combinations like *house and shop owners, wind and water mills* occur (Bloomfield, *Language,* 232, restricts them to German).

5.5. It is nevertheless often difficult to tell why in one case the language has created a compound while in another it has coined a syntactic group. Conceptually, *cóllege président* is in about the same position as *ópera diràctor,* but the first combination is a syntactic group, the second a compound. Form is one thing, concept is another. On the other hand, the same morphologic pattern does not necessarily involve the same degree of semantic unity: *lípstìck* is a closer unit than *recéption roòm.* The morphologic criterion of a compound enables us to do justice to both form and concept.

6.1. A few words are required about the problem of stress with regard to compounding. With Stanley S. Newman[12] we accept three degrees of phonemic stress: heavy stress (marked ´), middle stress (marked `), and weak stress (which is traditionally and perhaps more appropriately called absence of stress). As a combination of two independent words, basically speaking, a compound combines two elements which are characterized by presence of stress. Absence of stress in general indicates grammaticalization of a morphemic element (as in *políce-man, Mac Dónald, Fitz-gérald*). The determinant has the heavy, the determinatum the middle stress. Thus the usual pattern is ´ ` (e.g. *raínbòw*), which is also followed by combinations with a zero determinatum (*píckpòcket,* etc., see 1.2). All substantival compounds show this pattern, with the exception of those whose first elements are the pronouns *all* and *self.* Such compounds have double stress (e.g. *áll-soúl, áll-creátor, sélf-respéct, sélf-seéker*). Of adjectival compounds, only two types have the stable stress pattern heavy stress/middle stress: the type *cólor-blìnd,* i.e., adjectives determined by a preceding substantive (unless the underlying concept is that of emphatic comparison, as in *gráss-greén,* where double stress is the rule) and *heárt-breàking.* All other adjectival types are basically double stressed.

6.2. Bloch and Trager[13] posit four degrees of phonemic stress: loud stress, reduced loud stress, medial stress, and weak stress. They find reduced loud stress on the adjunct of a syntactic adjunct/primary group (*óld mán*) as well as on second elements of forestressed compounds (*bláckbìrd, élevator-òperator*) which are obviously not on the same level. But it seems to be more correct to say that the reduced stress on *old* is rhythmically conditioned by the position of *old* before a likewise heavy stressed word to which *old* stands in the subordinate relation of adjunct. This is a syntactic phenomenon of stress reduction. No change of the underlying concept is in-

[12] Stanley S. Newman, "On the Stress System of English," *Word* 2. 171–187 (1946).
[13] B. Bloch and G. L. Trager, *op. cit.,* 48.

volved in a shift from reduced to loud stress, as no oppositional stress pattern ′ ′ ∾ ` ′ exists in the case of adjective/substantive combinations. So *óld mán* is really a free variant of *óld mán*. *Bláckbìrd* is different: we cannot oppose *bláckbìrd* to *bláck bìrd* without changing the underlying concept. The stress pattern ′ ` of *bláckbìrd* is morphophonemic. The case of *élevator-òperator* is similar. A combination of the type *hoúsehòlder* (discussed in 1.3) implies the stress pattern ′ ` as morphophonemically relevant. Though in the particular case of *élevator-òperator* we cannot oppose the heavy/middle stress to a heavy/heavy stress combination, we can conceive of other pairs where change of stress implies change of the underlying concept, as *Frénch teàcher* 'a teacher of French' ∾ *Frénch teácher* 'a teacher who is French' *réd hùnter* 'one who hunts reds' ∾ *réd húnter* 'a hunter who is red', *fát prodùcer* 'one producing fat' ∾ *fát prodúcer* 'a producer who is fat'.

We must therefore assume a relevant degree of stress which distinguishes the phonemic non-heavy stress of *bláckbìrd* and *élevator òperator* from the non-phonemic non-heavy stress of *óld mán*. While we interpret the reduced loud stress as a positional variant of the heavy stress, we must consider the phonemic secondary stress of *bìrd* and *òperator* as a middle stress. On the other hand, the degree of stress on the third syllable of independent *élevàtor* and *óperàtor* is not different from that on *bird* in *bláckbìrd*: in either case we have a full middle stress. When these words become second elements of compounds, the intensity of the full middle stress is lessened and shifted to a light middle stress (which, for the sake of convenience, I will here mark ˘): *élevător òperător*. This light middle stress is non-phonemic. We interpret it as the rhythmically predictable form assumed by the full middle stress in a position before or after a morpho-phonemic full middle stress. In composition, it chiefly occurs with compounds of type *aírcrăft-càrrier* (see 1.6) on the second element of the determinant, the full middle stress being morpho-phonemically reserved for the determinatum. That full middle stress on the determinatum is morpho-phonemic is also manifest in the behavior of German compounds: those having a compound determinant are stressed as in *Ráthaŭskèller* whereas those with a compound determinatum are stressed as in *Stádt-baùrăt*.

An Exploratory Inquiry into Lexical Clusters*

Edward M. Anthony, Jr.

The stimulus for this paper arose out of the writer's dissertation in linguistics at the University of Michigan.[1] The dissertation attempted to describe the structure of the so-called 'two-word verb,' using as a basis some twenty-three hours of spoken English. The discussion which follows, however, does not apply solely to that class of constructions.

In one group of two-word verbs it was found that, although by structural criteria the members should have been ambiguous, they were not. Some examples, together with a word or phrase indicating the meaning in which they were grasped, stand below:

I'm glad you brought that up.	'introduce into the discussion'
Button your coat up.	'fasten completely'
I called her up six or eight times.	'telephone'
I'd certainly follow it up.	'pursue a subject'
They put it up on the shore of the lake.	'erect'

In these examples *up* occurs in a position that can be occupied by either a Class 4 *up*[2] as in *It took a hop up*, or a function word *up* as in *He climbed up the ladder*. None of these cases in the materials, however, showed the divided response which characterizes ambiguity. This phenomenon appears in utterances which bear no other relation to the problem which provided the impetus for this paper, and it is the general problem of the lack of expected ambiguity which concerns us here.

Before discussing any suspicious lack of ambiguity, it becomes necessary to describe various types of ambiguity which are founnd in English and some of the kinds of signals which the language employs in resolving these ambiguties. Some ambiguities which arise do not depend on the language itself for the divided response which they elicit. *The Yankees beat the Dodgers* receives an entirely different response in Brooklyn than it does in the Bronx. One must, however, go to nonlinguistic sources for information which will clarify these responses. This type of ambiguity is social or cultural.

---

* Reprinted with permission from *American Speech*, 29.174–180 (October, 1954).

[1] Edward Mason Anthony, Jr., 'Test Frames for Stuctures with *Up* in Modern American English' (unpublished doctoral dissertation, University of Michigan, 1954).

[2] These form classes are taken from Charles C. Fries, *The Structure of English: An Introduction to the Construction of English Sentences* (New York: Harcourt, Brace, 1952). Chapters V and VII treat the matter in detail.

Again, one hears *Look at the cat* and cannot predict whether the response will be characterized by loathing, delight, or indifference. Information pertinent to the problems of individual meanings must be sought outside the language.

Bloomfield states that the fundamental assumption of linguistic science is that 'in certain communities (speech-communities) some speech-utterances are alike as to form and meaning.'[3] Later, after presenting examples which show the difficulties of deciding whether two forms are homonyms or have a single meaning, he adds, 'our basic assumption is true only within limits, even though its general truth is presupposed not only in linguistic study, but by all our actual use of language.'[4] It has been, in fact, extremely difficult to classify the same phonetic shape into mutually exclusive lexical meanings. One might say that every lexical item is ambiguous. The following sentences, with some possible meanings appended, illustrate the point:

I have a *book*. 'dictionary,' 'book of tickets,' 'telephone book'

She used the *pencil*. 'eyebrow——,' 'lead——,' 'grease——'

He's sitting on the *bench*. 'judge's——,' 'substitute players'——,' 'bus depot's——'

He gave her a *ring*. 'telephone call,' 'engagement——'

John broke the *record*. 'track——,' 'phonograph——'

Do you want the *spoon*? 'golfer's——,' 'cook's——'

One might say that some of these examples seem more ambiguous than others, but objective criteria for deciding which are and why are difficult to set up. If other lexical items are present in near-by sentences, certain meanings are excluded, at least partially. For example, if the answer to *Do you want the spoon?* is either *No, I want the driver* or *No, I want the fork*, the probability of the other meaning cited decreases greatly. Such examples lead to the formulation of a valid, though necessarily vague, description of lexical ambiguity: Lexical ambiguity occurs when a phonetic shape having two or more lexical meanings appears with other lexical items that are compatible with these same meanings, and no nonlexical clues indicate the meaning intended.

Sometimes a lexical item appears which has 'one' lexical meaning and yet appears in more than one form class. Note the following examples:

The representative votes.
The motor(')s idle.

In the first example *representative* can be Class 3 (a 'representative' selection), or Class 1 (the 'representatives'). *Votes* can be Class 1 (a million 'votes') or Class 2 (he 'votes'). In the second example *idle* can be Class 2

[3] Leonard Bloomfield, *Language* (New York: Henry Holt, 1933), p. 144.
[4] *Ibid.*, p. 145.

(they 'idle') or Class 3 (they are 'idle'). This type of ambiguity depends structurally upon the lack of a signal of form, a pattern arrangement, or a function word.

If one chooses to believe that these particular lexical items have different lexical meanings when they appear as members of more than one form class, the above examples may simply be placed in the category which follows. One can, of course, make the assumption that every phonetic shape which appears in more than one form class has a different lexical meaning correlating to each form class. In effect, this denies the existence of this type of structural ambiguity.

Structural ambiguity may also come from an arrangement which shows a lack of clear correlation signals:

> A. The sisters of the boys who were there.
> B. The sisters of the boy who were there.
> C. The sisters of the boy who was there.

A lacks a signal to show with which Class 1 word *who* correlates. In B *who* clearly correlates with *sisters* and in C with *boy*.

A phonetic shape sometimes appears which has not only 'more than one' lexical meaning but also membership in more than one form class. This situation leads to lexico-structural ambiguity. The following examples illustrate:

> Duck feathers are *down*.
> *Direct* traffic.
> He looked *hard*.

Down as Class 4 has a meaning of 'lower position' and as Class 1, 'a certain kind of feathers.' The position directly after a Class 2 word can be occupied by either form class. *Direct* in the second example has a pre-Class 1 position that can be filled by either Class 2 'control' or Class 3 'straight.' *Hard* occupies a position that either Class 3 or Class 4 can fill, and the meanings are, respectively, 'sinister' and 'intently.' Structural clues that clarify these ambiguities appear below:

> Duck feathers are duck *down*. (Class 1)
> Duck feathers are *down* in price. (Class 4)
> The *direct* traffic. (Class 3)
> *Direct* the traffic. (Class 2)
> He looked *hard* and intent. (Class 3)
> He looked *hard* and intently. (Class 4)

In the second paragraph of this article six examples were given of what should have constituted lexico-structural ambiguity but did not do so in a particular body of material examined. In these examples or in similar ones it becomes necessary to seek further evidence outside the utterances themselves. Sometimes cultural and individual meanings are a factor, but are nonlinguistic. Frequency of appearance in the language is a factor. An example from Spanish will illustrate. Two verbs, *arar* 'plow' and *hacer* 'do' have the same phonetic shape when *arar* appears as a past form, (*aré* 'I plowed') and *hacer* appears as a future form (*haré* 'I will do'). If a sentence *Aré lo que pude* is submitted to a Spanish speaker, he will almost invariably change *pude* to *pueda*, using the subjunctive which ordinarily would be used in this situation after *hacer*. And yet *Aré lo que pude* is perfectly correct in its meaning 'I plowed what I could.' The much higher frequency of *hacer* is probably responsible for this correcting of an already correct sentence and supersedes the structural clue given by an indicative form *pude*. Thus homonyms will be interpreted in terms of the most common meaning, *ceteris paribus*, assuming a significant disparity in the frequency of the variant meanings.

In English, clarification of expected ambiguities is often explained by a reference to the context in which a word appears. These contexts are susceptible of further analysis. A context may be structural—*direct traffic* is ambiguous, but a structural clue in the position of *the* may be part of the context which will make the meaning clear—either *the direct traffic* or *direct the traffic* results.

It is, however, in the analysis of lexical context that the notion of lexical clusters[5] proves useful. The lexical items *foul, ball, score,* and *coach* are terms in baseball, football, and basketball. With no clues telling which sport is referred to, the meanings are hazy. But if one adds *inning* to the list, not only do we know that baseball is the sport but also that *foul* describes, not an action contrary to the rules, but simply a batted ball that is outside the play. *Ball* is now narrowed to a particular kind, *score* is interpreted in runs, and *coach* is one of several managerial assistants. If, in place of *inning*, we add *goal line*, the ball is now known to be oval, *score* is counted in touchdowns, and *foul* includes actions contrary to the rules of the game. *Basket*, if used to replace *goal line*, shifts the focus to a large spherical ball and a different interpretation of *foul*. Lexical items tend to group together in clusters in which they are mutually influential.

It can probably be assumed that every lexical item belongs to more than one cluster. *Foul, ball, score,* and *coach* have been shown to belong to several. If the lexical items in an utterance all share the same memberships, the result will show lexical ambiguity. If any one of the items has membership in only one of the possible clusters, the resultant utterance will not be lexically ambiguous because all other possible clusters will be negated. *The coach told the player to throw the ball* is ambiguous, for *coach, player, throw,* and *ball* all have several lexical cluster memberships in common. *The coach told the player to bunt the ball* is unambiguous, for

---

[5] Charles C. Fries, in his article 'Meaning and Linguistic Analysis' (*Language*, XXX [1954], 57–68), briefly discusses the problems of lexical distribution. [In this book pp. 101–113.]

bunt has membership in only one of the three clusters discussed above. *Kick,* substituted for *bunt,* is equally unambiguous. If, for convenience, we label the three lexical clusters *baseball, football,* and *basketball,* it is apparent that these belong to a larger cluster that we may label *sport.* And certain lexical items belong to smaller clusters within baseball, for example. *Bat* (used in offense) and *glove* (used in defense) belong to different subclusters, whereas *inning* includes both. Lexical clusters can be said to overlap.

The process of definition consists of placing a particular lexical item within a cluster. The cluster may be large or small, according to the needs and purposes of the definition. Scientific definitions seek to place an item in the smallest possible lexical cluster. Legal definitions give an impression of wordiness and redundancy largely because of the necessity of placing each word in a suitably small lexical cluster.

In a given lexical cluster, some items (specifics) are more limiting than others (generals). This is a relative, not an absolute statement. In our example above, *inning* was more limiting than *foul, score,* or *coach.* In our subclusters (*offense* and *defense*), *inning* was not so limiting as *glove* or *bat,* however. Some lexical items seem to 'set' a lexical cluster. If a specific appears before a general lexical item, the cluster has been 'set' early and the hearer perhaps grasps the meaning earlier. If a general occurs before a specific item, there is a possibility of a slower grasp on the part of the responder. One understands example *B* below more quickly than example *A:*

A. The *player* threw the ball across the field. It was dropped, but picked up in time to put the runner out.

B. The *pitcher* threw the ball across the field. It was dropped, but picked up in time to put the runner out.

Player here is a general and *pitcher* a specific. An awareness of general and specific items and their efficient handling could lead to the improvement of speaking and writing styles.

The notion of lexical clusters is helpful in teaching English to foreigners. A lexical item in one language may belong to a cluster different from that of its so-called 'equivalent' in another. *Banco* in Spanish is either *bench* or *bank* in English. *Bank* in English is either *banco* or *orilla* ('river bank') in Spanish. The teaching of vocabulary is largely a process of placing lexical items within lexical clusters peculiar to the language being taught and making those lexical clusters habitual with the learner when he is speaking the new language.[6] The selection of vocabulary to teach is largely a matter of selecting clusters significant in frequency and usefulness, and conveniently and efficiently limited in size.

[6] For some practice techniques in making the use of lexical items automatic for learners of English, see my article 'The Pattern Practice of Meanings,' *Language Learning,* II, No. 3 (1949), 83.

Many nonstructural aspects of style may be explained in terms of lexical clusters. If a nonambiguous utterance contains a lexical item that is not ordinarily found in the particular cluster involved, 'imaginative language' or 'slang' or a 'figure of speech' results. *That jazz is really solid; When asked the question on the quiz program, he struck out;* 'The Assyrian came down like the wolf on the fold,/ And his cohorts were gleaming in purple and gold' show *solid, struck out, wolf, fold* as lexical items which do not ordinarily appear in the lexical clusters previously 'set.' If an excessive number of such items appears and there is still understanding, the result is a 'mixed metaphor.' *The British lion will never pull in its horns nor retreat into its shell* is a classic example where *lion*, which frequently occurs in the same lexical cluster as *British*, infrequently occurs with *horns* or *shell* and even less frequently with both. The extreme case results in gibberish which, deprived of a common cluster, elicits classifiable response only to structural signals: *The elephants wrote a chair to the duck.*

It is hoped that the above outline, with its implications, may prove to be a basis for further investigation of what Bloomfield has called 'the weak point in language study,'[7] and that linguists may yet be able to approach scientifically the problems of lexical meanings.

Language for Everybody: A Book Review*

William Buell

Language for Everybody: What It Is and How to Master It is the most recent of several books on language and languages which Mario Pei, Professor of Romance Philology at Columbia University, has addressed to the general public. Its twofold purpose, to acquaint the reader having no previous linguistic knowledge with some fundamental facts and ideas concerning man's basic means of communication, and to give practical guidance to that reader in acquiring foreign languages and increasing his effectiveness in the use of his own, is wholly admirable. Unfortunately, *Language for Everybody* cannot be called successful in fulfilling that purpose.

The book is organized into six parts. Part I, "Language in Your Daily

[7] Bloomfield, *op. cit.*, p. 140.

* Reprinted by permission from *Language Learning*, 7.139–142 (1956–1957). The review is of Mario Pei's *Language for Everybody: What It Is and How to Master It* (New York, 1956). The best-known of his other books are *The Story of Language* (1949) and *The Story of English* (1952). For a similar adverse criticism of *The Story of Language* see H. B. Allen, "All is Not Gold," College English, 12.106–107 (Nov., 1950).

Life," is introductory. Part II, "Language in the Laboratory," contains the little that Pei says about linguistic structure. Part III, "History of Language," has more to do with the external history of languages than with internal structural change. Part IV, "Sociological Implications of Language," is concerned with such assorted topics as "the language community," "language minorities," and "what makes a language important?" Part V, "Languages in Comparison," touches on both comparative linguistics and linguistic typology. Part VI, "Some Practical Language Hints," purports to tell the reader how to identify languages he hears spoken or sees written, how to learn to speak a foreign language, and how to improve the use of his native language. Throughout the book, illustrative material, often lengthy lists of forms, words, or sentences, is set off from the main text by horizontal lines across the page. Examples, chosen at random, are "Permissible and Nonpermissible Groups of Consonants at Beginning and End of Words in Various Languages,"[1] a list of "The World's 106 Languages Having the Largest Speaking Populations,"[2] "Samples of Constructed Languages for International Use,"[3] and "Samples of Arabic Structure."[4] All too often, this material is merely presented and is not discussed in such a way as to make it meaningful for the reader.

It would be simple to fill several pages with statements from the book, both general and specific, which would strike the careful student of language as either misinformed, or badly reasoned, or both. For instance, Pei lists as two examples of "pure nationwide slang" a colorless, straightforward statement in non-Standard English, "I ain't got none," and a spelling representation of ordinary conversational pronunciation, "Jeet? No, joo?"[5] The first example could be accounted for by Pei's own definition of slang as "a substandard form of speech that is generally intelligible to the entire population . . . whether they choose to use it or not,"[6] but the second certainly could not. Even the best of books, of course, contain errors of fact and statements to which a critic may take exception; Pei's book, however, contains far too many statements to which linguistic scholars would take exception.

Merely cataloging such vulnerable statements, however, would never get to the real reasons why *Languages for Everybody* is an unsatisfactory book, for these reasons are more general. The first of them is a failure to fully utilize the methods and results of the structural approach to language. Such basic structural concepts as the phoneme and the morpheme are scantily and imprecisely treated in Part II and are never referred to again. Pei defines the phoneme and illustrates the principle of complementary

[1] pp. 112–14.
[2] pp. 223–25.
[3] pp. 242–43.
[4] p. 282.
[5] p. 61.
[6] p. 59.

distribution; but he immediately proceeds to violate the principle by listing the vowel of "the" and the vowel of "but" as different phonemes.[7] His entire treatment of English syllabics is inconsistent. Instead of either considering the syllabics of "beat" and "bait" as both being diphthongs, as Pike does, or as both being diphthongs, as Trager and Smith do, he considers "beat" as having a monophthong and "bait" as having a diphthong.[8] When he comes to stress and intonation, he neglects the phonemic principle altogether. The best he can do with intonation is to represent it with musical notes on a staff and to say that "there are no precise rules governing it."[9]

The morpheme comes in for even more cursory treatment. It is defined, rather inaccurately, between parentheses— ". . . morphemes (independent units of forms, like the -s of "birds," which convey significant accessory notions) . . ."[10]—and then forgotten entirely. Referential meaning is resorted to in defining parts of speech: "Verbs are action words or indicate states . . ."[11] There is no systematic attempt to discuss syntax. All that Pei has to say about Modern English might just as well have been written before the appearance of such books as Pike's *The Intonation of American English,*[12] Fries' *The Structure of English,*[13] and Trager and Smith's *An Outline of English Structure.*[14]

A second reason for the inadequacy of *Language for Everybody,* one perhaps even more basic than the ignoring of the structural approach, is the general attitude which underlies the book, and which permeates it throughout. The study of language is approached not primarily as a means to intellectual enrichment and satisfaction but as something which will pay off:

> Ignorance of improper use of language can easily interfere with your success and advancement. It can take money out of your pocket.[15]

> The person who speaks, easily and correctly, the standard speech of the broad language community to which he belongs will normally find himself better off all around. He will be able to express his ideas and personality and get what he wants. He will be able to make friends and influence people.[16]

Thus does Pei present language study as a sort of panacea. And a panacea, of course, must be easy. Perhaps a desire to make his subject matter easy is partly responsible for Pei's avoidance of the concepts of structural linguistics. Perhaps such a desire is also responsible for his failure to use standard phonetic or phonemic transcriptions any place in the book. Ironi-

[7] p. 82.
[8] *Ibid.*
[9] p. 100.
[10] p. 93.
[11] p. 93.
[12] University of Michigan Press, 1945.
[13] Harcourt, Brace and Company, 1952.
[14] Norman, Oklahoma: Battenburg Press, 1951.
[15] p. 5.
[16] p. 7.

cally enough, such avoidances make much that is in the volume more difficult. Without transcription, forms from foreign languages must be cited in
conventional orthography, which is meaningless to a person who does not
know the spelling system of the language involved, or in makeshift "phonetic spellings" which are as confusing as helpful. Structural concepts and
terminology may be difficult for a learner at first, but in a long run they can
make discussion of language clearer and simpler. The lack of such concepts
vitiates the sections on language learning and makes them little more than
casual conversation on the subject. . . . The continued popularity of books
like *Language for Everybody* presents a challenge for the linguist and the
language teacher. One of the responsibilities of the linguist is to write better
books presenting his discipline to the layman. One of the responsibilities
of language teachers, including those teaching English to native speakers,
is to direct their students toward such sound books about language as already exist within lay comprehension. . . .

Part III

LINGUISTIC GEOGRAPHY

INTRODUCTION

IN LESS THAN three-quarters of a century one field of applied linguistics, that called linguistic or dialect geography, has yielded a rich harvest in the understanding of relationships between language-users and where language-users live.

Linguistic geography, the study of the regional distribution of language forms and their variants, has attained its maturity in Europe, where for some time there have been in existence completed studies of dialect speech in France, Belgium, The Netherlands, Switzerland, Italy, and some other areas. Indeed, one great pioneering project, the *Atlas linguistique de la France* (1902–1910) has been finished for so long that a second survey is proceeding, since such a study desirably should be repeated every fifty years.

In the United States a projected Linguistic Atlas of the United States and Canada was begun with a pilot investigation in New England, the results of which have been published as the *Linguistic Atlas of New England* (1939–1943). No other regional atlases have yet been published, but data from field records are available for the entire Atlantic Coast, for the northern part of the country as far west as Montana and Wyoming, for Colorado, for New Mexico, and for the Pacific Coast, with some additional materials from Louisiana and Texas.

Marckwardt opens the present Part with a statement of the value of dialect atlas findings for the teaching of English to college freshmen; Allen follows with an article showing more specifically what kinds of information the teacher can expect to utilize from the files of records made by trained field workers.

The succeeding five articles report on the investigation of the occurrence of specific language items, and at the same time they serve as examples of the summarizing of evidence which is useful to the student and teacher of English. Ives reports on the variant pronunciations of *can't*, with little support for the notion that the so-called broad "a" pronunciation is better than any other. Atwood offers evidence to confirm and more sharply define the long-suspected social and geographical distribution of the two pronunciations of *grease* and *greasy*. In two articles McDavid offers data on controversial matters of pronunciation and grammar. A controverted pronunciation of *catch* actually turns out to be in quite fair repute among speakers of Standard English. Distribution of *hadn't ought,* he finds, suggests that textbooks may do the user a disservice by implying that a non-Standard usage is general instead of regional. A usage academically considered non-Standard, Allen's study indicates, will have to be rejudged in light of the atlas evidence for the frequency of *have drank* among cultivated speakers.

McDavid then adduces evidence for a number of phonological items in the atlas files to draw several conclusions about the various social and geographical relations of certain variants. Of special interest, in the light of popular belief and dictionary transcriptions, is his point that a prestige pronunciation in one area may be the non-Standard form in another.

Ives concludes the chapter with a report of his own supplementary investigation of the relationship between pronunciation and social status. This study may point the way to utilization of linguistic data in sociological research, a direction predicted earlier by McDavid in his article, "Dialect Geography and Social Science Problems," *Social Forces,* 25.168–172 (1946).

Linguistic Geography and Freshman English*

ALBERT H. MARCKWARDT

EVERY AUTUMN approximately half a million students enter the colleges and universities of the country. Virtually all of them are required to take a course in freshman English. Over a ten-year period their number mounts to a total of five or six million. Year in and year out several thousand instructors in English devote most of their time to teaching these students.

In one sense this is a thumbnail sketch of the most amazing linguistic enterprise in the history of the civilized world. Varied as are the aims and outlines of freshman English the country over, the hundreds of courses which fall into this category have one element in common: they seek to give the individual student a mastery of standard American English as a medium of communication. Never before has any educational system com-

* Originally a talk made at the Rocky Mountain Modern Language Association conference, Boulder, Colorado, October, 1951, this paper is here reprinted by permission from the *CEA Critic* (College English Association), 14.1 (January, 1952).

mitted itself to the teaching of a national standard, that is to say a prestige dialect, on so vast a scale.

This common aim poses certain problems. First, it is still true that many high school and college students come from homes where standard English is not habitually spoken or written. For these, this phase of the English program of school and college means that the individual student must be trained to forego his habitual use of certain language features characteristic of the regional and social dialects of English and to substitute for these, features of that prestige dialect which we call Standard English.

At the same time we must recognize that this so-called Standard English is not absolutely identical the country over, although most college handbooks and rhetorics are blandly written upon the assumption that it is. To select just a single instance, the use of *for* in "I would like for you to write me a letter," is characteristic of cultivated speech and writing over large parts of the South and totally absent from most other sections of the country, yet college textbooks often quite unreasonably legislate against this particular construction. I recall very vividly my own bewilderment when, as an undergraduate, I read in the textbook we used in those days that the use of *taken* as an active past-tense form—*I taken it*—was one of the worst errors that anyone could make. As I learned much later, this statement undoubtedly made a great deal of sense to students in some parts of the country, but to my classmates and me, with our particular regional linguistic background, it was wholly meaningless. We simply couldn't imagine anyone's doing it.

The situation is similar, if not even more aggravated, in the speech field with respect to matters of pronunciation. I say more aggravated because a good many manuals of speech are written from a more rigid, authoritarian point of view than are the best hand-books of composition. For example, when even a usually careful and competent phonetician applies the label "substandard" to the voiced *t* in better, the diphthongal pronunciation of the vowel in *bird,* the *w* of *somewhat,* and the voiceless initial fricative of *thither,* one feels the need of a body of objective fact to put these impressionistic judgments to the test. We have only to remember that even today, all candidates for teaching positions in New York City must demonstrate by examination that they have mastered the south-eastern British—so-called Received Standard—pronunciations recorded in Daniel Jones's *Pronouncing Dictionary of the English Language,* for which the editor claims no validity whatsoever outside of the particular area from which they were gathered.

The problem then becomes one of securing authoritative data about standard American English, as it exists in various parts of the country. One source of such data is to be found in the materials which have been collected for the Linguistic Atlas of the United States and Canada. At present this consists of the published *Linguistic Atlas of New England,* the completely collected field records of the Linguistic Atlas of the South-Atlantic States and of the Linguistic Atlas of the Middle Atlantic States, together with the fragmentary materials of at least four other linguistic atlas projects in various stages of completion throughout the country.

There is no question that these materials, even in their present incomplete state, present a more complete body of carefully gathered information concerning pronunciation than the most authoritative dictionaries are based on today. The second edition—still the current one—of *Webster's New International Dictionary* employed 104 consultants on pronunciation, and subsequent analysis showed these to be very unevenly distributed throughout the country. The cultured informants represented in the three coastal atlases alone comprise more than half again that number. When the country is completely covered, there will undoubtedly be from two to three times as many. Moreover, the atlas will contain affirmative evidence of substandard speech in quantity. That is to say, the evidence will be there and will not have to be guessed at negatively in terms of whatever does not happen to be known to, or habitually used by, the author or lexicographer. Finally, the wide variety of pronunciation characteristic of the cultured informants should serve to check some of the excessive dogmatism found in speech classes.

With respect to problems of vocabulary, morphology, and syntax the situation is much the same. Any examination of a dozen or more college textbooks in composition will demonstrate that in large measure the authors of these books have copied one another as assiduously as have the lexicographers. Or even if they have gone to the current factual sources of the language on many moot points, what help can they expect to get? A dictionary label of "colloquial" or a classification of "popular English" in a standard work on syntax is, after all, just another man's subjective judgment, often based upon somewhat meager evidence. It is reasonable to maintain that the selective sampling technique employed by the atlases and the sheer mass of evidence they have collected impart a greater validity to their findings than most collections of fact relative to current use of the language.

Early in 1951 a minor furore was created in one of the pedagogical journals when someone insisted that the apparent relaxation of standards in English grammars and handbooks over the past quarter-century could be accounted for by the fact that the linguistic habits of the freshmen were influencing, and indeed overcoming, those of the instructors. This somewhat startling conclusion was purportedly based upon a comparison covering twenty points of form and syntax between the 1949 Norman Lewis survey of the language of college professors, editors, lexicographers, authors, etc., and a presumably similar survey of the usage of a group of freshmen.

What the author of the article overlooked, and what so far few of his critics have pointed out, was that the instructions given to the two groups

differed so radically that the results of the surveys simply did not admit
of a valid comparison. To make his point, the author might much more
profitably have consulted the atlas materials for the normal usage of the
cultured informants. Had he done so, however, his point might well have
vanished, for a spot check of one or two items considered in the study
shows the cultured informants closer to the reported usage of the freshmen
than to the so-called authorities consulted by Mr. Lewis.

There is still another way in which atlas findings can be of considerable
service. In our attempt to assure our students, on the secondary as well as
the college level, of a habitual command of standard English equal to the
demands of any situation in which their abilities may place them, we must
operate with a high degree of efficiency. Language habits are formed only
by dint of constant repetition. Even in the twelve or sixteen years of schooling through the high school and college levels, the number of new habits
which can be formed and of the old ones which may be eradicated is not
too great. This calls for a highly judicious selection of the particular language features to be attacked and replaced by new habits. It demands careful curriculum planning.

We know now that it can no longer be assumed that all substandard
forms and syntactical patterns are alike the country over. Professor E.
Bagby Atwood, of the University of Texas, in analyzing the field records
of the three coastal atlases, has found sharp lines of demarcation in the inflectional forms of folk speech. The same is also true with such syntactical
matters as the choice of preposition in "sick (to) (at) or (in) one's stomach." If it is decided that there is enough prejudice against, or social stigma
connected with *sick to his stomach* to make the substitution of *at* a justifiable item somewhere in the language curriculum, in those areas where
sick at his stomach is the characteristic folk form, this item may be safely
omitted. It does not constitute a problem. The same conclusion will apply
to *all the farther, dog-bit* as a past participle, or *taken* as a past-tense form.
Atlas results merit the attention of those who are charged with framing
courses of English instruction at virtually all levels of schooling.

There are, of course, many broader implications of the splendid work
that has been done and that which is now under way in determining the
regional features of American English. My only purpose here is to suggest
that since so many of us are concerned with the teaching of the English
language on a practical level, the work of the linguistic geographer is by
no means merely a remote endeavor, presenting a few research scholars
with an opportunity to demonstrate their virtuosity, but rather an activity
that can touch intimately and affect profoundly our everyday classroom
practices.

The Linguistic Atlases: Our New Resource*

HAROLD B. ALLEN

A FEW YEARS AGO a teacher in South Carolina was pushing her less than enthusiastic pupils through a grammar drill book, painfully but relentlessly. The class struggled on to an exercise intended to teach the correct use of the negative of *ought*. Here the students found sentences with the approved construction *ought not*. But they found also some sentences with a construction they were supposed to cross out, *hadn't ought*. This the pupils had never seen or heard before, and they were delighted with it. True, the book said it was wrong, and teacher, as always, agreed with the book. But there it was—in the book—as plain as anything could be; and somehow it seemed marvelously sensible. *He hadn't intended to do it: He hadn't ought to do it. I hadn't wanted to go: I hadn't ought to go.* Why not? So within a week or two the puzzled teacher began to find more and more of her pupils using *hadn't ought*, pupils who up until then had used *ought not* with unconscious ease.

Such an incident can not happen in the future if teachers and textbook writers know and use the new data now becoming accessible to them. This is the body of facts about American English coming from the great research projects collectively designated the Linguistic Atlas of the United States and Canada.

Of course, this is not the first mass of information about American usage available to teachers of English. During the past forty years an increasing number of studies have effectively demonstrated the unreliability of much that had been accepted as truth. The NCTE itself has led in the publication of the significant and familiar studies by Sterling Andrus Leonard, Albert H. Marckwardt and Fred Walcott, and Charles C. Fries. Dozens of articles on specific items of usage have appeared in our own Council publications as well as in *Language, American Speech*, and a few other periodicals. Also there have been published the increasingly reliable commercial dictionaries and our first pronouncing lexicon, Kenyon and Knott's *Pronouncing Dictionary of American English*.

Now all this weight of evidence has had its clearly perceptible effects upon the handbooks and the school grammars. A comparison of those pub-

* Reprinted by permission from *The English Journal*, 45.188–94 (April, 1956). This article is adapted from a paper read at the convention of the National Council of Teachers of English, New York, November, 1955.

lished in 1920 and those appearing since 1950 reveals a much higher proportion of sweet reasonableness, of honest recognition of the facts of linguistic life. But influential as this evidence has been, it generally has had
one important limitation. On the whole, these studies and investigations
of usage have assumed the validity of the criterion of national use, a criterion enunciated by the Scottish rhetorician Alexander Campbell in the late
eighteenth century. Campbell insisted that national use must be one of
the determinants of what is good usage. Following him, these studies assume that what is true in the determination of usage in a smaller country
like England or France, with one cultural capital, is equally true for the
vast United States with its cultural diversification and many cultural
centers.

A second limitation of these studies is that generally they ignore the lexical and grammatical usage of the normal everyday, informal speech of cultivated people (though Leonard did record opinions classifying forms as
"colloquial"). Part of this limitation, of course, is also the fact that these
studies generally have not treated matters of pronunciation in informal
speech. An exception, again, is Kenyon and Knott's dictionary, which
did record conversational pronunciations reported by independent mail
surveys.

These limitations are reflected naturally enough in the contents of the
textbooks. The laudable improvement in the general treatment of usage
is accompanied by conspicuous inadequacy in the treatment of any language matters having variations which correlate with geographical distribution. This improvement, furthermore, is offset also by the persistence
of considerable misapprehension concerning various matters of pronunciation whether regional or not.

But any textbook or reference book with these inadequacies will soon
be obsolete. Already valuable evidence about regional usage in words and
grammar and pronunciation is beginning to emerge from the tremendous
research activity within the framework of the Linguistic Atlas of the
United States. Already enough evidence from this source is available so
that textbook-makers will shirk responsibility if they do not take these
new facts into account.

DATA ON PRONUNCIATION

What is the Linguistic Atlas of the United States? It is not a single project; it is a number of regional research projects using similar procedures
and collecting the same kinds of evidence, hence producing results that can
be added together and compared.

Essentially this evidence is gathered like this. Using a tested selective
sampling technique, linguistically trained fieldworkers interview native
residents representing three groups, older and uneducated speakers, mid-
dle-aged secondary school graduates, and younger college graduates. From

each of these persons information is sought about more than 800 language items (in the first project there were 1200). Each response is recorded in a finely graded phonetic transcription, so that all responses have value as pronunciation evidence. Some items are included for that reason only; others are included for their lexical or grammatical or syntactic significance. The basic list of items in the questionnaire is usually modified slightly in each area through the dropping of some which are irrelevant there and the adding of others significant there. (It is pointless to ask a North Dakota farmer what he calls the Atlantic round clam, a /kwáhɑg/, /kwɔhɔ́g/, or /kwəhɔ́g/. He never heard of it by any name!) But this basic list is essentially the same countrywide, so that national comparative studies will be possible when the fieldwork is finished.

At present, organizations to gather this evidence have been effected in eight different areas: New England, Middle Atlantic States, South Atlantic States, North Central States, Upper Midwest, Rocky Mountain States, Pacific Coast, and Louisiana. The New England Atlas has been completed and published. From it and the unpublished materials of the other eastern surveys has come the evidence presented by Hans Kurath in 1949 in his *Word Geography of the Eastern United States* and by E. B. Atwood in 1953 in his *Verb Forms of the Eastern United States*. Derivative articles by Raven I. McDavid, Jr., Atwood, Alva Davis, Walter Avis, Thomas Pearce, David Reed, Marjorie Kimmerle, and others have made public additional usage evidence in *American Speech, College English* and *The English Journal, Orbis, Language,* and *Language Learning*. The volume by Kurath and McDavid on the pronunciation of the Eastern United States is shortly to appear, and Mrs. McDavid is about to complete her dissertation on the verb forms of the North Central and Upper Midwest regions. These publications, together with the Atlas files, constitute a vast accumulation of data for the use of teachers and textbook writers.

When we look at the information now available about regional usage we find that probably the most important single fact is the reconstruction of the picture of American language areas. It has been assumed for years that we have Eastern, Southern, and Northern (sometimes called General American) dialect divisions in this country. But evidence from the Atlantic field records presented by Kurath has led to the recognition of a quite different structure consisting of Eastern New England, Northern, Midland, and Southern, with various subdivisions in each region and, of course, with some overlapping of regions. Midland is the speech of the Pennsylvania-Delaware settlement area and of its derivative areas in central Ohio, northern Indiana, central Illinois, southern Iowa, and so on. It exists also in the variety called South Midland, which extends south along the Appalachians as "Mountain English" and into southern Illinois, Missouri, Arkansas, eastern Oklahoma, and eastern Texas.

For significant matters of pronunciation I would suggest reference to McDavid's excellent article, "Some Social Differences in Pronunciation," in *Language Learning* in 1953.[1] McDavid's thesis here is that, although certain pronunciations may lack recognition or distribution nationally, they can enjoy high prestige in a given region through the influence of such a focal center as Boston, New York, Philadelphia, Richmond, or Charleston. Differences in pronunciation, in other words, are not merely a matter of social and educational background; they may also be related to geographical differences.

For example, despite the tendency of the schools toward spelling-pronunciation, the unaspirated forms /wɪp/ "whip," /wilbæro/ "wheelbarrow," and /wɔrf/ "wharf" are in common cultured use in the Midland area and, as a matter of fact, occur sporadically elsewhere among cultured speakers. A few years ago a teacher in Utica, N.Y., yielding to the probably normal impulse to consider one's own speech or that of a textbook as the proper one, wrote to *College English* that she had never observed a person of true culture who lacked the /hw/ cluster in such words. Yet, as McDavid has observed, this teacher would have had to go only a few miles south to central Pennsylvania to observe thousands of cultivated speakers who say /wɪp/ and /wilbæro/; indeed, even in her own community the Atlas's cultivated informant is recorded as having /w/ and not /hw/ in these words. In the function words, of course, the customary lack of stress has resulted in the loss of aspiration everywhere, not just in certain areas; yet in my own state of Minnesota the new guide for instruction in the language arts enjoins the teacher to insist upon distinguishing /wɪč/ "witch" and /hwɪč/ "which" and /wɛðər/ "weather" and /hwɛðər/ "whether."

Similarly, the /hy/ consonant cluster in *humor* reveals primary geographical distribution. This cluster commonly occurs in Northern speech, but elsewhere in the nation the usual form among all speakers is simply /yumər/.

In Northern American English and in South Carolina, probably in some other sections, a restressing of the second vowel in *because* has led to the form /bɪkɔ́z/ as usual among cultivated speakers. Yet many teachers, likely influenced by spelling and lacking the information forthcoming from the Atlas studies, insist punctiliously upon /bɪkɔz/.

The sounds represented by the letter *o* in *orange, horrid,* and *forest* also vary according to region. In much of New York state and in eastern Pennsylvania, for example, an unround /ɑ/ appears instead of the more common /ɔ/. Not long ago a teacher came to Minnesota from New York state and promptly began insisting that her pupils say only /ɑrmj/ and /fɑrɪst/; and recently a textbook came out with the same injunction, that the only correct form is /ɑrmj/.

[1] IV, 102–16.

The diphthong /ɪu/, mistakenly called "long *u*," offers another case in point. In the South, as in British English, a strongly consonantal /y/ beginning is heard in this diphthong in post-alveolar contexts, as in *newspaper, tube,* and *due* or *dew.* But in the North this beginning is quite weak, often almost imperceptible, and it is gone completely in northeastern New England and in Midland. Yet many teachers in the Middle West diligently drill their pupils in the pronunciation /nyuz/ instead of their normal /nuz/. More than half my own students each year report that this was their high school experience, although on only a few of them did the attempted inoculation "take." (To prevent misunderstanding, it should be clear that there can of course be no objection to the form /nyuz/ where it is the normal prestige form. What is objectionable is well-meaning but unenlightened tampering with acceptable speech.)

The same kind of thing, but with a much more complicated geographical picture, occurs with the pronunciation of a group of words spelled with *oo.* I should be surprised if many of the readers of this article, or of the original audience hearing it read, would have for all of these words the same pronunciation which I, a native of southern Michigan, have: /ruf, rut, huf, hup, hupɪŋ kɔf, kup, rum, brum, fud, spuk/ (with /ʊ/ as in *put* and /u/ as in *moon*). But I should also be surprised if you have not sometime been in a situation—on either the giving or the receiving end—where someone was being instructed to pronounce *root* and *roof,* perhaps even *soot,* with /u/ rather than /ʊ/. The Atlas files reveal a complicated distribution of these forms, each word having its own distinctive regional pattern; and nothing in this information supports the familiar injunctions.

Another vowel dilemma with historical roots in Middle English is that offered by *creek.* Many Northern teachers, probably swayed by the double *ee* spelling, for years have insisted upon their pupils learning the Southern standard pronunciation /krik/ despite the fact, which should be obvious to an objective listener in a Northern community and which is fully attested by the Atlas records, that the basic Northern form is /krɪk/. Even in Battle Creek, Michigan, I am informed, there is this attempt to lift at least the school population to the cultural heaven, Southern division, where /krik/ is the shibboleth.

There are numerous other moot matters of pronunciation upon which Atlas research now can provide information making possible an enlightened approach. I think, for instance, of such *loci critici* as /hɑg/ and /hɔg/, /rɑzbɛriz/ and /ræzbɛriz/, /grisi/ and /grizi/, /iðər/ and /ɑiðər/, /kɑfi/ and /kɔfi/, /kɑnt/ and /kænt/ and /kent/ "can't," /ves/ and /vɑz/, /kɛč/ and /kæč/, /wɑtər/ and /wɔtər/, /tord/ and /təwɔrd/, /sɝˑəp/ and /sɪrəp/, /təmetoz/ and /təmɑtoz/, /rædɪš/ and /rɛdɪš/, and /dɪfθɪryə/ and /dɪpθɪryə/—for information about which the Atlas sources are invaluable.

DATA ON GRAMMAR AND IDIOM

Then the category of grammar and idiom is another in which Atlas materials contribute to our knowledge about usage. As with pronunciation we quite humanly yield to the notion that what is standard or customary for us either is, or ought to be, standard for others. A recent rhetoric textbook for the college freshman course was written by two authors of southern background. They say, "*Bucket* is more likely to be the ordinary word *pail* . . . a little more old-fashioned and endowed with more 'poetic' suggestions." Any freshman speaking Northern English who finds this statement on page 372 must find it rather puzzling, for to him *bucket* refers to some unfamiliar wooden vessel in a well and is a word invariably preceded by *old oaken*. The Atlas files provide evidence for a much more objective statement about the relationship between *bucket* and *pail*.

Again, more than one textbook writer has condemned *sick to one's stomach* in favor of *sick at one's stomach*, but the Atlas findings reveal *sick to* as the usual Northern locution and *sick at* as a Midland variant, along with *sick from* and *sick with* and *sick in*.

Even those who have confidently relied upon the data in the 1932 Leonard report will now need to revise their statements in the light of what Atlas evidence tells them about *depot* (~railroad station), *in back of* (~behind), *mad* (~angry), *off of* (~from), and *like* (~as if)—all of them rated as disputable usages by Leonard—as well as about the expressions *the dog wants in* and *all the further*, both of which actually are rated there as illiterate.

Now such matters of pronunciation and of vocabulary may readily be accepted by the teacher as likely to be clarified by research in regional language. We are accustomed to thinking of dialect as consisting of differences in sounds and words. Actually, regional linguistic studies may also considerably illumine certain other matters of high importance to the teacher, those in the field of grammar.

At least seven of the grammatical items that Leonard's monograph listed as disputable were included in the Atlas worksheets. These are *dived~ dove, I'll~I shall, eat~et, aren't I?~ain't I?~am I not?, it (he) don't ~doesn't, these kind~those kind,* and *sang~sung*. At least eight more Atlas items appeared in the group classified by Leonard as illiterate: *have drank~have drunk, began~begun, lay down~lie down, a orange~an orange, hadn't you ought~ought not you, run~ran, set down~sit down,* and *you was~you were*.

The Atlas records offer data, some of it surprising, about these items. For instance, the frequently found textbook admonition about the preterit *dove* implies that this is non-standard in contrast with the historical form *dived*. But the records show plainly that *dove* is the usual form among speakers of

Northern English and *dived* is Midland and Southern. In other words, the present-day distinction is regional and not social.

But besides these items the Atlas files include comprehensive information about the social and regional distribution of many others that have been in controversy, such as the preterit forms *give* and *gave, did* and *done, dreamed* and *dremt, swam* and *swum, fitted* and *fit, shrank* and *shrunk, saw* and *seen, kneeled* and *knelt, taught* and *learned;* the participial forms *worn out* and *wore out, have taken* and *have took, I been thinking* and *I've been thinking, spoiled* and *spoilt, was bitten* and *was bit, have drove* and *have driven;* together with *you* and *you-all* and *it wasn't me* and *it wasn't I.*

APPLICATION OF THE DATA

For teachers of English, clearly the immediate application of this new source of information about our language is in the revision of previous statements about usage. In the simple interest of accuracy this revision is demanded. Those of us who have anything to do with the training of future teachers have the responsibility of using such revision in attention paid to usage items in our language and methods classes. The class room teacher has the special responsibility of using the new information in class drills, in class discussion, and in the evaluation of student oral and written language. As the experience of the South Carolina teacher with *hadn't ought* indicates, the teaching of standard forms must be done in full awareness of frequency and distribution of the contrasting non-standard forms.

But the teacher's application ordinarily must result from revision of usage statements in books of reference and in textbooks. Those who prepare texts, workbooks, drill exercises, and the like cannot in all conscience ignore the findings of the Atlases. Such revision is normal, of course, in the editing procedure of the main dictionaries, which constantly note the new evidence in published research. Full use of Atlas evidence is being made in the Council's own projected dictionary, the *Dictonary of Current American Usage.*

Here is an example. Preliminary treatments of various items are sent by McMillan to members of the advisory committee. In a recent batch of treatments appeared this tentative statement about the phrase *all the farther:* "In the sense of 'as far as,' this phrase is often heard, especially in the popular speech of the West. Cultivated speakers and writers, however, still avoid it. The preferred locution, therefore, is *as far as.*"

After checking the Atlas record for the Upper Midwest, I was able to write McMillan that the imputation of western popularity to this expression, if not incorrect, needs clarification, for actually the incidence of its occurrence drops from about forty percent in Iowa and twenty percent in Minnesota to about four percent in the area settled by the next wave of migration in the Dakotas and Nebraska. I could write him also that at least in the eastern half of the Upper Midwest area fifty percent of the cultivated speakers use *all the farther*. When he receives additional data from the other regional atlases, he will be able to revise the treatment of this locution so as to represent much more accurately just where and by whom it is used.

But we may look forward to a second kind of application of Atlas materials in the classroom. It is high time to recognize the validity of some regional speech in the scope of standard American English. There *are* standard forms which are regional and not national. The label *dial.* in a dictionary does not necessarily consign a linguistic form to either the linguistic slums or the linguistic backwoods. If you want to refer to the strip of grass between the sidewalk and the street, you are driven to awkward circumlocution unless you use a dialect word; there simply is no national word for it. But the cultivated speakers who in various parts of the country call this strip of grass the *boulevard, berm, tree-lawn, curb, parking, terrace, curb strip, sidewalk plot,* or any of several other names would be surprised, if not disgruntled, to be told that they were not speaking standard English.

Recognizing the validity of our own regional speech as standard means also that we recognize the validity of the standard speech of other regions. The time is surely long past when we need to take seriously such an unenlightened statement as this which appeared in a speech textbook several years ago: "There is perhaps no deviation from standard English that sounds as provincial and uncultivated as [the retroflex or inverted r-sound]. . . . Inverted sounds are not used in standard English pronunciation. They will do more to make one's speech sound uncultivated than any other one thing."

Students can be helped toward recognition of this regional validity through various kinds of inductive exercises, especially in the vocabulary. Through such an exercise students for the first time approach objectively the language of their family, their neighbors, the community leaders, and speakers of other areas whom they hear. This particular investigative activity, it may be observed, fits naturally also into a language arts program that seeks to draw upon community resources.

Then, finally, a further utilization of the Atlas data, possible in both college and secondary school, would be for the aim of developing awareness that language is a complex, changing, and always relative structure, not a set of absolutes. The use of regional language information can help our students attain a desirable degree of objectivity in their observation of language matters, can help them see that language is essentially a system of habits related at every point to non-language habits of behavior. And this kind of awareness, this kind of objectivity, is at the heart of a disciplined and informed ability to use language effectively for the communication of meaning.

Pronunciation of *Can't* in the Eastern States*

Sumner Ives

THAT THE NEGATIVE contraction *can't* is pronounced in different ways in different parts of the country is well known; and most people know that it has, in some areas, the vowel of *father*, in others the vowel of *paint*,[1] and in the country at large some variation of what is called 'short *a*.' The first pronunciation is associated with New England and is sometimes considered to be more elegant than the others. The second pronunciation is usually associated with the South. Opinions regarding its distribution and status vary in accordance with opinions concerning the extent of that speech region and with attitudes toward its individual characteristics. The approximately fourteen hundred field records of the *Linguistic Atlas of the United States and Canada* which have been gathered in the Atlantic states allow more precise statements concerning the pronunciation of the stressed vowel in *can't*. This is a report, on the phonetic level, of the vowel types and their distribution as revealed by these records.[2]

In interpreting the information which will be given, certain facts about the *Atlas* survey should be kept in mind. First, although the number of informants is considerable, there are not enough in proportion to the total population for conclusive decisions as to the exact frequencies of speech traits in the general population, considered locally or regionally. Secondly, the informants generally were older than the population average, and they represented the most stable elements among the local residents. It is possible, therefore, that the *Atlas* information is not definitive for younger individuals and more transient elements in some communities, for the speech of one generation is never in all particulars that of another. Thirdly,

---

* Reprinted by permission from *American Speech*, 28.149–157 (October, 1953).
[1] This pronunciation is not listed in the standard desk dictionaries, nor in the Kenyon-Knott *Pronouncing Dictionary of American English* (Springfield, Mass., 1944). It is, however, found in Harold Wentworth, *American Dialect Dictionary* (New York, 1944), in H. L. Mencken, *The American Language; Supplement II* (New York, 1948), p. 122, and in several studies on the speech of the Southern states.

[2] These records were examined during the summer of 1951 through the courtesy of Hans Kurath. For details of the *Atlas* procedure and the phonetic symbols used see his *Handbook of the Linguistic Geography of New England* (Providence, R.I., 1939). On the use of *Atlas* material see E. Bagby Atwood, 'Grease and Greasy—a Study of Geographical Variation,' *Texas Studies in English*, XXIX (1950), 249–60.

the field work was done by different people. Hence, such matters as differences in transcription practice and in the selection of informants must be considered in the evaluation of the data. The field work for the area between South Carolina and upper New York State, and some other regions, was done by Guy Lowman. In seeking out older and less educated informants (Type I), he normally reached less accessible places and sought out more primitive types than the other field workers. Some differences in transcription practices can be found in very detailed studies of some features; however, those which are found in the stressed vowel of *can't* do not, I think, seriously affect the general conclusions which will be given.

An additional factor in using the *Atlas* evidence is the nature of the informants. Three types were interviewed. Type I consisted of older, less educated, and more isolated persons, whose usage could be expected to show the highest contemporary retention of archaic features and the least influence of school instruction. These constituted approximately one half of the informants, although persons of this type certainly are not that common in the population as a whole. Type II consisted of persons with the average schooling for the locality. These were generally somewhat older than the population average but younger than Type I informants. The usage of these two groups, when it agrees, can probably be regarded as representative of the popular speech of a region, although somewhat old-fashioned. Type III represented those whose education was clearly superior and whose social contacts were primarily with others of educational and social advantage. Their speech traits can be regarded as broadly typical of usage among the older generation of educated people. This group constituted approximately 10 percent of the total number of informants.

The material for New England has already been published, and the pronunciation of *can't* appears on Map 695.[3] The other material has been neither edited nor published. It was gathered by two field workers, Lowman, whose area has already been given, and Raven I. McDavid, Jr., who covered the rest of the area outside New England, namely, South Carolina and parts of New York, Georgia, and Florida. Since these field records have not been reviewed, evaluated, and classified, conclusions based on them are subject to later verification. However, I consider it unlikely that the generalizations here will be seriously modified, for I have limited them to what is sufficiently clear even in the present state of the evidence.

The pronunciation of *can't* was secured in the statement 'I can't,' and the field workers were to record it as spoken with full stress.

In describing the distribution of vowel types in *can't*, I have organized the discussion according to three major differences. Transcriptions with [a] and [ɑ], regardless of diacritics, are treated as one type, called 'broad

---

[3] In Hans Kurath and Bernard Bloch, *Linguistic Atlas of New England,* 3 vols. (Providence, R.I., 1938–42).

a.'[4] Evidence for doing this is the fact that records which indicated broad
a in *can't* almost without exception had the same transcription for the
stressed vowel of *father*. Transcriptions with an upgliding diphthong having [e] or [ɛ] as the first element are regarded as another type, called 'long
a.' In verifying this grouping, I checked against transcriptions in the same
records for the vowel of *strain*. Occurrences of [e], monophthongal or ingliding, would also have been considered as this type, but none was found.
For temporary identification, occurrences of [æ], regardless of diphthong-
ization or other modification, are referred to as varieties of short *a*. It is
reasonably clear that the broad *a* type and the long *a* type are phonemically
distinct, both from each other and from the varieties of short *a*.

In the pronunciation of *can't* there is no significant difference between
the usage of Type I and Type II informants; however, there are some
local differences between the usage of Type III informants and that of
others which should be noted. In
the region where broad *a* is found,
shown on Figure 1, it appears in
approximately two thirds of the
records, regardless of type, but elsewhere occurrences of broad *a* are
almost exclusively limited to Type
III records. Only two occurrences,
and these are in upstate and western
New York, are found in other than
Type III records. On the other
hand, it appears in three of four
Type III records from New York
City, in two of three from Philadelphia, in three of twelve from eastern
Virginia, and in one of one from
southeast Ohio, originally settled
from New England. At the same
time, this is less than 10 percent of
the Type III records from outside
New England. This does not mean,
of course, that broad *a* would be
heard in this word only in these

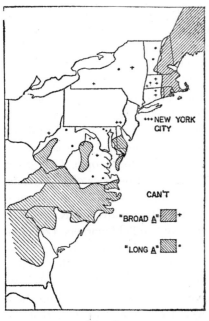

Fig. 1

places or from educated people, for there is evidence apart from the *Linguistic Atlas* that it has at least some currency among older and less educated people in eastern Virginia and elsewhere.[5] However, the frequency

[4] See also Herbert Penzl, 'Vowel Phonemes in *Father, Man, Dance* in Dictionaries
and New England Speech,' *Journal of English and Germanic Philology*, XXXIX (1940),
31.

[5] The speech of this state has been much discussed. For a fairly complete list of
studies see Mencken, *op. cit.*, pp. 223–24.

was apparently not great enough for the *Atlas* sampling to reveal it in the speech of these people. One can, I think, conclude that this pronunciation of *can't* is regarded as elegant among at least some people in New York, Philadelphia, and eastern Virgina.

The pronunciation with long *a*, however, seems to have a different status, even where it is the most common usage in popular speech. From the region where this pronunciation is found, shown on Figure 1, there are twenty-five records which the field workers classified as Type III. Only four of these twenty-five have long *a* in *can't*. In interpreting this evidence, one should realize that educated people in this region, as in other places, often use forms which they regard as incorrect in everyday, familiar speech, although they know and use those they regard as correct when they wish.[6] This evidence, therefore, does not prove that the pronunciation with long *a* is as limited in currency among educated people as the figures suggest. It does, however, suggest that the use of long *a* is regarded as incorrect or careless among most educated people of the region. As a former resident of the long *a* region, I think one is likely to hear both this pronunciation and some other from most native educated people, depending on the circumstances.

The most noticeable differences in the occurrence of vowel types are geographical. Figure 1 shows the distribution of broad *a*. The shaded area in New England limits the region in which this pronunciation is indicated for adjoining communities; hence there are a few occurrences, represented by crosses, west of the boundary, indicating less common usage. This boundary agrees with several other speech boundaries which mark off eastern New England as a distinct dialect region. One should note, however, that there is a small unshaded area which includes the coast of New Hampshire. The pronunciation here is some variety of short *a*.

Within this broad *a* region, some differences in distribution between [a] and [ɑ] can be observed. In general, [ɑ] is limited to the Boston vicinity and to Maine; but [a] is very common alongside [ɑ] except along the western half of the Maine coast and along the eastern boundary of the state adjoining Canada, where occurrences of [a] are relatively rare. It should be noted, however, that in and near areas where [ɑ] predominates, [a] is often written with a shift sign for retraction and [ɑ] with a sign for fronting. In the western part of the broad *a* region, [a] is often fronted. Nevertheless, the phonemic separation from forms written with [æ], even when lowered, can be assumed, pending a more careful study of phonemic patterns in this region, for a retracted vowel is consistently written for *father* in records which have lowered [æ] for *can't*.

Occurrences of long *a* are also shown on Figure 1. The shaded area in-

6 Allen Tate, *The Fathers* (New York, 1938), p. 17, has an interesting footnote describing levels of usage in the speech of the last generation.

dicates occurrences of this vowel type in adjacent communities, and isolated occurrences are shown by a black dot. The boundary of this region is particularly interesting. In West Virginia, it corresponds generally with the northern limit of some other features of Southern speech. In Virginia, it does not include, except in the interior, the area for the typical eastern Virginia traits.[7] In South Carolina and Georgia it does not include the area of low country speech, nor does it include Florida. This distribution, together with the population history, indicates dissemination from the mountain country. But the occurrence of the islands in central Virginia and the Delmarva Peninsula and the relative infrequency of occurrence in Type III records indicate that this is a recessive feature, although this evidence is not, of course, conclusive.

The frequency of occurrence is greatest in the mountain portion of North Carolina, long *a* being almost universal in Type I and II records. North and south of there, in the adjoining states, it is found in about half the Type I and II records. Toward the coast of North Carolina, it becomes progressively less frequent, although it remains common except along the coast near Wilmington.

Varieties with both [e] and [ɛ] are found, but all have a distinct upglide, generally written with [ɨ], superior or level. Those with the open beginning are predominant in Delaware, along the North Carolina coast north of Wilmington and in a narrow band inland, and in the western tip of Virginia and a narrow band southward. A few occurrences with the open beginning are also found in South Carolina and Georgia. Elsewhere, a close beginning [e] is indicated. The distribution of open and close beginnings in *can't* is quite similar to the distribution of these forms in *strain*.

The incidence of varieties written with some modification of [æ] is extremely complicated, and several maps or charts would be required to show these varieties in detail. The distribution of a type characterized by having a following upglide is, however, quite clear and probably of dialectal significance. The distribution of a lengthened type is sufficiently clear for representation on a map, although it is not so clear as that of the dipthongal type. In order, therefore, to make the best use of the map, only these are shown on Figure 2.

Although the phonemic status of the long *a* and broad *a* types seems to be clear, that of the various varieties of short *a* cannot be satisfactorily determined from the study of a single word in which these varieties appear. Nor would it be advisable to draw conclusions from a comparison with any other single word. The existence of two phonemes in short *a* has been

[7] E. Bagby Atwood, 'Some Eastern Virginia Pronunciation Features,' *English Studies in Honor of James Southall Wilson* (University of Virginia Studies, Charlottesville, 1951), pp. 111–24.

proved for some types of American English;[8] however, the exact distribution, both geographically and socially, of each phoneme and the phonetic characteristics of each for the various regions where it may occur is not sufficiently clear for present decision without phonemic analyses of individual records. And whether phonemic analyses of individual *Atlas* field records would be definitive is open to question.

For convenience in discussion, the type with the upglide is written here as [æy]. In this writing, the first symbol represents any modification of [æ], raised or lowered, short or long, and the second symbol represents any upglide, whether written with [i] or with [ɛ] and whether written superior or level. For the same reason, the lengthened type is here written [æ·]. This symbolization includes all transcriptions with length, whether raised or lowered, and whether or not an inglide release is indicated by a superior schwa.

In Figure 2, the distribution of [æy] is shown. The indicated area includes all but quite isolated occurrences of this type, which are shown by solid triangles. An interesting feature of this distribution is the fact that [æy] occurs in Virginia in an area which has several other distinguishing features and is generally regarded as a distinct dialect region. In the northern part of this dialect region, it occurs alongside other pronunciations, especially [æ·], but in the southern portion, it is clearly the predominant usage. In the other Southern states, its area generally overlaps the area of long *a* and popular usage seems to be about equally divided between the two forms; however, all Type III records in this area of mixed usage show [æy], and in northeast Florida all records of any type, except one, show [æy].

It should be noted that upper South Carolina and most of Georgia have a mixture of the Virginia and mountain types, but that lower South Carolina and coastal Georgia are clearly outlined. This distribution agrees with what is known of the settlement history, especially of Georgia.[9] That this diphthongal type is not entirely a Southern feature, however, is shown by the number of occurrences, in all types of records, in the Genesee Valley of western New York.

In most transcriptions which are generalized under this vowel type, the first element [æ] is written as raised and lengthened, although other modifications except lowering and centering are sometimes found. The raised and lengthened transcriptions are particularly common in the records made by McDavid. His records also show a great preponderance of [ɛ] as the second element, but both Lowman and McDavid recorded the first element with and without raising, with and without length, and with

[8] George L. Trager, 'One Phonemic Entity Becomes Two: the Case of "Short A," ' *American Speech*, XV (1940), 256.

[9] J. E. Callaway, *The Early Settlement of Georgia* (Athens, Ga., 1948).

both types of upglide. It is likely, therefore, that the upglide characteristic is less prominent outside the Virginia region than within it, although such a question cannot be answered conclusively on present evidence.

The distribution of [æ·] is likewise shown on Figure 2. This vowel type is found in nearly half of the over fourteen hundred field records examined for this study, and it is the predominant type in the very populous Middle Atlantic region. Its distribution clearly sets off an area which begins with

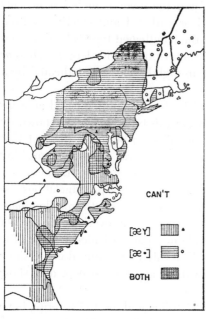

CAN'T

[æʏ] ▦ ▲

[æ·] ▤ ◦

BOTH ▦

Fig. 2

the eastern boundary of New York, extends south nearly to Norfolk, and extends west as far as the *Atlas* records which were used in this study. It includes the area which has been given for a contrast between two phonemes in short *a;* in fact, its northeast and south boundaries are approximately the same as this region. However, its western extent goes beyond it, for the western limit of the contrast is reported as a line roughly between Pittsburgh, Pennsylvania, and Albany, New York.[10] The next largest area where [æ·] is predominant is the coast of South Carolina and Georgia. Other small areas are in Connecticut and North Carolina, and there are many isolated occurrences, especially in eastern New England.

Within the main [æ·] region there are quite a few isolated occurrences of [æ] without length, and they are particularly common in central New Jersey, eastern and northern Pennsylvania, western New York, and along the North Carolina coast, although they are more common than [æ·] (in the [æ·] region) only in the Pennsylvania German locality. The type with unlengthened [æ] is, however, by far the predominant type in western New England, and it is more common than [æ·] in the rest of New England, where the predominant type is, of course, broad *a*.

There are two further distributions of phonetic types which may have importance in the study of American English. The first of these is the incidence of lengthened [æ] with inglide release. This form is almost universal in the low country of South Carolina and Georgia. The importance

---

[10] Henry Lee Smith, Jr., in review of Hans Kurath, *A Word Geography of the Eastern United States,* in *Studies in Linguistics,* IX (1951), 11.

of this is the fact that it is surrounded by areas in which some type of up-gliding diphthong is found, and further that it is the area which has an ingliding release in long *a* and long *o*, which are upgliding diphthongs in the surrounding regions. That is, the vowels of *late, road,* and *can't* are ingliding in this region and upgliding around it. This ingliding type of [æ·] is likewise the almost universal type in extreme western Pennsylvania, eastern Ohio, and northern West Virginia, and it is extremely common in New Jersey and eastern Maryland and Virginia. In New York state and the rest of Pennsylvania, ingliding types occur, but transcriptions without inglide are more common.

Another vowel type which is important in American English is that written with [æ] raised and lengthened, for this is the description given the short *a* phonemic which is written /eh/ in the Trager-Smith system.[11] This is the vowel of *can* (metal container) when it contrasts with the vowel of *can* (be able). In the *Atlas* records, a few, widely scattered occurrences of raised [æ·] were recorded in many places, but there are some concentrations which may have significance. Seven occurrences are found in the South Carolina low country dialect region, six of these at the boundaries of the region. Nine are in eastern Virginia, with four in or near Richmond. Eleven are in central Maryland north and east of Washington, which is rather heavy concentration, and occurrences are fairly common in a northeast band which extends into the lower Hudson Valley and includes New York City. There are also concentrations of this type in upstate New York,[12] and occurrences are fairly common in most of western New York State. There are none recorded in New England, although [æ·] without raising is found sporadically.

The information which has been given concerning varieties of short *a* in *can't* neither confirms nor denies the existence of phonemic contrast between one variety and another. It does, however, reveal a condition in which phonemic change is a distinct possibility. A raised and lengthened, presumably more tense, allophone is potentially a separate phoneme, especially if there is pattern pressure by analogy with other front vowel contrasts and/or if this allophone is eliminated by teaching from some words in which it would normally occur. By the same reasoning, an upgliding allophone, especially with a raised, tense, or lengthened beginning, is likewise potentially a separate phoneme. This is, of course, extrapolation, but there seems to be enough evidence to indicate that an extended study of the problem, supplementing the *Atlas* material, would be a worth-while project.

---

11 *Ibid.,* also George L. Trager and Henry Lee Smith, Jr., *Outline of English Structure* (Studies in Linguistics: Occasional Papers No. 3, 1951).

12 C. K. Thomas, 'Prouniation in Up-State New York,' *American Speech,* X (1935), 296, finds no [ɑ] or [a] in *can't* but some occurrences of raised [æ].

A review of the distributions of the various vowel types in *can't* shows that some of the already recognized dialect regions of American English are further marked by pronunciations of this word. Thus eastern New England, eastern Virginia, and the South Carolina–Georgia low country are clearly set off.[13] The usual line bounding Southern and South Midland as one area agrees closely with the southern boundary of [æ·], unmixed with either long *a* or [æy], the distribution of long *a* gives a general Southern exclusive of Florida and the subregions mentioned above, and the distribution of [æy] gives a general Southern exclusive of North Carolina and the South Carolina–Georgia low country. These divisions all agree with some facts of regional settlement.[14] The distribution of [æ·], in the main, sets off a central Atlantic region with some common cultural traits, although it includes certain areas which are clearly set off as separate by other criteria. The pronunciation of *can't* is also confirming evidence that the geographical South is far from homogeneous as a dialect region.

Grease and *Greasy:*
A Study of Geographical Variation*

E. BAGBY ATWOOD

THE FACT THAT the verb *to grease* and the adjective *greasy* are pronounced by some Americans with [s] and by others with [z] has long been well known even to amateur observers of speech.[1] It has also been pretty well

---

[13] For regional demarcations which, as far as they go, agree with these see Kurath, *A Word Geography of the Eastern United States* (Studies in American English I, Ann Arbor, Mich., 1949), and C. K. Thomas, *An Introduction to the Phonetics of American English* (New York, 1947), p. 145.

[14] Callaway, *op. cit.;* T. J. Wertenbacker, *The Old South* ('The Founding of American Civilization,' Vol. II, New York, 1942).

* Reprinted with permission from the University of Texas *Studies in English,* 29.249–260 (1950).

[1] Webster's *New International Dictionary* states that [z] in *grease* is found "esp. Brit. and Southern U.S."; [z] in *greasy* is "perhaps more general in England and the southern U.S. than in the North and East." Kenyon and Knott, *Pronouncing Dictionary* (Springfield, Mass., 1944), give [s] and [z] for the country as a whole, only [z] for the South. *The Century, Funk and Wagnalls New Standard,* and the *American College Dictionary* merely give [s] or [z] for both words. Kenyon and Knott state that "['grizɪ] and [tə griz] are phonetically normal; ['grisɪ] and [tə gris] imitate the noun *grease* [gris]." Certainly many verbs since Middle English times have been distinguished from the corresponding nouns by voicing the final fricative; cf. *house: to house, proof: to prove,*

accepted that the incidence of [s] or [z] in the words in question is primarily dependent on the geographical location of the speaker rather than on his social or educational level—that [s] is, in general, "Northern," [z] "Southern."

As early as 1896, George Hempl published a study[2] of these two words, based on a rather widely circulated written questionnaire. His returns enabled him to divide the country into four major areas, according to the percentages of [s] in *to grease* and *greasy* respectively. The "North"[3]—extending from New England to the Dakotas—showed 88 and 82 per cent of [s] pronunciations; the "Midland," comprising a fairly narrow strip extending from New York City to St. Louis,[4] 42 and 34 per cent; the "South,"[5] 12 and 12 per cent; and the "West"—an ever-widening area extending westward from St. Louis—56 and 47 per cent. The material which Hempl was able to collect was admittedly "insufficient";[6] moreover, he had no means of selecting strictly representative informants;[7] and the answers may not always have been correct, since, it seems to me, an understanding of the questions would have required a certain degree of linguistic sophistication.[8] Still, in spite of these handicaps, Hempl's study has not been greatly improved upon by later writers. Most authorities content themselves by stating that [z] in *to grease* and *greasy* is predominantly Southern, and that either [s] or [z] may occur elsewhere.[9] Few investigators

---

wreath: to wreathe, abuse: to abuse—and with vowel change) *bath: to bathe, breath: to breathe, grass: to graze*, etc. This paper will not be concerned with the origin or history of the feature.

The pronunciation of the vowels is of no significance in our study. For convenience I am using the symbol [i] for both the stressed and the unstressed vowels in *greasy*.

[2] *"Grease* and *Greasy," Dialect Notes*, I (1896), 438–44.

[3] In addition to New England, this area includes New Brunswick, Quebec, Ontario, New York, Michigan, Wisconsin, North Dakota, South Dakota, Minnesota, and the northern portions of Pennsylvania, Ohio, Indiana, Illinois, and Iowa.

[4] This includes New York City, New Jersey, Delaware, the District of Columbia, southern Pennsylvania, southern Ohio, northern West Virginia, middle Indiana, middle Illinois, and St. Louis, Missouri.

[5] This includes everything to the south of the Midland, as far west as Texas.

[6] *Op. cit.*, p. 438.

[7] For example, he urged his colleagues, especially "teachers of English in colleges, normal schools, and young ladies' seminaries to use the questions as an exercise in English. (*Ibid.*, p. 444.)

[8] Question 45 reads: "In which (if any) of the following does *s* have the sound of *z*: 'the grease,' 'to grease,' 'greasy'?" (Hempl, "American Speech Maps," *Dialect Notes*, I [1896], 317.) Judging from my experience in teaching phonetic transcription to college seniors and graduate students, a considerable proportion of a class would simply not know whether [s] or [z] was used in such words; certainly many students unhesitatingly write [s] in words like *rose* and *has* simply because the *letter s* is used in standard spelling.

[9] See footnote 1. It is sometimes pointed out that the same speaker may use both ['grisi] and ['grizi] with a distinction in meaning. This point will be discussed below.

have gathered material that would enable them to draw clearer lines between [s] and [z] than Hempl was able to do.[10]

The field records that have been gathered for the *Linguistic Atlas of the United States and Canada*[11] provide us with an excellent basis for delimiting the geographical and social spread of speech forms in the eastern United States. A number of features of the *Atlas* methodology[12] are conducive to an accurate picture of native and normal speech. The informants, though relatively few,[13] were carefully chosen, each being both native to and representative of his community. The answers to questions were elicited, so far as possible, in a conversational atmosphere, and thus the occurrence of ungenuine forms was minimized. Finally, the forms were recorded by trained phoneticians, who would be very unlikely to make such errors as to write [s] when the informant actually uttered [z].

A few words should be said regarding the cartographical representation of linguistic atlas data. In such works as the *Atlas Linguistique de la France*,[14] in which each community, or "point" on the map, is represented by a single speaker, it is usually possible to draw lines, or *isoglosses*, separating those communities where a form occurs from those where it does not occur. Often these isoglosses set off a large block of "points," forming a solid area—as, for example, the southern French territory marked by initial [k] in the word *chandelle*.[15] A more complex presentation is sometimes re-

---

[10] A. H. Marckwardt was able to draw a fairly clear line through Ohio, Indiana, and Illinois, though on the basis of relatively little data. See "Folk Speech in Indiana and Adjacent States," *Indiana History Bulletin*, XVII (1940), 120–140. Henry L. Smith has long been using the word *greasy* as a test word in his demonstrations of regional variation and to determine the origins of speakers, though he has not published his material. I presume that Dr. Smith's observations are the source of Mario Pei's statement: " 'greazy' . . . would place the speaker south of Philadelphia, while "greassy" would place him north of Trenton." (*The Story of Language* [Philadelphia and New York, 1949], p. 51.) C. K. Thomas considers the word *greasy* in his survey of the regional speech types, but comes to the strange conclusion that "the choice between [s] and [z] in words like *discern, desolate, absord, absurd,* and *greasy* seems to be more personal than regional." (*An Introduction to the Phonetics of American English* [New York, 1947], p. 154.) G. P. Krapp is likewise at fault when he states that, in *greasy*, "popular usage and, in general, standard speech have only the form with [z]." (*The Pronunciation of Standard English in America* [New York, 1919], p. 119.)

[11] The New England materials have been published as the *Linguistic Atlas of New England,* ed. Hans Kurath and Bernard Bloch, 3 vols. (Providence, R.I., 1939–43). Field records for most of the Middle Atlantic and South Atlantic states were gathered by the late Guy S. Lowman; recently (summer, 1949) Dr. Raven I. McDavid, Jr., completed the work for the eastern seaboard. The records, in an unedited but usable state, are filed at the University of Michigan, where they were made available to me through the courtesy of Professor Kurath.

[12] See *Handbook of the Linguistic Geography of New England,* ed. H. Kurath and others (Providence, R.I., 1939), for a complete account of the *Atlas* methodology.

[13] Something like 1600 informants have been interviewed, representing communities from New Brunswick to northern Florida, approximately as far west as Lake Erie.

[14] Ed. J. Gilliéron and E. Edmont, 7 vols. (Paris, 1902–1910).

[15] See Karl Jaberg, "Sprachgeographie," *Siebenunddreissigstes Jahresheft des Vereins Schweiz. Gymnasiallehrer* (Aarau, 1908), pp. 16–42; also Plate III.

quired, as in the case of the northern French occurrences of [k] in this same word: after setting off our solid area we find outside it a number of scattered communities where the feature in question occurs; these must be indicated by additional lines encircling the "points" where the form is found.[16] In still other cases, the communities where a given speech form occurs (for example, *conin* for 'rabbit') are so scattered that it is impossible to connect them; in such cases our isoglosses must consist merely of scattered circles here and there on the map.[17] When this situation obtains we would probably do better to assign a symbol (say, a cross, a dot, or a triangle) to the scattered form in question, lest the labyrinth of lines becomes too much for the reader to cope with.

Now, in presenting data from the American *Atlas*, we are faced with all these complications, plus others arising from the fact that more than one informant was chosen to represent each community. That is, at nearly every "point" the American field workers recorded the usage of one elderly, poorly educated informant and one younger, more modern informant. In certain key communities, a third type was included—a well educated, or "cultured," speaker who presumably represented the cultivated usage of the area. Thus, at the same point on the map we often find such variants as *sot down* (preterite), representing rustic usage, *set* or *sit down*, representing more modern popular usage, and *sat down*, representing cultivated usage.[18] It is obviously impossible to draw isoglosses separating *sot* from *set* or *sat;* it is even impractical to set off the *sot* areas, since the form occurs in about every other community through considerable areas. In other cases, of course, it is quite easy to mark off an area where a certain form is current. *Holp* (for *helped*), for example, occupies a very clear-cut area south of the Potomac.[19] Yet a line marking off this area would by no means constitute a dividing line between *holp* and *helped,* since most of the younger informants within the *holp* area use the standard form *helped.* My point is that an isogloss based on American *Atlas* materials *should in all cases be regarded as an outer limit, not as a dividing line between two speech forms.*

The examples hitherto adduced have, of course, illustrated the incidence of "non-standard" as against "standard" speech forms. What of those instances of two forms which are equally "standard," each within its area? Kurath's map of *pail* and *bucket* provides an example.[20] Here too we must

---

16 *Ibid.,* Plate III.

17 *Ibid.,* Plate X.

18 In addition, the same informant often uses more than one form; all of these are of course entered at that point on the map. On at least one occasion McDavid picked up from the same informant, as the preterite of *see, I seen, I seed, I see,* and *I saw.*

19 This verb, as well as the others mentioned, is treated in my *Survey of Verb Forms in the Eastern United States,* to be published soon.

20 *A Word Geography of the Eastern United States* (Ann Arbor, Mich., 1949), Figure 66.

follow the same principle: we must first draw the outer limit of one form, then that of the other. The two lines will lap over each other at some points, enclosing certain communities of mixed usage.[21] Thus, *a dividing line is a double isogloss*, each line being the outer limit of one of the two speech forms in question. The areas of overlapping between the two lines may be wide or narrow, depending on many social, geographical, and historical considerations.

Let us return to *grease* and *greazy*. The variation between [s] and [z] in these words furnishes an almost ideal example of geographical (as against social) distribution. Consider first the verb *grease*. It is unnecessary to describe in detail the incidence of [s] and [z], since the accompanying map tells its own story. The northern line of the [z]-form, it may be observed, takes in the southwestern corner of Connecticut (west of the Housatonic); from there it passes westward just to the north of New Jersey; then it dips sharply southward to Philadelphia, to the west of which it again rises gradually northward to the northwestern corner of Pennsylvania. The transition area (where both [s] and [z] are used), is relatively narrow to the west of Philadelphia; to the northeast, however, it widens considerably so as to include most of northern New Jersey, as well as New York City and eastern Long Island.

Outside our pair of isoglosses there is a surprisingly small number of "stray" forms. All together, there are only six occurrences of [z] in the [s] area and only six of [s] in the [z] area.[22] (It will be observed, of course, that there is a second area, or island, of [s] along the Ohio River extending northeastward from the vicinity of Marietta, Ohio.) There is no sign whatever of social variation within the solid [s] and [z] areas; cultivated usage is in strict agreement with popular usage.[23] Within the areas of overlapping there is naturally some variation between older and more modern informants—yet the general trend is not at all clear. In the communities of divided usage to the west of Philadelphia the more modern informant uses [s] in six out of eight instances; in such communities to the northeast of Philadelphia the modern preference is for [s] in six instances, for [z] in six others. As for cultured informants within the areas of overlapping, ten

[21] Even after drawing the lines we would find a good many scattered, or "stray," occurrences of *pail* within the *bucket* area and vice versa. Kurath's lines, which are all outer limits, do not attempt to indicate the presence of stray forms or small patches which occur outside the main area; however, since he also publishes maps on which each occurrence of each word is recorded by a symbol, the reader can easily check and interpret his isoglosses.

[22] This amounts to less than one per cent of the informants. Most of the informants who show exceptional usage also give the "normal" form; that is, they use both [s] and [z] forms.

[23] Although the preterite form of the verb was not called for in the work sheets, Lowman picked up some five instances of *grez* [grɛz] in the [z] area; and a number of other informants reported having heard this form.

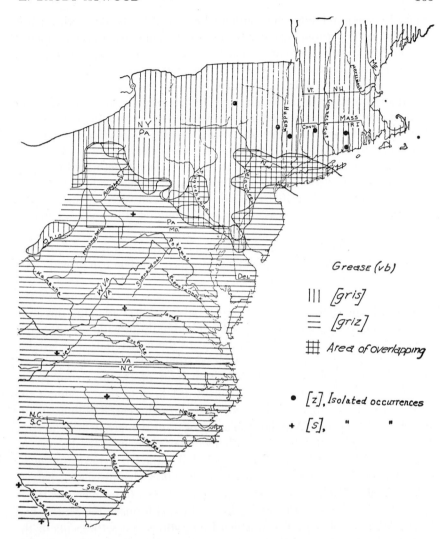

Grease (vb)

||| [gris]

≡ [griz]

▦ Area of overlapping

• [z], Isolated occurrences

+ [s],   "   "

MAP SHOWING THE DISTRIBUTION OF [s] AND [z] IN *GREASE* (VERB)

Northern Maine and Eastern Georgia (not shown on the map) show the same usage as the adjoining areas. At the time of this study, no field records were available for Northern New York.

use [griz], five use [gris], and one offers both [s] and [z] forms. One might state, very tentatively, that cultivated usage has tended to favor [griz], particularly in New York City and northern New Jersey.

For the adjective *greasy*, the pronunciations [grisi] and [grizi] show almost precisely the same isoglosses as those for [gris] and [griz]. The northern limit of [z] pushes further northward at three points in Pennsylvania;[24] correspondingly, the southern limit of [s] retreats northward at one point in Ohio, three in Pennsylvania, and two in northern New Jersey.[25] Within the [s] area, there are ten stray forms with [z], scattered through New England and the Hudson Valley; six of these occur in the cultured type of informant. Within the [z] area, we again find six stray occurrences of [s]; and precisely the same island of [s] occurs along the Ohio River. In short, a few more eastern informants use [z] in *greasy* than in *grease*, though the difference is not great. Within the areas of overlapping we find almost exactly the same social distribution as in the case of *grease*. Cultured informants prefer [grizi] by eleven to four; this fact, together with the six "stray" northern uses of [z] in the cultured type, inclines us to believe that [z] in *greasy* has penetrated into northeastern cultivated speech a little more palpably than in the case of *grease*—though still to a very slight extent.

After describing the incidence of the speech forms in question, we are still faced with a number of questions, to which our data can provide only partial answers.

What becomes of our isoglosses in the areas west of Pennsylvania? The materials being gathered for the Great Lakes atlas (under the direction of Professor A. H. Marckwardt) will undoubtedly provide an answer. I have not been able to examine the latest of these materials; but judging from preliminary information, as well as from a map already published by Professor Marckwardt,[26] the northern limit of [z] in *greasy* passes through central Ohio, then swings northward so as to take in almost the whole of Indiana, then bends southward through central Illinois in the direction of St. Louis. Whether the areas of transition are wide or narrow we can probably not determine with accuracy, since, in general, only one social type (the elderly, or rustic) is included in the Great Lakes survey.

Why should the isoglosses run where they do? The answer, in part, is relatively simple. Of the two sets of variants, the [s] forms were evidently generalized in the New England colonies, the [z] forms in the Middle and South Atlantic colonies. The westward migrations and settlements of the New Englanders covered New York (State), northern Pennsylvania, Michigan, Wisconsin, and the northern portions of Ohio, Indiana, and Illinois.[27] Many speech features mark off this Northern area from the "Midland"—

---

[24] Lehigh, Columbia, and Lancaster counties.

[25] Columbia, Armstrong, Blair, Cumberland, Hunterdon, and Morris counties.

[26] "Folk Speech of Indiana and Adjacent States," *op. cit.*, p. 128. [EDITOR'S NOTE: for a later statement based upon the completed study involving all three types of informants see A. H. Marckwardt: "Principal and Subsidiary Dialect Areas in the North-Central States," *Publication of the American Dialect Society*, No. 27 (April, 1957), pp. 3–15, with a map on page 10 showing the *greasy* isogloss.]

[27] Kurath, *Word Geography*, pp. 1–7; see also Lois K. M. Rosenberry, *The Expansion of New England* (Boston and New York, 1909). Even the island of [s] forms around Marietta, Ohio, is to be explained on the basis of early settlement; this area was first settled by New Englanders as early as the 1780's. See Rosenberry, pp. 175ff.

the area occupied primarily by Pennsylvania.[28] Most of the northern lines, to be sure, pass further to the north in Pennsylvania than do those of the [s] in *grease* and *greasy*. Yet the penetration of northern forms to the area of Philadelphia is occasionally to be observed in other instances; for example, the line of Northern *clapboards* (as against Midland and Southern *weatherboards*) dips sharply southward so as to take in Philadelphia and northern Delaware. Another explanation for the prevalence of [gris] and ['grisi] in east central Pennsylvania might be the fact that much of the area was occupied in the early 18th century by Palatine Germans, whose native dialect had no [z] phoneme at all[29] and who may, for this reason, have favored [s] in any English words where variation between [s] and [z] occurred.

What is the British practice with regard to the pronunciation of *grease* and *greasy*? No complete survey has been made; but there seems no doubt that London usage, as well as "Received Standard" usage throughout southern England, is mixed.[30] The questionnaires which Hempl circulated in England (for his study cited above) showed that in London only 25 and 33 per cent of the informants used [s] in *grease* and *greasy;* but that in England exclusive of London the percentages of [s] were 84 and 74.[31] We have no ground, even yet, for rejecting these figures; but it should be pointed out that folk speech in England, just as in the United States, shows its isoglosses. A survey of the linguistic atlas type conducted by Guy S. Lowman in 1934[32] shows that the [z] in *grease* (I have no information on *greasy*) occupies East Anglia and a small adjoining area; that [s] is universal in the remainder of southern England (we are speaking strictly of the rustic type of speaker). Since the line passes through (or very near) London, it is easy to see why the metropolitan area should show a mixture of usage.

Is there any evidence of a differentiation in meaning between ['grisi] and ['grizi]? The *Atlas* provides no answer to this question, since, in the interest of obtaining comparable data, the words were always called for in the same context ("grease the car, axle, etc." and "my hands are greasy"). In general, such differentiations in meaning are characteristics of areas of mixed usage, not of those where one pronunciation or another is definitely

---

[28] Examples of Northern words (from Kurath) are *whiffletree, pail, darning needle* ('dragonfly'), and *co, boss!* (cow call). Verb forms which I have found to have similar distributions are *hadn't ought* ('oughtn't'), *how be you?, clim* ('climbed'), and *see* as a preterite of *to see.* Note that Kurath's definition of "Midland" does not coincide with that of Hempl; the area, according to the former, extends much farther to the southwestward of Pennsylvania than Hempl indicated. (See *Word Geography*, pp. 27–37). [EDITOR'S NOTE: see also Atwood's own later study, *A Survey of Verb Forms in the Eastern United States* (University of Michigan Press, Ann Arbor, 1953).]

[29] See Carroll E. Reed, *The Pennsylvania German Dialect Spoken in the Counties of Lehigh and Berks: Phonology and Morphology* (Seattle, Wash., 1949), pp. 20 and 29.

[30] See Daniel Jones, *An English Pronouncing Dictionary*, 9th ed. (London, 1948).

[31] Hempl, *op. cit.*, pp. 442–43.

[32] Lowman's British field records are filed in an unedited state at the University of Michigan.

established. The distinction usually given in dictionaries is that ['grisi] may mean literally 'covered with grease,' while ['grizi] may be used with less literal, and sometimes unpleasant, connotations.[33] What we can say with confidence is that speakers to the south of our isoglosses do not follow this practice: ['grizi] is universal with the meaning 'covered with grease'; whether or not speakers in the area of overlapping, and to the north of it, would have used ['grizi] had the context been different we are unable to determine.

How should we evaluate the *Atlas* data as a picture of reality? What is most important to realize is that the *Atlas* makes no attempt whatever to record the usage of non-native speakers, or even of those natives who have resided for long periods outside their home communities. Such speakers are rather uncommon in some communities, fairly numerous in others; in a few of the latter, the *Atlas* may even reflect the usage of a minority of old-timers. In view of this, we might be inclined to wonder whether the percentage method might not give a truer picture of prevalent usage than the isogloss method. The proportion of non-native speech forms in a community would, of course, roughly correspond to the proportion of non-native residents; such data would certainly be valuable, though to collect it on a large enough scale (say, 100 or so informants from each county) would be so difficult as to be practically impossible. Few investigators are qualified to make extensive phonetic observations, and those few must take their informants from such captive groups as college classes whose usage may or may not be spontaneous or representative. Another feature of the *Atlas* that must be considered is the preponderance of rather old informants. Since the interviews were conducted several years ago, many of the forms shown to be current among the aged may now be rare or even obsolete; moreover, the *Atlas* records would not reflect the most recent trends, fads, and innovations—some of which are extremely rapid, others extremely slow. It seems unlikely to me that the lines on *grease* and *greasy* have shifted radically in the last few years, yet I have no doubt that usage may have shifted in certain individual communities.[34] All things considered, the *Linguistic Atlas* offers the most

---

[33] Daniel Jones, *English Pronouncing Dictionary:* "Some speakers use the forms . . . with a difference of meaning, ['gri:si] having reference merely to the presence of grease and ['gri:zi] having reference to the slipperiness caused by grease." *Webster's NID* states: ". . . many people in all sections use ['grisi] in some connotations and ['grizi] in others, the first esp. in the literal sense, covered with grease." Cf. Kenyon and Knott: "Some distinguish ['grisi] 'covered with grease' from ['grizi] 'slimy' " (*op. cit.*). G. P. Krapp states: "A distinction is sometimes made in the meaning of ['gri:si] and ['gri:zi], the latter being regarded as a word of unpleasant connotation" (*op. cit.*, p. 119). Webster's implies that this distinction is fairly general throughout the country—a very dubious proposition. T. Larsen and F. C. Walker simply prescribe [s] for the meaning 'sticky' and [z] for the meaning 'slippery'—as though this feature were standard and universal. (See *Pronunciation*, Oxford Press, 1931, p. 92.)

[34] Dr. Smith expresses the opinion that the younger generation in New York City has gone over almost entirely to the [s] in *greasy*.

reliable body of data as yet assembled, or likely to be assembled in the near future, on American speech; isoglosses based on it reffect the usage of a highly important segment of our population, and they are, moreover, of the highest value in a study of our cultural and settlement history.

The Pronunciation of *Catch**

RAVEN I. McDAVID, JR.

Catch IS A favorite shibboleth for those with a normative attitude toward differences in pronunciation. The fairly widespread notion that the pronunciation rhyming with *fetch* is socially inferior has been succinctly put by Professor C. C. Fries in his *American English Grammar:*

> Pronunciations such as "ketch" for *catch* and "git" for *get* . . . are not the characteristic modes of speech of university professors, or of the clergymen who preach from the pulpits in our large city churches, or of the judges of the supreme court, or of the presidents of our most important banks, or even of those who habitually patronize the opera [p. 10].

One who regularly says *ketch* but says *git* only in jest or in commands to animals is shocked to discover Fries attributing the same social status to *ketch* and *git;* such a reaction, however, is only marginally relevant. Observations that Episcopal bishops have said *ketch* in formal addresses are only slightly more pertinent. What is needed is comparable data from a large number of speakers, of various social backgrounds, representative of a large number of communities. Such data can be found in the records of the Linguistic Atlas of the United States and Canada. This summary on the pronunciation of *catch* is derived from research toward *The Pronunciation of English in the Eastern United States,* which Professor Hans Kurath, director of the Linguistic Atlas, and I hope to complete within the next year. It represents the usage of over fifteen hundred informants, including the entire Atlantic Seaboard area from southern New Brunswick to northern Florida, plus West Virginia, Ohio, Michigan, and southern Ontario.

Pronunciations of *catch* are of two types: major varieties and minor varieties. The major varieties include /ɛ/, the vowel of *fetch,* and /æ/, the vowel of *hatch.* The minor varieties include /a/, the vowel of *father,* /e/, the vowel of *hate,* and /ɪ/, the vowel of *hit.*

Minor varieties:

/a/: 2 occurrences, 1 in southern Ohio, 1 in southern Georgia
/e/: 2 occurrences, 1 in central New Hampshire, 1 in northern Vermont
/ɪ/: 26 occurrences: 4 in Maine, 7 in New Hampshire, 2 in Vermont, 4 in

* Reprinted by permission from *College English,* 14.290–291 (February, 1953).

Massachusetts, 3 in Connecticut, 1 in New York, 1 in New Jersey, 1 in Maryland, 2 in North Carolina, and 1 in South Carolina; the majority of these informants were also recorded using /ɛ/

The major varieties, /ɛ/ and /æ/, were recorded from all states, except that all Florida informants used only /ɛ/. A number of informants used both /ɛ/ and /æ/, and some apparently attempted a compromise pronunciation, which is indicated in the table below with a question mark.

Only in Ohio, the New York metropolitan area, central Pennsylvania, and central Massachusetts does majority usage favor /æ/. In northern New England, upstate New York, Michigan, and the South Atlantic States, /ɛ/ is the normal pronunciation. Over three-fourths of the informants interviewed use only /ɛ/, and less than a fifth clearly use only /æ/. Even if we add to this last group all the doubtful recordings—and I am inclined to think we should—the general preponderance of /ɛ/ is still overwhelming.

Where cultured informants are concerned, the picture is somewhat different. No cultured informant uses /a/, /e/, or /ɪ/. For the major varieties, we have the following picture of cultured usage:

Area	/ɛ/	/æ/	Both	?
N.B.	0	0	1	0
Me.	3	1	1	0
N.H.	1	2	0	0
Vt.	0	0	0	1
Mass.	2	13	0	0
R.I.	1	4	0	0
Conn.	5	4	1	0
N.Y. City	1	5	0	0
N.Y. State	9	7	2	1
Ont.	2	2	1	0
Mich.	3	0	0	1
Ohio	1	5	0	0
Pa.	3	12	0	0
N.J.	0	5	0	0
Del.	0	2	0	0
Md.	3	3	1	0
W.Va.	3	3	1	0
Va.	2	10	1	0
N.C.	4	7	0	0
S.C.	17	9	0	0
Ga.	6	2	1	0
Fla.	2	0	0	0
Total	68	85	10	3

The heaviest preponderance of /æ/ in cultured speech is found in those areas where /æ/ is strongest in the usage of all informants—Ohio, Massachusetts, Pennsylvania, and metropolitan New York—and in Virginia, where the traditions of the plantation class seem to favor /æ/ as a polite pronunciation. It is possible that the prestige of /æ/ in the South may be due to its occurrence in British Received Pronunciation, since most of the southern informants who have /æ/ in *catch* also rhyme *vase* with *days* and have /v/ as the second consonant in *nephew.*

It is always dangerous to speculate on linguistic tendencies. It may be that the pronunciation with /æ/ is on its way to general acceptance. On the other hand, since /æ/ in the South is associated with the prerogatives of an older social order, it could come about that in the South the spread of economic and educational opportunities may bring greater prestige for /ɛ/ rather than a tendency to acquire /æ/. If one recalls the popular middle western scorn for the "broad *a*," it is not utterly fantastic that some nativist movement in the American heartland might stigmatize /æ/ as an effete Briticism or as a pronunciation which educational bureaucrats are attempting to impose upon red-blooded American individualists. Happily, there is no need to react violently; we have ample justification for pronouncing *catch* to rhyme with either *hatch* or *fetch,* depending on our personal taste and the region we came from.

Oughtn't and *Hadn't Ought**

Raven I. McDavid, Jr.

In *College English,* VII (April, 1952), 398–99, Miss Margaret M. Bryant discussed the negative forms of *ought* and reached the conclusion any South Carolinian would reach—that *oughtn't* is a much more natural form than *hadn't ought.* The records of the *Linguistic Atlas* and associated projects give us further evidence on which we may base our judgments. A full discussion of the data from the Atlantic Seaboard is found in E. Bagby Atwood's *A Survey of Verb Forms in the Eastern United States;* this is a summary of his conclusions and an interpretation of data from England and from the Middle West as covered by the regional surveys under A. H. Marckwardt and Harold B. Allen.

Along the Atlantic Seaboard *oughtn't* is practically universal south of the Mason-Dixon Line and in Pennsylvania south of the New England settlements in the northernmost counties. It was recorded from about half the informants interviewed in New Jersey but is very rare in New York

* Reprinted by permission from *College English,* 14.472–473 (May, 1953).

State and in New England. Only 6 New Yorkers (3 in New York City) of 160 interviewed and only 18 New Englanders of 416 offered the phrase spontaneously or used it in conversation. Since 5 of the 18 New Englanders who used *oughtn't* were cultured informants, it probably has some social standing in that section; but 5 of the 6 New Yorkers who used it were of the most old-fashioned type. Farther west, *oughtn't* is very rare in Michigan (1 occurrence), slightly less rare in Wisconsin (6 occurrences, mostly in the Mississippi Valley and in the southern counties), and fairly common in the southern counties of Ohio, Indiana, and Illinois, though not nearly so common as in the Midland and Southern areas of the Atlantic Seaboard.

Hadn't ought, on the other hand, is characteristically a northern form, found almost exclusively in New England, the Hudson Valley, and settlements derivative from those areas. Except for the very conservative area between Chesapeake Bay and the Neuse River, North Carolina, there are hardly half-a-dozen instances of *hadn't ought* south of the Mason-Dixon Line. However, early settlements from New England have made *hadn't ought* common in southern New Jersey. A majority of Michigan and Wisconsin informants use it, as one would expect from the New York and New England origins of the earliest settlements in these states. Thanks to the important New England settlements in the Western Reserve and the Marietta area, *hadn't ought* seems to occur throughout Ohio; it occurs relatively far south in Indiana and Illinois, even in communities of Southern derivation. In the Upper Mississippi Valley it appears to be relatively less common than in New England or New York State but is still more frequent than *oughtn't.* Informants who hesitate to use *hadn't ought* seldom replace it with *oughtn't* but either substitute *shouldn't* or use the uncontracted *ought not.* Except for the South, where it is clearly a relic, *hadn't ought* is not restricted to any social group; in New England, New York State, and the Middle West it is used by many cultured informants.[1]

In the folk speech of southern England, both *oughtn't* and *hadn't ought* were recorded for the Atlas. *Oughtn't* occurs 7 times, in records from Middlesex, Cambridge, Worcester, Leicester, Rutland, and Lincoln; *hadn't ought* 19 times, from Kent, Sussex, Somerset, Gloucester, Oxford, Warwick, Northampton, Buckingham, Bedford, and Huntington. In East Anglia the prevailing form is *don't ought* (14 occurrences); in the southern and southwestern countries *didn't ought* (15 occurrences, plus one in Suffolk); 1 Lincoln informant uses both *don't ought* and *didn't ought,* with a difference in time. The American records so far contain no examples of *don't ought* and only 4 of *didn't ought* (2 in New England, 1 in northern Illinois, 1 in northern Michigan), plus 5 of *shouldn't ought* (Wisconsin, Michigan, Ohio, central Illinois, and southern Ontario), 1 of *hadn't*

---

[1] Some cultured speakers who do not use *hadn't ought* apparently have it as an underlying form, which is reflected in the statement-question expecting an affirmative answer: *I ought to do it, hadn't I?*

oughtn't (central Indiana), and 1 of *oughtn't ought* (eastern North Carolina). Occasionally, one encounters *had oughtn't*.

In the preliminary investigation of the speech of the Maritime Provinces, Henry M. Alexander did not elicit this item from all informants. Of those from whom he recorded it, 7 used *oughtn't*, 2 *hadn't ought*, 6 *didn't ought*, and 1 *should ought to not*. From 6 informants in southern New Brunswick, including a cultured informant, Guy S. Lowman recorded only *hadn't ought*.

The affirmative *ought* or *had ought* was systematically investigated only in the Middle and South Atlantic States, though occasional examples were recorded in New England. From the evidence it appears that *had ought* is much more restricted than *hadn't ought*, both geographically and socially. It occurs only in eastern North Carolina and in the New England settlement area within the areas where *hadn't ought* occurs, but it is far less common; none of those who were recorded as using it were cultured informants. One informant in eastern Ontario and another in eastern North Carolina used *should ought*.

The evidence suggests that in evaluating *hadn't ought* and *oughtn't* we are dealing with regional variants rather than with social variants. While each of us is naturally predisposed in favor of the form we grew up with, there is nothing to be gained by stigmatizing the other form as substandard or spending a great deal of time on the problem. If a student comes to college using one of these variants, it is almost certainly in good standing in his community; and, if he doesn't use it, he needs to learn only that it is part of the language habits of people as well educated as he is.

On Accepting Participial *Drank**

HAROLD B. ALLEN

As ADDITIONAL FIELDWORK is completed for the regional atlases associated in *The Linguistic Atlas of the United States,* additional evidence accumulates about numerous grammatical forms long adjudged controversial. A case in point is provided by the new data for the past participle *drank.*

The verb *drink* has come down to us from that interesting third class of Old English strong verb with two stem vowels in the past tense forms: one (*a*) peculiar to the past and found in the first and third persons singular; the other (*u*) used in the second person singular and in the plural but also identical with the stem vowel of the past participle. In this class the subtle power of analogy, operating with increasing strength in Middle

* Reprinted by permission from *College English,* 18.283–285 (February, 1957).

English as inflectional changes lost their phonetic distinctiveness, also inevitably favored the more frequently occurring *u* in the process of simplifying the verb patterns.

By the eighteenth century this process had gone so far that the *u* vowel was comfortably and exclusively established in the preterit of the following third class strong verbs: *bind, cling, fight, fling, grind, slink, spin, sting, string, swing, win, wind,* and *wring.*[1] In the other surviving members of this class the process was now to be retarded, though not blocked, by the prestigious pronouncement of Dr. Johnson in the Grammar prefaced to his *Dictionary* in 1755. Reflecting the philosophy of the ancient Greek Analogists, Johnson believed that every grammatical function should have its own overt grammatical form, and accordingly declared: "He shall seldom err who remembers, that when a verb has a participle distinct from its preterite, as *write, wrote, written,* that distinct participle is more proper and elegant, as *The book is written,* is better than *The book is wrote,* though *wrote* may be used in poetry."

Although even the prestige of Johnson's *Dictionary* and the authoritative copying of his dictum in scores of school grammars were unable to stop the trend toward the simple *u* in the preterit, a great many cultivated speakers were undoubtedly influenced by the bald injunction that nothing but *a* can be the proper preterit vowel. As a result, for the past one hundred and fifty years there actually has been divided usage among cultivated speakers.

We may look at *shrink* as typical of the larger group of those strong verbs which in moving toward a single form for past and participle have popularly used the vowel common to both. Although the textbooks list the contrast between *shrank* as preterit and *shrunk* as participle, actually the findings of the fieldwork for *The Linguistic Atlas of the Upper Midwest* indicate that 86.5% of all informants responding to this item use *shrunk* as the preterit. Nor do the findings reveal the existence of a small educated minority clinging to a favored *shrank,* for the relative frequency of *u* is nearly the same in all three groups: 89% of the uneducated, 89% of the high school graduates, and 86% of the college graduates.

Some regional variation, hardly enough to be significant, may be suggested by the slightly lower frequency in Midland than in Northern speech areas: Minnesota, 96%; North Dakota, 92%; Iowa, 86%; South Dakota, 81% and Nebraska, 72%. But within the divided usage the general dominance of *shrunk* is certain, despite the contrary statements of the textbooks.

The inaccuracy of the textbooks with respect to the past of *shrink* and of other verbs exhibiting the tendency toward the *u* vowel in the preterit is matched by their inaccuracy with respect to the one verb which stands

---

[1] Because the original Old English *u* underwent phonetic change through the influence of certain neighboring sounds, some of the past tense forms now in use, such as *fought* and *ground,* do not immediately betray their historical membership in the class.

out in exception to the trend. The verb *drink* is the only verb in this group that in moving toward simplicity has tended not only to retain the original *a* vowel in the preterit but also to entrench it in the past participle. Indeed, Professor Walter S. Avis has recently suggested that "we cannot refuse to accept the participle *drank* as Standard American English, at least in the regions where the evidence argues for its acceptance."[2]

It is true that even without Avis's evidence some grammarians have not been as dogmatic as the textbook writers in their attitude toward participial *drank*. Even Goold Brown, back in the mid-nineteenth century, said in his many-editioned and voluminous *Grammar of English Grammars* that "*drank* seems to be a word of greater delicacy, and perhaps it is sufficiently authorized." Among recent linguistic grammarians, Curme in his *Parts of Speech and Accidence* (1935) said of *drank* as a participle, "sometimes used in older English in the literary language. It survives in popular speech." And Jespersen, in the sixth volume of his *Modern English Grammar* (1942), wrote, ". . . a participle *drank* has been in frequent use for centuries, possibly to avoid misunderstanding with *drunk* 'intoxicated.' It is now getting rare, but instances occur in all the best-known authors from Bunyan down to our time." He cited Scott, Shelley, Keats, Trollope, and Kingsley, and referred to Mencken as listing *drank* as a participle.

Nor are current dictionaries more accurate in describing contemporary usage. The Merriam-Webster *NID* (2nd ed.) offers *drunk*. Similarly with the Thorndike-Barnhart dictionaries, although the Barnhart-edited *ACD*, less pressed for space, takes room to admit cagily, "sometimes *drank*." The *NWW* does give *drank* as participle but labels it "archaic."

Yet such recognition as that by Curme and the *ACD* is nothing like Avis's bold statement based upon Atlas evidence. This evidence is that even in New England, "the citadel of the prestige dialect," 38% of the cultivated informants regularly use *drank* as the participle and an additional 11.9% use it along with *drunk*, while in New York 27.7% of such speakers use it, in West Virginia 83.3%, and in Pennsylvania 43.7%. For the North Central states (except Kentucky, where fieldwork is still in process) revised figures later than Avis's are now provided by Virginia McDavid (Mrs. Raven I. McDavid, Jr.) in her recent unpublished Minnesota dissertation. In the North Central area, 54% of the interrogated high school graduates and 33% of the college graduates use the participle *drank*.

To all this evidence there now can be added a whole new set of data from the recently completed field records of *The Linguistic Atlas of the Upper Midwest*.[3] In this large five-state area Avis's conclusion finds even stronger corroboration. Here 80.5% of the interviewed high school graduates use *drank* as the past participle, and nearly half (47%) of the cul-

[2] Walter S. Avis, *American Speech*, XXVIII (May 1953), 106–111.
[3] For significance of such records in the field of usage see H. B. Allen, *English Journal*, XLV (April 1956), 188–194 [pp. 142–149 in this book].

tivated speakers. There is no significant regional variation within the Upper Midwest, almost the same relative frequencies being found in Minnesota, Iowa, the Dakotas, and Nebraska. Certainly it would appear that in this area, as well as in New England and the North Central states, *drank* is an accepted standard form of the past participle.

Explanation of the exceptional development with *drink* usually coincides with that offered by Jespersen, namely, that there is an aversion to the historical *drunk* because of the link with intoxication. On the supposition that women might feel greater hesitation on this score than men would, a further breakdown of the Upper Midwest figures was made. The complete picture, including the data for uneducated speakers, is of some interest. Of the 9.7% of uneducated informants who use *drunk* as the participle not one is a woman. Of the male high school graduates 12% use *drunk;* of the female high school graduates, 28.3%. Of the male college graduates 60% use *drunk;* of the female college graduates, 40%. Certainly there is aversion by women to the use of *drunk*, but chiefly among the uneducated. Among cultivated speakers the distinction by sex is hardly significant. But since linguistic taboos of this type seem to be stronger among uneducated people, it may well be that the association with intoxication is the ultimate cause for the preference for participial *drank*.

Whatever the cause of the large-scale rejection of *drunk*, however, the general acceptance of competing *drank* by from one-third to one-half of the cultivated speakers in New England, the North Central states, the Midland area, and the Upper Midwest supports the conclusion that we have here a condition of divided usage, with no sound basis for present objection to either *drank* or *drunk* as the single exclusive form in standard spoken English.

Some Social Differences in Pronunciation*

Raven I. McDavid, Jr.

When we compare varieties of American English, we generally assume that differences in grammar reflect social differences, and that differences in vocabulary or pronunciation reflect regional differences. Yet we must often modify this useful practical rule. The word *bastard* occurs every-

* Reprinted by permission from *Language Learning*, 4.102–116 (1952–1953).] This paper was originally presented at the meeting of the Michigan Linguistic Society, December 8, 1951. Most of the information on which it is based comes from the Atlantic seaboard records of the Linguistic Atlas of the United States and from the records of the Linguistic Atlas of the North Central States. Occasional examples come from the records of the Linguistic Atlas of the Upper Midwest, the Linguistic Atlas of the Rocky

where, but everywhere it seems to be a cruder term than *illegitimate child*. In all regions where *jacket* and *vest* are synonymous, *jacket* is apparently more rustic and old-fashioned. Conversely, Atwood's monograph[1] shows that the differences in status between the preterites *dove* and *dived*, *woke up* and *waked up*, *sweat* and *sweated*, are more regional than social. Moreover, though /klɪm, kləm, klom, klæm, klam, klum/ all have less prestige as preterites than *climbed*, at least three of these forms occur in definite regional patterns: /klɪm/ in the North and South, /kləm/ in the Midland, /klom/ in eastern Virginia.[2] Even /ɛt/ as the preterite of *eat*—a social shibboleth to many speakers—turns out to be the socially elegant form in Charleston, South Carolina, where the use of /ɛt/ (and of *ain't* in informal speech) sets off those who belong to the best Charlestonian society from those who would like to belong but don't.

We should therefore not be surprised if some pronunciations carry connotations of social prestige or lack of it. We can discuss a few of these pronunciations by examining the evidence collected for the Linguistic Atlas of the United States and Canada. This evidence has been collected in the field by trained investigators using a finely graded phonetic alphabet and a questionnaire of selected items dealing with everyday experience. The persons interviewed are strongly rooted natives of their communities, typical of various age or social groups. Usually there is one person, as unsophisticated as possible, from the oldest generation, and another either younger or more sophisticated or both. Besides, there are enough cultured informants to indicate the local or regional standards. For the Atlantic seaboard states alone, the field workers for the Atlas interviewed over 150

Mountain States, and from other research in American English. Professors Hans Kurath and A. H. Marckwardt of Michigan, H. B. Allen of Minnesota, and Marjorie Kimmerle of Colorado have made it possible to use these records.

The American Council of Learned Societies provided a scholarship for 1951–52 to make it possible for me to investigate the relationship between dialect differences and social differences. Many of the details in this paper will be expanded in *The Pronunciation of the Eastern United States* by Hans Kurath and Raven I. McDavid, Jr.

[1] E. B. Atwood, *The Verb Forms of the Eastern United States* (Ann Arbor: University of Michigan Press, 1952).

[2] The regional designations are those found in H. Kurath, *A Word Geography of the Eastern United States* (Ann Arbor: University of Michigan Press, 1949), and in articles by Kurath, E. B. Atwood, Raven McDavid, and A. L. Davis. Linguistically the North includes New England, the Hudson Valley (including New York City) and derivative settlements in upstate New York, Pennsylvania, and further west. The Inland North is the northern area exclusive of the Hudson Valley and eastern New England. The Midland includes most of New Jersey and Pennsylvania, with derivative settlements to the west and south. The North Midland includes most of New Jersey and Pennsylvania, plus northern West Virginia. The South Midland includes the Shenandoah Valley, southern West Virginia, southwest Virginia, and the mountain and upper Piedmont areas of the Carolinas and Georgia. The South includes the older plantation areas of eastern Virginia and the coastal plain and lower Piedmont of the Carolinas and Georgia. The boundaries between these sections are much less sharp west of the Appalachians than along the Atlantic Seaboard.

cultured informants—a greater number of cultured informants than even the largest standard dictionary has utilized for the entire United States.

Besides the relative status of informants in their own communities (indicated by the field worker after he has completed the interviews), one must evaluate communities, or groups of communities, against the whole body of American English. Previous work in linguistic geography, especially Kurath's *Word Geography of the Eastern United States,* enables us to judge pronunciations by the type of dialect areas in which they occur.

Focal areas are those areas whose economic, social, or cultural prestige has led to the spread of their linguistic forms into other areas. Examples are eastern New England (Boston), eastern Pennsylvania (Philadelphia), the Hudson Valley (New York City), the Virginia Piedmont (Richmond), and the South Carolina Low-Country (Charleston). Pronunciations characteristic of focal areas are likely to have prestige, especially when used by the younger and more sophisticated speakers.

Relic areas, on the other hand, are those whose geographical or cultural isolation, and relative lack of prestige, has caused the retention of older forms or prevented the spread of forms characteristic of these areas. Examples are northeastern New England, the eastern shore of Chesapeake Bay, and eastern North Carolina. Pronunciations characteristic of relic areas are likely to lack prestige, especially if they are chiefly used by the older and less sophisticated speakers.

A third problem we must consider is the attitude of speakers towards particular pronunciations—whether we call them "secondary responses" with Bloomfield or "metalinguistic details" with Trager. Here, incidental comments of the informants are of great value. For instance, the American *vase* /ves/ is a /vaz/ in Southern British Received Pronunciation. We might expect /vaz/ to have prestige in the United States, especially in those areas of New England and the Old South where British customs are admired and British speech forms are often adopted into local cultured speech. However, not only is /vaz/ rare as a spontaneous pronunciation, but the frequent comments of informants that "if it costs over $2.98 it's a /vaz/" suggest that many people who say /vaz/ are judged as parvenus who have acquired the pronunciation during a recent exposure to culture and who wish to use it to impress their neighbors. Judgments that pronunciations are characteristic of less privileged social groups—Negroes, unsuccessful farmers, recent immigrants—indicate for such pronunciations a lack of prestige in the community, regardless of their status elsewhere or their occurrence in the informant's unguarded conversation.

Finally, some informants may deliberately stick to pronunciations they know are considered old-fashioned, unprivileged, or simply peculiar. New Yorkers generally consider it substandard to pronounce a curl of hair and a coil of rope the same way, yet I know at least one prosperous and well-educated New Yorker of colonial stock who does not distinguish such pairs.

The most sophisticated informant interviewed in Charleston proclaimed that she personally said /tə'mætəz/, though she knew other people said /tə'metəz/ or /tə'matəz/—"because Grandmother H—— always said /tə'mætəz/, and what Grandmother H—— said is good enough for me." One cultured informant near Galt, Ontario consistently says /bul, pul/ for *bull, pull,* instead of /bʊl, pʊl/ because these pronunciations have come down in his Scotch-Canadian family. Such examples of "rugged individualism," family pride, or personal stubbornness do not give us patterns of prestige, but they warn us to go slow in condemning what we do not say ourselves.

As Kurath has often pointed out, there are three types of differences in pronunciation:

(1) Differences in the pronunciation of the individual phonemes.

(2) Differences in the occurrence of the individual phonemes.

(3) Differences in the system of phonemes.[3]

Differences in the pronunciation of the individual phonemes are hardest to detect and evaluate. Some of these pronunciations are fairly striking, and do denote social status:

1. The ingliding diphthongal pronunciation of *date* and *boat,* as [deət] and [boət] is generally confined to the Charleston area.

2. The fronted [ʉ] in *two, boot* is very common in the Midland and the South.

[3] The particular type of analysis one favors will often determine the category to which he assigns these differences. The analysis here used is basically that of *The Pronunciation of the Eastern United States* as adapted to the system of transcription generally used in *Language Learning.* Phonetic symbols are enclosed in brackets; phonemic symbols in slanting lines. Phonemic equivalents are as follows:

Vowels:
/i/ as in *beet*
/ɪ/ as in *bit*
/e/ as in *bait*
/ɛ/ as in *bet*
/æ/ as in *bat*
/a/ as in *hot, father*
/ɔ/ as in *bought*
/o/ as in *boat*
/ô/ the New England "short o" as in *coat, road, home*
/ʊ/ as in *put*
/u/ as in *boot*

Diphthongs:
/ai/ as in *write*
/au/ as in *rout*
/ɔi/ as in *oil*
/æi/ as in the common Southern and South Midland *bag, half*
/ɔu/ as in the common Southern and South Midland *law, hog.* This diphthong also occurs in New Hampshire.
/iu/ as in the common New England *beautiful, music.* This diphthong also occurs along the south Atlantic coast.
/ˈ/ primary stress
/ˌ/ secondary stress

3. The monophthongal or near monophthongal variety of /ai/ occurring finally and before voiced consonants in *high, hide*. This type of pronunciation is chiefly found in Southern and South Midland dialects. Though sometimes ridiculed by speakers from other regions, it is rarely considered an unprivileged form in the areas where it occurs—and then only if the speaker does not differentiate *high* from *hah, blind* from *blond, hide* from *hod* or *hard*.

4. The fronted beginning of /au/ ([æu, ɛu]) in such words as *cow* is found in northern New England and the New England settlement area, and in the South and South Midland. In the North they are generally considered old-fashioned or rustic, and are disappearing. They are very common in the Richmond area and seem to be spreading nearly everywhere in the South except in South Carolina.

5. The centralized beginning of /ai, au/ ([əɪ, əu]) in *rite, ride, lout, loud*. Sometimes this occurs only when the diphthong is followed by a voiceless consonant, sometimes in all positions. In the inland North the centralized beginning may occur regardless of the consonant following the diphthong, but in this region the centralized beginning is often considered somewhat old-fashioned and rustic, though it is used by many cultured informants. The centralized beginning when the diphthong is followed by a voiceless consonant, but not otherwise, is characteristic of the speech of three well-defined areas: Canada (especially Ontario), the Virginia Piedmont, and the Atlantic Tidewater area from Georgetown, South Carolina, to St. Augustine, Florida. In view of the social prestige of the Richmond and Charleston areas, the pronunciations of *light* and *lout* as [ləɪt, ləut] probably have privileged status.

6. An ingliding vowel with a rather high beginning sometimes occurs for /æ/ in such words as *calf, bad* [æˆə, ɛə] or for /ɔ/ in *law* [ɔˆə, oˇə]. These pronunciations are most common in such cities as New York, Philadelphia, and Baltimore. They are especially common in families with a central or eastern European background, and the more extreme varieties are often considered substandard.[4]

There are relatively few differences in the system of phonemes that all students would agree upon.

1. For some speakers the "New England short *o*," /ŏ/, occurs alongside /o/ in such words as *coat, road, home, whole*. It probably is found everywhere in the New England settlement area since it has been recorded as far west as Montana. On the other hand, even in New England it is losing ground, since it is found chiefly in smaller and relatively isolated communities and in the speech of the older and less sophisticated informants.

2. A falling diphthong /iu/ occurs alongside /yu/ (or /u/) in such

---

[4] These differences in the pronunciation of the individual phonemes are sometimes analyzed as phonemic or systematic differences. See George L. Trager and Henry Lee Smith, Jr., *An Outline of English Structure* (Norman, Oklahoma: Battenburg Press, 1951).

words as *puke, beautiful, music, tube, due, new, suit, sumach, grew, blew*. It is found chiefly in the New England settlement area, but also occurs along Chesapeake Bay and the Carolina and Georgia coast. It is slightly old-fashioned, especially in the North (it occurs most frequently in *puke*, which does not have a "schoolroom pronunciation"); yet it still occurs in cultured speech.

3. In the Pittsburgh area the vowel /a/ occurs only before /-r/, with both *cot* and *caught, collar* and *caller* having /ɔ/. This feature also seems to occur frequently in western Canada and in the Minneapolis area. If anything, it seems to be spreading among younger and better educated speakers.

Differences in the occurrence of individual phonemes are most common and easiest to evaluate. They may be grouped according to several social types, though we must remember that these groupings are only tentative ones.

1. Some differences are purely regional:

In such words as *whip, wharf*, and *whoa*, some speakers have /hw-/, others /w-/.[5]

For *humor*, the pronunciation /hyumər/ occurs sporadically and chiefly in the Northern area, though elsewhere there are indications it is being sponsored by the schools as a spelling pronunciation. /yumər/ is far more common, at all levels of usage. For other words of this group, however, (though the evidence is less adequate) the forms with /yu-/ seem to be less widespread and somewhat lacking in prestige.

For *without*, the middle consonant may be either /θ/ or /ð/ at any social level. In the North and eastern North Carolina /ð/ is overwhelmingly predominant; in Canada, the Midland area, eastern Virginia, South Carolina, and Georgia /θ/ is very frequent.

Ewe is /yo/ in most of the country where people have knowledge of sheep. Since this pronunciation is never heard from those who have not lived where sheep were raised, it may be considered an occupational pronunciation among sheep herders.

Bleat, the cry of a calf, is prevailingly /blæt/ in the North and /blet/ in the South, being replaced by *bawl* in the Midland; /blit/ is almost exclusively a city pronunciation.

Because is frequently pronounced /bɪ'kəz/ in the North and in South Carolina, but rarely in other regions. Where this pronunciation occurs it is used by speakers of all degrees of sophistication.

The unstressed vowel of *without* is always /ɪ/ in the North and the South, but usually /ə/ in the Midland.

Beside the usual /ču-/, Massa*chu*setts is often /ju-/ in New England, but /tyu-/ or /tu-/ in the South and south Midland.

[5] Raven I. McDavid, Jr. and Virginia Glenn McDavid, "h before semi vowels in Eastern United States." *Language*, Vol. 28, 1952, pp. 41–62.

Instead of /wɔnt/ (or the common Southern /wɔunt/) *want* is very often /want/ in Massachusetts and Vermont, /wənt/ in New Jersey and Western Pennsylvania. Both of these pronunciations occur sporadically in western areas settled ultimately from New England.

Words such as *orange, Florida, borrow,* and *tomorrow* may have either /a/ or /ɔ/ before /-r-/. In the Atlantic seaboard states /ɔ/ is most likely to occur in these words in northern New England, western Pennsylvania, and the Charleston area. For such words as *Florida* and *oranges,* /ɔ/ is practically universal in the North Central States and westward, but in these same areas /a/ or /ɔ/ may occur in *borrow* and *tomorrow.*

For *bulge, bulk,* and *budget,* both /ʊ/ and /ə/ occur: /ə/ in the North and North Midland, /ʊ/ in the South Midland, eastern Virginia, and the Piedmont of the Carolinas and Georgia, /ə/ again along the southern coast south of Chesapeake Bay.

For *won't,* /wont/ occurs everywhere. In addition there are four forms with regional distribution: (1) /wənt/ in the North, outside of the Hudson Valley; (2) /wɔnt/ in North Carolina; (3) /wunt, wʊnt/ in Canada, New York City, the Hudson Valley, Chesapeake Bay, eastern North Carolina, and the Charleston area. All of these forms occur in cultured speech.

For many of the words derived from Middle English /oː/—and some borrowings that have fallen into the pattern—both /u/ and /ʊ/ occur, without social distinction but with sharply differing regional patterns. This is true of *coop, cooper, hoop, goobers, room, broom, root, cooter, food, hoof, roof, spooks,* and probably others. For instance, I—a native of upper South Carolina—normally have /u/ in *root, cooter, food, roof, spooks,* and *goober,* /ʊ/ in *coop, cooper, hoop,* and either /u/ or /ʊ/ in *room, broom, hoof.*

For such words as *tube, dew, new,* we find /iu/ in the North and occasionally along the southern coast, although it is somewhat old-fashioned in both areas. In the South and South Midland, /yu/ is predominant. It occurs as a prestige form in some communities in the North and North Midland. In northeastern New England, the Hudson Valley, and the North Midland, /u/ is almost universal and is spreading in other parts of the North.

Such pairs as *horse* and *hoarse, morning* and *mourning, border* and *boarder* are usually distinguished in the North, the South, and the South Midland, but not in the North Midland. In many parts of the Inland North and in Canada the distinction is disappearing.

2. A few pronunciations seem to lack prestige everywhere. *Italian* as /ˌai ˈtælyən/ is generally looked down upon; /dif/ (instead of /dɛf/) for *deaf* and /ˈwaundɪd/ (instead of /ˈwundɪd/) for wounded are generally considered old-fashioned.

3. Other pronunciations lack prestige, but occur in limited regions.

Along Chesapeake Bay, *fog* and *hog* occasionally have /o/.

Rinse is rarely /rɪnč, rɛnč/ in the North, but these pronunciations are common in the Midland and the South. They are slightly old-fashioned, but not uncommon in cultured speech. The hyper-form /rɪnz/ is less common, limited to the same areas, and chiefly found in the speech of the half educated.

Coop occurs with /-b/ on Delaware Bay and along the southern coast south of Chesapeake Bay. This pronunciation is not common in cities, is slightly old-fashioned, but is used by many cultured speakers.

In parts of the South Midland and the South (but not in the Virginia Piedmont) *took, roof,* and *hoof* frequently have /ə/ in uneducated speech.

In much of the South and South Midland, the less educated speakers have /ə/ in *put,* to rime with *cut.*

For *loam* and *gums,* the pronunciations with /u,ʊ/ are confined to the New England settlement area, with /ʊ/ more common in Maine and New Hampshire than elsewhere. Although generally lacking in prestige, /gʊmz/ and /lʊm/ sometimes occur in cultured speech in Maine and New Hampshire. In other areas cultured speakers occasionally say /gumz/ and /lum/.

Two pronunciations of *can't*—/kent/ and /kæmt/—occur chiefly in parts of the South and South Midland. Although both pronunciations seem to have spread from the Virginia Piedmont, /kent/ seems to be the older and /kæmt/ the more recent form. Consequently, although both forms occur in the speech of all types of informants, /kent/ is often considered just a little more old-fashioned.

4. Several pronunciations may lack prestige in one region but be acceptable in another:

In the South and South Midland the pronunciation of *creek* as /krɪk/ is usually considered very quaint and lacking in prestige, since it is largely confined to the uneducated Negroes of the Carolina and Georgia coast. Even in the South, however, /krɪk/ may occur in the speech of cultured Charlestonians. In the North both /krik/ and /krɪk/ occur, with some pressure from the public schools to enforce /krik/ as a spelling pronunciation. However, /krɪk/ is very common in northern cultured speech. In the North Midland, especially in Pennsylvania, /krɪk/ is practically universal.

In the Atlantic seaboard states, *farm* and *form* are rarely homonymous, and where this homonymy occurs, as occasionally in South Carolina and Georgia, it is only in uneducated speech, and consequently frowned upon. In parts of Louisiana and Texas, however, this homonymy is normal among all classes of speakers.

Soot is most frequently pronounced as /sət/, except in Pennsylvania. In many parts of the country /sət/ is looked upon as old-fashioned, rustic, or uneducated. In the South, however, it is the pronunciation used by a majority of cultured speakers.

Many scholars, even C. C. Fries,[6] have labeled the pronunciation of

---

[6] Charles C. Fries, *American English Grammar* (New York and London: Appleton-Century-Crofts, 1940), p. 10.

catch with /ɛ/ as lacking in prestige. However, /kɛč/ is overwhelmingly the normal pronunciation, for the nation as a whole and for all regions except southern New England, the Hudson Valley, Pennsylvania, and the city of Charleston, where /kæč/ is the majority usage. In the areas where /kæč/ is the usual pronunciation, it is naturally preferred by educated speakers. In Virginia, and to some extent in North Carolina, /kæč/ is a prestige pronunciation, used by a majority of the cultured informants but by few others. In other parts of the country, however, a majority of the cultured informants say /kɛč/.

5. For some words, one pronunciation may have prestige in one region and another pronunciation have prestige somewhere else.

For *raspberries,* the "broad *a*" pronunciation with /a/ seems to have some prestige in eastern New England, and to a lesser extent in New York City and eastern Virginia. In other parts of the country, however,—particularly in the Inland North—the pronunciation with /æ/ is socially preferred, and the /a/ pronunciation considered old-fashioned or rustic.

For such words, as *hog* and *fog,* pronunciations with /a,ɔ,ɔu/ have been recorded from speakers on all social levels. The /a/ pronunciations seem to have social prestige in Boston, New York City, Philadelphia, Charleston, Richmond (but not in smaller communities in the Virginia Piedmont), western North Carolina, northwestern South Carolina, and northern Georgia. In other southern communities the cultured informants have /ɔ,ɔu/. It is probable that /ɔu/ is an older prestige pronunciation that has spread from the Virginia Piedmont, with /a/ replacing it in cultured Richmond speech and in the cultured speech of other metropolitan centers.

Almost everyone knows that the two pronunciations of *greasy* sharply divide the eastern United States, with /-s-/ more common in the North and North Midland but /-z-/ usual in the South and South Midland. In some areas where both pronunciations occur, they are associated with different social levels or social contexts. Trager has frequently pointed out that among his boyhood playmates in Newark the /-z-/ pronunciation was confined to such derogatory phrases as a *greasy grind.* In South Carolina and Georgia the /-s-/ pronunciation is regular among the Gullah Negroes but almost never occurs in the speech of whites.

6. Occasionally a pronunciation may have social prestige in one area but elsewhere be only one of several acceptable pronunciations. For instance, *office* with /a/ has social prestige in eastern Pennsylvania and eastern Virginia; in other areas /a/ or /ɔ/ or /ɔu/ may occur without any implication of social distinction.

7. Some pronunciations have prestige in the limited areas in which they occur.

The pronunciation of *can't* with /a/ is the socially preferred form in eastern New England, and to a lesser extent in New York City, Philadelphia, and eastern Virginia. Elsewhere it is extremely rare.

The pronunciation of *soot* as /sut/ is largely confined to the northern areas. Wherever it occurs, it is likely to be found in the speech of the moderately or better educated.

The lack of constriction of post-vocalic /-r/ (the so-called "loss of /r/") in *burn, barn, beard* occurs mostly in eastern New England, New York City, and the South Atlantic States. In the areas where it occurs, it is most likely to appear in the speech of the younger and better educated informants. In some communities in the South Atlantic States the rustic and uneducated white speakers preserve the constriction of /-r/, while Negroes and the more sophisticated whites lack constriction. In such communities visitors from the Inland North or the North Central States, where the constriction of /-r/ occurs in the speech of all classes, are likely to be at a social disadvantage. Conversely, in some Inland Northern communities, the only residents who lack constriction of /-r/ are the Negroes who have come from the South in the last generation. In these communities, Southern students have had difficulty securing rooms. In telephone conversations, landladies may identify the lack of consideration of /-r/ as a Negro characteristic and announce that no rooms are available.

8. A few pronunciations are always somewhat prestigious since they occur most frequently in cities and in the speech of the younger and better educated informants. However, if the group of informants using such a pronunciation is very small, the prestige of the pronunciation may be lost since the pronunciation will be interpreted as a mark of conscious snobbery.

The pronunciation of *soot* as /sʊt/ always has social prestige, not only in Pennsylvania where /sʊt/ is the usual pronunciation but in the North where /sut/ is a common pronunciation among educated speakers and in the South where /sət/ is the usual pronunciation among speakers of all classes.

The pronunciation of *vase* as /vez/, |less frequently /vaz/) and of *nephew* as /'nɛvyə,-yu/ (much less commonly /'nɛvi/) are largely confined to cultured informants—chiefly in Southern Ontario, Boston, New York City, Philadelphia, Richmond and Charleston, where British speech forms are likely to have prestige. Inland informants who say /vez/ or /'nɛvyə/ usually have strong family or cultural ties to one of those centers.

The pronunciation of *sumach* with /su-/ instead of the more common /su-/ is also largely confined to the larger coastal cities and to a relatively few inland cultured informants.

Such words as *suit, blew, threw* are normally pronounced with /u/. Although the pronunciations with /yu/ have social prestige in England they are extremely rare in this country, occurring almost exclusively in the North. Most Americans consider them unnatural and affected.

9. Sometimes the pronunciation of a word may involve a number of intricately related cultural, historical, and political facts. One of the most

complex of these is *Negro,* where the pronunciations involve not only the status and the attitudes of those who use them, but the reactions of those the pronunciations designate. The historical pronunciation /'nɪgər/ is by far the most common, and in many communities it is the normal pronunciation used by speakers of both races. However, since it is used by many people as a term of contempt, it is actively resented by Negro spokesmen —regardless of the intent behind it. The spelling pronunciation /'nigro/ is comparatively new, but it has been actively sponsored as a polite pronunciation and is so used by most cultured speakers of the North and North Midland. However, /'nigro/ is very rare south of the Mason-Dixon line, partly because it is recognized as a Northern pronunciation of a word about which most Southerners have strong prejudices, partly because it violates the normal Southern tendency to have /ə/ in unstressed syllables. The pronunciation /'nɪgro/ is also a common polite form in the North and North Midland, but relatively uncommon in the South. The normal polite form in the South (and occasionally in other sections) is /'nɪgrə/. Most cultured informants in the South do not use /'nɪgər/, which they feel is both derogatory to the Negro and characteristic of poor white speech. The difference in status and implication of /'nɪgrə/ and /'nɪgər/ is very sharply maintained in the South, though frequently outsiders do not understand the distinction and wonder why the Southerner does not say /'nigro/, which to the Southerner seems unnatural.

Even such a limited approach to the problem of social differences in pronunciation indicates that it is very complex and that the person who attempts to label the status of a pronunciation must have information about such social forces as trading areas, educational practices, and community structure. Nor will it be a simple matter for teachers to apply the knowledge gained from studies such as this. Yet one may suggest certain procedures.

Those who teach English in the public schools should be fully aware of the socially preferred pronunciations in the communities in which they are teaching. They should not waste time and energy attempting to force exotic pronunciations upon their students, regardless of how desirable or elegant such pronunciations seem. They should also be aware that other types of pronunciation may be acceptable in other communities. Such awareness will not only make it easier for teachers to deal with the student who has moved to the community from another region, it will also make it easier for them to teach in communities outside their own dialect area.

Teachers of English to foreign students must also recognize this problem. In universities with a cosmopolitan student body, the instructors and drill-masters may speak any one of several varieties of American English. Even if it is possible to choose instructors and drillmasters from one dialect area, or require them to use something like a uniform dialect in their classes, as soon as the foreign student goes into his regular classes he will hear other types of pronunciation from the professors and his fellow students. The problem would be less difficult at smaller colleges where the faculty and the student body are predominantly from one region. Even here, however, the students will occasionally encounter other varieties of English. The longer they are in the United States and the broader their contacts—by travel, movies, radio, or television—the more frequently they will hear other pronunciations than those they have learned. How much attention the teacher should pay to variant pronunciations is a matter of practical pedagogy, depending on circumstances—it is much more important for the student to master one American pronunciation of *can't* than to learn a little about several pronunciations—but certainly the advanced students should know that speakers may differ markedly in the details of their pronunciation, and yet all speak socially acceptable American English.

Use of Field Materials in the Determination of Dialect Groupings*

SUMNER IVES

THE TERM dialect could be used as a horrible example in a lecture on semantics, for the meanings and attitudes which this word signifies are very nearly as diverse as the people who use it. To some, what they say is the language, and what other people say is dialect. Once, in fact, after I had lectured on pronunciation, a member of the audience from New York expressed surprise that a Southerner could show any knowledge of "correct speech." A more scholarly view regards the language as something of an abstraction; it is manifested, that is, spoken or written, in a variety of forms which are called dialects. If one wishes to be very precise, he speaks also of idiolects. The linguist, as a student of language, is interested in all varieties of the language, living or dead, even though as a teacher he might promote those particular forms which are associated with education and prestige.

Any actual utterance, or stretch of language, can be broken down into at least three simultaneous elements. We can study language, in part, by focusing our attention, in turn, on these elements. The utterance has individual sounds; these are used to form words; and these words are put together according to the rules of grammar peculiar to the language of the utterance. There may be dialectal differences in all three elements. Thus a person may use different vowels or the same vowel in *horse* and *hoarse*,

* Reprinted by permission from *Quarterly Journal of Speech*, 41.359–364 (December, 1955).

he may call a certain container for liquids a *pail* or a *bucket*, and he may say *hadn't ought* or *ought not*. However, I shall here talk only about differences in pronunciation.

It has been customary to divide pronunciation differences into three categories. There may be variety in the sound of single phonemes such as the pronunciation of *night* as [na:t] or as [naɪt]; there may be differences in the distribution of phonemes such as the use of the same or different vowels in *marry* and *merry* or in the choice of vowels for *wash* and *water;* and there may be variation in the total number of phonemic contrasts such as having one sound in *tin can* [kɛ:n] and another in *I think I can* [kæn], or having the same vowel in all words like *cot* and *caught.*

These dialectal differences are all within the province of segmental phonology. But there are also dialectal differences which are in the province of supra-segmental phonology, such matters as voice qualifying, tempo, pitch pattern, and stress pattern. For example, in some sections people stress *are* in *how are you* and in other sections they stress *you*. These supra-segmental characteristics have not been studied very thoroughly, and there is no standard methodology for dealing with all of them, although symbolizations for pitch, stress, and juncture seem to be in process of establishment. This delay is partly due to the difficulties inherent in the collection of field material or basic data and partly to the fact that the segmental characteristics should be studied first.

Differences in pronunciation may correlate with social factors or with geographical areas; generally there are both social and geographical limitations on the occurrence of particular pronunciations. The social differences may agree with one or more of several circumstances. One of these is age. There are always some pronunciations which are moving towards disappearance, and there are some innovations which are moving towards acceptance. This consequence of language growth makes, at any given time, differences in language habits which correlate roughly with the generation to which the individuals belong. For example, the habit of pronouncing *horse* and *hoarse* alike seems to be gaining ground in New York State, and the use of a somewhat centralized beginning for the diphthong in *night* seems to be losing out. This sort of thing makes it possible, often, to mark dialect limits which agree with age rather than with social class or geographical area, or to find age limitations in addition to the others. Since such changes operate more rapidly in some localities than in others of a different type, the dialect picture is often very complex.

The most commonly observed social factor agreeing with speech differences is education, but often the effect of education is not so great as we think. We speak of speech as being educated or uneducated; or we might use such terms as folk speech, common or popular speech, and cultivated speech, regarding these terms as applicable to levels or hierarchies of esteem. However, the more we learn about class structure, and about linguistic habits which correlate with class structure, the more reluctant we are to accept the number of years in school as a definitive criterion. When I listened to some of the tape recordings of the speech of college students in Georgia collected by C. K. Thomas, I noticed pronunciations which are, in Georgia, regarded as typical of lower or middle class speech. In my own study of pronunciation in New Orleans, both of white and negro informants, I see that education is but one of several factors correlating with dialect difference and that there are consistent differences in the pronunciation of people with equivalent formal education. Social mobility, or movement from one cultural group to another, the spread of educational opportunity, and the existence of groupings based on the local criteria for social esteem all tend to limit the value of education as a distinguishing mark of social class.

These social differences in dialect are most obvious in sections of the country where family tradition shares responsibility with the school in the development of the cultural attitudes, where the consciousness of class is more compelling, sometimes, than the textbook. This influence of tradition generally operates more strongly at the extreme ends of the social scale than in the middle. Thus, there is sharp consciousness of social dialect in areas like the Southeast, where there is historically a local aristocracy based on birth and a class whose members have had relatively little opportunity for social or economic betterment. There, an elderly man who was confident of his status as a gentleman might use *ain't* freely in conversation, but he would not pronounce *police* with accent on the first syllable or *night* with the same long vowel he would use in *five*.

In spite of the actual complexity found in the speech habits of the United States, we can speak of dialects, both social and geographical, provided we do not imply or assume complete homogeneity within each class or region. In practice we define dialects by specifying the occurrence of particular pronunciations, but the naming of these particular pronunciations should not be taken as implying that the identified dialect differs from other dialects in all the characteristics which have not been named. In practice, we get the best results by using the occurrence of more than one feature. For example, the general dialect which Hans Kurath calls South Midland and C. K. Thomas calls Southern Mountain is characterized by having the retroflex variety of postvocalic *r*, by the use of a different vowel in *four* and *forty*, and by the pronunciation [grizɪ] rather than [grisɪ]. All these features are found outside the region of this dialect, but when they all occur together the combination defines the dialect. Calling the speech so defined a dialect does not, however, imply that it differs from other American English in all its characteristics, or that it is homogeneous within its limits. Some such procedure as this has served to define General American, although a linguist can discover very nearly as many differences among the speakers of this dialect as there are between this dialect and others spoken in this country.

Such a method of associating particular definitive characteristics of speech with areas or classes which have other elements of homogeneity has been very useful in the study of American English. The major product from the examination of field materials is the isogloss—more properly, when talking about pronunciation, the isophone. And it is the observation and selection of isoglosses which give order to the study of dialects. Two basic procedures for drawing them have been implicit in publications on the subject.

Kurath and those who have worked with the Linguistic Atlas look for the outer limits of occurrence of pronunciations which are significant. For example, E. Bagby Atwood, in his study of eastern Virginia speech, selected pronunciations at that region and then charted the instances of each pronunciation which were found in the field material. His isoglosses were lines drawn around the outer limits of these instances, although a widely isolated instance might not be included in the line. When contrasting pronunciations of the same item are studied, as for example [ɑn] rather than [ɔn] for the preposition *on*, two lines are derived. One is the outer limit of [ɑn]; the other is the outer limit of [ɔn]. These lines will show that there is an area where both pronunciations are in use. Isoglosses of this type are always based on the presence of something rather than the absence of something, for it should never be assumed that a sample contains everything which exists in the region.

The field material of the Linguistic Atlas consists of phonetic transcriptions of the responses made by selected informants to a questionnaire of over 700 items. The field worker tried to secure the desired item without himself pronouncing the word in question. Since the circumstances of the investigation limited the field worker to about three interviews each two weeks, the sampling is rather thin, there being about 2,000 for the Atlantic states. Moreover, about half the records were secured from the oldest and least educated people available in the communities studied, and this fact must be remembered in drawing conclusions from the results of the survey.

The Atlas materials are particularly useful for problems of history—such matters as the development of English phonology, changes in the distribution of particular features, the survival of relics, the delimitation of culturally isolated areas, the tracing of settlement movements, and the spread of culture elements like the plantation system. In phonemic analysis and in the determination of prestige characteristics, the Atlas materials must be used with caution. Although a skillful student can get a great deal from them on these points, he must know exactly what he is doing. Aside from the limitations of coverage, the major lack in the Atlas materials derives from the difficulty in transcribing extended utterances, free conversation, and such matters as pitch and stress. Consequently, their usefulness in investigating supra-segmental phonology is limited.

A different procedure has been used by Thomas. His basic method is to make a tape recording as the informant reads a text prepared to bring out those features which Thomas has found useful in defining dialects. By this method, he does not require a trained phonetician in gathering his material, nor does he have to contend with differences in transcription habits, which complicate the analysis when more than one field worker is used. Also, he is able to accumulate speech samples from more people in a shorter time than required when the Atlas method is used. At the same time, his text does not contain the number of items found in the Atlas questionnaire.

It is my understanding, too, that Thomas uses a different method in determining speech boundaries. He has secured large maps of the United States on which each county is marked. On these maps, he notes occurrences of the different pronunciations. Boundaries are located where majority usage shifts. By this method, Thomas is able to say something about the density of occurrence—that is, what the majority usage is—and about the prestige value of the pronunciations he studies. Moreover, a tape recording preserves more of the phonological characteristics than even the most skillful phonetic transcription, although this evidence must be used carefully, for the gross characteristics of reading aloud are seldom quite the same as those of free conversation. I think therefore, that the records being accumulated by Thomas will be useful in studying some supra-segmental characteristics—most of those relevant to grammar—but not in studying all of them.

These represent, so far as I know, the largest accumulations of field material gathered specifically for the study of American dialects, although some more limited bodies of material have been gathered, notably the collection of Middle South speech being made by C. M. Wise. There is, however, another study of American pronunciation which should be mentioned. George Trager, working now with Henry Lee Smith, Jr., has published a phonemic analysis, or rather a series of analyses, for English. Trager's interest is less in the determination of dialect boundaries than in the development of a procedure for representing the phonemic structure of any variety of American English. His material is particularly useful for such purposes as the preparation of textbooks in English for foreigners and as the representation of English morphology. It includes symbolization for pitch, stress, and juncture, those supra-segmental components of the utterance which are known to be relevant to grammar. I have said nothing about his field material or how he uses it, for his publications are not explicit on those points.

I shall say a few words now about my own current research in phonology, for some of the study differs from that already described. Last summer I began working with the Urban Life Research Institute at Tulane University. This is a group of sociologists, social workers, and psychologists, whose function is the study of various aspects of class structure and mobility in an urban area. One of the constant problems is finding a means of defining or delimiting class or cultural group and for estimating social mobility, or the movement of the individual from one culture group to another. Employment of such criteria as income, education, and the use of leisure time does not give the desired sharpness of demarkation, for such matters are generally in continuum; moreover, since these are also the object of study, their use as defining criteria admits the danger of circularity in the results.

Last summer I made detailed transcriptions of several tape recordings of interviews with negro subjects. These interviews were only partially directed, and no attempt was made to elicit the pronunciation of particular words. They were, for all practical purposes, the normal conversation of the subjects, except for the fact that some passages were rather long. I was able to isolate a number of words whose pronunciation was significantly different in the body of records and to make a tentative grouping of the records into two classes, with one class showing two dialects. My estimates as to the cultural grouping, and even to the mobility of one informant, agreed with the grouping made according to non-linguistic criteria. My grouping fitted into the hypothesis about class structure among New Orleans negroes which a member of the Institute had already formulated on other evidence.

Since then, using these records as a basis but adding other items to insure adequate coverage, I have developed a questionnaire designed particularly for this problem in this area. Since this type of questionnaire could be useful in other localities, I shall describe it briefly. It is presented to the informant as a simple verbal efficiency test, and we hope that he will not realize his pronunciation is being sampled. In the first part, the informant is asked to list such things as the days of the week and the months of the year. In the second part he supplies the missing word in such sentences as "Dairies have (   ) which give milk." He is expected to say "cow," but actually the words *dairies* and *milk* are the important items in the sentence. The third part has logical sequences like *inch, foot, yard, mile.* One item is omitted, and the informant is asked to supply it. The last part contains simple analogies like *boy-girl* paired with *father-mother.* One of the terms is omitted and to be supplied. The entire questionnaire is read by the informant and recorded on tape. There is enough duplication so that no great harm is done if the informant misses some of the items which he is to supply. This test is to give the segmental characteristics of his speech.

The supra-segmental characteristics are derived from study of other recorded material. All informants in the current project are interviewed at some length, and at least one of the individual interviews is recorded.

Since these interviews lead the subject to talk more or less at will on a variety of subjects, they contain a great deal of evidence.

I have already discovered that there are some phonological characteristics which occur consistently in the speech of the negroes whose social status is lowest. I have not yet heard them in the speech of white people whose economic and educational status is the same, nor have I heard them in the speech of other negroes of higher status. I have also observed some interesting correlations between the base pitch from which grammatically significant shifts are made and the emotional accompaniments to the content of the sentence. That is, this base pitch is not basic to all the speech but shifts from one to another of, I think, three points, according to the subject of the discourse and the speaker's reaction to it. However, I have not examined enough material, as yet, to know just what is phonetic and what is phonemic. Morover, the nature of the interviews is such that distinctly different voice qualifiers can be detected. These are especially interesting in one interview, for the circumstances and subject matter are such that the emotional overtones fluctuate during the course of the interview. Some striking correlations between voice qualifier—especially whine—and the subject matter are evident. The dialectal significance of this lies in the fact that the social status of the informant affects the relationship between voice qualifier and subject matter.

When this aspect of dialect study is more mature, I think that the linguists will have something useful not only for other scholars and for teachers of language but for all fields dealing with class structure and with the individual's adjustment to society. Who knows, we might be able to spot a person's social status as accurately as can an experienced clubwoman and tell as much about their insecurities as a good cop.

Part IV

LINGUISTICS AND USAGE

INTRODUCTION

To MOST PERSONS, the general public as well as many teachers of English, the study of English means the teaching of correctness. For them *grammar* and *usage* are synonyms. This fact is warrant enough for including in this chapter several articles which seek to explain the relation between linguistic study and usage and to clarify different attitudes toward usage.

As a cool and stable platform from which to view the subject of usage this Part offers first the article by Bloomfield, who found himself vastly entertained—and yet deeply concerned—by the phenomena of popular reactions to certain language matters and especially by popular reaction to linguists' statments about language matters.

McMillan and Hill tackle in their respective articles the rather difficult assignment of making persuasively clear some important distinctions. McMillan seeks to clarify the distinction between grammar and usage by treating usage as a function of rhetoric, quite another discipline. Hill, motivated by a previous article by Morton W. Bloomfield advocating a certain degree of dogmatism in the teaching of style and usage, would clear the air of misunderstandings by avoiding a direct clash and trying to find a common ground in the purpose of teaching.

Pedagogical recognition of actual usage as the basis for statements about English pronunciation, grammar, and syntax is really quite recent. Neither of the articles by McMillan and Hill would likely have been written thirty years ago, and neither would make so much sense to a teacher of English today had the Sterling Andrus Leonard monograph, *Current English Usage*, not appeared in 1934 nor Fries's *American English Grammar* in 1940. These studies, along with the first "liberal" handbook, Perrin's *Index to English* (1939), helped to popularize the concept of levels of usage. But that this concept itself is inherently fallacious is the burden of the article by Kenyon, probably the most significant single statement about English usage yet to be published. He finds that while it is possible to recognize "levels," each level then must in turn be recognized as including a wide range of usage from formal to informal. He calls attention to the easily attested but previously unrecognized existence of nonstandard formal usage alongside formal nonstandard.

Consonant with the relativism of Kenyon's position is Dykema's concern with the shift in standards through the years and his tentative inference that in some respects the rate of change may well be accelerating recently, an inference at odds with the general notion that printing and schools have just about blocked further change in language.

Pinpointing the recognition of language change is the article by Lehmann, who perhaps not too technically says that in certain positions /t/ and /d/ are beginning to merge for some American speakers. If this is true —and some readers may be able to confirm this in their own communities —then here is evidence for an important development in our language, a phonemic change.

But to recognize a fact of change, to say nothing of describing the existence of nonstandard forms, is apparently enough to cause some persons to leap to a presumably opposite position and charge the linguist with having no standards at all and with allowing that anything which anybody says at any time is always perfectly acceptable. Stated so crassly their interpretation seems obviously untenable; yet a great many people seek, with straight face and the zeal of martyrdom, to maintain it behind their wall of misunderstanding. As Geist says, in seeking to elucidate the linguists' real contention, this interpretation was at once inferred by many guardians of good English upon perceiving the title *Leave Your Language Alone!* even though no linguist, let alone the author of that book, would ever defend the purists' straw man named "Anything Goes."

It may well be observed that I. A. Richards, approvingly quoted by Hartung, also misunderstands the linguist's position by implying that it is the linguist who says, "If it's widely in use, it's OK." This is, of course, the same misunderstanding Hill dealt with in his reply to Morton Bloomfield. That Hartung himself shares some of this misunderstanding may be suspected, since he ends his interesting and useful analysis of different "doctrines" of English usage by advocating a somewhat nebulous "linguistic norm" which he discerns in the arguments of the oddly-grouped Richards, Otto Jespersen, and Edward Sapir. Curiously, Hartung not only does not even mention Kenyon (an omission something like neglecting to name Einstein in a history of modern science) but refers to Kenyon's theory of functional varieties as if it had been a proposal of Fries.

But after all, says Dobbins, most arguments about usage can be resolved by the ascertainment of the facts of usage among cultivated people. Succeeding articles in this part illustrate (as did several in the section on Linguistic Geography) the step by step growth of a body of information about that usage. Thomas, from his own collection, writes about *showed;* Berkeley finds handbooks far from reliable in their statements about the verb form following initial *There;* and Christensen, with a somewhat related problem of verb agreement, finds the handbooks similarly unhelpful in their attention to the verb form between *what* and a following plural.

Kenyon then deals with a usage which, while admittedly old, is presumably on the increase today and hence, because it controverts a handbook rule, has become a minor crux. Here the rule of grammatical agreement, like a traffic regulation, is frequently broken by normally law-abiding citizens, often without awareness of their infraction. Kenyon attempts to analyze this oddly anomalous construction and to provide a reason for it. Coincidentally Thomas had been collecting evidence of the frequency of this same construction and his own article, appearing elsewhere but simultaneously with that by Kenyon, offers nearly identical conclusions. (See Thomas, "Concord of the Verb in Relative Clauses after 'one of'," *English Journal,* 40. 452 (October, 1951).

Another syntactic problem is the subject of Roberts's article, in which the textbooks again are charged with being sadly unrealistic and incomplete. With respect to the uses of *this,* too, it would seem that Dobbins is right in asking for more evidence before definitive assertions are made about usage. Likewise with the sentence-ending "preposition" (which might often better be classed as an adverb on the basis of stress differentiation), Charnley offers a perspicuous analysis which is at odds with the familiar but now rarely-honored dictum. Then Thomas again—with an article that serves well as a model for comparable student investigations—offers evidence for a moot item, the inflected genitive which the manuals declare just is not supposed to be used with impersonal objects.

Finally Geist moves into the area of semantic usage with a concise presentation of the facts of semantic diversity and the consequent need for some deliberation before being too assertive about the debasement of *disinterested.* The chapter on linguistics and the dictionary will offer more on this general point.

Secondary and Tertiary Responses to Language*

Leonard Bloomfield

Utterances about language may be called secondary responses to language. For us, the most important are those which are made in the systematic study of language—the utterances, above all, which, recorded in books

* Reprinted by permission from *Language,* 20.45–55 (April–June, 1944). Only the portion to the top of page 51 appears here.

and essays, embody the past results of linguistic science. They will not concern us here; to the extent that we succeed in working scientifically, the verbal phase of our work takes on the general characteristics of scientific utterance.

On other than a scientific level, our culture maintains a loosely organized but fairly uniform system of pronouncements about language. Deviant speech forms in dialects other than the standard dialect are described as corruptions of the standard forms ('mistakes', 'bad grammar') or branded as entirely out of bounds, on a par with the solecisms of a foreign speaker ('not English'). The forms of the standard dialect are justified on grounds of 'logic'. Either on the strength of logical consistency or in pursuance of largely conventional authoritative rules, which constitute a minor tradition within the main one (for instance, the rules about *shall* and *will*), certain forms are theoretically prescribed for the standard dialect. When it is noticed that speakers of the standard dialect do not use these forms or use others beside them, these deviations are again branded as 'mistakes' or, less often, attributed to 'usage', which appears here only as a special and limited factor, mentioned doubtfully as interfering with more legitimate controls.

Traditional lore of this kind is occasionally put into literary form and developed in detail, as in the well-known treatise of Richard Grant White, *Words and Their Uses, Past and Present: A Study of the English Language* (New York, 1870).[1]

The speaker is able to discourse also upon more remote topics. In spite of the degenerative character of dialects other than the standard one, some distant local dialects are said to maintain pure Elizabethan English.[2] As a dim reflex of statements concerning linguistic relationships, one hears that the Finnish and Hungarian (or the Bengali and Lithuanian, or the Basque and Malayalam) languages are mutually intelligible. Some ignorant people and some savage tribes are said to have a vocabulary of only a few hundred words. This may be attributed to illiteracy, for 'spoken language' fleetingly renders the forms which have their basic and permanent existence in the 'written language'. The latter 'fixes' and 'preserves' linguistic tradition. Operations upon the system of writing immediately affect a language. The following press releases embody various other phases of popular linguis-

---

[1] Contemporary with Whitney's *Language and the Study of Language* (1867) and *Life and Growth of Language* (1874). Our undergraduate instructors advised us to read Richard Grant White; Whitney was not mentioned.

[2] An Associated Press dispatch (*New York Times*, November 26, 1939) is headed 'Fishermen speak in Middle English'. Part of the wording is as follows: 'A touch of Elizabethan England still flourishes on the "outer banks," a serpentine strand off North Carolina's coast. . . . one hears on the "outer banks" words and phrases so similar to the language of Queen Elizabeth's day that philologists and historians see a distinct connection.'

For this and most of the following citations, as well as for much kind help and criticism, I am indebted to Bernard Bloch.

tics, but are especially illuminating on the matter of language and writing.
From the *Tulsa Daily World* of February 27, 1941:

TULSAN WANTS SEQUOYAH'S ALPHABET TAUGHT IN PUBLIC SCHOOLS

Sequoyah's alphabet should become a part of the standard equipment in
Oklahoma schools, a Tulsan declared Tuesday as he mailed letters to officials
at the state capitol proposing that the Cherokee language be made a part of
the regular curriculum in all state high schools.

"It's the only native tongue conceived and taught as a language in America,"
Dr. C. Sterling Cooley, 415 South Guthrie, wrote A. L. Crable, Oklahoma
superintendent of public instruction. Copies were sent to Senator Henry Tim-
mons and Representative W. H. Langley of the state legislature which is now
in session at Oklahoma City. . . .

Possibility that Sequoyah's languages could fool the Germans again, however, was just a minor point in the doctor's contention the Cherokee tongue
should be taught in school like English, French or Latin.

"Oklahoma schools have taught a lot of subjects a lot more useless," Doctor
Cooley said. . . .

Doctor Cooley said the 86 characters of Sequoyah's famous alphabet were
memorized by some Cherokees in as little time as three days.

"One-semester course should be sufficient for Oklahoma students to learn
the subject," he said.

Doctor Cooley's letter to Superintendent Crable follows:

"Dear Sir:

"To perpetuate a beautiful language that would prove uniquely useful in
time of war; to preserve the only native tongue conceived and taught as a language in America; to offer something better than the "trial of tears" as a memory of our treatment of them and to honor a great leader of an historic people
I believe Oklahoma ought to make it possible for its citizens to choose the
syllabus of Sequoyah as an elective study in the curriculum of any public
school where languages in addition to English are taught.

"I propose this to you because you are logically the one who can best open
the door of opportunity to any and all who wish to learn the tongue of the
Cherokees, the language of Indians everywhere, and I shall be grateful to you
if you will advise how others and myself may help to make it possible for our
schools to perpetuate a language that is solely American in origin."

Doctor Cooley said he sent a copy of the letter to Representative Langley
because, to his knowledge he is the nearest full-blood Cherokee Indian in the
legislature and might be interested in furthering the proposal.

From the *Tulsa Daily World* of April 2, 1941:

CRABLE INDORSES SEQUOYAH'S LANGUAGE AS COLLEGE COURSE

Indorsement of a proposal for teaching Sequoyah's alphabet in public
schools, coupled with a recommendation as to where the subject might be ex-
perimented with was received here Tuesday from A. L. Crable, state superintendent of public instruction.

In a letter to Dr. C. Sterling Cooley, originator of the proposal which has grown, more or less, into a movement, Crable said, "I am in thorough sympathy with your interest in the syllabary of Sequoyah," and suggest that the State Teachers College in Tahlequah would be the school in which the course should be instituted as an elective study.

"Probably all the colleges of the state would be interested in the effort to perpetuate the great work of Sequoyah, in the way you suggest," the state superintendent's letter to Doctor Cooley read. However, the education executive specifically recommended that the Tulsan take the matter to the president of Northeastern State College in Tahlequah, capital of the Cherokee Nation. This Doctor Cooley indicated he would do.

The movement to perpetuate Sequoyah's alphabet and tongue has reached into states other than Oklahoma. Doctor Cooley pointed out after receiving a letter Tuesday from a Mrs. F. P. Arthurs who wrote in behalf of the department of modern languages at Western State College of Colorado at Gunnison. Mrs. Arthurs, who Doctor Cooley believes to be officially connected with the college, asked for references on the life of Sequoyah and inquired about the progress of the Sequoyah movement in Oklahoma.

"I shall write her," said the Tulsan, "that the movement has plenty of encouragement, but no official action—as yet."

Turning back pages of history to 1917, at which time the unveiling of Sequoyah's statue took place in the national capitol's hall of fame, Doctor Cooley found the kind of praise for the Cherokee Indian he has been looking for.

"Sequoyah invented the only sensible alphabet in the world," the Tulsan quoted the late Speaker Chomp Clark,[3] of Missouri as saying at the unveiling ceremonies. "It has one letter for each and every sound the human throat can make," the speaker added in praising phonetics of the language. "If he (Sequoyah) had lived 2,000 years ago, one-fifth of the usual time of life could be saved." Here Clark said that it took years of schooling to acquire even a fair command of the English language, while the Sequoyah alphabet could be learned in only a few days.

On the same occasion, the late Senator Owen of Oklahoma said: "It is a strange thing that no alphabet in all the world reaches the dignity, the simplicity, and the value of the Cherogee[3] alphabet, the Cherokee could learn to spell in one day."

The alphabet, containing 85 characters, was invented in 1821 by the Cherokee, whose name it bears, after 12 years of study. Sequoyah could neither speak nor write the English language.

For release September 3, 1941:

Tulsa, Oklahoma:—Bookkeeping, Typing, Shorthand and kindred subjects for business people, will move over slightly, to make room for a subject never before taught the white man. An Indian language, the tongue of the Cherokees, from the syllabus of Sequoyah, is to be offered as a special course with real Indian full-bloods as teachers.

To preserve the only native tongue in America before it is too late, Leon E. Crawford, President of the American Business College here, announced today

[3] So spelled in our reprint of the release.

he had made arrangements to bring an octogenarian from out of the hills of eastern Oklahoma, the only Indian alive who can set Cherokee type, to Tulsa to start work on grammars and dictionaries, necessary for classroom instruction. Crawford explained ordinary adults can learn the tongue in a couple of semesters of easy lessons, which he plans to give at night, to scores of business and professional men and women, who have expressed a desire to study Cherokee, in an endeavor to perpetuate it.

Levi Gritts, last elected Chief of the Cherokees, and his wife, together with J. B. Shunatonna, Chief of the Otoe tribe, all Oklahoma Indians, will supervise the classroom attempt to have Indians teach the white man how to speak and write the only printable language indigenous to North America.

In more abstruse matters our tradition gives the speaker some freedom of improvisation, but even here the pattern is fairly uniform. Theories about the origin of language and suggestions for research on this problem run along certain well-fixed lines.[4] The speaker has the right to improvise etymologies; these, however, adhere to a rather simple scheme.[5] This phase of popular lore also is capable of development in literary hands.[6]

The speaker who discourses about language sometimes adds that he himself has not a perfect command of his native language—the reasons differ with biographic details—but is aware of his weakness and tries to overcome it; he alludes patronizingly to other speakers who do not know enough to make a similar effort. In fact, it soon appears that the speaker

[4] The following, from a reader's letter to the *New York Times*, dated August 6, 1937, is quite characteristic.
'Some years ago a scientist lived in a land of monkeys to learn their language. I suggest that the study of language begin there with the primitive sounds of animals, followed by a survey of what is known of the speech of savages. After this might come a review of the most ancient fragments of recorded tongues, tracing them down into the developed languages of Egypt, Mesopotamia, Persia, India, China and elsewhere. Some idea of a dispersal of tongues from a common Asiatic center might thus be had and the earliest roots of our commonest words be learned. A brief survey, in translation, of the recorded literature of these dispersal tongues would bring us down through the ancient classics in all lands to the Greek and Roman cultures, where we should learn not merely a few pages of Xenophon and Homer; of Caesar, Cicero, Virgil and Horace, but, in translations, the whole glorious range of Greek and Latin literary, poetic, scientific and philosophic accomplishment, and the bearing of it all on our modern thought.'
[5] A letter to the *New York Times*, dated Caracas, Venezuela, November 18, 1939, contains the following characteristic passage: 'But from what root did the word "Reich" grow up? Certainly not from the same as the world "realm." I rather believe that "Reich" has something to do with the German word "reichen" (i.e., reach). On this basis I think I have a more satisfactory explanation of the designation of "Deutsches Reich" and "Frankreich," as those countries or lands that "reach" (or embrace within their respective boundaries, present or former) the Germans, respectively the French (or Franks, originally). . . . a long time ago, probably after the division of Charlemagne's Holy Roman Empire, the western part (chiefly present-day France) came to be designated by the German word Frankreich (although probably spelled in the then prevailing German), i.e., the realm, or rather the land within which "reached" the Franks, from which word afterward a new word, France, resulted.'
Cf. the discussion of a similar instance by R. G. Kent, *JAOS*, 55.115–9 (1935).
[6] Thus, a fairly elaborate theory is built up by Burton Rascoe, *Titans of Literature: From Homer to the Present*, pp. 48 ff. (New York, 1932).

possesses a fairly extensive stock of authoritative knowledge which enables him to condemn many forms that are used by other speakers.

Several peculiarities of these secondary responses deserve further study. The speaker, when making the secondary response, shows alertness. His eyes are bright, and he seems to be enjoying himself. No matter how closely his statement adheres to tradition, it proffers it as something new, often as his own observation or as that of some acquaintance, and he is likely to describe it as interesting. If he knows that he is talking to a professional student of language, he first alleges ignorance and alludes modestly to the status of his own speech, but then advances the traditional lore in a fully authoritative tone. The whole process is, as we say, pleasurable.[7]

The linguist's cue in this situation is to observe; but if, giving in to a natural impulse (or else, by way of experiment), he tries to enlighten the speaker, he encounters a TERTIARY RESPONSE to language. The tertiary response occurs almost inevitably when the conventional secondary response is subjected to question. The tertiary response is hostile; the speaker grows contemptuous or angry. He will impatiently reaffirm the secondary response, or, more often, he will resort to one of a few well-fixed formulas of confutation.

Invariably, in my experience, the linguist's counter-statements are treated as eccentric personal notions—even by speakers who otherwise are aware of the cumulative character of science.[8] The knowledge that the linguist has in person investigated the topic under discussion does not alter this response.[9] Statements about the relation of standard and non-standard forms are likely to be interpreted as 'defense' or 'advocacy' of the latter.[10] Especially, linguistic statements about the relation of writing to language conflict so violently with self-evident truth that they can be interpreted

[7] Undefined popular terms, such as *pleasure* or *anger,* are here used because there is not (or I have not) enough physiology and sociology to redefine them. See, for the rest, A. P. Weiss, *A Theoretical Basis of Human Behavior,* revised edition 419 ff. (Columbus, 1929). Similarly, I use terms like *mechanist* or *non-mentalist:* in a community where nearly everyone believed that the moon is made of green cheese, students who constructed nautical almanacs without reference to cheese, would have to be designated by some special term, such as *non-cheesists.*

[8] After I had outlined the relation of writing to speech, with explicit reference to the history of our science, before a group of educationists who were interested in elementary reading instruction, I was finally refuted by the statement that 'you'll have to SHOW the modern educationist'.

[9] A physician, of good general background and education, who had been hunting in the north woods, told me that the Chippewa language contains only a few hundred words. Upon question, he said that he got this information from his guide, a Chippewa Indian. When I tried to state the diagnostic setting, the physician, our host, briefly and with signs of displeasure repeated his statement and then turned his back to me. A third person, observing this discourtesy, explained that I had some experience of the language in question. This information had no effect.

[10] 'You surely don't expect me (You wouldn't want your children) to go around saying things like *I seen it* or *I done it.*' A college administrator expressed his wonder at the very 'liberal' attitude of linguists in matters of 'grammar'.

only as a perverse refusal to consider certain facts.[11] A cultured speaker, in confuting the linguist's statements, is likely to appeal, without making clear the connection, to the existence of great writers in his language.[12]

A literary instance of the irate tertiary response is the controversy between George Washington Moon and Dean Alford. Neither contestant had any knowledge of the subject, but one had questioned the other's secondary response.[13]

The ordinary speaker makes a response of the tertiary type only when some secondary response of his is questioned or contradicted; but, on a higher and semi-learned plane, a tertiary response may be aroused in a speaker who merely hears or reads linguistic statements and possesses enough sophistication to see that they conflict with his habitual secondary responses. Thus, Oscar Cargill, *Intellectual America*, p. 521 (New York, 1941), writes:

> One cannot ignore the weight of Freeman's essay, "Race and Language" (1885), upon the efforts of these pure scholars. His praise of philology and his use of it as a test of nationality tickled the egos of these new scientists who fancied that their researchers would be of the utmost consequence to society. Further and further back into German forests, up Scandinavian fjords, and over Icelandic barriers they pushed their quests for the origin of words. Now, while it is true that the commonest words in English speech have Anglo-Saxon originals and these in turn have Gothic counterparts, not one of these scholars

[11] Having read a few sentences about the difference between language and writing, a philosopher concludes that the linguistic author refuses to talk about writing. This conclusion is not shaken by a following fairly wordy passage about the use of graphic signs. To say that writing is not the central and basic form of language is simply to ignore writing altogether. See *Journal of Philosophy*, 36.613 (1939).

Naïve invention of phonetic alphabets is not uncommon. The inventor usually believes that he has made an important discovery. Usually, also, he views this discovery as capable of immediately affecting language—removing language barriers or the like. Thus, Senator Robert L. Owen of Oklahoma invented a 'global alphabet' (78th Congress, 1st Session; Senate Document No. 49, Government Printing Office, 1943). The *New York Times* (July 29, 1943) quotes Senator Owen as follows: 'Through it I can teach any reasonably intelligent man Chinese in two months,' he asserted. 'It is a means by which we can teach the English language to all the world at high speed and negligible cost. It will pay its own way.'

[12] A Russian savant was shocked, in the classical manner described by Jespersen, *Grundfragen der Phonetik*, p. 56 (Leipzig, 1904), at the sight of the transcriptions used in an elementary Russian course for American students, transcriptions which deviate from the conventional orthography, such as /trúpka/ for graphic *trubka*, /sát/ for graphic *sad*, /búdjit/ for graphic *budet*. In his complaint to an administrative officer he alluded at some length to 'the written and spoken language . . . of Turgeniev, Tolstoy and Chekhov', and to the circumstance that one of his schoolmates later became well-known as a poet.

[13] Henry Alford, *The Queen's English* (London, 1864 [1863]); George Washington Moon, *A Defence of the Queen's English* (London, 1863); *The Dean's English* (London, 1864). These books went into several editions, taking the shape of a polemic; see the entries in A. G. Kennedy, *A Bibliography of Writings on the English Language* (New York, 1927). Alford and Moon develop the art of finding 'errors' in English to a point where probably no utterance could escape censure. On Alford, see W. D. Whitney, *Oriental and Linguistic Studies*, 2.166 (New York, 1874).

has demonstrated that the ideational content of these limited Northern vocabularies was a heavy burden for the intellect of a moron. Words like *the, is, have, sleep, drink* and *eat* represent the profundity of primitive Anglo-Saxon thought. Pundits, of whom the revered Walter W. Skeat, Litt.D., LL.D., D.C.L., Ph.D., F.B.A., of the University of Cambridge, is typical, have laboriously traced *Ha* (interj. E.) back to Old Friesic *haha* to denote laughter!) and to German *he;* but it is said that Caligula quite unethically uttered a similar sound when he ordered Pomposo, the philologist, thrown to the lions. In all the northern vocabularies there are no equivalents for such words as *democracy, politics, morals, aesthetics,* and—horror of horrors—*scholarship!* The wolfish pursuit of moronic vocabularies and the ghoulish unearthing of the kennings and pennings of the Northern barbarians diverted young students from the true historical fount of wisdom—the Greek and Roman classics, which fell into the greatest disuse in Western history. There was treachery, alas, among the teachers of classics themselves; for under the leadership of Basil Gildersleeve (educated at Berlin, Bonn, and Göttingen, though a graduate of Princeton), who was appointed Professor of Greek at Hopkins in 1876 and editor of *The American Journal of Philology* in 1880, American classical scholars turned away from the teaching of concepts to the venal study of syntax and word origins. Before long there were no classical scholars in the old sense in America but only philologists, papyri readers, and robbers of tombs. On every front save that of history the triumph of *Kultur* over culture was complete.

The following remarks are briefer, but perhaps diagnostically even more significant:[14]

> The study of language today is not the learning to speak and write or even read: it is a technical subject, excessively dry, largely wrong, and thoroughly repellent. Yet an appreciation of language and its uses may be about as enlightening as any discipline we have. Enlightenment, however, is not a matter of accidence, morphology, and other technical aspects so dear to the German-trained and inspired. We give pretty much the same course in "English" from the grades through a couple of years of college—and yet we insist that we enlighten our students. Truly, we are fatuous as well as conceited!

It is only in recent years that I have learned to observe these secondary and tertiary responses in anything like a systematic manner, and I confess that I cannot explain them—that is, correlate them with anything else. The explanation will doubtless be a matter of psychology and sociology.

[14] S. A. Nock of the Kansas State College of Agriculture and Mechanic Arts, in the Bulletin of the American Association of University Professors, 29.202 (1943).

A Philosophy of Language*

JAMES B. McMILLAN

DURING THE LAST FIFTY YEARS the discipline which we call "linguistic science" has developed a considerable body of knowledge and a trustworthy methodology; likewise the study of aesthetics has made productive use of comparative and historical facts and the findings of relevant sciences. Yet the study of the English language in our schools (which one would naïvely suppose to be based on linguistics and aesthetics as biology is based on chemistry, physics, and genetics) has gone its own way, changing, it is true, but never aligning itself with the kindred disciplines. In fact, a remarkable dichotomy has occurred, with the specialists in language operating almost completely outside the sphere of the teachers and textbook writers in grammar, composition, and rhetoric.

In spite of this anomaly, the kinship of the matters discussed in the various kinds of English language classes suggests that an integrated philosophy of language (grammar, composition, rhetoric) can be formulated; such a formulation is the purpose of this paper. Since it is a philosophy for use and not for ornament, it will be called *a* philosophy, not *the* philosophy. Just as people who want to measure a rug do not argue the fundamental validity of the meter or the foot but agree to use meters or feet and proceed with their measuring, so I propose to state certain basic postulates and proceed to derive from them several useful sequiturs and implications. And just as use of the foot requires the measurer to use feet and inches throughout his job, and to divide feet into inches, not centimeters, so the use of particular postulates requires the writer to limit his derivations to those legitimately entailed by the postulates. The basic premises will not be defended. The dissenter is welcome to reject them and choose others or to choose none at all. Eclecticism is practiced, sometimes knowingly, by many people.

The first premise is the assumption that the job of the student or teacher of grammar, composition, or rhetoric is to make statements about language. The second premise is that we expect such statements to be true, according to the speaker's definition of truth. And the final premise is that there are recognized in this context two kinds of truth: (1) objective truth and (2) subjective truth.

Two factors determine the speaker's choice of one or the other kind of truth: (*a*) the purpose of the speaker and (*b*) the nature of the matter

* Reprinted by permission from *College English*, 9.385–390 (April, 1948).

discussed. If the speaker wishes to make his statements verifiable by other competent observers, he uses objective truth. His statements are thus independent of his personal authority; they stand or fall as they are observationally verified. Being hypotheses, they are subject to revision, and they claim no finality. If, however, the speaker wishes to base his statements on private authority, he uses subjective truth. He validates his asseverations by his personal prestige, eloquence, high motives, conformity to a selected tradition, or superior desk-pounding. Being descriptive of his private attitudes, such statements pertain in whole or in part to the speaker's interior bodily activities and to his history, not to the subjects mentioned in his sentences.

But a desire for objectivity does not alone make statements objective. The data discussed must have tangible, sensory reality. Only matters which can be quantitatively measured or described in physical terms can be the subject of objectively true statements. Metaphysics is thus ruled out, as is poetry,[1] theology, and ethics.

Now back to the grammarian. If he proposes to write literature, if to him grammar is a species of poetry or fiction, he is welcome to utilize subjective statements. There is no law against it. But he should be fair to his readers and announce that he depends for truth primarily on his private impulses. He is not operating within a learned discipline, and he should no more condescend to debate his assertions than should a poet or a prophet. In the very nature of his activity he can do nothing but assert his views and reinforce them by some sort of external authority. The reader cannot test the validity of a subjective statement; he can only test his willingness to be bound by the authority of the speaker or the extent of his accidental agreement with the speaker. This condition is true in grammar no less than in aesthetics.

If we make the arbitrary assumption that the grammarian wants to use objective truth wherever he can, we turn to his data to find when and where he can be a scientist. We discover that the facts pertaining to language fall into two groups, one made up of measurable data, and the other made up of imponderables. The first we shall call "grammar"; it can be a science. The second we shall call "rhetoric"; limited by present knowledge, it is an art. This division is not arbitrary; it is made automatically by the objectivity or subjectivity of the relevant data. The division does not bind the grammarian who does not desire objectivity.

The province of the grammarian qua scientist is twofold, because the facts with which he operates fall into two categories: (1) linguistic and (2) sociological. The linguistic facts concern the phonology, morphology, syntax, and lexicon of the language. The sociological facts concern the at-

---

[1] This does not mean that literature is all lies; it means that the writer of literature, in order to discuss some subjects, may go beyond the bounds of sensible reality, giving up objective verifiability but counting it no loss.

titudes toward locutions held by people in various societal situations. Each
of these two categories has two subdivisions: (a) present-day facts and
(b) historical facts.

Linguistic facts are statements severely limited to description of the
forms of the language and are derived from actual observation of speech
and writing. The objective of the grammarian qua linguist in this subprov-
ince is the objective of any scientist: the collection, classification, and
analysis of all relevant data and the formulation of "laws" (descriptive
hypotheses). His goal is "understanding" language. Sociological facts concern the folklore of language, the beliefs of people about specific words
and constructions. Such facts are usually records of the situations in which
certain locutions are disfavored and the situations in which locutions are
used without disfavor. The objective of the scientific grammarian in this
field is to label language forms according to their usage and so to provide
a useful information service which helps citizens "win friends and influence people" by using the "right" locutions.

If the grammarian as student of the language proposes to state what
should be rather than what *is* in the language, he leaves the confines of
objective verifiable truth; this course is perfectly all right, provided he
knows that he is making unverifiable statements. If the grammarian as student of language etiquette proposes to define what *should be* called "bad
English" rather than to say what expressions *are actually treated* as "bad
English," he likewise becomes a subjective moralist. Moralizing instead of
describing is, of course, legitimate, but the honest moralizer labels his
statements personal assertions, and he renounces any claim to verifiability.

This insistence that moralizing statements in grammar be clearly recognized as personal assertions is not a pedantic vagary; it is a necessary implication of comparative and historical language study. There is not a
single philologist, living or dead, who has been able to adduce a single
iota of objective factual evidence for saying that *are not* is more legitimately English than *ain't*. Philologists can, however, find evidence that
people in some social contexts punish the user of *ain't*. The reason for such
punishment is nonlinguistic. If the language habits of one group of people
are respected or disliked by other people, the respect or dislike is a matter
of social psychology, not of grammar. In language "whatever is, is right"
simply because there is no discovered source of knowledge about language
except language itself. And, in sociology, that which a group of people consider right is, to that group, right. From his objective study the grammarian knows that there is nothing ambiguous or inefficient about the common
double negative; but, if some people taboo the construction and others
want to emulate those who taboo it, the job of the grammarian is, perforce,
to record the taboo.

The grammarian (linguist) in his function of "understanding" language
as an intellectual discipline records the plain facts that *It's me* and *It's I*

are alternative forms in present-day English, just as *can't* and *cannot* are alternative forms. The grammarian in his function as an Emily Post of language records the treatment accorded *It's me* and *It's I* by various social groups.

Textbook writers are frequently betrayed into confusing linguistic and sociological provinces because the nomenclature of the two fields is the same, because "laws" of etiquette are phrased exactly as are "laws" of language, and because certain social prejudices have been traditionally stated as grammatical laws. For instance, the linguist finds English-speaking people saying *It's me* and *It's I*, but not *It's my*. He proceeds to state the law that the case of a pronoun which is a complement after *is* is nominative or objective, not possessive. He knows that any case can follow *is* which actually follows it, and he states his rule as a description of what he finds. The usage student may find *It's me* taboo in formal written English, along with *It's her*, *It's them*, etc., and may state the generalized rule that the nominative is required after *is*. But his statement applies only to formal written English, and it is a rule only as long as it is true to the observed facts. It is not true of the English language that *is* must be followed by a nominative; it will be true of formal written English only as long as such is the practice, and the law will apply only to the societal situations in which it actually obtains. Formal written English is not the language; it is merely one type of English. Its rules are pertinent only to people studying or writing formal written English; other types of English have their own rules.

It is the duty of the grammarian to announce publicly which of his functions he is performing, just as it is his duty to announce what kind of truth he is using. (The confusion of grammar and language etiquette is epidemic in conventional handbooks, where there is a superstition that analysis of the language has something to do with "speaking and writing correctly.")

The rhetorician has likewise two provinces: (1) the useful art of communication and (2) the fine art of speaking and writing beautifully. Our present ignorance of biosociology makes it impossible for the rhetorician to be a scientist.

In the practical art of communication, the rhetorician can be objective only as far as semantics is a science. In practice most rhetoricians use the lexicographer's common-knowledge and synonymy tests to determine whether an expression serves as an efficient means of communication, and so operate with a good deal of practical objectivity. (This statement does not apply to the grammarians and rhetoricians who talk about the "essential" meaning of a word; they are moralists.) In this field the rhetorician may choose to use the statements of the grammarian, but he is not a grammarian, because he does not deal solely with language forms.

In the fine art of composition the rhetorician is an aesthetician and is thus obliged to set up and use aesthetic standards. Such standards are necessarily at bottom subjective, as the history of aesthetics so insistently shows. The rhetorician *may* hold as one of his tenets that artistic composition must be in idiomatic English, and he may therefore make use of grammar; he *may* hold that in certain contexts the language of certain social groups is desirable, and in such cases may use the statements of usage students; he *may* be concerned with efficiency of communication as a factor in art and, if so, may make use of the statements of practical rhetoric. But, in addition, the rhetorician legitimately talks about the desirability or undesirability of words and constructions without being concerned with idiom, usage, or denotation. For example, he may prefer the word *carmine* to the word *red* in a particular sentence because his taste dictates *carmine*. No objective standard for such preferences can be required of the rhetorician, since "beauty" in language is not a simple tangible entity or quality. It may be any quality liked or approved by any person. The presence of beauty cannot be demonstrated; it can only be asserted. Competent aestheticians, like competent critics, poets, spiritualists, and theologians, can be flatly contradicted without suffering any disadvantage.

The important point for our analysis is this: a grammarian who is ostensibly discussing grammar cannot legitimately drag in rhetorical criteria and values. When he sets out to describe objectively the language or the etiquette of the language, he is expected to do just what he proposes; if he covertly slips in aesthetic statements, he misrepresents the facts he is supposed to be presenting. This is no disparagement of rhetoric; I am merely insisting that, because it is by nature subjective, its practitioners should carefully avoid being mistaken for grammarians and that grammarians should carefully leave rhetoric out of grammar.

It is obvious that the textbook and instructor in discussing the English language must at times make evaluative statements. It is useful to recognize two sharply distinct kinds of value: (1) instrumental and (2) terminal. Anything having instrumental value is useful as a means to an end. Anything having terminal value is good as an end in itself. It is not possible to debate questions of value. If a discussion concerns an instrumental value, the disagreement cannot be settled by logical argument but must be settled by getting the requisite information. That is, one simply finds out, by observation, whether the thing actually serves as a means and accomplishes its end. If a discussion concerns a terminal value, there can be no debate because there is no way to settle such a dispute. No objective moot question is raised. What is "bad" to one person (for instance, homely idioms or precious writing) may be "good" to another. Is peppermint or cinnamon a "better" flavor? Since terminal evaluations are descriptive of the speaker's taste, they cannot be debated as if they were objective; they can only be asserted.

When the grammarian is a scientist speaking in his function as an understander of the language, he makes no evaluative statements whatsoever (although he accepts the basic social premise of all the sciences that "understanding" is valuable); he merely describes the language as he finds it. Like any scientist, he is interested in what is, not in what ought to be.

In his function as a student of language etiquette, the grammarian must use evaluations, but he cannot make them. This fact is obscured by the grammarian's habit of using the terms "good" and "bad" in labeling expressions. When one of these adjectives is applied to a language form by a scientific grammarian, it is not in reality an evaluative term; it is a shorthand label meaning something like "This locution is favored (or disfavored) by so-and-so people in such-and-such contexts." When we translate "good English" and "bad English" into these meanings, it is clear that the phrases are not judgments of value, as they appear to be, but are simple descriptive statements. Since they merely record the presence or absence of specific locutions in specific contexts (the existence of taboo or or disfavor being presumed when a popular expression is regularly avoided in a given context), the labels are completely objective and can be verified by anybody who can read or head.

The evaluations used (not made) by the grammarian in this province are made by society. The social groups whose language is considered "right" in certain contexts are selected by nonlinguistic criteria. The avoidance of expressions which are disliked by a "superior" group may be a good-in-itself or it may be a means to an end. The grammarian is not concerned with the basis of the evaluation, since it is not a linguistic matter; he simply uses it, confining himself to facts about the usage. Because professional writers of belles-lettres use words as their stock-in-trade, they have been commonly supposed to have some mysterious genius-knowledge of language, and conformity to their grammatical habits has come to be for some people a terminal value. In the same way, grammarians (rhetoricians) have in the past acquired a spurious reputation of knowing what is "good" in grammar, and people have attached a terminal value to speaking and writing according to certain dogmatic rules. But values in language etiquette are usually instrumental; most people want to talk and write like the socially and economically successful as a means of identifying themselves with the "upper classes." Likewise they want to avoid resemblance to the socially unsuccessful, the "illiterate." Such evaluations are made precisely as are evaluations in dress and manners.

The scientific student of usage is a servant of society. He can describe the usage of any group that interests his audience, or he can describe the usage of all groups; but he cannot arrogate linguistic "superiority" to any particular group.

The rhetorician also deals with evaluations. In the useful art of writing and speaking, communication is assumed to be valuable, and whatever further instrumental values are necessary to effect communication are legitimate. In the fine art of literature, the rhetorician must set up terminal values according to aesthetic criteria, and objective instrumental values may be derived from the terminal values.

It is sufficient for our purposes to note that rhetorical values are proper and legitimate as long as they are labeled rhetorical values. The grammarian cannot be a scientist and assume that an aesthetic "good" is an objective reality pertinent to grammar. Church windows are frequently much admired, but they are not the sole standard for judging residence and museum windows.

If the three basic postulates of this exposition are acceptable and valid, the following conclusions appear to be justifiable:

First, it is possible for the English teacher to hold an integrated, consistent philosophy of grammar and rhetoric which is based on and makes use of the relevant underlying disciplines, and which allows him as much practical objectivity as most of the learned disciplines permit. It seems to be true that most of our colleagues in other fields have renounced authoritarianism and are encouraging students to demand reasons which they can verify instead of dogmas which they must swallow; it is not likely that the English teacher can long claim exemption from this tendency, and it is likely that he will be much happier when he can be as objective as a psychologist or a sociologist.

Second, if the English instructor chooses to use scientific methodology, then he will have to divorce the study and teaching of "correct" usage from the study and teaching of grammar. This means that in usage he must follow the general principles of modern scientific language study. If the study of grammar as an intellectual discipline is to be included in a curriculum (and the curriculum-maker must decide whether it is or not), then the course must be different from what passes for grammar today. Conventional formal grammar, which is an eclectic application of certain rules of Latin grammar to arbitrarily selected segments of English morphology and syntax, must give way to a thorough-going inductive study of the English language. The traditional superstitious identification of the "rules" of English grammar with the "rules" of a mythical "good English" must go.

Third, the present dichotomy between the specialists and the teachers (including the textbook writers) appears to have little excuse for existence and little hope for survival. It cannot be long that English teachers who hold scholarly research in literature in high regard will persist in ignoring scholarly research in language. If the literature teachers were scornful of objectivity generally, then the objective study of language could hardly hope to attract them; but factual knowledge in literary history has become indispensable, and factual knowledge in language must surely become equally indispensable.

Prescriptivism and Linguistics in English Teaching*

ARCHIBALD A. HILL

IN A RECENT ARTICLE in *College English*[1] Morton W. Bloomfield presents a cogent, informed, and admirably good-natured account of the problem involved in teaching English to native speakers of the language, now that linguistic scientists (a notably prickly group of men) have begun to question many traditional attitudes and even to deny vehemently, not always wisely but sometimes certainly with good evidence, some of the things we all learned in the classroom as gospel truth. Professor Bloomfield comes to the conclusion that what is taught in an English class must be some form of wise and moderate prescriptivism, checked by the limits of fact as established by linguistics. The reason for his position is that the teaching of English involves questions of value, which characteristically are not settled merely by the accumulation of facts.

It is probably natural that Bloomfield, as a man primarily interested in the discipline of English, though aware of linguistics, should lean in the direction of value, just as it is natural that a linguist, even though he be a practicing teacher of English, should lean in the direction of fact. I do not wish to question Bloomfield's central thesis or to add fuel to an already unfortunate blaze. Rather it seems to me possible, if a linguist states some modifications of what Bloomfield seems to believe the linguists' position to be, that the area of mutual understanding may be increased, with benefit to all.

Bloomfield defends prescriptivism first because it has social utility. That is, the public judges, and will continue to judge, our students by the language they use. Therefore, he says, the honest teacher must neither hinder nor hurry change but teach realities; an unwise liberalism will expose students to censure. With this position the majority of responsible linguists would agree. We are to blame for not having made ourselves clear on the point, though my own experience in the failure of serious attempts at explanation leads me to believe that perhaps not all the blame lies with the linguists. No intelligent linguist would think of denying that the use of a given linguistic form will have inevitable social consequences for the user —the position that language patterns are a part of larger patterns of social

* Reprinted by permission from *College English*, 15.395–399 (April, 1954).
[1] October, 1953.

behavior and that each reacts on the other is central to linguistics. In my own classes, as an example of social consequences from language use, I often tell a story told me by an old Charlestonian. She had brought a beau home for family inspection, and her father was proudly displaying his collection of art. "Now this," he said, "is called 'The Broken Pitcher.'"

"Yes," said the young man, "I see the corner's damaged." The suitor was never invited to the house again. The form "pitcher" cannot be ugly in itself—we use it as a perfectly good word. Nor can the confusion of two words, as the result of natural tendencies of change, be a very heinous sin. Millions probably confuse them, just as even more millions confuse *affect* and *effect*. The point, however, is not that it would be easy to defend the young man's misunderstanding. It is rather that the consequences of it were very real for him and presumably unpleasant. The nonlinguist often argues violently that there is something inherently wrong, ugly, or illogical in such a form as "pitcher" and equates any denial of the inherent "wrongness" of the form with a denial of the social consequences of using it.

The linguist maintains merely that in itself a form, say *golpet*, is as good as another form, say *thaltep;* the difference between them is merely one of attitudes, not of inherent qualities. I have chosen nonsense illustrations deliberately, in an effort to find forms to which the reader has not already learned to respond with conditioned attitudes of value. It seems to me that a linguist is performing a service in attempting to separate such conditioned value reactions from the inherent qualities of the stimulus and that we have a right to complain when our attempts to do so are received as further illustrations of the blindness of men who are supposed to believe that "anything goes."

Bloomfield's second reason for teaching a prescriptive grammar and usage is that it is an aid in understanding the past. Again a linguist cannot quarrel, at least with the aim. Yet it is to be doubted whether prescriptive grammar is always conservative. For instance, one of Bloomfield's examples of vulgate (the language of the majority) which he would rightly resist in classroom use is "I ain't got no dough." Two of the three objectionable forms in this sentence, *ain't* and the double negative, are older than the prescriptivist objection to them and are therefore more in line with past usage than are the modern condemnations. A linguist would hope to accomplish Bloomfield's aim of understanding past language structures not by reliance on prescriptivism but by knowing the structures of the present, with adequate recognition of the fact that different forms and structures are in use in the English-speaking community, in different places, on different social levels, and for different purposes. With such a background a student would, we hope, be ready to deal with the language of the past not as a primitive jargon less perfect than his own speech but as a structure to be respected and understood—a structure different from others, as all language structures are, and, by virtue of difference, capable of artistic effects as good as any open to Hemingway or Housman.

Bloomfield's third and fourth reasons for rejecting vulgate in favor of a prescriptive norm are that vulgate is deficient in all artistic qualities except vigor and is likewise deficient in intellectual breadth and depth. The two statements are closely related and should be discussed together. In a measure, a linguist can agree. If we listen to talk heard on street corners or in grocery stores, it is true that we hear little that is memorable for beauty or intellectual penetration. Language use is an art, and all can agree that great practitioners of any art are few in number. Similarly it is a truism that intellectual leaders are anything but numerous—otherwise they would not be leaders. Yet many linguists would feel that, when Bloomfield says that vulgate is deficient in beauty and intellectual qualities, he is confusing the language with its use. We can agree with him heartily that good models of language use should be given to our students, but we would maintain that the nature of an instrument is different from its employment.

Language structure, with which linguists are primarily concerned, remains relatively constant, and in all important ways is shared by all members of the community, both those who use the language well and those who use it ill. For instance, though it is not universally agreed to by all linguists, many would now say that English has four degrees of stress. If so, this is an example of an important structural feature shared by normal English contemporary speech on all levels and in all localities. Even if we grant that such structural characteristics can only be created by the habitual usage of the community and are further changed only as these habits change, the striking fact about such structural features is how slowly and how little they change. If English has four stresses, it has acquired the fourth at some time since the Norman Conquest; otherwise the stress system has apparently remained unchanged for approximately two thousand years. If there should be only three significant stresses in Modern English, there has been no change at all. If such structural features can remain so little changed in the face of all the social upheavals and linguistic rivalries of two millenniums, it would seem that we should not worry too much over such details as where a student stresses a word like *justifiable*. At most the choice can affect the student and this particular word; the system of stress distinctions will remain the same. It should be emphasized that structure in language is something more, and more important, than a collection of items. A change in the number or type of stress distinctions would be vastly more important (for good or ill) than the introduction or the loss of vocabulary items. I am aware, for instance, that confusion of *disinterested* and *uninterested* destroys a useful vocabulary item and one which I would have been glad to see preserved, even though nowadays I cannot talk of "disinterested judges" for fear of being misunderstood. But, though vocabulary items can be lost, others can be gained, and somehow we manage to carry on our necessary business with the vocabulary we have at any one time. Therefore, it seems to me that we need not fear that the whole of our language will be damaged by those who would say "bored, disinterested judges." For the individual and the community, structure is a broad, pervasive pattern, already determined, and capable of very little change. As such it is relatively neutral and colorless. Indeed, in large measure, it is something which escapes the user's conscious attention. The use he makes of his structure and the items within it is something different. Language use is important to the individual; he is highly conscious of it and rightly seeks advice and help in improving it.

For the reasons which I have tried to outline, when Bloomfield goes on to say that to accept the use made of our language by the majority would be to destroy the beauties of the language itself, I think it is necessary to disagree. He is here assuming that poor use is essentially the same thing as poor structure. I should rather say that the use of language is an area in which value judgments must indeed be made, and is an area in which English teachers should increase both their vigilance and their research, but that structure is different and is not subject to the same kind of criticism we would bring to bear in order to evaluate a paragraph by Winston Churchill or a sonnet by Shelley. Bloomfield goes so far as to say that one who does not recognize the beauty of "Forever wilt thou love and she be fair" is unfit to teach English. But the example belongs to art and is beautiful because it is a part of a literary work the totality of whose beauty we all admire. It is difficult to argue that the forms contained in the line—considered either as separate items or as a special dialect—are in themselves any better or more beautiful than the forms of vulgate. For instance, if *wilt* is more beautiful than *will*, does that lead us to the conclusion that the sequence *-lt* is beautiful, so that *kilt* is better than *killed?* Or if a dialect employing a distinction between singular and plural in second-person pronouns is better and more logical than one which does not, are we to defend the metropolitan low-class distinction between *you* singular, and *youse* plural? I wish, however, to be as clear as possible and therefore to say as emphatically as I can that I agree that anyone who cannot appreciate the beauty of the Keats poem is unfit to teach English. And I should add further that, if there is any student who has drawn from linguistics the idea that the poem is in a strange and inferior dialect because its vocabulary and forms differ from contemporary everyday usage, he holds a horrifying and absurd conclusion. If linguistics leads to such beliefs, it earns nothing but opposition. May I hope, however, should any student of literature be led into the equally horrifying and absurd idea that the dialect employed by Keats is better than vulgate in all social and even in all artistic situations, that Bloomfield would join me in giving such a fallacious conclusion as vigorous opposition as I am sure he would give the other?

Much the same sort of objection applies to Bloomfield's fear that too much liberalism would destroy intellectual activity. It is usual in our culture to write about intellectual matters in a very formal kind of English, which it is all too easy to identify with the intellectual activity itself. The same thing is true of other cultures, yet elsewhere in the world the disappearance or replacement of a special intellectual language or dialect has not meant the disappearance of intellectual activity. Such replacements have almost always been by the form of language originally regarded as an unintellectual vulgate. Yet, when the replacement takes place, the old vulgate quickly becomes the new intellectual language. For instance, no one would maintain that the body of intellectual writing in the vernacular tongues is inferior to that in Latin or that intellectual vigor has been circumscribed by the disuse of the scholar's language. For once, therefore, I think I am safe in denying one of Bloomfield's theses. If, by vulgate, Bloomfield means the language structure used by the majority, then I should oppose him with this statement: Good style, whether artistic or intellectual, is possible in any language structure. Mark Twain, in *Huckleberry Finn*, employed the vulgate structure of rural America in his day, yet Huck's descriptions of a village funeral and of a backwoods front parlor are among the classics of our literature. It seems to me that as teachers of English, whether with or without linguistic training, we should strive for clarity. If we assume that style and structure need no differentiation, we are in danger of obscuring both.

I have tried to equal Bloomfield's urbanity and his grasp of first things first. I may have failed, but I hope I may permit myself to believe that he as English teacher, I as linguist, might agree that all who teach the native language have a solemn duty in understanding language, its structure, its social implications, and the use, beautiful or otherwise, which men have put it to. Further, since literature is necessarily a part of language, all that a linguist can discover about his subject should not merely limit what the English teacher can say but is of positive though potential value to him in all his work.

Cultural Levels
and Functional Varieties of English*

JOHN S. KENYON

THE WORD *level*, when used to indicate different styles of language, is a metaphor, suggesting higher or lower position and, like the terms *higher* and *lower*, figuratively implies 'better' or 'worse,' 'more desirable' or 'less desirable,' and similar comparative degrees of excellence or inferiority in language.

The application of the term *level* to those different styles of language that are not properly distinguished as better or worse, desirable or undesirable, creates a false impression. I confess myself guilty of this error along with some other writers. What are frequently grouped together in one class as different levels of language are often in reality false combinations of two distinct and incommensurable categories, namely, *cultural levels* and *functional varieties*.

Among *cultural levels* may be included, on the lower levels, illiterate speech, narrowly local dialect, ungrammatical speech and writing, excessive and unskilful slang, slovenly and careless vocabulary and construction, exceptional pronunciation, and, on the higher level, language used generally by the cultivated, clear, grammatical writing, and pronunciations used by the cultivated over wide areas. The different cultural levels may be summarized in the two general classes *substandard* and *standard*.

Among *functional varieties* not depending on cultural levels may be mentioned colloquial language, itself existing in different degrees of familiarity or formality, as, for example, familiar conversation, private correspondence, formal conversation, familiar public address; formal platform or pulpit speech, public reading, public worship; legal, scientific, and other expository writing; prose and poetic belles-lettres. The different functional varieties may roughly be grouped together in the two classes *familiar* and *formal* writing or speaking.

The term *level*, then, does not properly belong at all to functional varieties of speech—colloquial, familiar, formal, scientific, literary language. They are equally "good" for their respective functions, and as classifications do not depend on the cultural status of the users.

* This paper was read before the College English Group of Northeastern Ohio (Modern Language Association) at its annual meeting at Oberlin College, October 25, 1947. Reprinted by permission from *College English*, 10.31–36 (October, 1948).

The two groupings *cultural levels* and *functional varieties* are not mutually exclusive categories. They are based on entirely separate principles of classification: *culture* and *function*. Although we are here principally concerned with the functional varieties of standard English (the highest cultural level), yet substandard English likewise has its functional varieties for its different occasions and purposes. Thus the functional variety colloquial English may occur on a substandard cultural level, but the term *colloquial* does not itself indicate a cultural level. So the functional variety formal writing or speaking may occur on a lower or on a higher cultural level according to the social status of writer or speaker, and sometimes of reader or audience. It follows, for instance, that the colloquial language of cultivated people is on a higher cultural level than the formal speech of the semiliterate or than some inept literary writing.

Semiliterate formal speech is sometimes heard from radio speakers. I recently heard one such speaker solemnly announce, "Sun day will be Mother's Day." Because the speaker, in his ignorance of good English, thought he was making himself plainer by using the distorted pronunciation *sun day* instead of the standard pronunciation *sundy*, he actually was misunderstood by some listeners to be saying, "Some day will be Mother's Day." About forty years ago the great English phonetician Henry Sweet used this very example to show that "we cannot make words more distinct by disguising them."[1] He was referring to the use, in this instance, of the full sound of vowels in unaccented syllables where standard English has obscure vowels. On the same page Sweet gives another example of the same blunder: "Thus in the sentence *I shall be at home from one to three* the substitution of **tuw** for **tə** [ə=the last sound in *sofa*] at once suggests a confusion between the preposition and the numeral." This was also verified on the radio. Not long ago I heard a radio speaker announce carefully, "This program will be heard again tomorrow from one two three." I have also recorded (among many others) the following such substandard forms from the radio: *presidEnt* for the standard form *presidənt*, the days of the week ending in the full word *day* instead of the standard English syllable *-dy*, *ay man*, for the correct *man*, *cahnsider* for *cənsider*, *tooday* for *təday*, *too go* for *tə go*, *Coalumbia* for *Cəlumbia*, etc. This is merely one sort among many of substandard features in the formal speech of the semiliterate.[2]

To begin my strictures at home, in *American Pronunciation* (9th ed., 4th printing, p. 17), I use the page heading "Levels of Speech." This should be "Functional Varieties of Standard Speech," for the reference is solely to the different uses of speech on the one cultivated level. Similarly, in the Kenyon-Knott *Pronouncing Dictionary of American English* (p. xvi, §2), I carelessly speak of "levels of the colloquial" where I mean "styles of the

---

[1] Henry Sweet, *The Sounds of English* (Oxford, 1910), p. 78.
[2] See further *American Speech*, VI, No. 5 (June, 1931), 368–72.

colloquial," as three lines above. For though there are different cultural levels of colloquial English, the reference here is only to standard colloquial.

S. A. Leonard and H. Y. Moffett, in their study, "Current Definition of Levels in English Usage,"[3] say (p. 348): "The levels of English usage have been most clearly described in Dr. Murray's Preface ["General Explanations," p. xvii] to the *New English Dictionary*. I have varied his diagram a little in order to illustrate better the overlapping between the categories." It appears to me that Leonard and Moffett have so varied the diagram as to obscure Murray's intention. For he is not here primarily exhibiting levels of speech but is showing the 'Anglicity,' or limits of the English vocabulary for the purposes of his dictionary.[4] The only topical divisions of his diagram that imply a cultural level are "slang" and "dialectal," and the only statement in his explanation of the diagram that could imply it is, "Slang words ascend through colloquial use." This may imply that slang is on a lower cultural level than "colloquial, literary, technical, scientific, foreign." We may also safely infer that Murray would place "Dialectal" on a lower level than colloquial and literary if he were here concerned with cultural levels. Murray's diagram rests consistently on the same basis of classification throughout ('Anglicity'), and he emphasizes that "there is absolutely no defining line in any direction [from the central nucleus of colloquial and literary]." Moreover, Murray's exposition here concerns only vocabulary, with no consideration of the other features that enter so largely into "levels" of language—grammatical form and structure, pronunciation, spelling, and meaning—of styles, in short, only so far as they are affected by vocabulary. These he treats of elsewhere but without reference to levels.

It is not quite clear just how far Leonard and Moffett intend their grouping "literary English," "standard, cultivated, colloquial English," and "naif, popular, or uncultivated English" to be identical with what they call Murray's "levels," his description of which they commend. But it is clear that they call their own grouping "three levels of usage" (p. 357) and classify them together as a single descending scale (cf. "the low end of the scale," p. 358). The inevitable impression that the average reader receives from such an arrangement of the scale is: Highest level, literary English; next lower level, colloquial English; lowest level, illiterate English; whereas, in fact, the first two "levels" are functional varieties of the one cultural level standard English, while the third ("illiterate or uncultivated," p. 358) is a cultural level.

Krapp has a chapter on "The Levels of English Speech,"[5] in which he

---

[3] *English Journal*, XVI, No. 5 (May, 1927), 345–59.

[4] The word *Anglicity* is a coinage of the *Oxford Dictionary*. They define it as 'English quality, as of speech or style; English idiom.'

[5] George Philip Krapp, *The Knowledge of English* (New York, 1927), pp. 55–76.

reveals some awareness of the confusion of cultural levels with functional varieties. He says:

> Among those who pay any heed at all to convention in social relationships, a difference of degree is implicit in all use of English. This difference of degree is usually thought of in terms of higher and lower, of upper levels of speech appropriate to certain occasions of more formal character, of lower levels existing, if not necessarily appropriate, among less elevated circumstances. These popular distinctions of level may be accepted without weighting them too heavily with significance in respect of good, better, and best in speech. A disputatious person might very well raise the question whether literary English, ordinarily regarded as being on a high level, is really any better than the spoken word, is really as good as the spoken word, warm with the breath of the living moment.

At the risk of having to own the hard impeachment of being disputatious, I must express the fear that the logical fallacy in treating of levels, which Krapp rather lightly waves aside, is having a serious effect on general ideas of speech levels, and especially of the significance of colloquial English in good usage. Krapp's grouping, frankly on a scale of "levels" throughout, constitutes a descending scale from the highest, "Literary English," through "Formal Colloquial," "General Colloquial," "Popular English," to the lowest, "Vulgar English." Here the fallacy is obvious: Literary English, Formal Colloquial, and General Colloquial are not cultural levels but only functional varieties of English all on the one cultural level of standard English. The last two, Popular English and Vulgar English, belong in a different order of classification, cultural levels, without regard to function.

So in his succeeding discussion *level* sometimes means the one, sometimes the other; now a functional variety of standard English, and now a cultural level of substandard or of standard English. It is functional on page 58 ("a choice between two levels") and on page 60 ("level of general colloquial"), cultural on page 62 ("popular level" and "cultivated level") and on pages 63–64 ("popular level," "level of popular speech"), functional on page 64 ("general colloquial level"), cultural again on the same page ("popular level," "still lower level"), cultural on page 67 ("vulgar . . . level of speech," "applying the term 'vulgar' to it at certain levels"), cultural on page 68 ("its own [popular] level"), cultural and functional in the same phrase on page 68 ("speakers from the popular and the general colloquial level meet and mix"), and so on most confusingly to page 75.

The same kind of mixture of cultural levels and functional varieties is thrown into one apparently continuous scale by Kennedy: "There is the formal and dignified language of the scholarly or scientific address or paper. . . . The precision and stateliness of this uppermost level . . . is a necessary accompaniment of thinking on a high plane."[6] Next in order he mentions colloquial speech, which he refers to as "the second level, . . .

---

[6] Arthur G. Kennedy, *Current English* (Boston, 1935), pp. 15–17: "Speech Levels."

generally acceptable to people of education and refinement." Clearly this is not a cultural level but a functional variety of standard English, like the "uppermost level." The third level is, however, a cultural one: "the latest slang," workmen's "technical slang and colloquialisms which other persons cannot comprehend," "grammatical solecisms." "The speech of this third level can fairly be ranked as lower in the social scale." His fourth level is also cultural: "At the bottom of the scale is the lingo, or cant, of criminals, hobos, and others of the lowest social level."

Finally, Kennedy fixes the false mental image of a continuous and logically consistent descent from "the cold and lonely heights of formal and highly specialized scientific and scholarly language" to "the stupid and slovenly level of grammatical abuses and insane slang." In reality there is no cultural descent until we reach his third "level," since "formal and dignified language" and "colloquial speech" are only functional varieties of English on the one cultural level of standard English.

In Perrin's excellent and useful *Index*,[7] under the heading "Levels of Usage," he names "three principal levels": "Formal English (likened to formal dress), "Informal English" (described as "the typical language of an educated person going about his everyday affairs"), and "Vulgate English." From his descriptions it appears clearly that Formal and Informal English are functional varieties of standard English, while Vulgate is a substandard cultural level. A similar classification appears in his table on page 365.

On page 19 Perrin uses level apparently in the sense of functional variety, not of cultural level: "Fundamentally, good English is speaking or writing in the level of English that is appropriate to the particular situation that faces the speaker or writer. It means making a right choice among the levels of usage." His advice, however, involves two choices: (1) choice of a standard cultural level and (2) choice of the appropriate functional variety of that level.

A clear instance of the inconsistent use of the term *level* is found in Robert C. Pooley's *Teaching English Usage* (New York, 1946), chapter iii, "Levels in English Usage." He names five levels: (1) the illiterate level; (2) the homely level; (3) standard English, informal level; (4) standard English, formal level; and (5) the literary level. In (1) and (2) *level* has an altogether different meaning from that in (3), (4), and (5). In the first two *level* plainly means 'cultural level'; in the last three it just as plainly means 'functional variety of standard English,' all three varieties being therefore on the one cultural level of standard English. So *level* in the two groups belongs to different orders of classification. All misunderstanding and wrong implication would be removed from this otherwise excellent treatment of levels if the last three groups were labeled "Standard English Level, Informal Variety"; "Standard English Level, Formal Variety"; and

[7] Porter G. Perrin, *An Index to English* (Chicago, 1939), pp. 364–65.

"Standard English Level, Literary Variety." Pooley's groups contain three cultural levels (illiterate, homely, standard) and three functional varieties of the standard cultural level (informal, formal, literary).

The misapplication to colloquial English of the term *level*, metaphorically appropriate only to cultural gradations, is expecially misleading. We often read of English that is "on the colloquial level." For example, Krapp writes: "*Who do you mean?* . . . has passed into current spoken use and may be accepted on the colloquial level."[8] This implies that colloquial English is on a different cultural level from formal English (literary, scientific, etc.), and a too frequent assumption, owing to this and other misuses of the term *colloquial*, is that its cultural level is below that of formal English. This supposition, tacit or explicit, that colloquial style is inferior to formal or literary style, leads inescapably to the absurd conclusion that, whenever scientists or literary artists turn from their formal writing to familiar conversation with their friends, they thereby degrade themselves to a lower social status.

This misuse of *level* encourages the fallacy frequently met with of contrasting colloquial with standard English, logically as fallacious as contrasting white men with tall men. For instance, Mencken writes: " 'I have no doubt *but* that' . . . seems to be very firmly lodged in colloquial American, and even to have respectable standing in the standard speech."[9] This contrast, not always specifically stated, is often implied. For example, Kennedy writes: "Colloquial English is, properly defined, the language of conversation, and especially of familiar conversation. As such it may approximate the standard speech of the better class of English speakers, or it may drop to the level of the illiterate and careless speaker."[10] *May approximate* should be replaced by *may be on the level of.*

Similarly, on page 440: "Some measure words [are] still used colloquially without any ending in the plural . . . ; but most of these are given the *s* ending in standard English usage." Here *standard* is confused with *formal.*

Kennedy (pp. 534, 616) several times contrasts colloquial English with "standard literary English." This implies that colloquial English is not standard, while literary English is. If he means to contrast standard colloquial with standard literary, well and good; but I fear that most readers would understand the contrast to be of colloquial with standard.[11]

---

[8] *A Comprehensive Guide to Good English* (New York, 1927), p. 641.

[9] H. L. Mencken, *The American Language* (4th ed.; New York, 1936), p. 203.

[10] Kennedy, *op. cit.*, p. 26.

[11] Greenough and Kittredge in *Words and Their Ways in English Speech* (New York, 1909), Chap. VII, only apparently treat literary English as the sole standard form: "What is the origin of standard or literary English?" (p. 80). They use *standard* in a special sense for their particular purpose, calling it "the common property of all but the absolutely illiterate," "the language which all educated users of English speak and write" (therefore including colloquial). For the usual current meaning, see the definitions of *standard* quoted in *American Pronunciation* (6th and subsequent eds.), pp. 14–15.

The term *colloquial* cannot properly designate a substandard cultural level of English. It designates a functional variety—that used chiefly in conversation—and in itself says nothing as to its cultural level, though this discussion, and the dictionary definitions, are chiefly concerned with cultivated colloquial, a functional variety of standard English. When writers of such standing as those I have mentioned slip into expressions that imply lower cultural status of colloquial English, it is not surprising that colloquialisms should not be represented as standard American speech. But the context of the statement indicated that its author was using *colloquialism* in the sense of 'localism.' I could hardly believe how frequent this gross error is, until I heard it from a well-known American broadcaster.[12]

The best dictionaries, at least in their definitions, give no warrant for the various misuses of *colloquial, colloquially, colloquialism, colloquiality.* I urge the reader to study carefully the definitions in the *Oxford English Dictionary* with its many apt examples from standard writers, and in *Webster's New International Dictionary, Second Edition,* with its quotations from George Lyman Kittredge. Kittredge's views on the standing of colloquail English are well known. It is said that somebody once asked him about the meaning of the label "Colloq." in dictionaries. He is reported to have replied, "I myself speak 'colloke' and often write it." I cannot verify the story, but it sounds authentic.

It seems to me inevitable that the frequent grouping of so-called "levels" such as "Literary, Colloquial, Illiterate," and the like, will lead the reader to suppose that just as Illiterate is culturally below Colloquial, so Colloquial is culturally below Literary. While I can scarcely hope that my humble remonstrance will reform all future writing on "levels of English," I believe that writers who confuse the meaning of the term *level* must accept some part of the responsibility for the popular misunderstanding of the true status of colloquial English; for I cannot avoid the belief that the popular idea of colloquial English as something to be looked down upon with disfavor is due in part to the failure of writers on the subject to distinguish between *cultural levels of English* and *functional varieties of standard English.*

[12] Leonard and Moffett also mention the frequency of this blunder (*op. cit.,* p. 351, n. 5).

How Fast Is
Standard English Changing?*

Karl W. Dykema

CHANGE IN LANGUAGE is a fact generally acknowledged, though with different feelings on the part of different groups. The purists accept it with regret as a necessary evil, the iconoclasts with delight as evolutionary progress, and the linguists with perhaps a slightly smug scientific detachment as a phenomenon. But it has to be accepted. And with its acceptance arises a curiosity as to the rate of the change, such queries as whether English changed faster right after the Norman Conquest than before, or whether Standard English is today changing faster than it did, say, fifty years ago. The purpose of this paper is to suggest that even with the wealth of material at our disposal for an examination of contemporary English, we are hardly in a position to make any confident statements about rate of change. Perhaps I should say rather that it is this very wealth of evidence which forces us to hesitate about making any positive assertions. For older stages of the language we are less embarrassed by such overwhelming evidence. In fact, the very paucity of the material often suggests a simplicity which can hardly have existed.

No discussion of change in language can be meaningful unless the signification of the terms *change* and *language* is restricted at the outset. For this brief discussion I shall therefore restrict the term *change* to alterations in form and structure, including, of course, phonology, ignoring as far as possible alterations in meaning. The term *language* I shall use, however, in the broad sense of a group of mutually intelligible dialects. This will prove, I believe, the most useful definition because it corresponds most nearly, I suspect, to what most people understand by the term.

This definition of language, however, immediately confronts us with a paradox. If a language is a complex of dialects, it is not a uniform thing, even though the dialects are mutually intelligible, for the term *dialect* is normally understood as a linguistic pattern which varies from that of the rest of the language. Therefore, in a language consisting of a number of dialects, there will be considerable variety in forms and structures; since no speaker of the language will have familiarity with all its dialectal varieties, each speaker will occasionally be confronted with patterns which differ from his own. These variants he will interpret, with the usual paro-

* Reprinted by permission from *American Speech*, 31.89–95 (May, 1956).

chialism of the linguistically naïve, as later deviations from his own original pattern. The paradox is, therefore, that what may appear to the individual speaker as a neologism may be in the total overview of the language a long-established form. Such variants as *don't* and *doesn't* in the third person singular are considered by speakers of Standard English as the recent innovation and the original contraction respectively, whereas it is probably more nearly the case that *don't* is the older form![1]

This paradox forces us to recognize that any discussion of rate of change in language based on the concept of language as a complex of dialects is futile. Linguistic change cannot be accurately measured except in a single uniform dialect. A hypothetical example should clarify this axiom. The preterit paradigm of *be* has had three developments in English: the survival of the *was-were* singular-plural distinction; the generalization of *was* to the plural; and the generalization of *were* to the singular. The latter two are restricted to nonstandard dialects.[2] This is the situation today. Suppose that a social revolution in 2000 brings the *was-was* dialect to cultural ascendancy, and another such revolution in 2045 replaces it with the *were-were* pattern. The chronology for the standard language is therefore: 1955, *was-were;* 2000, *was-was;* 2045, *were-were*. But the actual dates for generalizations from singular to plural and plural to singular in the nonstandard dialects themselves were many hundreds of years earlier. We would be justified in stating that in the Standard dialect, changes had occurred at forty-five-year intervals. But to extend this statement to the language as a whole would be meaningless because in the language as a whole, all three variants have existed for centuries, and it is now probably impossible to date accurately the introduction of the two regularized paradigms. Linguistic change cannot, then, be accurately measured except in a single uniform dialect.

In such a dialect the changes may be spontaneous or imposed from without. Examples of such changes can most easily be found in the earlier history of a language where we are not confused by an overabundance of evidence. The first Germanic Consonant Shift is, of course, a beautiful illustration of such a spontaneous change, especially striking in its uniformity because there is no documentary evidence extant from the period of the change itself to destroy its symmetry or to demonstrate any influence from outside the Primitive Germanic dialect, except, perhaps, a tenuous substratum hypothesis. An example of an imposed change would be the substitution of the Scandinavian plural personal pronouns for the English

---

[1] The sole *OED* quotation for *doesn't* is from a book published in 1864; the earliest for *don't* in the third singular is 1706; entry for *do,* B, 29. I have found an example of *don't* in the third singular as early as 1697 but none for *doesn't* before 1818; K. W. Dykema, 'An Example of Prescriptive Linguistic Change: "Don't" to "Doesn't," ' *English Journal* XXXVI (1947), 372.

[2] Joseph Wright, *The English Dialect Dictionary* (London, 1898), I, 199, *be,* II, 1. The examples cited by Wright show many other patterns of variation.

ones in Middle English. But already the symmetry begins to disappear because the substitution is gradual, and the Old English dative is said to survive even down to our own day.

It is, of course, quite impossible to find a uniform dialect in any culturally advanced modern society because such a dialect could exist only in a group so isolated that all speakers within it acquired their speech solely from other members of the group. Radio alone is a sufficient source of contamination to confirm this assertion. To be sure, the linguistic geographers find many isolated survivals of items which were presumably once more current in the total language; but these merely confirm the fact of change; they are of little use in determining rate of change because the practice of the present speakers cannot be compared with that of exactly comparable speakers a hundred or two hundred years ago.

We are driven therefore, for comparative purposes, to create a dialect group as a sort of statistical abstraction. That is what Fries did in his *American English Grammar*.[3] In fact, the body of evidence systematically presented there provides, I think, the sole starting point from which future studies of rate of change in Standard English might be made. By this I mean that parallel studies of comparable material made, say, twenty-five and fifty years after Fries's study would provide a genuine basis for determining rate of change. In fact, we probably do have a body of correspondence accumulated during the Second World War which would parallel that used by Fries from the First World War. Perhaps we can precipitate the Third World War in 1968 and assure ourselves of a third body of letters which will round out the material for a neat, tripartite, comparative study.

What Fries did was to create three statistical dialectal abstractions and then fit the real letters which were the raw material of his study into these frameworks. His Standard English dialect has, presumably, no regional limitations, which is perhaps unfortunate, but it does at least form a basis for comparisons—and also for conjectures as to what may have happened to Standard English in the last ten to fifteen years.

The rest of this discussion will be devoted to such conjectures.

The first conjecture is that those who now meet the requirements for Fries's Standard English dialect group are to a considerable extent not the direct cultural descendants of the group which provided the letters which Fries examined. By this I mean, to take the most sensational examples, that many of our present military officers and college teachers come from a social class other than that of the military officers and college teachers of 1917–18. It is these two professional groups which have shown the most remarkable increases over a period of thirty years. The maximum armed forces officer strength in the Second World War was approximately six times that in the First World War, an increase of 500 percent, though

---

[3] Charles Carpenter Fries, *American English Grammar* (New York, 1940).

the total population increased only 43 percent in the slightly longer period from 1920 to 1950. And the total number of college teachers rose from 33,000 in 1920 to 125,000 in 1950, an increase of 275 percent. The increases in clergymen, lawyers, and doctors were much less sensational. The lawyers just barely kept up with the general increase, while the doctors and clergymen lagged behind a bit.[4] Since the birth rate over this thirty-year period was not nearly high enough to provide a sufficient number of children from the professional groups themselves to supply this increase—also, the birth rate in the professional class during this period was notoriously lower than for the total population—it is evident that a considerable proportion of the officers of 1945 and the faculty members of 1950 must have been drawn from Fries's Groups II and III, the ones whose English he calls 'common' and 'vulgar.'

We must next conjecture whether an examination of letters such as Fries carried on, but based this time on letters from officers of 1945 and college teachers of 1950, would give the same results that Fries found or whether there would be significant changes. My guess is that there would be. To be sure, this great new crop of college teachers has been exposed to the normative teaching of a college freshman English course and, presumably, to the prescriptive strictures of college instructors throughout their undergraduate and graduate careers; and according to Fries's criteria, only military officers who were college graduates would be included among those providing Group I letters. But again my guess is that this teaching has had little permanent influence on the class dialect native to these new officers and teachers. There is perhaps some tangible evidence to support this guess in the material used by Fries in his *Structure of English*,[5] but again there is no comparable earlier study. The best evidence is, I suppose, the fairly obvious persisting discrepancy between the prescriptions of the

[4] The statistical basis for the statements in this paragraph will be found in U.S. Bureau of Foreign and Domestic Commerce, *Statistical Abstract of the United States: 1925* (Washington, D.C., 1926), pp. 54, 141, 142; and U.S. Bureau of the Census, *Statistical Abstract of the United States: 1954* (Washington, D.C., 1954), pp. 8, 134, 209, 240. As is usual with statistics, the ones on the pages cited could be manipulated to show somewhat different increases. For instance, in the 1954 *Abstract* there is a figure of 210,349 for total staff in institutions of higher education (p. 134) and a figure of 125,583 for total 'college presidents, professors, and instructors' (p. 209). The 1925 *Abstract* gives no figure for 'staff,' only for 'college presidents and professors,' but adds that the figure 'probably includes some teachers in schools below collegiate rank.' Are we to assume that the presidents and professors were essentially the staff in 1920, or that those who were not teachers were so few or so unimportant as not to be worth counting, or that now the nonteaching personnel (84,766, the difference between 210,349 and 125,583) is so significant that it deserves special mention? However the figures are interpreted, the increase in officers and college teachers appears to be much greater than the increase in total population. It may be argued that figures from the war years are too exceptional to be significant. But figures for the years after the two wars point to the same conclusion: officer strength in 1952 was more than ten times that in 1924 and almost double that in 1918.

[5] Charles Carpenter Fries, *The Structure of English* (New York, 1952).

school grammars of the past 200 years and the recorded practice in the standard literature, so beautifully exemplified, for example, in the enormous *Grammar of English Grammars* of Gould Brown (1851).

Of course, the impact of a different dialectal environment is bound to have some influence on the speech habits of those who are moving from one class to another. The result, we may assume, will be a new dialect combining elements of the speaker's childhood dialect with those of the previously existing standard dialect. This new dialect will be the new standard. This process is, of course, an ancient one, and has been going on wherever there has been class mobility. What I have tried to suggest is that there is statistical evidence which can be interpreted to mean that the process has been more rapid during the last dozen years.

Two other kinds of statistical evidence should be mentioned, though I shall not attempt to develop them. The first is the enormous increase in the volume of printed material, particularly periodicals. House organs, for instance, are now published by thousands of concerns,[6] and all of what is in them has to be written by somebody. The number of persons writing for publication would therefore appear to have increased far more rapidly than the total population.

The second statistical item is the acceleration of mechanization and the consequent increase in supervisory personnel. Spokesmen for industry say, for example, that one job in ten is now a management job. The managerial class has undergone a tremendous expansion. Because it is a well-paid and influential group in our society, its language habits are certainly having an effect on the standard dialect.

I hope I have now succeeded in calling attention to evidence which might well show that Standard English has been changing more rapidly in the past ten years than it did in earlier decades. But I suggest only that the evidence might show this if we had comparable data for those earlier decades. Before I conclude, however, I should like to make this hypothesis even more equivocal by a summary review of some of the difficulties in determining relative speed of linguistic change.

By 'linguistic change' I think we usually mean spontaneous, gradual, unconscious change within a single dialect, the kind of change whose slow steady progress seems to be pretty persuasively documented for the long vowels of Middle English in what is called the Great Vowel Shift. The delimitation of dialects as statistical abstractions will shed little light on changes of this sort. Yet even if some means could be found to examine the spontaneous changes in a uniform, isolated dialect, it is doubtful that any over-all rate of change could be established. Mathematically, there is

---

6 'A 1922 List of Employees' Magazines,' *Printers' Ink*, Jan. 12, Jan. 26, Feb. 9, March 2, 1922, pp. 67–72, 141–45, 149–53, 112–15 respectively, lists a total of only 580 titles; Harold E. Green, 'New Survey Shows Big Gain in House Organs,' *Printers' Ink*, Aug. 22, 1952, pp. 38–42, states that there were in 1952 'more than 6500 . . . publications having a . . . circulation of more than 90,000,000.'

perhaps no difficulty, as an article[7] in *Language* seems to indicate. The difficulty is, as careful mathematicians have pointed out, to determine whether the mathematics is applicable to the data. The basis of glotto-chronology, it seems, is 'the morpheme inventory of a language.' Morphemes are necessarily complexes of phonemes, and for the older stages of any language we are entirely dependent on written evidence for the phonemes of that language. This written evidence is always treacherous, as the transcription of modern English or French makes particularly clear, e.g., the orthographic *s* plural of French or our single spelling of two tenses of the verb *read* which could very well lead an unwary scholar of a thousand years hence to classify it among other verbs with zero tense inflection like *hit* or *cast*.

Spontaneous changes must have their origin in allophonic variation. The voicing of intervocalic *t* in some varieties of American English is a gradual process in which the brief period of voicelessness of the stop is slowly reduced still further as the vowels engulf the *t*. No system of spelling attempts to show this allophonic change. It is not until the writer classifies the variant as a *d* that that change will be reflected in the spelling, and even then only if the writer is shaky in his control of the scribal tradition—that is, a bad speller. Fortunately for historical linguistics, there were a good many bad spellers in the past.

Perhaps more bad spellers are getting into print today. At any rate, writers on linguistic matters are still using spelling as evidence of linguistic change, as witness the principal article in a 1955 issue of *Word Study*[8] in which the author uses spellings as evidence that the dental suffix of past participles is disappearing when these forms are used before a noun. His demonstration is entirely unconvincing for a variety of reasons, but especially because he presents no comparable data for an earlier period. He does, perhaps, demonstrate that proofreading is becoming more careless.[9] But since the loss of virtually all the dental suffixes he cites is obviously the result of assimilation under the influence of a following consonant of a type probably long current in speech, the present corroboration of the phenomenon in the naïve spellings proves only that the spellers have never been fully enslaved by the spelling tradition; it proves nothing as to the time such assimilations first became current.

There are many other difficulties in the way of establishing relative rates of linguistic change for past periods of a language. But for the Standard English of the United States during the past ten to fifteen years, I think we might cautiously assert that there has been some increase in rate of

---

[7] Robert B. Lees, 'The Basis of Glottochronology,' *Language*, XXIX (1953), 113–27.

[8] Ralph H. Lane, 'Passing Participles,' *Word Study*, February, 1955, pp. 1–3.

[9] In a single issue of the *Saturday Review*, March 20, 1954, *flaunted* is *flounted* [perhaps a solution of the *flaunt-flout* problem], in a letter from John R. Tunis, p. 25; and *pronunciation* is *pronounciation*, in a review of a dictionary, p. 38.

change provided we restrict the term *Standard English* to the kind of statistical abstraction which Fries created and understand by 'change' only alterations in the form and structure of that restricted dialect. This is, I fear, a rather too obvious statement on the one hand, and a rather meaningless one on the other. I hope, however, that there may be some value in suggesting that the only kind of change in language whose rate we can hope to determine accurately is that which occurs in such statistical abstractions as the one we call the standard language.[10]

A Note on the
Change of American English /t/*

W. P. LEHMANN

A CHANGE IN THE pronunciation of the allophones of /t/ in voiced surroundings has been noted in many recent descriptions of American English. John S. Kenyon, for example, says: 'In American English *t* is often voiced between voiced sounds, as in *better* [bɛtɚ·], *battle* [bætl]';[1] Victor A. Oswald, Jr., gives a detailed report on earlier publications in his article ' "Voiced *t*"—a Misnomer,' before presenting the results of his own investigations.[2] Apart from its importance for the development of American English, this phenomenon is of considerable interest because it is one of the first sound changes that is being observed and documented by linguists in its successive stages. Historical linguists who attempt to describe the course of earlier sound changes are forced to rely on random bits of evidence, such as misspellings, or the occasional observations of grammarians. A fully documented account of the change of American English /t/ would accordingly be of great value in further linguistic study. It is the purpose of this note to deal with the current situation among some speakers of American English, and to suggest that further documentation should now be undertaken.

Accounts other than Oswald's, describing the status of American English /t/ in voiced, unstressed surroundings, usually state that it is kept distinct from /d/ in some manner: by being shorter, or tenser, or through the

---

[10] This article in slightly different form was read before the Linguistics Section of the Eighth University of Kentucky Foreign Language Conference, Lexington, April 29, 1955.

* Reprinted by permission from *American Speech*, 28.270–275 (December, 1953).

[1] John S. Kenyon, *American Pronunciation* (8th ed.; Ann Arbor, Mich., 1940), p. 122.

[2] Victor A. Oswald, Jr., ' "Voiced *t*"—a Misnomer,' *American Speech*, XVIII (1943), 18–25.

greater duration of the preceding vowel. In this way Kenyon goes on with his description: 'Yet voiced *t* is not the same as *d;* and does not belong to the *d* phoneme, since Americans do not confuse such words as *latter* [lætɚ] —*ladder* [lædɚ], or *putting* [pʊt̬ɪŋ]—*pudding* [pʊdɪŋ]. It never occurs at the beginning or end of a phrase, nor at the beginning of an accented syllable. For example, it may be voiced in the word *at* in [nɑt ət ˈɔl], but not in [nɑt ə ˈtɔl].'[3] He continues with a more detailed discussion,[4] but for the sake of conciseness the phrase 'in voiced, unstressed surroundings' will be taken here as an adequate description of the environment of the changed allophones, as will 'voiced *t*' for the result of the shift. We may note already at this point from Kenyon's *not at all* example that a variation between [t] and [t̬] exists for some speakers in the same segmental environment when there is a variation in stress and syllable division. Another American phonetician, Heffner, describes voiced *t* on the basis of his experimental findings in his article 'An Adjunct to the Graphic Method':

> The phonograph record of *butter* in this case would probably give most observers the impression of a *voiced t;* what really happened is that the opening of the cords at the occlusion of *t* has been so quickly followed by the closure of the glottis for the final syllable that the 'residual vibrations' of the vocal bands occupy the very short interval taken up by the occlusion *t* as here pronounced. Whether or not this is the explanation of the 'voiced *t*' observed in the speech of many Americans I do not care to say.[5]

In his book, *General Phonetics*, Heffner gives a longer summary of his findings, which is possibly the most complete description of voiced *t* in relation to *t, d,* and other American English stops.[6]

The stage of development presented in these discussions accordingly shows a decrease in phonetic distinctiveness between some allophones of /t/ and /d/, a situation that may be the first step of a sound change. In a further stage of development the phonetic distinctiveness may decrease to such a point that speakers no longer distinguish between some allophones of the phoneme undergoing change and allophones of the phoneme with which they may be merging; at this stage of development the change is no longer merely phonetic, but has affected the phonemic system of the language. This is the stage described by Oswald in his article in *American Speech;* the speakers whose usage he investigated did not distinguish consistently between words like *bleating* and *bleeding* in sentences permitting

[3] Kenyon, *op. cit.*, p. 122.

[4] *Ibid.*, pp. 232–33.

[5] R.-M. S. Heffner, 'An Adjunct to the Graphic Method,' *American Speech*, XVI (1941), 37–38.

[6] R.-M. S. Heffner, *General Phonetics* (Madison, Wis., 1949), pp. 129–30. Allan F. Hubbell, *The Pronunciation of English in New York City* (New York, 1950), presents in great detail the relation of /t/ and /d/ in a circumscribed area of American speech and notes environments in which allophones, historically of the /t/ phoneme, have coalesced with the /d/ phoneme in some speakers; see especially pp. 23–24.

the use of either, as 'The injured lamb was ——.' On the basis of his experiment, Oswald concluded that the dental stop in voiced poststressed surroundings 'is a combinatory variant of both "t" and "d" '; whether or not we agree with this statement, his findings imply that a phonemic shift has taken place in this environment. Other scholars have published statements implying that the change has reached a phonemic level, as did Carroll E. Reed, who says of Washington speech: 'The medial consonant of words like *writing, waiter, water*, etc., may be pronounced as a [d] or a 'flapped *r*'.[7] Observations of some speakers, different from those Oswald made, suggest that they have passed beyond this step to a further stage of a sound change, a stage in which speakers confuse the phenomena even in other environments.

This further stage of a sound change may be marked by the use of analogical forms which indicate that the phoneme undergoing change is being grouped with another. If, for example, sound *x* is becoming more like *y* in some surroundings, speakers who wish to distinguish the two, restoring *x* to its former value (which may have for them a greater prestige), will also change some *y*'s to *x*'s. Americans who have lost the distinction between *due* [dju:] and *do* [du:] as part of the process of losing [-j-] between dental stops and high back vowels may introduce the [-j-] not only in *due* but also in *do* when some motives of elegance prompt them to introduce [j]-forms. This situation is often described in synchronic studies of speakers who attempt to substitute for their dialect a related dialect which has a different allophonic arrangement of its phonemes; it is then commonly referred to as hyperurbanization or hypercorrection, and the forms as hyper-forms. Examples are given in various handbooks.[8] They are usually drawn from attempts of dialect speakers to master the standard languages, as is Jespersen's example of Low German speakers who use *zeller* for *teller* 'plate' because they make a similar change in words like standard German *zahl* for Low German *tal* 'number.' Another well-known example is the use of rounded vowels by speakers of the Saxon dialect in words which have unrounded vowels in the standard language; some of these speakers, in attempting to change their pronunciation of *bühne* 'stage' from one homophonous with *biene* 'bee' may also round the vowel in *biene* and other words with front unrounded vowels in the standard language. Such aberrations indicate that the speakers have no mastery over a part of the allophonic distribution of the phonemes in question, but generally over only a part; the Low German speaker who uses *zeller* for *teller* would not be likely to make this substitution finally, as in *geht* 'goes,' but only in those positions in which *t* of Low German corresponds to *z* of standard German.

[7] Carroll E. Reed, 'The Pronunciation of English in the State of Washington,' *American Speech*, XXVII (1952), 188.

[8] E.g., Otto Jespersen, *Language* (London, 1922), pp. 293–94, and Leonard Bloomfield, *Language* (New York, 1933), p. 330 *et passim*.

Observations of confusion in such patterns have also been applied to diachronic study. One such, which was observed by Gamillscheg in Ladin of
the Rau Valley, is cited by Bloomfield,[9] whose transcriptions are reproduced here. In the Rau dialect of Ladin, Latin [wi-] had become [vi-]
through [u-], as in [vizin], compared with neighboring [užin] from
[wi'ki:num]; Latin [aw'kɛllum] 'bird' also appears in the Rau Valley as
[vičel], although in the neighboring Ladin it is [učel]. The explanation
offered for the aberrant form [vičel] is that speakers of the Rau dialect at
one time were replacing their [u-] with the more urbane Italian [vi-], and
replaced the [u-] from [au-] in [učel] just as they did the [u-] in [užin].
Through observation of speakers' use of hyper-forms in synchronic study
a problem in diachronic linguistics found a solution.

The assumption that such behavior can be expected was also made by
W. F. Twaddell in his article, 'The Inner Chronology of the Germanic
Consonant Shift.'[10] Noting that we have no instances of Germanic voiceless
spirants corresponding to PIE bh, Twaddell concludes that the shift from
bh to Gmc. β must have taken place after the shift of p' to f' to β'; for if the
alternation -f- : -β-' had been present in the language when hh was shifted
to β, Twaddell would have expected speakers to confuse some β from
PIE bh with β resulting from the shift described by Verner's law, and
to substitute for them f, on the pattern '-f-:-β-' ::x:-β-.[11] Otto Springer
also explains aberrant forms as hpyer-forms in his study, 'Pennsylvania
German *OCHDEM* "Atem" and the Problem of Hypercorrect Forms,' and
discusses at some length previous treatments of hyper-forms.[12] It is therefore no novelty in linguistic study to find hyper-forms as sound changes
are taking place. We may expect to find such forms some time after a
sound change has been initiated and before it is concluded, that is, before
the new structural alignment of the phonological system has been fixed.

We may now observe hyper-forms of this type in at least some areas of
American English. Numerous speakers in the central Texas area use a
voiceless [t] for [d], in voiced as well as in voiceless surroundings. Presumably, they have been taught that voiced t should be avoided in words
like *better*, or they have adopted this aim independently; in attempting
to apply this precept they devoice the dental stop also in words like *bidder*,
on the pattern [-t-] : [-t̬-] :: x : [-d-] (bɛtɚ : bɛt̬ɚ :: x : bɪdɚ). Illustrations are cited here from the speech of four speakers, all of whom betray
some tampering with their speech in patterns other than these.[13] An Austin

---

[9] Bloomfield, *op. cit.*, pp. 479–80.

[10] *Journal of English and Germanic Philology*, XXXVIII (1939), 337–59.

[11] It has been necessary to substitute β in this sentence and the preceding for Professor Lehmann's 'crossed b.'—ED.

[12] *Monatshefte für deutschen Unterricht*, XXXV (1943), 138–50.

[13] These and other examples have been observed by me and by Ruth P. Lehmann.
Professor E. Bagby Atwood, upon reading this paper, showed me a number of spellings
he has collected from students at the University of Texas which give graphic evidence
of t substituted for d.

sports announcer used a voiceless stop in *huddle*. A student uses a voiceless stop in *and* (even in *and-a*) when this is a sentence connective. Somewhat different is a public speaker who in an address of twenty minutes used a voiceless *d* in the following words when they were final in the sentence: *child, dead, God, word, world* but maintained a voiced dental in the sequences *called upon* and *hand upon*. This speaker seems to be making a realignment of the allophones of his noninitial poststressed *t* and *d* phonemes, using [t] in final position, [d] in medial, similar to that of Kenyon's *not at all* example.

A clear result of elementary school instruction is the use of voiceless stops in words like *middle* by a six-year-old girl in the first grade who is in process of learning to read. In a song which she was taught in school her pronunciation of *kitty, pretty,* and *ready* give further indication of the confusion of her *t* and *d* phonemes in voiced surroundings; in these three words she pronounced the dental stops as aspirated and voiceless:

> Kitty, my pretty white kitty,
> Why do you wander away?
> I've finished my work and my lessons,
> And now I am ready for play.

Presumably she had been taught to pronounce voiceless stops in *kitty* and *pretty* and since the unwanted stop in these words corresponded in her natural pronunciation to the stop in *ready*, she carefully unvoiced this too.

From these and further observations I conclude that some speakers of American English are beginning to confuse the allophones of their *t* and *d* phonemes when these occur in voiced surroundings in noninitial position. The confusion seems to exist among those speakers who have become aware of their voiced *t* sounds and attempt, or are taught, to restore the voiceless *t;* at present it is only sporadic and possibly temporary, especially among those speakers who are open to counterinstruction. But since some speakers now devoice sounds which are historically *d* sounds, the change of *t* is past the stage when 'Americans do not confuse such words as *latter* . . . *ladder,*' and even beyond the stage in which speakers do not distinguish between the allophones of /t/ and /d/ in voiced, unstressed surroundings. If information were collected about this development in various sections of the American English area as carefully as is that about innovations in vocabulary, it would be of great value to students of American English phonology and of linguistic change in general.

"Anything Goes"*

ROBERT J. GEIST

IT IS UNFORTUNATE, as Harold B. Allen has pointed out,[1] that Mario Pei in his *Story of Language*[2] takes a dim view of the doctrine of usage. Professor Pei seems to object especially to the twice-quoted statement that "language is what people speak, not what someone thinks they ought to speak." In Professor Pei's opinion, furthermore, recognizing that language is what people speak "gives *carte blanche* and free play to all slang, colloquialisms and substandard forms" (p. 409). Professor Allen has justly condemned this charge that advocates of a realistic standard based on usage lack all sense of discrimination. We have standards; and Professor Pei, as an educated and able writer, helps to form such a standard for educated writing. Realistically, his usage is good usage. Yet we know textbooks, tests, and teachers who would take a very dim view of these perfectly normal locutions, which he uses:

> . . . there was equal confusion and fluctuation . . . [p. 133].
>
> In addition to the original Chinese-English pidgin, there is the Melanesian variety . . . ; a variety used in New Guinea; one used by the Blackfellows of Australia; a *beche-la-mar* . . . that appears in Tahiti . . . [p. 302].
>
> [Cf. R. W. Pence, *A Grammar of Present-Day English* (1947), p. 209: "A verb agrees with its subject even when the subject follows the verb." For a more accurate statement see Albert H. Marckwardt, *Scribner's Handbook of English* (2d ed., 1948), p. 221.]
>
> Other writers . . . claim that "a language is . . ." [p. 409].
>
> [Cf. Sanders, Jordan, Limpus, and Magoon, *Unified English Composition* (1945), p. 176:
>
> "Incorrect: I *claim* that he's right. (Use *maintain*.)
>
> "Correct: I *claim* my inheritance. (*Claim* means to demand as due.)" See *The American College Dictionary*.]
>
> The word has gotten crossed . . . [p. 252].
>
> Some . . . have gotten into Brazilian dancing . . . [p. 253].
>
> [Cf. Jefferson, Peckham, and Wilson, *Freshman Rhetoric and Practice Book* (rev. ed., 1928), p. 647: "Gotten: obsolescent for the past participle *got*." See the dictionaries.]
>
> There are no inhibitions, no restraints, no holds barred, provided semantic transfer is accomplished, which it usually is [p. 425].

* Reprinted by permission from *College English*, 12.454–455 (May, 1951).
[1] "All Is Not Gold," *College English*, November, 1950, pp. 106–7.
[2] Philadelphia and New York: J. B. Lippincott Co., 1949.

[Cf. Summers and Patrick, *College Composition* (1946), p. 128: "The pronoun *has* a definite and single antecedent (not a clause or general idea). This antecedent is expressed (not implied) in a noun, another pronoun, a gerund, an infinitive, an noun clause." See *pronoun* in *Webster's New Collegiate*.]

Chinese, on the contrary, has carried the process of functional change farther than English [p. 120].

Other tongues carry the distinction much further [p. 128].

[Cf. Ralph B. Allen, *English Grammar* (1950), p. 142: "*Further* and *farthest* are, however, used only of distance or time that is real." See *The American College Dictionary*.]

The above, let me emphasize, is not intended to disparage Professor Pei's usage, which is good usage. It is not intended to disparage the specific texts cited, all of which are very useful. It is intended to disparage make-believe standards of correctness which do not accurately describe the language of educated persons, either in speaking or in writing.

That an advocate of usage need not give carte blanche even to an educated and able writer is illustrated by this sentence:

Translation of place-names are often curious [p. 68].

Whether Professor Pei or printer is responsible, *translation* is not normally construed as a plural.

Professor Pei's implication that a standard based on usage means "anything goes" would be less irksome if it were less common.[3] We advocates of a usage standard, however, are at least partially responsible for this opposition to a perfect reasonable idea. In opposing eighteenth-century precepts, we frequently lead others to believe that we advocate truck-drivers' English for everyone; we frequently fail to make clear that we advocate no such thing. When I first became acquainted with the idea that language *is*, and is not a mere bundle of prescriptions, the instructor made much of the slogan, "Whatever is, is right." Applying the quotation to language captured my fancy, but, two years later, the slogan did not serve as a useful bridge to the teaching of freshman composition. I too took, if not a dim, at least a perplexed view of the doctrine of usage. A more recent example is the title of Robert Hall's justly praised *Leave Your Language Alone!*[4] Professor Hall makes amply clear that one conforms to standards under social penalty (p. 13); he makes equally clear that he is writing journalistically in opposition to the commercial exploitation of linguistic insecurity (p. 9). Yet the title, which will be read by infinitely more people than will read the book, clearly implies that "anything goes." In summarizing, Professor Hall explains why he used the title:

But to return to our basic point: the message that linguistics has for our society at present is primarily the one that we have used as the title of this book:

---

[3] See, e.g., Kenneth L. Knickerbocker, "The Freshman Is King; or, Who Teaches Who?" *College Composition and Communication*, December, 1950, pp. 11–15.

[4] Ithaca, N.Y.: *Linguistica*, 1950.

LEAVE YOUR LANGUAGE ALONE! We put it this way on purpose, to emphasize that any meddling with our language, by ourselves or others, in the name of "correctness," of spelling, or of nationalism, is harmful [p. 248].

Sound as this passage, even out of context, is, the intelligent and determined purist is certain to object that Professor Hall is slighting the idea of social acceptability and the legitimate attempt to strive for greater clarity, forcefulness, or appeal.

It is impossible, of course, to find absolute lines to separate justifiable improvement of sentences and diction, the illusions most of us have about educated speech, and the pedantry of those who would keep eighteenth-century rules regardless. As we state our objections to pedantry, we should try to avoid overstatements that invite counterobjections.

Doctrines of English Usage*

CHARLES V. HARTUNG

THE TEACHER of English today may often be tempted to envy the teacher of a generation ago, who could turn to Woolley's handbook or its counterpart and find immediately an unqualified rule to answer questions about debatable usage. But the publication of the Leonard survey, *Current English Usage* (1932), ended the age of certainty for the teacher and ushered in the age of anxiety. There had of course been premonitory signs before the Leonard survey, notably in Krapp's *Modern English* (1909) and in Hall's *English Usage* (1917), but there had not been a systematic and thoroughly documented survey of current opinion. The Leonard survey definitely demonstrated the respectable standing of such locutions as *it is me, will you be at the Brown's this evening,* and *who are you looking for.* As a result the revised editions of prescriptive handbooks began to qualify their absolutism, and the English teacher's life became more complicated. Today the conscientious teacher must keep up with the latest developments in linguistic theory, weigh the results of various polls of English usage, and be constantly attentive to the language customs of his local community and of the wider community reflected in newspaper, radio, and television. There is even one school of opinion which holds that the teacher may well learn several versions of his language and use them appropriately to increase his popularity and effectiveness. Donald Lloyd gives clear and vivid expression to this view:

We say "he don't" and "ain't," not because we are stupid and stubborn, but because the people we live with and work with and play with—our closest

* Reprinted by permission from *The English Journal,* 45.517–525 (December, 1956).

friends—say them. We need, not to exclude these forms from our speech, but to learn to use them in alternation with "doesn't" and "isn't" or "aren't" with easy command in exactly the right circumstances. Then they help us make friends wherever we go. Then they enrich our speech; they do not impoverish it.[1]

This passage is extracted from an eloquent plea to banish prescriptivism from the classroom and is representative of the thinking of probably the most active school of linguists in this country today. Moreover, the relativism expressed here has been characterized as the "modern view of grammar and linguistics" and has been presented as the majority opinion of the Commission on the English Curriculum of the National Council of Teachers of English.[2] For those teachers who may not be familiar with the statement of the view in *The English Language Arts* here is a list of the basic concepts which are there attributed to modern linguists and advocated by the committee on language: (1) Language changes constantly; (2) Change is normal and represents not corruption but improvement; (3) Spoken language is the language; (4) Correctness rests upon usage; (5) All usage is relative. In the same place the point of view of the contemporary linguist is summarized as follows:

> 1. Correctness in modern English usage is not determined by appeals to logic, etymology, or the traditions of earlier days. It cannot be determined by rules of "right" and "wrong." It must be established by the needs of communication in every situation in which language is used.
> 2. Since correctness is a relative matter derived from the needs of communication, the teaching of correct English requires the development in pupils of a sensitivity to the requirements of language in all kinds of situations and the gradual development of skill to use English appropriately in each situation.
> 3. The teaching of correctness in school and college courses must shift in emphasis from the laying down of negative rules to the development of positive insights. Instead of teaching rules for the avoidance of error, pupils must be taught to observe and understand the way in which their language operates today for the various needs of communication.[3]

This is evidently the doctrine of the new orthodoxy. It comes with good credentials and presents a program that is in many ways attractive. And it has retained enough of the dogmatism of the old orthodoxy (note the words "must" and "requires") to appeal to those in need of authority. The dogmatism of the quoted passage may be partially explained by its polemical purpose, but a more qualified statement would doubtless be more accurate. Even among the linguistic experts cited as the authority for the new doctrine there is not the unanimity that is claimed; for one may find stu-

---

[1] "Let's Get Rid of Miss Driscoll," *The Educational Forum* (March 1954), p. 344.
[2] *The English Language Arts* (New York: Appleton-Century-Crofts, Inc., 1952), pp. 274–301.
[3] *Ibid.*, pp. 278–279.

dents of language advocating at least four currently respectable points of view from which English usage may be judged. It may serve to clarify the issues if we survey the main points of these four doctrines and make an appraisal of their claims.

Generally speaking, the four main doctrines current among those concerned with judging the propriety of language usage are: (1) the doctrine of rules; (2) the doctrine of general usage; (3) the doctrine of appropriate usage; (4) the doctrine of the linguistic norm. Rarely do those interested in language adhere consistently to any one of those doctrines. Instead there is the usual divergence between theory and practice; some linguists profess one doctrine and practice another. Also there is the usual eclectic compromise. Nevertheless, it is possible to make roughly approximate groupings of schools of opinion according to the degrees of emphasis given to these various doctrines.

THE DOCTRINE OF RULES

From the point of view of the modern school of linguistics the doctrine of rules is, or at least should be, moribund. But even a cursory glance at handbooks and grammars of recent date reveals what a tenacious hold it has on life. And even when the doctrine is disclaimed in theory, we find grammarians following it in spirit and practice. For example, in the preface to R. W. Pence's *A Grammar of Present-Day English,* we find the following statement: "Grammar is not a set of rules thought up by and imposed by some invisible godlike creature."[4] Yet the text itself consists of a set of prescriptions in the spirit of the eighteenth century grammarians and having the effect if not the form of the old rules. Here is an example:

> . . . inasmuch as an interrogative pronoun normally introduces a clause and so may not have the position that a noun of like function would have, the function of an interrogative pronoun may be easily mistaken. Care needs to be exercised to meet the demands of subjective complements of finite verbs and of infinitives. But especial care needs to be taken that the proper objective form is used when an interrogative pronoun coming first functions as the object of a preposition that is delayed.

1. Subjective complement
   Whom do you mean? [*Whom* is the object of *do mean.*]
2. Object of a preposition
   Whom were you with last night? [*Whom* is the object of the preposition *with. Not:* Who were you with last night?][5]

In a note some concession is made to the demands of spoken discourse: "Who are you looking for? [Accepted by some in spoken discourse.]" But

[4] New York: The Macmillan Co., 1947, p. v.
[5] *Ibid.,* pp. 204–205.

in the same note we find this comment: "This use of the nominative in informal spoken discourse is regarded by a few as acceptable, although the fastidious person will probably look upon it as sloppy speech." It is noteworthy that the text in which this judgment is to be found reached its seventh printing in 1953. Yet the sentence *Who are you looking for* is listed as *Accepted* in the Leonard survey printed in 1932.

It would be possible, of course, to multiply examples of the continuing hold that the doctrine of rules still has on a large proportion of present day students of language, but it is more to the point to examine the reasons for this hold. Probably the most important reason is that the doctrine has behind it the weight of over a century and a half of almost undisputed dominance. This is the result of two main sources of authority: the assumed correspondence of the rules of grammar with basic principles of reason and the supposed correspondence of the rules with the usage of the best writers. Some grammarians have assumed that reason has the prior claim and determines usage; others have placed usage first and have claimed that rules are inductively derived from the best usage. The eighteenth century grammarian William Ward gives typical expression to the view of the first group:

> Use and Custom are considered as the only Rules by which to judge of what is right or wrong in Process. But is the Custom which is observed in the Application of any Language the Effect of Chance? Is not such a Custom a consistent Plan of communicating the Conceptions and rational discursive Operations of one Man to another? And who will maintain, that this is, or can be, the Effect of unmeaning Accident? If then it be not so, it must be the Effect of the Reason of Man, adjusting certain means to a certain End: And it is the Business of Speculative or Rational Grammar to explain the Nature of the Means, and to show how they are applied to accomplish the End proposed. If this can be done with sufficient Evidence, the most simple of the Elements of Logic will become familiar to those who engage in a Course of Grammar, and Reason will go Hand in Hand with Practice.[6]

Ward's linking of grammar and logic was a common eighteenth century practice and carried over into the nineteenth century, receiving the approval of even such a great philosopher as John Stuart Mill. Mill says that "the principles and rules of grammar are the means by which forms of language are made to correspond with the universal forms of thought."[7] The weakness of this thesis was, of course, evident to the language experts of Mill's own time. Henry Sweet and A. H. Sayce brought to bear their great knowledge of comparative philology to show how little actual correspond-

[6] William Ward, *English Grammar* (1765). Quoted by C. C. Fries, *The Teaching of English* (Ann Arbor: The George Wahr Publishing Co., 1949), p. 13.
[7] See I. A. Richards, *Interpretation in Teaching* (London: Routledge & Kegan Paul, 1938), p. 280.

ence there is between logic and grammar, and modern linguists and semanticists have agreed with them. Probably the most judicious summation
of the problem is that of Otto Jespersen:

> Most linguists are against any attempt to apply a logical standard to lan-
> guage. Language, they say, is psychology, not logic; or "language is neither
> logical nor illogical, but a-logical." That is to say, language has nothing to do
> with logic. To many philologists the very word, logic, is like a red rag to a
> bull. . . . . It would be surprising however if language which serves to ex-
> press thoughts should be quite independent of the laws of correct thinking.[8]

As Jespersen demonstrates, however, what often has pretended to be
logic is no more than Latin grammar disguised, and arguments declaring
the correspondence of grammar with logic have often been little more
than the forcing of English into Latin syntactical patterns. For example,
the rule that the predicative must stand in the same case as the subject is
not, as has been claimed, an incontrovertible law of thought but merely
a rule of Latin grammar. Many languages of different types violate this
so-called incontrovertible law.

The authority that the rules have derived from deductive logic has never
been equal to the support given them by the belief that rules are inductively derived from examination of the best usage. George Campbell's dictum that reputable, national, and present usage determines correctness
has been cited with approval from the days of Lindley Murray, probably
the most popular of eighteenth century grammarians, to the present day.
Many writers on language have, in fact, cited Campbell's doctrine as liberalizing in effect, but it is difficult to see how such a belief can be accepted.
Campbell so restricted the field of acceptable usage that the doctrine of
rules lost little of the force it had held in the writings of such prescriptive
grammarians as Bishop Lowth and William Ward. Lowth had, of course,
declared the independence of grammar from the usage of even the best
writers, whereas Campbell paid lip service to the doctrine of usage. But
in practice Campbell, as S. A. Leonard has shown, repudiated the very
theory he had set up as a guide. We can see what the doctrine of usage
actually became when we examine the following statement from a latter
day follower of Cambell:

> By good usage is meant the usage generally observed in the writings of the
> best English authors and in the speech of well-educated people. Dictionaries,
> grammars, and books on rhetoric and composition record this usage, on the
> basis of wide observation and study.[9]

This definition follows a pattern dating from the eighteenth century and
repeated in scores of nineteenth century handbooks and grammars. The

---

[8] *Mankind, Nation and the Individual* (London: Geo. Allen, 1946), p. 114.
[9] Edwin C. Woolley, *Handbook of Composition*, Revised Edition (Boston: D. C.
Heath, 1920), p. 1.

doctrine of usage in the hands of the grammarians has been practically identical with the doctrine of rules.

THE DOCTRINE OF GENERAL USAGE

Joseph Priestly, the eighteenth century scientist and grammarian, was probably the first writer in English to show a consistent regard for the doctrine of general usage. But his views were neglected, and it was not until the rise of scientific linguistics in the late nineteenth century that the doctrine began to make headway against the doctrine of rules. Among the pioneers were W. D. Whitney, Fitzedward Hall, and Alexander Bain. The first full-fledged popular exposition and exemplification of the doctrine, J. Lesslie Hall's *English Usage* (1917), was not published until well into the twentieth century. In contrast with most of his predecessors, who only paid lip serve to the doctrine of usage, Hall is consistent and documents his opinion with particular examples. In his article, "Who for Whom," for instance, Hall cites the opinions of contemporary liberal grammarians in favor of *who* as the objective form in questions, and he gives a number of examples from usage, citing Shakespeare, Marlowe, Defoe, Kingsley, and Froude, as well as less well-known writers.

Comprehensive as it is, Hall's work is limited primarily to an examination of written documents, and it was not until Leonard's *Current English Usage* that there was a systematic survey of spoken usage to support Hall's findings. Strictly speaking, the Leonard report is not a survey of the facts of English usage but of opinion about the relative standing of various debatable items. The guiding principle of the survey is indicated succinctly in the statement that "allowable usage is based on the actual practice of cultivated people rather than on rules of syntax or logic."[10] In keeping with this principle, Leonard submitted a number of items of debatable usage to a jury consisting of linguistic specialists, editors, authors, business men, and teachers of English and speech. These judges were to decide the standing of the items according to what they thought the actual usage to be. Four levels of acceptability were indicated: "literary English," "standard, cultivated, colloquial English," "trade or technical English," and "naif, popular, or uncultivated English." The findings of the report provided evidence to demonstrate the discrepancy between actual usage and the rules of the common school grammar. Among the items indicated as *established,* or acceptable on the cultivated colloquial level by more than seventy-five percent of the judges, were *it is me, who are you looking for, I feel badly,* and many other locutions that had long been proscribed by the handbooks and grammars.

The Leonard report was not a survey of "general" usage but of "culti-

[10] Sterling Andrus Leonard, *Current English Usage* (Chicago: The National Council of Teachers of English, 1932), p. 95.

vated" usage. It is not until the research studies of C. C. Fries that we find a truly inclusive and adequately documented study of general usage. Eschewing the guidance of the grammars and even of polls of "educated" usage, Fries stated that "it is probably much more sound to decide that the spontaneous usage of that large group who are carrying on the affairs of English speaking people is the usage to be observed and to set the standard."[11] To provide evidence of actual usage, Fries has used letters and transcripts of telephone conversations. Like other modern advocates of the doctrine of usage, Fries has not held to the theory that the standard of general usage should apply in all language situations. In concession to the demands of effective communication and to the practical problems of the teacher in the classroom he has given assent to the doctrine of appropriateness. The problem of the teacher, according to Fries, is to develop in the student the habits that will enable him to use freely the language appropriate to his ideas, the occasion of their expression, and the needs of his hearers. To bring about this end, the teacher needs to become sensitive to the different levels and functional varieties of usage and to develop a program of study designed to meet the particular needs of each class. Although the teacher must take into account the prevailing demand that he equip his pupils with the language habits that have attained the most social acceptability, he needs to develop also an intelligently liberal attitude toward the particular language habits of any group of students.

THE DOCTRINE OF APPROPRIATENESS

In its essentials the doctrine of appropriateness has not changed since the full exposition by George Philip Krapp in his *Modern English* (1909). Krapp introduces his exposition by making a distinction between "good" English and "conventional" or "standard" English. Good English, according to Krapp, is any language which "hits the mark." Since the purpose of language is the satisfactory communication of thought and feeling, any language which satisfactorily performs this function is good English. Standard English is that usage which is recognized and accepted as customary in any particular community. Such locutions as *he don't* or *these kind of people* or *I will* may be standard in one community and not standard in another. Custom is the only relevant determinant of the standard. Krapp's relativism is evident in the following statement:

> What is defended as customary use by a community, or even by a single speaker, to carry the matter to its final analysis, is standard, or conventional, or "right," or "correct," in that community or for that speaker.[12]

In analyzing the concept of "good" English, Krapp arrives at the doctrine of appropriateness. He describes three tendencies in English speech—

[11] *The Teaching of English*, p. 35.
[12] New York: Charles Scribners' Sons, 1909, p. 332.

"popular English," "colloquial English," and "formal or literary English"
—and declares that each of these has its appropriate uses. They are three
kinds of arrows by which the speaker attempts to hit the mark of good English. Whether the speaker hits the mark or not depends upon his skill and
upon his acumen in sizing up the particular speech situation:

> . . . the degree of colloquialism which one permits, in one's self or in others
> depends on the subject of conversation, on the intimacy of the acquaintance-
> ship of the persons speaking, and in general on all the attendant circumstances
> . . . language which may be adequately expressive, and therefore good, un-
> der one set of circumstances, under a different set of circumstances becomes
> inadequately expressive, because it says more or less than the speaker in-
> tended, and so becomes bad English. One learns thus the lesson of complete
> relativity of the value of language, that there is no such thing as an absolute
> English, but that language is valuable only as it effects the purpose one wishes
> to attain, that what is good at one time may be bad at another, and what is bad
> at one time may be good at another.[13]

This doctrine has been somewhat qualified by some of its recent exponents, particularly by Pooley and Perrin, but it has not been changed in its
essentials. And it is still subject to the same sort of objection that J. Lesslie
Hall made to Krapp's statement of it. Hall pointed out that Krapp's conception of "good" English was unprecedented and varied from the commonly
accepted meaning of the term. He also deprecated Krapp's advocacy of "a
sort of isolated, neighborhood English" and declared that the consistent
carrying out of Krapp's ideas would mean the decline of a *general* and reputable usage for which students of language had been struggling. Consistent application of the doctrine of appropriateness would mean that
every newcomer to a community would need to learn a new set of speech
habits and that every traveler would need to be sensitive to innumerable
local dialects and to cater to the personal language habits of his listeners.
This would finally result in the decline of a general standard of cultivated
speech understood everywhere and acceptable everywhere. In answer to
Hall's objections Krapp might very well have repeated what he had said
in *Modern English:* that the completely consistent adherence to the idea
of general usage would mean finally a fixed language inadmissive of improvement and that the interplay of standard English and good English
makes for a language constantly improving in expressiveness and effectiveness of communication.

THE DOCTRINE OF THE LINGUISTIC NORM

Under the heading of the linguistic norm may be grouped those concepts
which emphasize that language is above all responsible to an expressive
ideal. Some advocates of the normative approach hold that language

[13] *Ibid.,* pp. 327, 329–30.

of meaning which gives force to the doctrine of the linguistic norm. In its expressive aims it is similar to the doctrine of appropriateness, but whereas the doctrine of appropriateness emphasizes the social situation, particularly the effect on an audience, the doctrine of the linguistic norm holds in balance the intention of the speaker, the nature of the language itself, and the probable effect on the audience.

Because of its over-all point of view the doctrine of the linguistic norm is probably the best vantage ground for the teacher. It provides criteria by which to evaluate both the conservative and the liberalizing forces in language. It does not, to be sure, provide the sense of psychological security and social approval so long associated with the doctrine of rules. But submission to dogmatic authority merely out of a desire to gain security hardly seems a constructive attitude. Nor does it seem desirable to compromise personal conviction in the way so often demanded by consistent adherence to either the doctrine of general usage or the doctrine of appropriateness. The most suitable philosophy of language for the teacher would seem to be one calling for a disinterested and yet constantly critical evaluation of language as a means to maximum expression. And this is the point of view of the doctrine of the linguistic norm.

The Language of the Cultivated*

AUSTIN C. DOBBINS

IN VIRTUALLY all modern handbooks of composition, students are advised to confine their language choices in college themes to usages which are appropriate to the writing of cultivated people. The use of colloquialisms is to be avoided. Slang—dread thought—is perhaps better rejected entirely. More appropriately, college themes are to be clothed in language which is appropriate to "the highest level of usage and style" which students are capable of writing.

How is the student to follow this frequently expressed advice of his elders? To what authority is he to turn to determine which terms are or are not suitable to the highest level of usage and style which he is capable of writing? Perhaps study of the statements regarding usage in the handbooks will enable the student to achieve the desired standard. Unfortunately, unless he decides to accept the pronouncements of one particular text, the student who follows this suggestion faces difficulties. To Hodges (*Harbrace Handbook,* 1951) *ugly* (ill-tempered) is a colloquialism. To

* Reprinted by permission from *College English,* 18.46–47 (October, 1956).

Marckwardt (*Scribner Handbook*, 1948), however, employment of *ugly* in this sense is clearly sanctioned by literary use. *To fix* (to repair), according to McCrimmon (*Writing with a Purpose, 1950*), is a term which is inappropriate in formal style. Warfel (*American College English*, 1949) considers this a usage acceptable in all but the most formal writing. Kierzek (*Macmillan Handbook*, 1954) asserts that *complected* should not be used in any level of writing. Leggett (*Prentice-Hall Handbook*, 1954) suggests instead that *complected* is acceptable as a colloquialism. Foerster (*Writing and Thinking*, 1952) labels "to feature" (to give special prominence to) as colloquial or as business jargon. Gorrell (*Modern English Handbook*, 1953) states rather that while overused the term is becoming established usage. The list might well be extended. Considerable disagreement exists regarding the status of such words as *bunch, claim, contact, date, farther, humans, lend, mad, nice,* and *tough.*

If the dictionary, which "records the [actual] usage of the speakers and writers of our language," is accepted as the authority, the result is frequently even greater confusion. For example, the *American College Dictionary* ("the best dictionary the English language has ever had") terms colloquial such words as *cop, gripe, holdup,* and *pal. Webster's New Collegiate Dictionary* ("the supreme authority") labels these words slang.[1] *Webster's* in turn, maintains that *guy, kids, medico,* and *to neck* (words chosen almost at random) are colloquial. The *ACD* identifies these words as slang. Since both dictionaries claim to base their labels upon usage, the question inevitably arises as to which dictionary should be accepted as *the* authority.

Admittedly, the words in these lists belong to shifting classifications. In many cases the differences between slang and colloquial usages are more of degree than of kind. But what of such words as *boondoggle, corny, frisk, liquidate, pinhead, bonehead, carpetbagger, pleb, slush fund,* and *snide?* Which of these words ordinarily would be considered appropriate in themes written by cultivated people? According to the editors of the *ACD*, the first five of these words are slang; the second five are established usage. To the editors of *WNCD*, the first five of these words represent established usage; the second five are slang. Which authority is the student to follow?

Since the pronouncements both of handbooks and of dictionaries prove confusing, perhaps the use of "common sense" on the part of the instructor may resolve disagreement into agreement? But this suggestion also raises difficulties. The instructor is asked to comment upon the level of language found in the following "specimens" of college writing. Should the itali-

---

[1] The *American College Dictionary* (1953) and *Webster's New Collegiate Dictionary* (1953) are used primarily for convenience in reference. Similar disagreement may be found if the labels in other standard dictionaries are compared.

cized words in these selections be considered appropriate or inappropriate to the writing of cultivated people?

The *highbinders* took care properly *to grease the palms* of the police. They hired *shysters* who didn't give a *tinker's damn* for law or justice. And, although the other Mongoloids soon became *sick* of the obvious connections between *honky-tonk* and law, honest citizens of all races continued to be *turned down* at the city hall so long as bribery remained unchecked. *Yellow* though the crooks were said to be, no crook was found willing to *spill* enough information to keep the town from being known as a *push-over* for criminal elements.

Flophouse habitués, wrinkled and wary, *skewed* eyed delinquents with *smokes* dangling loosely from their lips, old men shaky from *bootleg* and lack of soda—one and all made *snide* remarks as they listened to the ancient *wheezes* of Rev. Sam. *"Bonehead"* was the least of the taunts they used. But Sam was set in his ways. He paid no attention to their *lip*.

What is the instructor to answer? If he objects to the italicized words, he may be asked to show cause and authority for his objection. If he tries to defend the use of words of this nature by suggesting that levels of language vary in accordance with the demands of speaker, subject, and audience (the doctrine of appropriateness), he may be referred to particular authorities who maintain that "careful writers avoid this usage" in cultivated writing. Then, after laboriously consulting the various authorities, if he is conscientious, the instructor will discover that the authorities disagree. The *ACD* classifies the italicized words in the first selection as slang (the type of language which usually is to be avoided in college compositions). *WNCD* regards each of these terms as established usage. The *ACD* considers the italicized words in the second selection as established. *WNCD* labels these terms as a mixture of dialect and slang.

Certain words are deemed inappropriate in college compositions. How is the student to recognize these terms which are inappropriate to the highest level of usage and style—inappropriate to the writing of cultivated people? Perhaps the answer is to advise students to study only one handbook, consult one dictionary, listen to one instructor. An alternate suggestion, of course, is for our textbooks more accurately to base their labels upon studies of usage.

Showed as Past Participle*

RUSSELL THOMAS

THE USE OF *showed* as an alternate form of the past participle has an interesting history. In OE the verb (*scéawian*) belonged to the weak conjugation, but, according to the *OED:*

> From early ME the verb has had a strong conjugation (after *Know v.*, etc.) by the side of the original weak conjugation; in the pa. t. this survives only in dialects; but for the pa. pple *shown* is now the usual form; but the older *showed* is still sometimes used in the perfect tenses active (chiefly with material object); but in the passive it is obs. exc. as a deliberate archaism.

In 1933 or 1934 I began to jot down any examples of *showed* used as a past participle which came to my attention during the course of the day's reading. By March, 1937, I had found some in the King James Version of the Bible and one in Dryden's dedication to the *Aeneid*. However, I had only three examples from contemporary English, one of which was taken from Breasted's *The Conquest of Civilization* (1926), another from a book review by C. G. Poore in the *New York Times* (December 22, 1935), and the third from one of the issues of the *English Journal* (in either 1933 or 1934), for which I failed to make an accurate record as to the date.

I then decided to write the editor of Webster's *New International Dictionary* for information concerning the data which were in the dictionary files for this usage. About two weeks later I received a reply, from which I quote in part:

> . . . we have preferred the form *shown* for the past participle, and this preference is supported in contemporary use *by our lack of examples in modern literature for the alternative form "showed."*[1]

In his *Dictionary of Modern English Usage*, Mr. H. W. Fowler, page 532, states "The past participle is generally *shown*, rarely *showed*." In his *Comprehensive Guide to Good English*, G. P. Krapp, under the entry *show*, *verb*, writes "Past Participle *shown*, sometimes *showed*." In his book *How To Say It*, published by Putnam's Sons, 1927, Mr. C. N. Lurie comments as follows:

> "*Showed* or *Shown*
> "In the editorial columns of a newspaper the following sentence appeared:

---

* Reprinted by permission from *College English*, 11.157–158 (December, 1949).
[1] Italics mine.

'Suspicion and abuse have at once showed their heads, even as against the highest dignitaries of the church.'

"Either 'have showed' or 'have shown' is correct, according to good authority. It is difficult to say which is in more common use. Probably persons who pay attention to the matter of speaking and writing correctly say 'have shown,' while the ordinary speaker says 'have showed.' But he must not be accused of error for doing so. . . ."

The citations which we have on hand are of rather ancient date. . . .

I concluded that this information, together with the very scanty data which I had found, scarcely justified the listing of *showed* as an alternate form of the past participle. If listed at all, it should be marked either "rare" or "very rare."

At any rate, I continued on the alert. It seemed incredible that the strong form *shown* would continue to be preferred to the weak, and regular, pattern *showed*. Nevertheless, at the present writing it appears that the weak form is still rarely used in Standard Written English, for since 1937 I have run across no more than ten examples, taken from the following publications:

1935: *The Teaching of Literature in the High School*, by Reed Smith

1937: *Pedlar's Progress*, by Odell Shepard

1938: *Harper's Magazine*, January, "Business Finds Its Voice," by S. H. Walker and Paul Sklar

1944: *Ideas in America*, by Howard Mumford Jones

1946: *Association of American Colleges Bulletin*, March, "We Shall Honor Them," by F. P. Gaines
The Mining Journal (Marquette, Michigan), September 24, Walter Lippmann's column

1948: *The Contemporary Review* (London), January, "The Competitive Order," by Diana Spearman
The *New York Times*, August 1, editorial
The *Milwaukee Journal*, December 19, editorial

1949: *The Trying-out of Moby Dick*, by Howard Vincent

Thirteen examples, collected over a period of from sixteen to seventeen years, do not constitute sufficient data to justify the listing of *showed* as an alternate form of the past participle. It would seem, therefore, that, unless the staff of the *New International* has collected a pretty good batch of examples since 1937 (at which time it had no examples from contemporary English), and unless some "harmless drudge" other than myself has pertinent data other than that which has been presented in this article, the use of *showed* as a past participle in Standard Written English is still rare. I note that the *American College Dictionary* also lists *showed* as an alternate form. It would be interesting to know what data are in the files of this dictionary.

In conclusion, it is interesting to point out that in my observations of the present-day speech of the so-called "educated" group and of the speech of that broader group whom Fries calls "those who are carrying on the affairs of the community" strong pressure is being exerted by "showed" upon "shown."

An Agreement of Subject and Verb in Anticipatory *There* Clauses*

David S. Berkeley

English handbooks generally recommend that after the expletive *there* the verb is singular or plural according to the number of the subject that follows. Thus Smart; Greever and Jones; Foerster and Steadman; Davidson; Thomas, Manchester, and Scott; Kierzek; Wykoff and Shaw; and this list might be considerably enlarged. Of the descriptive grammarians who have treated this matter Jespersen states that *there is* before a plural subject is colloquial in modern English. Fries finds this construction frequently used in standard American English.[1] Robert C. Pooley comments on the construction:

> When a compound subject follows the verb, the verb is very often in the singular, as in 'There is wealth and glory for the man who will do this.' This usage is more common after 'there is,' 'there exists,' and so forth, as Curme remarks: 'Survivals still occasionally occur also in literary language after *there is, there exists*, etc., i.e., in certain set expressions where the mind is not on the alert'; although the explanation probably lies more in the accepted pattern of 'there is' plus a plural subject than in any lack of alertness of mind. Since the 'there is' combination is followed in the great majority of sentences by a singular subject it has become a standard way of introducing a subject, whether singular or plural, another example of the victory of usage over logical grammar.[2]

Professor Pooley would revise the rule in this fashion: 'Two or more subjects joined by *and* when felt to be plural are followed by a plural verb; when the subject, though plural in form, is felt to be a single entity, the singular form may be used; when the compound subject follows the verb, the verb is frequently in the singular, especially in the patterns *there is, there exists*.'[3]

---

* Reprinted by permission from *American Speech*, 28.92–96 (May, 1953).

[1] Otto Jespersen, *A Modern English Grammar* (Heidelberg, 1936), II, 182; Charles C. Fries, *American English Grammar* (New York, 1940), pp. 56–57.

[2] Robert C. Pooley, *Teaching English Usage* (New York, 1946), p. 81.

[3] Robert C. Pooley, 'Subject-Verb Agreement,' *American Speech*, IX (1934), 33.

The purpose of this article is to classify and exhibit certain plural subject patterns following *there is* in modern usage. The first usage has the
implicit approval of the handbooks generally; the second is noticed by
Perrin; the remaining six have not been treated by prescriptive or descriptive grammarians within my purview.

The handbooks sanction a singular verb with subjects plural in form but
singular in meaning, e.g., 'If international law and order *is* to be restored,
we must take action at once.' If this rule is combined with the rule concerning *there is, there are*, the result, 'If there *is* to be law and order . . . ,'
would, I think, satisfy a purist. In the example that follows, the author
evidently considered his subject to be singular in meaning, though plural
in form: 'There was little fuel and little food, and the British fought pitched
battles with the German mercenaries for what there was' (Sir John Fortescue, *Wellington* [London, 1925], p. 17).

One must also observe that Perrin, well known among handbook writers
for his recognition of levels of usage, remarks that 'there is' followed by a
plural subject is frequent on the colloquial level.[4] Thus we should have no
trouble in accounting for *there is* in this bit of conversation from John Buch-
an (later Lord Tweedsmuir), *The Half-Hearted* (London, 1900), p. 21:
'There is tennis and golf and fishing; but perhaps you don't like those
things.'

A frequent pattern of *there is* followed by a plural subject has this
formula: *there is* + modifier + substantive + modifier repeated + substantive, extending to an indefinite number of similarly modified substantives. The repeated modifier may be expressed or implied. Examples
of expressed repeated modifiers:

'With this Spartan ferocity there was mingled *the* glamour and *the* mystery
of the East.' Lytton Strachey, *Eminent Victorians* (New York, n.d.), p. 276.[5]

'Then there was *his* dauntless courage, *his* untiring energy, *his* oratory, persuasive, provocative, now grave, now gay.' *Victory: War Speeches of the Right
Hon. Winston S. Churchill,* compiled by Charles Eade (Boston, 1946) and
quoted in *The Saturday Review of Literature*, Sept. 21, 1946, p. 8.

'There is *too much* explosiveness and disaster, *too much* terror and "manip-
ulation of the masses," *too much* imitation of Bolshevik techniques in Nazism
to call it "basically conservative." ' *The Saturday Review of Literature*, Feb.
25, 1950, p. 14.

'. . . there was *little* joy and *little* pride which they could have felt in their
country . . .' Richard C. Trench, *On the Study of Words* (New York, 1914),
p. 115.

'From Long Island to San Francisco, from Florida Bay to Vancouver's Island, there is *one* dominant race and civilisation, *one* language, *one* type of

---

[4] Porter G. Perrin, *Writer's Guide and Index to English* (rev. ed., Chicago, 1950),
p. 793.

[5] My italics mark points under consideration in this paper.

law, *one* sense of nationality.' Frederic Harrison, *Memories and Thoughts* (New York, 1906), p. 176.

'Thus there was *every* facility for slackness on the part of the officers, and *every* difficulty in the way of a commander who disapproved of such slackness.' Sir John Fortescue, *Wellington* (London, 1925), p. 6.

'At Valenciennes, where there was *a* review and *a* great dinner . . .' Lytton Strachey, *Queen Victoria* (New York, 1921), p. 22.

'There was *an* earlier Graeco-Turkish war in 1897–98, and *an* Italo-Turkish war in 1911.' Howard Mumford Jones, 'Education and World Tragedy,' *Modern Minds,* compiled by H. M. Jones, R. M. Ludwig, and M. B. Perry (Boston, 1949), p. 323.

Examples of implied repeated modifiers:

'But there is still a revolutionary atmosphere and pride in the achievements of the government.' The New York *Times,* June 30, 1952, p. 3.

'There is plainly a wide curiosity and delight in words.' Ivor Brown, *Having the Last Word* (London, 1950), p. 5.

'There was too much trampling and rifle fire to hear any bullets.' Winston Churchill, *A Roving Commission* (New York, 1940), p. 190.

'There was so much interest and excitement . . .' *Ibid.,* p. 334

'There has been so much interest and speculation whether in our talks in Washington we entered into any new commitments.' Quotation from Anthony Eden in 'The Churchill-Eden-Atlee Debate,' *U.S. News and World Report,* Feb. 15, 1952, p. 97.

'There is so much baseness and duplicity in the story of Jacobitism that it is pleasant to be able to award praise for a generous act . . .' Sir Charles Petrie, *The Stuart Pretenders* (Boston, 1933), pp. 104–5.

'There is much manganese and chrome, and enough uranium in the slag heaps of the Johannesburg gold mines to make its extraction worth while.' *Harper's Magazine,* July, 1952, p. 54.

In the last example 'much,' the implied repeated modifier, accounts for the singular verb, but not for the third subject, 'enough uranium.' Here, I believe, the reader is expected to supply 'there is,' understood by the writer. A clearer example of understood *there is* preceding the second subject is this sentence: '. . . for there was hay-making all the way, and now and then a burst of lime-blossom.' E. V. Lucas, *A Fronded Isle, and Other Essays* (New York, 1928), p. 99. In this sentence the distance between the two subjects makes it unnatural to employ *were:* the reader supplies 'there was.' This observation may be applied to the second quotation from Fortescue above and to the quotation from H. M. Jones above. These and other examples elude rigid classification.

Another occasion for ignoring the rule of the handbooks is found in the usage of repeated subjects. Examples:

'There was *rioting* in French streets and *rioting* in the French mind.' Rebecca West, 'Whittaker Chambers,' *Atlantic Monthly* (June, 1952), p. 34.

'There is a *time* to be silent and a *time* to speak, a *time* for study and a *time* for resignation or action.' *The Saturday Review of Literature,* July 20, 1946, p. 16. In this example one also notes repeated articles.

Another departure from rule frequently occurs when correlative adjectives connect the two subjects, e.g., 'too much . . . not enough,' 'one . . . another,' 'more . . . less,' 'too much . . . too little.' Examples:

'In its essence the Renaissance is a protest against the time when there was *too much* divinity and *not enough* humanity. . . .' Irving Babbitt, *Literature and the American College* (Boston, 1908), p. 13.

'There was *one* code for the drawing room and *another* code for the foundry and the mill.' J. B. Priestley, 'Shaw As Social Critic,' *The Saturday Review of Literature,* July 27, 1946, p. 6.

'. . . but here there is *more* grace and *less* carelessness.' *Journal of English and Germanic Philology,* XLIV (1945), 329.

'In the average elementary class in English today there is already *too much* talking around and about *Hamlet* and *too little* emphasis upon the student's own perception of form and expression.' *Ibid.,* XLIII (1944), 259.

'. . . but on the other hand there is *much* good in the present and *more* hope in the future.' G. M. Trevelyan, *Clio, a Muse, and Other Essays* (London, 1913), p. 53.

One must take cognizance of a tendency of some good writers to employ 'there is' to introduce lists. Whether this is always done advisedly in formal prose is questionable, but it is done, both in lists of single items and in lists of single items with modifiers. Adherence to the handbook rule would, I think, cause awkwardness especially in sentences three, four, five, and six below.

'There was Sparta and even Aetolia; Pythagoras and the Oracle at Delphi.' Gilbert Murray, *Essays and Addresses* (London, 1921), p. 58.

'There was danger and excitement, the necessity of decision, the opportunity for action, on every hand.' Lytton Strachey, *Queen Victoria* (New York, 1921), p. 219.

'For him, there is always and everywhere the ruler, the philosopher, the mob, the aristocrat, the fanatic and the augur, alike in ancient Rome or in modern France and England.' G. M. Trevelyan, *Clio, a Muse, and Other Essays* (London, 1913), p. 38.

'There was a rumbling murmur, a groan, a shriek, a sound of distant thunder.' *Speeches of Benjamin Disraeli, Earl of Beaconsfield,* ed. T. E. Kebbel, II, 487 seq. Quoted by J. A. R. Marriott, *England Since Waterloo* (London, 1950), p. 251.

In the two preceding examples one also notes repeated articles.

'There was Codrington, gallant young soldier and lover of letters, Governor in the West Indies, munificent founder of the great Library; the curious and brilliant genius of Edward Young, poet, author of *Night Thoughts*, which so fascinates the surrealists; above all, Blackstone, the great lawyer.' A. L. Rowse, *The English Past* (London, 1951), p. 12.

'In addition to the original Chinese-English pidgin, there is the Melanesian variety . . . ; a variety used in New Guinea; one used by the Blackfellows of Australia; a *beche-la-mar* . . . that appears in Tahiti. . . .' Mario Pei, *The Story of Language* (New York, 1949), p. 302.

Yet another occasion for departing from the rule may be illustrated by this sentence: '. . . there was challenge, and a threat of triumph, in his steely black-browed fearless eyes. . . .' (Willard Connely, *Sir Richard Steele* [London, 1937], p. 90). Here Connely makes 'and a threat of triumph' more pointed and more unexpected than it would be by using the plural to signal a second subject. Besides, I must remark that to my mind the revision of this sentence (and many others quoted in this article) according to rule is awkward.

Most of these subject patterns are in my opinion sufficiently common and established to warrant notice from the more comprehensive type of handbook represented by the names of Kierzek and Perrin.

Number Concord with *What*-Clauses*

Francis Christensen

When so much effort has been spent on confining the language within hedgerows, and clipping the hedgerows, it is a strange sensation to come upon a little line of sportive wood run wild. Such is the *what*-clause in the subject position, where usage has not been constrained by rule and one can see natural linguistic processes at work. The usual run of school and college grammars and handbooks and popular reference books do not discuss it under the expected heads of number concord or agreement. Of the books widely used by public and teachers only Fowler's *Modern English Usage* treats it, under *what* with the subheads 'Wrong number attraction' and 'What singular and *what* plural.' Fowler points out that in such a sentence as 'What is required *are* houses at rents that people can pay,' *what* as subject of the noun clause is construed as singular (=*which* in *that which*, as he explains it) and is then (as *that* in *that which*) construed by the verb *are* as plural. The verb *are*, he says, has been attracted to the plural by the plural predicate noun *rents* and should be corrected to *is*.

Even the standard grammars are perfunctory in treating this particular

* Reprinted by permission from *American Speech*, 30.30–37 (February, 1955).

problem of concord. In Curme,[1] Jespersen,[2] Poutsma,[3] and Kruisinga,[4] I have found only eleven sentences that illustrate the problem. I list them here, in two groups according to the predicate of the main clause.

Type I. Any predicate except one with a plural predicate complement:

1. Whoever *allow* themselves much of that indulgence *incur* the risk of something worse.[5]
2. What *have* been censured as Shakespeare's conceits *are* completely justifiable.
3. Indeed, *what mistakes* she made *were* due to wisdom rather than folly.
4. There are few paths through the great forests of Poland and what there *are*, *are* usually cut straight.

Type II. Predicate consisting of copula followed by plural complement:

1. What *appear* . . . to be its shortcomings *are* emphatically the shortcomings of its type. . . . .
2. . . . to point out when what *were* once truths *are* truths no longer.
3. What *are* wanted *are* immigrants of British origin.
4. What chiefly *count* at the elections . . . *are* the shibboleths of party.
5. What it unquestionably did contain *were* carbon monoxide gas and prussic acid gas.
6. What the Russians really want *are* better roads, more railways, better housing, better sanitation, better schools.
7. What I want *are* details.

The collectors of these examples never come to grips with the question the sentences clearly raise—the question of whether we must recognize the plural clause as a grammatical category. Curme says that a verb is in the singular if its subject is a clause.[6] Jespersen only says, of the third sentence above, that 'the whole combination *what mistakes she made* is naturally treated as a plural idea.'[7] Curme[8] and Kruisinga[9] remark that when the verb is a colorless copula it is often diffcult to distinguish between subject and predicate.

I have not seen this problem discussed in print, but John S. Kenyon

[1] *Syntax*, pp. 50, 214–15.
[2] *A Modern English Grammar*, II, 58–59, 168; III, 41.
[3] *A Grammar of Late Modern English*, Part II, Sec. IA, 279; IB, 1336.
[4] *A Handbook of Present-Day English*, III, 307.
[5] The problem is the same with all the indefinites; cf. this sentence from Byron's *Don Juan* (4, 12) cited by Jespersen: 'Whom the Gods love die young.' I found no further examples except this, from *Venice Preserved* (II, 60–61), where the second verb is probably subjunctive: 'Give order that whoever in my name comes here, receive attendance.'
[6] *Op. cit.*, p. 59.
[7] *Op. cit.*, III, 53.
[8] *Op. cit.*, p. 50.
[9] *Loc. cit.*

raised it in an unpublished paper which he graciously turned over to me to use when I wrote about a sentence of his own Type II, namely 'What are frequently grouped together in one class as different levels of language *are* often in reality false combinations of two different and incommensurable categories . . .' For his data he used sentences 1 and 2 above and three others of Type I:

1. I went to market to buy some *vegetables,* but what I found *were* stale.
2. The Revolution made a complete sweep of all the old *endowments;* what exist *date* from a time since the Revolution.
3. *What of the votes* we have seen *are* equally divided.

Professor Kenyon rejects the analysis of *what* implied in Fowler's resolving it to *that/those which;* this is to analyze a substitute construction, 'and it does not follow that sentences of like meaning have the same syntax.' But he also rejects the analysis supported by Jespersen[10] that assigns it a single function (in the noun clause) and makes the noun clause the subject of the plural verb:

> Observe that if we say that the subjects of the main clauses in these sentences are the dependent clauses *what I found,* etc., then we must admit into grammar a hitherto unrecognized category, namely, a plural clause; for the verbs are plural in agreement with their subjects. These plural verbs cannot be explained as due to attraction, for singular verbs would not here be tolerated.

Kenyon's own analysis assigns *what* a double construction: 'In sentence 1 [of the three immediately preceding this paragraph] *what* is object of *found* and also subject of *were stale.* For the native user of English the pattern of concord is determined solely by whether *what* is singular or plural (as shown by its antecedent),[11] not by the whole clause. In accord with this pattern the single word *what* is felt to be the subject of the main clause.' He bases this analysis giving *what* a double construction 'on the analogy of the contact clause, such as "That is the *man* I saw yesterday," in which *man* is both predicate complement of *is* and object of *saw;* or "There's a man below wants to speak to you" (Swift), in which *man* is the subject both of *is* and of *wants;* or "I saw him the *day* he arrived," in which *day* is adverbial objective in both clauses. As Jespersen and others have pointed out, it is not necessary to assume omission of a relative pronoun.'

So much for the present state of the discussion. I started with a sentence of Type II—'But what interests Sutter above all others *are* stories brought him by travelers,' quoted by Pooley—with the curious comment

---

[10] *Philosophy of Grammar,* pp. 103–04.

[11] This is true of only two of Professor Kenyon's examples. In No. 3 of his three additional sentences *what of the votes* equals *what votes;* in the first sentence listed under the heading 'Type I,' *whoever* is shown to be plural only by *allow;* in the sentence that follows it *what* is "passive subject' and is plural in agreement with the 'retained' objective complement *conceits.*

that the 'overmeticulous plural' is 'uncomfortably conspicuous.'[12] I began
to observe all sentences I met in reading and listening with a *what*-clause
in the subject position and soon found that a plural verb in the main clause
is almost invariably a copula followed by a plural predicate complement,
Type II. So I shifted focus and began collecting (a) all sentences with a
what-clause in the subject position followed by a plural verb regardless
of the form of the rest of the predicate and (b) all such sentences with a
plural predicate complement regardless of the number of the verb. It
took about five years to collect the 100 sentences analyzed in this paper.

Contrary to my expectation, I came out with 62 sentences with plural
copula and 38 with singular. This distribution is not wholly reliable, however, since the sentences came not only from close reading but also from
casual reading and listening where the usual form, the plural, would leap
to my attention. But if usage on this point could be accurately assessed I
believe the plurals would still hold the majority of the stock.

One type of plural predicate can be eliminated at the start as an influence on the copula. The predicates of singulars and plurals fall into
four groups, thus: (1) passive verb—plurals 3, singulars 1; (2) predicate
adjective—no examples (3) plural predicate noun—plurals 56, singulars
23; (4) compound predicate nouns—plurals 1, singulars 15. The sharp
difference in the fourth group shows that in sentences like 'What is most
striking about Johnson *is* the vigor of his ideas, the variety of his knowledge, the forcefulness of his conversation, and the dignity with which
. . . he maintained his position,' the series of nouns in the predicate
do not add up to a plural to affect the preceding copula. Even a series of
plural nouns do not necessarily do so: '. . . and what is smuggled *is* not
guns but medicines and nylons.' Examples come from Henry James, Mari-
anne Moore, Van Wyck Brooks, Bertrand Russell, Bonamy Dobree, Ernest
Bernbaum, Crane Brinton, John W. Clark, J. C. Maxwell, Robert C. Hall,
Eric Bentley, Hollis Alpert, and others.[13]

We turn next to the 62 plurals and divide them into three groups, based
on the number of *what:* (1) *what* plural; (2) *what* singular; (3) *what*
undetermined.

'*What plural.*—In all these sentences *what* is established as plural by
formal evidence within the noun clause itself, not by an antecedent as in
two of Professor Kenyon's examples:

1. What storms *lie* ahead *are* not indicated.
2. Sometimes what *appear* to be disciplinary problems *are* easily solved by
   very elementary applied psychology.

---

[12] *Teaching English Usage*, p. 91.
[13] The same appears to be true of tandem noun clauses in the subject position: 'What
you say and how you say it, therefore, *is* wholly to be determined by the effect it will
have.' Cf. 'Why and how "the wave of scientific curiosity began to mount" *are*, of
course, among the most fascinating and difficult of historical questions.'

3. What might have been attributes and powers *were* perverted there . . .
4. What *appear* to be large windows in the second story *are* glass heat collectors.
5. What you call Shakespeare's 'effective word pictures' *are* the materials of Brutus's thinking.
6. Professor Olson thinks that what Professor Ransom, also long ago, called Mr. Empson's 'muddles' *are* the necessary products of bad and confused theory.
7. Science has shown us in many instances that what we have regarded as facts *were* not really facts at all but merely hearsay and superstition.
8. What *are* frequently grouped together in one class as different levels of language *are* often in reality false combinations of two distinct and incommensurable categories.

In No. 1 *what* is an adjective and *storms* selects the plural *lie*. In Nos. 2, 3, 4, and 8, *what* is subject and selects the plural verb in the noun clause, except for the auxiliary in No. 3; in Nos. 5–7 *what* is object. Except for No. 1, the number of *what* itself is determined by a plural complement—subjective complement (2–4) and objective complement (5–8). The only difference between sentences 5–7 and 8 is in the passive voice of the noun clause in No. 8. Sentences 1–3 are Type I; with the four drawn from the grammarians and the three added by Professor Kenyon, they bring to ten the examples of Type I. The rest are Type II, and the plural complements *collectors, materials, muddles, facts, combinations* may be thought to have affected the copulas. But if the plural predicate complement is replaced by a predicate adjective or a passive or progressive verb form (and if this is a legitimate test) the plural copula remains: 'What appear to be large windows in the second story *are* [not *is*] designed to collect heat.' Thus in every sentence, eight in a hundred, where *what* of the noun clause is plural the verb of the main clause is plural.[14] To my ear, the only one that would tolerate a singular verb is the first on this list: "What storms lie ahead *is* not indicated.'

'*What*-singular.—In these sentences, all belonging to Type II, *what* is the subject of the noun clause and is shown to be signular by its own verb:

1. What *is* not going to change in this Congress *are* the issues it must face.
2. What *impresses* them *are* planes and divisions and ships.
3. In brief, what's wrong with our foreign broadcasting media *are* not some alleged subversives.
4. What *makes* each division different *are* a few simple things—time, place, tradition, and leadership.
5. What *interests* and a little *confuses* me *are* the names he chose to call.

[14] I found this sentence in our freshman syllabus too late to include it in the 100 sentences: 'What Watt, following Perrin, calls the first two levels of usage *are* best thought of as two styles, formal and informal.'

6. What *looks* to the foreigner like arrogance and conceit *are* simply the over-compensatory devices . . .

7. What *is* most discussed, the *Times* went on to say, *are* the implications of this policy.

8. What *is* needed *are* methods of imparting some knowledge of the Tactics and Strategies of Scientists . . .

9. What *happens* to Maggie Verver in *The Golden Bowl,* to Milly Theale in *The Wings of the Dove,* to Isabel Archer in *The Portrait of a Lady,* to George Stransom in 'The Altar of the Dead,' *are* examples of religious experience outside a creed, just as what *happens* to John Marcher in 'The Beast in the Jungle' *is* an example of the privation of religious experience . . .

It may be pointed out, first, that these sentences range from a high level of radio speech, through daily and weekly journalism, to the carefully edited writing of the learned caste—the president of Harvard, published by Yale. They are the products of reflection and correction as well as of impulse—a topic we shall return to later. It would be hard to contend that *what* has a double construction here, singular subject of the dependent clause and plural subject of the main clause. The plural verb must be owing to the plural in the complement position of the main clause, *issues,* etc. Give these clauses any other form of predicate, I believe, and the plural verb would go: 'What is not going to change in this Congress *is* [not *are*] going to stay put.' In every sentence but No. 9 a singular copula would be idiomatic. In sentence 9, one could say 'What happens . . . happens because they' but not 'What happens . . . is examples.'

'*What undetermined.*—There were 43 examples—4 with *what* as subject of a preterit verb, 39 as object in the noun clause, all therefore without a formal mark of plurality, and all with plural copula and plural predicate complement in the main clause. Two examples will suffice:

1. What they want *are* promises.

2. . . . what he shows us here (as in *Epsom Wells*) *are* Londoners on a holiday.

These can be compared with 14 other sentences where the same conditions produced singular copulas:

1. What they hate and fear *is* their own neighbors who try to think.

2. Accordingly, what we want *is* not terms that avoid ambiguity . . .

It is possible, of course, that *what* may be felt as plural even though it has no plural antecedent and there is no formal sign of plurality within the clause. Sentences such as 'What I want to show you are some teacups' take shape with the teacups within the field of attention, the purpose of the sentence being to bring them into relation with the verbal idea of *show you.* The simple statment 'I want to show you some teacups' will not serve the purpose, because the purpose is not simple, but complex, with two stages: 'I have in mind something I want to show you' and 'That something is some teacups.' But, although this explanation is possible (and it gives plural *what* a double construction as subject or object in the noun clause and subject of the main clause), it does not answer to my subjective feeling about the *what* clause—that it is *indefinite*. I had to say just now *something* (indefinite) not *some things* (definite and therefore plural).

The closest study of these 57 sentences, together with the 8 from the group with singular *what,* gives me no basis for a generalization to account for the choice. If the plural is acceptable in one it is almost equally acceptable in all, and the same for the singular. If the cards were recopied with *is/are* or *was/were,* I am sure no one could re-sort them. In short, here is absolutely divided usage, with more than three to one in favor of the plural. There is no question, either, of social level. If you think only the singular is correct, then you differ with many professors of English—Ernest Bernbaum, George Sherburn, Thomas C. Pollock, Chauncey Sanders, Basil Willey, A. L. Rowse, and three of my colleagues; literary figures like Thomas Hardy, Stephen Spender, Edmund Wilson, Margaret Marshall; the *Saturday Review, Time, Fortune;* radiomen Collingwood, Vandercook, Murrow; Averell Harriman, the American Meat Institute, and cartoonist Jo Fischer; and thrice with my wife and twice with the 1949 Ivy Orator at Amherst College. If you prefer the plural, you differ with three other professors; with Robinson Jeffers, Malcolm Cowley, Kenneth Burke; with Elmer and H. L. Davis; with the *Saturday Review* and *New Yorker;* with Whittaker Chambers and with me, in some old papers I was sorting over.

With this summary of the hundred sentences, we shall try next to see why it is that plurals in the predicate complement position are associated with plural copulas. We are concerned primarily with the 52 plural copulas where *what* in the noun clause is singular or undetermined. There seem to be two explanations, the first of which assumes that the noun clause, although in the subject position, is not in fact the subject, that the subject is the plural noun in the predicate position. This assumption can rest either on the little learning in grammatical matters that inspires such strange confidence in those that have it, or on grammatical theory too subtle for human nature's daily food.

Many of these sentences are from printed sources and therefore edited sources, some written and edited by professors of English, and some edited in publishers' offices by the nice girls good in English whom Jacques Barzun recently took to task. There is no question but some of the plurals in the predicate complement position have been consciously taken for subjects and the copulas adjusted accordingly.

The too subtle theory stems from Jespersen's *Philosophy of Grammar.* In Chapter V he attempts to distinguish between substantive and adjective and in Chapter XI uses the same principle to distinguish between subject and predicate noun: "The subject is comparatively definite and special, while the predicate is less definite, and thus applicable to a greater number of things."[15] Jespersen does not apply this principle to the kind of sentence we are examining—he regards the noun clauses as subject; but Curme includes one in the examples he cites to illustrate the principle: 'What it unquestionably did contain were carbon monoxide gas and prussic acid gas.'[16] Since *what* in all its functions is indefinite, according to this theory all the *what*-clauses in sentences of Type II should be regarded as predicate complements rather than as subjects and all the singular copulas should be changed to plurals. Curme goes on to say, however, that in common practice many find it difficult to distinguish in this way between subject and complement, and so "the present tendency is to avoid a decision on this perplexing point by regulating the number of the copula by a mere formal principle'—the principle of position.[17] But this, as we have seen, is not the present tendency.

The next explanation applies to all our sentences but those where *what* is plural. It assumes that the noun clause is subject and that where the verb is plural it is plural by attraction of the plural complement. This, of course, is Fowler's analysis, and since he rejects attraction as a principle of English grammar, he changes the plurals to singulars. The interesting question about attraction, though, is how it operates and why it operates irregularly. I assume that the principle at work is anticipation—the kind that gave us the variants *foot/feet, food/feed* and caused me a moment ago when I let my attention run too far ahead in writing *carbon monoxide* to write *carbonide*. For me, in the few times I have surprised myself in the act of putting together sentences of this sort, the copula is the turning point of the sentence. If my attention is not too far ahead, if I do not look beyond the verb, the indefiniteness of *what* results in a singular verb. But if I do go ahead, the concreteness of a plural noun in the predicate is likely to result in a plural copula—by attraction, I take it, rather than by Jespersen's theory. The process in operation can be illustrated by a sentence a student, Eli Jenkins, brought me, in which Arthur Godfrey stopped and corrected himself: 'What they want us to tell you about *is—uh—are* these things.' In writing we can go back over our first drafts and correct with more deliberation. I once found, in a paragraph which I had recast, the following pair of sentences: 'What the parents liked best in their children *were* traits that showed them to be . . .' and 'What parents liked least in their children *was* traits that showed them to be . . .' Taking the noun clause for the subject and preferring, maybe, though it has nothing to do with grammar, the crispness of the singular form, I changed *were* to *was*.

[15] P. 150.
[16] *Op. cit.,* p. 50.
[17] *Ibid.*

What this all adds up to, finally, is/are a set of rules rather than a single one, accounted for by a set of principles rather than a single one: (1) Plural *what* regularly selects a plural verb in the main clause, but singular or undetermined *what* does not regularly select a singular verb. (2) A plural form (not a plural by compounding) in the predicate complement position controls the copula—whether by attraction or by being taken for the subject—more often by far than does the noun clause in the subject position. In this situation one cannot say with Professor Kenyon that *what* has a double construction without admitting that *what* does not control the pattern of concord except when it is plural. On the other hand, the notion of a plural clause merely recognizes a fact and gives it a name without explaining it.

In this seesaw between the elements in the preverb and postverb position, with the uncertainty as to which is the subject, we seem to have evidence that the principle of word order is not yet established firmly enough in the language to override the influence of a form with such a marked grammatical character as the inflected plural.

"One of Those Who Is . . ." *

John S. Kenyon

Joseph Addison, famous exemplar of excellent prose style, writes (*Spectator* No. 122, 1711),

> My worthy Friend Sir Roger is *one of those who is* not only at Peace within *himself*, but beloved and esteemed by all about *him*.

Here the relative clause *who is . . . him* is a clear example of a restrictive, limiting, or defining clause. It defines the character of *those* and tells us, by means of the partitive genitive *of those*, that Sir Roger is one of the group so defined. In another place (*Spectator* No. 203, 1711) Addison writes,

> I am *one of those People who* by the general Opinion of the World *are* counted both Infamous and Unhappy.

Here the *who*-clause performs the same function as in the first example. But here the verb *are* is plural, agreeing in number with *those*, the antecedent of *who*, while in the first example the corresponding verb is singular, as are also the pronouns *himself* and *him*, although their antecedent is the plural *those*. The plural verb agrees with logic and conventional

* Reprinted by permission from *American Speech*, 26.161–165 (October, 1951).

grammar. Before we consider the grammar of it, let us see if the first type of sentence with singular verb and/or singular pronoun in the *who*-clause is common enough in good writers to make the question important.

In the tenth-century Old English Gospel of John (XII. 2) we find a sentence that may be accurately modernized thus: 'Lazarus was *one of those who was sitting* with him.' The singular verb (*sæt*) was evidently native English idiom, for the Latin original was different ('one of those reclining with him'). A closely analogous construction is found in the same Old English Gospel (III. 15): 'That not *one of those* shall perish who *believes* in him.'

Similar examples are very common from the earliest Old English, sometimes with plural verb in the relative clause but very often with the verb in the singular. It is not certain that the modern English examples can be regarded as a continuation in popular speech of the Old English habit of expression, but the underlying mental tendency to shift from the plural to the singular appears to be the same. A similar shift is also found in Old French and in German.

Following are modern examples showing a singular verb or a singular pronoun, often both, in the relative clause that modifies *those* or equivalent partitive expression, such as *one of the best, largest,* etc.:

> You are *one of those* that will not serve God if the devil bid *you* [not *them*]. —*Othello*, I. i. 108.

Observe also that Kittredge's paraphrase of this shows the same construction:

> 'You are *one of those men* that will not take the best advice in the world if it comes from a person that *you* [not *they*] do not like.'[1]
>
> Yet his brother is reputed *one of the best that is.*—*All's Well That Ends Well*, IV. iii. 322.
>
> He is *one of those* that must lose *his* employment.—Swift (quoted by Jespersen, *Grammar*, II, 181).
>
> The Sunday school is *one of the noblest institutions* which *has been seen* in Europe for some centuries.—John Wesley (quoted in *Reader's Digest*, November, 1948, p. 90).
>
> It was *one of the largest* that ever *was seen.*—Cowper, letter, December 11, 1786.
>
> *One of the most valuable books* for the improvement of young minds that *has appeared* in any language.—Boswell, *Johnson* (Oxford, 1904), I, 129.
>
> Dr. Johnson: Are you, Sir, one of those enthusiasts who believe *yourself* transformed into the very character *you* represent?—*Ibid.*, II, 512. [Ed. note: This quotation, not in the original article, has been inserted at the author's request.]

[1] George Lyman Kittredge, *Othello* (Boston, 1941), p. 126.

This would be thought a hard condition to *those* who still *wish* for reunion with *their* parent country. I am sincerely *one of those*, . . . but I am *one of those* too who rather than submit to the right of legislation for us assumed by the British Parliament . . . would lend *my hand* to sink the whole island in the ocean . . . Th: Jefferson.—*The Papers of Thomas Jefferson* (Princeton, 1950), I,242. [Note that Jefferson holds to the plural in agreement with *those* until well removed from it before shifting to the singular.]

Your uncle is *one of those* to whom the least lamb in *his own* folds is dearer than the whole Christian flock.—Scott, *Old Mortality* (Everyman ed.), p. 47.

Henry Morton was *one of those gifted characters,* which *possess* a force of talent unsuspected by the *owner himself.—Ibid.,* p. 138.

Oliver is *one of those* whose *mind is* better known by *his* actions than by *his* words.—Scott, *Woodstock* (Everyman ed.), p. 80.

I confess that I am *one of those* who *am* unable to refuse *my* assent to . . . those philosophers who assert that nothing exists but as it is perceived.—Shelley (quoted by W. M. Rossetti, *Adonais* [Oxford, 1903], p. 57, with the comment, 'This phrase [*one . . . assent*] is lumbering and not grammatical.') [Note that *of those philosophers who assert* is grammatical.]

He effected *one of the most extensive, difficult, and salutary reforms* that ever *was accomplished* by any statesman.—Macaulay (quoted by Jespersen, *Grammar,* II, 181).

This plain anchorite had been *one of those* whom sorrow made . . . too timid to front the simple world *she* knew.—Sarah Orne Jewett, *The Country of the Pointed Firs,* p. 131.

His voice was *one of those strange instruments* that filled every building with *its* finest tone . . .—Thomas Nelson Page, *Red Rock,* p. 41.

He seems to have been *one of those temperaments* born to take risks and never to let *his* imagination daunt *him.—*T. C. Smith, *Garfield,* I, 16.

My Aunt Connie was *one of those amiable people* who *had* it in for the world because it hadn't given *her* what *she* wanted.—Dorothy Canfield Fisher, *The Deepening Stream,* p. 26. [Here the past tense *had,* though not distinctive in number, suits with the singulars *her* and *she.* Strict concord would call for *people* who *have* it in for the world because it *hasn't* given *them* what *they* want. Cf. *filled* in the example from Page.]

She was *one of those women* who, by *her* carriage and the thrust of *her head,* could invest even a Mother Hubbard with style.—Louis Bromfield, *Pleasant Valley,* p. 86.

It was a comic, clownish trick, *one of those* which at times *convinces* me that animals know far more than we suspect.—*Ibid.,* p. 88.

He *was one of those fools* who *funks* going to a doctor.—Carol Carnac (pseud.), *Upstairs and Downstairs,* p. 145. [Spoken by a research physician.]

He's *one of those chaps who's* easy to check up on.—E. C. R. Lorac (pseud.), *Place for a Poisoner,* p. 170. [Spoken by an intelligent police officer.]

He is *one of the finest students* who *has* ever studied at Harvard during my time.—Quoted from Felix Frankfurter in *A Man Called White*, p. 156.

Mrs. Brownlow was *one of those assured women* who *thinks herself* divinely appointed to manage the lives of *her* neighbors.—Ben Ames Williams, *House Divided*, p. 253.

She's *one of those people* who instinctively *tries* to put things off.—*Ibid.*, p. 271.

Art Young is *one of those people* whom everybody adores, pays tribute to in the form of . . . breakfasts in honor of *his* latest publication, farewell lunches upon *his* departure . . . cocktail parties to signalize *his* return . . . —Max Eastman in the *New Yorker*, March 2, 1935.

I am *one of those rare birds* who *believes* that Roosevelt may not run for a fourth term.—William Allen White, newspaper.

I am *one of those* who *calls herself* a 'meanser.'—Dorothy Thompson, recording of radio broadcast, transcribed in *American Speech*, XIII (1938), 198–99.

His . . . book is *one of the most readable and entertaining works* on the theory of poetry which *has appeared* in recent years.—Frederick A. Pottle, *The Idiom of Poetry*, p. 182.

This is *one of those novels* which *begins* with an idea for which the writer must find time, place and characters.—Horace Reynolds, New York *Times Book Rev.*, September 28, 1947, p. 14.

Jane Austen is *one of the few English writers* who *has become* a cult. (Cf. She is *one of the few novelists* who *take* indiscretion seriously.) Edwin Muir, *ibid.*, August 28, 1949, p. 1.

This is *one of those rare books* that *accomplishes* several important things at once.—C. A. Robinson, Jr., *Sat. Rev. of Lit.*, March 4, 1950, p. 21.

Tugwell has written *one of the most significant books* which *has been* published in recent years.—Sumner Welles, *ibid.*, December 28, 1946, p. 9.

He is an efficient and well-organized man, certainly *one of the best fitted* . . . who *has aspired* to the presidency.—Fred Smith, *ibid.*, November 15, 1947, p. 33.

These instances, which I have found only incidentally in not very extensive reading, are enough to exclude the view held by some purists that they are mere mistakes, not representative of good usage.

What accounts for this 'ungrammatical' construction found in the oldest English and increasingly frequent today, in which a plural *those who,* or equivalent, is followed by a singular verb or a singular pronoun? Jespersen (*Grammar*, II, 181) suggests that the singular verb or pronoun is 'attracted' to *one*. Perhaps this is but saying in grammatical terminology what may be otherwise expressed by saying that the writer or speaker is more immediately concerned with the *one* than with *those,* the whole group to which the *one* belongs. So he switches from the plural *those* to the single person or thing that he is most interested in.

This is aptly illustrated by the following passage from *Romeo and Juliet* (III. i. 5 ff.):

> Thou art like *one of these fellows* that, when *he enters* the confines of a tavern, *claps me his sword* upon the table and *says* 'God send *me* no need of thee!' and by the operation of the second cup *draws him* on the drawer, when indeed there is no need.

The vivid effectiveness of the singular, following the plural *these fellows*, stands out strikingly if we restate this in 'correct' grammatical form:

> Thou art like *one of these fellows* that, when *he enters* the confines of a tavern, *claps me his sword* upon the table and *says* 'God send *me* no need of thee!' and by the operation of the second cup *draw them* on the drawer.

Here 'correct' grammar reduces the passage to downright absurdity. Shakespeare's dramatic imagination could be trusted to present a vivid picture of a hothead though the grammar should halt for it.

Note also the tame and flat result of replacing the singular with the plural in this passage from Howells:

> He was *one of those men* of whom the country people say when *he is gone* that the *woman gets* along better without *him.—A Hazard of New Fortunes*, p. 135.

The attempt to rescue the grammar by simply taking *one* instead of *those* as the antecedent of the relative reveals a dull sense of syntactical relations and forces *those* to do a greater crime of dangling than any participle ever committed.

The late Edwin Meade Robinson, literary critic and columnist of the Cleveland *Plain Dealer,* had very clear ideas of conventional grammar, but at the same time a fine sense of idiomatic English that led him often inadvertently to use the locution in question. For example, he wrote, 'The word *executive* as a noun . . . is *one of the Americanisms* that *has been* made popular in business jargon by people who like big words.' On another occasion he wrote, 'This is *one of the jokes* that *sticks* in the mind.' Several correspondents accused him of an error in grammar. But one correspondent, who dimly sensed the real reason for the 'error,' wrote him, 'It was one joke you were speaking of, one that "sticks in the mind." Were you not right after all when you used the singular verb?' Robinson replied, 'No. I was wrong. I was speaking of one joke, but I was designating it as one of the many that stick in the mind. . . . Logic and the grammar books are both against the singular verb.'

What, then, shall we say of the grammar of this locution as it stands, plainly evidenced as an established feature of English from the earliest times? Let us compare two widely contrasting definitions of grammar. In Lindley Murray's famous *English Grammar* we find: 'English Grammar is the art of speaking and writing the English language with propriety.'[2] This shows a typical eighteenth-century attitude toward English grammar, which still largely prevails in run-of-the-mine school grammars and in the popular mind, as well as in the minds of most of the fairly well educated.

In contrast, I recall the following incident. Some forty-five years ago in a class at Harvard under the great French and English scholar Edward Stevens Sheldon, a student remarked about a passage in Old French, 'Professor, that sentence is not very grammatical, is it?' Sheldon characteristically cocked an eye toward an upper corner of the room and said quietly, 'Grammar is a description of the facts of language.'

When we say of the construction here in question that it is ungrammatical, we can only mean that it fails to conform to our notion of grammar, mostly inherited from the eighteenth century before the existence of a true science of language, and ultimately derived from Latin grammar, which differs greatly from the grammar of English. If this construction does not conform to our ideas of grammar, then our description of the locution is not complete and needs revision. The facts are clear and abundant, and if there is no 'rule' of grammar to allow for them, such rule should be made. But it should describe the facts, not prescribe what is supposed to be proper, like the rules of Lindley Murray.[3]

Pronominal *This:* A Quantitative Analysis*

PAUL ROBERTS

THE QUESTION of how one knows what English is 'good English' continues to be vexing. I do not suppose that there are now any linguists who hold that 'good English,' 'Standard English,' must fit some logical or metaphysical or historical scheme apart from the test of usage. Everyone agrees that Standard English is the English spoken or written by the group taken as setting the standard. But at this point obvious difficulties and notable divergences arise.

---

[2] I quote from the fifth edition (London and York, 1824), p. 25.

[3] The eighteenth-century conception of grammar as an external system imposed upon English, and best found in Latin, is clearly shown in Dr. Johnson's statement, 'I always said, Shakespeare had Latin enough to grammaticise his English.'—Boswell, *The Life of Samuel Johnson* (Oxford, 1904), II, 346. Note also his reference to English as 'a language subjected so little and so lately to grammar.'—*A Grammar of the English Tongue,* under 'Of Adjectives.'

* Reprinted with permission from *American Speech,* 27.170–178 (October, 1952).

It has been frequently pointed out that there are, in fact, many standards within what we think of casually as a single language. For example, a
child in elementary school may be confronted with a playground standard
that is quite different from the standard of his dinner table at home; he may
consequently alternate between two standards, saying 'I did it' so as not
to be conspicuous at the dinner table, but 'I done it' so as not to be conspicuous on the playground. We must therefore say what standard we are
talking about. I shall be concerned here with the standard of written American English of the middle of the twentieth century, the English that American English teachers intend to teach, the English reported in handbooks
used currently in American colleges.

Our first question may be stated thus: How do authors of handbooks
know what to set down as Standard English?

The cynical reader will reply: 'By reading what has been set down in
other handbooks.' And no doubt there is some truth in this, that some
writers of handbooks have no great concern for the facts of the language
but merely reshape whatever fact and fiction have previously proved welcome to English teachers. We may dismiss this type of handbook from the
present discussion, pausing only long enough to deplore its existence.

There is another kind of handbook that is less deplorable than the first
but probably no more satisfactory. This is the book which is simply an
aggregate of the author's impressions and intuitions about the language.
The author, presumably, wishes to report the language as it is, but he feels
that to this end scientific investigation is unnecessary. Instead, he operates
as a sensitized plate, develops his own linguistic consciousness, puts it in
a book, and calls it Standard English. There are those who feel that this is
as good a way as any to get at the facts of the language, but I am not one
of them and I dismiss this kind of handbook also from the present discussion.

We come then to a third variety: the handbook intended as an accurate
report of Standard English and based on study and investigation. The authors of such handbooks will presumably agree that the criterion of correctness is usage and that knowledge about usage must be gained through
observation. They differ, however, on whose usage to observe and on how
to observe it.

The first question is a crucial one, and at the same time it is something
upon which agreement is neither necessary nor even desirable. Each of us
finds his own standard, in language as in other fashions. It seems to be
a common belief among nonlinguists that all linguists are wild radicals,
eager to embrace any vulgarism and call it Standard English. Not so, of
course. Many linguists are as puristic as one could wish, turning quite pale
in the presence of 'the reason is because.' The difference between the puristic linguist and the 'liberal' linguist is that the former chooses to imitate

or hold up for imitation the language of a highly select group, whereas the latter is comfortable with the language of a larger and more heterogeneous group.

It is not required, then, of authors of handbooks that they agree on being liberal or puristic. What is, or should be, required is this: (1) that they report somebody's language and not just language; (2) that they define for the reader as best they can the group that they have taken as setting the standard.

Having decided whose English he will report as Standard English, the handbook writer has then the problem of ascertaining what that English is. Here he will of course be assisted by the existing collections of linguistic facts—the grammars, the dictionaries, the articles in the journals. But I believe that he will find these collections quite inadequate for the settlement of dozens of troublesome and controversial points, and I wish to suggest for this hypothetical writer of handbooks another recourse, one which would shock him if he were not hypothetical. I am going to suggest that he count.

I shall take, for example, the pronoun *this*. Pronominal *this* is controversial in the sense that handbooks disagree on whether it should or need not have as antecedent a noun or noun-equivalent. If we read professional linguists on this point, we find general agreement but nothing that we can accept as evidence. Grammarians are more or less in accord that Standard English does not require a substantive antecedent for pronominal *this*. Indeed, the grammarians are inclined to inveigh against the textbooks which rule otherwise. Such pronouncements may awe the textbook man into submission, but they hardly amount to a demonstration of the truth.

We are told, for example, that pronominal *this* is used by so-and-so and so-and-so and four times by so-and-so, all reputable writers and God-fearing men. Very well! But how shall we know that these are not merely aberrations, occasional freedoms taken by experienced writers? We are not writing such a large book that we can report everything that happens in our Standard English; we must confine ourselves to what happens customarily. And we have so far no light on what is usual.

We are told next that Professor Curme (or Perrin or Fries or Jespersen) approves the construction. Here is irony indeed! Professor Curme stands where Richard Grant White stood fifty years ago, and the wheel has come full circle. Professor Curme (and all the scholars named) are surely worthy of our admiration and emulation, and we may freely acknowledge that their linguistic perceptions are more likely to be accurate than our own. But the major lesson we learn from reading the works of these very men is that in language one should beware *ipse dixits*.

Or we are told that someone queried 625 competent judges and that 419 of them gave it as their opinion that it is all right to use pronominal *this* with vague reference. This is interesting. But we are still in the fog of opinion. We want to know what the facts are, not what various people, however competent, think the facts may be. Is there no way to get at the facts?

It happens that once we decide what English we are calling Standard English the facts are ascertainable and are not even very hard to ascertain. First we define the criterion of the standard. We are working on present-day, written, American English, and within these limits we may choose as exemplary whatever seems to us fit for emulation. Suppose we decide to report what is standard in nationally circulated 'slick' and 'quality' magazines. Since fiction has caprices of its own, let us limit ourselves to the nonfiction in such magazines. This standard will seem properly respectable to many readers; some, of course, will think it too high or too low.

Next we take a sampling of the magazines in the group. The sample should be large enough that numerous authors will be represented and that the count will be statistically reliable. Then we count and classify the occurrences of pronominal *this*.

I took the following magazine issues: *American Scholar,* Summer, 1949; *Atlantic Monthly,* August, 1949; *Harper's,* August, 1949; *McCall's,* August, 1949; *New Yorker,* August 6, 1949; *Saturday Evening Post,* August 6, 1949. I think it will be agreed that the sample is large enough to give a reliable count. The nonfiction consists of 79 articles, editorials, and departments, 67 of which are signed. Two articles were written in collaboration, and one writer signed two articles. I estimate the number of words to be 222,000, distributed as follows: *American Scholar,* 40,000; *Atlantic,* 50,000; *Harper's,* 51,000; *McCall's,* 27,000; *New Yorker,* 24,000; *Post,* 30,000. But the best testimony of the reliability of the sample lies in the fact that, as will be seen, the percentage figures for each magazine do not deviate very much from the figures for the group as a whole.

There must be a mark against which to measure the magazine usages. I set up a hypothetical handbook rule: The pronoun *this* should not be used with vague reference. That is, when it refers to something which precedes it, the antecedent must be a noun or a noun-equivalent which may be substituted for the pronoun without injury to sense or idiom.

In these six magazine issues the pronoun *this* occurred 296 times. These occurrences may be divided into three groups according as they relate to the hypothetical handbook rule:

1. Those which adhere to the rule: 75 occurrences
2. Those which break the rule: 195 occurrences
3. Those to which the rule does not apply: 26 occurrences

These three groups may be divided into subclasses according to the kind of reference. I shall define and illustrate each subclass and give page references for all occurrences.

1. REFERENCES WHICH ADHERE TO THE RULE

a) Reference to a preceding noun:

> Immediately at issue was the super-aircraft-carrier. As the weeks went by this became for the Navy the end and be-all of existence. (Marquis W. Childs, *Harper's*, p. 49.)

Thirty-eight occurrences.[1]

b) Probable reference to a preceding noun, other analysis possible:

> Every now and then a cab driver gets into a situation which calls for gallantry. Every man knows that this can be embarrassing. (Robert M. Yoder, *Post*, p. 74.)

Eleven occurrences.[2]

c) Reference to a preceding gerund that can be substituted for the pronoun:

> Any liberal who has had the experience of working in any community agencies also supported by Communists knows that this is a time-consuming and often difficult activity. (Helen M. Lynd, *American Scholar*, p. 352.)

This was the only occurrence.

d) Reference to a preceding infinitive or infinitive phrase that can be substituted for the pronoun:

> . . . that it is easier to say no to invitations and seek diversion in such solitary pursuits as movies, books, and concerts.
> This is a dangerous habit. (Virginia Lee, *McCall's*, p. 82.)

Seven occurrences.[3]

e) Reference to a preceding noun clause that can be substituted for the pronoun:

> The point is that the same caution should apply to consumers, but does not. At any rate, this is the conclusion of . . . ('The Atlantic Report on the World Today,' *Atlantic*, p. 6.)

Four occurrences.[4]

---

[1] *American Scholar*, pp. 287, 302, 306, 337, 364; *Atlantic*, pp. 5, 6, 35, 40, 52, 74, 75, 82; *Harper's*, pp. 32, 41, 43, 48, 49, 50, 53, 67, 84, 85, 86; *McCall's*, pp. 7, 81, 83, 123; *New Yorker*, pp. 16, 26, 53, 54, 57; *Post*, pp. 78, 78, 84, 86, 87.

[2] *American Scholar*, pp. 338, 346; *Atlantic*, p. 11; *Harper's*, pp. 21, 22, 43, 99; *Post*, pp. 55, 74, 78, 88.

[3] *American Scholar*, p. 340; *Harper's*, p. 107; *McCall's*, pp. 82, 94, 116, 116; *Post*, p. 74.

[4] *American Scholar*, p. 326; *Atlantic*, pp. 6, 72; *New Yorker*, p. 46.

f) Reference to a preceding quotation:

> . . . from the very fountain of its sweetness bubbles up something bitter that stings in the midst of the flowers.' Lucretius, in saying this, was . . . (George Santayana, *American Scholar*, p. 279.)

Fourteen occurrences.[5]

2. REFERENCES WHICH BREAK THE RULE

a) Reference to a preceding main clause or sentence, the idea not summed up in a noun following the pronoun:

> Eighty per cent of Connecticut's industry is in the three counties of Fairfield, Hartford, and New Haven. This explains why New England still has great open spaces. (C. Hartley Grattan, *Harper's*, p. 37.)

Ninety-five occurrences.[6]

b) Reference to an idea in a preceding adjective or adverb clause:

> When he is the Sophisticate Abroad, who should know better, and when this results in a reactionary credo of class lines unhistorically restored, then the tour becomes . . . (Peter Viereck, *Harper's*, p. 63.)

Three occurrences.[7]

c) Reference to more than one preceding sentence; in thirteen of the twenty-four passages the construction is 'all this' or 'all of this':

> The children under 12 years old received a personal gift and each employee a money present and a cornucopia of candy. We usually gave the police guards a tie or a hankerchief, a fruit cake and a cornucopia of Christmas candy.
>
> Of course, this meant a great deal of organizing and planning . . . (Eleanor Roosevelt, *McCall's*, p. 111.)

Twenty-four occurrences.[8]

d) Reference to preceding main clause, sentence, or sentences, but with the idea summed up in a predicate noun or equivalent following the pronoun. (This construction is not a vague reference in quite the same way that the three preceding are, and therefore I have separated it; but of course it also breaks the hypothetical handbook rule.)

---

[5] *American Scholar*, pp. 275, 279, 292, 340, 352; *Atlantic*, pp. 36, 88; *Harper's*, pp. 72, 102; *McCall's*, pp. 28, 94; *New Yorker*, p. 33; *Post*, pp. 52, 52.

[6] *American Scholar*, pp. 267, 270, 274, 286, 287, 295, 297, 300, 301, 309, 330, 332, 334, 334, 343, 348, 348, 363, 364, 368; *Atlantic*, pp. 6, 6, 13, 37, 52, 53, 53, 54, 55, 55, 56, 60, 61, 71, 73, 74, 75, 76, 77, 78, 89, 89, 94; *Harper's*, pp. 7, 23, 28, 32, 35, 37, 38, 39, 39, 39, 41, 61, 62, 65, 66, 67, 81, 83, 84, 85, 87, 99, 101, 104, 106; *McCall's*, pp. 8, 68, 80, 101, 109, 112, 113, 116, 123, 123, 123, 127; *New Yorker*, pp. 14, 15, 17, 34, 34, 51, 60; *Post*, pp. 21, 27, 74, 77, 77, 78, 78, 84.

[7] *American Scholar*, p. 368; *Atlantic*, p. 83; *Harper's*, p. 63.

[8] *American Scholar*, pp. 285, 343, 353; *Atlantic*, pp. 13, 17, 18, 36, 55, 73, 77, 84; *Harper's*, pp. 39, 44, 44, 51, 52, 84, 98, 106; *McCall's*, p. 111; *Post*, pp. 10, 12, 48, 50.

In short, New England is an export-import region within a huge and highly dynamic national economy. This is its strength and its weakness. (C. Hartley Grattan, *Harper's*, p. 36.)

Forty-five occurrences.[9]

e) Reference to preceding sentences, with the idea summed up in an objective complement following the pronoun:

A huge cast and elaborate sets make this a handsome production. (Frankie McKee Robbins, *McCall's*, p. 7.)

f) Reference to a preceding plural noun:

Suddenly I saw them—her panties! They were blue cotton-jersey affairs, standard all over Russia. It was for this the speculators had risked their lives and the women of Kiev had paid one hundred and eighty rubles. (Margaret K. Webb, *Harper's*, p. 79.)

This was the only occurrence.

g) Reference to a preceding gerund that cannot be substituted for the pronoun:

The second aims at stabilizing politically and economically the Atlantic Pact countries of Western Europe. This cannot be done until . . . [Idiom would hardly permit '. . . stabilizing . . . cannot be done . . .'] ('The Atlantic Report on the World Today,' *Atlantic*, p. 7.)

Two occurrences.[10]

h) Reference to a preceding infinitive or infinitive phrase that cannot be substituted for the pronoun. In this group and the next the reference is not really to the substantive but to a verbal idea expressed therein. Often a corresponding gerund might be substituted:

If a yacht-owner decides to wander into foreign waters during a war and wants coverage on this, he gets, for an additional fee, a third clause, reinstating the war perils. ('The Talk of the Town,' *New Yorker*, p. 16.)

Eight occurrences.[11]

i) Reference to a preceding noun clause that cannot be substituted for the pronoun:

It is enough that through judicial proceedings and under continued regard for due and public process, the case was disposed of (subject to subsequent

---

[9] *American Scholar*, pp. 269, 272, 273, 277, 297, 315, 327, 327, 327, 328, 333, 339, 339, 340; *Atlantic*, pp. 6, 36, 52, 52, 55, 61, 81; *Harper's*, pp. 9, 24, 36, 38, 45, 46, 48, 49, 51, 52, 53, 67, 85, 100; *McCall's*, pp. 8, 94, 111; *New Yorker*, p. 13; *Post*, pp. 20, 29, 77, 84, 87, 88.

[10] *Atlantic*, p. 7; *Harper's*, p. 33.

[11] *American Scholar*, p. 308; *Atlantic*, pp. 11, 39, 72; *Harper's*, pp. 33, 51; *New Yorker*, p. 16; *Post*, p. 88.

court action). To ask more than this is to ask too much . . . (T. V. Smith, *American Scholar*, p. 346.)

Sixteen occurrences.[12]

3. REFERENCES TO WHICH THE RULE DOES NOT APPLY

a) Reference to a following noun, phrase, clause, sentence, or sentences. Typically, the pronoun is followed by a colon:

But understand this: since there is no regulation prohibiting their entry, these were brought in legally. (Albert R. Mead, *Atlantic*, p. 42.)

Fifteen occurrences.[13]

b) Adjectival *this* used substantively; here the pronoun is often equivalent to 'this one':

After an evening like this no American ever . . . (Ann Leighton, *Atlantic*, p. 62.)

Five occurrences.[14]

c) Reference to time:

This was a bad winter in the Arctic. (Thomas R. Henry, *Post*, p. 29.)

Two occurrences.[15]

d) Reference to the author's own piece of writing:

. . . at the date of writing this it is a question which is before the Federal courts for judicial determination. (Arthur O. Lovejoy, *American Scholar*, p. 43.)

Three occurrences.[16]

e) Completely indefinite reference:

. . . the instinctive expert whose metal formula is based on a little pinch of this and a little pinch of that. (Herbert Coggins, *Atlantic*, p. 91.)

This was the only occurrence.

Adding these figures we get the following statistics:

Class 1: *American Scholar*, 15; *Atlantic*, 13; *Harper's*, 18; *McCall's*, 10; *New Yorker*, 7; *Post*, 12; total, 75.

[12] *American Scholar*, pp. 329, 340, 346, 352, 364; *Atlantic*, pp. 4, 71, 75, 79, 85, 93; *Harper's*, pp. 65, 100; *McCall's*, pp. 99, 113; *Post*, p. 110.
[13] *American Scholar*, pp. 273, 285; *Atlantic*, pp. 42, 78; *Harper's*, pp. 7, 26, 27, 27, 43, 73; *McCall's*, pp. 82, 83; *Post*, pp. 36, 37, 88.
[14] *American Scholar*, p. 320; *Atlantic*, pp. 42, 62, 82; *McCall's*, p. 7.
[15] *New Yorker*, p. 44; *Post*, p. 29.
[16] *American Scholar*, p. 333; *Harper's*, pp. 6, 35.

Class 2: *American Scholar,* 44; *Atlantic,* 49; *Harper's,* 54; *McCall's,* 19; *New Yorker,* 9; *Post,* 20; total, 195.

Percentage of vague references (Class 2) in the occurrences to which the rule applies (Classes 1 and 2): *American Scholar,* 0.74; *Atlantic,* 0.79; *Harper's,* 0.75; *McCall's,* 0.65; *New Yorker,* 0.56; *Post,* 0.63.

Our initial problem is no longer a problem. It is clear from these figures that in the material we have taken to represent Standard American English vague-reference *this* is the norm. We cannot possibly term it an aberration or an occasional freedom taken by the experienced writer. The chances are heavy that whenever an experienced writer types out the word *this* he will be referring not to a substantive antecedent, but to an idea, a main clause, a sentence, or sentences.

The fact that the percentages for the separate magazines are none of them more than 16 percentage points off the group percentage indicates a satisfactory reliability for the study. Further counting would probably fix the group percentage somewhere between 60 and 80, the mathematical chances that it would ever go outside those figures being small. Probably the sample is not large enough to warrant remarks about the meaning of the differences among the several magazines; but one point is quite clear. Quality writing is as fond of vague-reference *this* as mass-circulation writing is—evidently more so. It is of at least ironic interest that the *Atlantic Monthly,* that splendid old citadel of linguistic propriety, appears in this study most abandoned of all in its attitude toward *this.*

Counting, I am aware, will not solve all problems, not even all handbook problems. But it will solve many, and it does seem absurd to argue about what the facts may be when it is possible to know what the facts are. If we were indeed writing a handbook of English usage and if we set down the information that in the national magazines pronominal *this* is generally used without a substantive antecedent, our readers might disapprove of our choice of standard, but they could not disagree with what we say about the standard. That is fact.

The Syntax of Deferred Prepositions*

M. BERTENS CHARNLEY

A PREPOSITION is held to be no word to end a sentence with. It is a usage that writers like Dr. Johnson would carefully avoid: one would have to go through many pages of his *Lives of the Poets* before encountering half a dozen. The idiomatic smack of the construction is evident in writers of a

* Reprinted by permission from *American Speech,* 24.268–277 (December, 1949).

more spontaneous nature. When Motteux came across an untranslatable saying in the exceedingly colloquial *Don Quixote,* he consistently tried to render the atmosphere by resorting to a staggering preposition:

What a woeful condition would they be in! (*No le arrendara la ganancia.*)

All I aim at, is only to make the world sensible (*sólo me fatigo*).

If the difficulties of his medium become unsurmountable, and he expands his text in order to compensate, it is again his resource:

Having asked the governor what condition the graduate was in.

A language which, like English, relies so largely on the forcefulness of its particles, often pregnant at that, but manacled on the other hand by a rigid word order, gains in the end by the resulting conciseness:

The huge sea-wall of Istrian stone, with cunning breathing-places for the waves to wreak their fury on and foam their force away in fretful waste [Symonds].

The eloquent adverb is correlated with, and balanced by, the preposition. Cacophony is often avoided by the device, as in

Desperately tired of the babies he seemed to think she alone was responsible for [Newspaper].

This order is vastly superior to the cumbrous 'the babies for which he seemed to think that she alone was responsible.'

When the preposition has to be repeated, a pleasant modulation of its stress is permitted:

The difference between the price he sells at and the price at which he obtains the stock himself [Wheeler].

The antithesis has been reinforced by cross order.

In the orthodox 'in his last moments he found he had no one to whom to give or to esteem,' the three *to's* jar a little on the ear. The logical parallelism of 'to give' and 'to esteem' is furthermore grammatically belied by the first *to,* seemingly implying that you 'esteem to someone' as well as you 'give to someone.' By leaving out the unnecessary relative and by placing the first *to* enclitically after the only one of the two infinitives it is intended to qualify, we at the same time gain in brevity: 'no one to give to or to esteem.'

The rigidity of English word order is gracefully overcome when the prominence of a subject is kept in the sequence by not having to make it an object, particularly when two coupled statements are made:

The movement known as the revival of learning was accomplished before the end of the xv century, and all investigators are agreed that *it* was very largely *contributed to* by Greek exiles [Pears].

The balance is maintained in Spanish, for instance, through the flexibility of word order: *el movimiento se completó . . . contribuyeron a él los griegos;* but the continuity is not impaired, and the concentrated effect is greater, in

> His appearance, some of his written words, what certain others said about him, his publications, his money affairs—all these we are duly informed of [Newspaper].

Not the least advantage is seen in the possibility of having one relative to introduce two or more coördinate relative clauses, when they contain different prepositions:

> I looked now upon the world as a thing remote, which I had nothing to do with, no expectation from, and, indeed, no desires about [De Foe].

The relative has to be repeated every time in other languages, as an object for the varying prepositions. The device may be carried into the field of subordination:

> The degeneracy of human nature, which, though I had heard of often, yet I never had so near a view of before [De Foe].

No amount of typographical refinement could in translation reproduce the studied contrast in

> He was very sorry that Dr. Channing—a man to whom he looked *up*—no, to say that he looked *up* to him would be to speak falsely; but a man whom he looked *at* with so much interest—should embrace such views [Emerson].

To sum up, practice has been right in departing from the school-grammarians' rule that prepositions always must be preposed. English has thereby overcome to a degree the disadvantages derived from its rigid word order and, literally making a virtue of necessity, has in some respects surpassed other languages in brevity and vividness.

The highly idiomatic preposition at the end of a clause is, possibly, the last collocation to be used by foreigners learning English. In reading, they usually apprehend their purport because the sentences containing them are seldom so involved as to set them very widely apart from their object, so that the latter is still present in the reader's mind when the anastrophic preposition is arrived at. Instances like the following are, however, rather puzzling to the beginner:

> A landfall, good or bad, is made and done with with the first cry of 'Land ho!' [Conrad].

It is a very difficult matter to learn how to use prepositions in this way, except after an extensive acquaintance with the language. And I do not know of any systematic treatment of the circumstances under which idiom allows them. The *Oxford English Dictionary* states, under the heading

'Preposition,' that they are relegated to the end when their object is a relative or interrogative pronoun. Under *To*, II, *7aa* 11*a* (*d*), 11*b* (*d*), and 11*c* (*d*), it speaks of an infinitive followed by a preposition, the substantive being the implicit object of the preposition. I do not want to impeach the *Dictionary* for not being a grammar, although it is the work coming nearest to a complete grammar of English without pretending to be so, but even there no consistency is observed in this regard; under *Which, Who, What,* and *Where,* mention is made of a preposition standing at the end of a clause, always branded as a colloquialism, and accounted for as an occasional occurrence. Nothing to the point is to be found under *Be* as the passive auxiliary, nor under *Than* or *Worth,* nor under *Have.*

An analysis of the different patterns wherein a straggling preposition is idiomatically justified proves that the object which is naturally expected to follow it is in every case dislodged from its position owing to some kind of inversion, either rhetorical or syntactical, or to a combination of these. 'Straggling' is perhaps too strong a term to apply to them. But they cannot be called 'final' as finality is only denoted by the *to* of some gerundials; or 'terminal' without conflicting with the nomenclature of, let us say, Spanish —a preposition is inconceivable without its *término.* Fowler has 'preposition at end.' But since its object is, explicitly or implicitly, always anticipated, 'deferred' is in my opinion the best designation.

RHETORICAL INVERSION

In the opening chapters of *Roderick Random,* Smollett makes his hero say: 'I resolved to apply myself with great care to my studies; this I did with such success, that, in the space of three years I *understood Greek* very well . . .' Further on, the object is related to its verb through a preposition, which lags at the end of the clause: '. . . *logic* I made no account *of.*'

The front position is seen to be unimpaired by what ought logically to be preposed, so that we have a clear-cut detachment of the psychological subject. Grammars speak of intransitive verbs being made into transitives through a preposition being tacked on to them, so that the latter must be parsed together with them; this is the case with

The humble calling of her female parent Miss Sharp never alluded to [Thackeray].

But no such explanation would hold good for the verb in

All this labour I was at the expense of purely from my apprehensions [De Foe].

More elaborate instances of rhetorical inversion are:

My father and mother, since they are both dead, I shall be no nearer to in Essendean than in the Kingdom of Hungary [Stevenson].

A drinking cup of some precious metal was found; and this cup, fashioned no doubt by elfin skill, but rendered harmless by the purification with fire, the sons and daughters of Sandy Macharg and his wife drink out of to this very day [Cunningham].

INTERROGATIVES

The emphatic nature of questions necessitates the initial position for the interrogative, which is at the same time the object of the preposition:

'*Where* are going *to?*' asked Mr. Smeeth [Priestley].

Needless to say, this is the inverted 'you are going to where?' The same initial position of the interrogative with a deferred preposition is found if they are merely part of an adjunct intended to carry the greatest weight:

He had mistrusted the idea from the first. What did he want to go into the country for? [Galsworthy].

What did he want to tell her she was wicked for? What did he tell her that God hated her for? If God hated her, what did she want to go to Sabbath school for? [Hawthorne].

The interrogative may also be used adjectively:

Do not enumerate his talents or his feats, but ask thyself, what spirit is he of? [Emerson].

RELATIVES

The relative pronouns, as hinted above, have sprung historically from the interrogatives. They must head dependent clauses by reason of their having at the same time to connect them with the main clauses, but they may be the object of the verb in the predicate, and of the preposition, if any:

The character that Seneca gives of this hyperbolical fop, *whom* we stand amazed at [Cowley].

That's *what* a honeymoon is for, but now we've got to get down to work [Somerset Maugham].

A happy union of our families by marriage; a thing *which* the equality of our births and fortunes did indeed of itself almost invite us to [Motteux].

'Anybody keep goats around here?' 'Not *that* I know of' [Jerome].

In this last quotation, the antecedent is elliptic; compare 'not a single circumstance [that] I know of.' So long as the antecedent is explicit, the relative may be omitted:

The other pieces of ground I had worked so hard at [De Foe].

The relative is usually expressed when its omission might be confusing:

> You know what I mean—the sort of girl that you turn round to look after [Jerome].

(It is not the girl that is turned round!) It may be suppressed even when not a direct object:

> We must work our utmost at the thing we are in [Walpole].

With a verb that is merely copulative:

> That manager only saw him in 'Candida.' It's the only part he's half way decent in [Somerset Maugham].

The preposition dependent on a noun complementing the verb:

> Rights, that we are obliged to no power, under heaven, for the enjoyment of [Emerson].

This specimen borders on Browning's forced

> The Michaels and Raphaels you hum and buzz round the works of.

The compound (Sweet's condensed) relative behaves in like manner, provided it is an objective, and not solely a subject ('who gets at my purse'):

> *What* we wish *for* in youth comes in heaps on us in old age [Emerson].
>
> Modern, no less than ancient history, supplies us with many most painful examples *of what* I refer *to* [Wilde].

As, when a relative, likewise causes a preposition to straggle:

> I'll have a glass of rum from this dear child here, *as* I've took such a liking *to* [Stevenson].

Here *as* is used dialectally instead of one of the current relatives. A literary example is

> His activity was employed in observations such as no thinker would ever have engaged in [Buckle].

Constructions like the ones explained under rhetorical inversion may, in all likelihood, have been facilitated by clauses in which the relative has been omitted, due to their identity in form on the one hand, and on the other to the fact that both types exhibit subordination, of psychological emphasis in one case, and of the qualifying function in the second:

> This way of life the first serious reflection put a period to [Fielding].

(This way of life [which] the first serious reflection . . .)

'THAN'

Akin in origin to relative conjunctives is the comparative of inequality *than:*

> . . . tire my imagination and give me an inclination to a repose more profound than I was at that time capable of [Steele].

Just as the *such* preceding the *as* discussed above is pregnant ('such observations'), so also *than* implies *repose.*

> More things are wrought by prayer
> Than this world dreams of [Tennyson].

(More things than things that . . .) The pronoun is felt to be redundant after *than* in this passage:

> Cargo-carriers that would know no glory other than of a long service, no victory but that of an endless contest with the sea [Conrad].

PASSIVAL

There are more kinds of fools than one can guard against [Conrad].

'There are more things in heaven and earth, Horatio, than you dream of.' But the liberally indulged-in English passive, an inversion resulting from ignoring the irrelevant or subdued active subject, wills it thus: 'More things than *are dreamt of* in your philosophy.' The object having assumed the role of subject, the preposition governing it stands now necessarily—and not as often formerly, at pleasure—at the end. Shakespeare's preposition lags for a double reason: the clause is passive as well as relative. But a purely passive sentence prescribes the same:

> In such marine shore-talk as this is the name of a ship slowly established, her fame made for her, the tales of her qualities and her defects kept, her idiosyncrasies *commented upon* with the zest of personal gossip, her achievements made much *of,* her faults glossed *over* as things that, being without remedy in our imperfect world, should not be dwelt *upon* too much by men who, with the help of ships, wrest out a bitter living from the rough grasp of the sea [Conrad].

Similarly, after a passive infinitive:

> You don't know what it is to fall into the pit, to be despised, mocked, abandoned, sneered at—to be an outcast [Wilde],

or after a complement:

> Tricked by Gad, that's what I was, tricked by life and made a fool of [Sherwood Anderson],

or after an adverbial particle:

> Consider the number of trades that would be thrown out of employment if it were done away with [Hazlitt].

The deferred preposition is invited by adjectives construed with *to—apt, liable, likely:*

> Towards the interior of the country, where we can hide for a time and are less likely to be looked for [Hardy].

Besides *to be,* other intransitives of incomplete predication may serve to form passives with a resulting end preposition:

> She did not *feel* called upon to point out to him the obvious facts [Somerset Maugham].

The passive is implicit in the second member of

> When Isabella was young and Prim unthought of [Lytton Strachey],

and is altogether dispensed with in

> He thought of the old house and the woman who lived there with him as things departed and done for [Sherwood Anderson].

The elliptic

> A letter addressed to himself and directed to be left till called for [Dickens].

leads insensibly—by detaching the qualifier—to

> Looked back on, the Atomic War was a deliverance [Armitage].

PARTICIPIAL

The next step is to treat the past participle and preposition as an adjectival attribute:

> The number of unofficially but very largely *dealt in* securities has been greatly swollen [Wheeler].

Here belong the large number of negative qualifiers of the type represented in

> We discard all *uncalled-for* evidence [Hazlitt].

The word order in the following, where *infringed upon* is a not yet stereotyped phrase, shows that what is felt to be a syncopated passive adjective clause helps to establish the idiom:

> Our thanks for every rational measure they have taken for the preservation or recovery of our invaluable rights and liberties infringed upon [Emerson].

This pattern is suitable to the brevity requisite in definitions:

> PRIVILEGE: an advantage not shared in by all [Hugon].

'WORTH'

The passive sense imposed by *worth* relegates the preposition:

That Kit should inherit an England *worth* living *in* was of more intrinsic importance [Galsworthy].

Similarly with *except, save, past*, of participial origin:

If she's quarrelsome now, she'll be *past* living *with* if you're not careful [Priestley].

DISRUPTED PERFECT

The causative and receptive verbs construed with a direct object and a passive participle call for a deferred preposition:

He would *have* no person sent *for* [Dickens].

Old Acton *had* his house broken *into* last Monday [Conan Doyle].

On their analogy, we find a similar construction with verbs of perception:

A hundred times he had *heard* the old man spoken *of* as a little off his head [Sherwood Anderson].

GERUNDIALS

It has been laid down that a passive rules the end preposition, as in this dictum of Antisthenes:

It is a princely thing to do well and *to be* ill-*spoken* of.

In the following, the infinitive is no longer a subject, but a modifier:

It refuses to appear, it is too small to be seen, too obscure *to be spoken of* [Emerson].

The form is, nevertheless, identical; the same happens whether we are qualifying a noun, as in

This age is not *to be trifled with* [Emerson],

or an adjective, as in

Books too good *to be trifled with*, yawned over in a train [Priestley].

However, I do not intend to prove that it is the identity in form, but rather that it is the similarity in envisaging the notion when modified that prescribes the deferred preposition. The avowedly passive form cited above is a late development; the earlier form made no use of the verb *to be*, thus:

He had just come out of the marvellous Tweed, a ship, I have heard, heavy to look at [Conrad].

That the import is passive appears clearly in Rupert Brooke's 'Say, is there Beauty yet to find?' The characteristic *by* of the active subject turned adjunct in the passive is seen in

> A false step to be particularly guarded against by those who converse with monarchs [Scott].

Compare the Latin *res iucunda auditu;* and the Spanish *cosa digna de ver,* also *verse,* the impersonal passive. But when modifying a noun, the gerundial is adjectival, and now the equivalent of an elliptic relative clause, which explains the following instances, whose verbs cannot possibly be labeled as passival:

> What a chap to be out with, to be smiling at! [Priestley].

> I had no floor to thrash it on, or instrument to thrash it with [De Foe].

The adverb *too* demands either *to* or *for,* or both, and so falls in with the above:

> A power *too* mighty *for* reason *to* grapple with [Anson's Voyages].

We have a case wherein the gerundial is found to be absolute, namely, when introducing a parenthesis:

> I haven't the smallest intention of doing anything of the sort. *To* begin *with,* I dined there on Monday [Wilde],

which may be interpreted as a quasi-relative: 'I dined there on Monday (wherewith to begin) . . .'
There are ellipsis, inversion, and passivity in

> On mature reflection, I think the music was most to blame. Except to dance to, I always loathed American music [Lockhart].

RESTRICTIONS

Although 'no other construction is possible' with the relative *that,* it may be worth while to consider several instances in which the preposition, for some reason or other, does not lag at the end. It must precede the relative when it joins the phrase or clause introduced by it:

> Little as I like the *sound of what* I heard, and slow as I began to travel [Stevenson].

> Everything in the world to her might *depend on what* that note contained [Trollope].

The preposition must not run the risk of being taken as depending on the verb in the other clause, should it thus make sense: 'get to what he pointed; get what he pointed to.'

A verb without any possibility of assuming an active sense makes the deferred construction impossible:

> She bent her steps towards the end of the village at which the parental cottage *lay* [Hardy].

Confusion is also to be avoided when the governing preposition is *to,* and a gerundial is involved:

> Have a care to whom thou givest it to read [Motteux].

But when the preposition is dependent on the gerundial, no such risk is incurred:

> This is not the door to speak to me at [Wells].

ADVERBIALS

In collocations like 'all the country over,' 'all night through,' none of the syntactical reasons so far given is the explanation:

> Why, yes, they were famous eyes, famous the diocese *through* [Walpole].

They are half adverbs, and consequently do not fall within the province of the present paper. The same is the case with *round, around, notwithstanding, over,* and similar words. The elliptic object of the preposition, itself half adverbial, in

> A thing called 'one's honor' which included money and women and something beyond [Newspaper],

paralleled by *within, without,* etc., is the link carrying us to the verbal phrase we find in

> In this bustle many men have to go *without* [Newspaper].

Further yet, in

> A person capable of giving a seaman a talking-to [Clark Russell],

the particle is on its way to becoming a mere affix: compare Anglo-Saxon *tōcyme,* German *Zukunft* or *Zurede.*

The Inflected Genitive
in Modern American Prose*

RUSSELL THOMAS

SEVERAL YEARS AGO Professor C. C. Fries showed that the inflective genitive in present-day American English is not confined to the "possessive" meaning.[1] And, after reading his article, I wondered about the status of the inflected genitive when the word inflected names something other than a human being, for, in those examples which Professor Fries lists (except for some which represent either a genitive of measure or the genitive with gerund), the word inflected denotes a human being. Furthermore, inasmuch as many grammarians have condemned the use of this genitive for inanimate objects, I decided to investigate the problem beyond the limits of my previous study[2] as well as those by Fries, Jespersen, Hall, Curme, and other historical grammarians. My results are based upon an examination of, roughly, 10,000–12,000 pages of material, the far greater portion of which dates from 1930 to 1952. It includes works of fiction, critical essays and books, scientific essays and books, book reviews, editorials, news stories, and informal essays.[3]

I have classified my materials (with the exception of one group) on the basis of the meaning of the inflected word, instead of on that which Fries used as indicated in note 1 above. Although my procedure is open to some criticism, I have decided to use it because I feel it clarifies further the whole problem of the construction.[4]

* Reprinted by permission from *College English*, 14.236–239 (January, 1953).

[1] In "Some Notes on the Inflected Genitive in Present-Day English," *Language*, XIV (April–June, 1938), 121–33. His materials consisted of "some three thousand personal letters copied from those in the files of one of the government bureaus at Washington" and revealed that the inflected genitives of nouns were distributed as follows: "Possessive genitive (liberally interpreted)—40%; Subjective genitive—23%; Genitive of origin—6%; Objective genitive—17%; Descriptive genitive—10%; and one example each of the Genitive with gerund and the Absolute Genitive."

[2] "Syntactic Processes Involved in the Development of the Adnominal Periphrastic Genitive in the English Language" (unpublished doctoral dissertation, University of Michigan, Ann Arbor, 1931).

[3] I excluded all poetry because exigencies of meter very often force the poet to use the inflected genitive. Some of the periodicals which I examined are the *Yale Review*, *PLMA*, *Atlantic Monthly*, *Nation*, *Harper's Magazine*, *Saturday Review of Literature*, *New England Quarterly*, *Sewanee Review*, *New Republic*, *Kenyon Review*, et al.

[4] One of the earliest studies of the problem was published in J. Lesslie Hall's *English Usage* (Chicago: Scott, Foresman & Co., 1917), pp. 202–7. His study of the "possessive

Most readers of this article will be interested at once, I suppose, in what I found concerning the inflected genitive with inanimate objects.[5] I have 47 examples, most of which date within the last ten years. Some of these are "the bed's head," "the building's roof," "a car's axle," "the clock's tick," "the hat's crown," "the big hall's location," "the arrow's shank," "the bomb's angle of contact," etc.

The next group consist of examples where the inflected genitive denotes, as stated in note 5, the general name for an individual publication, such as *book, novel, poem, play,* etc. I have 96 examples, ranging from 1926 to the present, but the greater portion date from within the last six years. This locution seems to be favored by college and university professors and by others who write book reviews for our leading periodicals. I examined certain issues of three periodicals (*Yale Review, Nation,* and *Harper's Magazine*) in the 1930's and early 1940's and found that there were fewer examples in these early issues than in those within the last six years, thus leading me to conclude that locutions of the type included in this group are beginning to encroach upon the phrasal genitive.[6] Examples are "the story's genesis," "the play's philosophy," "a poem's sources," "the book's true importance," "this book's intention," "the novel's rhythm," etc.

In the next group, consisting of 18 excerpts which range from 1940 to the present, the inflected genitive names some branch of knowledge, such as "modern poetry's desertion of the genteel tradition," "fiction's two possible worlds," "art's frontal attacks," "science's influence on society," "archeology's job," and "history's ugliest marauder."

The inflected genitive is used fairly frequently when the writer has in mind some geographic and/or political areas or units, such as "world," "country," "nation," "city," "town," and "region." I have 71 examples of this type, all but one of which date anywhere from 1950 to 1952, the one lone exception dating from 1915. The following is a sampling: "the world's life," "the world's economic organization," "the nation's chief waterways," "the

---

case of inanimate objects" is based on "87 authorities and 700 passages" selected from literature dating from John Mandeville down to Stevenson and Chesterton and also includes American authors. However, outside of a few quotations, he makes no attempt to classify his material. For example, he lumps together such locutions as Matthew Arnold's "the creative power's exercise," Poe's "the world's view," Hawthorne's "tomorrow's dinner," Emerson's "life's book," and Ruskin's "his table's head."

[5] I have placed in a separate group all inflected words which designate certain publications, such as *books, novels, poems, stories,* etc., because my data show that there has been a slight encroachment of the inflected genitive on the periphrastic (phrasal) genitive with these particular words within the last thirty years.

[6] This locution is not, furthermore, an Americanism, for I picked up examples of it from recent British periodicals, such as the *Times* (London) *Literary Supplement* and *The Nineteenth Century* and from essays in criticism by such scholars as E. M. W. Tillyard and Lord David Cecil. This same comment applies also to some of the other groups of locutions discussed in this article.

region's lack," "the earth's interior," "the country's name," "the town's foreign flavor," "the city's beauty," "the city's working maelstrom," etc.[7]

Words which denote a certain period of time have shown genitival inflection for centuries. I have 63 examples of this type, varying stylistically from such expressions as "a day's work" to "the next year's baptisms," "the decade's post-mortem," "today's cold war," "a winter's program of reading," "at the year's turn," "November's voters," "the future's course," "today's and tomorrow's business," and "this summer's suspense novels."

The next group, for which I have 104 examples, has a kind of homogeneity in that it includes words which designate a group or body of people more or less closely united—most of them for some purpose. But these purposes are of a heterogeneous nature, as will be seen from the following examples: "the Church's corruption," "communism's aims," "Christianity's attackers," "democracy's probable course," "a government's conviction," "the majority's platform," "the right's President," "the court's action," "the party's elder statesmen," "the agency's outlook," "in labor's ranks," "the company's working capital," "the trust's profits," "the railroad's past exploitation," "the law school's failure," etc. I have also included in this group 17 examples of words which denote large blocks or divisions of people who are not united for any specific purpose. Examples: "society's oscillation," "the public's convenience," "the race's oldest and strongest institutions," "humanity's orations," "youth's problems," "childhood's comprehension," etc.

During my reading I collected a small number of examples for each of the words "war," "life," and "mind." For the word "war," I have 12 examples, dating from 1940 to 1952. Examples: "war's growing indecisiveness," "the war's outbreak," "the war's end," "war's cruelty." The data for the word "life" are interesting. I have nine examples from American usage and also one each from an Icelander (the novelist, Anne Crone), a Dane (the late Professor Jespersen), and an Englishman (the Honorable Winston Churchill). The Americans represented come from varied walks of life; a private in the United States Army (in a letter to the London *Times Literary Supplement*), a former dean of women of Brown University, a Methodist pastor, a professor of philosophy at Yale, a columnist, etc. Variety, thy name is human! Some examples are: "life's open air," "life's struggles," "life's security," and "life's purpose." I have but three examples of the word "mind," all from recent material. Examples: "with the mind's general development," "through the mind's last mode of beautiful sound," and "the mind's knowledge of its objects."

The next group consists of 20 examples of expressions which may be classed as "stock formulas," where the important word is the noun which

---

[7] I have omitted all examples where the inflected genitive designates specific cities, towns, rivers, countries, etc., such as "Los Angeles's story," "Minnesota's placards," "America's future," "Japan's guilt." They occur so frequently that to include them would be as superfluous as shipping iron ore to Upper Michigan.

the genitive modifies. These are examples of the influence of analogy. They range from 1915 to the present, but the majority are fairly recent. Some examples follow: "for war's sake," "for experience's sake," "for authority's sake," "for my soul's sake," "for pure virility's sake," "the water's edge," "the valley's edge," "the cliff's edge," "sheep's clothing," "a finger's breadth," "the lion's share," etc.

I found only 14 instances of genitive inflection with the names of animals. One of these dates from 1926, while the others are from the last three years. A few examples are: "the rat's brain," "the bird's leg," "a horse's skeleton," "the dog's collar."

The last group consists of 32 examples which I am unable to classify. Again, the greater portion dates from the last two decades. I list these in alphabetical order:

battle—in the battle's front
benefit—for the benefit's time
bill—the bill's introduction
body—the body's descent
cardboard—the cardboard's time
death—death's tomb
desert—the desert's nature
dollar—four hundred dollars' difference
fleet—our fleet's spectacular cruise
freedom—in freedom's name
garden—the garden's vitality
law—the law's existence
mile—a mile's distance
operation—the operation's end
personality—the personality's urge
polio—polio's behavior
program—the insurance program's failure
project—the project's editors
radio—radio's most human contributions
rain—the rain's midst
rainbow—the rainbow's arch
stock—the stock's descent
strike—the strike's end
sun—the sun's exterior
telegraph—the telegraph's report
television—television's future
thought—a thought's meaning
treaty—the treaty's ratification
valley—the valley's forests
water—the water's uses
wind—the wind's last dissolving sigh
word—a word's function

Table 1 summarizes the data gathered for this study.

TABLE 1

Type or Group	No. of Examples
1. Inanimate objects	47
2. Publications	96
3. Branch of knowledge	18
4. Geographic and political areas	71
5. Periods of time	63
6. Groups of people	104
7. Three isolated words ("war," "life," "mind")	24
8. Stock formulas	20
9. Animals	14
10. Miscellaneous (unclassified) words	32
Total	489

In concluding this article, I should like to make a few comments as to the reasons for the use of these inflected genitives, several of which no doubt strike a harsh stylistic note. In the first place, all of them can be traced back to similar examples in the Old English period, when the inflected genitive was used 99.5 per cent of the time, as I demonstrated in my doctoral thesis. Another reason why some of the locutions are present today is that their use lends itself to the practice of piling up pre-noun modifiers, as, for example, in these two excerpts:

Added to the American public's then moral attitude to such subjects. . . .

There are in the Lockwood Library's Spender notebook, six. . . .

Then, too, I found an occasional example where euphony seemed to demand the inflected genitive. On the other hand, there were instances where the phrasal genitive could have been used just as effectively. Occasionally I found an excerpt, such as the one given below, where the writer used both types in successive sentences, thus:

What are these things which endanger the position of our colleges? What are these things which jeopardize the college's position?

Of course, it is possible to use an uninflected adjective instead of either type of genitive, as was done by a minister recently, who said, "These are times when religion's flame burns low." And a few minutes later he spoke of "the flame of religion," and then of "the religious flame."

By and large, I do not see that much can be done about ostracizing these constructions. A large portion of my data is from writers who cannot exactly be classed as "skimmed milk." Such novelists as Faulkner, Hemingway, Evelyn Eaton, and Sherwood Anderson, such literary figures as Louis Untermeyer and Archibald MacLeish, such scholars and critics as David Daiches, Howard M. Jones, O. J. Campbell, John Mason Brown, and the *New York Times*—to mention a few sources for my materials—presumably know something about style. In fact, when I sent at inquiry to Professor Campbell about his use of the locution "the play's structure," I received—pronto—a red-hot reply in defense of it.

Usage and Meaning*

ROBERT J. GEIST

BEFORE THE "usage vs. correctness" battle gives way entirely to the "structure vs. traditional grammar" battle, I should like to scout an area where "correctness" appears to have "usage" on the defensive. This area includes the concern over the "correct" meaning of *disinterested* as well as this engaging sentence: "Accuracy in the use of these [foreign] terms is determined not by careless oral expression but by appeal to written usage . . ."[1] Since *careless* slightly prejudices the issue, one is tempted to retort that accuracy is not determined by careless written expression either. But a retort here will not do, for the statement expresses the honest fear of many teachers that the nonauthoritarian ideas of "usage people" will undermine the precise use of words, that a doctrine of usage condones or actively promotes fuzzy diction and fuzzy meanings. I cannot share this fear.

At the risk of getting stuck on the sticky subject of meaning, I think it can safely be stated that a word means what a speaker intends it to mean and what a hearer interprets it to mean.[2] In the event intention and interpretation differ, a realistic appeal can be made only to the intention and interpretation of people—in other words, to usage. One can assume, I suppose, that there is a "real" meaning which has no relation to what people intend or interpret, but I find nothing to support this assumption and no usefulness in it. In reconciling differing intentions and interpretations, one may make the startling discovery that a meaning can be very vague

---

* Reprinted by permission from *College Composition and Communication*, 6.88–91 (May, 1955).

[1] *College English*, XIV (Oct., 1952), 37.

[2] This statement, of course, says only that the meaning of a word is the meaning of that word. A more significant definition may be quoted from Bloch and Trager's *Outline of Linguistic Analysis* (1942), p. 6: "The meaning of a linguistic form . . . is the feature common to all the situations in which it is used." Since, however, the present paper merely objects to the proposition that the meaning of a word is *not* the meaning of that word, the statement as given will do. A further quotation from Bloch and Trager (p. 7) states the essential thesis of this paper: "All these words [*horse, cheval, Pferd; bowwow, gnaf-gnaf, wanwan*] are equally appropriate, since all are equally arbitrary. It is convention alone—a kind of tacit agreement among the members of a social group—that gives any word its meaning. This elementary truth, which no one disputes after a moment's reflection, is nevertheless often forgotten by students of a foreign language." And, we may add, sometimes by others intent on the *real* meaning of a word.

or very specific or that a single word may have several meanings. One can make the same discovery on almost any page of a dictionary. The word *phoneme,* for example, has a very specific meaning because it is used with this meaning by linguists. The word *work* is used with specific meanings by physicists; it is used with more general meanings by physicists and others in nonphysics contexts. A person who observes the actual usage of people will no more advocate the general meaning of *work* in a physics context—or an anomalous meaning of *phoneme* in a linguistic context—than he will advocate a nonstandard *ain't* in a paper that is intended to pass as standard English.

To elaborate a bit, if a hearer takes a word to mean what the speaker intends, the idea "gets across," the two persons understand one another. A hearer, obviously, may take the word to mean something other than what the speaker intends. The two do not understand one another. Now how do we decide who is "right" about the meaning? In a given situation, of course, both can be right or both can be wrong. Learning the right meaning is of practical importance. That is, unless misunderstanding is the goal (as it sometimes is), hearer and speaker must get together regarding meaning. Hearer or speaker may take a very authoritarian view—"my meaning is the right meaning"—and the chances of their getting together are reasonably negligible. For a while one may "pull rank" on his children or very young students, but he beguiles only himself if he thinks the process attacks the problem of meaning realistically or effectively—in or out of the classroom. It was Humpty Dumpty, we may recall, who answered Alice's objection to his definition of *glory* by replying that a word meant just what he chose it to mean and it was simply a question of who was to be master, that's all.

Or, as previously noted, one may assume that there is a "real" meaning which has no relation to what people intend or interpret. The assumption is sometimes used pedagogically—with baneful results. About twenty-five years ago I was first told that if I said, "If I couldn't swim and tipped over my canoe three miles from shore, I would drown," I would *really* be saying, "I want to drown." I heard this assertion most recently about two years ago. Nonsense dies hard. No speaker I know would so intend the sentence and no hearer so interpret it. Incidentally, the *should* being sought in this sentence in the name of correctness has two possible meanings—which speech will keep separate, and hence unambiguous, far more successfully than writing will.

Finally, one may—and in practice usually does—look for the right meaning in the intention of the speaker and the interpretation of the hearer. In a given situation speaker and hearer may actually try to get together— "Just what do you mean by—?" Or they may appeal to other persons— especially the people who compile dictionaries. In these compendiums of usage speaker and hearer may find the common meaning they need in order to understand one another. Again they may not—since a word or meaning may have come into being since the dictionary went to press and since the people compiling dictionaries are fallible like the rest of us. Speaker and hearer may also find that the originally divergent intention and interpretation are both recorded—hardly a surprising discovery, since multiple meanings for a single word are frequent. Apparently when one becomes insistent about the *real* meaning, he is likely to forget what he otherwise knows very well—that a word often has several meanings. Is the usage advocate guilty of urging vagueness and woolliness of diction then simply because he recognizes that various meanings are actually used? He's being just about as wildly romantic, it seems to me, as dictionaries are.

The word *disinterested* is a present shibboleth of "correctness." How present is indicated by a paragraph in a recent *Atlantic Monthly* (September, 1954, p. 56), where the use of *disinterested* as a synonym for *uninterested* is belabored in strong language: "the wickedest of steals," "this crime . . . committed . . . by 'intellectuals' who know better," "this unscrupulous steal," and "outrages." *Disinterested* means *impartial,* so the argument goes, and anyone who uses it to mean *uninterested* or *bored* just doesn't know what the real meaning is and, what's worse, he's corrupting the language. Some of us get dreadfully worried about the possible ambiguity of the phrase *a disinterested judge.* Before one decides that this word has only one meaning—or one *real* meaning and a debased recent meaning—one would do well to look at various dictionaries, including the ACD, various Webster's, Samuel Johnson's and the OED. The original vocabulary of the OED, for example, cites quotations from about 1612 (Donne), 1684, and 1767 for the meaning "not interested, unconcerned"; it labels the meaning as questionably obsolete. The Supplement, with three quotations from 1928, tells us to remove obsolete from the original entry. Incidentally, since the first quotation for the meaning "impartial" is dated 1659, one wonders about the direction of "this unscrupulous steal."

If we grant that both *impartial* and *bored* are real and current meanings, we can at least avoid the ridiculousness of a *'tis-'tain't* controversy between equally well-educated and intelligent persons. We may also see that ambiguity does exist in *a disinterested judge,* just as it exists in *curious university scientists* and a multitude of other phrases. But let's agree that the ambiguity in *a disinterested judge* is undesirable. What shall we do about it? To insist that *disinterested* can or does have only one meaning is to insist on what simply isn't true; to insist that others accept my meaning and reject their own simply because I insist is to invite objection. (I use *disinterested* to mean *impartial* only.) If this word requires more attention than countless other words with multiple, even contradictory meanings (and it doesn't), one can simply recognize that, when speaking the word, he runs the risk of being misinterpreted and, when hearing the word, of misinterpreting. As a speaker he can avoid the word if he feels the risk too great; as a hearer, he's certainly better off for knowing that ambiguity is possible.

Perhaps one can put *disinterested* back in proper perspective, first, by recognizing that many words have multiple meanings; the ACD, for example, lists 104 meanings for *run*, and Irving Lorge reportedly assigns the word 832 meanings.[3] Somehow we manage to make our way through these meanings so that *run* remains a useful word. And pity the poor punster if he were deprived of multiple meanings. Then, too, *disinterested* is far from being alone in having extremely divergent meanings. "He rents his house," "Gus didn't mind," "The prisoner was in charge of the lieutenant," "He married her," "He wants nothing," "since he was eight" are all, unhappily, ambiguous[4] although no one seems to have become unduly upset about the conditions of the language here. Not always, but usually, context clarifies the ambiguity in these expressions. So too, usually, with *disinterested:*

> The administration could find grounds for real concern over the apathy shown by Illinois Republicans . . . The implications of this disinterest . . . But the current Republican boredom in Illinois . . . In this disinterested atmosphere . . .[5]

Possibly it is worth noting that ambiguity may spring not only from the meaning of a given word but from grammatical structure as well. The phrase *John's betrayal,* for example, is ambiguous. We can and sometimes do misinterpret a subjective for an objective genitive, or an objective for a subjective; but the remedy hardly lies in insisting that a genitive can have only one meaning. Similarly no one has insisted on strait-jacketing the structure substantive—verb—substantive—substantive, even though this structure is capable of varied meanings, including the ambiguity in Othello's ". . . . she wish'd that heaven had made her such a man" (I.iii.162-3). Nor will a strait jacket resolve the delightful ambiguity in an advertisement for Disney's *Alice in Wonderland:* ". . . and an army whose soldiers are playing cards." Not the least of the virtues of C. C. Fries' *Structure of English*, it seems to me, lies in the attention given to structural ambiguity. It is in the language; we cannot argue or decree it out of the language. Recognizing its existence, we are better equipped to handle a given ambiguity in either speaking or hearing, writing or reading. So too with the varied meanings of words.

In epilog, I may note the occasional objection that "usage" says little or nothing about the inventive or imaginative use of words. The proper reply, of course, is that "correctness" says less.

---

[3] *Inside the ACD*, Feb., 1953, p. 4.

[4] This phenomenon is hardly recent or exclusively English if one can judge by the definition of *onwendan* in Clark Hall's *Concise Anglo-Saxon Dictionary* and of *olim* in White's Latin Dictionary.

[5] *Christian Science Monitor*, April 5, 1954, p. 1.

Part V

LINGUISTICS AND THE TEACHING OF GRAMMAR AND COMPOSITION

INTRODUCTION

PRECEDING PARTS have already implied or suggested relevance of linguistic analysis and information to the teaching of English in schools and colleges. In this chapter several linguists and classroom instructors of composition look specifically at this subject.

A kind of introduction is provided by the brief statement of assumptions by Hackett, who would insist that the teaching of English recognize the language not as an independent entity to be analyzed in a vacuum but as part of the general culture in which the student lives and to the changes of which he must adjust. Here he seems to draw upon the theories of Whorf, and perhaps also those of the sociologist, George Herbert Meade. Accepting these assumptions, Hackett presumably would argue, would considerably alter the content of English teaching.

Ives, a linguist, while iterating some of the ideas appearing in earlier chapters, here deals with them specifically with respect to the work of the classroom teacher in improving students' ability to communicate. Walker, such a teacher, studies the dilemma of the normative and the objective approaches and decides that a realistic acceptance of relativism, as in regional diversity, must be the answer.

McMillan treats briefly a familiar classroom problem of the relation between spelling and pronunciation, with a warning against putting the cart before the horse.

Carroll, a psychologist who for some time has been studying linguistics and its relationships to other disciplines, finds hope in the use of structural grammar as a means of improving students' written style.

Lloyd, a pioneer in linguistic applications in the composition class, relates the ideas of structure in grammar and structure in usage, offers in the next article specific help by showing how parts of speech can be treated

e classroom, and then finally describes a particular class operation in
)wn institution.

ᴸurnet, following Fries's structural analysis more closely than Lloyd
does, likewise offers specific classroom help upon the basis of his own experience at Maryland State Teachers College. Gates, in proposing his own
method for helping students, does nevertheless operate with structural
units for which complex replacements may be made—the essential feature
of English structure. Sledd, a linguist, opens a new door for the composition
teacher who has accepted the familiar handbook principle that a main
idea requires express in a main clause and a subordinate idea in a subordinate construction.

Geist, having accepted the value of teaching structural patterns in college composition classes, asks whether this approach is not possible in the
last years of the elementary school. The linguist would answer yes; the
elementary teacher probably would say that the answer must be found in
the availability of teaching materials as well as in the preparation of the
teacher.

At present there is only one such textbook for the secondary school,
Roberts's *Patterns of English* (Harcourt, Brace, 1956), which has found
some use in the eighth grade as well as in senior high school; there is no
textbook like it for the fifth and sixth grades. But in the meantime, until
textbooks and other materials are ready, the linguist would say that the
properly prepared elementary teacher can do much to give pupils a sound
orientation toward their use of language toward their use of language
through individually devised exercises and through supplementing dis-
creetly statements in existing textbooks.

Some Assumptions . . . To Be Examined*

Herbert Hackett

I would like to state some assumptions, drawn from a variety of fields,
about the nature and function of language, assumptions which I think are
defensible on the evidence but all of which need further study.

1. Language is behavior and must be taught on behavioral principles.

2. Language is first of all a functioning tool of interaction and only
relatively rarely a means of reflective thought; as such it has no meaning
apart from the total context of situation; meaning is context.

3. Language operates within a cultural context and is limited by it.

* This letter to the editor is reprinted in part by permission from *College English,*
16.452–453 (April, 1955).

4. Language is not only dependent on its culture, but in turn structures reality for this culture. The individual cannot operate outside the limits set by this language, nor see the world except as it is given structure by his language. This structure will vary from culture to culture.

5. As behavior, language is measured by effectiveness in terms of purpose; it must adopt to the situation, the user, the audience, the subject matter.

6. As behavior it must be studied in terms of group norms, the expectations of the group as to usage, content and purpose. These expectations must be found by observation, they cannot be prescribed on the authority of historical or theoretical considerations.

7. Language cannot be taught prescriptively, since the prescription may fail to keep up with the actual practice of the culture; rather, the student must be taught to observe and to fit his communication to accepted good usage.

8. The unit of language is not the part—the word, sentence or paragraph—but is the total perception to be transmitted, to which the parts are bound. Thus, the approach to teaching communication skills is the teaching of a total perception.

9. The end of language is not language but content, leading to better perception by the audience. The teaching of skills, then, will be concerned with what is said, in its context; how it is said will develop from this.

10. Language as social behavior has social responsibility, including proper recognition of bias, accurate use of data, and a positive acceptance of the opinion of others and of the relativity of knowledge.[1]

These are a few of the assumptions about language and the process of communication which many of us make, with or without consciously phrasing them. None of these has been sufficiently examined by teachers of skills, although a substantial body of data in other disciplines supports them. Some are over-simplifications, *all are to be doubted.*

And yet these assumptions and many related to them indicate the direction in which our thinking about the teaching of skills must go. They are not the final formulations of a discipline but must be reexamined, restated, framed into hypotheses, observed, tested, rehypothesized. . . . Only then may we sit in the circle of language scientists and from them learn, because we will know what they are talking about.

[1] Some of the wording and emphasis of the above assumptions is borrowed from Frederic Reeve, "Toward a Philosophy of Communication," *Education* 72:445–455 (March 1952).

Linguistics in the Classroom*

SUMNER IVES

ANYONE WHO has been reading periodicals for English teachers or who has been attending conventions of English teachers must be aware of the controversy over linguistics and its relevance to the teaching of composition. As one whose research is primarily in descriptive linguistics, but whose teaching includes at least one composition class each semester, I have a personal interest in the interaction of linguistics and the practical use of language. I am somewhat disturbed by what appears to be a conflict between linguists and teachers of writing when I can detect no valid reason for such a conflict.

I suspect, both from reading the exchanges and from listening to the discussions, that much of the disagreement comes from misunderstanding. I observe arguments which promote linguistics without showing an exact appreciation of the significance of its findings; I notice defences of positions which linguistics, properly understood, does not attack. Moreover, although many composition teachers have come to believe that traditional grammar is a very poor description of English structure, some of the more judicious have complained, rightly, that the arguments of the linguists have been largely negative, that they have given little to replace that which they have attacked. This, then, is the situation with which this paper deals.

In order to accomplish its purpose, the discussion must be both general and specific, for the usefulness of linguistics is two-fold. One contribution is a valid and useful theory of what language is and how it works. The other is a description of the specific forms and constructions which are used in a particular language for the expression of meaning.

In general academic usage, the term linguist includes those who teach the language courses in an English or other modern language department. However, the criticisms of traditional grammar have come chiefly from those who have made particular study of descriptive or structural linguistics, and the counterattacks have been made against this group. In this discussion, therefore, linguistics means descriptive linguistics, and linguists are those who work in this branch of language study. In his study of language, the linguist uses the standard methods of observation and classification common to all systematic studies of human behavior and the natural world. In describing the structure of a language, he is guided by the forms of words and their characteristic patterns of use. His criteria of defi-

* Reprinted with permission from *College English,* 17.165–172 (December, 1955).

nition and classification are therefore very much the same as those of the anthropologist or the chemist.

The major aims of the linguist are the discovery of the principles true of all living languages and the accumulation of detailed and systematic descriptions of the phonology and the grammar of these languages. Both these major goals have relevance to promoting facility in the native language and to teaching the use of a second language. Hence, as a methodology of investigation, linguistics is one of the social sciences, but the nature of its subject matter and the application of its results give it primary association with the humanities. The study of the forms of language is a science; the proper and effective use of language is an art.

The difficulty which many persons trained in the humanities seem to have with linguistics is due primarily to our intellectual climate. Most of the notions which underlie our common vocabulary for talking about language are survivals from a pre-objective period of language study. The words in our vocabulary reflect an orientation on language matters which is very different from that which is derived through direct observation of individual languages. When a non-linguist reads what a linguist has written about language, there is often a break-down in the communication, even when familiar terms are used, for the non-linguist is often interpreting the discussion in a frame of reference which differs from that in which it was written. This difficulty is compounded when the linguist uses terms from the technical jargon of his field. Yet such a technical vocabulary is necessary and is no more exotic than those in other fields. Physicians, for example, no longer use such terms as "humorous" and "sanguine" in their medieval sense, for these terms reflect a theory of disease which they no longer hold.

The consequences of this misunderstanding, which is often greater than either party realizes, are most easily observed in the extrapolations from linguistics which persons without training in its methods attempt to make. Any statement in any field is only a partial expression; it must be interpreted within the restrictions imposed by the nature of what is talked about, by the context, and by all the assumptions, postulates, and qualifications which are part of the accumulated knowledge in the field. This does not mean that linguists talk only with each other, though they are as prone to this as anyone, but it does mean that the statements of linguists should be accepted and applied only to the extent that they are explicit, that conclusions should be drawn only within the limits of the primary statements and only about that aspect of the subject concerning which they are made. When, for example, a linguist uses stretches of actual speech as material for grammatical analysis, his purpose does not include the establishment of a standard dialect, and his results apply only to his sample.

Aside from this difficulty, which is concomitant to every major advance in fundamental knowledge, linguistics is not a hard subject. Its subject matter is all around us. Ordinary people have mastered and use quite easily all the forms, constructions, and sound patterns it deals with. Its results, whenever a particular language is described, can be checked by any native speaker who will believe what he observes and not what he has been taught to expect. And any native speaker who has the necessary perseverance and mental discipline can learn and use its methods to extend his conscious understanding of the form and constructions of his own language.

But at the present time, direct provision for the development of an adequate theory of language and for the accumulation of knowledge about the actual constructions of English is seldom made in the training of English teachers. Virtually all their upper division and graduate courses are in literature. When language courses are required, and they are seldom taken unless required, they generally consist of reading more literature, this time in a stage of the language which is no longer current, or they consist primarily of tracing individual sound changes, with some attention to resulting changes in morphology, and some checking on etymologies. This language program undoubtedly has cultural value, but it has little direct bearing on the teaching of composition. It is possible for a student to go through such a program with excellent marks and yet remain basically ignorant of the nature of language as a socially directed activity, unaware of the difference yet interaction between a language and its written symbolization, blind to the operation of its grammatical devices, and unprepared even to read many of the basic publications which describe the current characteristics of his own language or to analyze that language for himself.

This has not been said in any spirit of superiority or condemnation. It is the simple truth. Any blame is general. It is up to linguists to relate their findings to the larger aims of education. But they have the same right to attention and trust as the zoologist, the political-scientist, or the specialist in the pastoral elegy. The problem is the familiar one of cultural lag. A solution will come only with time, careful explanations, and a decent regard for human feelings and fallibility on all sides.

Much of the misunderstanding about what the linguist does and says comes from his insistence on two of his basic principles and their corollaries. One of these is the primacy of speech as the language, with writing as a secondary and derivative manifestation of speech. The other is the dynamic, changing nature of language, with its corollaries about stability and standardization. Both principles are derived from studying languages as physically observable structures; neither is a threat to the basic aims of the composition course—namely, to teach students to write their own language as clearly and effectively as they can, and with full regard for the conventions of usage observable in the products of recognized masters.

In explaining his attention to speech, the linguist points out that all systems of writing are based on the prior existence of speech, that all alphabetic systems depend ultimately on the sound system of the language, even though, as in English, the correspondence between sound and spelling is very complex and difficult to describe. The linguist realizes that the writing system, even with its marks of punctuation, never quite symbolizes all the components which contribute to meaning in speech. He comes to see the teaching that English has five vowels as nonsense and the mother of error, and the designation of long and short vowels in English as little better. And he learns to dismiss such questions as whether English is a phonetic language as meaningless. These lessons may not have direct bearing on the teaching of good composition, but they are vital if one is to understand the relationship of writing to the language, of spelling to pronunciation, or of reading to speaking.

On the other hand, distinct from the alphabetic representation of words on paper, speaking and writing are different but interacting activities. They are not the same, do not follow all of the same conventions, and are not done for the same list of purposes. Neither is finally and fully determinative for the other. No competent linguist would suggest that the teacher of written English should accept in student writing all of the conventions and the same characteristics of style as are customary in speech, even that of the most cultivated. The notion that linguists make speech determinative for writing is one of the false extrapolations made by people who interpret the findings of linguistics without knowing what they mean. They are failing to distinguish between writing as a graphic representation of a linguistic expression (which is secondary to speech) and writing as a special kind of communicative activity (which differs in style and purpose from speech).

The fundamental reason why the linguist gives his primary attention to speech is the fact that only in speech does he find all the signals which convey information. For example, the two phrases, "a stone wall" and "a race horse," are not spoken with the same patterns of stress. In the first phrase, "stone" is functionally an adjective, just as "high" would be in the same place. In the second, "race" is functionally a part of a compound noun, in spite of the orthography, like "black-" in "blackberry." It is the difference in the patterns of stress which makes the grammar clear. With the grammatical importance of stress in mind, read the following sentences aloud and then parse "drinking" and "water" in all of them. (1) Our drinking water fortunately remained fresh. (2) Drinking water from our canteens rather than from open streams kept us from getting dysentery. (3) Drinking water rather than wine made the boys healthy.

Another practical result of investigation into these "supra-segmental" characteristics of speech is the recognition of the relationship between pitch patterns and structural unity. In ordinary prose, the ends of statements and of most questions are marked by a quick rise in pitch, followed by a quick drop to a level below that of the bulk of the sentence. A sentence which has the word order of a statement can be made into a question by a quick rise of pitch at the end. When there is a quick rise and then a drop back to the basic level, a shift in constructions within a sentence is marked. These pitch signals mark the places where punctuation decisions are to be made if the speech is set down in writing. A student can often clarify his constructions and rectify his punctuation simply by reading his themes aloud, for he will generally find that an unEnglish construction cannot be read with the English supra-segmental patterns—what are popularly called intonation patterns—and he has used these since childhood.

For these reasons, any analysis of English grammar which is not based ultimately on the signals of speech is necessarily incomplete. The other basic principle which is sometimes misunderstood is corollary to the fact that language is a social institution with the same counteracting tendencies towards stability and adaptability as other social institutions.

A typical expression of the linguist's view is found on page 177 of W. D. Whitney's *Language and the Study of Languages,* published as long ago as 1867. "Language is an institution founded in man's social nature, wrought out for the satisfaction of his social wants; and hence, while individuals are ultimate agents in the formation and modification of every word and every meaning of a word, it is still the community that makes and changes its language."

The relevance which this principle has for the composition teacher is its bearing on the formation and continuity of the conventions which he should teach as part of the standard language. That dialect of English which we now call edited written English is the product of changes resulting from the interaction of individuals as agents of the community. The dialect whose modern development we teach originally had no discernible virtues as a language which made it superior to other local forms of English. Its selection for cultivation was almost surely the result of socio-economic factors. Nonetheless its fortuitous origin does not invalidate its claim to superiority today. But these claims rest in part on the growth and refinement of special vocabularies, in part on the great store of literature which is written in it, in part to the social prestige which is granted to those who use it, and in part to the size and importance of the territory over which it is spread. These reasons are fully adequate to demand that it be taught as a school subject.

Yet, this standard English cannot be exactly defined, nor does it remain constantly the same, in spite of the factors which give it stability. No complete, definitive, and final dictionary of English usage can be made so long as English is in active use, although the list of disputed usages is never large at any one time. A teacher of writing simply has to maintain the same kind of contact with changes in his basic material as that maintained by doctors and lawyers.

A special problem in dealing with usage is the presence of shibboleths.

So long as overt marks of social and educational status are considered useful by society, some of these will be linguistic. For example, the adequacy
of one's education is often judged by his ability to spell, or by whether he
splits infinitives, or by whether he says "eyether" or "eether." It is in the
area of shibboleths that the purist feels most authority, for he is usually
their custodian. To the linguist, however, most of these have the status of
myth, as the term is used in sociology. Nevertheless, a rather large part of
one's acceptance in society is his adjustment to myths of this type. Hence, it
is, I think, the duty of the school teacher to point out the current shibboleths, for they change, and to advise how much they are observed and by
which people.

Language is thus a social institution. It has the same kind of stability and
adaptability as other social institutions, from table manners to democratic
government, and its conventions are just as obligatory while they last. The
scholar should remember that the major purpose of language is not to preserve for the future, but to serve the exigencies of now. To ask for a static
language makes just as much sense, and no more, as to ask for a static society. There are, of course, people who do this. To put the language in the
hands of a self-appointed few is just as reasonable, and no more, as to put
the regulation of government in the hands of a similarly appointed group.
There are people who want to do this too.

These principles constitute the major elements in a theory of language
which is valid and which should assist the composition teacher to deal
more intelligently with his basic subject matter. The major tool which linguists can give to the teachers of composition is a true and adequate description of the forms and constructions which are used in English for the
expression of grammatical meaning, in short, an English grammar. Such a
grammar will retain some of the categories and their terms which are in
traditional grammar, but its methods of classification and definition will
be fundamentally different.

When we attempt to relate the terminology, with its implied classification, of traditional grammar to the actual forms of English and their behavior, at least four major defects appear. Some terms, e.g., grammar, have
more than one referent; some terms, e.g., passive voice and tense, have
referents which are not, by their very nature, susceptible to sharp definition in English; some terms, e.g., adverb and pronoun, are in use without
a genuine referent (the supposed referents of these terms lack identity as
single classes or categories of items); finally, some terms, e.g., noun and
verb, are identified, not by definitions, but by statements which may well
be true, but which do not name the particularizing characteristics of the
classes which the terms refer to.

In traditional grammar, an adverb is defined as a word which modifies
a verb, adjective, or other adverb. However, the "adverbs" *quite* and *very*
simply do not obey the same rules of syntax as the "adverbs" *usually* and

soon, for *quite* and *very* do not modify verbs. Another false classification is that which includes *he* and *few* in the same category, for one is inflected and the other is not, one can be modified by *very* and the other cannot, and one has a noun antecedent and the other does not. It is true that both can act as subjects, but then, so can adjectives. The concept of tense in traditional grammar is complicated by the fact that verb phrases made with *will* are called a future tense, yet these phrases have the same formal characteristics as those made with *must* and other modal auxiliaries.

I am, admittedly, judging a grammatical description according to criteria of form and usefulness. To be valuable in teaching a language or in promoting facility in its use, a description of its grammar should isolate those classes about which statements need to be made. These statements may be rules for word order, for the formation of phrases, for derivational change, for functional change, for inflectional concord, and so on. There is obviously very little which one can say about word order which will be true of both *very* and *soon,* of both *he* and *few.*

A classification must select out and associate in identity a group of items which, so far as the purpose of the classification is concerned, are equivalent. These items must be, within the purpose for which the class is isolated, freely substitutable for each other. In defining this class, a property must be named which is tangible, which is present in all members of the class, and which is absent from all items not in the class. If this definition is part of a taxonomy, it must be one of a set. The definitions in a set must contrast with each other and must conjointly exhaust all items in the same division and level of analysis. These sets must each have a common factor which excludes members of other sets, and so on until the entire classification is complete. A properly developed taxonomy, therefore, has the outward design of a genetic tree.

In framing definitions, one must enumerate a list of attributes generally agreed upon, or one must name one or more characteristics whose presence or absence can be verified by direct observation. Many of the terms in literary criticism, e.g., "romanticism," rest upon agreement to associate the term with a list of attributes. Other terms, such as those in the taxonomy of botany, are defined by direct appeal to nature. Anyone who has good eyesight and the proper instruments can count the cotyledons in a seed. One may have more trouble with "hirsute" and "pubescent," but the degree of fuzziness which they denote can be easily distinguished after a little experience. Since Linnaeus, the botanists have had a way to bring order to the apparently limitless variety of nature; they had a classification system for what is, to the layman, infinite discreteness. The objective of the descriptive grammarian is to do for the forms of individual languages what the botanist has done for plant life.

In popular usage, grammar is often considered to be a crystallization of human logic, a set of concepts and distinctions in terms of which all lan-

guages should be described, a set of formal characteristics and correspondences to which all languages should conform. In this view, which is that
implied in some recent articles and found in most older books on language,
the most convenient expression of grammar is one based on Latin. When
it was shown that a knowledge of traditional grammar had little correlation with an ability to use English correctly and effectively, the result was
a belief that grammar need not be studied as a prerequisite to training in
composition. This view, is, I think, wrong. I think that, on the contrary,
an adequate knowledge of the forms of English and of the rules for their
use should be a very valuable pre-requisite to instruction in composition.
Arguments based on current experience are irrelevant, for the grammar has
not been English grammar.

Now the linguist studies a language by analyzing, in turn, its levels of
complexity. These correspond only roughly to the levels indicated by the
common terms phonology, morphology, and syntax. In this division into
which deals with the combination of the smallest meaningful units into
the largest self-sufficient and independent constructions is grammar. These
smallest meaningful units are called morphemes. They may be affixes like
-ness, -ed, and non-; they may be words like *kind, his,* and *the;* they may be
stress patterns like those which make a word like *subject* into a noun or into
a verb. Every utterance consists of segmental morphemes, like words,
stems, and affixes, and of supra-segmental morphemes, which include
what the layman means by intonation. Grammar classifies these morphemes
into groups according to similarities of form and grammatical meaning. It
includes the rules by which morphemes are combined into constructions
and the rules governing the formation of still larger constructions until the
ultimate limit of strict structural relationship has been reached. The units
at the limit of strict structural relationship are sentences.

Grammar as conformity to the conventions of the standard dialect becomes a matter of comparative grammar. The dialects of English which
comprise vulgate English all have grammars, as the term is defined in the
preceding paragraph, but the rules and forms of these grammars differ in
some ways from those of the standard dialect. The teaching problem is the
correlation of equivalent expressions and the substitutions of standard for
nonstandard forms and constructions. The only inherent source of confusion is the presentation by the teacher of conventions which differ from
those which the student observes in his academic reading.

A more serious cause for confusion is a failure to distinguish between
grammar and style. The rules which govern the combination of morphemes into sentences are imposed on the individual; the words and constructions which he uses, out of those which conform to the rules, are matters of choice. This area of language choice is style, or rhetoric. For example, after "individual," just above, I could have used a period or a
semicolon, for both show the boundary between structurally complete

units. But I could not have used either mark before that word, for it is grammatically related to those which immediately precede. Such matters as the selection of words and constructions, the length of sentences and their complexity, and the organization of the total expression are matters of style. Such matters as consistency in parallel structure, reference of pronouns, and agreement of subject and verb are matters of grammar. These matters of grammar are finite; they can be discovered and described.

An example of confusion arising from a failure to make this distinction clear is the trouble students have with "sentence recognition." The customary definition of the sentence as the verbal expression of a complete thought does not, by itself, separate the sentence from the paragraph or from larger sections which are supposed to have unity. As the term is applied in most handbook discussions of punctuation, it designates a unit in style but not necessarily in grammar. The crucial information—that there is an identifiable unit in grammar, that, in connected prose, the juxtapositions of these units must be marked, and that one of the ways to make these juxtapositions is with a period—does not follow from the traditional definition.

In English structure, the sentence, the independent unit in connected discourse, has the following characteristics: (1) it must contain at least one finite verb or verb phrase; (2) all words must be structurally related; (3) it must not, as a unit, have a grammatical function in a larger construction. There are three types of such units in English. In the statement, the subject normally precedes the verb, unless it begins with a word of the class of "never." In the question, the subject is normally inserted inside the verb phrase. (If the verb is not a phrase, it is made into one with a form of "do.") In the request, there is no subject. The verb may come first, or it may be preceded by a word to get attention or to show courtesy.

There are two other types of constructions which are marked by end punctuation or intonation. One is the response; the other is the exclamation. Both of these constructions get their "incompleteness" from something which has been said or is physically close enough to be pointed out by a gesture. Thus, we can use a construction which is structurally not a sentence when we reply to a question, stated or implied, or when we react to an automobile accident, or when we point to something and comment on it.

The most common error in student themes is the failure to mark the juxtapositions of structurally complete units, or the habit of marking as sentences groups of words which are not structurally units. But difficulty with "sentence recognition" can be virtually eliminated by teaching what is in the preceding paragraphs, listing the devices for marking the juxtapositions, and giving the following suggestions. As the beginning of a sentence, structural relationship points forward; at the end it points backward. If the student reads what he has written, aloud and phrase by phrase, he can detect the point where there is a break, where the shift from backward to forward relationship occurs. "Sentence fragments" ordinarily result from one of two causes. One is the insertion of an end sign where no structural end exists; the other is the failure to keep the structural patterns clear enough so that a structural unit can be isolated. In this case, a break in communication will almost be noticed. It has been my experience that native speakers of English can determine the presence or absence of grammatical relationship even when they cannot give a name to the type which exists.

In so far as their academic functions are concerned, linguists and composition teachers are related in somewhat the same way as botanists and gardeners and related in raising plants. Their duties do not conflict; they complement. The botanist identifies plants, groups them in families, analyzes their physiology, and observes the ecological factors which promote or retard growth. The gardener uses such information and adds to it his knowledge of the virtues of different fertilizers and methods of cultivation. If he has good soil and healthy stock, he may get good results regardless of how little he knows. But if his soil is not good, his stock is poor, or his experience is little, there is much he can learn from the botanist, although the botanist cannot teach him all he needs to know. There is, of course, nothing to prevent the botanist from becoming a gardener or to keep the gardener from gaining through experience a great deal of useful but uncoordinated knowledge.

What this means is that the students whose environment has provided them with habitual use of good English are likely to do well whether their teacher knows much about language or not. On the other hand, in so far as the students do not have these habits, the teacher will find useful what the linguist has to say. Even if he does not have this preparation for formal and systematic teaching, he may still get acceptable results with some students by requiring practice, making corrections, and insisting on revision, provided he is himself a reasonably competent craftsman.

I should confess, nay insist, that linguistics simply gives the teacher additional or more effective tools and a better understanding of what he is working with. Any improvement he makes in his knowledge of language, any details he learns about the actual forms and constructions of English, will make him a more expert instructor. But at the present time, although linguists know and can teach information which is more accurate than the traditional notions, they still have to learn much about the details of English, and some of what they have learned is not ready for publication. Moreover, the field itself does not cover all the things that the composition teacher needs to know. There is still no royal road to good writing, no magic method that will turn out skilled writers, and neither linguistics nor any other field is likely to provide one.

What Language Shall We Teach?*

A. J. WALKER

LET US LOOK AT the speech process, for we speak before we write and consequently begin to write as we speak. The child learns to speak, whether through imitation or the play instinct or any of several reasons hotly debated by linguists in the eighteenth century and now relegated to the psychologists. The child talks baby talk because his vocabulary is limited. Grammar he knows only as grammar of position: "Me want a drink of water."

He may be so unfortunate as to go through the first few years of his life without meeting an English teacher, yet he moves unerringly to the impeccable "I want a drink of water." He imitates and at the same time outgrows. As a big boy of five he no longer talks like a baby. He talks in a manner appropriate to his age and thereby wins the approval of those whose approval he values. He will continue to talk, as he inevitably must, like those around him—or, to be more exact, like those around him whom he wishes to talk like. I don't want to be too narrow; those whom he wishes to imitate may be a single person or may be the great and mighty dead known through books or may even be the creatures of his fancy living with him in this world of dreams. This process of change does not stop when he enters school; it does not stop when he leaves school.

Perhaps the most and best we can do is to help our students see language as a changing thing, with many levels attainable. Some students, we know, will strive too hard, will become overprecise, will demand that we be Miss Post and prescribe niceties far beyond any need. Others will reject us entirely, for our attempts to change their language they will consider, and rightly consider, an attempt to change their whole way of life and a covert insult to their heritage. Ours is a job requiring tact. We must walk carefully as we show them that certain language peculiarities (I did not say errors) separate us from the people we would become and should be put away as we put away the water bucket with the single dipper and go instead to the fountain in the corridor.

I believe we can study with our students the language peculiarities of our region or our age group and discover together at what point we in Atlanta or in Dublin or in Mountain City depart from the general language of America. We can be happy that there is a considerable homogeneity of

* This excerpt, constituting the second half of the presidential address to the Georgia Council of Teachers of English, Atlanta, March, 1953, is here reprinted by permission from *The English Journal,* 42.431–436 (November, 1953).

our people in Georgia. We are more fortunate than the English teachers in rural Pennsylvania, in urban Brooklyn, or in the great German or Swedish areas of the Middle West. But we do not talk exactly alike. One teacher told me of her efforts in one school in Georgia to eradicate the phrase "in back of" from the vocabulary of her students. Then she moved to another part of the state, prepared to continue the dubious battle, only to discover that none of the students in the new locality used the phrase.

This teacher who had observed that one language habit marked one section of Georgia but not another was on the track of an exciting possibility in teaching language. Should not an English teacher know the language habits of the region just as surely as the botany teacher knows what the plants in the locality are? Neither should be textbook teachers. To carry the idea even further, could not the language teacher ask the students to bring in specimens of language habits? Notice that I did *not* say "errors," and the teacher should not. She may destroy her usefulness and lose her friends if she does. But students can discover that *holp*, still common in Georgia, is but a strong form of what has become the weak verb *help*, and that *hit* is a variant of *it*. They can struggle with *hain't* and *ain't*, which I believe Georgia usage indicates come from *have not* and not from *am not*. Let them learn what "Lawsy mussy" means; I doubt that they know. Let them discover the southern habit of using the present for the past tense, both in strong and weak verbs, a habit that led Mr. Sparkman to say to Mr. Stevenson on election eve, "We run a good race." Mr. Sparkman is not illiterate; he is a Phi Beta Kappa from the University of Alabama. Students may also be amused to find around the "hyperurban" school the overprecise schoolgirl language of "Aren't I?" and "Harry took Susie and I to the show."

Before I go further, let me take refuge in quoting someone much wiser in the ways of language than I. Edward Weeks in the *Peabody Reflector* has some interesting comments to make about the advantage of directing the student's attention to language. After saying that as a boy he read many of George Ade's stories in slang, he adds:

> There is no harm, but rather an advantage in following up the lively use of idiom. Don't scoff at Pogo. Walt Kelly has the liveliest sense of fantasy and whimsy as he twists up the English langwich. Such things amuse young readers, and I think are better fare than some of the current thrillers and murder mysteries.

We in Georgia are peculiarly fortunate should we decide to follow Mr. Weeks's advice. For south Georgia there is Pogo and his friends. For a few days my life was brightened by Miz Angleworm. (By the way, how does your community pronounce Mrs.?) Miz Angleworm reports, "Pap and me got a young'un crawls through nothin' but sawdust." and leaves to go and "chaw mud pie."

For north Georgia there is Li'l Abner. Only a genuine southerner can pronounce "Li'l." Mammy Yokum, as you no doubt remember, tries to *drap* a picture over a cliff. Failing that, she buries it *whar* no one will find it, but she *heered* a noise while doing so. You and I know that Daisy Mae (Is that a typical mountain name?) *jest hain't* got the will power to resist and has *gotta* know *what* the picture looks like. It may please and comfort some students to be told that Abraham Lincoln at the age of twenty talked very much like Li'l Abner and called his parents "Mammy" and "Pappy."

And let us not overlook Aggie Mack, a high school girl whose language is appropriate to her age. Aggie reflects her English training by asking, "I'm his manager, aren't I?" Aggie is in high school. Her young friend Yum Yum is a grade school pupil and talks like one. And language as it is spoken is not confined to the comic pages. The sports pages, if your boys will read nothing else, burgeon with gems of tortured language. And our radio announcers constantly add to the collection of the seeker after language as it is but shouldn't be. Thousands in the South heard the announcer of the Sugar Bowl game do credit to his English teacher with the elegant sentence: "The tackle parted he and the ball."

As the student becomes aware of the peculiarities of his language, whether regional or social, he should also become aware of the limitations imposed on him by his peculiarities. He must be led to accept and acquiesce in the fact that what is locally acceptable is not always acceptable nationally. The teacher, with a broader background, should represent not the hidebound rules of a textbook but the generally accepted language of educated Americans. The student, however lacking in ambition, knows that ours is a country in which men move from area to area and mingle with others. He may anticipate a period in the army where he will mix with boys from Texas and Brooklyn, Vermont and Missouri. His knowledge of his own localisms will help him adjust his language to their understanding. It will also help him to understand the language peculiarities of others and to recognize them not as something foreign, strange, and un-American but as counterparts of his own peculiarities which he should strive to eradicate.

Perhaps all I have said can be summed up in a few words.

Let us never forget that language is alive and vital and changing. It is not dead and safely embalmed in rules in a textbook.

Let us be sensible in our approach to our problem and not waste time on minor matters or insist on questionable and sometimes personal rules. Let us respect language and be as perceptive and sensitive to it as we would have our students be.

Let us keep in mind our purpose—our great purpose in a democracy —that each person is, through us, to have access to an opportunity to learn a language which will not handicap him in finding his proper place in society.

Let us work toward a simplification of our rules of formal grammar and a consistency in terminology, regarding both as observations on usage, not as absolute controls over usage. We must recognize that there is at present very little value in the mere learning of definitions.

Finally, let us begin where we are and use the language of our region, our state, our locality, as a point of departure to lead our students toward a language acceptable by a national standard. It is not so important that we achieve our goal as that the student when he leaves us is aware of the goal and has the means and the desire to continue to strive toward it.

Correctness and Style in English Composition*

ARCHIBALD A. HILL

THE TEACHER OF ENGLISH is often accused by students of language of being unable to modify his teachings in accord with facts of usage no matter how well proved, and the linguist in turn seems to those of us who have to struggle with freshmen to be a wild libertarian who would accept the most shapeless writing on the ground that all linguistic forms are equally good. Perhaps, as with other disputes, some of the differences may be resolved if the basic terms are more clearly defined.

I shall begin with correctness, giving a few well-worn statements of what it is not.

Correctness is not logic, since all languages are largely illogical. English says, "I see him," as if sight were a positive act of will comparable to that in "I hit him." Yet all of us know enough optics to realize that, if there is any action involved, it starts with *him* and reaches and affects *me*. Languages which happen, like Eskimo, to avoid this particular illogicality fall into others as great.

The basis of correctness is not beauty inherent in the forms used. Beauty in linguistic forms is due to the associations they arouse. Such a form as "goil" is ugly only if the hearer happens to dislike Brooklyn. To realize the truth of this statement, one has only to consider variants where we have no such associations. If a child in the New Mexican pueblo of Santa Clara puts the sentence, "I am going to town," in the form *bupiyeummang*, the "ugly" pronunciation is immediately corrected to *bupijeummang*. The Tewa parents are not being merely arbitrary; they are objecting to an

* Reprinted by permission from *College English*, 12.280–285 (February, 1951).

unacceptable dialect. I doubt if any English speaker can seriously maintain that he finds one Tewa form more beautiful than the other.

The basis of correctness is not history; such a belief would contradict the results of linguistic science. Further, the belief that older forms are better then newer can readily be reduced to an absurdity. If only old forms are right, then we do not speak English but bad Old English—or bad Indo-Hittite.

Equally certainly correctness is not the result of an authoritative ruling by an individual or a book. A neat example of this last view is the statement of a columnist who once said that 98 per cent of Americans mispronounced a given word, since they failed to follow dictionary recommendations. Actually such a statement demonstrates that 2 per cent of America mispronounces the word or that the dictionaries had better catch up on usage.

A final view once widely held is that anything which is impossible in Latin is incorrect in English. The view hardly needs denial, baleful as its lingering influence may be on the analysis of English grammar. At least, no one would now seriously maintain that "Oh, father!" is a vocative case, incapable of being split into two words.

I can start my positive exposition with a quotation which puts clearly the idea that the composition teacher has a double task. Most of what will follow will be merely an attempt to sharpen the distinction set up in the quotation.

> Competence . . . has to do with the organization of ideas . . . with putting words together . . . in such a way as to convey meaning easily and clearly. Decency may be regarded as the manners of discourse, and bears the same relation to speaking and writing that good table manners have to eating. The schoolboy who declares, "We ain't goin' to have no baseball team this year" is using language with competence, for his meaning is perfectly clear, but he is not using it with decency.[1]

For these terms I should like to substitute "correctness" and "style." Any form is correct if it is current in the dialect—to be defined, of course, beforehand—that the writer is using. A form is incorrect only if it has no such currency. It follows that it is possible to be incorrect in the use of other dialects than the rather vaguely defined Standard Written English with which teachers concern themselves. Professor Thorpe's schoolboy was using language incorrectly if he was speaking in the formal atmosphere of the schoolroom; but, if he was speaking to playmates across the tracks, he was speaking correctly enough. A more serious illustration is that the English department of one of our leading universities was recently taken to task because its training did not equip graduates to communicate with workmen. The point was well taken: it is as serious an error to use the forms of Standard English where they are socially out of place as it is to use

[1] Clarence D. Thorpe (ed.), *Preparation for College English* (Ann Arbor: University of Michigan Press, 1945), p. 12 n.

Gullah in the pages of a learned article. Incorrectness can result also, not merely from the use of a dialect in an inappropriate situation, but as well from the mixture of dialects or the improper imitation of a dialect. Readers of Galsworthy may remember that he sometimes makes an American character say sentences like, "If you've gotten a sense of humor, you've gotten it jolly well hidden up." Such sentences are grossly un-American at the same time that they are un-British; they are therefore incorrect.

The second term was "style." If forms A and B both occur in a given dialect, it is impossible to say that either is incorrect in that dialect. It may, however, be possible to show that A is better than B in the particular context in which it occurs. Such an evaluation will be based on the positive qualities of the passage under criticism; that is, A is better than B if it is clearer, more in accord with artistic conventions, or fits better with the structure of the utterance in which it falls. It should be stated emphatically that good and bad style are both possible in any dialect—Professor Thorpe's schoolboy was speaking with excellent style, since his statement left no doubt of the vigor of his denial. It should also be pointed out that, if a stylistic variant is condemned in one passage, it is by no means implied that it should be condemned elsewhere.

A third form of variant also exists. These are the indifferent variants. If A and B both exist, and no stylistic reason can be found for preferring one over the other, the variation is indifferent. The existence of indifferent variants is of some importance, since somehow the idea has gotten abroad that, if there are two ways of saying a thing, one must always be better than the other. English teachers are all too often called on to adjudicate between six and a half-dozen, though to devote effort to such decisions can only falsify what we so much need to tell our students.

From these rather generalized examples we can pass to discussion of variants such as actually appear in student themes. We will begin with variants which involve correctness, the first group of them springing from insufficient knowledge of the way in which writing represents the forms of speech. It is characteristic of these forms that, if read aloud with normal pronunciation, they immediately become acceptable Spoken English.

He couldn't *of* had a worse introduction.

Sentences like this have a sort of currency in dialect writing but have no currency in Standard Written English. The mistake consists in selecting the wrong spelling for a weak form which is homonymous for *have* and *of*. It is odd that the reverse mistake as in "a pair *have* shoes" seems never to occur.

Rooms for *Tourist*.

This is a type of form which is common in much of the South. What is back of it is an assimilation of *-sts* to *-ss* or simply to *-s*. It occurs at all levels of regional speech, and even teachers of English use it quite unconsciously. The mistake can be explained to students by giving the conditions under which the assimilation occurs and by pointing out that written forms do not recognize the change.

The next group of variants are incorrect because they employ local or social dialect forms not found in the Standard language.

Youse had better not do it.

This sentence will be recognized as belonging to uncultured New York City speech. Its badness, however, is altogether the result of its lack of currency in standard dialects of any type—it cannot be condemned as illogical or out of keeping with the structure of the language, since it makes a contrast between singular and plural just as other pronouns do, and since it is parallel to the southern *you all.*

I want this *doing* immediately.

This sentence is not likely to occur in compositions by American students, but it is nonetheless instructive, since we are likely to think of anything British as all right. The form is northern British local dialect, which finds its way into occasional printed books, among them those of Hall Caine. It is certainly not correct in this country. Another local sentence type is the southern "I *might could* do it," which is common enough in colloquial speech, but which I have never seen in print. The sentence should be rejected in compositions, acceptable as it may be in less formal situations.

The next group of incorrect variants arises from an unsuccessful attempt to use the forms or vocabulary of a standard dialect and are thus comparable to the mistakes made by foreigners.

This phone broken. Do not *uses.*

This sentence appeared on a sign put up by a colored janitor in a government building. The writer presumably used a type of dialect in which the present forms of verbs are without variation. Knowing that an -*s* appears in many forms where he would not use it, he corrected a little too much.

Modern culture is *sadistic.* Its music, painting, and literature are all sad.

In these sentences from a doctoral examination it is amusing to watch what starts out to be a provocative statement evaporate into a merely unfortunate attempt at elegance. The mistake is parallel to the student habit of describing modern poetry as "mystic" under the belief that this word is a critical term meaning "hard to understand."

A final type of incorrect variation is of rather common occurrence in student themes. This is contamination of one construction by another, with consequent production of variants lacking currency. A convenient if somewhat mentalistic explanation is to say that the writer intended one construction and then shifted his intention to another. Readers can readily supply other examples than the one which follows.

> There are *a points* which I can make. . . .

The author of this phrase has mixed *are a few points* with *are points*, producing a mistake which at first sight seems quite improbable for a native speaker.

> John met Jack, and *his* wife spoke to *him*.

In English, as in many languages, we have no way of distinguishing the reference of pronouns when there are two nouns of the same class, so that ambiguity often results. The sentence above must be condemned as bad style, though similar sentences can be found by the hundreds in all sorts of writing.

> Record the pronunciation on the lists in capital letters.

This sentence is drawn from a set of directions made up by a professor of English, who will, I hope, pardon my use of it. The sentence seems clear enough, but unfortunately the intended meaning was: "Record the pronunciation of only those words which appear in capital letters on the lists." Such ambiguities pursue us all.

> This factory is two miles beyond Lynchburg, going south.

This sentence is the only really bad example of our friend the dangling participle which I collected in two sessions of theme-reading. You will note that I have called it bad style, not an example of incorrectness. First, it produces ambiguity, not perhaps of a sort dangerous to real understanding, but sufficient to give a comic effect. Thus the sentence has positive badness. Second, dangling participles are surprisingly common in Standard Written English, though the handbooks do not admit it. Generally, no matter what our rationalizations, we do not notice danglers unless the stylistic effect is bad.

The next sentence may strike the reader as wildly improbable, though it comes from an actual composition.

> Mrs. Jackson devoted many years of endeavor to establishing and supporting a home where unfortunate women who had made mistakes (which they often regretted) could go to have their bastards.

The stylistic fault is obvious, since the final word comes with a distinct shock, the stronger for the vaguely elegant verbiage which precedes it.

The next variants are some which seem to me indifferent, though occasionally a particularly puristic handbook condemns one or more of them.

He *dove,* or He *dived.*
It's *me,* or It's *I.*
We carried it in a *burlap* bag (or *croker sack,* or *gunny sack*).
Let him do it if he dares (or *dare*).

The first three of these are regional variants or are regional variants sometimes crossed with social variation. Yet since both forms appear in Standard writing, no matter what the origin, none of them can be condemned as incorrect. The second set is perhaps the most interesting, since *It's I* seems to occur as the natural form around Boston, though elsewhere it is a schoolmastered product not to be recommended. Shelley's line, "Be thou me, impetuous one!" is a helpful quotation in dealing with the overmeticulous, since, though it may be a trick, it is always possible to point out that no one would wish the line changed to "Be thou I." The last set shows variation between an older and a newer form, both of which occur in formal writing.

There follow some forms of wide currency, which seem to me also defensible stylistically, though they are nonetheless often condemned.

> The mail is all delivered by plane, *which* is not only remarkably efficient, but is the chief weekly excitement.

This sentence violates the frequently expressed rule that *which* must have a definite antecedent. Yet vague antecedents are common in modern writing and have been common at all periods of the language. There is no ambiguity in the sentence above, and *which* seems a convenient device for avoiding a clumsily exact rephrasing. The sentence comes from the *Saturday Evening Post.*

> We might assume that Standard Oil is going to sponsor a news program. *They* will select a commentator with political views which coincide with *their* own.

This example comes from a student theme discussed by a panel of English teachers, a majority of whom regarded the indefinite *they* as incorrect. The sentence is of a type similar to the one above, has wide currency, and is certainly convenient. The stylistic effect of *it* would be quite different in this passage, and some such periphrasis as "the board of directors of Standard Oil" would be awkward. In the opinion of one person at least, illogical suppleness has always been one of the beauties of English.

I hope that I have by now given enough examples to make it clear that skepticism toward handbook rules does not mean undue libertarianism. To sum up, that part of a composition teacher's activity which concerns itself with correctness is grammar—normative grammar if he is telling students what to use; descriptive grammar if he is himself finding out what forms are current. That part of his activity which concerns the excellence of forms is a part of literary criticism. Both activities are difficult, and both important. On the one hand, it requires investigation rather than mere acceptance of authority to determine whether a given form is right or wrong. For instance, I recently wanted to know whether students should be graded down for writing "the table's leg" or "the story's climax." I went to a national periodical and found there about a hundred examples of both the -s genitive and the of phrase, about equally divided between living beings and inanimate objects. The handbook rule is clearly false, and students should not be corrected for genitives which break it. As for stylistics, on the other hand, it is not my task to try to cover the subject, though is is obvious that we must bring to the reading of themes the same sort of detailed analysis which we give to understanding the literature we teach. I am aware that teachers are overworked and that it is perhaps too much to expect them to devote even an hour a week to investigating usage, or that they criticize their themes in the same spirit in which they analyze a paragraph of Swift or Arnold. There is only one answer to such an objection, arrogant as the answer may sound. It is surely better, and in the long run easier, to find the facts and teach them than to rely on a merely convenient myth.

Mispronunciation?*

JAMES B. McMILLAN

FRESHMAN-HANDBOOK WRITERS conventionally include a list of words said to be frequently misspelled because of mispronunciation, words like *athlete, length, irrelevant, lightning,* and *separate.* The student is advised to correct his pronunciation of such words to improve his spelling. This advice is probably good in some instances; I don't doubt that a list of misspellings taken from actual student papers would contain many forms like *athlete* and *drownded,* which reflect substandard variant pronunciations.

But the orthodox handbook treatment of this matter is deplorably uninformed and frequently harmful. When a textbook lists such spellings as *Artic, evry, intrested,* and *litrature* as results of "mispronunciation," it reveals either a questionable definition of mispronunciation or the author's failure to look up the words in modern dictionaries, in spite of the fact that a handbook usually contains a neat set of directions on "How To Use a Dictionary." Dictionaries are not identical in their handling of pronunciation, so that an unwary handbook writer may assume that a pronunciation is "incorrect" because he doesn't find it in the dictionary he is using; for example, the current *Webster's New International* doesn't show *Arctic*

* Reprinted by permission from *College English,* 10.480–481 (May, 1949).

without the first *k*-sound. But both the *American College Dictionary* and the Kenyon-Knott *Pronouncing Dictionary of American English* show it. Since all dictionaries are conservative, never entering a pronunciation until it is very widespread, I believe that a handbook should never call a pronunciation "incorrect" if even one modern reputable dictionary (e.g., *ACD*, *Century*, Funk and Wagnalls, Jones, Kenyon-Knott, *Oxford*, *Webster's*, *Winston*, Wyld) lists it. Students can certainly be taught to spell *Arctic* without an irrelevant argument about its pronunciation.

But even worse sins are committed: several popular textbooks explicitly or implicitly recommend that the student mispronounce words like *separate, despair, divide, restaurant,* and *existence* (substituting stressed vowels for unstressed vowels in reduced syllables). If this is a mere mnemonic device to be employed by the student when he is trying to recall a spelling, it may be useful, but it should be recommended only as such. No student should be told that it is incorrect to pronounce *accept* and *except* or *device* and *divide* with identical initial syllables. No instructor with even a bowing acquaintance with standard studies in English phonology can defend a textbook statement which blithely ignores and contradicts facts of phonology. And any instructor is likely to face students who have read the remarks on unstressed syllables by W. Cabell Greet on page xxii of the *ACD*.

Because one type of mispronunciation is the addition of consonants or vowels, it is common in the textbook tradition to assume that misspellings which involve the addition of letters reflect phonetic additions. Thus words like *disastrous, entrance, lightning,* and *suffrage* are old standbys in the spelling lists, along with genuine examples like *athletics* and *drowned*. If college freshmen put an extra *e* in *disastrous, lightning, suffrage,* and *entrance,* they are making a purely orthographic mistake by analogy with *disaster, lighten, suffer,* and *enter;* surely no freshman ever spoke these words with an extra syllable. Such words are out of place in a list of misspellings due to mispronunciation.

A prize howler is the advice sometimes given to spell such words as *accommodate, accumulate, defer, differ, writer,* and *written* with regard to the number of medial consonants pronounced, as if *accommodate* had two sounded *m*'s, *differ* two *f*'s and *written* two *t*'s. Any enterprising freshman who looks up the pronunciation of such words in any desk dictionary will discover the falsity of this notion, and most instructors who use handbooks know that English speakers never pronounce the same consonant twice in succession inside any English word except derived words like *meanness* and *penknife* (where the consonant is actually lengthened rather than doubled). Telling the student to pronounce *occasional* "correctly (with two *c*'s)" in an effort to get the word spelled with two *c*'s is bound to be confusing, since not one dictionary shows such a pronunciation. Somewhat similar is the advice to pronounce *tragedy* and *prejudice* correctly to avoid misspelling them with a *d* instead of the *g* and *j*. These misspellings may be due to mispronunciation, but it is not likely. The *d* is written at the end of the first syllable precisely because the writer hears and says a *d* at this point; the *j* sound is analyzed by phoneticians as a compound sound beginning with a brief *d*. Misspelling here is due to pronunciation, not mispronunciation. It is like *hiz, wuz,* and *wimin,* which are certainly not due to *mis*pronunciation.

Sometimes a misspelling is a result of the pronunciation of a particular variety of English. For example, *formerly* and *formally* are confused by college students, and *surprise* is sometimes listed as troublesome. Here again pronunciation, not mispronunciation, is the villain. There are millions of people to whom *formerly* and *formally* are identical; it is ridiculous for a mere freshman handbook to accuse these people of mispronunciation. Even in areas where the midwestern *r* survives before other consonants, assimilation has eliminated the first *r* in *surprise* quite generally (as reported by Hempl in 1893 and by many observers since). These examples can be multiplied by an examination of almost any handbook (with the notable exception of Perrin's and Marckwardt and Cassidy's); since traditional handbooks are so similar, it is pointless to cite them by title.

Spelling must be taught. It should be taught efficiently and effectively, since it is an accomplishment of a very low order, to leave as much time as possible for positive improvement in written expression and communication. The handbook can be very helpful to the hard-pressed instructor if it accurately distinguishes various types of misspellings as a diagnostic device. But the textbook writers cannot rely on older handbooks for information; they must go to studies of spelling-error frequency and to standard descriptions of present-day pronunciation.

Psycholinguistics and the Teaching of English Composition*

JOHN B. CARROLL

As I LOOK OVER what has been thought, said, or tried out in the teaching of English composition, I find a territory already extremely well traversed. The original inhabitants of this territory, of course, have lived there for a long time and have contributed their full share of highways, roads, paths, and trails. And some of the original inhabitants have been outside,—even into the strange, newly discovered land of Linguisticia—and have brought back what have seemed to be new ways of traveling. I think it is a little

* Reprinted by permission from *College Composition and Communication,* 7.188–193 (December, 1956).

impertinent for a person like myself,—from the even newer and stranger land of Psycholinguisticia—to think that we have any really new ways which could be exportable, partly because our land borders closely upon Linguisticia itself and has borrowed many of its ideas from linguistics, but also because—and here I become more serious—the chief task of psycholinguistics at the moment is to describe and explain what goes on in verbal behavior, let alone trying to tell anyone how to teach better verbal behavior.

In approaching my subject, I tried to find some way of breaking down the teaching of English composition into component parts so that they could be dealt with singly. One of my colleagues in psychology thinks that seven is a psychological magic number,—for example, it's about the average number of random digits a person can remember in immediate memory span; hence, I have arbitrarily decreed for myself seven interrelated problems in writing. They are:

1. Having something to say.
2. Gauging the audience.
3. Organizing one's thoughts.
4. Choosing the right words.
5. Constructing sentences and paragraphs.
6. Saying exactly what you mean.
7. Saying it with style.

I'd like to run through this list with a series of brief comments from the point of view of the psychology of language, provided that you understand that what I can say about them is not necessarily in proportion to what they may deserve.

1. *Having something to say.* To use ordinary language, we can say that writing or speaking (for that matter) is translating some kind of "thoughts" into words. The psychology of language is ordinarily concerned with how these "thoughts" get translated into words, but the college composition instructor may feel that his first problem is to arouse thoughts in his students. Occasionally we hear of a teacher who arrogantly says that he is not interested in teaching writing to people who have nothing to say, but I believe most of us prefer to assume, at least until we are proved wrong, that every one of our students has something to say, whether spontaneously,—from within, so to speak—or *in response to* something,—from without, so to speak. The problem, then, is to motivate thinking, and hence, writing.

Let me bring several things to your attention in this respect:

First, let us note that one of the motivating factors in verbal behavior is reinforcement, or reward. A person who is rewarded, somehow, for saying something is more likely to say it again, or to say more. I invite you to try this experiment, modeled after some recently published research. The next time you find yourself engaged in a conversation with a friend, take particular care to show agreement with any opinions he expresses, either by nodding assent, or better still, by rephrasing what he has said. In general, you can expect to find that the person you are talking to will be more likely to continue talking about his subject than if you show indifference, or even disagree. Is there any way of paralleling this finding in writing? The difficulty is that the reward for writing must inevitably be delayed, perhaps from Friday when the theme is passed in until the next Friday when it is returned to the student. Any means you can find for decreasing the time between actual writing and the reward that comes for it will contribute toward better motivation for writing.

But this has to do with eliciting the writing of whatever the person has to say. People must sometimes be helped to find what they have to say. Some psychologists studying creativity and originality think that highly creative people are distinguished by the fact that they are constantly "shuffling attributes," so to speak; that is to say, in considering any problem, idea, object, or event, the creative person thinks of it in more dimensions or from more points of view than the ordinary person. Propose some topic, like "A Holiday," and where your ordinary person will treat it very literally in terms of his own experiences, your creative person will think of this topic in terms of such aspects or dimensions as the uses of holidays, the history of holidays, the symbolic significance of special holidays, and so forth. The skill with which great writers invest rather ordinary topics or events with a great richness of detail, usually by considering these ordinary topics things from out-of-the-ordinary points of view, is often remarkable. The question, now, is whether this kind of creativity can be taught or otherwise encouraged, without, of course, doing so in an artificial and forced manner. I think it can; at least I would urge experimentation in this direction. For theme topics, propose not only the central ideas but some series of unusual points of view from which these can be considered.

2. *Gauging the audience.* Studies of the conditions for communication suggest that communication implies an audience, and that lacking an audience verbal behavior is stilted and unnatural. In the context of the freshman composition course, this means that writing must be *for* someone, and that "someone" must not necessarily be the instructor. In fact, it is useful and enlivening to try to write for different audiences and different occasions. An interesting class project might be the study and imitation of the style of the tabloids in contrast to that of the *New York Times.*

3. *Organizing one's thoughts.* This is a large topic, but here is at least one thought: Good writing shows a peculiar kind of interconnectedness which carries the reader along and allows him to fall into no traps unawares. As you very well know, this is accomplished by establishing in almost every sentence some expectancy of what sort of thing may come next, —perhaps an illustration, perhaps a contrasting idea, perhaps an explication of a novel idea just introduced. There is even the trick of establishing

an expectancy that *nothing* will come next. To teach students to appreciate these devices and perhaps to use them more effectively, I suggest applying to paragraph organization what has been sometimes called Shannon's guessing game. In the usual application, one has people guess each successive letter of a text. Here I propose having students guess each successive *sentence* of a text,—not the exact words, of course, but at least the idea, or the kind of function played by the sentence in carrying along the development of the thought. This game can be played with texts from either standard or, shall we say, non-standard authors, the students. And I'll wager that most standard authors write more guessably.

4. *Choosing the right words.* There are many problems here, including that of good usage. Time allows me only to make a suggestion similar to what I made above,—another guessing game, but of a somewhat different sort. The background of my suggestion is as follows: a journalistically-minded psychologist has worked out what he calls the "cloze" procedure for measuring the readability of a text, i.e., the ease with which it can be comprehended. You take the text which you are going to work with and subject it to a little delicate butchering,—cut out, say, every tenth word and leave a blank in its place. You then measure readability as a function of how readily people can guess the words you have extracted. Incidentally, this procedure seems to give more sensible results than some of the word-counting formulas like Flesch's, since this procedure shows Gertrude Stein to be a difficult writer while Flesch's formula makes her out to be easy. Now my suggestion is that this procedure be adapted to showing students how context should help to determine the "right word"; and on the way it may also show them something about writing understandably. This should be an illuminating exercise for the classroom; take a text by a standard author, strike out selected words, and see how readily students can guess those words. Then discuss the contextual clues which prompt their guesses. And finally, subject student products to this kind of analysis.

5. *Writing grammatical sentences.* This is the problem for which linguistic science has seemed to provide a long-sought solution, and I know that many of you have already tried, with considerable success, to apply structural grammar in your teaching. I have been impressed with several articles in *College English* by MacCurdy Burnet, who shows how the linguistic structure of a paragraph can be diagrammed on the blackboard, and how students can be taught to identify the parts of speech rapidly and with retention,—if they are led to employ Fries's form-classes rather than the traditional quasi-philosophical definitions of parts of speech. I have been doing quite a bit of experimentation and testing with an approach to grammar which has many similarities to the recent attempts of which I have just spoken. The difference, if any, is in my emphasis on the learning of grammar as a special case of concept learning.

Start with the earliest learning of one's native language. It must be obvious that the child is constantly learning the form-class allegiances of every new word he acquires. If he were to learn a word *niss*, say, meaning a kind of clay used in his play, he would very soon begin using this as what we technically term a mass noun, and he would automatically say, "Give me some niss . . . I like to play with niss," never: "Give me a niss . . . I like to play with the niss." But the pre-school period is not the time to try to make the child verbalize about such things, become conscious of form-classes and begin to label them. At what age do children start to be able to do this? Studies conducted under my direction at Harvard indicate that under the right conditions they can do it at an elementary level even by the third grade, and possibly earlier. We find this out by means of a rather conventional type of concept formation experiment: suppose we are interested in whether children can form the concept *verb*. We give a sentence like *The boy hit the ball* and ask the child to guess the word we are thinking of. After a few tries he guesses the word *hit*. "Fine," we say, and present another sentence: *I touched the sharp knife*. Again there is perhaps some fumbling, but we wait for the response *touched* and reward it. This goes on for quite a few more sentences; even third-grade children can pick out the verb in simple sentences like *Jim and Mary helped their mother*, or *Soft winds gently blow the little boat*. Notice, however, that we never mention the word *verb*. Nor do we even try to make the child verbalize how he arrives at the verb. This can come later. Next we give sentences like *A cudof biced the sitev*. The child will almost invariably pick *biced* as the verb. Even when we give a sentence like *Docib hegof gufed ripan tesor* many children will pick *fufed* because of its verbal ending. This is a nice demonstration of the linguist's point that the parts of speech are structural rather than semantic entities.

I have used the same approach in a group testing situation, both at the third, fourth, fifth, and sixth-grade level and at the adult level. For the elementary school children I have developed a test which teaches four grammatical ideas: subjects, objects, verbs, and adjectives. Here is the sample teaching material for *objects:*

1. Ned cut the APPLE.

2. I didn't mean to hurt YOU.

3. Do you like to eat PIE?

4. The policeman shot the THIEF.

5. I broke the WINDOW last night.

1. Peter fixed my DOLL.

   The cat killed the mouse.

2. The dentist pulled my TOOTH today.

   Fred wrote a long letter.

The explanation is in terms of the model sentences at the left; the practice exercises are at the right, and the children are asked to mark the word in the second sentence in each pair which "does the same job" as the word in CAPITALS in the first sentence. The test items are similar. I have found that third-grade children are able to identify subjects, objects, verbs, or adjectives if you give them one task at a time. They get confused, however, when these tasks come in scrambled order; the ability to identify these items when given in any order does not mature, apparently, until the sixth grade. But it is striking that at the sixth-grade level practically all children can do these simple tasks without trouble; in the samples I have studied, they can do them with about 90% accuracy, on the average.

What about the college-age level? We would expect these people to do more complicated tasks. Actually, they do not seem to do even quite as well as sixth-graders (though I must admit I have not tried them out on sixth-grade tasks). A few examples will show you precisely what kind of tasks college-age students can do, and how well.

In the test items which follow, the students are supposed to find the word or phrase in the second sentence which does the same job in *its* sentence as the word or phrases printed in CAPITAL LETTERS in the first sentence. The percentages placed next to each item are the percentages of students of college age able to find the right answer. All these items concern sentence subjects, but are drawn from a larger pool of items testing various grammatical concepts.

(96%) Many BIRDS go south during the winter.
       Most *infantry soldiers* during World *War* II carried *Garand rifles*.
               1   2   3   4   5
(74%) FEW come back.
       In the *middle* of the *lake* will be found a *small island* crowned with
               1   2   3   4
       a single *tree*.
                  5
(39%) Which color do YOU like best?
       This *one* suits *me* better than the *other*. It makes no *difference* to *me*.
              1   2   3   4   5

It is obvious that many students do not have any reliable sense of what constitutes a sentence subject when they are confronted with such confusion factors as can be seen in the second and third of the above items,— inverted sentence order and repeated words. But I believe the above items illustrate a type of teaching device which could be effective. It stresses patterning and structure rather than grammatical terminology, and encourages the formation of true concepts rather than mere verbalizations. Notice that the device completely avoids grammatical terminology. This type of device can in fact be used for teaching almost any type of grammatical concept. How much of this is relevant to English composition? I do not know, but I am reasonably sure that unless the student gets a feeling for sentence patterning, as he can do if he is given training in solving these "grammatical analogies" problems, his own sentence patterns will show many obvious defects. Research on the effectiveness of teaching English grammar in improving English composition has been mainly negative, but until this research has been repeated with improved methods of teaching English grammar, I will remain unconvinced that grammar is useless in this respect.

The reports of one of our student teachers at Harvard have given me considerable cause for optimisim about the structural approach to grammar, which turns out to be so clear and frustratingly simple that we wonder why it has not been tried before. Our student teacher took over a class of high-school seniors of widely dispersed abilities whose previous, regular teacher had thrown up her hands as far as the teaching of grammar was concerned. She started teaching with the "guessing game" approach I have described here—beginning with simple components like subjects and predicates, nouns and verbs. One thing she discovered rather early was that the technique did not work well with *printed* sentences. With *spoken* sentences, the students caught on much more quickly. Furthermore, this inexperienced student teacher discovered that the students were easily guided by pointing out the implications of their wrong answers. For example, if a student said that "blue" in the sentence "The sky was blue" was a verb, the teacher would ask, "Then would it make sense to say 'The sky was bluing' (or 'blued' or 'had blued')? At a later stage, sentence building rather than sentence analysis was stressed. Starting with a simple sentence proposed by a student, the teacher worked with her students to add various kinds of phrases and clauses, with a view to demonstrating how the various kinds of complex and compound sentences could be constructed. She claims that as a result of this the students' written work improved immeasurably, the students volunteered the comment that they very much enjoyed grammar now, and that they understood certain simple and basic facts for the first time. I am not quite sure how to evaluate this report, since I would like to see the technique tried by experienced teachers on classes of known ability, but I regard it as encouraging nevertheless.

6. *Saying exactly what you mean.* One of the most frequent faults in my graduate students' theses is the failure to use terms with their proper referential functions. This sort of thing comes out even in the simplest of all sentence patterns, the copulative sentence. A student will write, "Let *a* be a set of mutually exclusive classes," when he actually means "Let *a* be *any one of* a set of mutually exclusive classes." It is as if he wrote, "Tom was a group of boys at the camp," when he meant to say, "Tom was one of a group of boys at the camp." I am sure all of you could give me better examples. What to do about this frustrating state of affairs? The tendency towards abbreviation and ellipsis seems to be strong, and I think it would be effective for the instructor to collect many, many examples of this sort of thing, to help the student see this tendency in himself and others.

7. *Saying it with style.* Style is like personality; indeed, perhaps style can be equated with personality (though I feel this is stretching a point). Above all things, let us not dampen style when it is associated with a per-

sonality. In freshman English, there will be those whose personalities and styles are just forming; rather than dampening them, let us bring them out. This must be done in an atmosphere of freedom; it cannot be done with a constraining, copybook spirit. I have no special trick or gimmick to bring this about, except to suggest that any challenge, almost a dare, is worth making if it will make students feel free to develop in their own ways, to write about things as they themselves see them rather than with the imagined perspective of another.

The Uses of Structure and the Structure of Usage*

DONALD J. LLOYD

ONE OF THE GREAT IDEAS of our time, it seems to me, is the concept of structure, the vision of vast and apparently inchoate systems being reducible, in the ultimate, to units functioning with other units in arrangements, making up levels of organization which themselves are units in larger patterns. This concept, faithfully pursued, has fractured the infrangible atom and contained the expanding universe. It has also broken the sound-barriers of language and penetrated the mysteries of human speech. In every instance of its application, however fruitful, it has racked the presuppositions of mankind and forced a painful readjustment of thought. Matters once seen clearly fall into confusion; practitioners flounder aimlessly between systems, trying to apply new knowledge to ends which have themselves been negated.

As an English teacher who came to a simple decision some years ago that the rigorous methodology of linguistic scientists is valid, coherent, and fruitful, I have tried to understand the science in its relations, particularly in its relations to the teaching of English. We have lived through two eras —one in which linguistics seemed simply irrelevant, and one in which its effect was destructive. Linguistic critics, without seriously questioning correct writing as the object of English teaching, attacked the good of grammar and the unity of usage. I think we are now in a third era, in which linguistics offers more than a method and a base for criticism; it now offers a body of knowledge which can be put to use in the classroom.

Grammar and usage have traditionally been important elements in the teaching of English. Faith in grammar has become somewhat weakened, but our times have seen the concentration on usage develop almost into a new article of belief. Arthur G. Kennedy says in his *English Usage*, "What-

* Reprinted by permission from *The English Record,* 6.41–46 (Fall, 1955).

ever uniformity and degree of perfection our language now possesses is in large measure the result of the constant and agelong effort of the cultural aristocracy to keep the English language on a high level of usage. . . . A mere policy of *laissez faire*," he adds, "would almost certainly result in the degeneration of this great cultural medium to the level of an illiterate jargon, such as pidgin English . . ." Much knowledge about language has come to us since those lines were written, but their spirit lives on in recent letters and articles by such writers as Robert Withington, Morton Bloomfield, and Louis Salomon. To Salomon the English teacher is a grammatical policeman who tells us what we can do and what we can't do—a traffic cop of language.

The grammar of the English class has been the grammar of printed English, sketchily treated, and the usage has been the usage of writers present and past. The student has been expected not merely to learn to read and write, but to conform his speech to the model of standard writers. To the linguistically oriented English teacher, this seems like asking Narcissus to remodel his features according to the image he sees in the rippling pool—a possibility in myth, but not in real life. For grammar this teacher wishes to substitute a structural description of the language, and for the punitive enforcement of the usage of writers, an understanding of the speech and writing habits of living men and women. He has to face, then, two problems—the uses of structure, and the structure of usage.

Among the multitude of matters taken up in English classes—so multitudinous, in fact, that we may echo the dean who asked why we keep on the other faculties in the university, if we are going to handle everything in the freshman course in composition or communication—I am convinced that a structural display of the language has its place, and not in college only, but through the primary and secondary grades. Speech is central to human communication, and I can think of no more truly humane study than the exploration of its intricate architectonic, in broad and simple terms at first, and in progressively more discriminating sophistication as schooling proceeds. Writing is in no sense a primary system of symbols, and its derivative, printing, is even less so. Both writing and printing are mnemonic in their effect, reminding each native speaker of the infinitely more complex, more highly ordered, more ample, more spontaneous, and more intuitive signalling system he has learned to speak and hear. We have an obligation to expose for each youngster in the schools the methodical ordering of segmental phonemes, pitches, stresses, and junctures that are the building-blocks of human interaction.

We must, however, abandon the notion of using structure as a mere replacement for traditional grammar, to be employed in the same way for the same purpose. We must concede the "correctness" of the casual and spontaneous utterance, so long as it is a meaningful signal responded to by those who hear it. We must abandon all pretense of teaching the English language to youngsters whose integration into the give-and-take of common talk demonstrates their command of it. We must accept without quibbling the validity of the speech patterns they naturally speak, setting ourselves the task of developing in them a cultivated consciousness of what they do. For it has become obvious that a child's ear, responding to subtleties that have evaded analysis, is a better grammarian than the trained analyst.

Our model for procedure is the pattern-practice of the foreign language class, where utterances, varied internally by acceptable substitutions, are drilled by mouth to the level of automatism. We need not talk much about these patterns, but simply display them, limiting ourselves to those structures of speech which are employed in writing, but without invidious comment on that vast range of human expressions for which we have no standardized written or printed equivalents. Our object is to lift this selection of speech-patterns from unself-conscious spontaneity of production to the level of consciousness, so that they can be felt and understood as a storehouse of structural devices. Then by repetition and drill we may drive them down below consciousness again, available for automatic production and instantaneous recognition.

Primitive schoolboy writing does not represent ignorance of one's native language, but inability to transfer speech-patterns to the page of written symbolism that bears at best only a hop-skip-and-jump relation to them. The road to a style of one's own, apt and adequate to his needs, is by way first of a thorough and disciplined understanding of the primary system— speech—one of immanent order, and then of the secondary, comparatively disordered system—writing—in its relation to speech. Primitive reading represents a failure to grasp the mnemonic nature of writing and print, an inability to grasp the unit functions of words and word-groups. A good reading eye is not a young, alert, 20–20, sharply focused instrument of sight: it is an old, sophisticated, worldly, slightly blurred rounder of an eye, used to familiar words in familiar groupings, too lazy to bother with any but general outlines—unless some unfamiliarity of contour catches the attention. Some youngsters develop this eye naturally, long before their vocabularies are, taken item by item, very extensive—as early as eight or nine. Most have to be taught. Early drill with the pitch, stress, and juncture patterns of common talk, and plenty of extensive, lightly guided reading, would bring many youthful eyes to the degree of sophistication necessary for efficient reading. I have not beat the bushes for all the works in print, but I have yet to find a textbook which treats spelling in relation to the phonemes of English, or reading in relation to the structural organization of our speech.

So much for the uses of structure. That other much-vexed matter, usage (as traditionally approached) is a list of separate items beyond any man's control. But the ground of usage is in fact not that portion of written and printed English devoted to expository essays. The ground of usage is different for each person; for each the one fixed point of reference is not a compendious body of national, reputable, and current expressions, but the personal and social relations of his upbringing. So long as he is secure and integrated within his own speech-community, he has no problem of usage; his problems begin when he crosses the boundary of that community and mingles with the members of others. Now the multitude of men in the workaday world are not contemptible, and their speech ought not to be equated, as Morton Bloomfield equates it, with the ignorant, the thoughtless, the obscene. It may be news to him that they respond with equal disdain, with flat rejection of his judgments in general and in detail.

The mother of usage is the company we keep, and we keep the company we do because we like it. Usage further is a matter of habit; we speak the way we do because the speech springs lightly to the tongue. The teacher must approach with courtesy the usage of his students; each is in a sense a delegate from his own speech-community, whose emotions are interwoven with its ways. Much adjustment to different speechways goes on all the time in our lives, but rarely in an atmosphere of strain. We imitate what we admire and what strikes our fancy. The college student, adjusting over a term of four years to his fellows in the college community, wishing to belong, to be accepted, to disappear in the group, adjusts also to the accepted norms of the English they speak. But he does not necessarily abandon anything, and in moments of relaxation or of tension, falls back into the familiar language of his youth. All the thunders of the faculty have nowhere near the same force on his writing.

Here again we can borrow from the foreign-language class to help him. Teaching a student French we do not attempt to dislodge his English, but to supplement it; we simply add to what he knows a store of alternate locutions that will permit him to move in the society of the French. Explaining French expressions in terms of what he now says in English, factually and without bias, we find the points of contrast and develop them. And we give him guided practice in hearing, reading, speaking, and writing the locutions we expect him to learn.

The English-speaking world is a multitude of speech-communities, some defined geographically, some socially, and some in terms of occupation, age, sex, and common interests. Much is common to all of them; otherwise we could not understand each other. What is not common is systematically different. Phonology, morphology, syntax, and choice of vocabulary differ together. More than courtesy demands that the teacher bend a keen and sympathetic ear to his students' speech; simple pedagogical efficiency lays the responsibility on him. He has to find the points of contrast, present the alternatives in an atmosphere that makes them seem attractive, and set up circumstances that encourage their use. Every time he dwells in an invidious way in the locution he wishes to provide an alternative for, he provokes the demon that frustrates him.

We cannot package the language and its writing for our students and hand it to them in a bundle, because we cannot predict what their needs and the courses of their lives will be. Nor can we be that well and broadly versed in the language. We can acquaint them, however, with the social basis of usage, treating it not as a department of manners but as a facet of the separation of men and their clotting into groups. Just as we now acquaint them with the communal life of a village in Pakistan or France, teaching them to respect ways other than their own, we can teach them to observe with humane understanding the speech practices of other Americans, and to respect them. For it is a fact that Americans differ from one another in their speechways, as they differ in their modes of life and in their occupations. As for acceptable written usage, it is tied more closely to our divergent speechways than we have been led to think, to the force of personality and the accidents of prestige. There is room in the English class for a factual presentation of usage in general, so that the students can observe it for themselves, and choose to change or not as they will. But I think that we are under no obligation to impose conformity to any norm, even if we think we can find one.

Every act of speech or writing is a creative act rising out of some felt need for expression. Dictionaries, grammars, and linguistic descriptions are historical compendia gathered with loose and fallible nets. They are not much good for prediction. Like the barometer and thermometer, which don't affect the weather, they don't affect the language. I know that it is often held that they do, but studies seem to put the sources of linguistic influence elsewhere. These works have a proper limited use. But if our aim is to create literate people, people who read and write as a matter of habit and choice, we need to focus our effort, not on the history of the acts that literate people perform, but on the practice of those acts. Structure will serve us by exposing the resources that we call on and enforcing their patterns in our minds, so that we consciously read and actively write according to those patterns. Usage in detail is better left alone.

The original studies of usage—those of Leonard, Marckwardt and Walcott, and Fries—and the teaching theories based on them, such as Pooley's in *Teaching English Usage,* did not question correctness of usage as an aim of teaching. They did question the accuracy of current statements and they sought a more reliable description. From them the notion of "levels" of usage began to emerge—not abandoning correctness, but seeking it in a more complicated way. Perrin's thorough blurring of speech and writing practices offers three categories of usage: formal, informal, and vulgate. But as Kenyon points out, all men of all classes, including the vulgar commonality, adjust their language to the social situation they find themselves in. Those who are subject to power take their key from those who apply power, and express themselves formally or informally as they respond to cues from above. Formal English is not a segment of the language, but the self-conscious expression of persons who are ill-at-ease and a means also of keeping people at a distance while we do our business with them. (Ours is an age when brass-hatted generals decree a formal informality without altering the status relationship they cherish: *The order of the day is no ties and everybody will use first names.*) The result of the attempt to apply the doctrine of usage has been a watchful Emily Postism applied to weekly themes with a red pencil, with the real purpose of writing—making oneself understood—squeezed out of court. We need to attend more to *what* our students have to say and less to how we would like them to say it.

The phonemic, morphemic, and syntactic arrangements of speech, meticulously observed and thoughtfully exposed, lead to command of their written equivalents in reading and writing. These are the uses of structure in the English class. The permissives and negations—usually unspoken themselves—of community groups select for each group a related set of phonological, morphological and lexical terms. Each person's participation in one of more of these groups gives us some measure of his usage; his personal character and sensitivity to these things give us another. The sum is his style, properly his own, unique, different from the styles of other men and women, different, too, from each of its earlier stages of development. An understanding of the social structuring of usage will enhance his comprehension of what he reads and increase his pleasure in reading. It will help him control the implications of what he says and writes and increase his effectiveness. We can steal for it some of the class time now devoted to fragments lifted from psychology, history, the social sciences and the Great Books. Courteously, sympathetically, and professionally guided practice in reading and writing will fix these as habits laced with pleasure and satisfaction. We can then deliver him proudly to society—to business, or to industry, or to the other faculties in the college—as a literate citizen.

Grammar in Freshman English*

Donald J. Lloyd

THE PREVIOUS SPEAKERS have brought us a step beyond what we are used to; they have developed the nature of linguistics and its implications for the teaching of English. We now have to consider specifically how to use

* Originally a paper given at the Spring Meeting of the Conference on College Composition and Communication, St. Louis, 1954, this article is here reprinted by permission from *College Composition and Communication*, 5.162–166 (December, 1954).

a linguistic grammar in our teaching, and what to use it for. I agree with Sumner Ives that what the grammarian has to say is not the end of wisdom but a part of the beginning. How important a part I shall try to show.

We must not forget the rawness and recency of our present knowledge of English speech. I review some modern monuments: Bloomfield's *Language* (1933), a massive exposition of basic theory, Fries's *American English Grammar* (1940), Bloch and Trager's *Outline of Linguistic Analysis* (1942), Nida's *Synopsis of English Syntax* (1943), Pike's *Intonation of American English* (1945), Trager and Smith's *Outline of English Structure* (1951), and Fries's *Structure of English* (1952). This is the work of about twenty years, while English teachers generally, drunk with the wine of literary history and literary criticism, have slept like Rip van Winkle. Like Rip, we awake to find that a revolution has taken place; like Rip, we are not sure we like the looks of it. But if we accept it as a fact—as we must— we may advance boldly on the question what to do with it. I am going to try to outline a workable way to use a linguistic grammar of English for teaching reading and for teaching writing, two basic aims we all profess, being all professors.

As these studies reveal speech to us, we may conceive of it as a kind of drama with an actor and an audience, a speaker and a hearer. The hearer, as Fries has shown, is a part of the act; he is not inert. He responds. He responds to the performance of the speaker because it is such as he can perform himself, and he will, if a pause occurs long enough for him to edge into.

The central reality in language is conversation. The frequency and ease of conversation keep the members of a single speech-community sharing the same habits; on the other hand, all the barriers of distance, social groupings, and separated interests limit the conversational exchange and bring about differences in speech. Normal informal conversation is a complex dramatic performance. The speaker manipulates several communicative systems at once, to offer God's abundance of signals of meaning. Central to the performance is the linguistic system, which consists, as we now see, of a constantly changing, delicately modulated stream of sounds. In this flow the basic linguistic units are the phonemes—the vowels, semivowels, consonants, four levels of pitch, four of stress, and four kinds of complex pitch-pauses called junctures. The phonemes combine, by an architectonic as beautiful as any structure in man's work or nature's, into morphemes, and the morphemes into patterns of syntax. The phonetic, phonemic, morphemic, and syntactic strata of organization all strike the ear at once, in a total impression whose meaning is not settled until the speaker signals its end by one of the final junctures. The linguists have this structure of structures well in hand, with notations for all aspects of it.

Accompanying this linguistic flow of sound, the speaker manipulates at least two other systems which also have meaning for him and the hearer. One is body movement and gesture—or if you prefer a fancy word, kinesics —which we are beginning to understand as an organization of basic units, and for which we have the beginning of a system of notation. The other is a set of vocal qualifiers, five pairs of overriding modulations of the linguistic stream—named by the researchers overloudness and oversoftness or muting, drawling and clipping, rasp and openness or hollowness, breaking and whining, singing and whispering. These, as their discoverers point out, do not have encapsulated meaning; they combine with each other to convey attitudes as part of the total meaning of the whole performance.

This whole is the basic speech act—the conversation. A TV talk which we can hear but not join in is a limited abstraction—the responses of the hearers are omitted. The radio or phonograph abstracts further, giving us the linguistic part of the utterance and the vocal qualifiers, but not the movements of face and body that we usually see. With each cutting-away of a part of the whole entity, a greater burden falls upon what is left. The performer begins to fake a little, offering special tricks that stir us to imagine the signals being omitted. Art and artifice get into the act.

Writing and printing are further abstractions; they omit all but the linguistic system, and they translate this sequence of sounds emitted in time into a line of letters on the page. They omit stress, pitch, and juncture, and they introduce signals for the eye alone, such as capital letters, the spaces between words, and punctuation marks. In place of the massive mutual reinforcement of the three elements of speech—the linguistic flow, the kinesic pantomime, and the vocal qualifiers—words and their structural arrangements work almost alone to carry the load of meaning. Written English is mnemonic in its effect: it must remind us of our speech, or we cannot read it. It is, further, a traditional system in its own right, evolved through centuries to meet the needs of the eye. Precision of grammar and vocabulary is forced on it by what it lacks; far from being superior to speech, it is relatively new and crude; it is truncated, taboo-ridden, limited in its structural resources, altogether inferior as a communicating instrument to the old, mature, flexible, endlessly reinforced, subtly modulated, complex orchestration of common talk. Managing it is an art which has brought agony to creative spirits from Caedmon's day to ours.

Most of the concerns of the English teacher, where he deals with language, are not precisely linguistic; they fall into the area which the researchers in the Department of State have called "metalinguistic"—the relation of the language to the other structured patterns of activities in our community. We have to understand the relation of speech to writing, of language to literature, of words to what is named by words. Every other system of human communication is somehow derived from speech or based on it. Hence we must begin with a thorough knowledge of linguistics; anything less will not serve us. The grammar of speech is not the grammar of writing, but it has its equivalents in writing. Becoming literate is basically the job of learning to control the written equivalents to what we say, learning to write them and learning to read them, learning what to leave out and what to put in.

The linguists have made practical use of their science in the teaching of English as a second language, doing some things that help us and some that do not. One thing that they do does not help us is intrude meaning. They have to intrude meaning; their students begin with another language that uses different words, forms, and patterns to express a different analysis of experience. Our students already know and control our language; their manipulations of its signals and responses to the signals show an immediate, almost instinctive grasp of our meanings. We can thus revert to the classic linguistic presentation of the signals, describing them quite abstractly, getting at meaning by means of the signals, not at the signals, as traditional grammar sometimes does, by way of the meaning. One thing that the linguists do does help us: they practice patterns. They practice patterns until the student automatically speaks and hears and thinks patterns.

Our job, then, is to identify the signals of speech, find their written equivalents, and practice the two in relation to each other. We must work selectively, dealing with commonly recurrent elements, lifting them to consciousness, drilling them until they become automatic and are reduced once more below the level of consciousness. We need not bother with anomalies, differences of usage, or special cases of any kind; we deal only with the structural elements that let all of us, educated and uneducated, foreign and domestic, Northern, Eastern, and Southern, understand each other when we talk to each other. In the spirit of Poor Richard, who said, "Take care of the pennies and the pounds will take care of themselves," we must teach our students to manipulate the small-change of language, the common coinage of everyday talk. It is not the words that give meaning to the sentence; it is the sentence that assigns meanings to the words in it. We approach vocabulary by way of structure.

The grammatical signals of English work unnoticeably; they cradle the noun, verb, adjective, and adverb as water supports and sustains the fish that swim in it, and a word apart from these signals is as dead as a fish in a basket. Patterns of order in the utterance, relatively settled since Middle English times, are scarcely mentioned before our own day, so quietly do they do their work. Prosodic contours of pitch, stress, and juncture that segment the utterance into meaning-groups were almost unnoticed until Pike, pondering our inability to hear and reproduce the significant tones of tone languages, turned his attention to the tonal factors of English. Inflectional endings and what Fries has called function words fall modestly in unaccented syllables, inconspicuously cementing the stressed elements of vocabulary together. The child learns all these grammatical signals at such an early age that he is not conscious of them; they precede his sense of words as words; he knows them before he has built up an extensive vocabulary. The English lexicon is not the English language; these signals are; we learn them only by experience with the language. We learn words by experience with language and the world outside language—with men, things, qualities, and actions.

The order of utterance which is grammatically significant in speech appears in writing as word-order. For the delicate signals that define meaning-groups of words we have no real equivalent in writing; modern punctuation is far too sketchy to do this job, but in most cases the word that begins the group warns us of the characteristic span of the groups. *The, this, that, some,* or *any* guides the eye across any number of premodifiers to the noun-headword of the phrase. *Can, is, do,* or *has* defines a group ending in some form of the verb. *Who, which, that, where,* or *when* following a noun tell us to take the next span of words as a modifier of this noun. A preposition steers us forward to a noun, suppressing it within the function of the whole prepositional phrase—usually adverbial or adjectival. We reverse the usual approach to concord, and teach the student as reader and writer to take heed of what is to come, if we assume as a principle that words uttered first select the forms of words that follow. As for the function words, critics of the *Structure of English* who complain that Fries's fifteen groups are bewildering need only sort them in relation to the four great form-classes of words, to bring a good pedagogical order out of the raw order of his research. It is not hard for us to add more to the 155 words he lists; the important thing is for us to see that their recurrence is of the same pervasive kind as the recurrence of inflections and word-order patterns, and has the same effect.

If we are to work quickly and economically toward literacy in our students, we must lift these grammatical signals to consciousness, to an emphasis they do not have when we are thinking about what we are saying or writing. We must find ways of drilling the cluster of modifiers that attend the noun, regardless of particular word-items involved; we must practice substituting noun-phrase and noun-clause for the noun, verb-phrase for the verb, adjective-phrase and adjective-clause for the adjective, and adverb-phrase and adverb-clause for the adverb. And we must define and enforce by drill the conditioned substitution of the members of each form-class in the functions of each of the others—nouns as verbs, adjectives as nouns, verbs and verbals as nouns, adverbs and adjectives.

To determine usage is not the proper use of grammar. The matrix of usage is the company we keep, and as we bring our students to citizenship in the Republic of Letters, they will take on the usage of educated men and women. The proper use of grammar is to take apart the machinery of the language, exposing the signals by which meaning is conveyed in writing in relation to the signals by which meaning is conveyed in speech. We have to accept the primacy of speech; we have to face the subtlety, intricacy, and plenitude of speech-signals. High-flying students of logic, rhetoric, and literary criticism though we are, we have to get down off Pegasus and learn them. Then we have to apply our minds steadily to our problem (about which the linguists cannot as linguists give us much help), the mass education of our young people in the control, as readers and writers, of English writing.

Generally speaking, the students who come into remedial composition classes know little grammar of any kind, and both their reading and writing are inept. The students we promote directly into English 2 know very little more grammar, but their reading and writing are both more successful. I have given considerable thought to this matter. As I watch the children in the schools, it is clear that the difference begins to take shape quite early, often even before the youngsters get much English—and with little regard to whether they normally speak the grammar of educated or uneducated English. Somehow one child learns to use meaningful groups of words at an early age—even before he can tell you what individual words mean—and another does not, but moves his eyes or his pencil painfully from word to word. A good reader can reconstruct from what he reads the patterns of pitch, stress, and pause normal to English speech.

In my own practice, I build my teaching around the structures of speech. I give my freshmen five weeks of linguistic grammar, enforced by oral drill. I have them read aloud a good deal, sometimes phrase by phrase after me, sometimes in chorus. I push them into extensive outside reading of the books and periodicals that the educated read. I teach them how to use their eyes in reading, in large jumps, rather than small, according to the patterns we have drilled. I keep them writing constantly also; I press them to explore their thoughts with their pencils, to find out what they think about. The leap that their competence takes during the term is a large one, almost as large as their feeling of confidence. And yet, as I feel my way, I regret that nothing like this comes before or after in their experience, and that there are so few other teachers trading information with me about the practical everyday conduct of this kind of class.

In a nation which is more highly educated than ever before, in which the arts—music, architecture, design, painting, sculpture, the dance—have reached real popular acceptance, we have no reason as English teachers to be proud of our work. Literature and drama languish; we have fewer readers of books, fewer bookstores, fewer libraries in proportion to our numbers than any western nation. We are uncomprehending readers and unwilling writers. Now it is easy to scatter the blame like seed on the wind, on sports, radio, TV, the movies, and the colleges of education, but let us take a portion to ourselves. The nation learns its English from college departments of English; we teach all the English that teachers of English in all the schools get. We have not understood our language nor how to teach it.

What you think the language is determines how you teach it. Today, an adequate workable description of English is a commonplace in every department of Linguistics in the country. Whenever we take it into the classroom and base our teaching on it, our subject glows with light and interest. We have much to learn about making the best use of it; we have teachers to educate, textbooks to write, practical procedures to work out. A respectable and self-respecting future lies ahead of us, if we resolve to ground our teaching of Engish on a modern scientific description, in strict and conscientious adherence to the best that is known. Grammar is a ground only, but logic, rhetoric, and stylistics not based on the most adequate grammar known hang on the empty and echoing air.

A "Linguistic" Approach to English Composition*

Donald J. Lloyd

Let me say in the beginning that I mean by a "linguistic" approach something more than an application to the teaching of English Composition of the so-called "doctrine of usage" current in many English departments today, and certainly not a surrender to anyone's way of saying anything; something more, too, than semantics, valuable though semantics may be; and something more than the cultivation of skills, though I feel that the ability to read and write must be the main object of cultivation in English courses in the schools and colleges. I mean simply an approach based on modern studies of language and consistently informed by them. I should also say that my remarks will be colored by my experience in teaching segregated sections of students too poorly equipped in English to enter regular college composition classes.

First, as to the subject-matter of the course. In our effort to set up a situation in which students can express themselves, we have ranged widely looking for subject-matter. We have scoured the heavens, the earth, and the waters under the earth. We have constructed books of readings from anthropology, geopolitics, Marxism, psychoanalysis, and on through zoology; we have drawn from the oldest classics and the latest periodicals. In so doing, we have missed our proper subject-matter, which I believe to be simply the English language itself. It is always surprising to me and a little saddening to see how ignorant even our best students are about their mother tongue and about the complicated nexus of actions, knowledge,

* Reprinted by permission from *Language Learning,* 3.109–116 (July–December, 1950).

and habit they set in motion when they use it. I think that somewhere they should learn about these things, and that they should learn from us in our classes at the same time as they learn to express themselves. We are in a position to help protect them from the cant that circulates popularly in the community, and we should do it. We should give them information about language and language habits, and we should help them learn to observe language for themselves. We should be careful to make no statements about language that they cannot verify, and we should take care that we are well informed enough to be accurate. That is what a mathematician has to do in his field, and we should be no less rigorous in ours.

Second, we should keep ourselves aware of the complicated linguistic world in which our students live, and we should be ready to interpret it to them. They move today in a welter of dialects which bring to their ears many conflicting usages; they shift in a matter of moments from one social level to another and from situations of complete conventionalized formality to those of the most intimate familiarity, each involving its own consistent patterns of usage. Instead of knowing a few books thoroughly and lovingly, they have a slight and insignificant contact with a mass of writing in which they are for the most part only casually interested; and this writing presents them with a diversity of standards and practices which renders the firm pronouncements of our handbooks whimsical and nugatory. In their ears constantly is the sound of voices to which they listen sometimes and sometimes not; they have to deal with commands, pleas, exhortations, persuasions, slimy and unctuous suggestions; without moving from their chairs the young women hear themselves pressed to gird for love and the young men for war. If we do not help them find some sense, some order in all this, who will?

Recognizing an obligation, then, to explain and interpret their language to them in terms of the social world in which they use it, how shall we approach English composition so as to have the greatest effect on their ability to conduct themselves in the walks of life which we presume for them, and do it in the time that is available to us? This is what I wish to discuss. It is a problem toward whose solution I think that modern studies of language have some genuinely useful contributions to make. I shall touch occasionally on specific means which I have worked out for myself for use in my own classes.

In the first place, I think that we should approach our students in a relaxed and easy-going frame of mind. I think that the idea that our work should be disciplinary is illusory, and I think that a disciplinary approach fails us. Most of our students have had their fill of discipline in English classes, and many of them are thoroughly soured on the idea that any good can come of any English class, though if pressed for their prescription of what they think they need, they will prescribe what they have had. They think that it ought to hurt. With a beginning class, I am inclined to take about a month before I try to have them do much writing. We need that time to feel each other out. I find that a class writes as well at the end of that month as it would if I were calling for papers and flunking most of them, as I would have to.

Second, I think that our treatment of the language should be general, descriptive, and informative; we should prepare our students for divergence of usage in an easy way; we should encourage them to observe for themselves and try to make sense out of what they find. We should gradually build up a picture of standard written English as a cultivated instrument, a conventionalized means of expression varying in form according to time and place and circumstance, but being most like a representation—in a different medium—of a selection of the habits of the educated and prestige groups in their community, and least like the speech of the ignorant, the illiterate, and all that great mass of people whose needs in expression put no great burden on their language, either in precision or range.

With the standard language thus defined—and I can assure you that for most of the students this will be new material, because they have never clearly understood its status—we can consider its machinery. I think that a proper linguistic approach would distinguish between its graphics and its grammar. Each is a matter to be handled informatively, not prescriptively or in the spirit of the correcter, but descriptively. Our aim should be, I think, to give information, because it is only on the basis of knowledge that our students can develop the will or the ability to discipline themselves in their writing and seek more constant adherence to generally accepted standards. The graphics of English are ever a problem, because I am sure that it is only in Cloud-Cuckoo Land that we could find another system of writing so irregularly and inadequately representing the stream of speech, and so whimsically segmenting it. They yield best to description, and to a non-punitive use of the blue-pencil in the presence of the writer and with his understanding of the significance of the changes being made in his work. I use class sessions with the opaque projector and individual conferences for the correction of graphics, and these alone.

The question of the nature of the amount of grammar to include in a composition course is one much vexed these days, and over it modern scientific linguistics constantly looms. The word *grammar* has many meanings: to some it is simply the mechanism by which the language communicates meanings: in Engish the instruments of word-order, empty relational or function words, and some active inflections, all adjusted to each other in speech by familiar cadences of intonation and pace, but in writing standing alone or merely interpreted by the memory of spoken intonation. To others (and to most of the writers of textbooks) grammar is what seems to me—and I cannot conceal my attitude—the traditional categories of an inflected language misapplied to ours, and mingled with transitory items of usage, a ragtag and bobtail of rhetoric, and much personal favoring of the familiar. Some people treat all grammar under the heading usage; some people tackle contemporary usage as if it were basic grammar.

In my approach to grammar, I have come more and more to draw on the printed materials of the English Language Institute at Ann Arbor and on other Michigan publications such as *Language Learning,* and to observe the techniques used in foreign language laboratories such as the one we have at Wayne. At the risk of being misunderstood, I shall say that I now look for patterns: if something isn't reducible to a pattern I do not deal with it as grammar. I think an understanding of the patterns of our language is essential in reading and writing; and I think that the methods used in Michigan's intensive course are very effective in teaching those patterns, if the materials are selected and simplified to serve the needs of native speakers of English.

It is hard to give a quick description of what I now do in four weeks or so sometime about the middle of the term. I start having selected passages read aloud by different people until we come to a decent reading of them. Then I have all normal pauses marked, and I discuss the words which start the groups that must be spoken together—words like prepositions and articles, which, whatever else they mean, usually say in effect, "Noun coming up pretty soon." We mark a pause after the noun. Once we get the nouns we have the key to the rest, for the modifiers of nouns occur in an inflexible order which can be demonstrated and drilled orally until it is fixed in mind. We get the idea that the article signals a noun somewhere in the following group, that the noun may appear alone or with some or all of its possible modifiers, and that it usually appears as subject, as object, as complement, or suppressed to the function of a modifier by a preposition.

I treat the main patterns of simple sentences—and when I call a sentence simple it is simple: one word carries each function. I distinguish four functions: noun, verb, adjective, and adverb; I distinguish three units which operate as interchangeable bricks in performing these functions: the word, the phrase, and the clause—with one exception: I have never been able to make a clause work as a verb. (But Mr. Downer offers: "She's always I-told-you-so-ing me.") I find the functions by word-order—no word is really a noun or really a verb or really an adjective; it finds out what it is in the sentence in which it is used. Now we play with these three units performing the four functions, and we do it all orally. I say, "Let me have a sentence with each of the four functions carried by a single word. Now, modify the subject with a phrasal adjective. Now, into that phrasal adjective, put an adverbial clause." And so on. By the time I am finished with my treatment of grammar, I can call for some fantastic combinations and get instances of them: a noun clause as subject, three noun clauses as complement, with a single-word adjective and a phrasal adjective in each one. Verb, of course, a linking verb.

The last thing we take up is the verb with its complicated phrasal combinations and its delicately discriminated indications of tense and meaning.

This sort of practice and discussion reflects itself immediately in a startling improvement in reading ability and in a startling sophistication of sentence patterns in the papers I have to read. Some poor sentences, too, but we move with aplomb through all kinds of error to some genuine accomplishments, because when we make a mess in our efforts to express ourselves, we laugh and take another crack at it. We take error to be a natural accompaniment of learning, and when we do not find errors we do not feel we are moving far into new territory. I should point out again that this work with grammar is always descriptive and informative, never corrective, and that I urge my students when they are trying to give written form to an idea to forget direct concern with the languge and concentrate on the idea.

This is our basic subject-matter, the status of the standard written language and its machinery; it is essential, not only for those who come to us fumbling with it, but for those who already have a fair working facility with it. The informative approach concentrates on language when it is working as it should, not when it is failing, and it lights up the areas in which difficulties occur and offers a rationale for dealing with them. It offers at the same time a rough guide to punctuation, in terms of which specific practices can be discussed. It presumes, I may say, no prior knowledge whatever, a sad state that often faces us.

Now as to writing. Our limited objectives are to prepare our students to behave creditably in two situations: one, when they write on matters of their own choosing, and at leisure; the other, when they write on prescribed subjects on demand. Since language is a tool we use best when we think least about it, a linguistic approach seeks to provide a maximum amount of experience in speaking and writing under conditions not wholly detached from those we meet outside the English class, and in such a way as to offer the greatest satisfaction and pleasure. It concentrates on the process and on the experience of writing, not on the result. It seeks also to provide an audience, not a faceless, cryptic demon with a red pencil, but a living, reacting reader or readers. I think, then, that it is linguistically sound for the writer to write on what interests him and may well interest others, for writer and reader to concentrate on the idea, not on the language, for the finished paper to be given the largest possible audience, but to be otherwise lightly regarded, for corrections to be made casually and kindly in the presence of the writer, and for grades to be delayed as long as possible and minimized as far as possible.

In a linguistic approach, therefore, no writing needs to be done until class and teacher are adjusted to each other, and the occasional writing of short pieces begun on matters in which the writers are interested, these to be read and returned without comment, or read or shown to the class, until the students have had a chance to get the feel of writing and appraise the reactions they are likely to meet. Gradually the amount of writing can be increased—the reading can be handled, for if you don't have to mark every paper you see you can get through a good many of them—until by the end of the term you may be having a paper coming in practically every day and one or two or three impromptus a week. Most students complain about the work, but they enjoy it, too, and they are themselves capable of laying their first papers up against the last and measuring their accomplishment. With regular publication in the classroom by means of the opaque projector and with intermittent conferences, matters of rhetoric and stylistic, problems of organization, phrasing, propriety, meaning, spelling, emphasis, or any other problems get a good working-over.

Now I shall go out on a limb. I submit that such an approach as this will carry more students to a comfortable, knowledgeable command of standard written English than any other that I know of. Furthermore, I submit that it will pick students up in a darker state of ignorance and incapacity, and carry them, with intelligent cooperation from them, to the minimum competence demanded of entering college students more quickly and less painfully than any other method I know of.

This approach demands more knowledge of language than most of us get in our undergraduate and graduate preparation for the teaching of English, and it thus places two burdens upon us. It places a burden on our graduate schools to design a training in linguistics and in the English language for prospective teachers of English that will prepare us for the work that most of us find we have to do—teaching English composition. And it places a burden on us as individuals to inform ourselves and keep ourselves informed about the progress of modern studies of language, and to work out in the classroom ways of making those studies productive for us—in short, it obliges us to become professional about English composition. If we do our share, then it seems to me that college administrations should take steps to provide channels for promotion, so that a skilled and learned teacher of composition could find in this work the substance of a career.

You will notice what this approach excludes, but I would like to call some items to your attention: it excludes the common exercises and drills and all truck with workbooks; it excludes minute and cryptic symbols pencilled into the margins of papers returned to their writers; it excludes all lockstepping on whole classes, providing instead complete freedom for individual development; it excludes the traditional muddled and inaccurate "grammar" and the pipedreams of "intellectual discipline" often used to justify it; and it excludes the misery of theme grading, which has sent so many English teachers to a frustrated, sour, and embittered old age.

This approach is an application of linguistics to English Composition, not a teaching of linguistics—the structures of the language are treated only so far as their treatment leads to their more effective use, but no further. It is a civilized approach, embodying a genuine intellectual content, and thus it has a proper place in the university and the college.

Structural Syntax on the Blackboard*

MacCurdy Burnet

THE GRAMMARS of Charles C. Fries—especially his *Structure of English*[1]—have been used in composition courses at Maryland State Teachers College for the past several years.[2] The approach and techniques suggested have paid off in several ways: Better writing results, less time is taken up with grammar, and more grown-up attitudes toward language are adopted. More is learned in less time—more skills, more knowledge, more insight. This adds up to a phenomenally efficient way of talking about writing—and having more time to talk about other things.

I'm going to break an important rule in telling about the approach used: I'm going to use old fashioned terminology.

The first of these techniques, which involves "tracking structures" through stretches of prose longer than the sentence, can be presented on the blackboard in some such fashion as this:

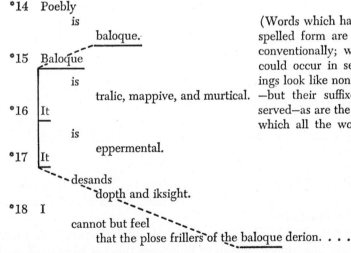

(Words which have only one spelled form are reproduced conventionally; words which could occur in several spellings look like nonsense words —but their suffixes are preserved—as are the positions in which all the words occur.)

* Reprinted with permission from *College English*, 16.38–43 (October, 1954). This article is adapted from a talk made to the Michigan Linguistic Society in Detroit, spring, 1954.

[1] *The Structure of English* (Harcourt Brace, 1952) and *American English Grammar* (Appleton-Century-Crofts, 1940).

[2] Special thanks are due to Dr. J. D. Blackwell, President of Maryland State Teachers College and to Dr. Howard E. Bosley, Dean of Instruction; and to Warner G. Rice, Chairman of the Department of English and John Weimer, Chairman of the Committee for Freshman English, University of Michigan. To men like these, teachers who are attempting to infuse aspects of linguistic method into classroom teaching owe a great deal.

In spite of the oddity of this material, we can, as readers of English, make certain statements about "baloque;" it includes "Poebly," whatever that is; it's tralic, mappive and murtical, and desands dopth and iksight, and there's a derion which is baloque, according to the writer. Although this little passage refers to nothing known on heaven or earth, it *does* have certain built-in signals of meaning, we feel.

The "step-format" is queer-looking, too, but that's beside the point at the moment.

And another parenthetical point can be made here, one that's really important in a composition course: Recurring similar words like "baloque" occur in just about nineteen out of twenty adjacent printed sentences. And so it seems practical in the classroom to assume that their recurrences constitute "links" of a sort, between sentences. Now more of these links occur between subject-areas in printed materials than in student papers; the ratio is approximately eight subject-links in print to three subject-links in passages from freshman themes.

The fact that these figures confirm what teachers of rhetoric have known for untold years is neither surprising nor important. What is important in a course in freshman composition is this: *Good-naturedly forcing students to look at the signs built into real language as a system of signals of meaning.*

This involves a firm yet merry tactfulness in distinguishing between "conventional grammar" and what we may choose to call "structural analysis," which, in turn, makes necessary a fresh set of names for parts of sentences —during the first class meeting perhaps "this area," "this word," "premodifier," "postmodifier," supplemented with gestures. Later, "nounform," "verbform," "complement," "punctuation unit," and "sequence signal" can be introduced, together with "adverbform" and "adjectiveform." It is useful in a survey, I think, to avoid definition as such entirely—and postpone classificatory techniques until several students are both interested and puzzled. Then the time is ripe for saying, "We'll call this word an 'adjectiveform'; what other words could occur in the same position?" Finally, a more generally useful test sentence with a hole or two in it can be provided —e.g., where the same word could plug up both spaces in the frame sentence: The *hot* thing's *hot*.

But showing the forms and positions which signal differences in meaning is of secondary importance. The most important thing is to present, and have students collect and examine real language—the materials not ordinarily brought to the classroom for analysis, like prose in periodicals or books of readings—genuine language in printed form which will both interest students and furnish some sort of a model for the writing the instructor wants them to submit in college.

Presenting sentences in some such form as the "step format" we looked at in the "baloque" passage has several advantages: It shows the positional

relations of "blocks of structures" which occur over and over again in
printed sentences. It exposes modificational patterns, too—and it helps to
hammer home the notion that sentences consist of "blocks of structure"
within which words are relatively incidental. The format, if a teacher
chooses to use it, need not be taught as such; students find that after blackboard demonstration they can transcribe nearly every sentence they encounter. I'd like to illustrate some of the commoner format patterns into
which nearly all printed sentences fall: First, let's take the utterance made
famous by Dr. Fries and put it through its paces on the page as if we had
found it in printed form. Conventionally, it would look like this:

1a   The uggle wogs a diggle.

In the "step format," it would look like this:

1b   The uggle
      wogs
         a diggle.

We have cut it into three strips and placed them on the page so that one
line includes the subject, the next line the verb, with the complement trail-
ing after. The format consists of nothing more or less than an eye-guide for
amateur grammarians.

Most sentences, though, come in longer strips. Let's add some modifiers:

1c   The uggle to the norp
      uffly wogs
         a seckly diggle of nerbal facks.

Here, we have indented the format so that the first words in the subject
structure, the verb structure, and the complement occur at different dis-
tances from the left margin. By asking students what words or groups of
words could be erased with a minimum of damage to whatever this sentence means, we can draw arrows showing the direction of modification:

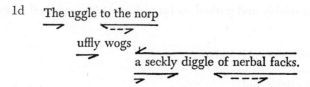

1d

Now we can take the sentence away and leave the arrows:

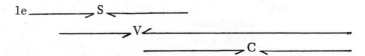

1e

What's left over is one of the most frequent modificational patterns of the
English sentence, with the different "layers of modification" chalked on the

blackboard. (The fact that students rather enjoy playing with a topological
gimmick like this is again incidental. I believe the primary value of this
exercise is that it tricks students into looking at real material analytically—
and teaches aspects of "structure" unconsciously.)

The above sentence-form is the most popular one in English—where a
form of "be" does not occur in the verb structure. The three other most
frequent ones all have the "be" form:

    2   A diggle
                is wogged
                        by the uggle.
            (Note the "ed" form)
    3   The uggle
                is
                    a vemp.
            (Note the "a" and lack of suffix)
    4   The uggle
                is
                    vemper.
        (Note the lack of "a" and suffix.)

The meanings of the above four sentences, in terms of their contrasts in
form, are "that which performs, (1); undergoes, (2); is identified, (3);
is described, (4)" respectively.

But about a fifth of the sentences which appear in print don't begin with
subjects but with "opener modifiers" which connect them somehow to
something that came before the sentence in question. If these structures
don't fit the patterns of subject premodifiers, the chances are that they
serve as "whole-sentence modifiers" and stand outside the sentence. Usually, they have the same kind of general meaning that "thus," "then," and
"there" have; usually they occur as prepositional phrases, single-word adverbs which may have modifiers, subordinate clauses, or participial phrases
—or any of these forms in combination. They can be identified by form
almost invariably and parked, as far as format is concerned, over in the left
margin:

    Into tenk and meckle and
    at the melk
    5   the uggle and
            his breep
                weg and
                fleb
                    a diggle and
                    a larg. . . .

Sentence 5 also illustrates a format treatment of several items within the
same block of structure. Words like "and" and "but" usually separate exchangeable structures; when they occur between blocks of structure, we

can place them at the end of a format-line; when they occur within blocks of structure, they can be buried in the interior of a line of text. (It is useful, I think, to consider them, with adjacent punctuation, as punctuation units in the form of words.)

Verbs are worrisome, too, when two forms occur separated by another word of structure:

6   The uggle
          wogs
                a diggle
          up.

(This is what happens to a prepositional adverb preceded by a complement.)

7   How
          can
     a diggle
          wog
                an uggle?

(Many questions can be treated like this.)

More than thirteen out of fourteen printed sentences can be dissected as shown in sentences 1-7. Others, usually where the subject structure is "longer" in relation to the complement, are these:

8   It
          is
                vemper
     that the uggle wogs a diggle.

("that . . . diggle" can occur in the same position as "It." See sentence 4.)

9   It
          is
                a vemp
     to wog a diggle so uffly.

("to . . . uffly" can be substituted for "It" See sentence 3. Subject structures in sentences like 8 and 9 can assume any substantive form.)

10   There
          is
     the uggle which wogs a diggle.

(If "There" is not a "gesture-word," "is" has the range of meaning of "exist.")

11   Into tenk
          wogs
     an uggle with a diggle.

(When a form which may be a whole-sentence-modifier stands first but is followed by a verb before its subject, the "modifier" is part of the complement.)

This takes us past two points of procedure which I have wanted to stress: First, the forms and positions of words in real material must be examined by students. Second, the form of transcription they use must illustrate rather than obscure the arrangements of blocks of structure which characterize English prose. If you feel that this format serves that purpose, I hope you'll experiment with it.

It's useful especially for laying out sentences which are to be examined in relation to each other. Here is the English of the "baloque" passage:

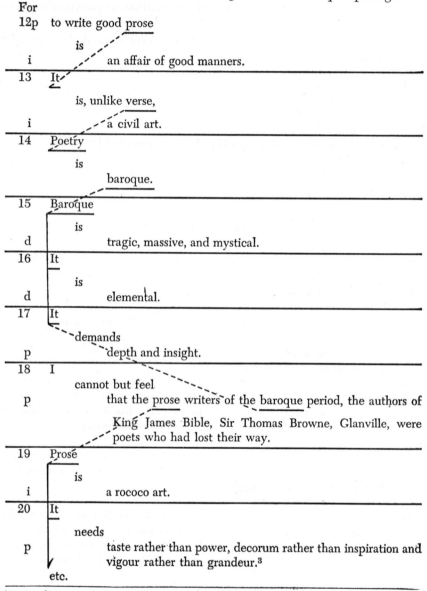

For
12p   to write good prose
            is
    i   an affair of good manners.
13   It
            is, unlike verse,
    i   a civil art.
14   Poetry
            is
                baroque.
15   Baroque
            is
    d   tragic, massive, and mystical.
16   It
            is
    d   elemental.
17   It
            demands
    p   depth and insight.
18   I
            cannot but feel
    p   that the prose writers of the baroque period, the authors of
                King James Bible, Sir Thomas Browne, Glanville, were
                poets who had lost their way.
19   Prose
            is
    i   a rococo art.
20   It
            needs
    p   taste rather than power, decorum rather than inspiration and
                vigour rather than grandeur.[3]
        etc.

Here, the nounforms or structures which could be shifted from one sentence to an adjacent one are underlined, and the underlined "sames" connected by lines. When these connecting lines cross lines separating sentences, we call the connecting lines hypothetical links between sentences.

[3] These sentences are quoted from W. Somerset Maugham's *The Summing Up* (Doubleday Doran, 1938), p. 37.

Other "sames" in adjacent sentences may be of interest: Sentence 12p, as indicated by the "p," occurs as the opening sentence in a paragraph. It is the only sentence in the extract which begins with a whole-sentence-modifier. And several adjacent sentences have the "same" general structural meaning: 12-13, "Identified;" 14-16, "Described;" 17-18, "Performer." In addition, sentences 12-16 have the same verbform. Sentences 15-16 end with the same two letters.

Similarities like these, since they occur frequently in adjacent sentences, probably constitute a kind of rhetorical "glue" which binds sentences together. If so, they furnish a suggestive starting point for a grammar which goes beyond the borders of the sentence—a descriptive rhetoric which might help students in composition courses to write papers that more people want to read.

From methods of classroom approach like the ones discussed here, students gain at least a subjective sense of what happens from one sentence to the next. They also gain a command of the forms in which the English sentence appears. They add to their vocabularies a set of terms which refer to language rather than to language superstition; this command of terms shortens the time spent both in conference and in class—and in correcting papers. And they gradually adopt a point of view toward language which makes it possible for them to grow in their freedom to use it more effectively. No teacher can ask for more.

Shortly after the two-week structural survey, the incidence of "graphic errors"[4] in themes—of the sort that instructors note with their red pencils —is reduced to a small and dwindling fraction. "Structural trouble,"[5] statable in technical terms, all but disappears from student writing. The practical result of an approach which fixes linguistic attention on real language can be summed up in one word: Efficiency. This means that more time in the composition course can be devoted to matters which are more important than the marks made on a sheet of paper.

[4] For example, misspellings and typographical slips.

[5] These are matters like agreement, case, coherence, coordination, emphasis, fragment, misrelated modifier, parallelism, principal parts, reference, subordination, tense and word order.

"Let's Teach Grammar Too"*

GEORGE G. GATES

As A PROCESS of language unity, grammar reveals the structural process of writing. The structural process of writing can be expedited by teaching five language blocks—each a basic element of the English sentence. To make the five language blocks function in the student's writing is a primary purpose of teaching the grammatical process.

Traditionalists who have made a fetish of Latin terminology and method of teaching the grammatical process will object vigorously to the foregoing propositions. Those who adhere to grammatical osmosis through writing question not only the propositions but also the methods. Those who subscribe to the patterns proposed by C. C. Fries in *The Structure of English* will take likewise a dubious view. But no one of these, it is hoped, will reject finally the proposal presented here until he and his students have found the principle, the idea, and the method false and unproductive. Those, however, who find in the proposal only new names for old structures will miss the fundamental idea.

The first, and the basic one, of the five language blocks, with which all others work, is the S-V-O, the old Subject Verb-Object triumvirate. Three of the blocks are given numbers—1's, 2's, 3's—numbers that have no virtue in themselves, but that aid in voiding the weight and error of conventional definition and terminology. The fifth block is the small s-v-o. These five language blocks are the means by which the structural process of writing is done. The ways these five language blocks work with each other are the "grammar" of the English sentence, and are of most use to the student in his writing and reading.

Examples of the 1's are: *by the library, on the wall, over the river, beyond the atomic era, in the Dark Ages, to run the race, to split the atom, to divide the spoils.* The Latinist will call these prepositional and infinitive phrases and will point out that if these modify the noun, they are adjective phrases, that if they modify the verb, they are adverbial phrases, and that if they function as the noun, they are noun or substantive phrases. But a student wishing to write doesn't need, it has always seemed to me, the "double-talk" of "now, this is really a prepositional phrase, but it modifies the subject and hence is called really an adjective phrase, for the subject is a noun and adjectives modify nouns." This "double-talk" is verbiage to

* Reprinted, by permission of author and publisher, from *College English*, 17.306–308 (February, 1956).

most students and to a few teachers. But its verbiage is not its worst fault.
The worst fault lies in the part-of-speech analysis of language that such a
labeling and such a method imply.

What a student needs to know, and to be taught if he doesn't know it, is
how to use *by the library, to split the atom, and beyond the horizon* to say
what he means and to get from another's writing the meaning conveyed
through this language block. He needs to know where this block may be
placed in relation to the S-V-O or to the s-v-o or to the 2's and the 3's. For
example, he may need to be shown the pattern:

S-V-O

1 1 1

Then he may write: The book *of old poems* brought *for a moment* memories *of his childhood.* He may try further to discover what happens to his
thought if he writes: "The book of a moment brought from his childhood
memories of old poems." Or this: "The book of his childhood brought of
old poems for a moment." Or: "The book brought for a moment memories
of old poems of his childhood." He may also try: "The hour to strike determines the moment to fight." But whatever he writes to discover for himself
where and how in the sentence the 1's work by position and function to
convey his meaning teaches him *directly* the structural process of writing.
Learning the structural process of writing teaches him what to do and how
to do it—two things he needs to know. Freeing the student from cumber-
some and erroneous terminology is like freeing a well man from crutches.
But more important is the idea of relation and unity and meaning the student gets: a respect for the grammatical process.

Examples of 2's are: *knowing the cause, wanting to be popular, writing
on the board, taking defeat, splitting the atom.* This language block works
with S's and O's (s's and o's, 1's and 3's) but not with V's unless the V is a
form of *to be* (and then, depending on the position or word order, of course,
it is not a 2; it is a verb). It is a 2 only if it works with the S's and O's (s's
and o's, 1's and 3's). The 2 some will insist on calling present participle or
gerund or verbal or verbal adjective or verbal noun, and it may still be all
these. But knowing simply that the 2 works with S's and O's (s's and o's)
helps the student to do two things: to link the 2 in his own writing with an
S and/or an O to avoid error in the sense and meaning ("dangling participles") and to read the 2 in other writing as working with the A and/or
O instead of taking it as the verb without the verb form ("is running,"
"was going"). One of the difficulties encountered in teaching students from
the seventh grade through the freshman year in college is the student's
insistence on the 2 as a verb. (His insistence may be the result of the definition of a "participle" given in many grammars and repeated in many class-
rooms: a participle is a VERB ending in "ing" and used as an ADJEC-

TIVE.) Because of this difficulty, the student needs to work directly with such patterns as this:

S-V-O
2   2

From this pattern he may write: "*Knowing the cause for their plight,* the colonies declared the motives *lying beneath their action.*" Or he may work with:

S-V-O
s-v-o
2   2

and write: "When the colonies knowing their plight declared the motives lying beneath their action, they startled the world." From such patterns the student can see and know directly the structural process of his own writing, and in knowing the structural process of his own writing will find other writing easier to follow and to comprehend. When he finds such words as "reading," "speaking," "singing," and "laughing," he does not try to read them as verbs unless he sees that they have a different form: "am reading," "was speaking," "will be singing," "have been laughing." Nor does he write "Wishing to leave now, the library closed."

Examples of 3's are: *defeated trying, broken in spirit, sold on the block, caught speeding, known on heaven or earth.* Many students are familiar with this block, and some use it with skill. But a few students, like Frost's farmer in "Mending Wall," once having learned the 3 as a *verb* won't go behind their teacher's teaching. At first such students write and read the 3 only as the verb. Such a sentence as "An army defeated in battle will always surrender" is meaningless its syntactical content—for some freshmen. They learned that "defeated" is a verb and so it is. With these students, telling them that "defeated" is a past participle and that past participles modify nouns and pronouns or substantives and thereby become adjectives seldom seems either to improve their skill in reading or to increase their knowledge of the structural process of their own writing. More important for the student is his experience in what he can do with the 3 in his own writing. For instance he may work with:

S-V-O
3   3

and get: "Prometheus, chained to a rock, endured the agony inflicted upon him by Zeus." (The 3 is most ambiguous structurally in many English sentences. In this sentence, "chained to a rock" points out Prometheus' condition as one meaning and as the place where he endured the agony as a second meaning. The two meanings are not antithetical, but the "Janus" nature of the structure causes the student to falter.) Further, the student may work with his pattern:

S-V-O

s-v-o

3   3

"Because Prometheus, chained to a rock, endured the agony inflicted upon him by Zeus, Prometheus gained man's love."

To show the interworkings of 3's with 1's and 2's; 1's with 2's and 3's; 2's with 3's and 1's would take more space than is available. But these interweaving patterns are a fruitful study, especially if the student is given the chance to work directly with his own structural process of writing. And to know these interweaving structures of the 1's, 2's, 3's is to increase speed of reading and power of comprehension.

The final structure is the small s-v-o. The small s-v-o works with the large S-V-O as in this pattern:

S	V	O
s-v-o	s-v-o	s-v-o

With the large S and O, the small s-v-o has such sign words as *who, which, that*. With the V's, the small s-v-o has such signal words as *when, if, since, until, because, although,* etc. At first the student may work with the simpler pattern:

S	V	O
s-v-o		

and write: "A nation that neglects morale invites defeat." Or he may work gradually to a more complex pattern:

S	V	O
s - v - o	s - v - o	s-v-o
s-v-o		

"A nation that neglects morale when that morale means victory invites defeat because a nation's morale provides the strength that insures that nation's triumph." And then the students may go on to such a pattern as:

(s-v-o)	V	(s-v-o)
s-v-o		s-v-o

Here the (s-v-o) is the subject and the object, grandma's old substantive clause. The student may write: "Why a nation invites defeat when its morale provides no strength does not explain why a nation neglects morale when that morale means victory."

What so often happens in the teaching of grammar is that the grammar is left out. We teach terms, we pick out subjects, we diagram the "prepositional phrase": we neglect the grammar, a process of language unity that reveals the structural process in writing.

Coordination (Faulty) and Subordination (Upside-Down)*

JAMES SLEDD

(This paper attributes certain opinions to the "the linguist," a fictitious in-dividual whose authority I find it convenient to cite for opinions of my own, and certain others to "the traditionalist," a hollow man who is never allowed to talk back. For these innocent inventions, perhaps no actual linguist liv-ing or dead would care to be responsible.)

THE FIRST AND MOST IMPORTANT WAY in which linguistics can serve us as teachers of composition is that it can help us see what we have to do and how we can best do it. The teacher who knows some linguistics sees the composition course in the light of his knowledge; and if he does not fool-ishly conclude that linguistics is a panacea, his introduction to linguistic science may be part of a general reorientation which is more valuable than any one specific use of linguistic methods or materials. Linguistics can teach us something about the relations between speech and writing—for example, that speech comes first in time and in importance, that writing is an incomplete but partially independent secondary representation of speech, that the kinds of speech which we normally write are very dif-ferent from plain talk, and that mastering these differences is a large part of our students' job. Linguistics can teach us something about the nature of style as choice; and when we are dealing with style in language, it can give us the necessary terms and distinctions to describe the choices that are open. Linguistics can teach us that grammatical structure is stylistically no less important than vocabulary and that structure must be described systematically, *as* a system and as a *formal* system, whose categories cannot be adequately defined in terms of meaning. And linguistics has already taught us that when we have specified the choices which the student can make in speech and writing, we should not ruin our work by upholding some silly standard of mechanical correctness. A good linguist is no *enemy* of standards, but he does believe that we should know what is before we try to say what ought to be. He can therefore help us, I think, to set higher ideals than we have often been contented with—and to reach them, too.

If this faith that is in me is more than the faith of an apprentice witch-

* This paper was one of three read in Panel I, Applying Structural Linguistics to Spe-cific Teaching Problems, 22 March 1956, CCCC Spring Meeting. Reprinted here by permission from *College Composition and Communication,* 7.181–187 (December, 1956).

doctor in a new and blacker magic, I must welcome the demand that the linguist and his converts put up or shut up. I do welcome it, and happily accept my share in the burden of proof that the principles of linguistics are directly relevant to problems of writing. Such proof, in one small area, is what I am here to offer.

A grammatical system, the linguist says, is a formal structure whose categories must be formally defined. His reason is not only that it is difficult to deal precisely and objectively with meaning. Grammatical and logical categories, he argues, do not always coincide; even if they did, the logical or semantic categories which would have to be recognized in the description of a particular language would still be determined by the number and nature of the formal distinctions in that language; and if grammar is to be a means of interpretation, the grammarian must start with the forms in order to avoid circularity. It is only by way of the forms that we can get at the meanings.

These propositions, if they are true, have the most immediate and far-reaching consequences for the teaching of composition. Both our descriptions and our prescriptions will have to be revised. With at least some of the necessary changes in description all of us are familiar. The conservative himself is now a little uneasy when he tells a class that a noun is the name of a person, place, or thing, that the subject of a sentence is what the sentence is about, or that a sentence itself is a group of words that expresses a complete thought. The junior witch-doctor, like me, is more than just uneasy. He begins his definition of the English noun by describing its inflections; he goes on to note the main positions which nouns occupy in phrases and sentences; he says something about the derivational patterns in which nouns occur; and he strictly subordinates his semantic descriptions to these matters of form. Happily or unhappily witch-hunters and witch-doctors both recognize that in description a revolution has begun.

Perhaps we have not yet recognized so clearly that the changes in grammatical description which have been forced upon us will force us also to change our statements of what is good and what is bad in our students' speech and writing. Ulitmately, we cannot escape that recognition. If we accept the linguist's doctrines, we will find that our whole treatment of diction must be modified, and modified at every level of our teaching, from the freshman classroom to the graduate seminar. A good example is our classification of clauses and our instructions for the use of coordination and subordination.

Our usual teaching about clauses rests, I think, on the false assumption that grammatical and semantic categories do coincide. Having made that assumption, we quite logically tell our students to put their main ideas into main clauses and their subordinate ideas into subordinate clauses. Principal clauses, we tell them, express principal ideas, so that compound sentences, consisting of two or more such clauses, give equal emphasis to equal thoughts but weaken unity or coherence. Between the clauses of a compound sentence, which we say are related just as separate sentences are related, there is then no logical advance; two ideas, or two expressions of the same idea (if two are possible), are merely juxtaposed. With complex sentences, we say, the case is altered. Since subordinate clauses express subordinate ideas, complex sentences rank and relate our thoughts in the order of their importance. The primary thought receives primary emphasis, and complex sentences are therefore more unified and more coherent than compound sentences.

I have been careful not to misrepresent the traditional theory of clauses, which I have found in learned histories of prose style as well as a variety of handbooks; and I think I am equally fair in saying that to a linguist, this theory seems to rest on a series of bad puns, the old confusion of grammatical and logical terms. Subordinate clauses, the linguist tells us, are grammatically subordinate; that is, they are used like single nouns, adjectives, or adverbs, often to expand smaller constructions. Just as we can say, for example, "The man is my uncle," so we can expand the nominal construction *the man* with a subordinate clause and say, "The man *whom you met is* my uncle." In this grammatical sense, *whom you met* is subordinate, precisely as we might say that *big* is subordinate in the sentence, "The big man is my nephew," or that *there* is subordinate in "The boy there is my nephew." Similarly, according to the linguist, independent or principal clauses are *grammatically* independent; they are subject-predicate combinations which do not expand smaller constructions and whose only *grammatical* equivalents are similar combinations. It does *not* follow that the same state of affairs *must* always be symbolized or *should* always be symbolized by the same clause-pattern. Principal clauses can and sometimes should express subordinate ideas, which need not be expressed by grammatical subordination; and the clauses of a compound sentence may be as unified and coherent and as precisely related as the clauses of a *complex* sentence. The traditional theory of clauses is simply untenable. When we teach it, we are teaching a rhetoric that is bad because we have confused our grammar with our logic.

The most obviously false statement in the traditional theory is the least generally accepted, that compound sentences, by comparison with complex sentences, lack unity, coherence, and precise articulation. I will not laboriously disprove this statement, either by analyzing the meanings of words like *and* or *but* or by citing the logician's rules for the transformation of propositions from one form to another; our everyday experience is ample refutation of an obvious absurdity.

Other propositions in the traditional theory turn out to be less clear, but more dangerous, because more plausible and more widely believed. One version might be summed up in the ambiguous platitude that form and meaning are inseparable. Thus when he lays down his rules about clauses, the traditionalist may mean that in their use we have no stylistic choice, because it is impossible to say the same thing in two different clause-patterns; "the writer's meaning *is* his language, and his language *is* his meaning."[1] We should therefore tell our students, when their use of subordination or coordination displeases us, only that they should re-think their material and say what they really mean.

If this is what the traditionalist intends, his theory is easily reduced to absurdity, for it denies the possibility of translation, paraphrase, summary, accurate indirect quotation, and deductive logic. Indeed, if there were no synonymous expressions, language and communication themselves would be impossible, since meanings would be inseparably bound to particular sequences of phones or graphs. If we asked a man what he meant, he could only repeat what he had said before, and if we did not understand him, he could give no further explanation.

The second step in the refutation of this wild notion is again the appeal to the logician's transformation-rules, which guarantee the possibility of expressing the same content in clauses of different form. So if we say, "Either it's not raining, or the streets are wet," we have uttered a compound sentence; but that compound sentence may be exactly translated by the *complex* sentence, "If it's raining, the streets are wet." Such transformations are the stock in trade of the logician, who puts his propositions into the form that best suits his purpose; and we do precisely the same thing unless we have lost our senses by reading the New Critics. Consider the following pairs of sentences:

1. Though he was tired, he still worked hard.
    He was tired, but he still worked hard.

2. Language would be impossible, since meanings would be inseparably bound to particular phones.
    Language would be impossible, for meanings would be inseparably bound to particular phones.

3. I won't write you, since I wouldn't have anything to say.
    ^{2}I won't ^{3}write you^2 | ^{2}I wouldn't have anything to ^{3}say^1 #

The members of each pair, though one sentence is complex and the other compound, are the same in meaning.

To my examples it may be objected that although two sentences may say the same thing, they say it with different emphases—that main clauses are by nature more emphatic than subordinate clauses. Such an objection would embody the traditional theory in its most limited but clearest, most persuasive, and most generally accepted form. For all that, I answer that the objection is preposterous; and the form of my answer proves that the answer is correct. The sentence "I answer that the objection is preposterous"

[1] This quotation is genuine, but no good purpose would be served by identifying its authors, who must have written it in their sleep.

does not emphasize the mere fact that I am meeting an objection, though that fact is stated in the main clause. Rather the emphasis is on the subordinate clause, "that the objection is preposterous," and as far as I can tell the sentence would not be improved by reversing this arrangement.

Better examples than my own are of course a dime a dozen. Turning the pages of Kruisinga's big grammar,[2] I quickly find numbers of good sentences in which a nominal clause is more emphatic than the main clause that it depends on:

> It was generally discovered that the maker of these splendid books was himself a splendid old man.
> The fact was that Yeobright's fame had spread to an awkward extent before he left home.
> A good deal of its importance consists in this, that it is minute and detailed.

As for adjectival clauses, Kruisinga actually sets up a special class among them, defined as giving additional information "which is not subordinate to the rest of the sentence but of equal weight." From his discussion, one can gather many convincing specimens:

> She was much attracted by the novels of Kingsley, between whose genius and his faults she drew a drastic contrast.
> Eustacia was indoors in the dining-room, which was really more like a kitchen, having a stone floor and a gaping chimney-corner.
> It is a point that we must exert our imaginations a little to understand.

To complete the roll call of cause-types, I will here just mention certain kinds of sentence where the main idea almost has to go in an adverbial clause in order to avoid absurdity:

> As the years passed, I grew wiser. When Lincoln was assassinated, my father was a young man.
> Before the war began, Joe went to America.

In most contexts it would be plain silly to write, "As I grew wiser, the year passed"; yet the passage of time is certainly more important than any individual's increase in wisdom. The traditionalist will have to say, when he is faced with these sentences, that coordination and subordination need not reflect the intrinsic importance of ideas, but only their importance to the writer.

The evasion will not save him from the ultimate necessity of junking his theory, deliberately writing bad sentences, or deliberately wrecking good ones: the most telling of all the instances in which the traditional theory fails to account for the facts are those where it would require damaging revision. Consistency would require the traditionalist, for example, to revise the following neat sentence from Kruisinga's collection:

[2] E. Kruisinga, *A Handbook of Present-Day English*, Part II, Vol. 3 (5th ed., Groningen, 1932), pp. 367, 373, 375, 376, 379, 381, etc.

The noise echoed terribly through the building, and then there was a silence that was even more terrible.

To my mind, that sentence emphasizes the fact that the silence was more terrible than the noise, and I assume that the professional who wrote it knew and wrote what he intended; but the traditionalist must spoil the sentence because he cannot leave the main idea in a subordinate clause. He will have to write something awful, like this:

The noise echoed terribly through the building, and then the silence was even more terrible.

In the same way, he will have to ruin my next example, where again an empty main clause actually contributes to emphasis:

It is not everybody that cares for early Staffordshire pottery.

The edge would be quite taken off of that admirable generalization if it were revised:

Not everybody cares for early Staffordshire pottery.

And so it goes, in sentence after sentence. The traditionalist, however, is determined to uphold standards even though he has none worth upholding. It is thus that he promotes vice in the name of virtue.

I suggest, then, in summarizing the critical part of this paper, that the linguist's general insistence on the formal nature of grammatical categories will force us to delete specific sections from our handbooks—namely all instructions to put main ideas in main clauses and subordinate ideas in subordinate clauses. "Determine the most important idea of the sentence," the typical handbook says, "and express it in the main clause. Put lesser ideas in subordinate clauses, phrases, or words."[3] I think I have shown that that rule will do more harm than good; and if I am right, the demonstration has positive value and cannot be dismissed as merely negative. I am still not content with the mere deletion of a bad rule. We will have to put something in its place if we are to teach the student anything about the use of principal and subordinate clauses; and I should like to offer some modest suggestions, centering on the analysis of a few sentences such as we typically use for horrible examples.

If grammatical and logical terms cannot be equated and if we can say the same thing in different clause-patterns, then the student must regularly face stylistic choices which cannot be made mechanically. He must learn that writing is purposeful, that good writing is writing that serves its purpose well, and that the real abnegation of standards is the assumption that a single kind of writing is the only correct kind for all purposes. He may then grasp the possibility of reasoned choice by various criteria, one of which, in the matter of clauses, is proper emphasis. An idea may be em-

---

[3] This quotation is also genuine, but too familiar to need identification.

phasized by making a separate sentence of the clause which expresses it, by giving that clause a certain position within a larger sentence, by balancing or contrasting its structure with that of other clauses, or in some cases (as my examples have shown) by subordinating the important clause. Sometimes different clause-patterns will be equally emphatic, and the choice of *for*, or *since, though* or *but, who* or *and he* will have to be made by some other standard—variety, rhythm, ease in transition, or the like.

Since stylistic choices are so complicated, and since we cannot trust the traditional rules to decide them, we will have to replace the old rules of thumb with a more detailed analysis, both formal and semantic, of the patterns of clause-connection and sentence-connection in English; and we must try to invent exercises which will turn the student's theoretical knowledge into active control of the resources of his language. For example, *but* and *though* may be synonymous; often they both indicate that the simultaneous truth of the two propositions which they connect is for some reason not to be expected or out of the ordinary. The differences between *but* and *though* are largely formal: *though*-clauses are grammatically subordinate and rather freely movable, while *but*-clauses are grammatically independent and must follow a *preceding* independent clause. These facts could easily be impressed on the student's mind by asking him to observe the effects of replacing *but* by *though* in a collection of sentences or throughout a single long passage.

I would add, however, that a great deal of our trouble with subordination and coordination is not grammatical at all, but logical or rhetorical; and here I come to my analysis of horrible examples: In the following sentence, all of us would object to the faulty coordination:

> The barometer's falling, and those clouds have wind in them, and we'd better put into harbor at once.

Certainly the sentence is bad, but not because it contains three independent clauses; we would not object to sentences like the following:

> He laughed, and he laughed, and he laughed.
>
> Fox singled, and Minoso doubled, and the game was won.
>
> In that one morning it rained, and it hailed, and it snowed.

Since the difference between the accepted and rejected sentences is not in their clause-patterns, which are identical, we must look for it elsewhere; and it is easy to see that the label "faulty coordination" we actually mean, in this instance, a failure in logic. In the sentence about the barometer, the suggested relation of premise and conclusion, situation and consequence, is not made clear; and any rewriting will be acceptable if it introduces the needed clarity. A first rewriting changes the one sentence into two and makes their relation clear by inference from their relative positions:

> The barometer's falling, and those clouds have wind in them. We'd better put into harbor at once.

Two other rewritings make the relation explicit, but in notably different patterns of coordination and subordination:

> We'd better put into harbor at once; for the barometer's falling, and those clouds have wind in them.

> Since the barometer's falling and those clouds have wind in them, we'd better put into harbor at once.

Unless the original sentence were placed in a determining context, there would be little to choose, for all their differences in clause-patterns, among the three corrections.

Of my next example, the usual criticism would be "upside-down subordination:"

> He had almost reached Gainesville when he saw the tornado that struck the town and killed two hundred people.

One man's arrival in town, most of us would say, is not so important as the death of two hundred people—which is no doubt true, but irrelevant to the judgment of the sentence. The sentence is bad because its first two clauses state that two things happened about the same time, while the third clause has nothing to do with this temporal relation; and the fault will remain if the unimportant first clause is subordinated and the important third clause is made independent and coordinate with the second:

> When he had almost reached Gainsville, he saw the tornado, and it struck the town and killed two hundred people.

As a matter of fact, it is almost indifferent which of the first two clauses is introduced by *when*, but in either case the third clause must be made a separate sentence:

> When he had almost reached Gainesville, he saw the tornado. It struck the town and killed two hudred people.

> He had almost reached Gainesville when he saw the tornado. It struck the town and killed two hundred people.

The really applicable rule would not be to avoid upside-down subordination, but to talk about one thing at a time.

I would conclude, from my two horrible examples, that when we have given a student a theoretical and practical knowledge of English clause-patterns, the best general advice that we can next give him is to use both coordination and subordination in such a way that the natural or logical relations in his material will be clear. When he puts one sentence after another, when he puts two clauses together in a single sentence, or when he chooses a conjunction or a pair of intonation-patterns to connect his clauses, he is building, at the same time, a pattern of meaning. Neither we nor the linguist can decide for the student what he wants that pattern to be; but we *can* show him any formal indications of contradiction or confusion in his finished product. We can insist that he talk sense; and though when we do so we have quite properly left the realm of grammar for those of logic and rhetoric, our insistence will be more effective if our grammar has been sensible—that is, if we have abandoned, among other delusions, the identification of main and subordinate ideas with main and subordinate clauses.

Structural Grammar and the Sixth Grade*

ROBERT J. GEIST

ROBERT C. POOLEY concludes his review of Charles Carpenter Fries's *Structure of English*[1] with the statement that, despite Fries, 'for a long time to come the grammar of the schools will plod the traditional path.'[2] One is forced to admit the probable truth of this dictum. Based on what Pooley himself calls 'the inconsistencies and false orientation of traditional grammar,' our dictionaries, foreign language texts, handbooks, and reference grammars will certainly keep traditional concepts of grammar alive for a long time to come. Perhaps more important than books, the varying present grammatical knowledge of students, teachers, editors, and the general populace (from eight to eighty) will retard any rapid change to a new system. Yet surely a start, however, humble and perhaps misguided, ought to be made in getting rid of admitted inconsistencies and false orientation —and the earlier in the school program the better. Pooley's statement, it seems to me, overlooks the very real help that 'structure' can provide at an elementary level—a conviction I was led to as much by a fifth-grader as by Fries's book.

From her teacher's dictation the fifth-grader had copied down definitions of some of the parts of speech—among others. 'The verb is a word of action.' When I saw the definitions, I wondered how ten- and eleven-year-olds could possibly apply these definitions to finding the parts of speech in sentences; and my wonder grew when the fifth-grader wanted to know if *football* and *baseball* were not words of action. I suggested that she could

* Read at a meeting of the Michigan Linguistic Society, East Lansing, May, 1955, and reprinted here by permission from *American Speech*, 31.5–12 (February, 1956).
    [1] New York, 1952.
    [2] 'Grammar in a New Key,' *American Speech*, XXVIII (1953), 40.

forget about action and spot verbs in anything she said by looking for the word that changed form for time,[3] that would be 'different' when she used *right now, yesterday,* or *tomorrow* with the word. Being asked to say something, anything, she offered utterances like *Mother does the dishes; I help; Rodney is five years old; Gee whiz.* In all the sentences she or I offered, she located the verb without difficulty. *Gee whiz,* she recognized, did not change with the addition of *right now, yesterday,* or *tomorrow.*

A grade teacher subsequently informed me that the definition 'A verb is a word of action' is used in the fifth grade;[4] since 'state of being' is a difficult concept, it is postponed until the sixth grade. Yet if we invoke the idea that function words, which include auxiliary verbs, are learned as individual items,[5] it certainly should be possible to inform fifth-grade or even younger students that they already know various forms of the verb *to be* and, to know some grammar, they need only label these words *verb.* In the early grades one might even point out that a word meaning a person or thing generally precedes the *am, are, is, was, were,* and *thus prepare* the way for discussing the sentence in a later grade.

For the purpose of seeing whether structural grammar might improve instruction at an elementary level, however, it may be well to leave personal experience and hypotheses about the early grades for a specific examination of a textbook aimed at students supposedly mature enough to grasp the concept of a 'state of being.' A sixth-grade text—*Improving Your Language,* by Paul McKee and Annie McCowen[6]—begins, after a chapter on discussion, with the concept of the complete sentence: 'If it [a group of words] tells or asks something *by itself,* it is a sentence. If it does not, it is not a sentence.[7] The easiest way out of the difficulty of the complete thought,' especially in the sixth grade, is simply not to bring it up.

---

[3] See Fries, p. 124. Including auxiliaries as part of the verb takes care of verbs like *hit* and *set—will hit, is going to set.* Fries sometimes labels the auxiliaries Class II, as on p. 159. The expanded form of the verb may also cause occasional trouble. If for a sentence like *He wrote a book,* a student replies, 'He is writing a book right now, he was writing a book yesterday, he will be writing a book tomorrow,' the student at least sees which word changed form in the test.

[4] For example, a fifth-grade text—Edna L. Sterling, Hannah M. Lindahl, and Katharine Koch, *English Is Our Language* (Boston, 1950)—summarizes its information on verbs and verb phrases (p. 306):

    1. An action word such as *swam* is called a verb.
        Sharks *swam* past Beebe.
    2. Not all *verbs* show action.
        A shark *is* a large fish.

[5] Fries, pp. 106–9.

[6] Boston, 1947. I use this text, not because it is better or worse than others available, but merely because a sixth-grade teacher, exposed to some Fries grammar in my class, asked me for specific suggestions in applying Fries to her teaching with this text. I prefaced the specific advice, detailed in this paper, with the general statement: Don't contradict the book needlessly, but try to add structural characteristics to what it says.

[7] *Ibid.,* p. 10.

To be realistic we ought to recognize that 'Especially in October'[8] does tell something *by itself*. 'Especially in October' is not, however, the kind of utterance with which persons—including sixth-graders—begin conversations.[9] Calls and greetings frequently begin conversations, of course,[10] but since, in the interests of writing, the teacher is looking for the subject-verb kind of sentence,[11] he might restrict himself to the conversation beginner that contains a word that will change its form when *right now, yesterday, and tomorrow* are successively used. Rather than asserting or arguing that one utterance tells something *by itself* and another does not, a teacher might, it sees to me, spend time profitably in eliciting from students utterances with which they have begun or would begin conversations, or utterances with which they have heard others begin conversations. Surely enough questions and statements could be elicited or supplied to illustrate the sentence desired: *Did you listen to the ball game? Is Jim home? The Tigers lost again; The Yanks always win.* The other 'situation' sentence likely to be elicited is the command: *Close the window; Open the door.* A discussion of this could be postponed,[12] or it could be explained as a kind of sentence that normally begins with the kind of word that—with the same meaning in related sentences like *They close the window; They open the door*—changes form with *right now, yesterday, tomorrow.*

This approach to a 'favorite form of the sentence' looks to the characteristic occurrence of such sentences at the opening of a conversation and to the verb as a key. It identifies the verb by a structural characteristic, not as the element that asserts action or state of being. Relying on the meaning content, the McKee-Cowen text arrives at the relationship between 'sentence' and verb rather late. It defines predicate on page 17 ('the part of a sentence that tells what it is about the subject') and verb on page 55 ('A word is a verb when it is used to show action'). On page 95 the text brings 'state of being' into the definition and first links the verb with the predicate ('The verb is the most important part of a predicate'). Incidentally, on page 96 the sentence 'You cannot tell by the looks of a word that it is a verb' obscures the fact that in utterances you can tell by their looks alone, as pre-

---

[8] *Ibid.*

[9] Fries, pp. 37–38, 164–65. The McKee-McCowen text approaches this idea on p. 11: 'In a discussion it is correct to use a group of words that is not a sentence if what has already been said or done makes it easy for others to know what you mean. If nothing has been said or done that helps others to know what you mean, you should use a sentence.' The idea of opening a conversation should not be a difficult approach in a chapter entitled 'Making and Using Good Sentences in Discussions.'

[10] Fries, pp. 42–44.

[11] Cf., for example, 'You know that a group of words must have a subject in order to be a sentence' (McKee-McCowen, p. 96) and 'You know that a sentence has a subject and a predicate' (*ibid.*, p. 152).

[12] Despite the necessary subject in a sentence (see n. 12), McKee and McCowen early talk about imperative 'sentences' (p. 12) while postponing an explanation of the 'subject' until p. 230.

viously suggested, some constantly recurring verbs (*am, is, are, etc.*).[13]

Perhaps at an early state in discussing the sentence one could be satisfied with the auxiliary of multiple-word verbs as the verb of the sentence. Or by reducing *is coming* to *comes, will go* tomorrow to *goes* today, etc., one might early indicate that the auxiliary 'belongs to' the verb.

The other key element in the sentence pattern described here—the subject—can be located, even in the sixth grade, it seems to me, by asking *who* or *what* before the verb. This rather familiar method of finding she subject does not appear in the McKee-McCowen text, though it is strikingly less vague than the definition given—'the part of a sentence that tells what is talked about'[14]—a definition that must perplex a sixth-grader when, without further clarification, he learns that a subject may be first in the sentence or last or between parts of the predicate.[15] He may well wonder why the sentence 'Out of the white house an angry man ran' is not 'talking about' the white house. The interest in varied sentence order is laudable, but surely it complicates the student's ability to recognize word order as an essential of English grammar.[16] *Who* or *what* before the verb relies upon word order[17] and the common correlation of *who* and *what* with nouns.[18]

In the interests of punctuation, the text early discusses the kinds of sentences—interrogative, declarative, imperative, exclamatory[19]—even before it discusses subject and predicate. Possibly the definitions given are adequate for their purpose, though one wonders whether 'strong emotion' is so frequently expressed in a subject-verb pattern that we need an exclamatory 'sentence' as a distinct type, even for punctuation. Furthermore, even a sixth-grader might be capable of understanding that a question is normally characterized by an oral response,[20] a command by an action response,[21] and a statement by neither, or by 'signals of attention.'[22] One might even illustrate signals of attention by means of telephone conversation. This approach might lay the groundwork for some subsequent insight into the 'ways in which they [sentences] tell or ask something,'[23] and even

[13] This emphasis on not being able to distinguish similar morphemes (*love*, verb, from *love*, noun) merely by looking at them perhaps shares some of the responsibility for obscuring the importance of prefixes and suffixes in distinguishing parts of speech. Cf. Fries, p. 112.

[14] McKee and McCowen, p. 17.

[15] *Ibid.*, p. 78.

[16] Fries, p. 189, *passim*.

[17] In an exercise in McKee and McCowen, p. 85, students are asked to supply subjects for predicates (*Made a snowman*) and predicates for subjects (*The snow and the wind*). In terms of 'what is talked about,' a student would be justified in writing 'I disliked the snow and the wind.' In terms of word order, he would not. A similar exercise occurs on p. 161.

[18] Fries, p. 167.

[19] *Ibid.*, p. 12.

[20] *Ibid.*, pp. 45–47.

[21] *Ibid.*, pp. 47–49.

[22] *Ibid.*, pp. 41–42, 49–50.

[23] McKee and McCowen, p. 13.

prevent the illusion—so difficult to eradicate later—that one does more than present a learned label in the standard definition: a sentence that asks a question is an interrogative sentence.

'A word is a noun when it is used to name something.'[24] This semantic definition is probably the earliest and perhaps the best elementary approach to nouns; yet it seems that one might profitably show that plurals and possessives, introduced later only for spelling,[25] are characteristic of nouns.[26] All the nouns used for illustration,[27] except *sagebrush* and the proper nouns, are readily made plural; and all can be made possessive with an appropriate noun—*Wyoming's capital; the sagebrush's color.* Furthermore, as a help in analysis, in utterances the function words *the, a, an* (learned as items) are almost foolproof signals that a noun will occur immediately or shortly thereafter.[28] McKee and McCowen say[29] that *race* in *Her horse won the race* is a noun, since it is used to name something; that *race* in *Joan decided to race the cowboys* is not a noun, since it is not used as a name. It would seem simpler to point out that, in the first sentence, *the* 'makes' *race* a noun, and that the plural *races* can be substituted. Thus we need not decide whether the infinitive in the second sentence 'names something.' The rather dull business of locating 'persons, places, and things'—which depends on our knowing the lexical meanings of the words —might, on occasion, be enlivened by a game in which the students find words like *race* which, when preceded by *the,* represent things and can be made plural; which, when preceded by *they,* will change for *right now, yesterday, tomorrow: the help, they help; the work, they work; the kid, they kid.* Thus the student may be prepared for eventually seeing that, grammatically, the important point is not that nouns name persons, places, and things, but that definite devices signal that certain words represent persons, places, and things—even when one does not know what the person, place, or thing is. Even a sixth-grader, who is unlikely to know what *mitosis* or *rhomboid* means, might be made aware that he considers them things as long as he sees such constructions as *Mitosis is carried on . . .* or *a rhomboid.*

The adjective is presented first on page 81 of McKee and McCowen: 'A word is an adjective when it is used to describe a noun,' and again on page 200: 'A word is an adjective when it modifies or makes clearer the meaning of a noun or a pronoun.' This semantic definition, like that for the noun, may be the easiest elementary approach; yet, if we use it, we ought to

[24] *Ibid.,* p. 29.
[25] *Ibid.,* pp. 93, 104.
[26] Fries, pp. 117–18.
[27] McKee and McCowen, pp. 91–93.
[28] Fries, p. 118. McKee and McCowen, pp. 200–201, merely call *a, an,* and *the* adjectives with a special name—articles—and thus, along with most of us, completely overlook their tremendous significance and usefulness as signals of structural meaning.
[29] McKee and McCowen, p. 92.

place safeguards around it lest we lead directly into the 'hopeless' state of the terms *adjective* and *adverb*.[30] The definition does not help to distinguish nouns from adjectives when we modify a noun with another noun (*a Ted Williams homer; the city streets; the drainage system*). We usually call the modifying noun an adjective; or, if we are pressed by a student who insists *Ted Williams* is the name of a person, we compromise with a 'noun used as an adjective.' The definition is even less helpful when we modify a noun with an 'adverb' (the tree *here,* the walk *home,* the game *tomorrow,* the confusion *everywhere, only* James). Here, despite our definitions, we hesitate to call the modifying word an adjective, probably because 'an adverb used as an adjective' just does not make sense in the light of our definitions. Furthermore, to be realistic, a verb often 'modifies or makes clearer the meaning of' or "is used to describe' a noun in sentences like *The girl blushed* or *The sky darkened.* We concede as much in the term *descriptive verb.* If we further concede, in all common sense, that the subject 'modifies or makes clearer the meaning of' both verb and object in *Ted Williams hit the ball* and *Ben Hogan hit the ball,* we may be willing to agree that 'a "modifier" as a "modifier" is not a part of speech.'[31]

If the easy approach—that a word that modifies a noun is an adjective— leads to ultimate confusion, what can we substitute for it or supplement it with—in the sixth grade? Perhaps we could safeguard the semantic approach by saying, not that 'a word is an adjective when it is used to describe a noun,' but that 'an adjective usually modifies a noun.' In then indicating what adjective is, perhaps without too much difficulty, one could point out that certain words are subject to comparison,[32] and that these words usually occur in two favorite positions: after the verb *to be* and before a noun, especially between *the* (or a subordinate) and the noun: *The* big *house was* big.[33] Significantly enough, all the illustrative 'adjectives' listed or italicized,[34] except *last* (which is already a superlative) and some of the past participles, readily compare. Except for the unitalicized phrase *as usual,* the story used in the lesson provides only examples of the favorite positions: *a* very hard *battle; the* smart *quarterback; their* worried *right* end; *with* extended arms; a quick *dash; the* last *moment the referee's* shrill *whistle;* Bob *was* alert and reliable.[35]

[30] Fries, p. 205, n. 4.

[31] *Ibid.,* p. 239.

[32] Fries, pp. 130–32. McKee and McCowen, p. 232, bring in comparison only in regard to using the correct form in comparing two.

[33] Fries, p. 82.

[34] McKee and McCowen, p. 81.

[35] Probably, since participles are verb forms, they are best omitted from an introduction to 'adjectives.' McKee and McCowen wisely do not illustrate 'nouns used as adjectives' in their initial discussion, but a later exercise (p. 201), contains 'heavy *rubber* pedals, six *model* planes, heavy *glass* door.' We may also note that in a later exercise for distinguishing adjectives and adverbs (p. 222), the favorite positions will serve to identify all the adjectives and (by elimination) all the adverbs.

Until terminology is better clarified and problems involving modification are more completely solved,[36] perhaps we can find no suitable label for the words which are subject to comparison and which fit both indicated positions in *The big house was big*. In all likelihood, however, we will continue to use the term *adjective* to label words like *big, little, beautiful, usual*; and probably no harm will be done if we recognize them as a separate group, not because they modify nouns—which other parts of speech do equally well—but because they have distinctive shapes (*wider, more beautiful*) and distinctive positions (*is wide, the beautiful song*). Sixth-graders, it seems to me, can comprehend these structural characteristics as readily as they can comprehend that 'a word that modifies a noun is an adjective.'[37] The problems raised by this approach (*the insane asylum, the perfect stranger*, among others) needs not be solved in the sixth grade, but can be postponed for an eventual solution more satisfying than our present solutions for *a Mickey Mantle homer* and *the noise there*.

McKee and McCowen present the conventional definition of the adverb full-blown: 'A word is an adverb when it modifies or makes clearer the meaning of a verb, an adjective, or another adverb.'[38] If we agree with Fries that a Class IV word ('adverb') is quite different from a Group D function word (*very* and substitutes), structural grammar suggests, at the very least, that we can simplify this conventional presentation by discussing the 'modifier of a verb' separately from the 'modifier of an adjective or adverb.' And we might begin to get away from modification, in a first presentation, by considering an adjective plus *-ly* as an adverb (which McKee and McCowen include in their discussion) and by pointing out the movability of many adverbs: (Then) *he* (then) *came* (then).

The discussion of compound subjects and predicates[39] offers a fine example, it seems to me, of needless complexity because of an insistence on meaning. 'A subject that names two or more persons or things separately is called a compound subject. . . . When the predicate tells more than one thing about the subject, it is called a compound predicate.' Although *and* is used in all the illustrations, McKee and McCowen do not mention the fact; yet sixth-graders have long since learned this function word as a specific item. *And* and substitutes for it make compound subjects and verbs. A zero substitution need hardly be invoked at this stage, although 'nothing at all' is a rather simply understood substitute for *and* between the first two members of the *a, b,* and *c* series used here as examples.

[36] Fries, p. 217, n. 12.

[37] McKee and McCowen's introductory examples (p. 200), *Jane has a dog* and *Jane has a big, black, shaggy dog*, can be readily adapted to a structural description. Instead of, or in addition to, 'Each adjective makes clearer the meaning of the noun *dog*,' we can say that each adjective occurs between *a* and a noun, each can fit into the position *The dog is big, the dog is black, the dog is shaggy*; and each can be compared—*bigger, blackier, shaggier*.

[38] *Ibid.*, p. 202.

[39] *Ibid.*, pp. 74–76.

Paradoxically, some sections on correctness come closest to using structural concepts. 'With the first word in each of the eight pairs of words [*saw, did, ran, ate,* etc.], it is never correct to use helping words such as *has, have, had, was, is, were, have been* and *had been.*'[40] This sentence approaches the idea that function words are learned—and presumably to be taught—as distinct items in the grammar of the language. Again, the section on 'Using Six Pronouns Correctly'[41] indicates that certain forms of pronouns are not to be used 'after such words as *between, by, for, from, into, on, to,* or *with.*' Here word order is invoked, as well as a list of familiar items that are called prepositions when nouns or pronouns follow. Perhaps the apparent paradox linking aged correctness and youthful structure has real significance. In the pursuit of correctness—so central to traditional grammar that it is frequently equated with it—we find 'meaning' definitions too vague to be useful. Without realizing it, we approximate the mysteries of structural grammar.

Speaking of mysteries, one may wonder which would be the more mysterious to a sixth-grader: the statement that *at, of, from* are prepositions in utterances like *They were at the park; the hat of the boy; absent from class,* or the statement 'A word is used as a preposition when it shows some relation or connection between two other words or ideas.'[42] The students already know the commonest prepositions as items; they can be shown the favorite position before nouns.

Finally, structural grammar can contribute to teaching at an elementary level, it seems to me, by enlivening a subject which, to the average sixth-grader (and college student), is forbidding at best. It has been suggested above that sixth-graders might find it sport to discover words that would fit equally well after *the* and after *they.* They might also find it sport to discover that they can tell that a word whose meaning they do not know is a noun or a subject or a verb. That sixth-graders could handle the structure of *A woggle ugged a diggle* or *An ugg woggles diggs,*[43] or the ideas that filled Alice's head when she heard the poem of the Jabberwocky,[44] or the lexically recondite *ontogeny recapitulates phylogeny* is open to question. Yet such problems could well be presented before students reach college. Age, I feel, was hardly essential to the college students who have responded excellently to *The Heffalumps eeyored a kanga; The trug was glimblufly nerbed by a bladgol;* PROFESSOR RAKES LEAVES AFTER COMMENCEMENT.

[40] *Ibid.,* p. 20.
[41] *Ibid.,* p. 119.
[42] *Ibid.,* p. 219.
[43] Fries, p. 71.
[44] *Ibid.,* p. 70.

Part VI

LINGUISTICS AND THE DICTIONARY

INTRODUCTION

MATHEWS, himself a lexicographer trained by Sir William Craigie, final editor of the *Oxford English Dictionary,* opens the chapter by describing deeper values of the dictionary for the freshman than the immediate satisfactions of ascertaining correct spelling or preferred pronunciation. Barnhart, also an editor of dictionaries, writes a letter in which the problem of indicating pronunciation is seen to be less simple than the student might suspect.

Hill's advice on how a dictionary may be used in language teaching is helpful both for the native users of English and for the teacher of English as a second language.

That modern lexicography, highly developed and specialized as it has become since the days of Nathan Bailey, is still subject to improvement is also indicated by Hill in his demonstration of a specific inadequacy in a college dictionary. Another type of weakness, one apparently common in dictionaries, is described by Kenyon, who, as a phonetician, would insist that accurate recording of pronunciation should recognize a linguistic fact of life, the normal existence of various syllabic consonants in standard speech.

Most handbooks and composition texts have a section on the use of the dictionary, usually quite superficial. Worth reading carefully is the best such treatment, Chapter XXIX of Lloyd and Warfel's *American English in Its Cultural Setting* (Knopf, New York, 1956). For a general understanding of the modern English dictionary the student should read J. R. Hulbert's concise study, *Dictionaries British and American* (Deutsch, London, 1955).

The Freshman and His Dictionary*

MITFORD M. MATHEWS

WHEN I WAS A SMALL BOY a carpenter once said in my presence that few workmen, even among master mechanics, knew more than a fraction of the uses of an ordinary steel square. The remark amazed me, as at that early age I thought a carpenter's square was a very simple tool. It certainly appeared so to me,—nothing more than two flat pieces of metal forming a right angle, and useful in marking a plank that one wished to saw in two in something like a workmanlike manner. True, the instrument has numerous markings and numbers on it, but I had never seen anyone making the slightest use of these, so I had concluded they might be ignored.

When I became older and found that large books have been written on the uses of the steel square, I changed my mind about the simplicity of the tool and the limited range of its usefulness. For many years as I have observed the use made of dictionaries by even good students, I have been reminded of that remark by the carpenter about steel squares.

Dictionaries are tools, and they are much more complicated, and capable of many more uses than students suspect. All of us know students need encouragement and guidance in the use of dictionaries, and perhaps there are few teachers of freshman composition but that devote a part of their program to an effort to help students form the habit of consulting dictionaries. Composition books for freshmen point out the need for instruction of this kind.

Despite what is being done, however, the fact is easily observable that few students are able to use their dictionaries with anything like efficiency. Certainly there must be very few of those who come up through the grades these days who are not familiar with the details of looking up words in dictionaries, but it is one thing to find a word in a dictionary and quite another to understand fully the information there given about it. It seems to me that college freshmen are fully prepared for and could profit by a well-planned introduction to the larger of the English dictionaries, and an acquaintance with what they contain. Such a program might well include material of the following kinds.

1. Students should know something about the large, unabridged dictionaries to which they have ready access in college. They might well be given brief sketches of the *Oxford English Dictionary*, the *English Dialect*

* Address at the annual luncheon, CCCC Spring Meeting, March 24–26, 1955, Chicago, Illinois. Reprinted here by permission from *College Composition and Communication*, 6.187–190 (December, 1955).

Dictionary, by Joseph Wright, the old *Century Dictionary* (12 volumes), and the modern unabridged *Webster*. These may be called the "Big Four" in the dictionary field, and while it is certainly not anticipated that the freshman will ever provide himself with all of them, it is a cultural experience for him to become acquainted with the circumstances under which each of them was produced, and with the special excellencies each exhibits.

An acquaintance with these larger works will not only make the student aware of what kind of information about words is available in them, but it will leave him much better prepared to make efficient use of the desk-size dictionary with which he has some familiarity.

Many years ago a graduate student inconvenienced himself greatly to come a long distance to see me to ask if I could help him secure some information about the term "poll tax." He was preparing a doctor's thesis, he told me, and needed to know how long this term had been in the language, what its basic meaning was, and what other meanings it may have had in the course of its use in English. He was most surprised when I opened the *OED* to the appropriate place and showed him that all he needed to know about this term had been available within a few feet of his desk in the school where he was studying. It is not at all likely that any but the exceptional student will ever need all the information about words that the larger dictionaries afford, but it is well worth the while of every student to become acquainted with the fact that such information is available for those who at any time need to make use of it.

It is to be hoped that in such general instruction as may be given about the different dictionaries, some emphasis will be placed on the fact that modern dictionaries do their utmost to *record* usage, not to *prescribe* it. The tendency to regard the lexicographer as a linguistic legislator is so deep-seated that it will probably never be entirely overcome. The habit of thought that is back of such expressions as "the dictionary now permits us to pronounce it thus," has been with us for a long time, and will continue. But every student should have the wholesome experience of being taught that dictionaries attempt to give commonly accepted usage, and that correctness in the use of language varies sometimes according to time and place.

2. Along with some information about the origin and scope of the large dictionaries mentioned, there should be given some elementary information about the history of the English language and the place it occupies with reference to the others of the Indo-European group. I am certainly not foolish enough to suggest that all teachers of freshman composition become instructors in Germanic philology. What I have in mind is nothing more detailed than could be easily covered in one, or at most two, class sessions, the over-all relationships of the languages being presented briefly,

with a few well chosen examples to indicate the relationship of a few of
them.

The desirability of this elementary acquaintance with the linguistic position occupied by English is brought out quite clearly by Professor Pei in his
Story of Language:

> Many years ago, I was requested to tutor in French a young girl who had
> to take College Entrance Examinations. Knowing that she had had four years
> of Latin as well as three years of French, I spared no occasion in the course
> of the tutoring to remind her that certain French words which she had diffi-
> culty in remembering came from Latin words which she knew. For a time she
> took it patiently, though with a somewhat bewildered air. But one day she
> finally blurted out: "Do you mean to tell me that there is a *connection* be-
> tween Latin and French?" In the course of four years of one language and
> three of the other, it had never occurred to any of her Latin teachers to inform
> her that Latin had descendants, or to her French teacher to tell her that French
> had a progenitor!

3. The attention usually devoted to instruction in the use of the dictionary apparently stresses spellings, meanings, and pronunciations somewhat
in the order here given. Certainly these are conspicuous features of any
dictionary, and it is altogether desirable for students to be encouraged to
turn to these works when they are confronted with a problem of the kind
indicated.

The impression, however, inevitably conveyed by instruction restricted
altogether to employing the dictionary as a problem-solver, is that such
a book is of no particular use unless there is a problem requiring immediate
attention. Students are sorely tempted to so manipulate things as to avoid
encountering problems that drive them to a dictionary. It is to be feared
that, for many of them, the dictionary is a form of medicine to be resorted
to only in time of unavoidable need. They associate it perhaps with castor
oil or some other undesirable, dynamic type of cathartic. It is a most helpful thing for the student to learn that dictionaries are filled with interesting
information from which one can derive much pleasure and instruction, even
though he may not be confronted with an urgent problem of any kind.

Students should be encouraged to develop a wholesome curiosity about
words that present no particular problem in spelling, pronunciation, or
meaning. As a rule, the words we know well do not rise to the surface of
our consciousness. It is only rarely that some common, everyday term forces
itself upon our attention so urgently that for the first time we turn to the
dictionary to see what lies back of it.

This use of the dictionary when there is no immediate, pressing need to
do so, this giving attention to words we have known for a long time but
have never grown curious about, is most rewarding. This kind of use of the
dictionary we may think of as the labor of free men; the forced use is more
properly likened to that of slaves.

On every hand there are words of fascinating backgrounds about which the dictionary has much to teach us. Certainly the name *Jesus*, that of the founder of Christianity, is well known to all those with whom you and I come in contact. Perhaps few of us have ever felt impelled to look the word up in a dictionary, or even realized that dictionaries contain it. An examination of the dictionary, however, reveals that the name his parents gave the Saviour was Joshua, and it was by this thoroughly Jewish name that He was known by those He lived among.

The first accounts of His life were written in Greek, and in these writings *Joshua* was transliterated into *Jesus,* a name that is certainly not Jewish in its present dress and at the same time appears odd as a Greek name.

Not even a grade-school pupil is likely to be baffled by *ostrich,* but one who is allergic to words may well become curious about it. Allow it to become the focus of your attention for a moment and see how odd the word appears. Make a guess as to where you think it might have come from, and then check up on yourself by turning to the dictionary. You may be surprised, as I was, to find the word is made up of two, one from Latin and one from Greek, which have so blended as to obscure altogether the fact that the expression signifies "bird-bird" or "bird-sparrow." It is a good term to bear in mind and use upon those of our brethren who insist that only "pure English" should be used, and profess to be pained by such obvious hybrids as *cablegram* and *electrocute.*

There may be few teachers who have discovered how rewarding it is to look curiously at the scientific terms used in dictionaries in the definitions of plants and animals. These expressions are usually hurried over by most of us as being the exclusive property of scientists and of very little interest for others.

It is surprisingly interesting to linger over such terms. It is a gratifying experience to discover one that yields its significance somewhat readily. Our common mocking bird, for instance, is *Mimus polyglottos.* The ingenuity needed for deciphering this expression is possessed by all of us. *Mimic* and *polyglot* are all we need to see that our expression means "the many-tongued mimic," a fitting description of the bird in question.

In the spring when the snow has melted, and the earth is warming up from its long cold sleep, the cheerful piping notes of a very small frog begin to be heard in the woods and marshes. People call this little creature a *spring peeper* because of the season when his little peeping notes are first heard, but scientists dub him *Hyla crucifer.* As we puzzle over this name we are likely to give up on *Hyla* for there is no other word in the English language with which we can, perhaps, associate it profitably. It has descendants among us, but we are not likely to be acquainted with them.

Crucifer though is easier. Even if we do not know that a *crucifer* is one who carries a cross, especially in a church procession, we can reason out the two elements in the word and see that it must have the meaning of one who carries a cross. Our ability to reason out this much of the scientific expression may increase our curiosity about the first element *Hyla*. Here is a helpful hint. As we all know, these scientific genus names are often from Greek. So we are reasoning sensibly when we suppose *Hyla* is Greek.

The fact is elementary that when we are confronted with a Greek word which begins with an *h*, i.e. with a rough breathing, it behooves us as cautious scouts to cast about in our minds for a possible Latin cognate beginning with an *s*. Substituting an *s* in *hyla* we come up with *syla*. Let us study *syla* a bit. It is almost a word. If we might be so bold as to insert a -v- and make it *sylva* we have a word that is in our dictionary, and one we met in a slightly different form, *silva*, when we studied first-year Latin.

The little detail of why this -v- is necessary need not bother us in the slightest at this point, because we are just having fun with no idea of becoming linguisticians. And this is it. *Hyla* and *sylva* go together and they both mean wood or forest. Now we can interpret this *Hyla crucifer* "the (little) fellow who lives in the woods and carries a cross," and when we find that this spring peeper has a dark marking on his back shaped like a cross, we are indeed gratified that now light is shining where previously all was darkness.

A teacher who is fortunate enough to have an assiduously cultivated curiosity about words will over and over again bring to a class gleanings of unexpected sorts from dictionaries. Such sharing of treasures will do more than anything else to bring home to students the fact that dictionaries are not dull, enlarged spelling books. They are filled with such a number of things that we can never exhaust their treasures but we can all be as happy as kings as we come time after time upon interesting nuggets of the kind just mentioned.

Establishing and Maintaining Standard Patterns of Speech*

Clarence L. Barnhart

To the Editor:

Between six and seven trillion words are uttered daily by about 160 million American people. The former figure is based on an estimate made in a recent program on linguistics given by Kemp Malone that the average American speaks around 40,000 words a day. We have a record of only a

* Reprinted by permission from *Quarterly Journal of Speech*, 43.73–74 (February, 1957).

minute percentage of this; more is obviously impossible. It is doubtful if more than a fraction of the speakers of these billions of utterances turn to dictionaries for any guidance. In the practical affairs of the day-to-day world, people speak as their mothers taught them to speak.

In this country we are so concerned with literacy as a requirement of education that we tend to forget the great importance of the spoken word. Harold Anderson, in a recent address to the National Council of Teachers of English, told the story of an American teacher and a Hindu teacher talking over the problem of literacy in India. The American teacher had high hopes for mass reading. The Hindu teacher listened carefully and then, after agreeing with the American teacher that the Americans had much to teach, the Hindu replied, "We should welcome your help. Perhaps, however, we have something to offer in return. For while I regret the inability of my people to read and write, yet we must consider further the meaning of literacy. In the United States you measure literacy by the written word. In India we have a literacy of the spoken word—thoughtfully spoken and thoughtfully listened to."

This, perhaps, is as clear a statement of the subject matter of speech and possibly also of the subject matter of dictionaries as any I have ever encountered. We are concerned with the spoken word thoughtfully spoken and thoughtfully listened to. But we cannot hope to cover all possible utterances.

In order to obtain sound information with regard to speech, we must depend upon the observation of trained and scientific workers called phoneticians. Their observations deal with the speech of groups, individuals, or regions. For obvious reasons, in the making of good dictionaries, we take the agreed knowledge of the phoneticians as a basis of the record of pronunciation. For, after all, the function of reference books is to make the knowledge of specialists accessible to the general public—not every minute detail of knowledge in a particular field, but that part of it which a person outside the field may need to know or want to know at any given time.

There are two agreed general principles among all scientific workers in the field:

(1) Pronunciation keys should not be spelling keys—that is, they should represent actual pronunciation so far as this is possible; and
(2) The pronunciations recorded in a dictionary should be educated colloquial in context, and not pronunciations of isolated words or artificial "platform English." Above all, pronunciations in dictionaries should be contemporary and reputable.

I have been corresponding for some time with Mr. Ladislas Országh in Budapest with regard to the Hungarian-English dictionary which he is making behind the Iron Curtain. (This correspondence, incidentally, has all had the approval of the State Department.) You may find interesting the statement he makes on pronunciation in his letter to me of March 5, 1951: "At the same time we are not harried by problems which face the compiler of every English dictionary: we have no need to indicate pronunciation, for our language is written with an orthography that is remarkably phonetic, just like Turkish or German or Finnish. In English-speaking countries people need dictionaries to tell them how a word is pronounced. Such problems do not exist here."

Not all languages are so irregular as to require pronunciation keys in dictionaries. For the pronunciation key is merely a device for giving regular and consistent directions to say the sounds of words. The letters of the alphabet are directions to say the sounds, but about 25 per cent of the time the English alphabet fails or misleads us in giving us directions on the pronunciations of words. There are, in English, over 230 spellings of approximately 40 different sounds. The first task of a dictionary from the standpoint of pronunciation, then, is to give clear directions to its users to say the proper sounds. The proper principles underlying a pronunciation key may, therefore, be said to call for (1) one symbol for each sound, and (2) the utilization (especially so in a school dictionary) of English speech habits, so as to produce a key that will be easy to use.

One of the important problems facing the speech teacher and the dictionary maker is to devise a system of pronunciation which will avoid over-stressing. According to Professor Cabell Greet, speech adviser for the Columbia Broadcasting System, one of his great difficulties is to get radio announcers to avoid over-stressing and artificially equalizing the pronunciation of English words. The International Phonetic Alphabet uses the symbol "schwa" for the unaccented vowel sound, and this symbol has now found its way into many, if not most, American dictionaries. Once this symbol is mastered, artificial distinctions made between the vowel sounds in unaccented syllables disappear and the pupil gets a natural iambic rhythm to his speech. However, this standard practice of using "schwa" is not everywhere understood and not everywhere accepted. Just the other day I received a query from a very sincere teacher with reference to "schwa." This letter reads as follows:

> Please explain the "inverted e" in phonetic spelling as an aid in the pronunciation of words. Please explain the tilde mark substitution by the dot above the e. I am meeting these for the first time in my classes in word study. I was surprised and alarmed because I wasn't aware of the change before this. Please help me all you can. I am very anxious to know what symbols for sounds I must understand so that I may be able to teach my group of pupils.

This teacher is simply unfamiliar with modern principles in linguistics and phonetics. Here we have a failure of the educational schools to take the knowledge in the field of phonetics and linguistics and make it a part of the teacher's daily life. I wrote to the teacher as follows:

The "inverted e" or schwa, as it is technically called by many phoneticians, is the symbol used by the International Phonetic Alphabet (IPA) to indicate the neutral sound of a vowel in an unaccented syllable. As I point out in the preface of the *Thorndike-Barnhart High School Dictionary,* on page vii, schwa represents "the sound of *a* in about, *e* in taken, *i* in pencil, *o* in lemon, and *u* in circus. The use of only one symbol for this sound is the approved practice of modern phonetics and has proved a valuable aid to speakers, teachers, and beginners in the use of English." This one symbol enables us to replace as many as thirteen symbols necessary in some other pronunciation keys and thereby reduces the teaching load.

You, as college teachers, have the clear duty to make sure that as many grade-school and high-school teachers as possible understand the scientific principles of language. And we, on our part, as reference-book makers, have a duty to reinforce your efforts and make this knowledge available to teachers.

In pronunciation, we try to give the pronunciations of hard words such as *arteriosclerosis, arsenical, arsenous,* and to indicate clearly the divided usage which is important nationally in such words as *ask, carburetor,* or *been.* We cannot indicate on a scientific basis the many, many varieties of pronunciations of a word. For example, Professor C. K. Thomas has found thirteen or more ways of pronouncing the word *oranges.* Even a pronouncing dictionary could not make a complete and accurate record of all the ways of pronouncing a particular word of this sort. We, therefore, try to present the important facts of pronunciation, especially such as are important nationally or from a contemporary point of view, or which indicate levels of usage. Of course, how many of our 160,000,000 citizens finally use this reference-book tool effectively is a matter of education, but this I am sure I can safely leave in your hands.

The Use of Dictionaries in
Language Teaching*

ARCHIBALD A. HILL

THE RECENT PUBLICATION of the *American College Dictionary*[1] has given us the best short dictionary the English language has ever had. It would be pure pleasure to praise its many improvements, as doubtless reviewers are

*Reprinted by permission from *Language Learning,* 1.9–13 (October, 1948).

[1] *The American College Dictionary* edited by Clarence L. Barnhart with the assistance of 355 authorities and specialists (Random House, New York). First printing, November, 1947; second printing, February, 1948. (Reviewed in *Language Learning,* Vol. I, No. 3, July, 1948.)

now doing. Instead I intend to discuss certain ways in which the *ACD* and other dictionaries fall short of the ideal reference work which we will never achieve, but which each new attempt ought to bring appreciably closer. Before I do so, however, I want to make it as clear as I can that I am not criticizing the *ACD*, for which no student of English can have anything but respect.

The practical necessities of dictionary making demand, first of all, that every dictionary give as much information as possible in three related but separate fields: the descriptive, the comparative, and the historical. Each dictionary places its emphasis differently within these three; the *New English Dictionary*[2] is mainly historical, dialect dictionaries are mainly comparative, while the *ACD* is mainly descriptive. However necessary such triple aims may be, they nonetheless make it inevitable that no one aim will be perfectly achieved. Accordingly I shall simplify the task of discussion by assuming a situation in which only one goal is striven for, the descriptive. I am envisaging a monolingual dictionary, whose usefulness would be limited to those who had a considerable, but still imperfect knowledge of English. In other words, the users would be foreign learners of English, or native children.

✻   ✿   ✿

We should expect these five kinds of information about words from the ideal dictionary. They are in ascending order of complexity: the phonemic structure of the word,[3] its morphemic structure,[4] the grammatical modifications it undergoes, its syntactic habits, and its meanings. It is worth while to review, with varying degrees of attention, how well dictionaries fulfill their share in giving information of these several types. I shall, however, omit consideration of meanings, since the problems of giving all the meanings of even one word is certainly impossible of ideal solution, and such a dictionary as the *ACD* does as well with solving the unsolvable as anyone has any right to expect. As to the first type of information, the phonemic structure, there is also nothing which I have to contribute, except to praise the *ACD* for being the first college level dictionary which gives a workable phonemic[5] transcription of American English.

---

[2] Murray, James A. H.; Bradley, Henry; Craigie, W. A.; Onions, C. T. *Oxford English Dictionary*, corrected re-issue (Clarendon Press, Oxford, 1933). 12 vols. and supplement. (Originally issued as *A New English Dictionary on Historical Principles*, 1884–1928, 10 vols.)

[3] The phonemes of a word are minimum contrastive sound units usually represented by single letters, accents, or other marks in phonemically spelled languages.

[4] The morphemes of a word are minimum meaningful elements, either a word, as *paint*, or part of a word, as *-er* in *painter.*

[5] Considered strictly, the pronunciation system of the *ACD* is not phonemic, but is rather a system of key words designed to reconcile dialect differences. Within the framework I have chosen, that is, an assumption that there are no dialect differences, such a system becomes phonemic.

As for the second type of information, morphemic structure, no dictionary gives more than incidental information on the morphemes of which words are made up, nor does the public demand that a dictionary should give more. It is true that if one looks at a series of words such as *con-struct, con-struc-tive,* the divisions given in the dictionaries will give a very rough idea of the morphemes. But such divisions are, of course, intended to tell the reader how to divide the letters when the written form runs over the end of a line, and only accidentally coincide with morphemes. For instance, the second form must surely end in a morpheme *-ive* rather than *-tive.* It may be objected that the practical user of a dictionary has no need for a morphemic analysis of words, but though he may not now demand such an analysis, it ought to be obvious that such information would be useful. We have assumed that the user of the dictionary is one who is imperfectly acquainted with English—typically a foreigner at a moderately advanced stage of learning. A morphemic analysis of a new word to such a reader, would immediately relate the new word to familiar words which contain the same morphemes. Further, a morphemic analysis would often clear up points which are now confused. Thus at least a part of the confusion which learners experience in handling the *-ics* words like acoustics (of which more later) is caused by the fact that no dictionary makes clear that the final *-s* in these words, no matter what its origin, is not identical with the familiar plural morpheme of nouns which happens to be homonymous with it. In short, it seems to me that a requirement for dictionaries ought some day to be that as well as the rewriting of the word in a phonemic notation, there should be a second rewriting which would show the morphemes it contains and point out their boundaries. Such a notation should at least remove the disguises morphemes undergo in automatic variation, though the description of the rules governing such alternation properly belongs in the grammar. Unfortunately such morphemic analysis must also await the growth of substantial agreement among morphologists.

The remaining two types of information about words, their inflectional and syntactic habits, can most easily be treated together. The handling of this information presupposes a thorough grammar which describes first the inflectional classes and subclasses of English words, and next the syntactic classes. The dictionary, as I have said earlier, would confine itself to showing to which classes words belong. Further, the method by which this designation of class can be given is not any longer new. There are already in existence various schemes of description and enumeration which can indicate conveniently and completely, by the use of symbols, the class to which a given word belongs.

It is not my purpose to go into details about how to construct such systems, but rather to point out certain conditions which must be fulfilled before any system can be safely applied in the pages of a dictionary. English inflectional classes must be described separately, and each word given a designation assigning it to its inflectional class and to its syntactic class separately. In present dictionary practice this is not done. If a foreign speaker goes to the *ACD* to look up *so*, he will find that it is classed as a pronoun, among other parts of speech. The reasons why *so* is called a pronoun must be either syntactic or semantic since *so* shares none of the inflectional characteristics which appear in pronouns. The reader is nowhere given this information, so that it seems to me that there is a real danger that he will construct some monstrous paradigm as *so * sor * sors * som*,[6] assuming that it has the inflectional characteristics of *they*. What is called for, then, in a completely adequate entry for such a word as *so*, is a statement that it belongs to an inflectional class which undergoes no modification, but a syntactic class sharing some of the characteristics of pronouns.

If such non-existent paradigms as that given above can be dismissed as somewhat unlikely dangers, there are other pitfalls in our dictionaries which are troublesomely real. The most important type of danger results, it seems to me, from an insufficiently rigid distinction between individual properties of words, which belong in the dictionary entry, and class properties, which do not. Among the individual properties of words are the forms which a given word may lack, and words lacking one or more of the normal paradigmatic set are spoken of as defective. The statement that defectiveness is an individual word property may not seem important in English nouns where the inflectional forms are few, and it would be relatively easy and economical to group together all defective nouns in classes in the grammar. But in any paradigm where the forms are numerous there will have to be a separate class for every word lacking a special form, and a separate class for every new combination of missing forms. It is obvious that the result would be unwieldy description, and that defectiveness is therefore best handled as a property of the individual word. Another not quite obvious distinction is that between words whose forms can be shown by their syntax to be constructed with a zero modification,[7] and words which are genuinely defective. A simple illustration is that *sheep* has a plural in zero, whereas *ethics* is defective in the plural. The importance of the distinction here is that forms having zero modifications are subclasses of the major form classes to which they belong, so that description of these subclasses belongs in the grammar, while I have suggested that defectiveness forms a part of the lexicon.

The *ACD* in common with other dictionaries, follows the practice of making no entries for words which are considered regular in their paradigms, listing the forms only for words which have some peculiarity. Now un-

---

[6] A star before a word indicates that the form is nonexistent in the language, or if existent, it does not appear in the given context.

[7] A hypothetical affix: "The Hindus hit upon the apparently artificial but in practice eminently serviceable device of speaking of a *zero element:* in *sheep: sheep* the plural-suffix is replaced by *zero*—that is, by nothing at all." Bloomfield, Leonard, *Language* (Henry Holt and Co., New York, 1933), p. 209.

fortunately the *ACD* also omits, in many instances, information as to defectiveness. The result is very real confusion, unless the reader already knows all about the paradigm. The learner can only assume that if an entry makes no comment on the grammatical forms of a word, that word has a full and normal paradigm. If one looks up such a word as *spaghetti*, he will find that there is nothing in the entry which indicates that such a sentence as "Please put some *spaghettis on my plate," is not possible in English. Even more confusing is the fact that in some uses the word has a normal paradigm, though it is usually defective. Thus though we cannot use the sentence I have given above, the sentence "The spaghettis made by Brown and Jones are equally good," is certainly acceptable. Indeed, if our user of the dictionary is really unwary, or has an Italian background, he may make a further mistake. A good deal of reading is necessary before he can infer that the general practice in the *ACD* is to assume that a noun is singular unless otherwise stated. In the entry for *spaghetti* the word is described as being derived from an Italian plural, and its final could easily suggest such plural forms as *banditti*. Thus it seems not unlikely that our foreigner might construct such phrases as "a *spaghet is" and "the spaghetti *are."

Some measure of the importance of this sort of difficulty is given by the fact that in the letter *A* alone I have counted no less than eighty nouns which for one reason or another left room for doubt as to whether their paradigms were full and normal, whether they had irregular forms, or whether they were defective in one or more forms. The *-ics* words like *ethics* are a typical class which will illustrate the whole group. The entry for *acoustics* is one of the fullest and clearest since it is stated that when the word is construed as a singular it means the science of sound, when construed as a plural it means acoustic properties. This is certainly true, but it suggests to the reader that he may form a plural *acoustics* for one meaning, and a singular *acoustic* for the other. You will remember that I said earlier that the *-s* of these words was not the plural morpheme. It is true that some of the difficulty with words of this sort might be removed if it were stated that this particular morpheme is a derivational element. Yet not even this would cure the difficulty since only the further statement that both forms of the word are defective, and making clear what forms each lacks, would completely clear up the trouble . . .

Syllabic Consonants in Dictionaries*

John S. Kenyon

In the following observations the descriptions are based on my own speech habits, and the reader must judge how far they represent practice sufficiently general to be regarded as valid. I define a syllabic consonant as one that forms a syllable without any vowel whatever, as described and illustrated in *American Pronunciation*[1] (*AP*) and in *PDAE*, §§24, 114.[2] In my speech only unstressed [l, m, n, ŋ] are syllabic. Examples are: *cattle* [kætl̩], *cradle* [kredl̩], *open* [opm̩], *ribbon* [rɪbm̩], *eaten* [itn̩], *Eden* [idn̩], *I can go* [aɪ kŋ̍ go], *bag and baggage* [bægŋ̍ bægɪdʒ].

The most unmistakable syllabic consonant occurs in the second of a homorganic pair: in [kætl̩, kredl̩] the tongue point remains on the teethridge from the beginning of [t] or [d] to the end of [l]; in [opm̩, rɪbm̩] the lips remain closed throughout [p] or [b] and [m̩]; in [itn̩, idn̩] the tongue point remains in contact throughout [t] or [d] and [n̩]; in [aɪ kŋ̍ go, bægŋ̍ bægɪdʒ] the tongue back remains in contact with the velum throughout [k] or [g] and [ŋ̍]. If even the slightest vowel separates the two homorganic

---

* Reprinted by permission from *American Speech*, 31.243–251 (December, 1956).

[1] By John S. Kenyon (10th ed., 4th printing; Ann Arbor, 1954, misdated 1951), §§88 ff.

[2] Designations of the dictionaries referred to in this paper:

ACD *American College Dictionary* (New York, 1947)
CDD *Comprehensive Desk Dictionary* (Chicago, New York, 1951)
CSD *College Standard Dictionary* (New York, 1940)
Hempl Robert Morris Pierce, *International French-English and English-French Dictionary* (New York, 1903); English pronunciations by George Hempl
Jones Daniel Jones, *English Pronouncing Dictionary* (11th ed.; London and New York, 1956)
NCD *New Century Dictionary* (New York, 1930)
NSD *New Standard Dictionary* (New York, 1947)
OED *Oxford English Dictionary* (Oxford, 1888–1933)
PDAE J. S. Kenyon and T. A. Knott, *Pronouncing Dictionary of American English* (Springfield, Mass., 1944; 6th printing, 1953)
TCS *Thorndike Century Senior Dictionary* (Chicago, New York, 1941)
WNID₂ *Webster's New International Dictionary, Second Edition* (Springfield, Mass., 1934)
WNW *Webster's New World Dictionary of the American Language, College Edition* (Cleveland and New York, 1953)
Wyld Henry Cecil Wyld, *Universal Dictionary of the English Language* (London, 1932)

Pronunciations in symbols of the International Phonetic Association (IPA) are enclosed in brackets; those otherwise indicated are put in parentheses. IPA symbols are sometimes used to show pronunciations from dictionaries that do not use the IPA alphabet.

consonants, that is, if the tongue or lips withdraw contact between the two consonants, then that vowel, usually [ə], becomes the syllabic, and the following consonant becomes nonsyllabic.

In some consonant pairs less closely related organically, the second consonant may still be syllabic, as in *mason* [ṃesn̩], *prison* [prɪzn̩], *often* [ɔfn̩], *oval* [ovl̩], *apple* [æpl̩], *bubble* [bʌbl̩], *buckle* [bʌkl̩], *regal* [rigl̩], *Jonathan* [dʒɑnəθn̩], *heathen* [hiðn̩].[3]

Besides the IPA subscript marker, another way of marking syllabic consonants is by the use of an apostrophe before them, as in (kat″l, hid″n).[4] But the apostrophe is sometimes used when there might be doubt whether the following consonant is syllabic or there is a vowel, however slight, between the two consonants; that is, whether the tongue point may be withdrawn between them. Thus in (kaz″m, mā′s′n) the apostrophe might indicate either [kæzm̩], or [kæzəm̩], [mesn̩] or [mesən̩].

The use of the apostrophe to mark a syllabic consonant undoubtedly arose from its use to indicate the omission of a vowel, as in the form of the possessive, and reflects the baseless assumption that a vowel is necessary to form a syllable. Just as this use was later extended to possessives that never had a vowel, as in *men's*, so its use to mark a syllabic consonant was sometimes extended to cases where the consonant need not be syllabic, as in *prison* (priz″n), in *WNID₂*, *OED*, and *WNW*.

Some dictionaries list pronunciation with syllabic [l̩, m̩, n̩] without the syllabic diacritic but in such positions that they would naturally be read as syllabic; as in (hud′l) *NCD*, (izm) *TCS*, (fat′n) *CSD*, *NSD*, [‖prɛzɪdnsɪ] *Hempl*. Jones's dictionary uses the IPA subscript marker, but omits it if no ambiguity results. But ambiguity is apt to sneak in unawares. To obviate all ambiguity, *PDAE* always uses the marker with syllabic [l, m, n]. In that book those symbols always mean consonantal syllables with no vowel whatever. (But it must be remembered that some words are currently pronounced either with [l̩, m̩, n̩] or with [əl, əm, ən].) Syllabic [ŋ] needs no marker, which is typographically inconvenient, for [ŋ] is always syllabic in the groups [kŋ] and [gŋ] but not elsewhere.

Some linguists regard syllabic [l, m, n] as phonemically identical with /əl/, /əm/, /ən/.[5] I have as yet seen no statement about the phonemic equivalence of syllabic [ŋ] to /əŋ/, though in some cases they might be

---

[3] For some of the phonetic conditions under which these latter may be syllabic, see *AP*, §§89f.

The pronunciation [ɔfn̩] should have been mentioned in *PDAE*.

[4] The apostrophe is so used in *OED*, *WNID₂*, and *WNW*. *OED* explains in the 'Key to Pronunciation' that the apostrophe represents a voice glide. There might be some sort of glide in its key word (eib′l, but there is none in its key word (it′n), for the voice does not begin till the [n] has begun.

[5] George L. Trager and Bernard Bloch, 'The Syllabic Phonemes of English,' *Language*, XVII (1941), 232; and George L. Trager and Henry Lee Smith, Jr., *An Outline of English Structure* (Norman, Okla., 1915), p. 41.

phonetically interchangeable in usage if [g] or [k] immediately followed [əŋ]. Thus [aɪ kŋ go] might alternate with [aɪ kəŋ go], or [dʒækŋ ket] with [dʒæk əŋ ket]. Nor have I seen [hæpəm, opəm, raɪpəm, rɪbəm, sɛbəm,[6] ʃɑrpəm] mentioned as phonemic equivalents of [hæpm̩, opm̩, raɪpm̩ rɪbm̩, sɛbm̩, ʃɑrpm̩], current colloquial pronunciations of *happen, open, ripen, ribbon, seven, sharpen.*

I have no reason to discuss such phonemic equivalence here, though I may need to refer to it in connection with some dictionaries. I will only explain that, when the *PDAE* was being planned, the advice of some members of the staff of the *Linguistic Atlas* agreed with my views that pronunciations should be given in phonetic terms rather than phonemic, as being the more practical method in a dictionary intended to be useful to consultants untrained in linguistics. In the pronunciation, therefore, I distinguish sharply between syllabic [l, m, n, ŋ] and [əl, əm, ən, əŋ]. It is true that a choice is often phonetically possible without violating English patterns, but not always without violating current usage.

For in a pronouncing dictionary prevailing spoken usage has to be considered. In *PDAE* I have expressed the opinion that the phonetic pronunciations [dɪdənt, kɪtən, kʊdənt, mʌtən, nidənt, ʃudənt, wʊdənt] are not in cultivated colloquial use in America. I believe the same is true of the pronunciations [kætəl, pædəl, hʌdəl, rætəl snek, bætəl dor, ʃʌtəl kɑk, sædəl bæg], if [ə] is given the sound described in the keys of *ACD*, *CDD*, and *TCS*, which list them. For *satin, bitten* these dictionaries record [sætən, bɪtən] with no indication that these are meant as the phonemic equivalents of [sætn̩ bɪtn̩].[7]

Some of the dictionaries mentioned in this paper fail to give the consultant a clear idea of their theory and practice regarding syllabic consonants. *CSD* (p. xi) states that 'no syllable can be formed without the aid of a vowel.' One example given, *chasm,* 'pronounced as it spelled *chas'um,* can not be divided because the second element [i.e., syllable] lacks the necessary vowel.'[8] However, at the entry *syllabic,* II, noun, is the definition 'A vowel sound, or its equivalent, necessary to the formation of a syllable.' Here perhaps we are expected to infer that 'equivalent' refers to a syllabic consonant, not mentioned in this connection, though *CSD* and *NSD* list many pronunciations with syllabic consonants and fully recognize them.

In their introductions to sounds and spellings both dictionaries say:

---

[6] The *Linguistic Atlas of New England* reveals that a significant number of cultivated speakers pronounce *seven* [sɛbm̩].

[7] It may be noted that in regions where [r] is sounded only before a vowel, *bittern* [bɪtən] is distinguished from *bitten* [bɪtn], and *Saturn* [sætən] is distinguished from *satin* (adj.) [sætn̩], the last so pronounced in Hempl, *PDAE, WNID₂, WNW.* See *AP* (10th ed.), §86.

[8] These statements in *CSD* occur in directions 'On the Division of Words.' They are replaced in *NSD* by rules of division with many examples that fail to mention such special cases as *prism, rhythm, area, abler, couldn't,* etc.

The final sounds in *able, prism, fasten, flour* are called syllabic *l, m, n, r,* it being a peculiarity of these open consonants that they may partake of the nature of a vowel and form a syllable. . . . In the ordinary spelling syllabic m appears as simple *m* in *-ism, chasm, prism,* and some other words, but as *-am* in *madam, Adams,* as *-om* in *bottom,* etc.

On this it should be observed that prevailing American usage in *prism* and the like, is not with syllabic [m], but with [əm]; and that *madam, Adams, bottom* do not usually have syllabic [m] either in spelling or pronunciation, but [əm] instead.

CSD and *NSD* continue: 'Syllabic r appears [in spelling] as *r* sometimes after a long vowel or diphthong, as in *flour,* but after a consonant always as *-ar, -er, -or,* etc.' It is important to distinguish spelling from sound, and consonant from vowel. First, the fact must be recognized that such words as *flour, flower, hour, power* are either one-syllabled or two-syllabled, and have long been so pronounced in rhymes by poets, and unconsciously by speakers. In early English, when spelling was less regularized, the difference was often shown in the spelling. Note:

The *fire* seven times tried this. [*Merchant of Venice,* II. ix. 63.]

Two syllables, spelled *fier* in the Folio.

Have I given *fire* and rifted Jove's stout oak. [*Tempest,* V. i. 45.]

One syllable, spelled *fire* in the Folio.

On the sixth *hour,* at which time, my lord. [*Ibid.,* V. i. 4.]

Two syllables, in the Folio spelled *hower.*

Wherefore did they not that *hour* destroy us? [*Ibid.,* I. ii. 138.]

One syllable, in the Folio spelled *howre.*

Inhabits heere: ſome heauenly *power* guide vs. [*Ibid.* (Folio), V. i. 105.]

Two syllables, so spelled.

And ev'n that *Powre* which gaue me firſt my oath. [*Two Gentlemen of Verona* (Folio), II. vi. 4.]

One syllable, so spelled.

Whose *power* hath a true consent. [*Il Penseroso,* l. 95.]

Two syllables.

His utmost *power* with adverse power oppos'd. [*Paradise Lost,* I. 103.[9]]

One syllable; both forms spelled alike.

The optional pronunciation is also shown in poetic rhymes: *briar: fire,* Ben Jonson; *power:hour* (spelled *hower*), Shakespeare; *tower:hour,*

---

[9] Cf. *AP* (10th ed.), §353, and Robert Bridges, *Milton's Prosody* (1921), pp. 20f.

higher:fire, Shelley; and many such rhymes as *fewer:pure, newer:cure*, etc.

Remembering that 'the pronunciation is the word itself' (Sir James A. H. Murray, in *OED*), note that in prevailing American speech the letter *r* in monosyllabic *flour* represents a nonsyllabic vowel (not a syllabic consonant), and that the letters *-er* in dissyllabic *flour*, *-ar* in *pillar*, and *-or* in *sailor* represent alike a single *r*-colored vowel although the facts are obscured for American speech by the well-nigh universal habit in dictionaries of representing the simple, single *r*-colored vowel in respelling for pronunciation by a digraph (êr) or [ər], thus encouraging the false view that the single vowel is a vowel followed by a consonant [r], as it had once been.

CSD and *NSD* show pronunciations with syllabic [l, m, n], but none with syllabic consonant [r]. Syllabic [r] as a consonant like [l, m̩, n̩] has no place in this paper.

The word *ism* and other two-syllable words, like *chasm, rhythm*, are somewhat confusing in those dictionaries that show syllable division in the entry spelling, either by an accent mark or other means, for the useful purpose of guiding typists and printers in dividing words at the ends of lines. So, to discourage such division of *chasm, prism, spasm, rhythm*, etc., the entry forms of such two-syllable words in many dictionaries are printed without syllable division; and in those that usually show accent in the entry spelling, such as *CSD, NSD, WNID₂*, these words, though dissyllabic, are not accented there, for that would divide them.

But even the separation of syllables in the entry spelling does not always prove to be a sufficient guide to an acceptable division of words at the end of a line. Common sense and a sense of proportion must sometimes decide. For instance, the three-syllable word *a're. a* cannot well be so divided: *a-/rea* or *a-/bler* would hardly do; a lonesome initial vowel looks awkward; and in a division at the end like *are-/a* the last *a* might as well replace the hyphen and avoid division. Likewise, an end division like *chas-/m*, though quite logical since the *m* is a second syllable, would be as futile as *are-/a* for the same reason. Moreover, most writers and printers would balk at any division of the familiar and useful words *could-n't, did-n't*, and the like.[10] Dictionaries could properly advise typists and printers by excepting a small group of the anomalous words like *prism, area, couldn't*, etc., with appropriate directions for division. This exception would thus confirm the rules of division in the cases not expected, leaving the troublesome words to be treated in the vocabulary as normal citizens with regular division and accentuation corresponding to the facts of usage.

In such words as *prism, rhythm* a question of current pronunciation is involved. The spelling naturally suggests syllabic [m]. But the articulatory

---

[10] I am indebted to Mr. Edward Artin of the Merriam-Webster editorial staff for valuable suggestions about division of words.

phonetic processes involved and the evidence of my proper ears convince me that [m̩] in these words is rare, and that [əm] greatly prevails. So I think *ACD* and *CDD* are right in pronouncing *prism, rhythm,* and the like, as (priz′əm, rith′əm), etc., with Hempl, Wyld, *PDAE,* and Jones.[11]

Although there may be the practical reason for not accenting the entry spelling, reputable dictionaries have an obligation to supply complete accurate information, including accent, in the pronunciation forms of the indisputably dissyllabic *prism, rhythm,* etc. Accent was omitted in the vocabulary of *WNID₂* (prĭz′m), but was permitted in the 'Guide to Pronunciation,' §172 (prɪz′əm). In *OED* the pronunciation is accented in (i·z′m, kæ·z′m, spæ·z′m), but not in (kriz′m, plæz′m, priz′m, siz′m). In Wyld it is accented in ['kæzəm, 'krɪzəm, 'prɪzəm, 'sɪzəm, 'spæzəm], but not in [ɪzəm, plæzəm]. The pronunciation of these words is regularly accented in Hempl, *ACD, CDD,* Jones, and *PDAE.* Accent is regularly omitted in *TCS, NCD, WNID₂, WNW, CSD,* and *NSD.*

The two-syllable colloquial contractions *couldn't, didn't, doesn't, durstn't, hadn't, hasn't, haven't, isn't, mightn't, mustn't, needn't, oughtn't, shouldn't, wasn't, wouldn't,* are in general cultivated colloquial use both in England (Jones) and in America (*PDAE*). With three exceptions they are pronounced with syllabic [n] in dictionaries: *TCS* has (-ənt) for all they give, omitting *mightn't, mustn't, oughtn't. CDD* has (-ənt) for all they give, omitting *couldn't, durstn't, mightn't, mustn't, oughtn't, wasn't, wouldn't. ACD* has (dŭz′ənt, hăv′ənt, hăz′ənt, ĭz′ənt, nēd′ənt, shŏŏd′ənt), but (dĭd′nt, kŏŏd′nt, wŏz′nt, wŏŏd′nt), correctly, perhaps by inspired oversight, and omits *hadn't, mightn't, mustn't, oughtn't.*

A complete list of the *couldn't–wouldn't* contractions is given with pronunciation in *AP,* ninth and subsequent editions, §137 at [nt] (after consonant), and adopted in *PDAE* 1944.[12] No other dictionary that I have seen contains all of them, and none of them are given in *OED,* Wyld, *NCD,* and *CSD. NSD* has only *didn't* (did′nt), *shouldn't* (shud′nt), *isn't* (no pronunciation).[13]

WNID₂ recognizes syllabic consonants, both in the 'Guide to Pronunciation'—in the keys to the symbols, at the descriptions of the sounds (*l,* §169; *m,* §172; *n,* §175)—and throughout the vocabulary, where they are marked with the apostrophe.

WNW ('Guide,' p. xi) says: "The apostrophe occurring before an *l, m,*

[11] Jones gives ['kæzm̩, 'kæzəm] as occurring 'with approximately equal frequency.' *PDAE* describes ['kæzm̩] as 'much less frequent.'

[12] Eight others with nonsyllabic [nt] (after vowel), [ɑrnt], etc., are also given *ibid.*

[13] At the entry *don't NSD* supplies the categorical information: 'The uncontracted forms [*do not, does not*] are preferred almost uniformly in literary use and *correct speech.*' Italics mine. Here we find the frequent erroneous assumption that colloquial speech is a sort of inferior English to be avoided at all cost, even the cost of intolerable bookishness in educated talk. See 'Levels of Speech and Colloquial English,' *English Journal,* XXXVII, No. 1 (1948), 25–31.

or *n* indicates that this consonant has become a sonant, or syllabic consonant; that is, it has formed a syllable with no appreciable vowel sound, as in
apple (ap″l) or *season* (sē′z̓n). In some persons' speech such syllabic consonants are often replaced with syllables containing neutralized vowels,
as (sē′zən); such variants . . . can be inferred."

But such variants are not unconditionally optional without violating
standard speech if the adjacent consonants are strictly homorganic. There
is not free choice between [katn̩] and [katən], or kudn̩'t] and [kudənt], as
I have shown above.

I think *WNW's* (fôl″n) for *fallen*, (stōl″n) for *stolen*, (swōl″n) for
swollen are wrong: [-ln] does not give [n̩] as [nl] gives [l̩]. These words
are either [fɔlən] or fɔln] (nonsyllabic [n]), [stolən] or [stoln], [swolən]
or [swoln]. Compare *swoln* in *Lycidas*, l. 126, and *swolne* in *Tempest*, II.
i. 115, in both of which the rhythm requires a monosyllable. *McClellan*
should not be (məklel″n), but (məklel′ən). *Stolen* at the entry *steal* is
given as (stōl″n), but at its own separate entry correctly as (stōl′ən),
better (stōl′ən). So *swollen* at the entry *swell* is given as (swōl″n), but
at its own separate entry correctly as (swō′lən).

TCS (1941), *ACD* (1947), and *CDD* (1951) in common avoid syllabic
[l, n], pronouncing *rattlesnake* [ˈrætəlˌsnek] instead of the current [ˈrætl̩-
ˌsnek]; *fiddlestick* [ˈfɪdəlˌstɪk] instead of current [ˈfɪdl̩ˌstɪk]; *cottontail*
[ˈkatənˌtel] instead of current [ˈkatn̩ˌtel]; *maidenhair* [ˈmedənˌhɛr]
instead of current [ˈmedn̩ˌhɛr].

Likewise the three agree on [bætəl, fætən, gatən, hʌdəl, kætəl, mɪdəl,
mɪtən, pædəl, pʌdəl, ratən, sʌdən, ˈwudənˌhɛdɪd, ˈfɪdəlˌfædəl], the last
with perhaps some onomatopoetic advantage; and on all analogous words
with homorganic [tl, tn, dl, dn], recorded with syllabic [l, n] in Jones,
Hempl, *WNID₂*, *WNW*, *OED*, Wyld, *CSD*, *NSD*, *NCD*, and *PDAE*.

Those three also agree in pronouncing the very common colloquial words
needn't, shouldn't, and the like, as [nidənt, ʃudənt,], etc., except that *ACD*
correctly pronounces [dɪdn't, kudnt, wɒznt, wudnt].

In *TCS* and *CDD* the only intimation I have discovered that syllabic
consonants exist in daily British and American usage, as duly recorded
throughout the vocabularies in Hempl, Jones, *OED*, Wyld, *NCD*, *CSD*,
NSD, *WNID₂*, *WNW*, and *PDAE*, is found at the vocabulary entry *syllabic*
in those two dictionaries: 'The second *l* in *little* is syllabic,' a statement
flatly denied by the pronunciation (lit′əl) given in all three books. In *ACD*
I do not find even this recognition of syllabic consonants.

In *TCS*, however, we find what appears to be syllabic [m] in the *-ism*
words, like *prism*, and in *rhythm*, respelled for pronunciation as [prizm,
rithm), without syllable division, accent, or further explanation.

So far as I have seen, *PDAE* is the only American dictionary that recognizes syllabic [ŋ]. It lists occasional instances of it as alternative to
[n̩, ən] after [k, g]: *bacon* [bekən, bekn̩ bekŋ] §114; *black-and-blue*

[blækən blu, blækŋ blu]; *wagon* [wægən, wægn̩, wægŋ] (§114); at the entry *and,* unstressed, [ən, n̩, ŋ] after [k, g]: *Jack and Gill* [dʒækŋ dʒɪl], *bag and baggage* [bægŋ bægɪdʒ]; at the entry *can,* unstressed, [kən, kn̩, kŋ]: *I can go* [aɪ kŋ go]; at the entry *-ing,* often replacing [-ɪŋ] after [k, g]: *making* [mekɪŋ, mekŋ], *dragging* [drægɪŋ, drægŋ].

Syllabic [ŋ] had also been shown in the first edition of *AP* (1924; p. 51, §55), and in subsequent editions.[14] Examples (10th ed.): [dʒækŋ dʒɪl], p. 73; [dʒækŋ ket], p. 105 at *and;* [aɪ kŋ kɔl ɪm], p. 106 at *can; aɪ kŋ go*], p. 30, §24.

All the foregoing and following instances in my speech have been corroborated as general in colloquial American by several linguistic scholars: *back and fill* [bækŋ fɪl], *back and forth* [bækŋ forθ], *broken glass* [brokŋ glæs], *chicken gravy* [tʃɪkŋ grevɪ],[15] *egg and coffee* [ɛgŋ kɔfɪ], *oak and pine* [okŋ pam], *old oaken bucket* [old okŋ bʌkɪt], *lock, stock, and barrel* [lɑk, stɑkŋ bærəl], *taken* [tekŋ], *weaken* [wikŋ].

Syllabic consonants are facts of current speech, not merely a point of view. But I fear the baseless view that 'no syllable can be formed without a vowel,' and that a consonant has to be 'the equivalent of a vowel' in order to become syllabic, is still in existence. The statement that it is a peculiarity of certain consonants 'that they may partake of the nature of a vowel and form a syllable' shows that the old idea is still lurking about and influencing some teachers and publishers of textbooks. In no other way can I account for such noncurrent pronunciations as [dɪdənt, kʊdənt, kɪtən, mʌtən], and the like, solemnly presented to us as actual living speech by scholarly editorial boards in dictionaries having innumerable other qualities of excellence.

Vowels are vowels and consonants are consonants in a practical and recognizable sense and, I believe, in a scientific and organic sense.[16] But

[14] So far as I can now determine, my recognition of syllabic [ŋ] was based on observation of my own speech. My first copy of *AP* was received May 5, 1924. My earliest edition of Jones is dated October, 1924, in which he records [kŋ] as weak form of *can,* with note: '[kŋ] only occurs before words beginning with [k] or [g]' (so also 11th ed., 1956). I regarded [ŋ] as due to preceding [k] or [g] as in [bægŋ bægɪdʒ] (1924). At entry *and* Jones (1924) has [ŋ], with note: 'only occurs next to [k] or [g]' (so 1956). He also gives *bacon* [beikŋ], *taken* [teikŋ]. I have not found syllabic [ŋ] described in Jones, nor in his *English Phonetics* (1956) where he treats of syllabic consonants (§§213–15). On page 223 he gives [beikŋ] for *bacon* as an example of assimilation of [n] to [ŋ].

[15] Possibly the dialectal form *chicking* (cf. Lowell, *Biglow Papers* [Boston, 1896], p. 43), explained by Robert J. Menner (*American Speech,* XII [1937], 167) as a hypercorrection, may instead be an instance of syllabic [ŋ], [tʃɪkŋ] by assimilation from [tʃɪkn].

[16] I believe that Bloomfield's articulatory definition of a vowel (*Language* [New York, 1933], p. 102), referred to by Pike, in *Phonetics* (Ann Arbor, 1943), p. 78, is phonetically defective; for my American [r] does involve contact of the sides of the tongue with the molars (*AP* [6th ed., 1935], §37, p. 44). Here the criterion of the vowel as cavity resonance (*ibid.,* §§67–72, or 1950, §§59–64) is more fitting. Pike (p. 145) agrees with me, I take it, in classing prevocal [r] (*rich*) as a semivowel along with [w] and [j] (*AP* [10th ed.], pp. 39, 54).

syllabic consonants are in no debt to vowels for their power to form syllables alone; they can be syllabic in their own right because of their own organic formation, as linguists have long known and the great dictionaries have recognized.

Part VII

LINGUISTICS AND THE STUDY OF LITERATURE

INTRODUCTION

IN THE PREPARATION of this collection this chapter has been included three times and dropped twice. Part of its content is from a rather tentative and controversial area of linguistic applications; activity in this area is quite recent; certainly much work must be done before students of English can generally feel that they have here any established methodology. Nevertheless I have yielded to the argument that since significant work is surely to be done within a short time the student should acquire some awareness of the potential value of linguistics in the teaching and understanding of literature.

Extrapolation of linguistic analysis to the study of poetry has so far been an activity of only a bare handful of scholars oriented to both linguistics and literature. This activity crystalized in the summer of 1953 in the work of the Language and Literature seminar during the Linguistic Institute at Indiana University. Whitehall and Hill offer here a synoptic report of that seminar.

Whitehall then reviews the Trager-Smith *Outline* from the standpoint of a linguist who is also a literary scholar and who sees in structural analysis material for closer interpretation of poetry. Hill, who had already published two earlier studies (see, e.g., his "An Analysis of *The Windhover*: An Experiment in Structural Method," *PMLA*, 70.968–978, December, 1955), next applies structural procedures in his study of Browning's familiar poem within a poem.

Chatman's article has a broader base insofar as he offers the student help in dealing with the complexities of any style different from that of ordinary colloquial English. Elsewhere he has given an example of how his approach works with a single poem ("Robert Frost's *Mowing*: An Enquiry into Prosodic Structure," *Kenyon Review*, summer of 1956, 421–438).

Finally a quite different application of linguistics in the study of literature is demonstrated by Ives with his investigation of the use of dialect
by Joel Chandler Harris to distinguish individuals.

A Report on the Language-Literature Seminar*

HAROLD WHITEHALL AND ARCHIBALD A. HILL

WE STARTED with what we believe to be a necessary series of assumptions
for any objective study of literature, even though we are aware that these
assumptions are necessarily limited, and may even be objected to by
several schools of literary criticism. We believe, however, that quarrel
over the asumptions given below is unnecessary and unfortunate, since
these assumptions merely constitute the necessary rules for a certain kind
of game—a very serious game, however, in which the only prize is increase
of human knowledge and understanding. In other games—again we use a
word which we do not wish to have understood in any flippant sense—the
rules would be different.

Our first assumption is that a work of literature, whether a full length
novel, or merely a triolet, is an utterance fully contained in the utterances
which make up human language. A piece of literature is therefore a language act, like other language acts, but differentiated from them by
characteristics of its own. As a further assumption, which in part necessarily follows from the first, we believe that a work of literature can be
behavioristically investigated as a language act having reality in the outside world like other language acts. It can not, contrariwise, be usefully
investigated if we make the assumption that it exists only in the mind of
the author, the mind of the reader, or in a sort of union of the two. In making this assumption, you will note, that we are not denying the reality of
what goes on in the mind of author and reader, but merely stating that we
can not usefully study it. Once the behaviorist assumption outlined above is
made, it then becomes possible to study the structure of a work of literature, secure in the belief that our study is throwing light on the object of
investigation, and that we are not merely describing our own subjective
reactions to it.

If then, literature is a type of language act, we believe that it follows that
it can not be studied with the fullest fruitfulness unless the student is
deeply versed in scientific linguistics, and is prepared to focus this knowledge on both the external and internal characteristics of literature, in hope
of finding, eventually, those particularly significant characteristics which

* Reprinted by the permission of the authors from the original mimeographed report.

define, in each culture, the difference between literature and mere every-day use of language. There is no phase of literature where there is a more intimate relation between the structure of language and the structure of the literary work than in metrics. As a result, the Seminar this summer set itself the primary task of re-examining English metrics in the light of phonemic theory. The results of this re-examination follow.

English, being a language in which stress differences are a basic and significant structural device—in contrast to many languages where stress differences may exist but are not significant—builds all its metrical patterns on stress differences. No matter whether the metre is that of Beowulf, Pope, or T. S. Eliot, there is always a pattern of alternating stronger and weaker stress. The metrics of such a language as Hungarian, on the other hand, makes no such fundamental use of stress, since there the pattern is often a merely symmetrical arrangement of syllables. The stress phonemes of English are four, though it is probable that there were only three in Old English. Metrical stress, however, recognizes only two stresses, a stronger and a weaker. It therefore follows, as we think we have been able to demonstrate, that there is a permissible range of stress variation within which variety is felt as one of the conventional ornaments of English, though variation beyond these limits is a blemish. The two extreme stresses, primary or weak, are poetically fixed, the first being necessarily always a poetic strong, the second always a poetic weak. The two middle stresses, secondary and tertiary, may be poetic strongs, or poetic weaks. The principle of poetic stress is that a syllable is strong if it is stronger than those which surround it, so that as indicated above, a tertiary stress followed by a weak may count as a poetic strong, while if followed by a secondary or primary stress, it may count as a poetic weak. Those English poets who are generally admired as metrists make use of these differences to produce variety, and we have tested enough poetry of all periods and types so that we are sure of this statement. It will be noted that this formulation, simple though it may be, is at least useful in imposing a theoretical limit on variation, and explains why some poets can make use of metrical variation without offending the reader, while others invariably produce the effect of lack of skill by stress conflicts.

Next, English has three phonemes of the type called terminal junctures. These are essentially pitch shapes which occur at the ends of (phonological) clauses and sentences. Two of them can be readily heard by pronouncing the sequence "one, two, three." After the first two numbers there is a slight rise, and after the third, a fall. These are the two junctures known as double bar, and double cross (//, and #). A third type, single bar (/), functions in much the same way as double bar, but does not have the rise of double bar. Instead it seems to have a continuation of the pitch level of the preceding material, whatever that level may be. It is important to note that these juncture phenomena are not pauses, since though pause may accompany them, it is not a necessary accompaniment. In all English poetry these junctures are made use of. In relatively unskilful and unvaried poetry there is a juncture placed at the end of each line, as a heavy reinforcement of the rhyme. In more skilful poetry, the juncture pattern is extremely varied in relation to the rhyme words. There is no better poet for the study of the subtle variations in juncture than Pope, who takes a rigid basic structure, and varies it continually with junctures within the line, and with junctures absent at the ends of lines. It is worth noting in passing that criticism has concerned itself a good deal with the "caesura" in Pope, believing it possible to explain his verse in terms of a relatively mechanically placed pause in the middle of each line. This form of statement now turns out to be largely irrelevant.

The third characteristic of English which is strikingly used in metre is a feature which is not a part of the significant structure, but is nonetheless a basic phonetic characteristic of the language. We owe knowledge of this feature to the phonetician Kenneth Pike of Michigan. This feature of English is the fact that the amount of time between two primary stresses tends to be the same, irrespective of the amount of material between them. This feature can be called isochronism, and it is intimately related to juncture, since isochronism is often secured by increasing or decreasing the pause which always may accompany a terminal juncture. In contrast to English, such a language as Spanish tends to make all syllables occupy the same amount of time, thus producing the effect that we have called isosyllabism. For those wishing to test the English characteristic of which we speak, the Pike drill sentences

> Énglish / is éasy #
> Énglish / is very éasy #
> The Énglish lesson / is very éasy #

will demonstrate what is meant.

We believe that a language having characteristics like English will almost necessarily create a metrical form in which what is counted is the number of strong stresses, and in which the number of weak stressed syllables is irrelevant. The whole of the material will be further arranged into the time units of the same length, marked off, not into feet, but into juncture units. It is just this type of verse which represents the native English tradition, beginning with the verse of Beowulf, continuing through ballads and proverbs, and nowadays once more practiced by selfconscious and highly sophisticated poets. This type of verse we call isochronous verse, and believe that it is to be identified with the type of verse imperfectly described but brilliantly practiced by the 19th century poets Hopkins, Bridges, and Patmore. The name given by this group to poetry of this sort is "dipodic verse" which we believe to be a name less useful, because less

accurately descriptive, than "isochronic verse." Two useful examples of isochronic verse may make these statements clearer.

> A stitch in tíme // saves níne.#
> Fát // bláck // búcks# (in a winebarrel room . . .)

It will be noted that the first is popular, the second literary. In each, the
material between junctures is clearly isochronous.

Beside the pattern of isochronous verse there exists also a borrowed form
which appears for the first time in the verse of Chaucer, which is isosyllabic or syllable-counting. The theory of English metre has always
recognized this type, and unfortunately all too often seems to assume that
it is the only type. We do not attempt to judge between the two types, but
could content ourselves with pointing out that Pope and Dryden belong
to this school, and that the usage of Milton seems to be a blend of this
school with isochronism. We believe further, that these two types exhaust
the forms practiced in English. The attempts, at several different periods, to
introduce quantitative classical metres are necessarily doomed to failure,
since though differences in quantity exist in English, they are not phonemic.

A word about metrical theory can conclude this portion of the report.
English metrical theory has generally been of two schools, a relatively
mechanical school which has taken over the terminology of classical metrics,
even to such terms as "long and short," which counts syllables, and breaks
verse up into units of various kinds of feet. This is usually the metrics of
school handbooks. It works reasonably well with isosyllabic verse, but
breaks down almost completely with isochronic verse. A second school,
largely founded by Lanier, insists that poetry is a kind of music, and records
isochronic verse with considerable success in musical notation. Both
schools, however, are pre-phonemic, and both attempt to explain English
verse by extraneous material—the structure of Latin verse in one school,
the structure of music in the other. We believe, then that our conscious
linguistic analysis of English verse can make use of stress units, juncture
units, and time units, in such a way as to give a coherent theory of verse
structure broad enough to take into account any form of English verse.
Neither of the two previously practiced types of analysis can do this.

From Linguistics to Criticism:
A Book Review*

HAROLD WHITEHALL

An Outline of English Structure. By *George L. Trager* and *Henry Lee Smith, Jr.* Studies in Linguistics: Occasional Papers 3. (Battenburg Press). $1.50

FENDING OFF political attack on one flank, the U.S. Department of State achieves quiet, significant gains on the other. This short treatise on contemporary English, written by two of the several distinguished linguists teaching in the Foreign Service Institute of the State Department, exemplifies the kind of advanced training in language, culture, and allied subjects now given our foreign service personnel. Although the authors regard their work as very tentative, or, in their own words as "a series of conclusions about English structure that constitute . . . the basis for further study and discussion," they are, it seems to me, dramatically over-modest. Whatever else this many-faceted book may claim to be, it is above all a brilliant attempt to apply to an Atlantic "cultural" language the methods of analysis and presentation so far chiefly used in describing so-called "primitive" languages. Considering the immense scope of English and the manner in which it reflects its recurrent instabilities of structure, its tortuous social history, and its pervasive literary tradition, Trager and Smith's results are amazingly coherent, both practically and societally. Their book is the first sketch of English structure really worthy of the term *descriptive*.

Back of the book, of course, are three decades of preliminary spadework by a score of investigating linguists. The basic problem, which was to objectify ("phonemicize") the telegraphic code of audible gestures constituting the signaling system of English, has been variously solved by workers as diverse in method as Bloomfield, Trnka, Trubetzkoy, Swadesh, and Bloch and Trager. In this country, at least, a continuum of agreement has gradually emerged; and if, as I think will happen, the Trager-Smith solution becomes accepted as standard, it is because the soil of assent is already fully prepared. Yet the authors of the *Outline*, whether dealing with phonemics, morphology, or syntax, are anything but blind followers of recent American linguistic theory, scholiasts of Bloomfield, re-interpreters of Pike. Their neatly dovetailed hierarchies of descriptive statement—many of them highly individualistic—are based on a twelve-

* Reprinted by permission from *The Kenyon Review*, 13.710–714 (1951).

years' observation of spoken English in all its principal varieties and are intended to hold good for modern spoken English as a whole, no varieties barred. In two areas at least—the treatment of "superfixes" and the whole approach to syntax—the originality is revolutionary.

The book starts with a highly systematized examination of English phonetic phenomena, possibly less adequate for certain dialects of the American South and the British Northwest than the authors would like to believe, but otherwise wholly admirable. The sounds revealed by this examination are then quantized into their phonemes by the usual American methods of phonetic similarity, complementary distribution, and pattern congruity. (European linguists would have proceeded somewhat differently but, on the basis of the same evidence, with much the same result.) The phonemic system of English turns out to consist of 33 items, roughly to be tiered as front, central, and back, of which 9 are vowels, three (y, h, w) semivowels, and 21 consonants. There is a convincing treatment here of the complex vowel nuclei (as in *bay, bough, bite, beet, boat, boot,* etc.) and a satisfactory argument for interpreting the "long" vowels in *dear, dare, palm, paw, war,* etc. as complexes of simple vowels with the semivowel /h/. Needless to say, no one variety of English employs the full range of this phonemic system, although the spread in the dialects specifically examined by the authors is surprisingly wide.

The next section of the book consists of a description of the constructive and prosodic features of the language—stress, transition, and pitch. Four degrees of relative stress (loud, secondary, tertiary, weak), four levels of pitch, and four kinds of transition (here called "junctures") are distinguished. That such a 4-4-4 pattern exists in English is, I think, undoubted, but whether *sui generis* and significantly, only further investigation will show. The point is possibly of secondary importance. What is important here is the careful working out of the integration between the three constructive features, of the manner in which they reinforce each other, of the grammatical and semantic implications that they carry. For the first time in the long history of English language studies, such matters are really made clear. Since the constructive features must necessarily serve a descriptive grammar as *segmentalizers*—they are our chief scissors of linguistic perception—the value of this part of the *Outline* can scarcely be exaggerated. The remainder of the volume depends completely upon it.

The subsequent treatment of English morphology is not and is not intended to be a complete coverage of that very vexed subject. On the whole, the authors have analysed only the situations which repay analysis. I sometimes wonder whether more is worth doing with a language which combines a word-order syntax with an active morphology predominantly of the type once called *agglutinative* and a passive morphology dependent upon the structures of French, Greek, Latin, and Old English. This section of the book, however, is a fine example of controlled morphological method, made

exciting by the description of word-elements ("morphemes") not as mere
linear recurrent partials semiotically charged but as phonemes or suc-
cessions of phonemes accompanied by distinctive stress-and-juncture features ("superfixes"). To use a musical analogy, these represent chords
rather than single notes or sequences of notes. When the "superfix" is
changed, the semantic spectrum of the morpheme or morphemes is
changed. Thus the collocation of linear phonemes in *light+house+keep+
er* can express, according to the particular superfixes applied to it, the three
semantic spectra "keeper of a lighthouse," "one who does lighthousekeep-
ing," and "a housekeeper who is not dark." This kind of thing is so common
in English that it must be regarded as a major structural characteristic of
the language—one which underlies our system of word order and makes
possible the free "conversion" of English morphemes and words from one
grammatical function to another. For clearly delimiting the linguistic features operative here and for demonstrating how they work, Trager and
Smith deserve the close attention of everyone concerned with English.

The *Outline* concludes with a rapid sketch of syntactical method and
a few suggestive notes on "metalinguistics." In the description of such
languages as French and English, segmentation into syntactic units would
seem to be the first logical analytical step. Unfortunately, descriptive linguistics, although expert in phonemic and adequate in morphological investigation, has done relatively little with syntactics. The authors of this
book use intonation and juncture as cutting tools, correlate the subject
closely with their treatment of morphology, and attempt a formal analysis
of formal units without the intervention of meaning. What they achieve
(the analysis of the English verb is their most important exhibit) combines
nicely with extant studies of word order and concord to provide a realistic
foundation for an objective English syntax.

An Outline of English Structure is not and is not intended to be the
critic's vade mecum to the English language. Nevertheless, it is a work that
literary criticism cannot afford to ignore. If, as Robert Fitzgerald recently
wrote, English poetry has a hunger for a sound metaphysics, criticism in
English ought to have a hunger for a sound linguistics. So far, where the
hunger has existed at all, it has had to go unsatisfied. Whatever the philological and etymological achievements of the 19th Century Neo-gram-
marian linguists, it cannot be said that they provided the critics of their
own time or this with a metrics that would analyse, a stylistics that would
reveal, a grammar that would describe, or even a history of English sounds
that would elucidate. In our own country, neither the Eastern European
formalist and structuralist critics (who certainly understood the European linguistics of their time) nor the behaviorist school of American linguists have had any perceptible effect on Anglo-Saxon literary criticism.
Yet as no science can go beyond mathematics, no criticism can go beyond
its linguistics. And the kind of linguistics needed by recent criticism for the

solution of its pressing problems of metrics and stylistics, in fact, for all problems of the linguistic surface of letters, is not semantics, either epistemological or communicative, but down-to-the-surface linguistics, microlinguistics not metalinguistics. In their *Outline,* Trager and Smith have unwittingly assembled for the critic some of the necessary linguistic tools. Their exposition of the superfix, for instance, throws immediate light on the distinction between the verse of Wyatt, Donne, the Coleridge of "Christabel," Hopkins, and Eliot in which superfix patterns function freely and naturally as part of the rhythm, and the verse of Surrey, Daniel, Waller, Dryden, Pope, Tennyson, in which the superfixes are frozen and partly entombed in the rhythm. Similarly, the interconnections between stress, pitch, and transitions analysed so carefully in the *Outline* allow us to envisage for the first time a really objective and fully descriptive English metrics, with a vertical as well as a horizontal dimension.

Not that one has to stop with Trager and Smith. Their book contains on the one hand an *embarras de richesses* for criticism, on the other a *défaut.* For the practical purpose of poetic analysis, their phonemic inventory could be reduced to twenty-seven items, their stress system from four degrees to three, their four pitch levels to three, and their junctural system to three simple functions of pause. Conversely, anyone engrossed with minute sound patterns (like Arnold Stein in his recent KR articles), will need to dissolve the phonemes of English, as Jakobson and Lotz have recently done for those of French, into their constituent bundles of distinctive features (based on the oppositions vowel/consonant, voiced/voiceless, nasal/oral, saturated/diluted, grave/acute, continuous/intercepted, tense/lax, strident/non-strident). He will also need to note how these features, from which phonemes are built, significantly persist or disperse in the chordal progression of the poetic texture.

As Roman Jakobson has recently pointed out, language, although constructed around simple dichotomic oppositions, involves both an axis of successiveness and an axis of simultaneity which cut its hierarchical structure even up to the complex connotational symbol itself. It is the craft of the poet to exploit them both; it is the craft of the critic to disengage them from the poem, in all occurrences, at all levels.

Pippa's Song:
Two Attempts at Structural Criticism*

ARCHIBALD A. HILL

The year's at the spring
And day's at the morn;
Morning's at seven;
The hill-side's dew-pearled;
The lark's on the wing;
The snail's on the thorn:
God's in his heaven—
All's right with the world!

JOHN CROWE RANSOM, in an able and important critical study, recently re-marked of "Pippa's Song" that its last two lines were "a tag of identification so pointed as to be embarrassing." Thereafter he went on to justify the statement:

> She spends three lines dating the occasion very precisely. . . . Then come three details which constitute the concrete: the hillside, the lark, the snail. . . . And that would be the poem; except that she must conclude by putting in her theological Universal. . . .[1]

Ransom's approach is structural. He sees in the poem a pattern of two three-line groups followed by a two-line conclusion. He condemns the conclusion because it does not seem to be properly related to the preceding material. It would appear that the units with which he has operated are essentially semantic: units of time, units of concrete experience, and a unit of abstract theological universality. If the operating units are valid, his statement of the structure and the resultant evaluation follow almost inevitably.

His units are not, however, the only ones that might be chosen. In metrical structure the poem is remarkably rigid, each line being ended by a terminal juncture, with no terminal junctures within the lines. Each juncture-group has the grammatical form of a sentence, with subject, verb, and complement. The lines of the poem therefore invite the interpretation that they are the normal first segments, since they are defined as units by their formal and grammatical structure. Even at this stage, divergence from Ransom's segmentation results. Ransom has taken the last two lines

---

* Reprinted by permission from The University of Texas *Studies in English*, 35.51–56 (1956).

[1] "The Concrete Universal, II" *Kenyon Review*, XVII (1955), 395.

as one unit, not two, because both are concerned with the "theological Universal." To group them thus, he must disregard the linguistic characteristics which mark line eight as separate from line seven.

Yet the eight separate lines cannot be presumed to be unrelated. A second task is therefore to search for and describe this relationship, since if the poem has a general pattern it must reside in its parts and their relationship to each other and to the whole. Because the parts are sentences, the relationships between them belong to the study of stylistics (which deals with relationships between sentencse) rather than linguistics (which deals with relationships within sentences). Typical stylistic relationships show themselves in the repetition of formal patterns from one sentence to the next.

The first three lines have the grammatical structure of noun, copula, and prepositional phrase headed by a noun. Line four, on the other hand, has the structure of noun, copula, and phrasal modifier. Lines five, six, and seven repeat the structure of the first three lines. Line eight has the structure found in line four: noun, copula, and modifying phrase. There is therefore a formal similarity between lines one, two, and three and lines five, six, and seven, and further similarity between line four and line eight. In form, then, line eight is related to line four, rather than primarily to line seven as Ransom stated. The formal similarity between lines four and eight is backed by their linkage in rhyme.

The relationships so far stated have been arrived at by study of formal characteristics. Such a procedure is similar to that of linguistic analysis. It is true that the subject of analysis is here a printed text, in contrast to the oral material with which linguistics habitually operates. The difference is more apparent than real. Browning's punctuation, like that of English written composition generally, does not give a clear picture of the phonological structure. In analysis of any printed text it is necessary to read it aloud, so that thereafter it can be treated as a spoken utterance. The reading given to the poem is not to be defended as the necessarily right interpretation. It has been checked with several other speakers of English, and can therefore be described as a natural and possible rendering, however it may differ in detail from others.

If formal characteristics have been exhausted, the next step is consideration of lexical meanings. The content of line one, "The year's at the spring," can be stated in general terms. *Year* is a large unit of time, and *spring* is a unit contained within it. Many readers would agree that, in human terms, *spring* is the best of the contained units. The statement that *spring* is the best unit within the year is not forced by the structure of this line. It is a hypothesis to be tested by its results in analysis of the rest of the poem.

Line two, "And day's at the morn," also contains a larger unit of time and a contained unit, though the larger unit of this line is smaller than the larger unit of the first line. When sentences are stylistically linked by structure, it is to be expected that there will be analogies in meaning as well. If the hypothesis about line one is correct, it is reasonable to suppose that *morn* is also the best of the contained entities.

In line three, "Morning's at seven," there is once more a larger unit of time, and a contained unit. By stylistic implication, the contained unit is again the best of its group. There is, moreover, an additional fact which emerges from line three. *Morning* is a form exchangeable with *morn*, so that the contained unit of line two is the containing unit of line three. In stylistic relations, particularly those in the relatively permanent form of literature, spans of interpretation can spread backward as well as forward, and it is therefore possible to reinterpret the relationships in the earlier lines. The entities in the first three lines descend in a general order from larger to smaller. Yet it is possible that the pattern is even more precisely parallel and that *spring* and *day* are in the same relationship to each other as *morn* and *morning*. The point cannot be settled, since it is obvious that *spring* and *day* are not exchangeable, but the suggestion is certainly there. A reasonable reading might therefore assume that the structure of the poem has equated the two words. The first three lines can now be given in a schematic statement of the stylistic structure which emerges from lexical examination:

> Large A is at contained B (its best)
> Smaller B is at contained C (its best)
> Still smaller C is at contained D (its best).

In the grammatically different line four, "The hill-side's dew-pearled," *hill-side* can be defined as a part of the physical scene. In contrast to a unit like *world*, in line eight, it is a small and immediate part. The phrasal modifier, *dew-pearled*, indicates a state in which the hillside is certainly attractive. A generalized statement is "Little X is good Y." Line four, though related to line eight, is also related to the lines which precede. Carrying forward the hypothesis that the contained units are the best of the several groups, it is possible to see in the attractive state of the hillside a similar excellence: being dew-pearled is its best state. The formulaic statement should therefore be revised to "little X is good Y (its best)." Further relationships between the first three lines and line four are not explicitly indicated, but as stated earlier there is a change in grammatical form and content with line four. The tightly knit sequence of the first three lines is broken by a statement of a different sort, though one which is related to the preceding. In linguistic analysis, as in the everyday interpretation of speech, it is a sensible procedure to settle on the interpretation of highest probability and disregard all others. There is no reason why this technique should not be used here. The most probable interpretation of the meaning of such an incremental change is that the relationship is one of cause and result. *Post hoc ergo propter hoc* may not be good logic, but it is a good probabilistic interpretation of stylistic sequences. A final statement of line four is then: "Therefore small X is Y (its best)."

Now that the lexical and stylistic pattern has been tentatively established, the rest of the poem can be more quickly described. Lines five, six, and seven move in general from small objects to large. The objects are living beings, and the prepositional phrases which follow the copulas are, by analogy from the content of the first four lines, the proper and best place for each of these beings. It is true that *wing* is not strictly a place in the same sense as *thorn* or *heaven*, but the minor difference is overridden by stylistic similarity to the surrounding sentences. The order from small to large is a reversal of the order in the first group of lines. Yet this ascending order is itself reversed by lines five and six, where *snail* is smaller than *lark*. The break has a startling result in that it brings the extremes of the scale, *snail* and *God*, into immediate juxtaposition. We can therefore represent lines five, six, and seven thus:

> Small E is on F (its best place)
> Smaller G is on H (its best place)
> Large I is in J (its best place).

Line eight is also readily describable. It is, like line four, a result—"therefore the large scene is at its best." The statement that the poem deals with best entities and states has up to this time been a hypothesis—not contradicted at any point, but without confirmation. The last line furnishes explicit confirmation in the words "all's right." A final statement of the pattern of the poem is now: three analogically related descending statements and their results on a small scale, then three analogically related ascending statements and their results on a large scale. The surprise in structure is the departure from order which brings the smallest entities of the second part into contiguity.

The analysis of this poem has been thus labored only partly because of a desire to arrive at an interpretation, and not at all because of a fondness for elaboration. The attempt has been to work out an orderly critical procedure having a maximum of rigor at each step. The method should therefore be defined. It might at first sight seem to be linguistic, since linguistic data have been used at a number of points. Such a description would not be accurate. The method falls wholly within the area of the metalinguistic— those portions of the communication situation beyond the fields of phonology, morphology, and syntax. The linguistic data (phonology and grammar) were used as a tool for the first segmentation of the poem into components, in a fashion similar to the use of phonetic data for a preliminary segmenting of the sounds of speech into phonemic units.

I have elsewhere said that the whole of microliterary study belongs on the metalinguistic level, while microlinguistic data fall, as here, onto the preliterary level.[2] The parallel with linguistic analysis is made even closer by the fact that the preliminary (microlinguistic) units, once segmented out, were analyzed for recurrent component parts, just as phonemic units are analyzed for their recurrent components—the distinctive features. The result of this examination of preliterary segments and their components was a statement of the first level of microliterary structure, the grammatical similarities between the several sets of lines within the poem. As in linguistic analysis, analysis then moved to a level higher in the structural hierarchy, in this instance the lexical. Lexical examination resulted in further insight into stylistic relationships; from full exploitation of them the statement of the total pattern of the poem finally emerged. When such a pattern is reached it can be said that microliterary analysis breaks off. Any further statements of meaning are in the metaliterary sphere of correlation between the literary structure and known facts of patterned cultural behavior and values. One such statement is worth making. Ransom has called the last two lines a well-schooled theological tag. Pippa breaks her strict analogical pattern to bring *snail* and *God* together. The juxtaposition does not correlate with the way we expect theologians to talk about God. It correlates, instead, with the way we expect children to talk of Him, in concrete and simple terms. Pippa's statement also correlates with our belief that simplicity like hers often contains insights somehow better than those found in the words of the most philosophically sophisticated. One is tempted to find, in the breaking of the pattern Browning has established for her, a sort of model of the cultural contradiction in our attitudes toward children. We treat them as not yet perfected human beings, yet we remember the Biblical "out of the mouths of babes and sucklings."

It remains only to state the differences between Ransom's method and that used here. Ransom is structural in his approach, but uses semantically defined units without having worked through the formal linguistic differentia. His method is therefore similar to that of traditional grammar, where a formal word-class, such as nouns, is defined in terms of the semantic count of the class. In contrast, the analysis given here rests on one of the most basic assumptions in linguistics, that it is form which gives meaning and not meaning which gives form. Ransom's assumptions are commonly used by critics, those used here by linguists. Since the two sets of assumptions are correlated with differing kinds of activity, it is impractical to measure which set is the more reasonable. Fortunately the two analyses can be measured otherwise. They must be assumed to be significantly different, since one cannot be mechanically translated into the other. If different, both cannot be true; one must be more complete, more consistent, and more simple than the other. Evaluation may be left to the reader.

[2] "An Analysis of *The Windhover:* An Experiment in Structural Method," *PMLA,* LXX (1955), 972–73.

Linguistics
and Teaching Introductory Literature*

SEYMOUR B. CHATMAN

I ASSUME THAT THE PURPOSE of introductory courses in English literature is to teach students how to read it. Yet many college students, in spite of the best intentions, never *do* learn to read the masterpieces of our language with even elementary comprehension. One reason for their failure is that the basic skill of interpretation is all too easily assumed by the instructor, whose anxiety is to prove the value of literature or whose scholarly interests may insulate him from the beginner's major problems. The kind of English which we want our students to learn to read differs strikingly from the kind they are used to. For the first time, they must try to make plain sense out of a dialect which is infinitely more subtle in lexical distinction and more complex in structure than any they have ever known; and there is no use in minimizing the size and dangers of the linguistic gap that yawns before them.

The central problem in the teaching of literature is to bridge the gap: to show students how to expand and refine their disturbingly narrow grasp of potential structures, to develop a whole new syntactic and lexical musculature for dealing with the complexities of Milton, Shakespeare, and Pope. One way to accomplish this is to treat the text almost as if it were a foreign language (for it is at least a foreign dialect), to be parsed and worked over until pattern and meaning are learned and overlearned. All the devices that linguistics has developed for teaching foreign languages might be tried: substitution within a frame, imitative oral drill (with particular attention to stress, pitch, and juncture), restructuring for analysis, expansion, and omission, etc. Furthermore, the instructor must be aware at every moment of the specific linguistic complexities of the piece he is teaching in relation to the level of his class. This is as important to his immediate job as a knowledge of mythic patterns in the Modern English novel or what nasty fellows Elizabethan printers were. He must attempt—and it is a painful job—to uncover the multifoliate layers of his own literary sophistication and put himself in the students' position. He must realize that students are unable to move with the linguistic facility that he has developed in himself, that they are not alert to the lexical and structural possibilities of language and are quickly reduced to helplessness if the

* Reprinted by permission from *Language Learning,* 7.3–10 (1956–1957).

first meaning which comes to mind proves untenable. Nor are they willing
to pore over a passage until it makes sense, because they know that more
than poring will be needed to help *them*.

Let us consider the three areas where linguistics might be helpful.

I. *Lexicon.* We must be careful not to shrug our shoulders over the lexical problem and say, 'It's all in the dictionary.' First of all, the facts of
American college life are such that we cannot count on a student to *buy*
a decent dictionary, let alone use one. This bit of student pathology, of
course, is not our problem. What *is* disturbing is that even where a student
shows a willingness to use the dictionary, it is all too clear that he often
doesn't know *when*. Most students dutifully look up words that they don't
'know'; that is, *words that they've never seen before.* But it isn't the unusual
word that causes the trouble. Even lazy students can be expected to look
up 'incarnadine' and 'multitudinous' if threatened with quizzes. The real
danger lies with relatively simple words that are known in one—but the
wrong—definition. Not only doesn't the student understand the word, but
far worse, he doesn't even *know* that he doesn't understand it. And the
astonishment and disbelief in his eyes when you tell him that words *often*
have more than one meaning! Here are a few rather obvious instances
that have troubled my students:

> I only hear
> Its melancholy, long, withdrawing roar,
> Retreating, to the breath
> Of the night wind, down the vast edges drear
> And naked *shingles* of the world.   (small beach stones)

> From this descent
> Celestial *virtues* rising will appear
> More glorious than from no fall.   (angelic host)

> . . . leaving the tumultuous throng,
> To cut across the *reflex* of a star
> That fled, and flying still before me, gleamed
> Upon the glassy plain . . .   (reflection)

> Love's not Time's fool, though rosy lips and cheeks
> Within his bending sickle's *compass* come.   (range)

> I sigh the lack of many a thing I sought
> And with old woes new wail my *dear* time's waste.   (precious)

Becoming *aware* of a lexical difficulty is far more than half the battle,
for it is precisely the skill of recognition that students lack so desperately.
And it is obviously the teacher's affair, for even the most heavily glossed
text-book will not help students whose real problem is that they refuse to
admit that they do not 'know' rather simple words. The teacher must demonstrate with semantic exercises the perniciousness of taking the first
meaning that comes to mind if his students are ever to become competent

and self-dependent readers. Those students who have successfully studied foreign languages will be the first to believe him; anyone who has had to look up *facio* or *affaire* or *Bestimmung* a dozen times for a dozen different contexts will readily accept the principle of semantic diversity in English. It is the monolithic monolingual who will be hardest to convince, just as he is the hardest to teach to write decent compositions. This is basically a problem in sensitizing students to a higher degree of semantic awareness than they have ever known, and they may offer fierce resistance. The whole drift of their lives in the culture which nurtured them may go against recognizing the possibility of finely wrought discrimination of meaning. But it is a vital job of pedagogy and worthy of more scientific interest among linguists than it has so far aroused.

II. *Form-class identification.* Separate from the lexical problem (which is self-evident and a little removed from my major concerns) is the difficulty the beginner frequently encounters in identifying a word's part-of-speech. Students are accustomed to taking the path of least resistance: they only know how to identify a word's structure in terms of its most *frequent* assignment, and are reluctant to analyze the specific syntactic demands which the environment makes upon it. For example:

> The Sea of Faith
> Was once, too, at the full, and *round* earth's shore
> Lay like the folds of a bright girdle furled.

I have had all eighteen students in a class of eighteen tell me that 'round' is an adjective modifying 'shore.' The reason is obviously quantitative: 'round' occurs more frequently in their idiolects as an adjective than as a preposition, and its occurrence immediately before 'earth' seems to have utterly incapacited these readers from making any other form-class identification. ('Full,' too, is easier for them to take as an adjective modifying 'earth' than as a nominal, the axis of 'at the . . . ' .)

But we are more competent to handle this problem than the lexical problem, for we have the signals to help us. Rather than *tell* the student that 'round' should be taken as a preposition, we can make him *hear* his mistake. After convincing him that his reading is meaningless ('What then is the subject of "lay"?'), we contrast his superfixes with our own.

His:

> The Sea of Faith
> Was once, too | ²at the ³fùll and rôund êarth's shóre²
> Lay like the folds of a bright girdle furled.

Ours:

> The Sea of Faith
> Was once, too| ²at the ³fúll¹ #² and ròund êarth's ³shóre²
> Lay like the folds of a bright girdle furled.

The insertion of $\#$ between 'full' and 'round' and the substitution of tertiary for secondary on 'round' will be enough for three out of four students, simply because the signals are stronger than any abstract grammatical explanation could be. (And, of course, if Smith's new syntactic views are correct, the phonological *is* the grammatical explanation. The less astute fourth student will not understand the difference, but for non-linguistic reasons; either because he has never heard the expression 'at the full' before, or 'round' used as a preposition, but *not* because he is unprepared to interpret the comma as $\#$ and the tertiary on 'round' as the signal of a preposition.

Another example:

> Me though just right, and the fixed laws of heaven,
> Did first create your leader, next free choice . . .

Most students take 'just right' to modify "me," thus tertiary on 'just' (and in some idiolects /jist/ instead of /jəst/), and secondary on 'right':

$$^3\text{Mé though jùst rîght}^2$$

But if forced to imitate another reading, many grasp the structure immediately:

$$^3\text{Mé}^1 \mid {}^2\text{thòugh } {}^3\text{jûst rîght}^2 \mid {}^2\text{and the } {}^3\text{fîxed lâws of héaven}^2$$

('Although righteousness and heaven's laws first created me your leader . . .') Here are some other lines from the same passage:

> from this descent
> Celestial virtues rising will appear
> More glorious than from no fall.

Several students, after learning that 'virtues' refers to the fallen host, took 'celestial virtues' as a vocative, and 'rising' as a gerund, rather than as a post-positional participial modifier (with 'from this descent' as adverbial object):

$$^2\text{from thìs de}^3\text{scént}^3\mid$$
$$^2\text{Celêstial vir}^3\text{tues} \mid\mid {}^3\text{rising}^1 \mid {}^2\text{will appêar}$$
$$\text{Mòre } {}^3\text{glórious}^1 \mid {}^2\text{than from } {}^3\text{nó fâll}^1 \#$$
$$\text{(and trust themselves to fear no second fate.)}$$

('From this descent, o ye virtues, your rising will appear more glorious than from no fall.') But this reading is only superficially possible, for 'trust,' then, has no subject. We ask them to imitate the following:

$$\text{from } {}^3\text{thìs descént}^2\mid$$
$$^2\text{Ce}^3\text{lêstiàl vírtues} \mid\mid \text{rìsing}^2 \text{ }^2\text{will ap}^3\text{péar}^3 \mid$$
$$^3\text{Mòre glórious}^2 \mid {}^2\text{than from}^3 \text{ nó fâll}^2\mid$$

('Celestial virtues, rising from this descent, will appear more glorious than from no fall and will trust themselves to fear no second fate.')

A final example: one student, reading it this way

O bright-eyed Hope, ²my ³mòrbid fâncy chéer¹#

wondered how Hope could be at the same time 'bright-eyed,' 'fancy,' and 'morbid.' Her embarrassment knew no bounds when she heard the following reading and immediately saw her error:

O bright-eyed Hope, my ²mòrbid ³fáncy¹ | ¹chéer¹#
('O hope, please cheer up my morbid fancy.')

III. *Word Order.* Word order is so vital in Modern English structure that inversions[1] offer perhaps the most difficult syntactic adjustment that a student has to make. What he needs is basically a re-education is signalling potential. There is no use saying that this comes with reading experience, because all too often even graduate students appear unable to parse locutions like Johnson's

> Behold surrounding kings their pow'r combine,
> And one capitulate and one resign;

or Milton's

> to consult how we may best
> With what may be devis'd of honours new
> Receive him coming to receive from us
> Knee-tribute yet unpaid, prostration vile,
> Too much to one, but double how endur'd
> To one and to his image now proclaim'd?

Since inversions are easily analyzed and catalogued,[2] it is strange that no one has ever compiled a primer or drill-book to develop among novice readers the essential skill of interpreting them. It would seem that the very act of going through several examples of the same type would prove eminently useful as 'pattern practice.' An example is the difficult inversion of Object-Imperative (for Imperative-Object), which the tremendous pressures of the *usual* meaning of the NV pattern often lead students to interpret as Subject-Predicate, particularly where signals of potential subject-predicate agreement are lacking: 'Then, pilgrim, turn; thy cares forego' or 'Here subterranean works and cities see,' or 'Round my true heart thine arms entwine.' The student must be taught to search for *other* clues than he

---

[1] I use the term in the broad sense to mean any order of words not usual in normal spoken English.

[2] The job has been done excellently by Mats Redin, *Word Order in English Verse from Pope to Sassoon* (Uppsala: Universiteits Arsskrift, II, 1925), from whom most of my examples are taken. I am grateful to Professor Josephine Miles for calling this study to my attention.

could normally count on; for example, in the Object-Imperative pattern, he could use previous straightforward imperatives as a hint ('turn,' in 'in . . . turn'). The important thing, however, as in all pattern practice, would be to set the model and then to fill it with numerous confirmatory examples.

Here are some of the kinds of poetic inversions that cause students trouble[3]:

SOV	Bright Thames the brightest beauties yield
Prep SOV	With hairy springes we the birds betray
OSV	What though no credit doubting wits may give
OVS	Among the Shepherd-grooms no mate / Hath he
SAuxOV	Gums and pomatums shall his flight restrain
SprepV	Not fierce Othello in so loud a strain
	Roared for the handkerchief that caused his pain
SVprepO	The God who darts around the world his rays
OConjSV	But fortune's gifts if each alike possessed
AdvSV	Unless aside thy purple had been thrown
AdvPrepVS	Swift on his sooty pinions flits the gnome
SAuxPrepV	There all the Learn'd shall at the labour stand
PrepImp	Hope humbly then; with trembling pinion soar
PrepP	A vile conceit in pompous words expressed
PrepInf	What moved my mind with youthful lords to roam
SPredNV	Some figures monstrous and mis-shaped appear.
	For I thy own dear mother am.
ObjCompOSV	Modes of Self-love the passions we may call
PrepN	O thou! Of Bu'ness the directing Soul.
NAdj	Not tyrants fierce that unrepenting die
AxisPrep	She talked and sung the words among.
	I went my work about.

The teacher has no business assuming that his beginning students have either the initiative or the ability to learn how to interpret poetic inversions on their own. What they need is the same kind of intensive drill that has proven so effective in foreign language instruction—drill within the pattern, in this case with instances drawn from all periods of English poetry. The alternative is a continuing incapacity to handle any other structure than SVO or its standard variations—in short, incompetence as a reader of poetry.

It would be fatuous to suggest that all the problems of teaching introductory literature can be solved by linguistics, for the obvious reason that literature can never be defined in terms of language alone. Obviously our methods do nothing to develop the vital poetic prerequisites of emotional maturity, esthetic sensitivity, and general culture. Yet, as important as these qualities are, they do not even *become* problems until the student has succeeded in piecing together the plain syntactic sense of a poem. Let

---

[3] S = subject, O = object, V = verb, Prep = prepositional phrase, Conj. = conjunction, Adv = adverb, P = participle, Inf = infinitive, PredN = predicate noun.

us not evade our linguistic responsibilities. Let us try to solve linguistic problems with linguistic methods, and let the other things take care of themselves.

Dialect Differentiation
in the Stories of Joel Chandler Harris*

SUMNER IVES

DESPITE THE WIDESPREAD USE of literary dialect by American authors, this device for realism has been studied very little. True, George Philip Krapp included an extensive discussion of dialect writing in his *English Language in America*, published in 1925, but aside from this, very little original work has been done. And twenty years later E. H. Sturtevant and H. L. Mencken were simply repeating his conclusions: that all of our literary dialects are essentially alike, that authors did not succeed in differentiating them, and "that there are no true dialects in America . . . so far as dialects have been utilized for literary purposes. One may say that there have been only two forms of speech in America, the more or less formal standard and the more or less informal colloquial."[1]

I have already argued at some length that these conclusions have been unjust to many authors, especially such men as James Russell Lowell, Mark Twain, and Joel Chandler Harris.[2] This discussion is an extension of the arguments advanced then and a fuller demonstration of just how one of them, Harris, was able to use various white and Negro dialects in his stories and to show systematic differences between them. But first some review is necessary, for the recognition of differences between literary representations of dialects depends on agreement as to how dialects themselves are different.

We may apply the term *dialect* to the speech of any group, limited socially or geographically, which has certain language habits in common, enough so that there is an appearance of homogeneity within the group and an appearance of difference between this group and other groups. These distinguishing language habits, however, have individually their own separate and distinct distributions. The isoglosses, or lines bounding their distribution, extend horizontally across the country and vertically through the social structure of every region. Consequently, the social status of many nonstandard items is often different in different sections. For example, both

* Reprinted by permission from *American Literature,* 17.88–96 (March, 1955).
[1] I, 243.
[2] "A Theory of Literary Dialect," *Tulane Studies in English,* II, 137–182 (1950).

it don't and *you was* are found nearly everywhere in popular speech. But all educated people know that both are condemned by guides to correct usage. However, a great many Southerners, knowing this textbook rule, use *it don't* in ordinary conversation, although the same people would not say *you was.* Thus the social implications of *it don't* in the dialogue of a story would differ according to the native region of the speaker. But *you was* in the dialogue of any character would at least separate him from the company of the educated or their more successful imitators. Another form, *it do,* is practically limited to the rural South and even there it implies a less educated or more rustic speech than does *you was.*[3] It is through the careful management of such items as these, with their different social and regional associations, that Harris was able to distinguish his dialects from each other and from other popular speech.

When all the characters of a story are residents of the same locality, use of dialect, or nonstandard speech forms, serves chiefly to identify the characters as members of different social groups. These social distinctions are indicated by two devices. One is the density or frequency of the nonstandard forms; the other is the choice of nonstandard forms. In general, the greater the density, the greater the rusticity or the lower the class. Thus, in Harris's stories, the speech of a "poor white" farmer has in it not only the nonstandard forms found in the speech of a middle-class tradesman but many others as well.

But just as the choice of certain dialectal forms can show a difference in social status, so can the selection of other forms give some indication as to the generation to which the character belongs. An elderly plantation owner may use archaisms which would not appear in the speech of a younger person, regardless of his social status.

Harris could indicate such differences in dialect in his stories of Middle Georgia because many distinct speech patterns actually existed there. Middle Georgia was a relatively isolated town and country section. Settlers had come in well after the American Revolution from both the lowland South and the mountain South.[4] These differences in origin must have been reflected in the local speechways, for they can still be discovered in field records of the Linguistic Atlas.[5] And differences in family origin correlated to some extent with occupation and economic standing. Thus there were distinct social classes in town and in country, and town and country differed from each from each other. Both had their "poor whites" and their local aristocrats, with gradations between. And there were also the Ne-

---

[3] E. Bagby Atwood, *A Survey of Verb Forms in the Eastern United States* (Ann Arbor, 1953), pp. 27, 28, 41.

[4] J. E. Callaway, *The Early Settlement of Georgia* (Athens, Ga., 1948).

[5] For a general description of the Linguistic Atlas and its methodology, see Hans Kurath, and others, *Handbook of the Linguistic Geography of New England* (Providence, 1939). All forms which have been cited from the Harris stories have been verified by examination of unpublished Atlas records.

groes.[6] Thus the local speech mores were more complex than those of other areas with less diversity in settlement and culture. Harris must have had a keen ear and exact memory, for he used the distinguishing marks of the several dialects in his characterizations. Whether this use was based on deliberate and systematic analysis, I would not say.

Much of this social dialect is also regional. It is well known that all forms of popular speech are derived from earlier popular and cultured speech through the operation of the same linguistic processes as those which give standard speech. At the same time, each change of each word in each region and in each class is a unique event, and these changes are not necessarily consistent with each other. For example, in some dialects of eastern New England, the form *be* is generalized throughout the present indicative, regardless of the subject. On the other hand, the form *is* has been similarly generalized in parts of the rural South.[7] Thus, when Uncle Remus says *I is*, he is using both social and regional dialect. Such internal causes of dialect difference have been reinforced by education and other enemies of the local folkways. These have not been nationally uniform in their effect. Consequently, "relic areas" appear with distinctive traits, although these same traits might not have been regionally definitive a few generations earlier.

The grammar and vocabulary of local speech can be shown rather fully and with little difficulty, for the conventional alphabet will spell its forms, and the meanings are relatively clear. But the representation of pronunciations is another matter. The function of orthography is to identify the phonemes, or distinctive vowels and consonants, of a language. For it to show regional differences in the pronunciation of these vowels and consonants would be redundant. Although English spelling is defective and awkward, even in its representation of the distinctive sounds, an author is generally able to show which of the traditionally recognized vowels and consonants are used in particular words. Nevertheless, he very seldom shows purely regional pronunciations in the speech of educated people, even when he could do so, unless there is some immediate reason for showing that the character is not native to the locale of the story. He varies from the standard spelling only to show pronunciations which differ from standard speech in the region of the story. At the same time, pronunciations correlating with social class are nearly always circumscribed geographically, just as nearly all social differences in grammar are geographically limited.

In summary, then, an author employs dialect writing to identify a character as a member of some social group to which neither author nor reader

---

[6] The Negroes in Middle Georgia had been born in this country, with rare exceptions. Negro slaves were brought in from the lowland plantations at the time of settlement, and the plantation culture was fully established within a generation of the time when the land was first thrown open for occupancy.

[7] Atwood, *op. cit.*, p. 27.

is presumed to belong. By exploiting the diverse occurrence and density of nonstandard forms, he is able to distinguish between social groups with some sureness. In dialect writing, structural, lexical, and rhetorical items can be shown rather fully, and generally are; for they clearly contrast with equivalent forms in the literary standard. However, this literary standard is not uniformly pronounced, and variations in the standard pronunciation are not ordinarily shown, even to the extent they could be. Only when pronunciations are socially indicative does an author represent them. Nevertheless, these socially distinct pronunciations, like socially distinct grammatical items, generally have regional as well as social limits to their occurrence.

The best known of all the dialects which Harris used is the Negro dialect of the Uncle Remus stories. I have shown elsewhere some details of how this dialect differed from rustic white speech, as Harris represented it, and shall give here only a few generalizations.[8] There are, it is true, many items which appear in both his Negro and his rustic white speech, but there are others which appear only in his representation of Negro speech. Among them are the use of *d* for *th* when it indicates a voiced sound, as in *the, that, them,* and *whether;* the use of final *f* for voiceless *th* in words like *mouth* and *tooth;* the omission of *r* in words like *before* and *sure;* and the omission of *h* in words like *what* and *why*. Also, the Uncle Remus speech shows far more assimilation, more loss of initial unstressed syllables, more leveling of preterit and past participle forms, and a greater density of archaic forms. Uncle Remus himself has a peculiarly ornate use of words, with such exotic formations as *sollumcholly, sustonished,* and *rekermember*. He has a rich imagery, with such expressions as *leg-bail* for escape by flight and *you'er thumpin' de wrong watermillion* for barking up the wrong tree. Furthermore, his speech is larded with such proverbs as *'oman tongue ain't got no Sunday* and such comparisons as *ez ca'm ez a dead pig in de sunshine*.[9]

Actually the field records of the Linguistic Atlas, aside from a very few Gullah records, show hardly any usages in Negro speech which cannot also be found in rustic white speech. And there are many similarities in usage as Harris wrote the dialects. However, the peculiarity of his Negro speech, in addition to the features already listed, consists in the greater density of nonstandard forms, and in the fact that the nonstandard items include, in greater number, features which are associated with Southern plantation speech rather than with Southern mountain speech. Since the same features can actually be found in the speech of both Negro and rustic white, Harris could more justly be accused of exaggerating the actual difference than of failing to indicate it. One additional point should, however, be mentioned.

[8] *Op. cit.,* pp. 165–167.

[9] For many similar expressions, see the list compiled by Stella Brewer Brookes, *Joel Chandler Harris—Folklorist* (Athens, Ga., 1950), pp. 97–110.

Some of the Atlas field records of rustic white speech show much closer agreement with the Uncle Remus dialect than do others. These other records show features which are neither in the records of cultured informants of the region nor in the records of Negro speech. Instead, they show characteristics of South Midland[10] or Southern mountain speech, and in this respect, their usage agrees substantially with that of the "poor white" as Harris wrote it. Although most of the animal fables are told by Uncle Remus, a few of those in *Nights with Uncle Remus* are told by Daddy Jack, who represents the Gullah Negroes of the coast. The dialect is quite different, in fact so different that any one complete line of text is enough to tell them apart. I shall be able to give only a few of these differences.

According to Lorenzo Turner,[11] Gullah speech has the same vowel in words like *pat* as in words like *pot*, and it has no post vocalic *r*. Thus *pat*, *pot*, and *part* would all have the same vowel. This characteristic is suggested by Harris in Daddy Jack's speech. For example, he spells *laugh* and other words normally pronounced with "short *a*" with *ah*, sometimes with *ar*. At the same time, he omits the letter *r* from those words which, like *smart* and *part*, have *ar* in their normal spelling, or he spells them too with *ah*. This spelling practice shows that Harris heard the same vowel in all these words.[12] In writing the dialect of Uncle Remus, Harris indicated no dialectal pronunciation for these words.

Another of the peculiarities in the representation of Daddy Jack's speech is the use of a spelling for "short *e*" as in *met* for words which have "long *a*" in the speech of most Southerners, including Uncle Remus. Examples are *shekky* for *shake*, *yent* for *ain't*, *bre'k* for *break*, and *sem* for *same*. According to Turner,[13] *met* and *make* have different vowels, but the vowel of *make*, which is a diphthong in Southern standard speech, is a short monophthong in Gullah. There was no way by which Harris could show the actual facts with the conventional alphabet. But of course he may have thought that the two monophthongs were actually the same vowel.

Three consonant features will do for illustration, although there are many others. All these are corroborated by Turner's study and differ from the usage of Uncle Remus. One is the use of *t* for voiceless *th* in all positions. For example: *troo* for *through*, *nuttin'* for *nothing*, and *mout'* for *mouth*. Second is the use of *f* for final *v*, as in *drife* for *drive* and *lif* for *live*. The third is the spelling of *young* as *noung*. This word occurs in one of Turner's illustrative texts with an initial palatal nasal,[14] a sound for which there is no precedent in native English.

[10] For the limits of this speech region, see Hans Kurath, *A Word Geography of the Eastern United States* (Ann Arbor, 1949), p. 36.

[11] *Africanisms in the Gullah Dialect* (Chicago, 1949), pp. 16, 17.

[12] This vowel was probably intermediate between the vowels of *pat* and *pot*, something like that in French *la*.

[13] *Op. cit.*, p. 16.

[14] *Ibid.*, p. 263. This sound is similar to that of *gn* in French *agneau*.

Differences in grammar and rhetoric are quite obvious, but I shall illustrate them only by giving a portion of a conversation between Daddy Jack and Uncle Remus. Regarding one of the young plantation women, Daddy Jack said, "Da' gal do holler un lahf un stomp 'e fut dey-dey, un dun I shum done gone pidjin-toe. Oona bin know da' 'Tildy gal?"[15]

Uncle Remus replied, "I bin a-knowin' dat gal now gwine on since she 'uz knee-high ter one or dese yer puddle ducks; en I bin noticin' lately dat she mightly likely nigger."[16]

In giving examples to show how Harris differentiated between his white dialects, I shall draw from *Sister Jane,* a novel telling, in the person of William Wornum, the activities of Wornum's sister, Jane, and her associates. In it, some characters use consistently the standard colloquial of literature, deviating only in so far as consistent with occupation and personality. For example, the dialogue of the narrator, a mild and bookish man, is rather formal and old-fashioned.

On the other hand, the dialogue of Sister Jane herself has in it many nonstandard forms and local expressions which do not appear in the speech of her brother or in that of Colonel Bullard and members of his family. For example, she says *he don't, fetch* for *carry, chany* for *china,* uses *ain't* with subjects in all persons, and has such expressions as *it would look a heap better.* Next is a group of Jane's friends, middle-class townswomen, of whom Mrs. Beshears is representative. She uses all the monstandard forms which are found in the speech of Sister Jane and many more. Examples of these additional usages are *done took; don't never up and tell me; I ups and says, says I; teetotal;* and pronunciations of the *ee* sound in *guardian, oblige, scare,* and *care; cuss* for *curse;* and *purty* for *pretty.* Such spellings as *bekase* for *because* and *natur'* for *nature* occasionally appear, but the standard spelling for many of these is more common. Next, there is the speech of Jincy Matthews, son of a well-to-do plantation family, but popularly regarded as a half-wit and vagabond. Some forms he uses, in addition to those of the persons already mentioned, are *ast,* preterit of *ask; I seen, I taken,* and *I know'd; jine* and *spile* for *join* and *spoil; allers* for *always; tech* for *touch, drapped* for *dropped,* and *hoss* for *horse.*

There are two further dialects which have all these features and many more. One is that of two elderly gentlemen, Grandsir Roach and Uncle Jimmy Cosby, about whom it is said: "They owned land and negroes, horses and carriages; but back of their prosperity were the experience of the pioneer and the spirit of true democracy." The other is that of Mandy Satterlee, a young girl from a "poor white" settlement who is befriended by Sister Jane, and her brother, Bud Satterlee, of whom Sister Jane said, "He was born trifling and he's stayed so." Both dialects have a heavier con-

[15] Translated, this means: 'That girl shouts and laughs and stamps her foot right here, and then I see her walk pigeon-toed. Do you know that Tildy girl?"
[16] *Mighty likely* here means *well-favored* and *desirable.*

centration of nonstandard forms than is found in other white dialects of the story. That of the older people includes *holp* for *helped, mought* for *might,* and in general a greater density of other archaic items such as *ax* for *ask* and *desarve* for *deserve.* Additional forms which appear in their dialogue but not in that of the younger Satterlees are *nother* for *neither, oneasy* for *uneasy; hyearn* for *heard, her'n* for *hers, gwine* for *going,* and *cotch* for *caught.* Both they and the Satterlees have such features in their dialogue as *hain't; hisse'f; out'n* for *out of; e'en about* for *just about; a-nigh* for *near;* and the following phonetic spellings: *ef* for *if; hender* for *hinder; yan* for *yon; quare* for *queer; whar* for *where; arter* for *after; shore* for *sure;* and *creetur* for *creature.* These examples, of course, are only a few of the non-standard usages found in each dialect.

The mere listing of specific items which occur in one literary dialect but not in others does not, of course, exhaust the distinctions between them. There are differences in syntax and idiom which are not revealed by this type of analysis; moreover an author puts more of such spellings as *sez* for *says,* which indicate no more than the normal pronunciation, into his writing of nonstandard dialogue.

From one point of view, this is an exaggeration of the dialect, an insinuation that it is further removed from the standard than it is. However, such exaggeration is probably defensible, for it adds to the illusion that actual conversation has been reproduced. Once the literary standard has been left behind, the author tends to suggest the actual rhythm and flow of speech as closely as he can. In doing this he is apt to indicate by spelling changes what probably occurs also in the speech of those whose conversation is not represented as dialect. Thus the dialects in literary transcription may actually appear more different from the regional standard than in truth they were.

But if this is a fault it is, so far as Harris is concerned, a happy one, for his writing of conversation in literary dialect seems truer and more natural than his writing of it in the literary standard. In fact, the more one examines the speech of Harris's folk characters, the more one admires the skill with which he worked. He has, in truth, done more than write a more or less informal colloquial, as Krapp put it. A shy man himself, he must have listened keenly and sympathetically, for he caught the various patterns of folk speech in great detail. And whatever his narrative ability, he handled the dialogue of his folk characters with skilful discrimination.

Index